WHAT DO YOU CALL A SOCIOPATH IN A CUBICLE?

(ANSWER: A COWORKER)

Other DILBERT books from Andrews McMeel Publishing

Another Day in Cubicle Paradise
ISBN: 0-7407-2194-6

Random Acts of Management
ISBN: 0-7407-0453-2

Dilbert Gives You the Business
ISBN: 0-7407-0338-2 hardcover
ISBN: 0-7407-0003-0 paperback

Don't Step in the Leadership
ISBN: 0-8362-7844-5

Journey to Cubeville
ISBN: 0-8362-7175-0 hardcover
ISBN: 0-8362-6745-1 paperback

I'm Not Anti-Business, I'm Anti-Idiot
ISBN: 0-8362-5182-2

Seven Years of Highly Defective People
ISBN: 0-8362-5129-6 hardcover
ISBN: 0-8362-3668-8 paperback

Casual Day Has Gone Too Far
ISBN: 0-8362-2899-5

Fugitive from the Cubicle Police
ISBN: 0-8362-2119-2

Still Pumped from Using the Mouse
ISBN: 0-8362-1026-3

It's Obvious You Won't Survive by Your Wits Alone
ISBN: 0-8362-0415-8

Bring Me the Head of Willy the Mailboy!
ISBN: 0-8362-1779-9

Shave the Whales
ISBN: 0-8362-1740-3

Dogbert's Clues for the Clueless
ISBN: 0-8362-1737-3

Build a Better Life by Stealing Office Supplies
ISBN: 0-8362-1757-8

Always Postpone Meetings with Time-Wasting Morons
ISBN: 0-8362-1758-6

For ordering information, call 1-800-642-6480.

WHAT DO YOU CALL A SOCIOPATH IN A CUBICLE?

(ANSWER: A COWORKER)

A DILBERT BOOK
BY SCOTT ADAMS

Andrews McMeel
Publishing

Kansas City

www.dilbert.com

03 04 05 06 DUB 10 9 8 7 6 5 4 3 2

ISBN: 0-7407-2663-3

Library of Congress Control Number: 2002102229

ATTENTION: SCHOOLS AND BUSINESSES

Yes, Pam, it's for you.

Introduction

I'm often asked if I think there are more sociopaths, morons, and lunatics in the workplace than anywhere else. It's a fair question, because it seems as if cubicles attract more than their fair share. But I have a different theory. I believe that everyone is a sociopath waiting to be discovered. Normally you can control your evil impulses. In fact, outside of work, you have to control yourself or you'll be beaten, disinherited, or jailed.

But at work, chances are you're already experiencing life at its worst. It's important to inject some entertainment into your day. And if that means making life miserable for your coworkers, many people seem willing to yank that thread. The only danger in being a workplace sociopath is that you can't be evil to your boss, your boss's secretary, customers, or anyone who is having an affair with your boss, because it'll come back to bite you. But anyone else is fair game, especially vendors and coworkers. Even if they complain, no one will listen. There's no downside to being a sociopath if you pick your targets carefully, and the entertainment value can be considerable.

Traditionally, every workgroup has at least one flaming @$$hole, one interminable bore, and one person who needs a metronome to remember to breathe. But thanks to technology, many new breeds of sociopaths have evolved. Far and away the most popular type is the guy who uses his speakerphone in the cubicle. I hear more complaints about that than about any other workplace issue. To the uninformed observer it might seem as though the speakerphone sociopath is oblivious to the anguish he causes to nearby cubicle dwellers. My theory is that he knows, and he enjoys making the people around him suffer. This is the same guy who raises new, unsolvable issues at the end of three-hour meetings. On some level, he thinks it's funny. There's no other way to explain it.

Speaking of abusing other people for entertainment, there's still time to join Dogbert's New Ruling Class (DNRC) and be by his side when he conquers the world and makes everyone else our domestic servants. To join, all you need to do is sign up for the free *Dilbert Newsletter* that's published approximately whenever I feel like it—about five times a year.

To subscribe or unsubscribe, go to www.dilbert.com. If you have problems with the automated subscription method, write to newsletter@unitedmedia.com.

S. Adams

Scott Adams

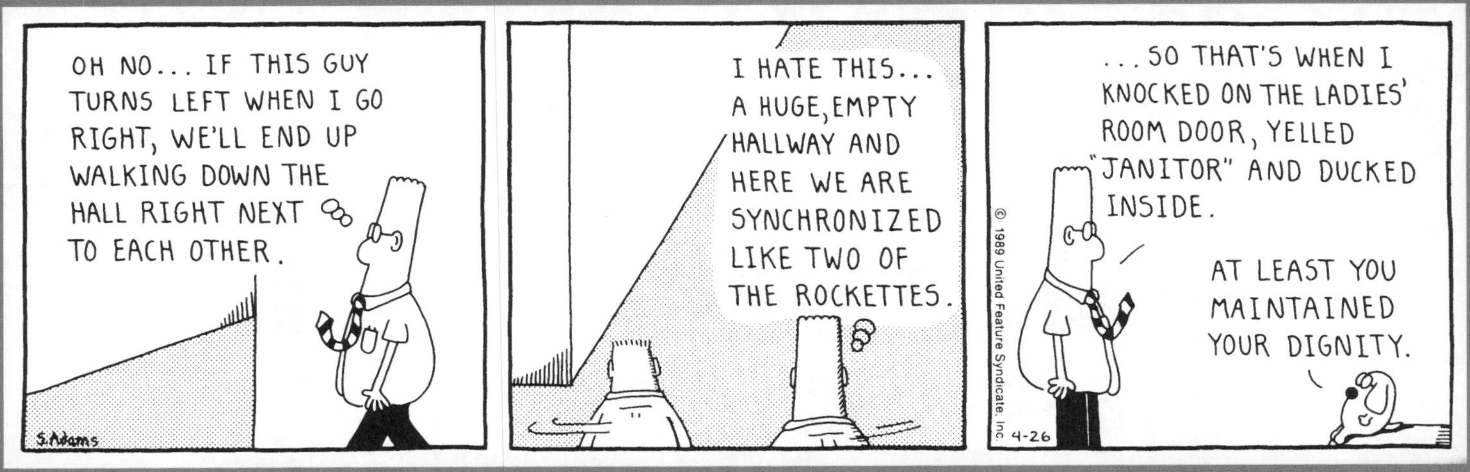
OH NO... IF THIS GUY TURNS LEFT WHEN I GO RIGHT, WE'LL END UP WALKING DOWN THE HALL RIGHT NEXT TO EACH OTHER.
S.Adams
I HATE THIS... A HUGE, EMPTY HALLWAY AND HERE WE ARE SYNCHRONIZED LIKE TWO OF THE ROCKETTES.
© 1989 United Feature Syndicate, Inc.
4-26
...SO THAT'S WHEN I KNOCKED ON THE LADIES' ROOM DOOR, YELLED "JANITOR" AND DUCKED INSIDE.
AT LEAST YOU MAINTAINED YOUR DIGNITY.

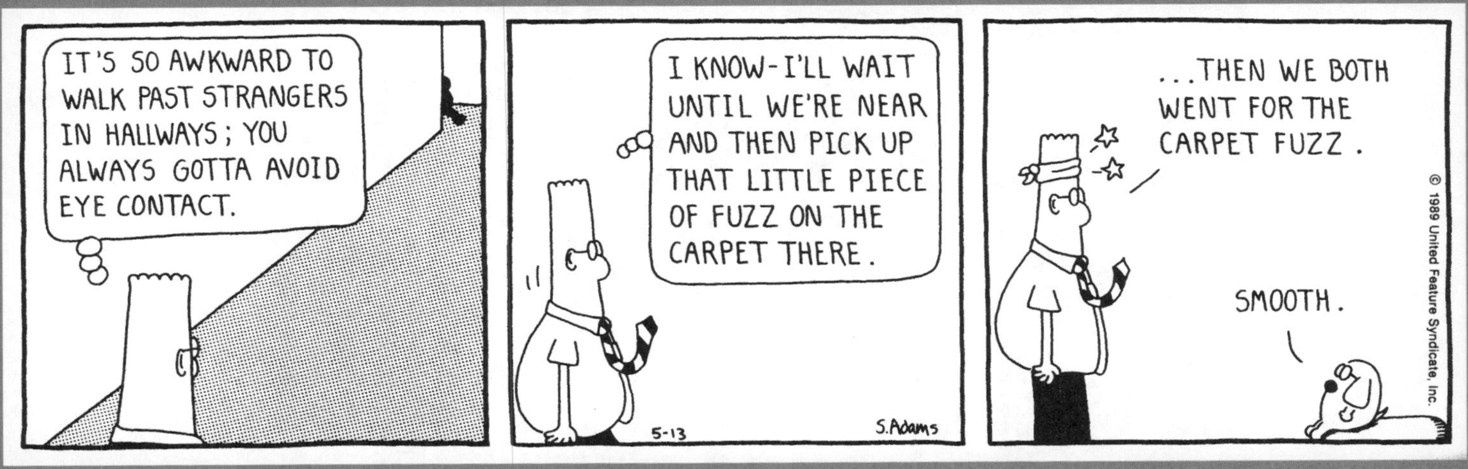
IT'S SO AWKWARD TO WALK PAST STRANGERS IN HALLWAYS; YOU ALWAYS GOTTA AVOID EYE CONTACT.
I KNOW-I'LL WAIT UNTIL WE'RE NEAR AND THEN PICK UP THAT LITTLE PIECE OF FUZZ ON THE CARPET THERE.
5-13
S.Adams
...THEN WE BOTH WENT FOR THE CARPET FUZZ.
SMOOTH.
© 1989 United Feature Syndicate, Inc.

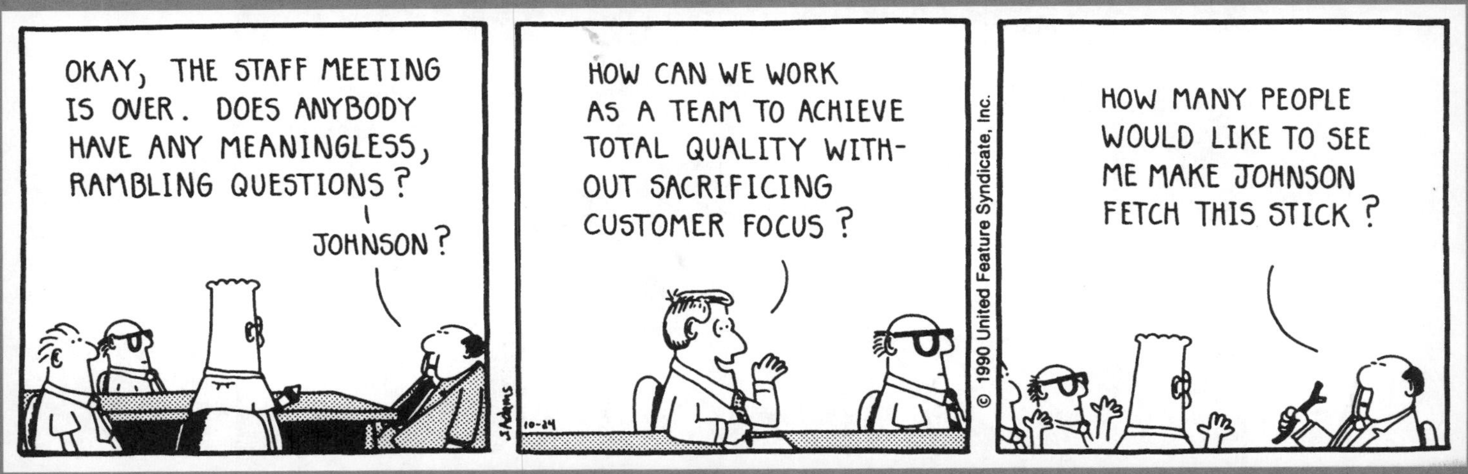
OKAY, THE STAFF MEETING IS OVER. DOES ANYBODY HAVE ANY MEANINGLESS, RAMBLING QUESTIONS?
JOHNSON?
S.Adams
10-24
HOW CAN WE WORK AS A TEAM TO ACHIEVE TOTAL QUALITY WITH-OUT SACRIFICING CUSTOMER FOCUS?
© 1990 United Feature Syndicate, Inc.
HOW MANY PEOPLE WOULD LIKE TO SEE ME MAKE JOHNSON FETCH THIS STICK?

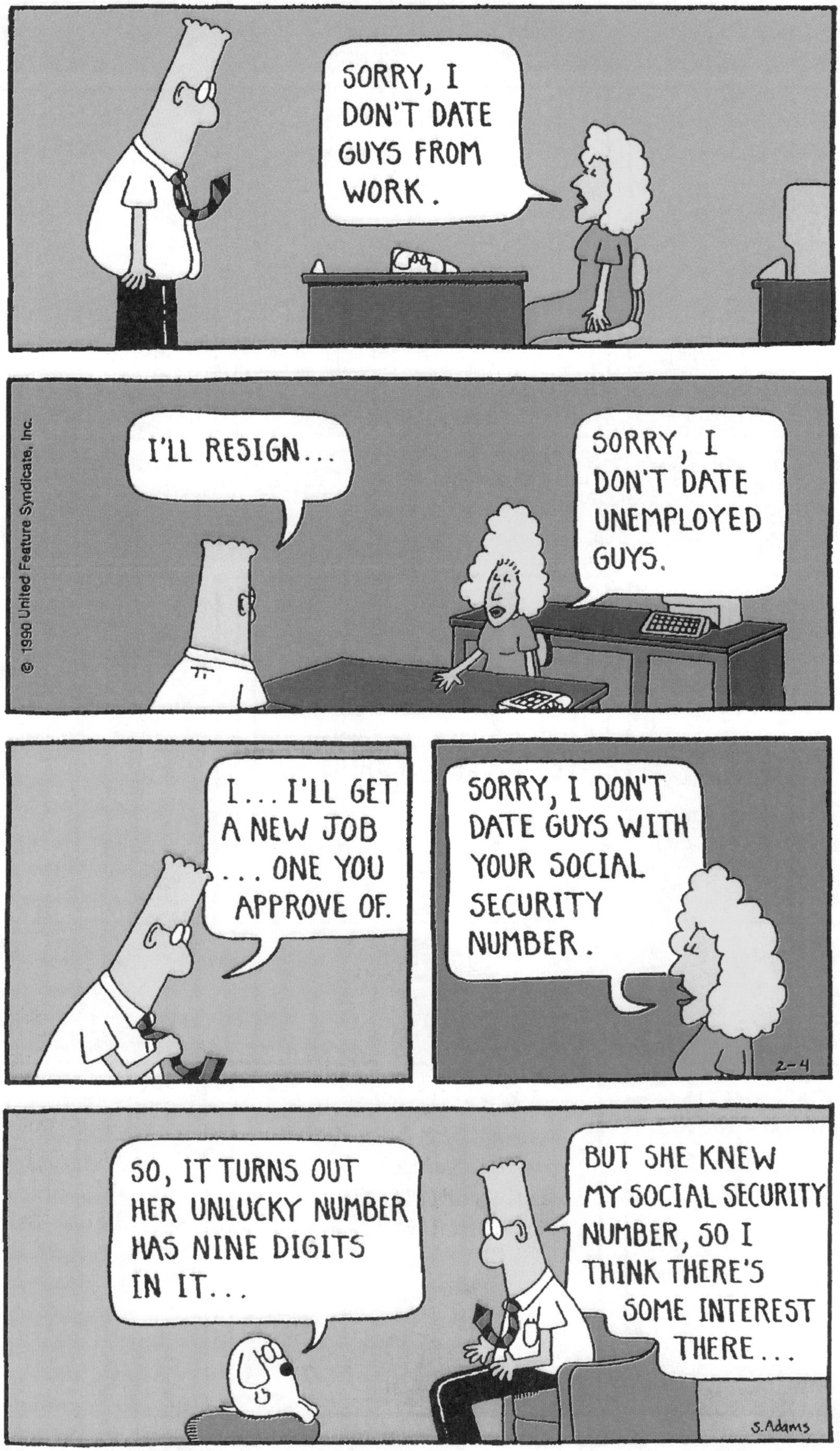
SORRY, I DON'T DATE GUYS FROM WORK.
I'LL RESIGN...
SORRY, I DON'T DATE UNEMPLOYED GUYS.
I... I'LL GET A NEW JOB ... ONE YOU APPROVE OF.
SORRY, I DON'T DATE GUYS WITH YOUR SOCIAL SECURITY NUMBER.
2-4
SO, IT TURNS OUT HER UNLUCKY NUMBER HAS NINE DIGITS IN IT...
BUT SHE KNEW MY SOCIAL SECURITY NUMBER, SO I THINK THERE'S SOME INTEREST THERE...
S. Adams

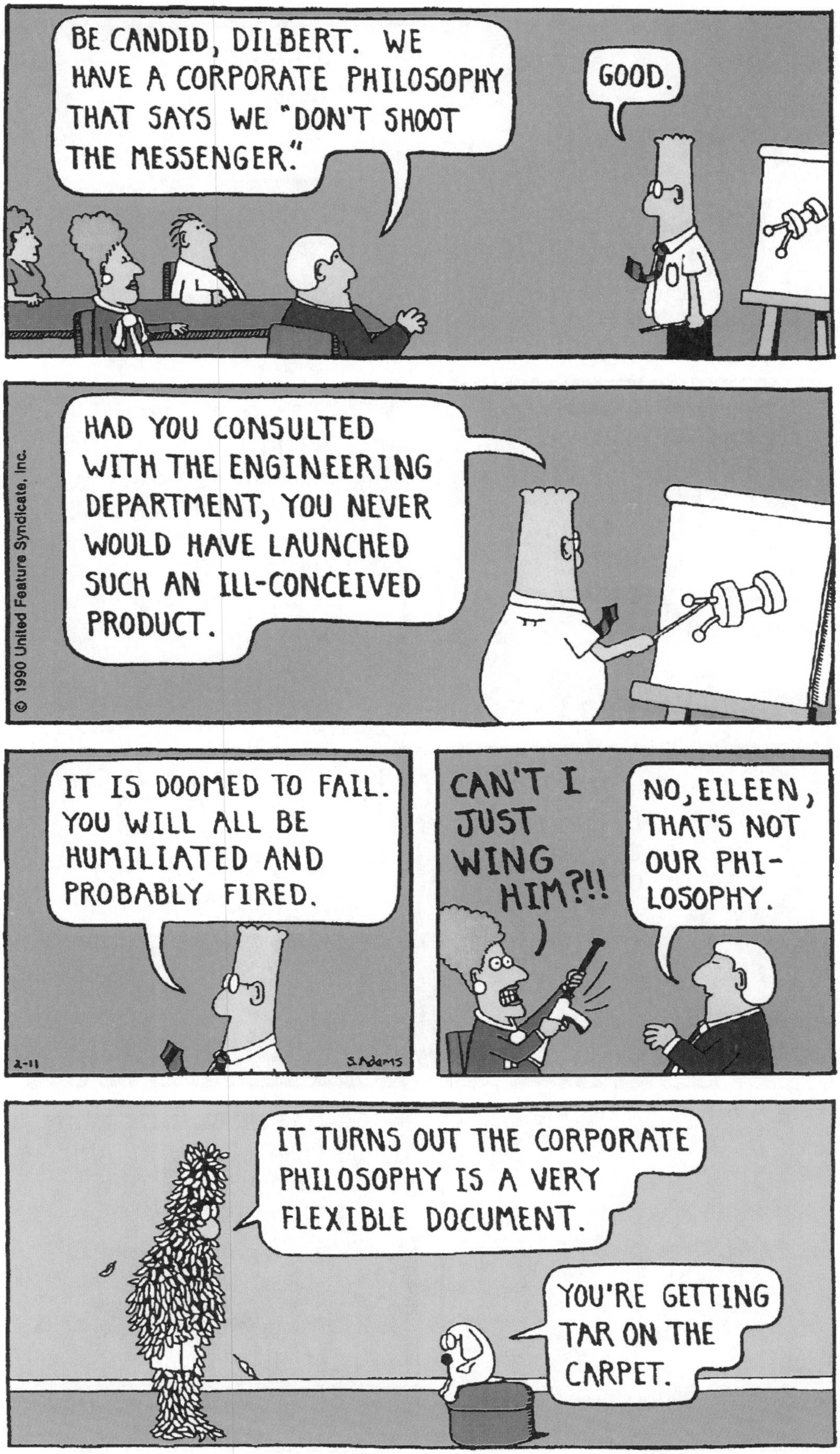
BE CANDID, DILBERT. WE HAVE A CORPORATE PHILOSOPHY THAT SAYS WE "DON'T SHOOT THE MESSENGER."
GOOD.
HAD YOU CONSULTED WITH THE ENGINEERING DEPARTMENT, YOU NEVER WOULD HAVE LAUNCHED SUCH AN ILL-CONCEIVED PRODUCT.
© 1990 United Feature Syndicate, Inc.
IT IS DOOMED TO FAIL. YOU WILL ALL BE HUMILIATED AND PROBABLY FIRED.
2-11
S.Adams
CAN'T I JUST WING HIM?!!
NO, EILEEN, THAT'S NOT OUR PHI-LOSOPHY.
IT TURNS OUT THE CORPORATE PHILOSOPHY IS A VERY FLEXIBLE DOCUMENT.
YOU'RE GETTING TAR ON THE CARPET.

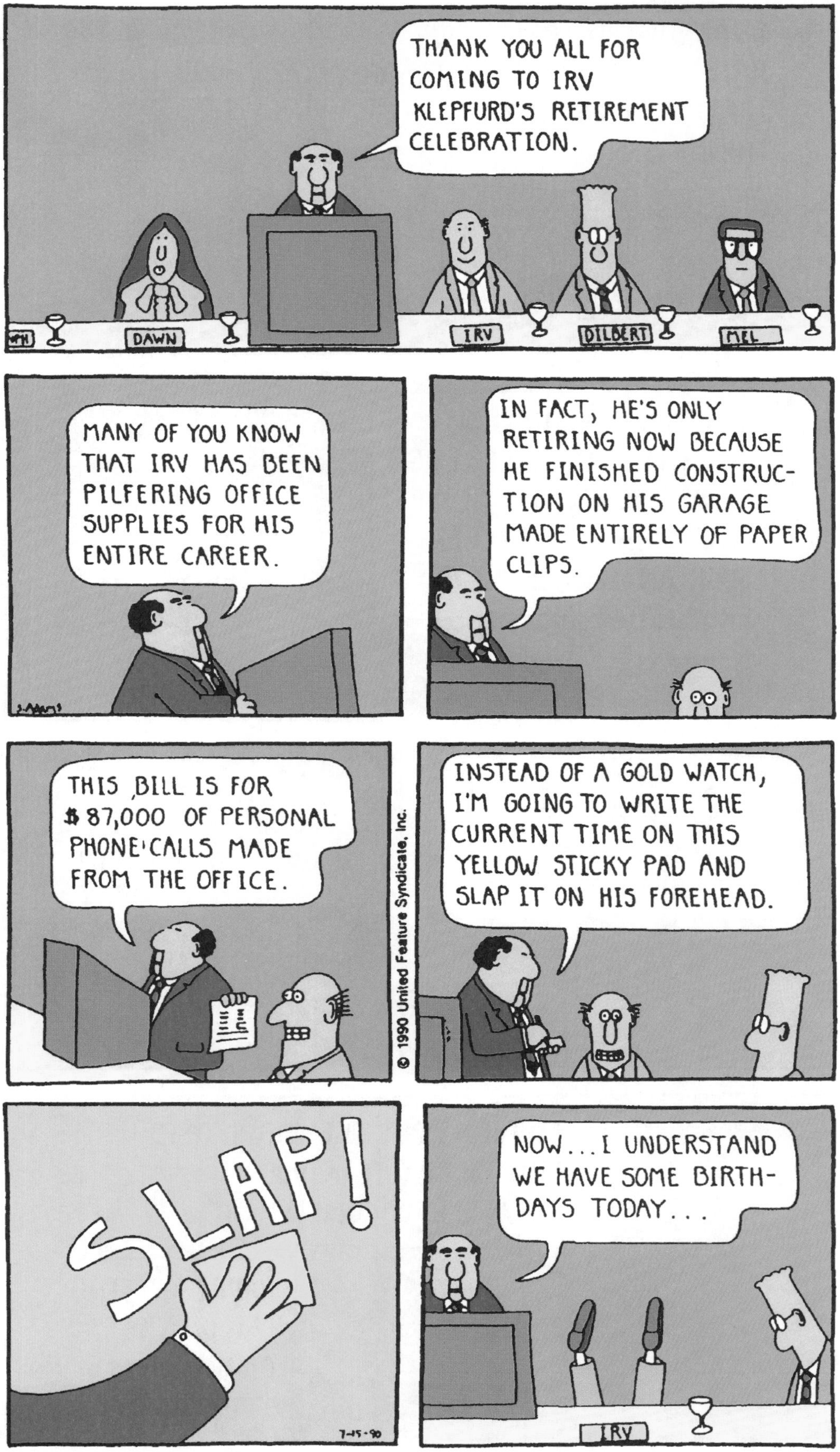
THANK YOU ALL FOR COMING TO IRV KLEPFURD'S RETIREMENT CELEBRATION.
DAWN
IRV
DILBERT
MEL
MANY OF YOU KNOW THAT IRV HAS BEEN PILFERING OFFICE SUPPLIES FOR HIS ENTIRE CAREER.
IN FACT, HE'S ONLY RETIRING NOW BECAUSE HE FINISHED CONSTRUCTION ON HIS GARAGE MADE ENTIRELY OF PAPER CLIPS.
THIS BILL IS FOR $87,000 OF PERSONAL PHONE CALLS MADE FROM THE OFFICE.
© 1990 United Feature Syndicate, Inc.
INSTEAD OF A GOLD WATCH, I'M GOING TO WRITE THE CURRENT TIME ON THIS YELLOW STICKY PAD AND SLAP IT ON HIS FOREHEAD.
SLAP!
7-15-90
NOW... I UNDERSTAND WE HAVE SOME BIRTHDAYS TODAY...
IRV

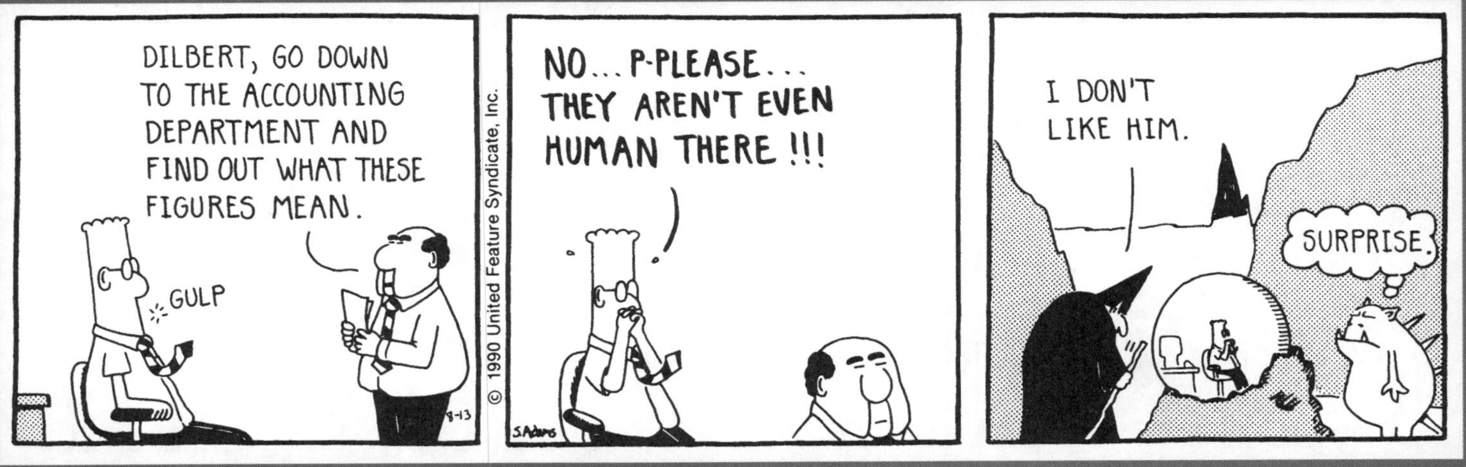
DILBERT, GO DOWN TO THE ACCOUNTING DEPARTMENT AND FIND OUT WHAT THESE FIGURES MEAN.
GULP
© 1990 United Feature Syndicate, Inc.
NO... P-PLEASE... THEY AREN'T EVEN HUMAN THERE !!!
I DON'T LIKE HIM.
SURPRISE.

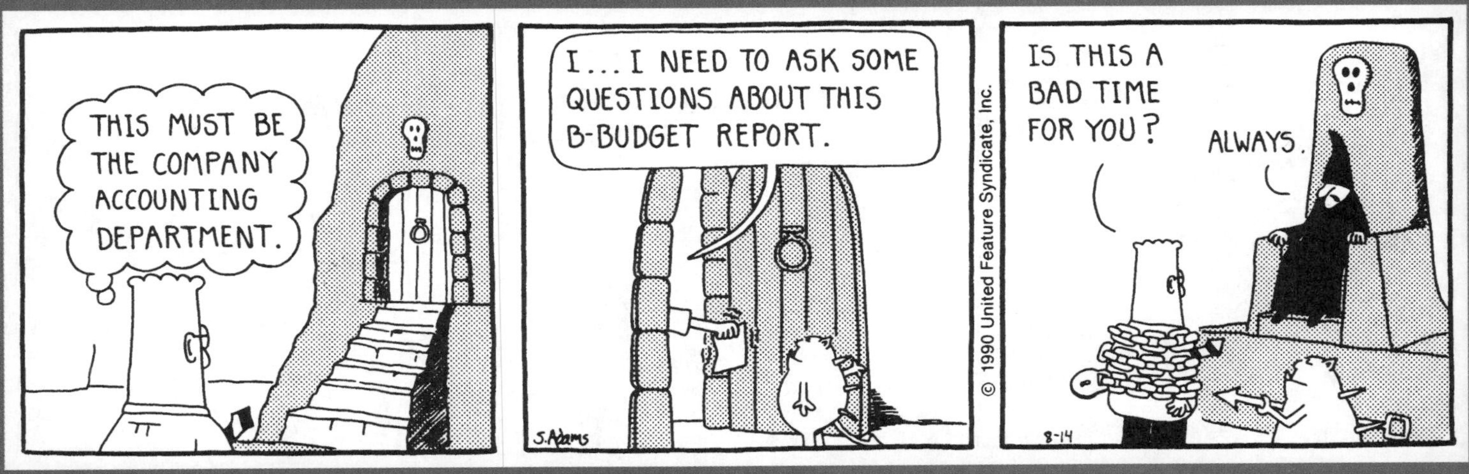
THIS MUST BE THE COMPANY ACCOUNTING DEPARTMENT.
I... I NEED TO ASK SOME QUESTIONS ABOUT THIS B-BUDGET REPORT.
© 1990 United Feature Syndicate, Inc.
IS THIS A BAD TIME FOR YOU?
ALWAYS.

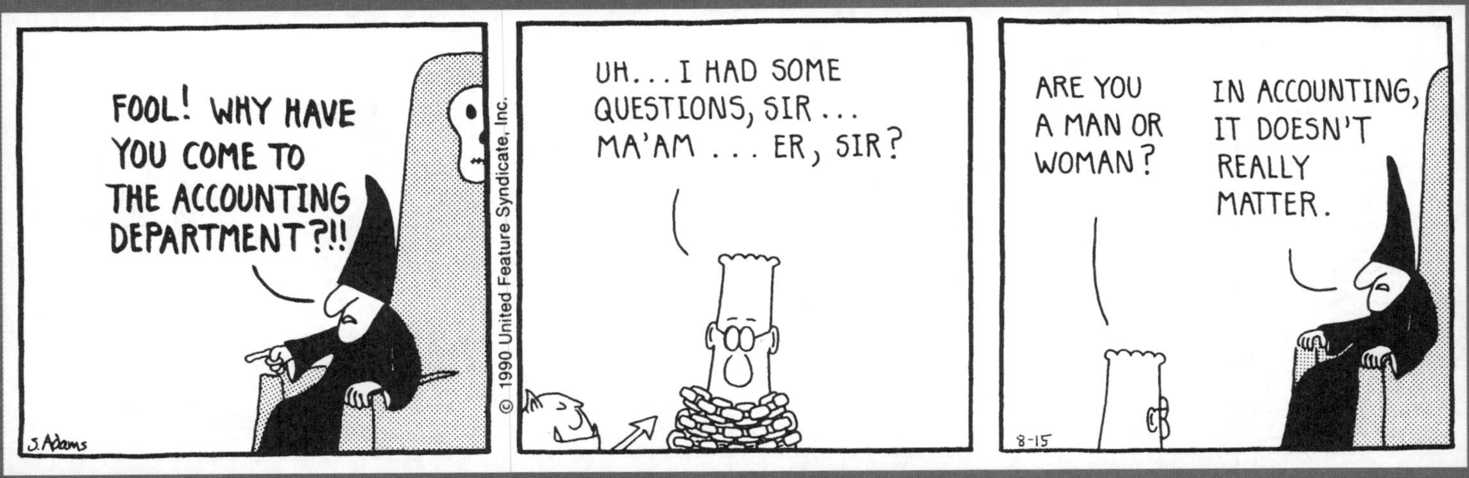
FOOL! WHY HAVE YOU COME TO THE ACCOUNTING DEPARTMENT?!!
© 1990 United Feature Syndicate, Inc.
UH... I HAD SOME QUESTIONS, SIR... MA'AM ... ER, SIR?
ARE YOU A MAN OR WOMAN?
IN ACCOUNTING, IT DOESN'T REALLY MATTER.

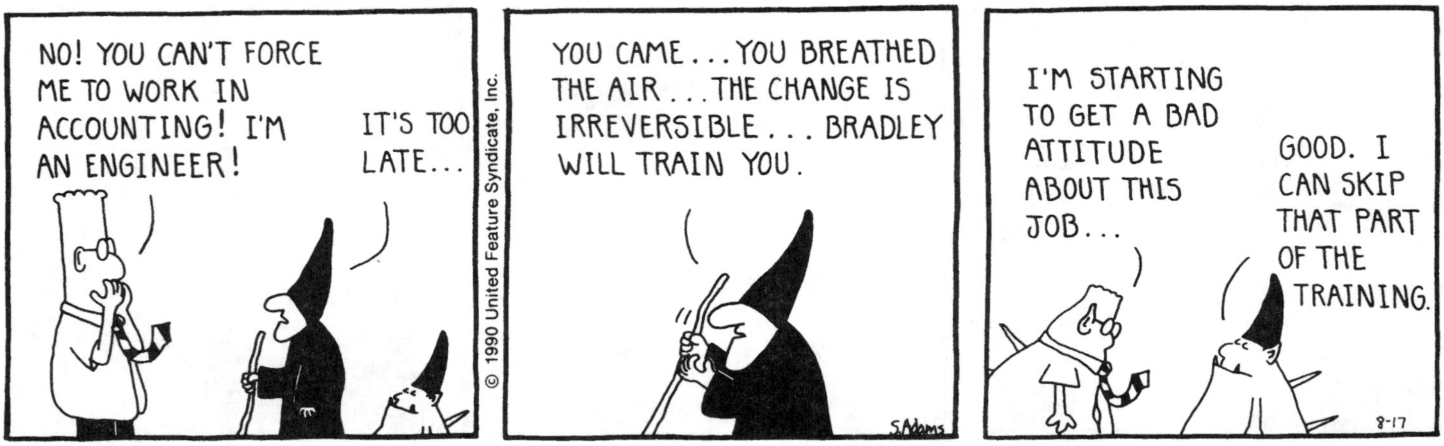
NO! YOU CAN'T FORCE ME TO WORK IN ACCOUNTING! I'M AN ENGINEER!
IT'S TOO LATE...
© 1990 United Feature Syndicate, Inc.
YOU CAME... YOU BREATHED THE AIR... THE CHANGE IS IRREVERSIBLE... BRADLEY WILL TRAIN YOU.
S.Adams
I'M STARTING TO GET A BAD ATTITUDE ABOUT THIS JOB...
GOOD. I CAN SKIP THAT PART OF THE TRAINING.
8-17

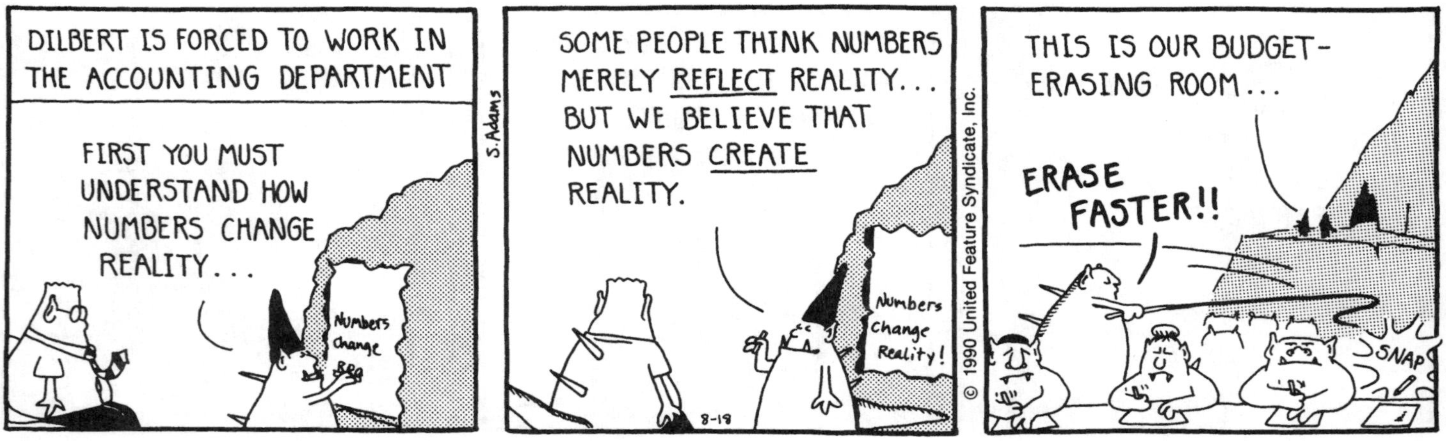
DILBERT IS FORCED TO WORK IN THE ACCOUNTING DEPARTMENT
FIRST YOU MUST UNDERSTAND HOW NUMBERS CHANGE REALITY...
Numbers Change
S.Adams
SOME PEOPLE THINK NUMBERS MERELY REFLECT REALITY... BUT WE BELIEVE THAT NUMBERS CREATE REALITY.
Numbers Change Reality!
8-18
© 1990 United Feature Syndicate, Inc.
THIS IS OUR BUDGET-ERASING ROOM...
ERASE FASTER!!
SNAP

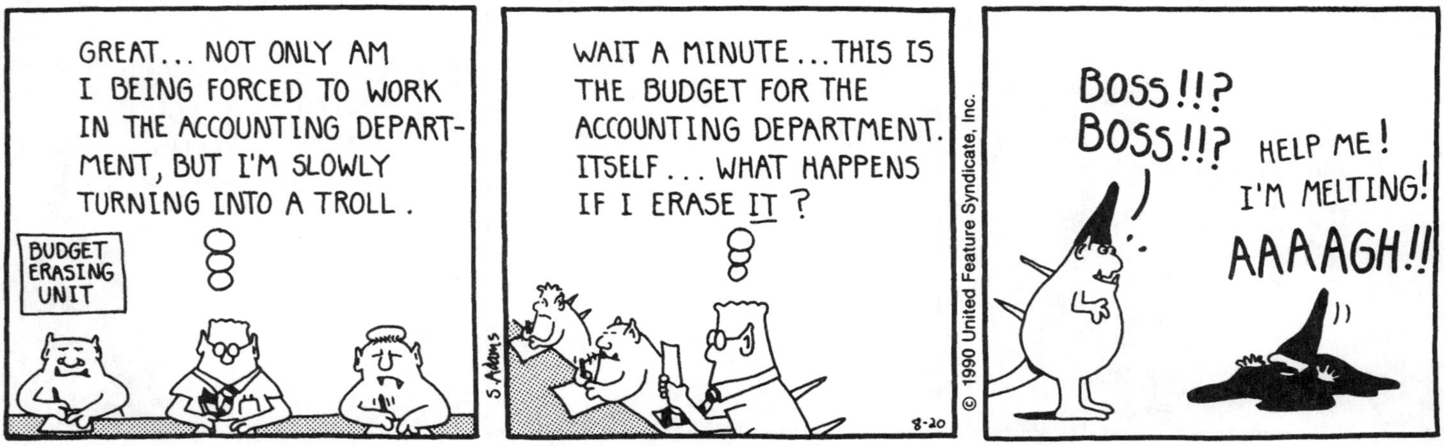
GREAT... NOT ONLY AM I BEING FORCED TO WORK IN THE ACCOUNTING DEPARTMENT, BUT I'M SLOWLY TURNING INTO A TROLL.
BUDGET ERASING UNIT
S.Adams
WAIT A MINUTE... THIS IS THE BUDGET FOR THE ACCOUNTING DEPARTMENT. ITSELF... WHAT HAPPENS IF I ERASE IT?
8-20
© 1990 United Feature Syndicate, Inc.
BOSS!!? BOSS!!?
HELP ME! I'M MELTING!
AAAAGH!!

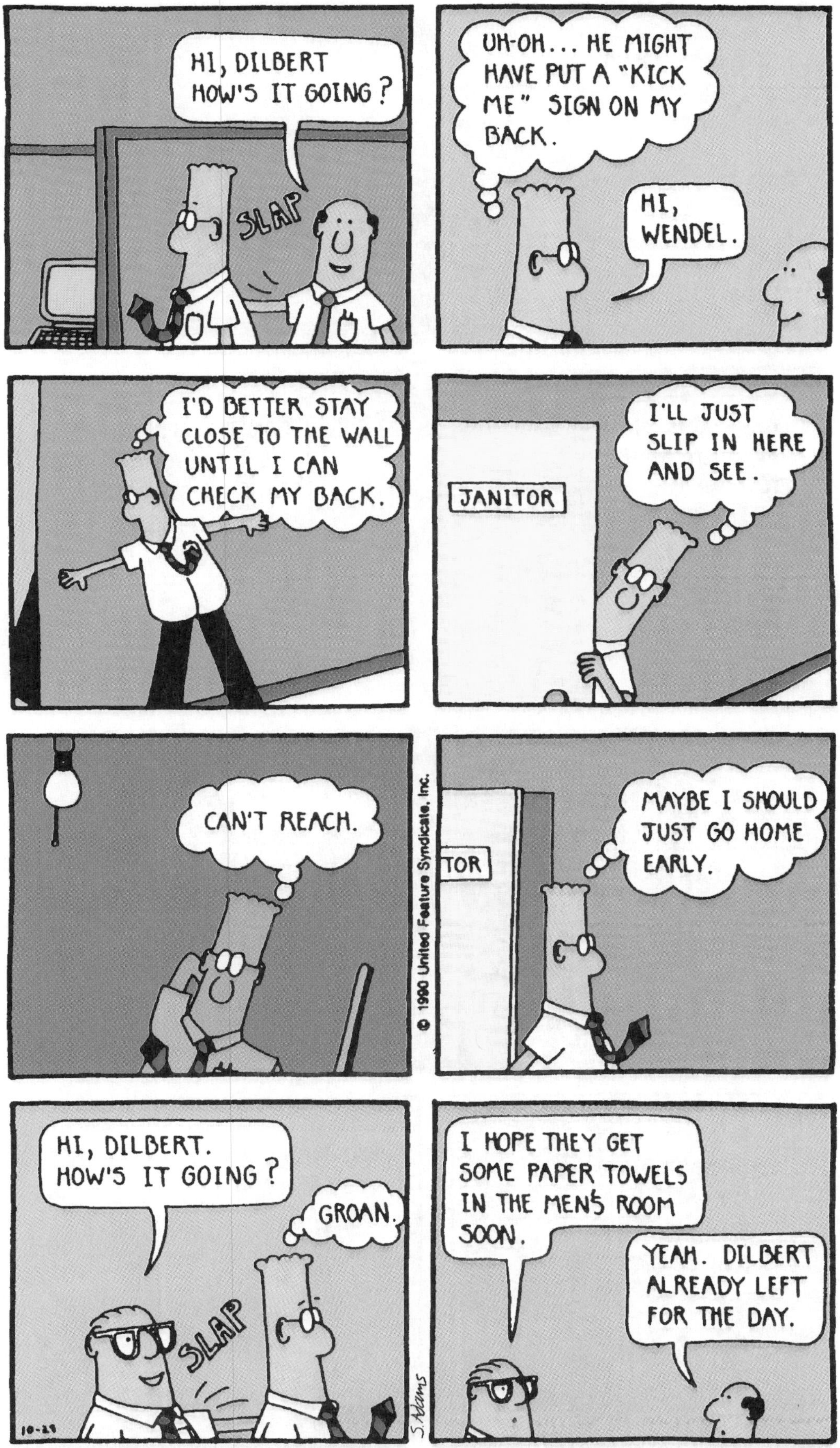
HI, DILBERT
HOW'S IT GOING?
SLAP
UH-OH... HE MIGHT HAVE PUT A "KICK ME" SIGN ON MY BACK.
HI, WENDEL.
I'D BETTER STAY CLOSE TO THE WALL UNTIL I CAN CHECK MY BACK.
JANITOR
I'LL JUST SLIP IN HERE AND SEE.
CAN'T REACH.
© 1990 United Feature Syndicate, Inc.
TOR
MAYBE I SHOULD JUST GO HOME EARLY.
HI, DILBERT.
HOW'S IT GOING?
GROAN.
SLAP
S. Adams
I HOPE THEY GET SOME PAPER TOWELS IN THE MEN'S ROOM SOON.
YEAH. DILBERT ALREADY LEFT FOR THE DAY.

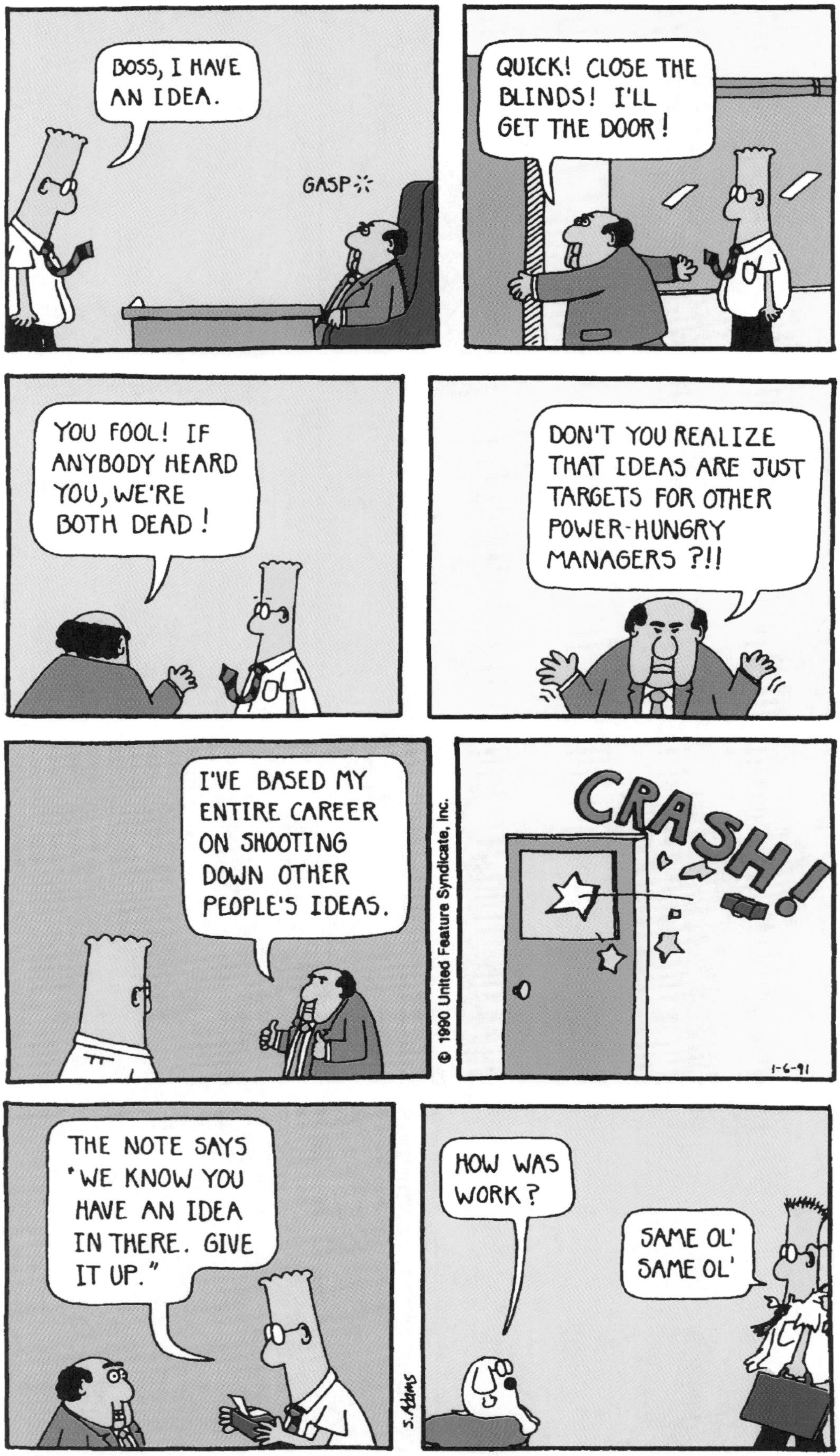
BOSS, I HAVE AN IDEA.
GASP
QUICK! CLOSE THE BLINDS! I'LL GET THE DOOR!
YOU FOOL! IF ANYBODY HEARD YOU, WE'RE BOTH DEAD!
DON'T YOU REALIZE THAT IDEAS ARE JUST TARGETS FOR OTHER POWER-HUNGRY MANAGERS ?!!
I'VE BASED MY ENTIRE CAREER ON SHOOTING DOWN OTHER PEOPLE'S IDEAS.
© 1990 United Feature Syndicate, Inc.
CRASH!
1-6-91
THE NOTE SAYS "WE KNOW YOU HAVE AN IDEA IN THERE. GIVE IT UP."
S. Adams
HOW WAS WORK?
SAME OL' SAME OL'

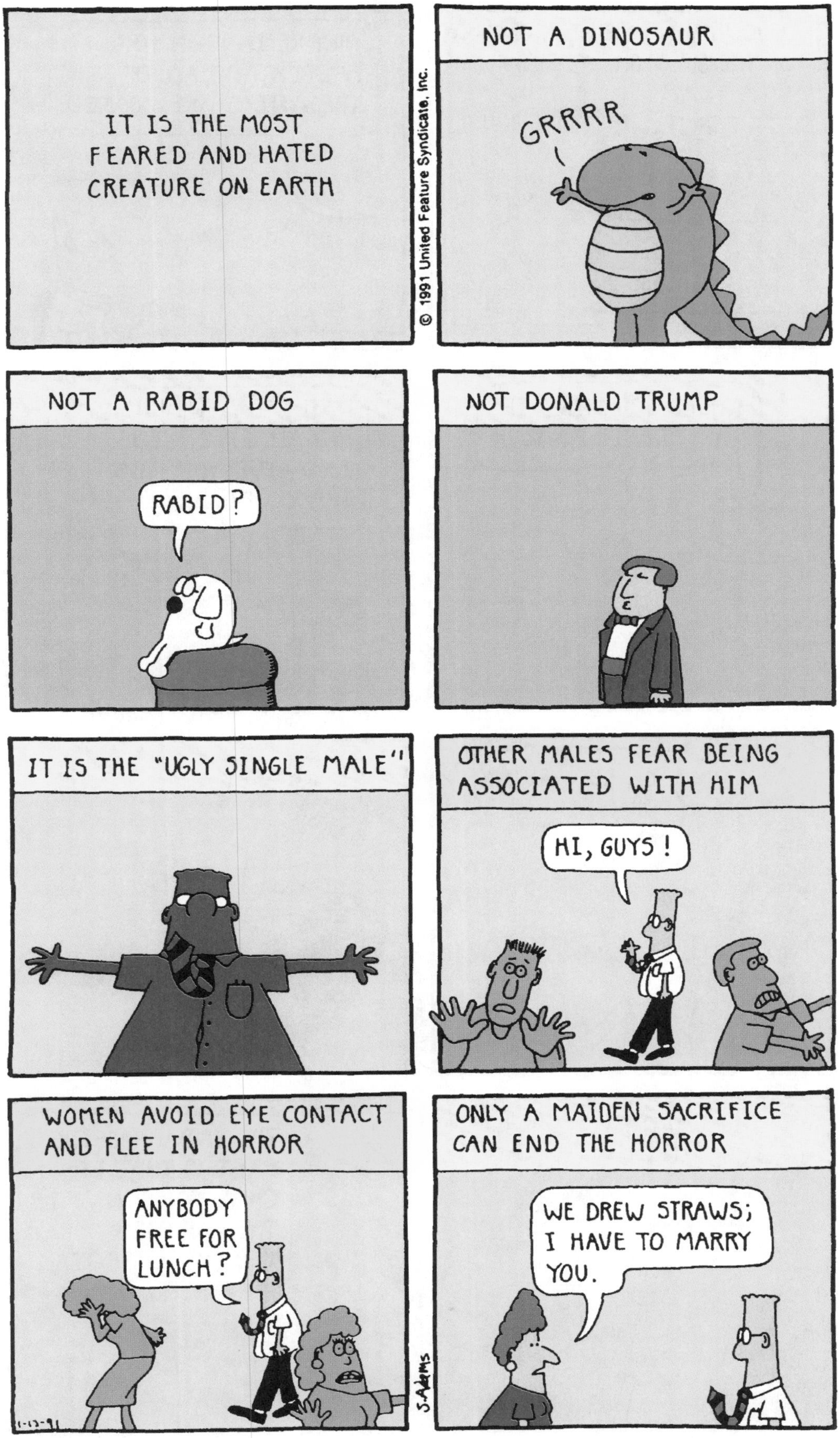
IT IS THE MOST FEARED AND HATED CREATURE ON EARTH
© 1991 United Feature Syndicate, Inc.
NOT A DINOSAUR
GRRRR
NOT A RABID DOG
RABID?
NOT DONALD TRUMP
IT IS THE "UGLY SINGLE MALE"
OTHER MALES FEAR BEING ASSOCIATED WITH HIM
HI, GUYS!
WOMEN AVOID EYE CONTACT AND FLEE IN HORROR
ANYBODY FREE FOR LUNCH?
S. Adams
ONLY A MAIDEN SACRIFICE CAN END THE HORROR
WE DREW STRAWS; I HAVE TO MARRY YOU.

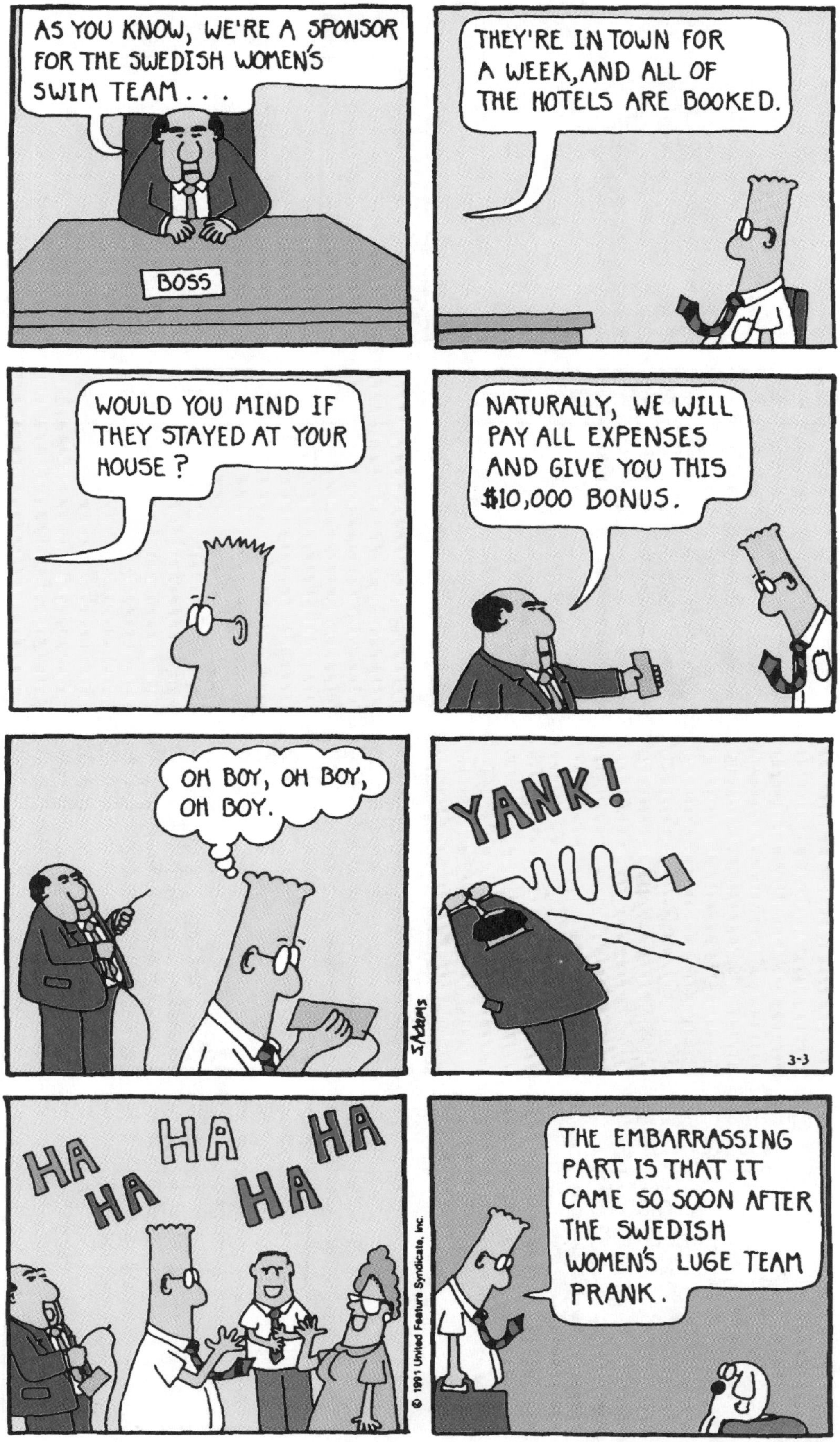
AS YOU KNOW, WE'RE A SPONSOR FOR THE SWEDISH WOMEN'S SWIM TEAM . . .
BOSS
THEY'RE IN TOWN FOR A WEEK, AND ALL OF THE HOTELS ARE BOOKED.
WOULD YOU MIND IF THEY STAYED AT YOUR HOUSE?
NATURALLY, WE WILL PAY ALL EXPENSES AND GIVE YOU THIS $10,000 BONUS.
OH BOY, OH BOY, OH BOY.
S. Adams
YANK!
3-3
HA HA HA HA HA HA
© 1991 United Feature Syndicate, Inc.
THE EMBARRASSING PART IS THAT IT CAME SO SOON AFTER THE SWEDISH WOMEN'S LUGE TEAM PRANK.

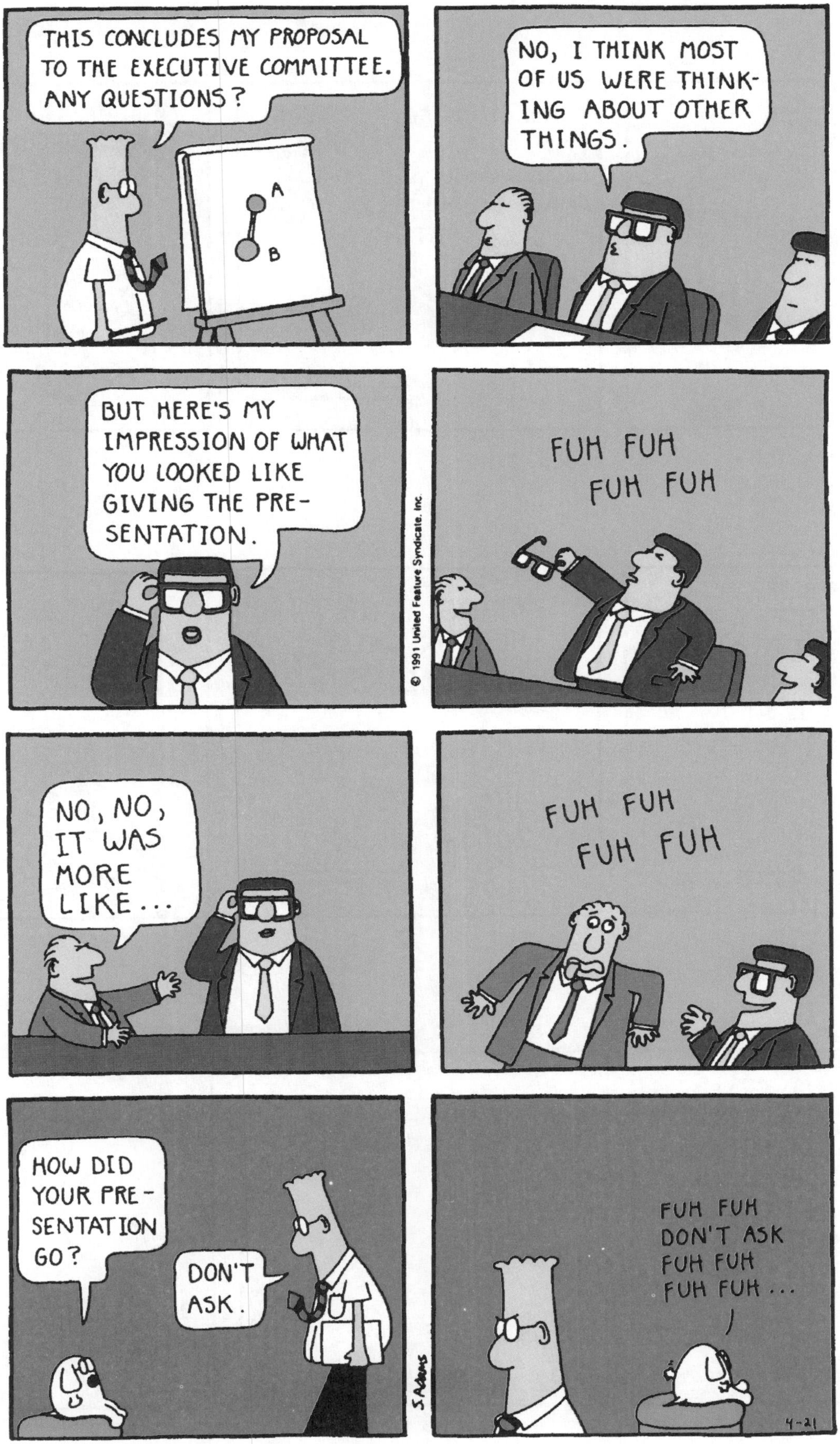
THIS CONCLUDES MY PROPOSAL TO THE EXECUTIVE COMMITTEE. ANY QUESTIONS?
A
B
NO, I THINK MOST OF US WERE THINKING ABOUT OTHER THINGS.
BUT HERE'S MY IMPRESSION OF WHAT YOU LOOKED LIKE GIVING THE PRESENTATION.
© 1991 United Feature Syndicate, Inc.
FUH FUH FUH FUH
NO, NO, IT WAS MORE LIKE...
FUH FUH FUH FUH
HOW DID YOUR PRESENTATION GO?
DON'T ASK.
S. Adams
FUH FUH DON'T ASK FUH FUH FUH FUH...
4-21

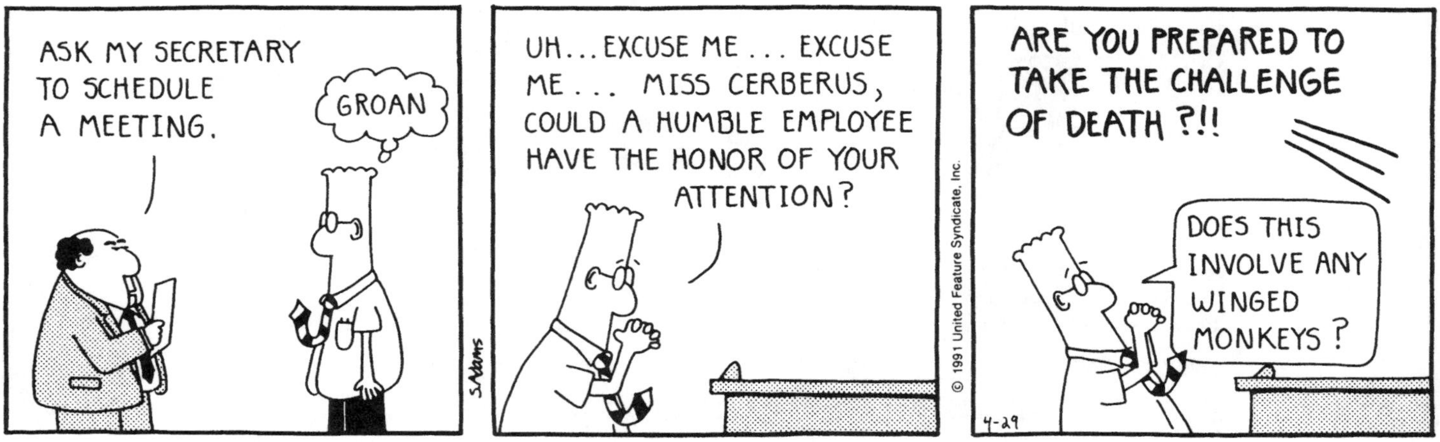
ASK MY SECRETARY TO SCHEDULE A MEETING.
GROAN
UH... EXCUSE ME ... EXCUSE ME ... MISS CERBERUS, COULD A HUMBLE EMPLOYEE HAVE THE HONOR OF YOUR ATTENTION?
© 1991 United Feature Syndicate, Inc.
ARE YOU PREPARED TO TAKE THE CHALLENGE OF DEATH ?!!
DOES THIS INVOLVE ANY WINGED MONKEYS ?

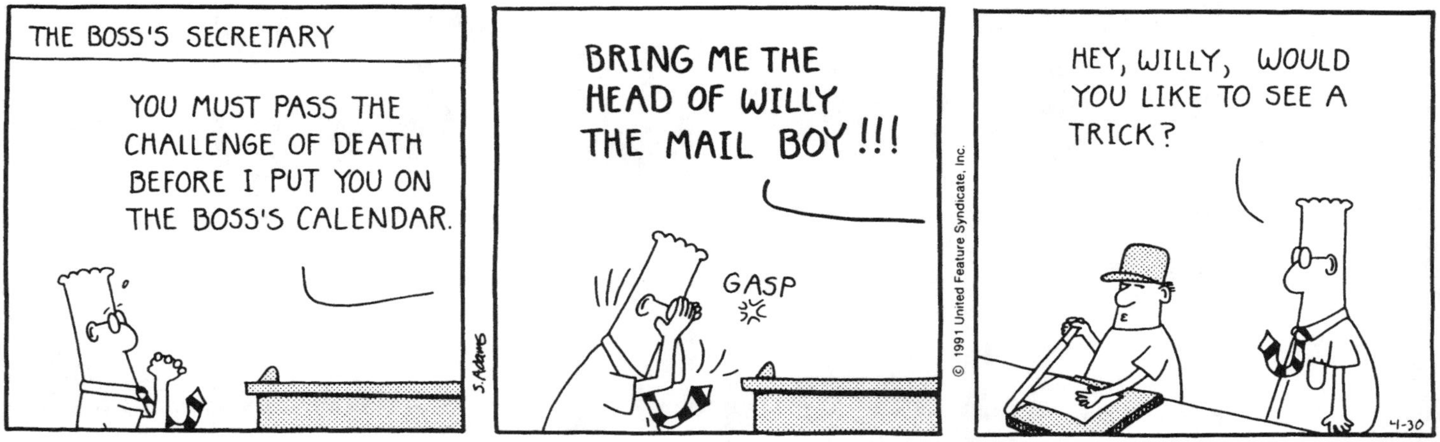
THE BOSS'S SECRETARY
YOU MUST PASS THE CHALLENGE OF DEATH BEFORE I PUT YOU ON THE BOSS'S CALENDAR.
BRING ME THE HEAD OF WILLY THE MAIL BOY !!!
GASP
© 1991 United Feature Syndicate, Inc.
HEY, WILLY, WOULD YOU LIKE TO SEE A TRICK?

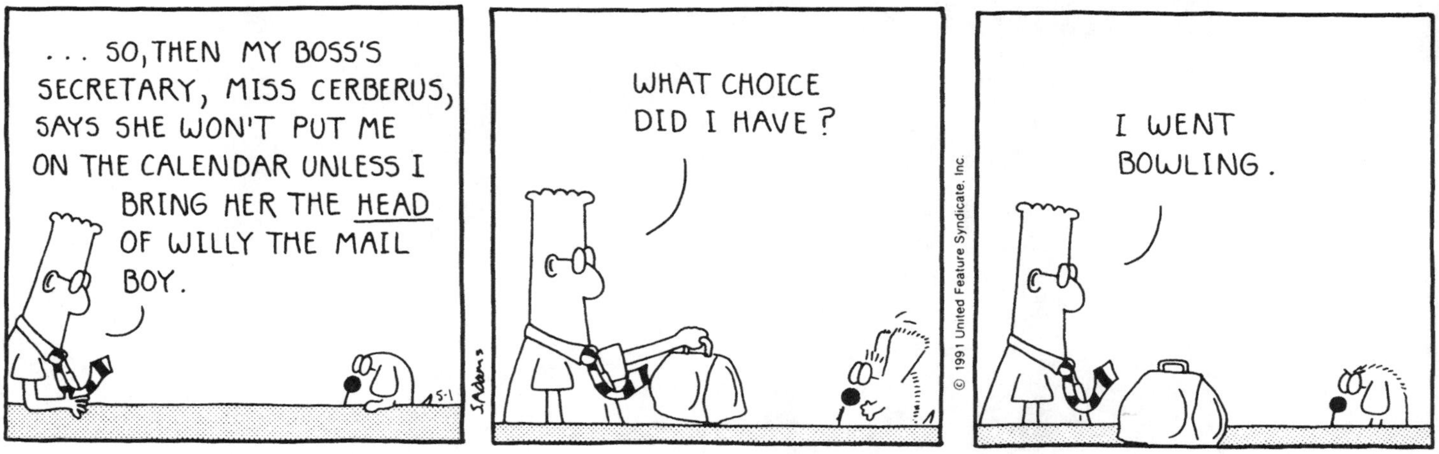
... SO, THEN MY BOSS'S SECRETARY, MISS CERBERUS, SAYS SHE WON'T PUT ME ON THE CALENDAR UNLESS I BRING HER THE HEAD OF WILLY THE MAIL BOY.
WHAT CHOICE DID I HAVE?
© 1991 United Feature Syndicate, Inc.
I WENT BOWLING.

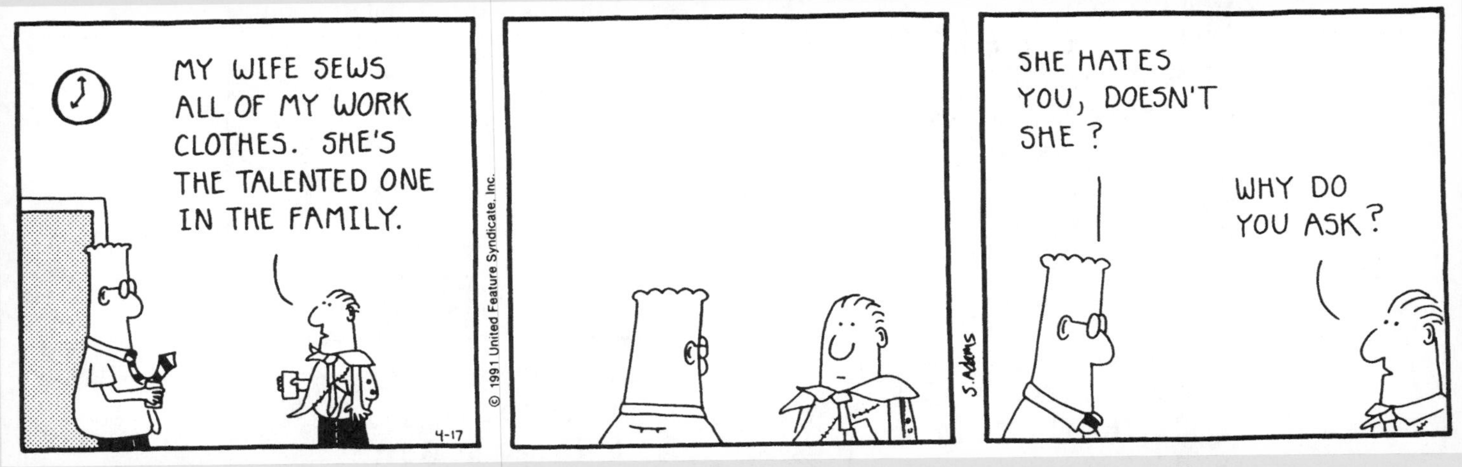
MY WIFE SEWS ALL OF MY WORK CLOTHES. SHE'S THE TALENTED ONE IN THE FAMILY.
© 1991 United Feature Syndicate, Inc.
SHE HATES YOU, DOESN'T SHE?
WHY DO YOU ASK?

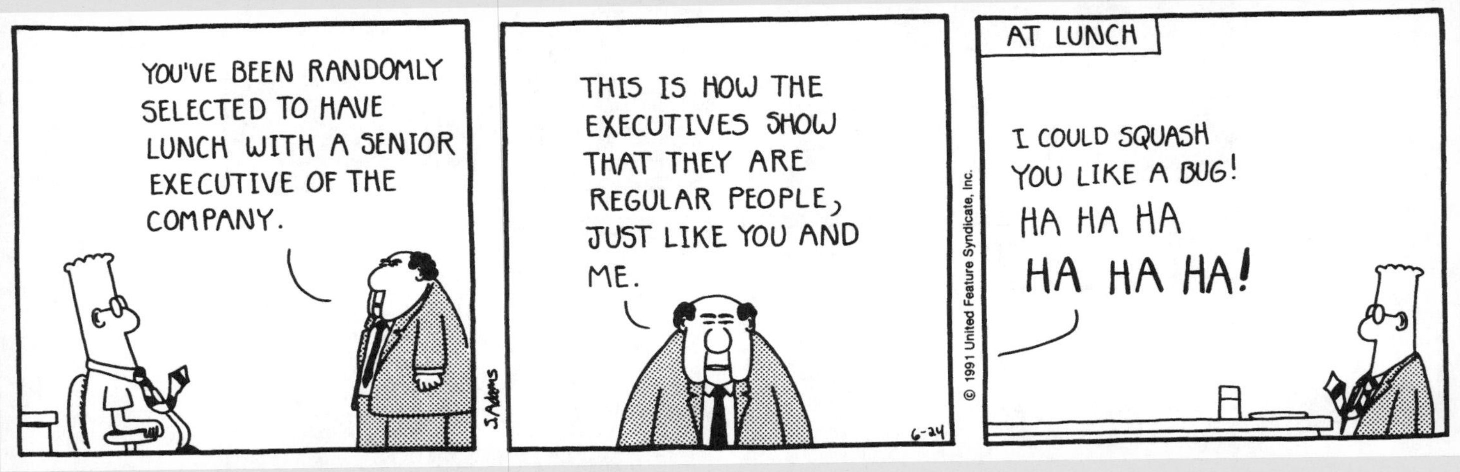
YOU'VE BEEN RANDOMLY SELECTED TO HAVE LUNCH WITH A SENIOR EXECUTIVE OF THE COMPANY.
THIS IS HOW THE EXECUTIVES SHOW THAT THEY ARE REGULAR PEOPLE, JUST LIKE YOU AND ME.
© 1991 United Feature Syndicate, Inc.
AT LUNCH
I COULD SQUASH YOU LIKE A BUG! HA HA HA HA HA HA!

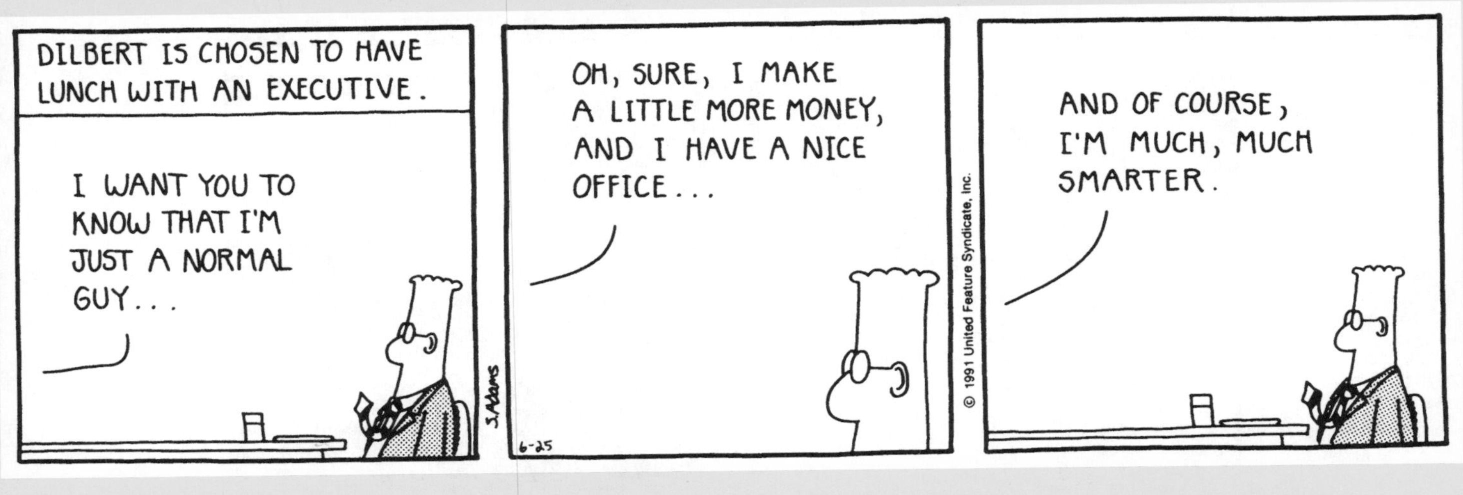
DILBERT IS CHOSEN TO HAVE LUNCH WITH AN EXECUTIVE.
I WANT YOU TO KNOW THAT I'M JUST A NORMAL GUY...
OH, SURE, I MAKE A LITTLE MORE MONEY, AND I HAVE A NICE OFFICE...
© 1991 United Feature Syndicate, Inc.
AND OF COURSE, I'M MUCH, MUCH SMARTER.

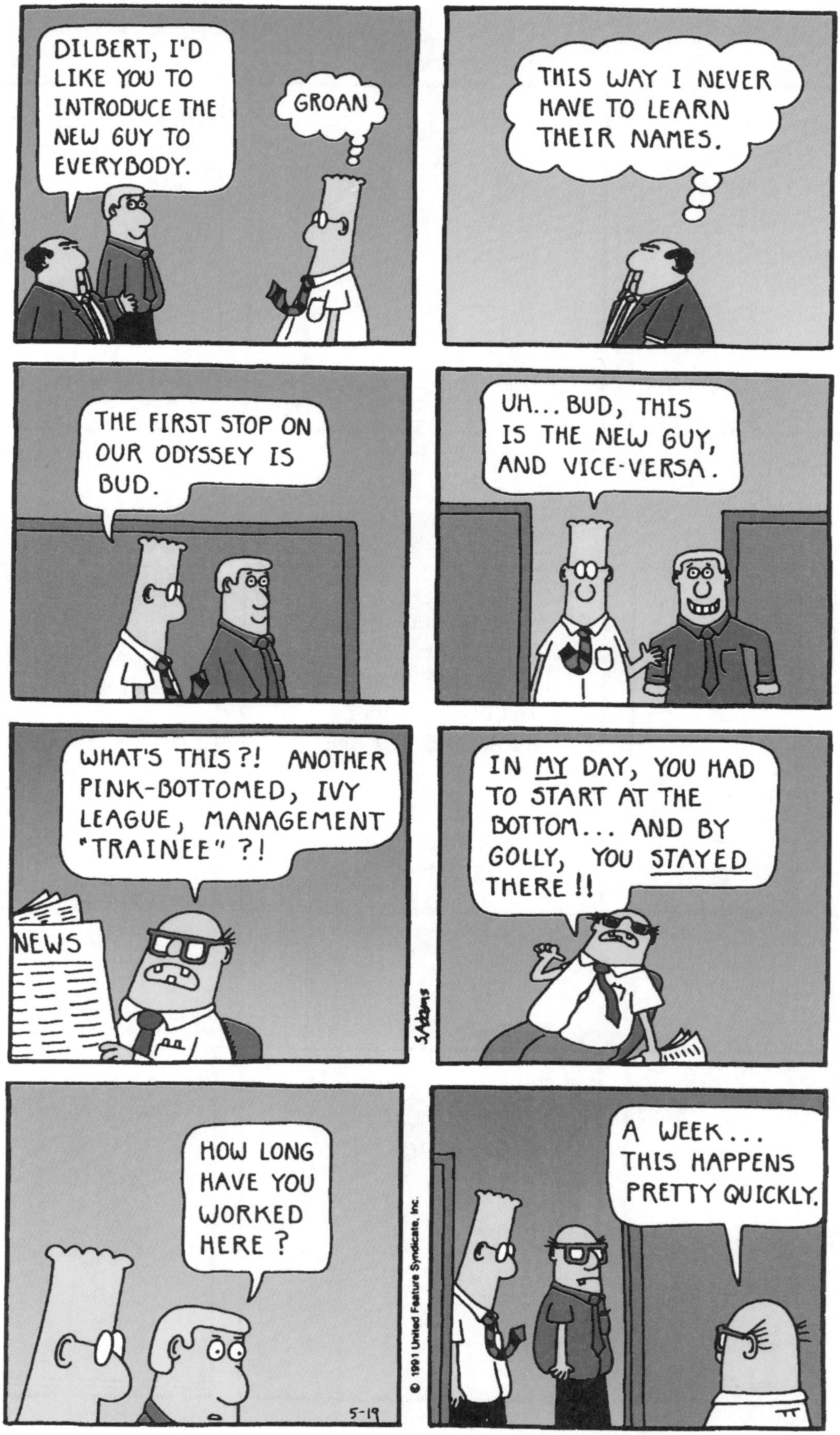
DILBERT, I'D LIKE YOU TO INTRODUCE THE NEW GUY TO EVERYBODY.
GROAN
THIS WAY I NEVER HAVE TO LEARN THEIR NAMES.
THE FIRST STOP ON OUR ODYSSEY IS BUD.
UH... BUD, THIS IS THE NEW GUY, AND VICE-VERSA.
WHAT'S THIS?! ANOTHER PINK-BOTTOMED, IVY LEAGUE, MANAGEMENT "TRAINEE"?!
NEWS
IN MY DAY, YOU HAD TO START AT THE BOTTOM... AND BY GOLLY, YOU STAYED THERE!!
S.Adams
HOW LONG HAVE YOU WORKED HERE?
5-19
© 1991 United Feature Syndicate, Inc.
A WEEK... THIS HAPPENS PRETTY QUICKLY.

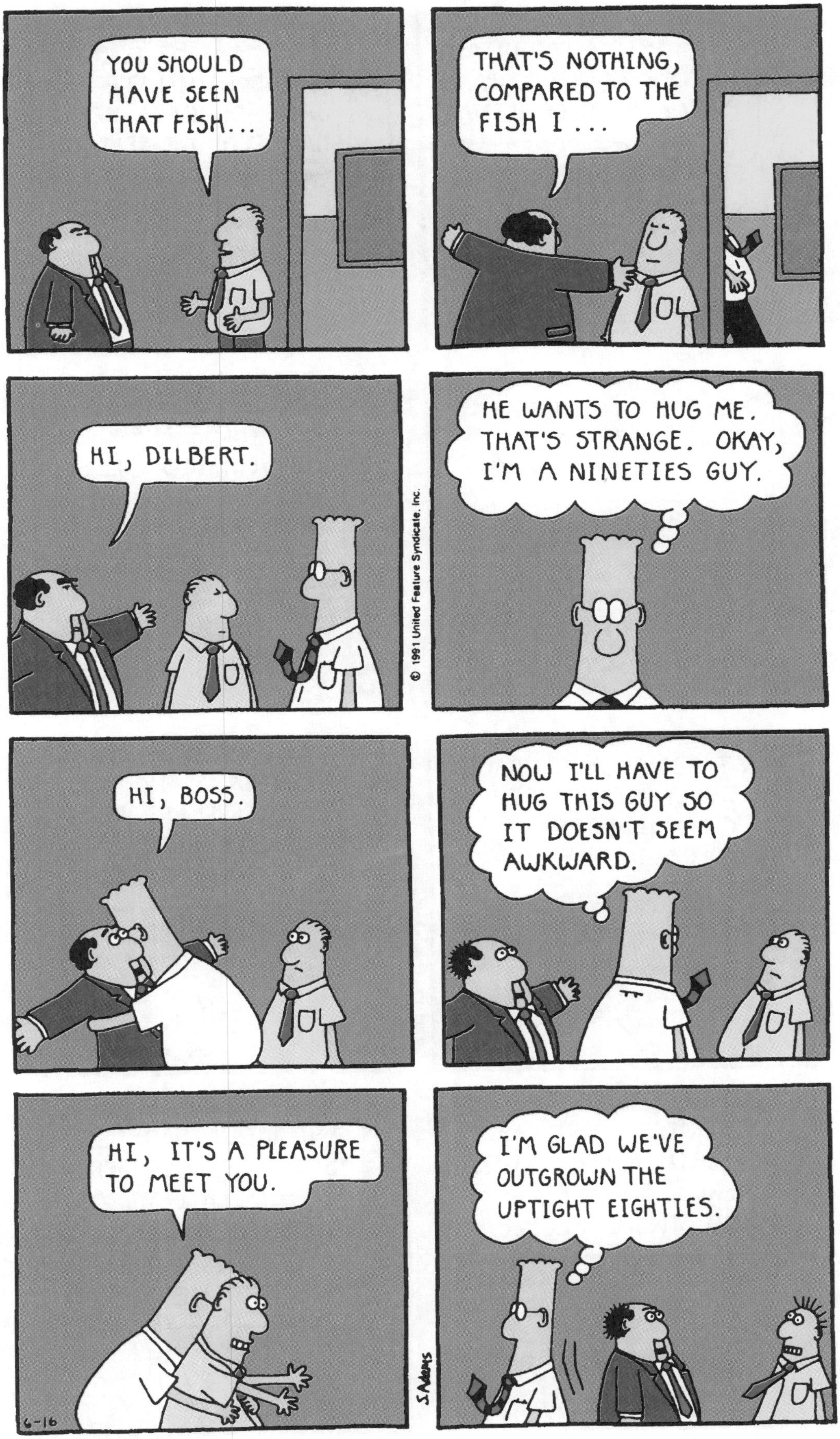
YOU SHOULD HAVE SEEN THAT FISH...
THAT'S NOTHING, COMPARED TO THE FISH I ...
HI, DILBERT.
HE WANTS TO HUG ME. THAT'S STRANGE. OKAY, I'M A NINETIES GUY.
HI, BOSS.
NOW I'LL HAVE TO HUG THIS GUY SO IT DOESN'T SEEM AWKWARD.
HI, IT'S A PLEASURE TO MEET YOU.
I'M GLAD WE'VE OUTGROWN THE UPTIGHT EIGHTIES.
6-16
S. ADAMS

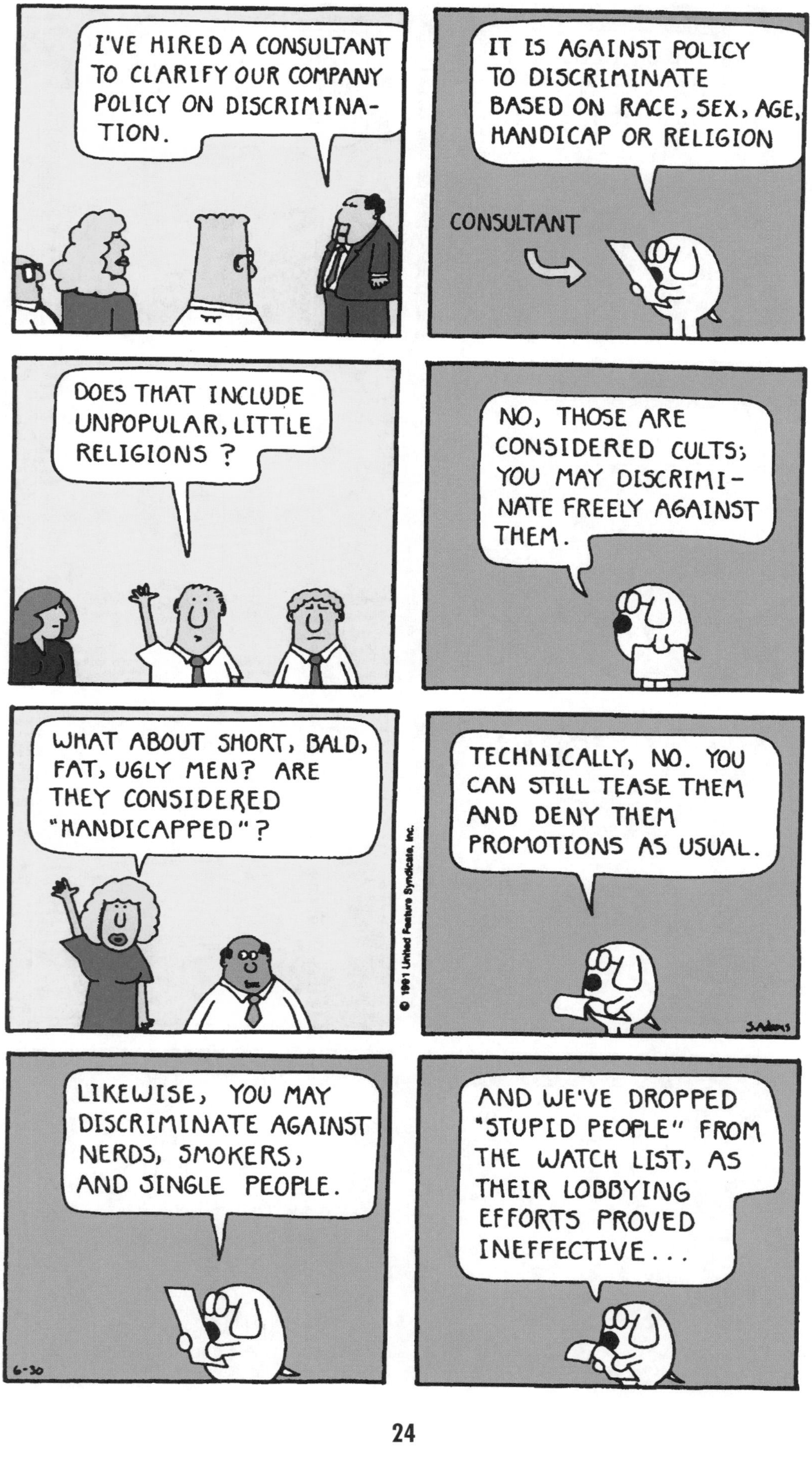
I'VE HIRED A CONSULTANT TO CLARIFY OUR COMPANY POLICY ON DISCRIMINATION.
IT IS AGAINST POLICY TO DISCRIMINATE BASED ON RACE, SEX, AGE, HANDICAP OR RELIGION
CONSULTANT
DOES THAT INCLUDE UNPOPULAR, LITTLE RELIGIONS ?
NO, THOSE ARE CONSIDERED CULTS; YOU MAY DISCRIMINATE FREELY AGAINST THEM.
WHAT ABOUT SHORT, BALD, FAT, UGLY MEN? ARE THEY CONSIDERED "HANDICAPPED"?
TECHNICALLY, NO. YOU CAN STILL TEASE THEM AND DENY THEM PROMOTIONS AS USUAL.
LIKEWISE, YOU MAY DISCRIMINATE AGAINST NERDS, SMOKERS, AND SINGLE PEOPLE.
AND WE'VE DROPPED "STUPID PEOPLE" FROM THE WATCH LIST, AS THEIR LOBBYING EFFORTS PROVED INEFFECTIVE...
6-30

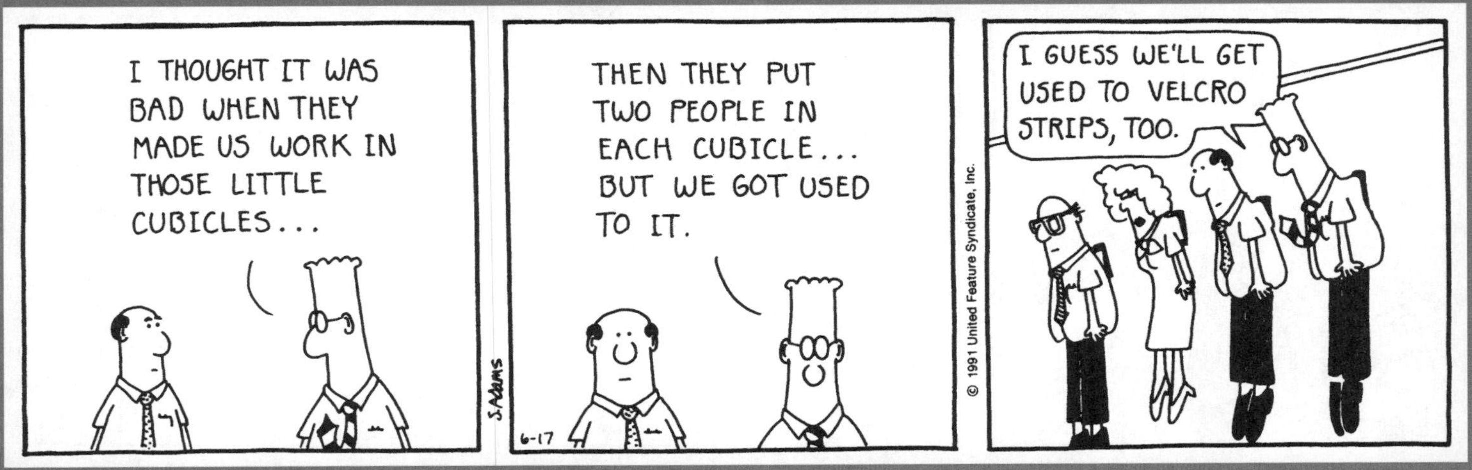
I THOUGHT IT WAS BAD WHEN THEY MADE US WORK IN THOSE LITTLE CUBICLES...
THEN THEY PUT TWO PEOPLE IN EACH CUBICLE... BUT WE GOT USED TO IT.
I GUESS WE'LL GET USED TO VELCRO STRIPS, TOO.
© 1991 United Feature Syndicate, Inc.

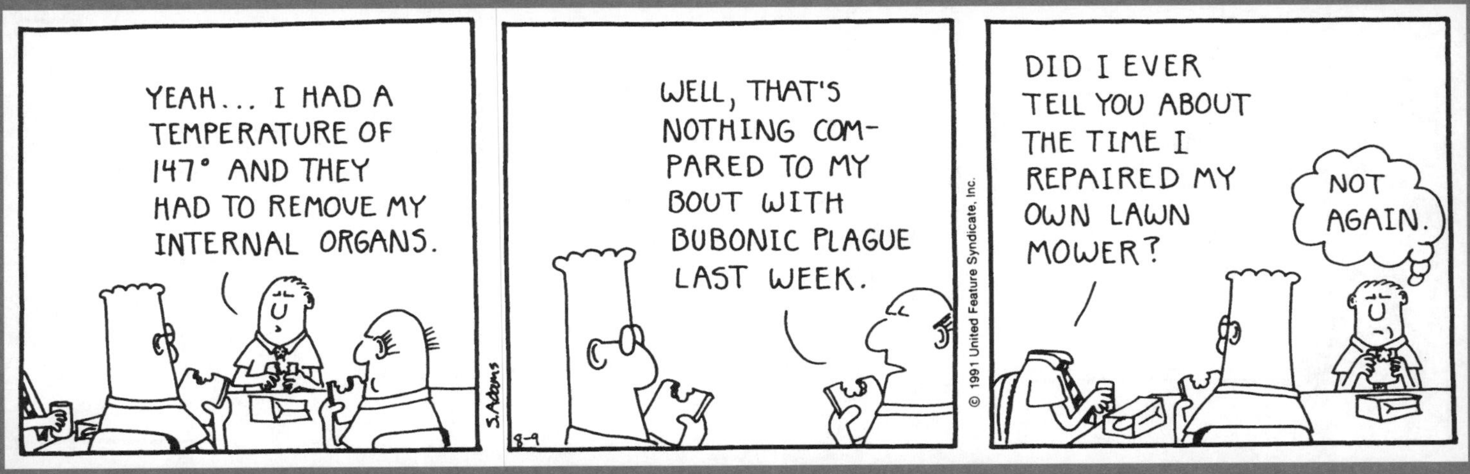
YEAH... I HAD A TEMPERATURE OF 147° AND THEY HAD TO REMOVE MY INTERNAL ORGANS.
WELL, THAT'S NOTHING COM-PARED TO MY BOUT WITH BUBONIC PLAGUE LAST WEEK.
DID I EVER TELL YOU ABOUT THE TIME I REPAIRED MY OWN LAWN MOWER?
NOT AGAIN.
© 1991 United Feature Syndicate, Inc.

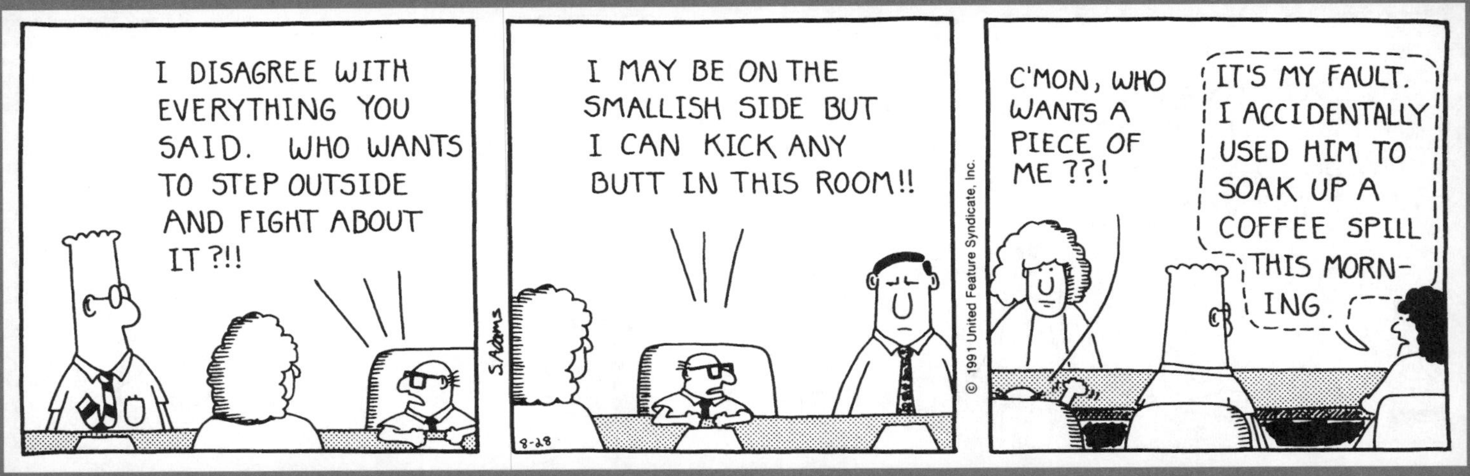
I DISAGREE WITH EVERYTHING YOU SAID. WHO WANTS TO STEP OUTSIDE AND FIGHT ABOUT IT ?!!
I MAY BE ON THE SMALLISH SIDE BUT I CAN KICK ANY BUTT IN THIS ROOM!!
C'MON, WHO WANTS A PIECE OF ME ??!
IT'S MY FAULT. I ACCIDENTALLY USED HIM TO SOAK UP A COFFEE SPILL THIS MORN-ING.
© 1991 United Feature Syndicate, Inc.

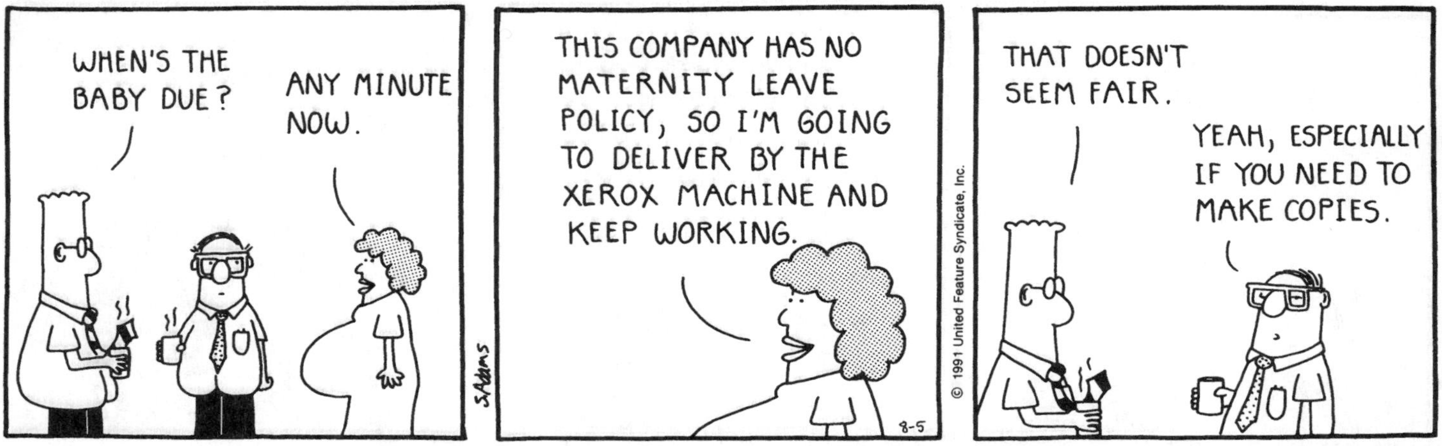
WHEN'S THE BABY DUE?
ANY MINUTE NOW.
THIS COMPANY HAS NO MATERNITY LEAVE POLICY, SO I'M GOING TO DELIVER BY THE XEROX MACHINE AND KEEP WORKING.
THAT DOESN'T SEEM FAIR.
YEAH, ESPECIALLY IF YOU NEED TO MAKE COPIES.
© 1991 United Feature Syndicate, Inc.

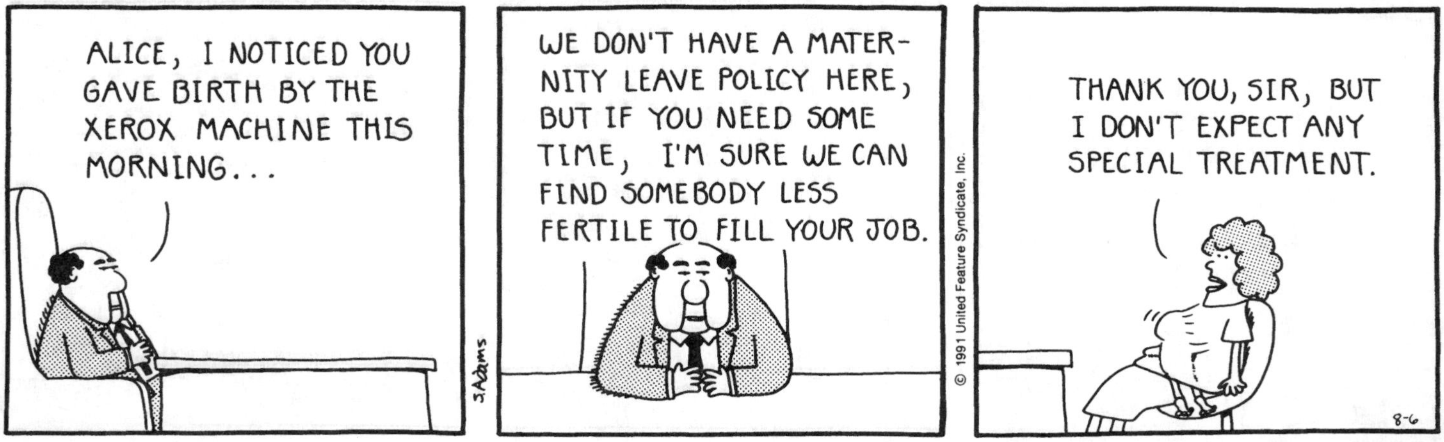
ALICE, I NOTICED YOU GAVE BIRTH BY THE XEROX MACHINE THIS MORNING...
WE DON'T HAVE A MATERNITY LEAVE POLICY HERE, BUT IF YOU NEED SOME TIME, I'M SURE WE CAN FIND SOMEBODY LESS FERTILE TO FILL YOUR JOB.
THANK YOU, SIR, BUT I DON'T EXPECT ANY SPECIAL TREATMENT.
© 1991 United Feature Syndicate, Inc.

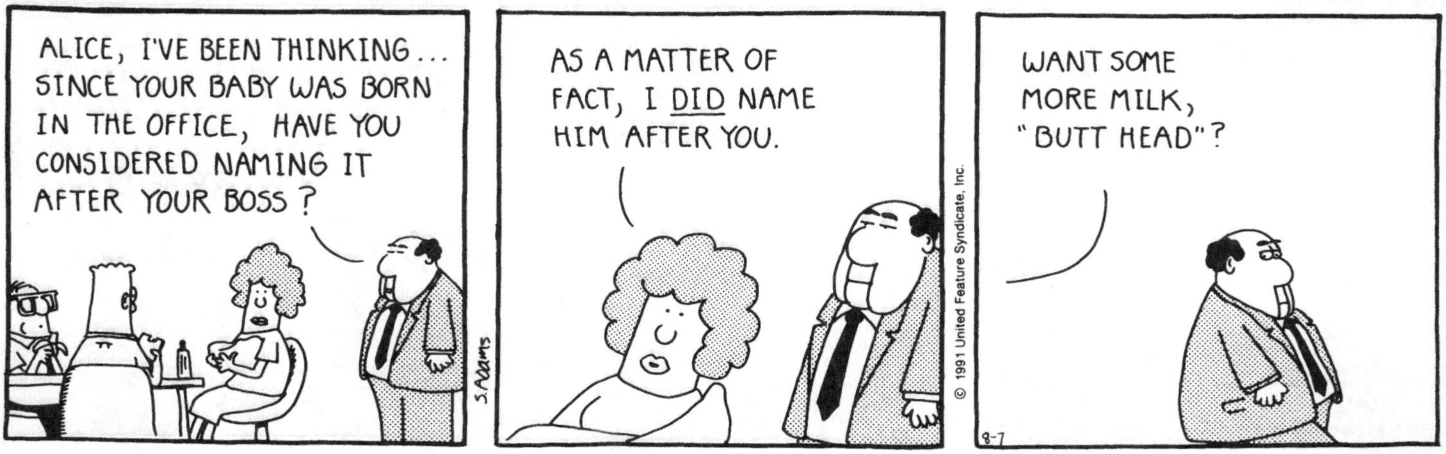
ALICE, I'VE BEEN THINKING... SINCE YOUR BABY WAS BORN IN THE OFFICE, HAVE YOU CONSIDERED NAMING IT AFTER YOUR BOSS?
AS A MATTER OF FACT, I DID NAME HIM AFTER YOU.
WANT SOME MORE MILK, "BUTT HEAD"?
© 1991 United Feature Syndicate, Inc.

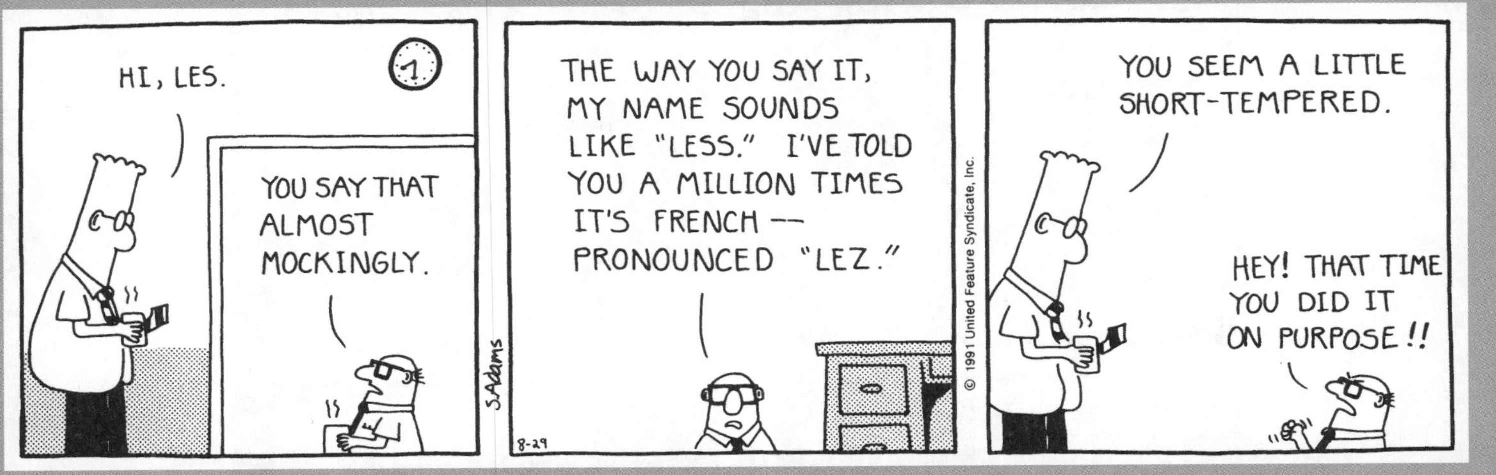
HI, LES.
YOU SAY THAT ALMOST MOCKINGLY.
THE WAY YOU SAY IT, MY NAME SOUNDS LIKE "LESS." I'VE TOLD YOU A MILLION TIMES IT'S FRENCH -- PRONOUNCED "LEZ."
YOU SEEM A LITTLE SHORT-TEMPERED.
HEY! THAT TIME YOU DID IT ON PURPOSE!!
© 1991 United Feature Syndicate, Inc.

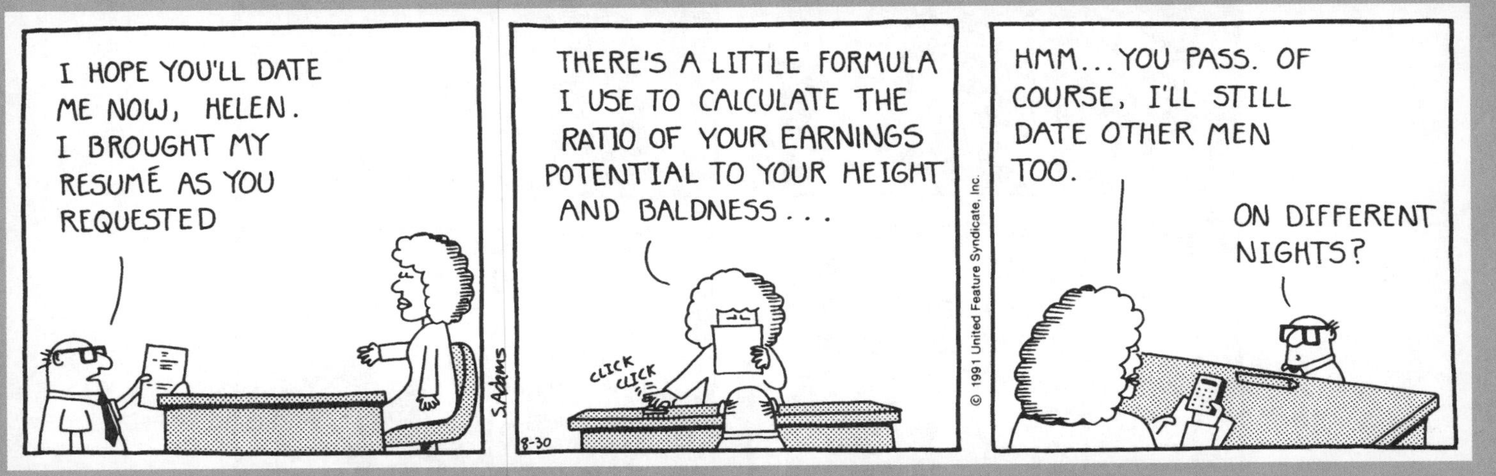
I HOPE YOU'LL DATE ME NOW, HELEN. I BROUGHT MY RESUMÉ AS YOU REQUESTED
THERE'S A LITTLE FORMULA I USE TO CALCULATE THE RATIO OF YOUR EARNINGS POTENTIAL TO YOUR HEIGHT AND BALDNESS . . .
CLICK CLICK
HMM... YOU PASS. OF COURSE, I'LL STILL DATE OTHER MEN TOO.
ON DIFFERENT NIGHTS?
© 1991 United Feature Syndicate, Inc.

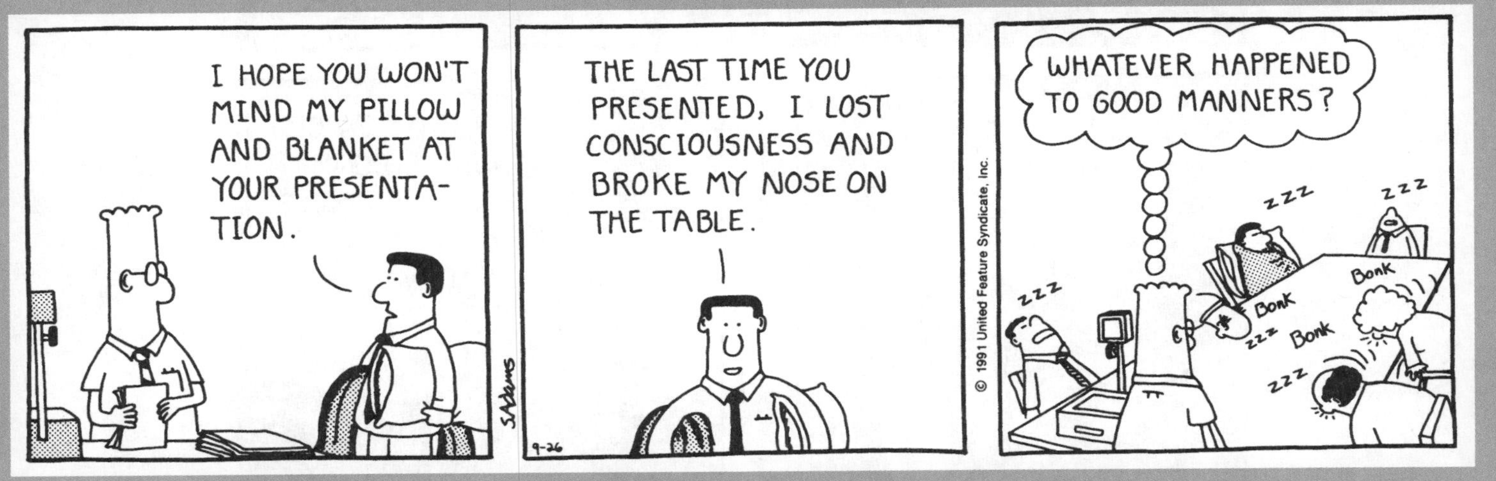
I HOPE YOU WON'T MIND MY PILLOW AND BLANKET AT YOUR PRESENTATION.
THE LAST TIME YOU PRESENTED, I LOST CONSCIOUSNESS AND BROKE MY NOSE ON THE TABLE.
WHATEVER HAPPENED TO GOOD MANNERS?
ZZZ
Bonk
© 1991 United Feature Syndicate, Inc.

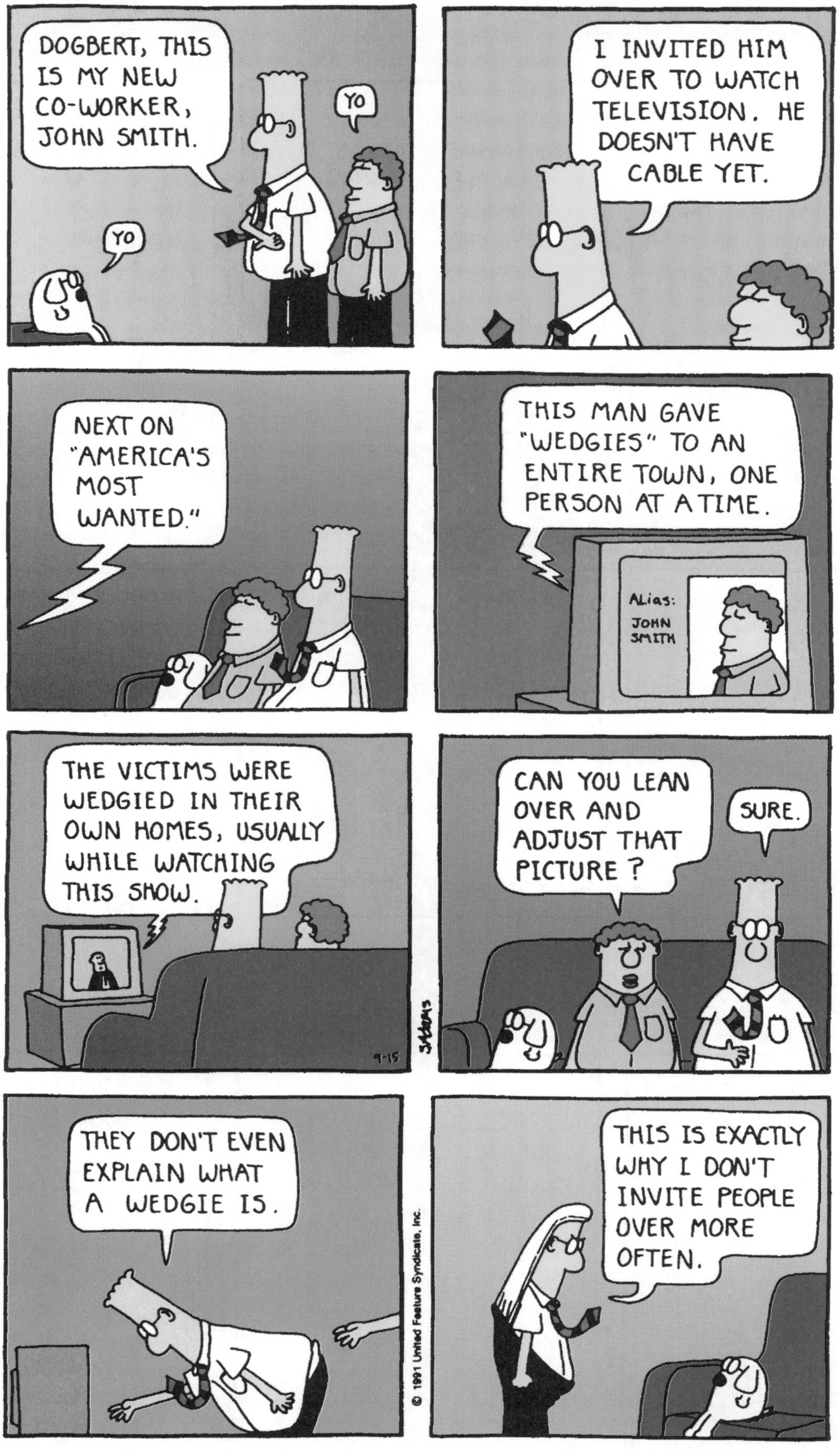
DOGBERT, THIS IS MY NEW CO-WORKER, JOHN SMITH.
YO
YO
I INVITED HIM OVER TO WATCH TELEVISION. HE DOESN'T HAVE CABLE YET.
NEXT ON "AMERICA'S MOST WANTED."
THIS MAN GAVE "WEDGIES" TO AN ENTIRE TOWN, ONE PERSON AT A TIME.
ALias: JOHN SMITH
THE VICTIMS WERE WEDGIED IN THEIR OWN HOMES, USUALLY WHILE WATCHING THIS SHOW.
CAN YOU LEAN OVER AND ADJUST THAT PICTURE?
SURE.
9-15
THEY DON'T EVEN EXPLAIN WHAT A WEDGIE IS.
THIS IS EXACTLY WHY I DON'T INVITE PEOPLE OVER MORE OFTEN.
© 1991 United Feature Syndicate, Inc.

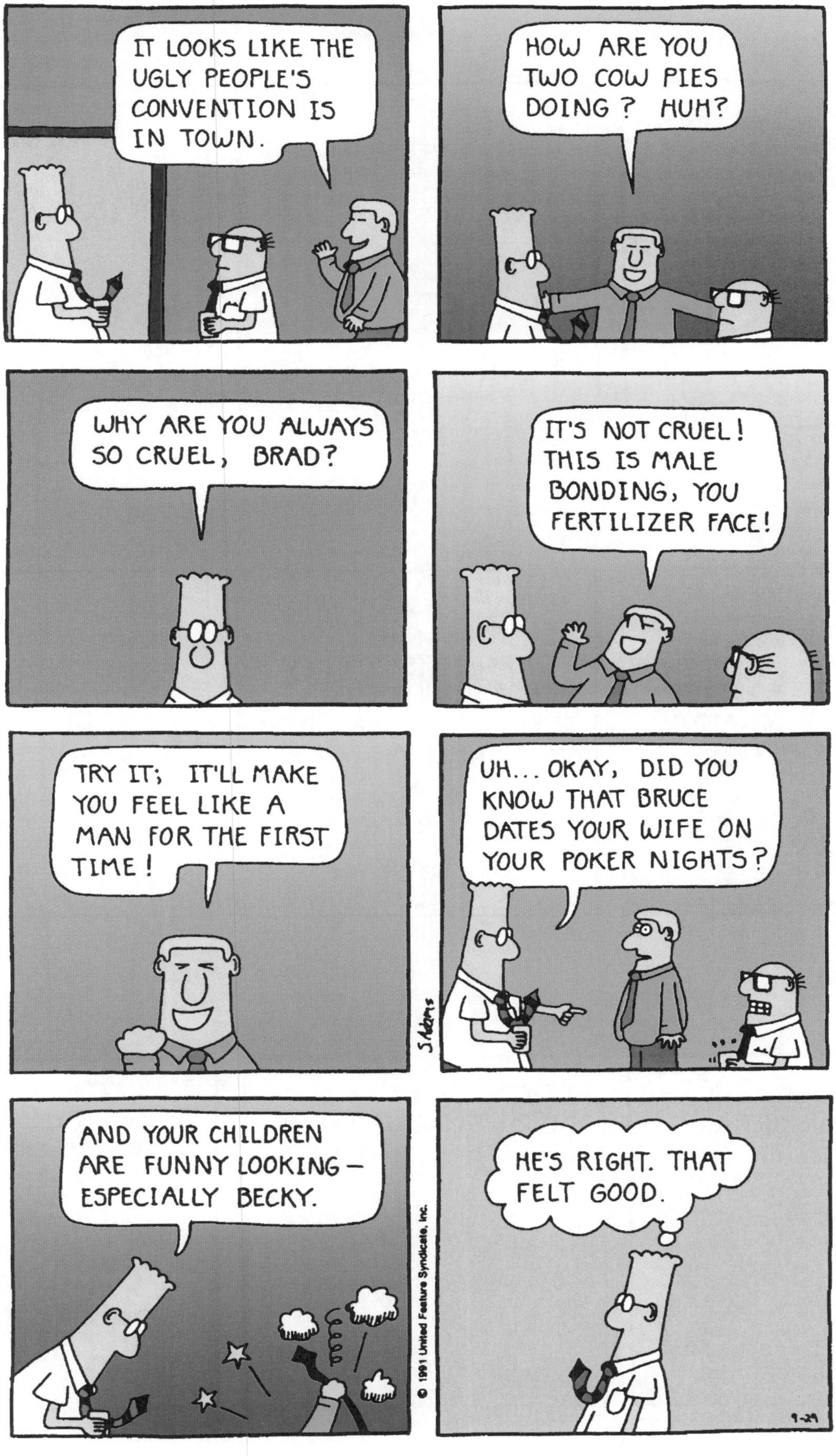
IT LOOKS LIKE THE UGLY PEOPLE'S CONVENTION IS IN TOWN.
HOW ARE YOU TWO COW PIES DOING? HUH?
WHY ARE YOU ALWAYS SO CRUEL, BRAD?
IT'S NOT CRUEL! THIS IS MALE BONDING, YOU FERTILIZER FACE!
TRY IT; IT'LL MAKE YOU FEEL LIKE A MAN FOR THE FIRST TIME!
UH... OKAY, DID YOU KNOW THAT BRUCE DATES YOUR WIFE ON YOUR POKER NIGHTS?
S. Adams
AND YOUR CHILDREN ARE FUNNY LOOKING — ESPECIALLY BECKY.
© 1991 United Feature Syndicate, Inc.
HE'S RIGHT. THAT FELT GOOD.
9-29

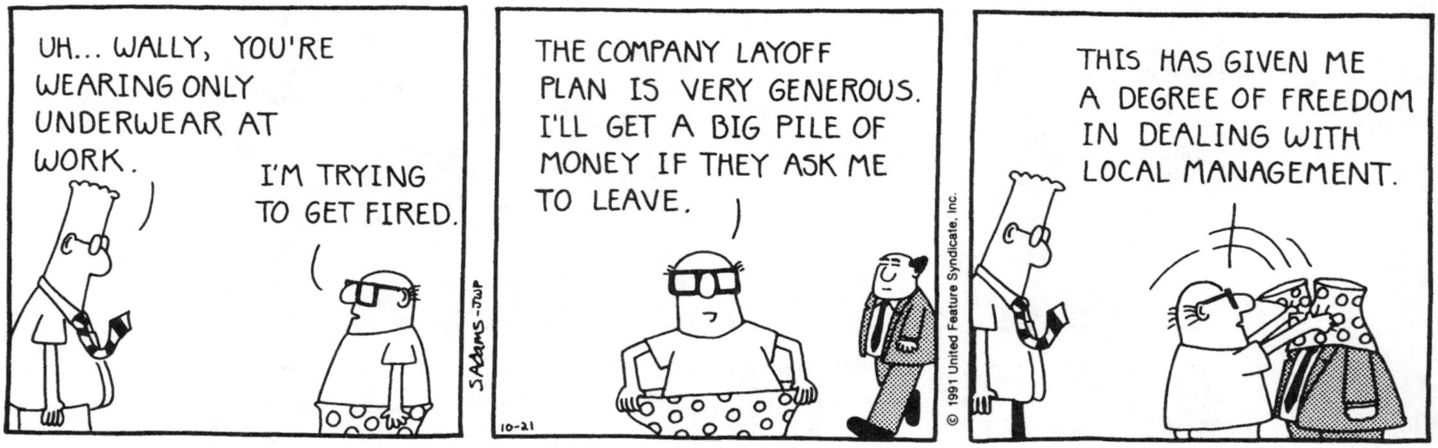
UH... WALLY, YOU'RE WEARING ONLY UNDERWEAR AT WORK.
I'M TRYING TO GET FIRED.
THE COMPANY LAYOFF PLAN IS VERY GENEROUS. I'LL GET A BIG PILE OF MONEY IF THEY ASK ME TO LEAVE.
THIS HAS GIVEN ME A DEGREE OF FREEDOM IN DEALING WITH LOCAL MANAGEMENT.
© 1991 United Feature Syndicate, Inc.

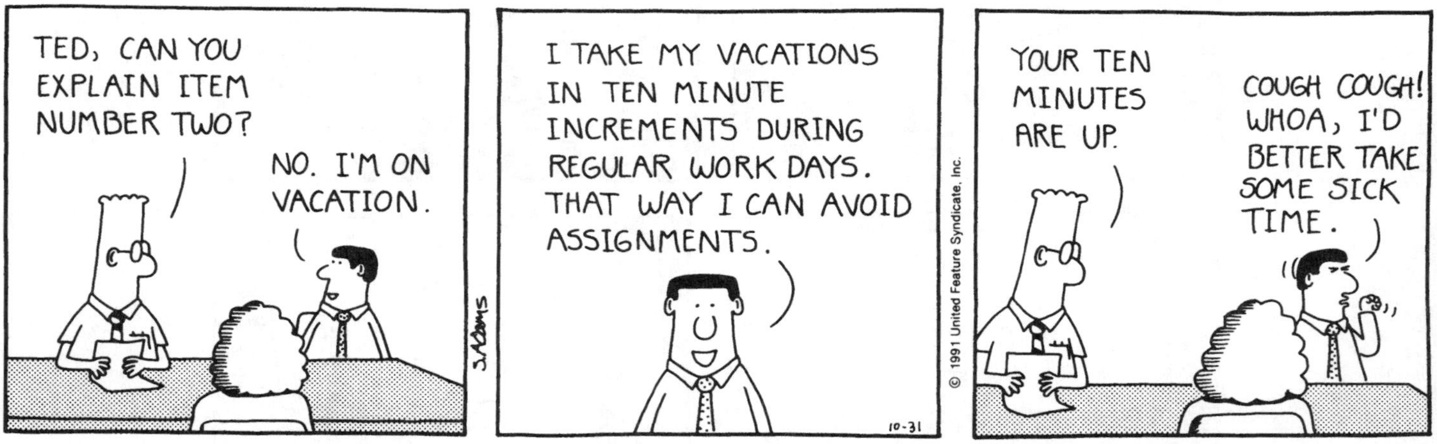
TED, CAN YOU EXPLAIN ITEM NUMBER TWO?
NO. I'M ON VACATION.
I TAKE MY VACATIONS IN TEN MINUTE INCREMENTS DURING REGULAR WORK DAYS. THAT WAY I CAN AVOID ASSIGNMENTS.
YOUR TEN MINUTES ARE UP.
COUGH COUGH! WHOA, I'D BETTER TAKE SOME SICK TIME.
© 1991 United Feature Syndicate, Inc.

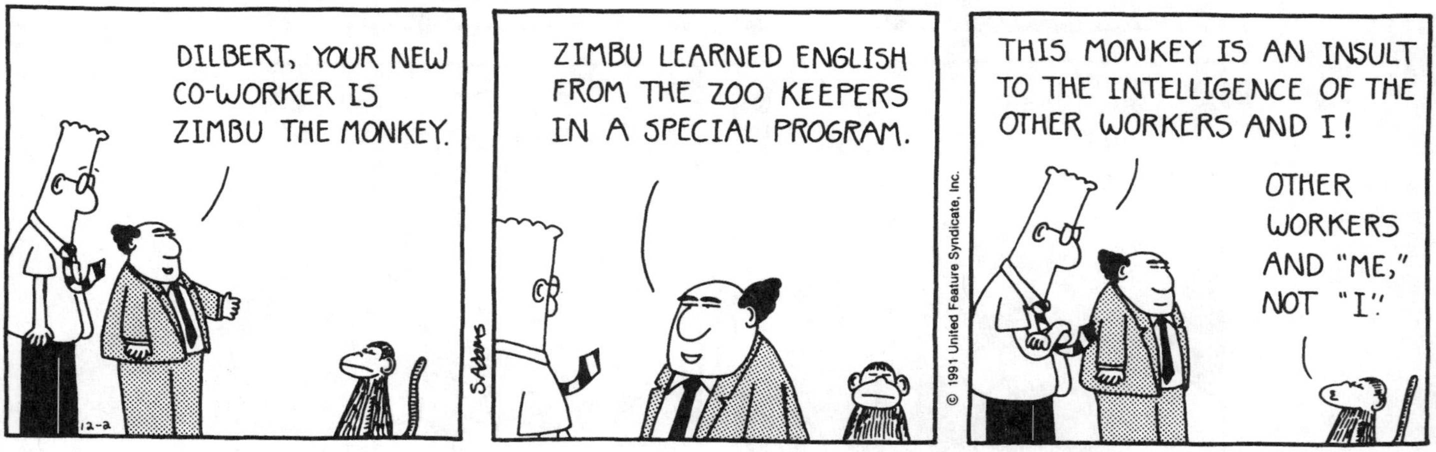
DILBERT, YOUR NEW CO-WORKER IS ZIMBU THE MONKEY.
ZIMBU LEARNED ENGLISH FROM THE ZOO KEEPERS IN A SPECIAL PROGRAM.
THIS MONKEY IS AN INSULT TO THE INTELLIGENCE OF THE OTHER WORKERS AND I!
OTHER WORKERS AND "ME," NOT "I".
© 1991 United Feature Syndicate, Inc.

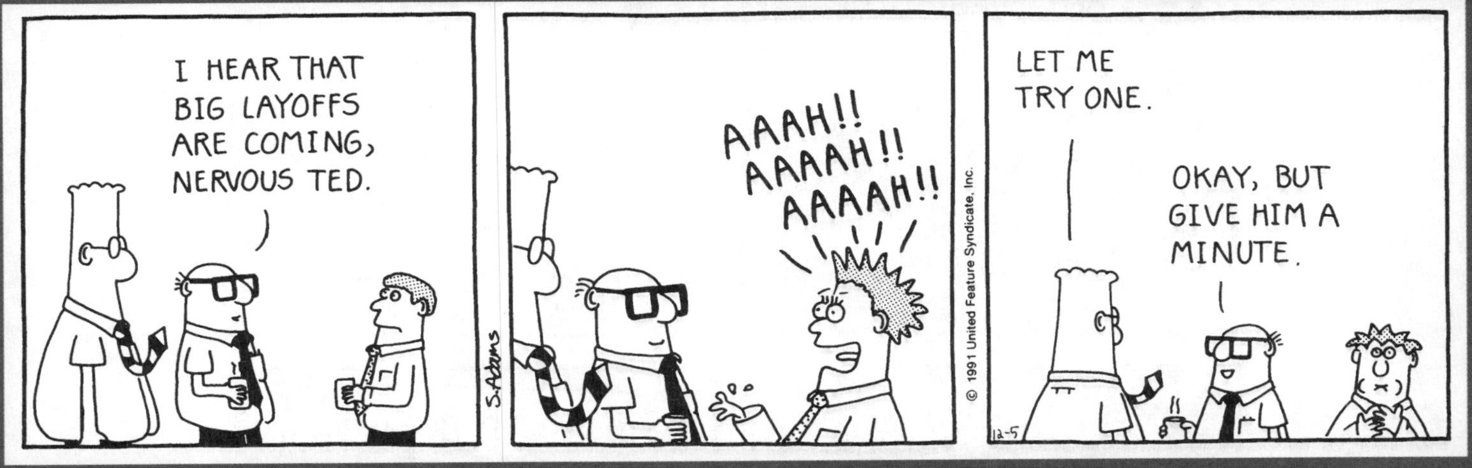
I HEAR THAT BIG LAYOFFS ARE COMING, NERVOUS TED.
AAAH!! AAAAH!! AAAAH!!
LET ME TRY ONE.
OKAY, BUT GIVE HIM A MINUTE.
© 1991 United Feature Syndicate, Inc.

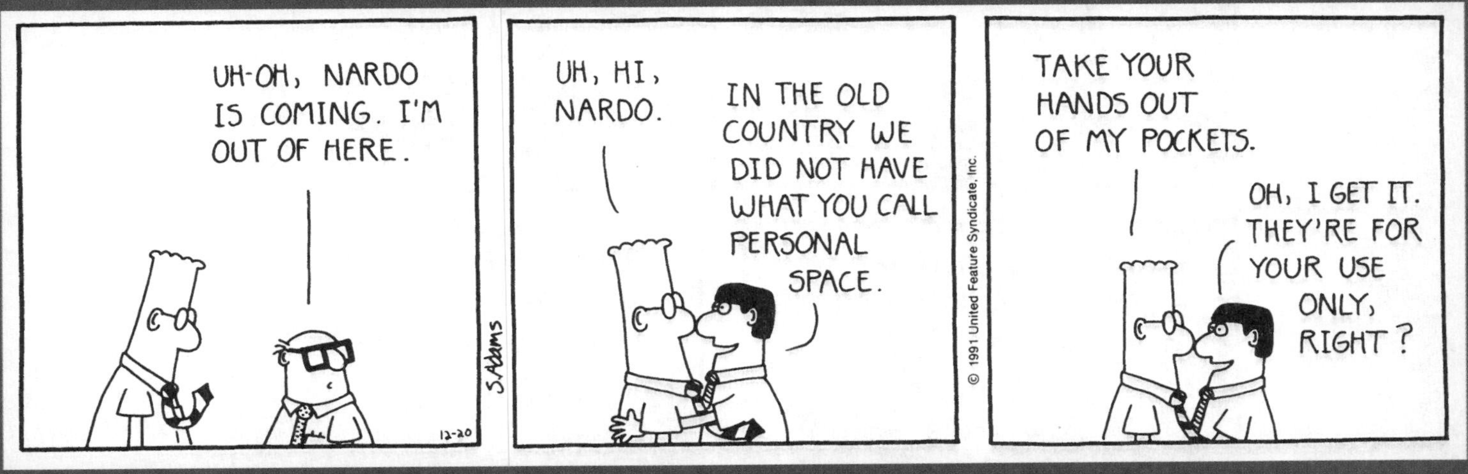
UH-OH, NARDO IS COMING. I'M OUT OF HERE.
UH, HI, NARDO.
IN THE OLD COUNTRY WE DID NOT HAVE WHAT YOU CALL PERSONAL SPACE.
TAKE YOUR HANDS OUT OF MY POCKETS.
OH, I GET IT. THEY'RE FOR YOUR USE ONLY, RIGHT?
© 1991 United Feature Syndicate, Inc.

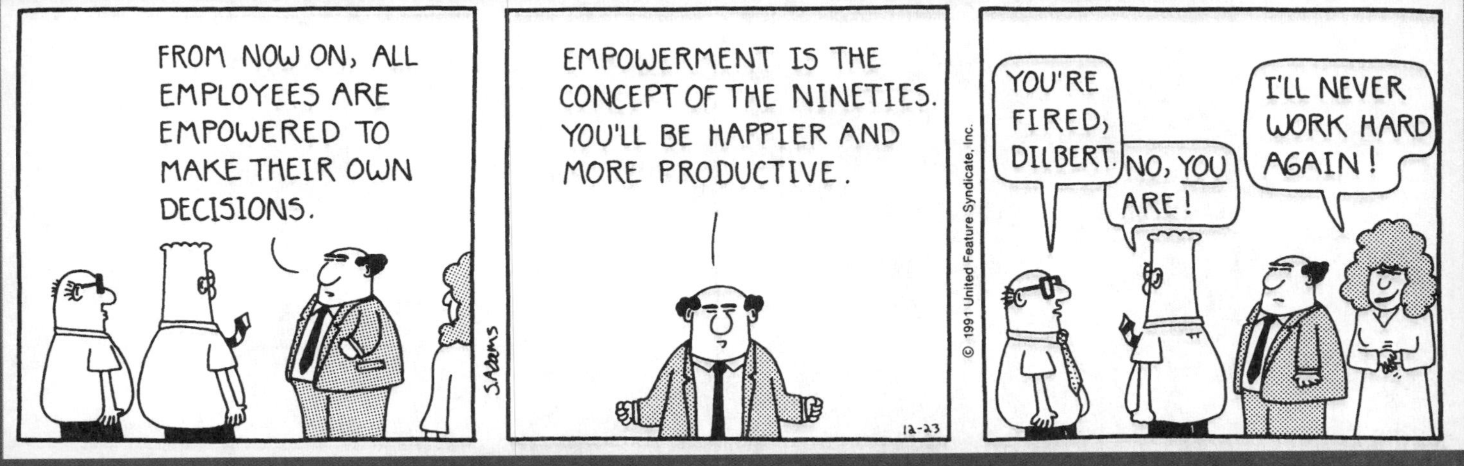
FROM NOW ON, ALL EMPLOYEES ARE EMPOWERED TO MAKE THEIR OWN DECISIONS.
EMPOWERMENT IS THE CONCEPT OF THE NINETIES. YOU'LL BE HAPPIER AND MORE PRODUCTIVE.
YOU'RE FIRED, DILBERT.
NO, YOU ARE!
I'LL NEVER WORK HARD AGAIN!
© 1991 United Feature Syndicate, Inc.

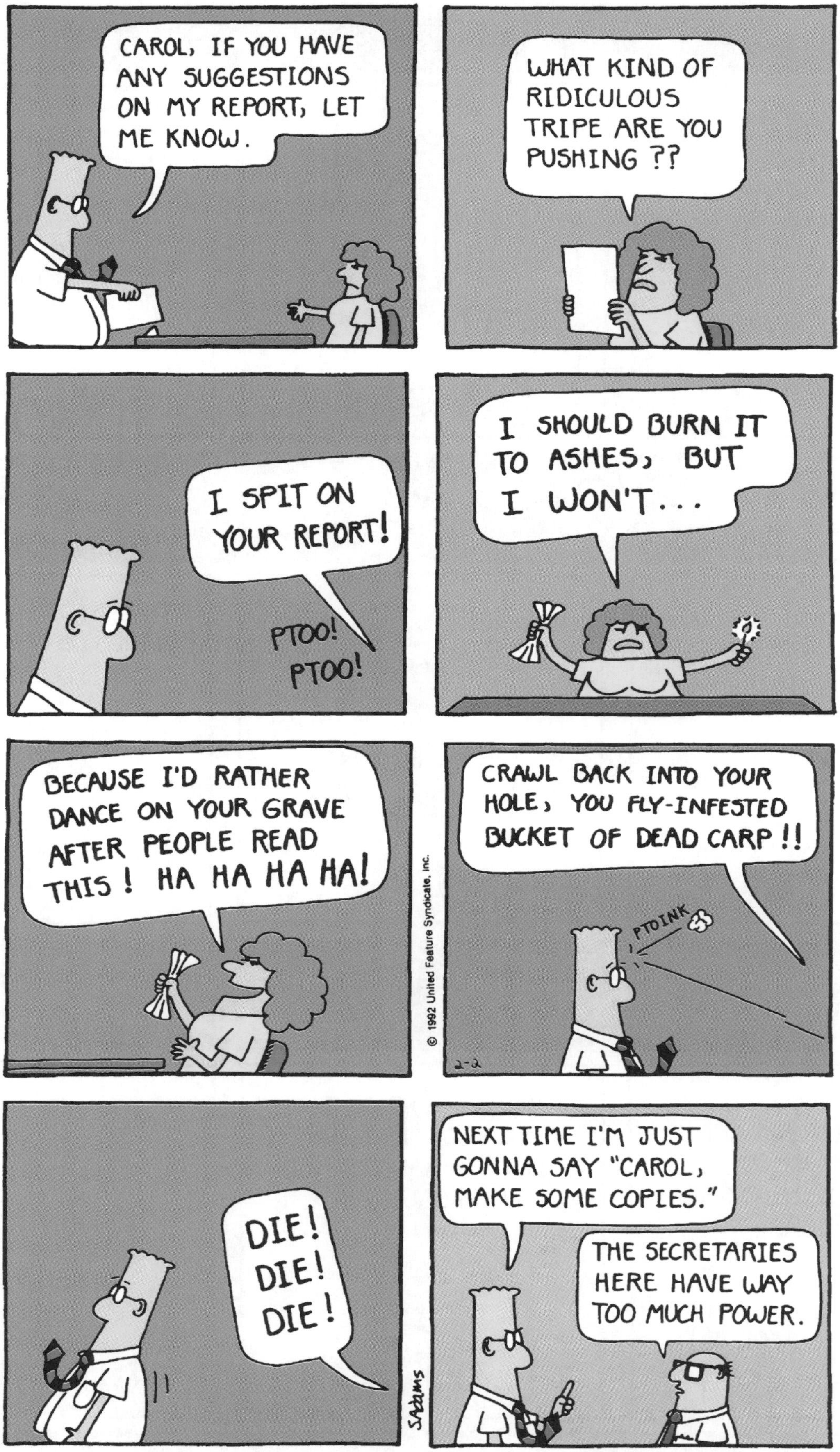
CAROL, IF YOU HAVE ANY SUGGESTIONS ON MY REPORT, LET ME KNOW.
WHAT KIND OF RIDICULOUS TRIPE ARE YOU PUSHING ??
I SPIT ON YOUR REPORT!
PTOO! PTOO!
I SHOULD BURN IT TO ASHES, BUT I WON'T...
BECAUSE I'D RATHER DANCE ON YOUR GRAVE AFTER PEOPLE READ THIS! HA HA HA HA!
CRAWL BACK INTO YOUR HOLE, YOU FLY-INFESTED BUCKET OF DEAD CARP !!
PTOINK
DIE! DIE! DIE!
NEXT TIME I'M JUST GONNA SAY "CAROL, MAKE SOME COPIES."
THE SECRETARIES HERE HAVE WAY TOO MUCH POWER.

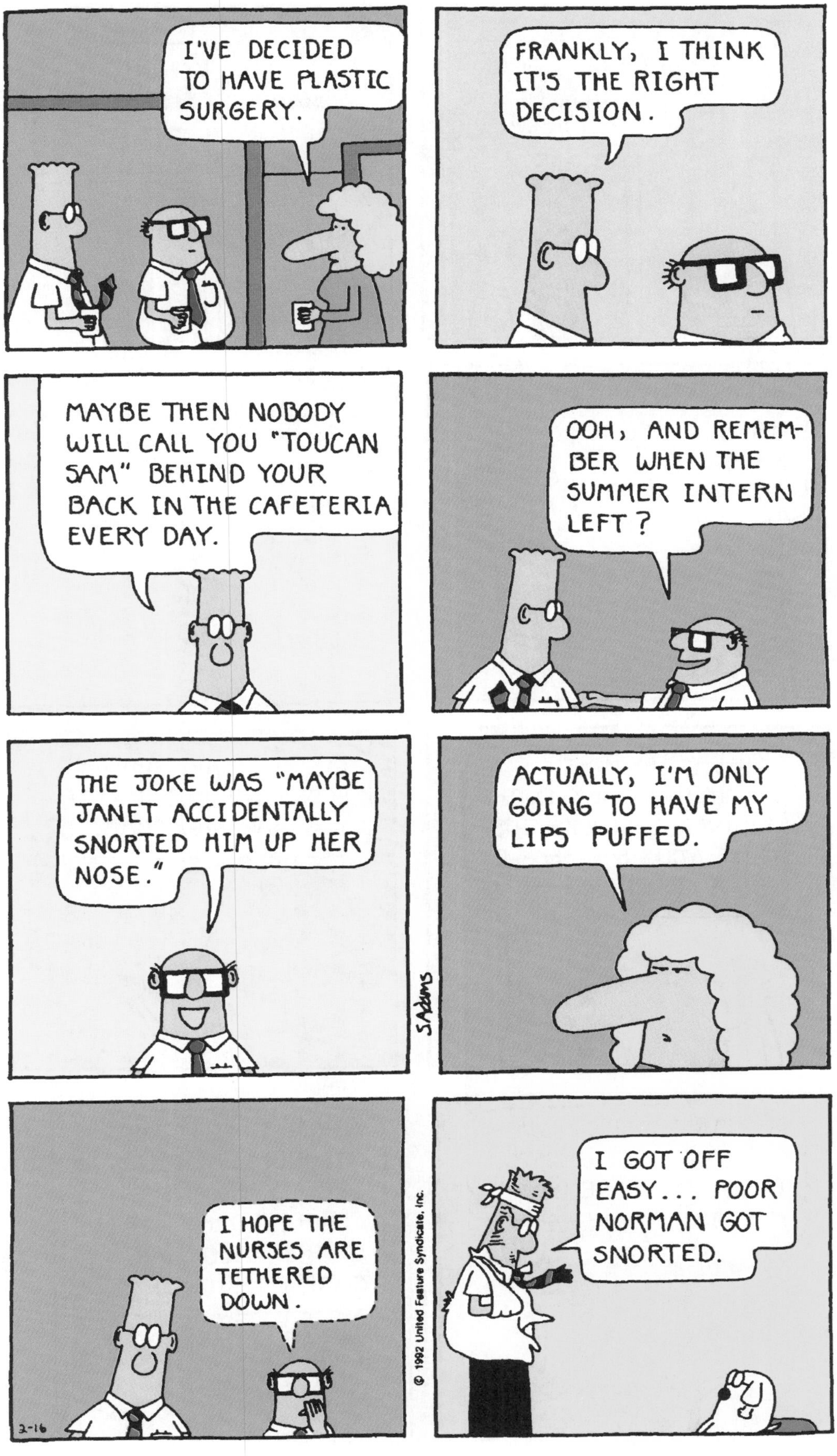
I'VE DECIDED TO HAVE PLASTIC SURGERY.
FRANKLY, I THINK IT'S THE RIGHT DECISION.
MAYBE THEN NOBODY WILL CALL YOU "TOUCAN SAM" BEHIND YOUR BACK IN THE CAFETERIA EVERY DAY.
OOH, AND REMEMBER WHEN THE SUMMER INTERN LEFT?
THE JOKE WAS "MAYBE JANET ACCIDENTALLY SNORTED HIM UP HER NOSE."
S.Adams
ACTUALLY, I'M ONLY GOING TO HAVE MY LIPS PUFFED.
2-16
I HOPE THE NURSES ARE TETHERED DOWN.
© 1992 United Feature Syndicate, Inc.
I GOT OFF EASY... POOR NORMAN GOT SNORTED.

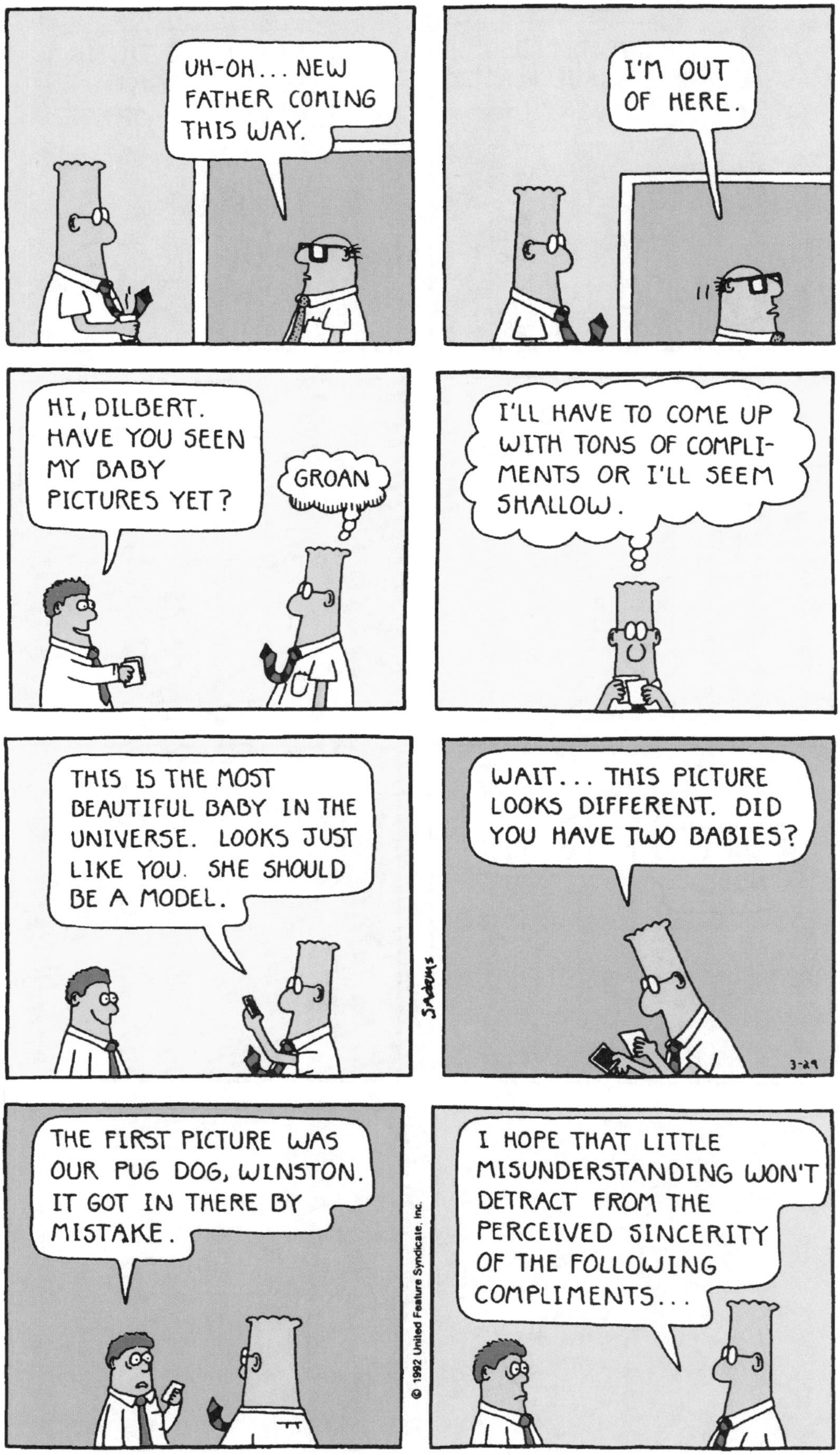
UH-OH... NEW FATHER COMING THIS WAY.
I'M OUT OF HERE.
HI, DILBERT. HAVE YOU SEEN MY BABY PICTURES YET?
GROAN
I'LL HAVE TO COME UP WITH TONS OF COMPLI-MENTS OR I'LL SEEM SHALLOW.
THIS IS THE MOST BEAUTIFUL BABY IN THE UNIVERSE. LOOKS JUST LIKE YOU. SHE SHOULD BE A MODEL.
WAIT... THIS PICTURE LOOKS DIFFERENT. DID YOU HAVE TWO BABIES?
3-29
THE FIRST PICTURE WAS OUR PUG DOG, WINSTON. IT GOT IN THERE BY MISTAKE.
I HOPE THAT LITTLE MISUNDERSTANDING WON'T DETRACT FROM THE PERCEIVED SINCERITY OF THE FOLLOWING COMPLIMENTS...
© 1992 United Feature Syndicate, Inc.

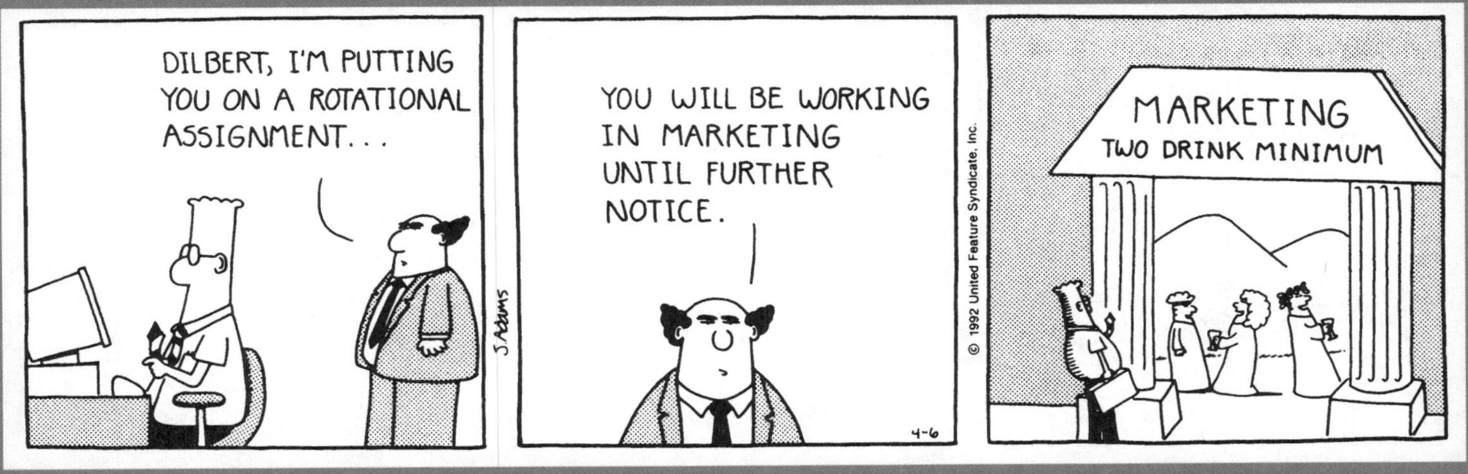
DILBERT, I'M PUTTING YOU ON A ROTATIONAL ASSIGNMENT...
S.Adams
YOU WILL BE WORKING IN MARKETING UNTIL FURTHER NOTICE.
4-6
© 1992 United Feature Syndicate, Inc.
MARKETING
TWO DRINK MINIMUM

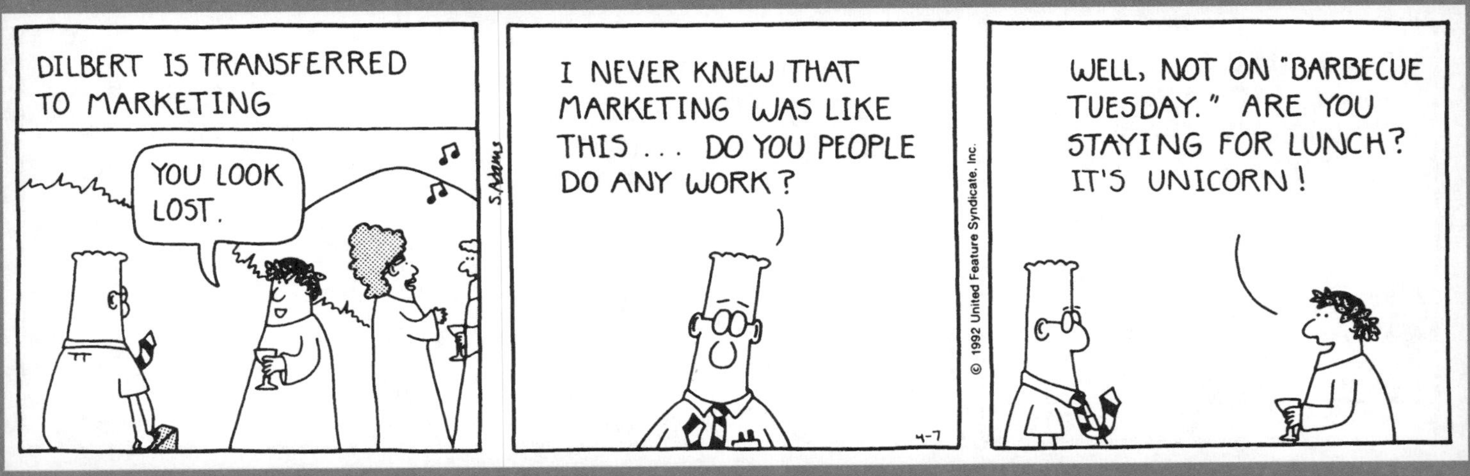
DILBERT IS TRANSFERRED TO MARKETING
YOU LOOK LOST.
S.Adams
I NEVER KNEW THAT MARKETING WAS LIKE THIS ... DO YOU PEOPLE DO ANY WORK?
4-7
© 1992 United Feature Syndicate, Inc.
WELL, NOT ON "BARBECUE TUESDAY." ARE YOU STAYING FOR LUNCH? IT'S UNICORN!

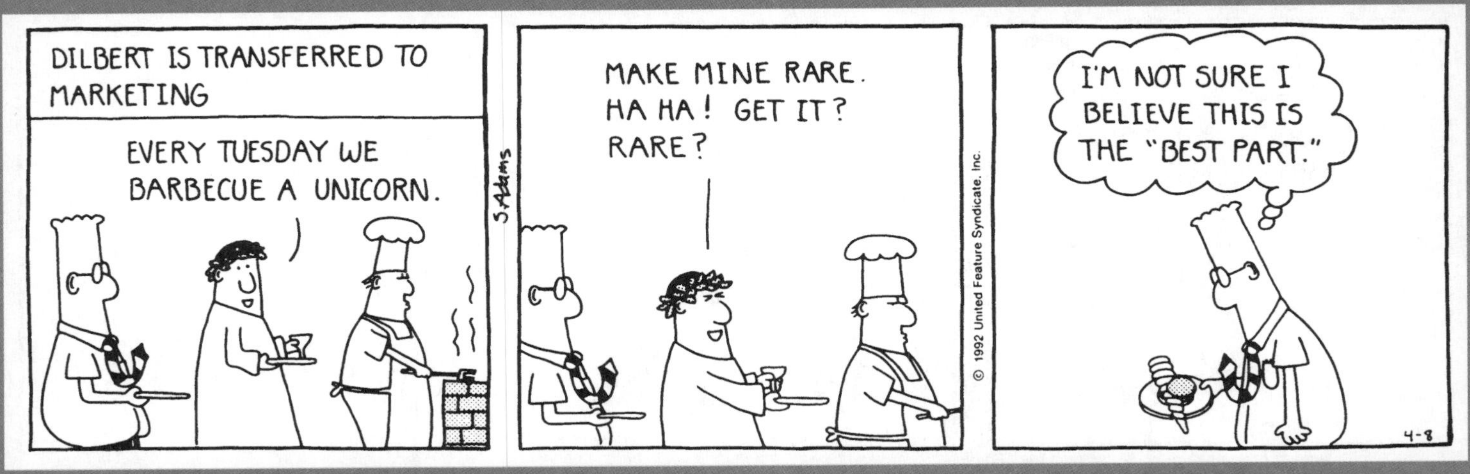
DILBERT IS TRANSFERRED TO MARKETING
EVERY TUESDAY WE BARBECUE A UNICORN.
S.Adams
MAKE MINE RARE. HA HA! GET IT? RARE?
© 1992 United Feature Syndicate, Inc.
I'M NOT SURE I BELIEVE THIS IS THE "BEST PART."
4-8

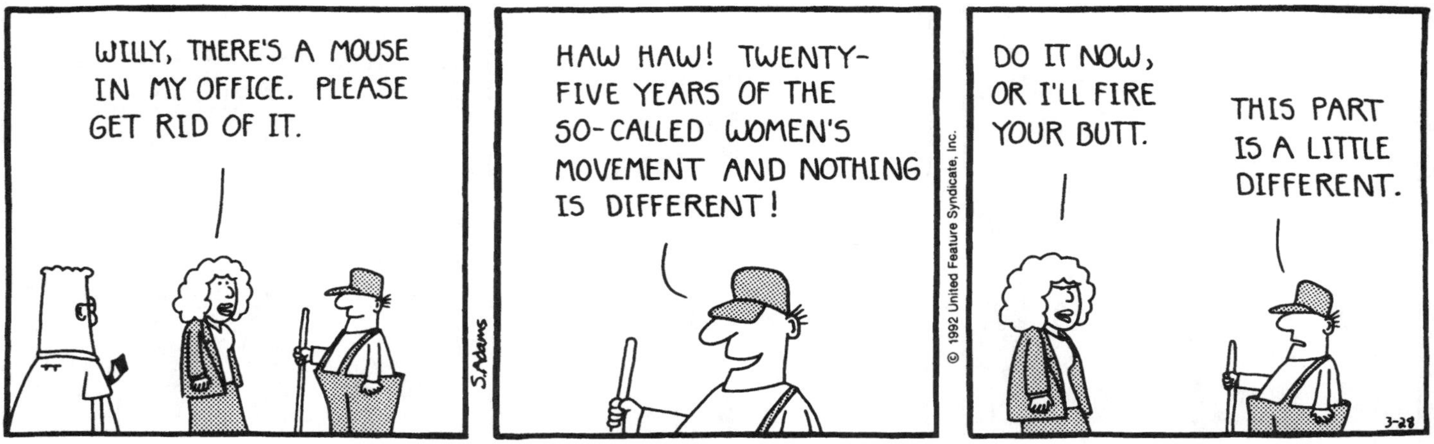
WILLY, THERE'S A MOUSE IN MY OFFICE. PLEASE GET RID OF IT.
S. Adams
HAW HAW! TWENTY-FIVE YEARS OF THE SO-CALLED WOMEN'S MOVEMENT AND NOTHING IS DIFFERENT!
© 1992 United Feature Syndicate, Inc.
DO IT NOW, OR I'LL FIRE YOUR BUTT.
THIS PART IS A LITTLE DIFFERENT.
3-28

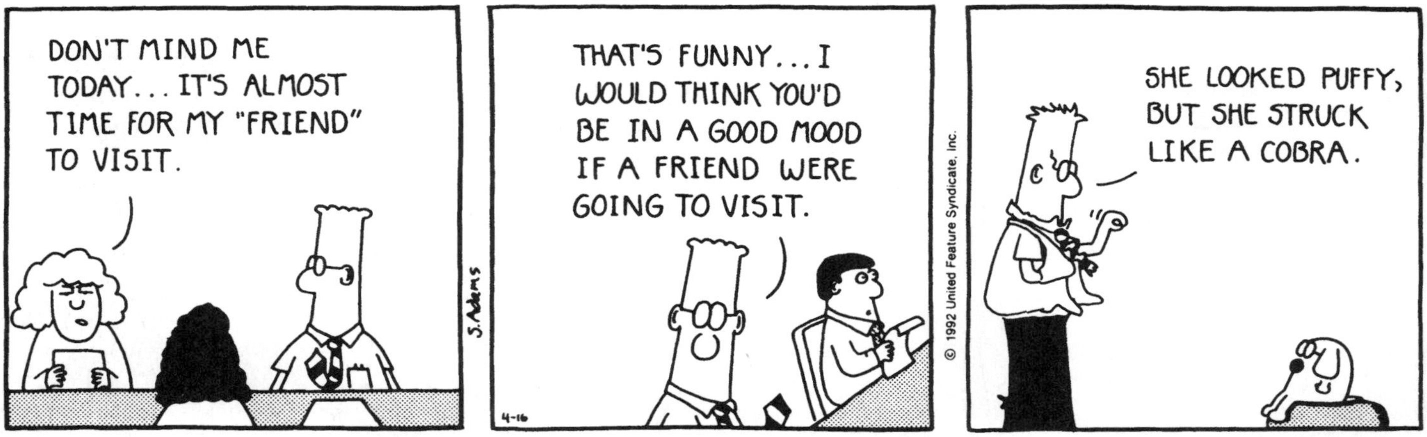
DON'T MIND ME TODAY... IT'S ALMOST TIME FOR MY "FRIEND" TO VISIT.
S. Adams
4-16
THAT'S FUNNY... I WOULD THINK YOU'D BE IN A GOOD MOOD IF A FRIEND WERE GOING TO VISIT.
© 1992 United Feature Syndicate, Inc.
SHE LOOKED PUFFY, BUT SHE STRUCK LIKE A COBRA.

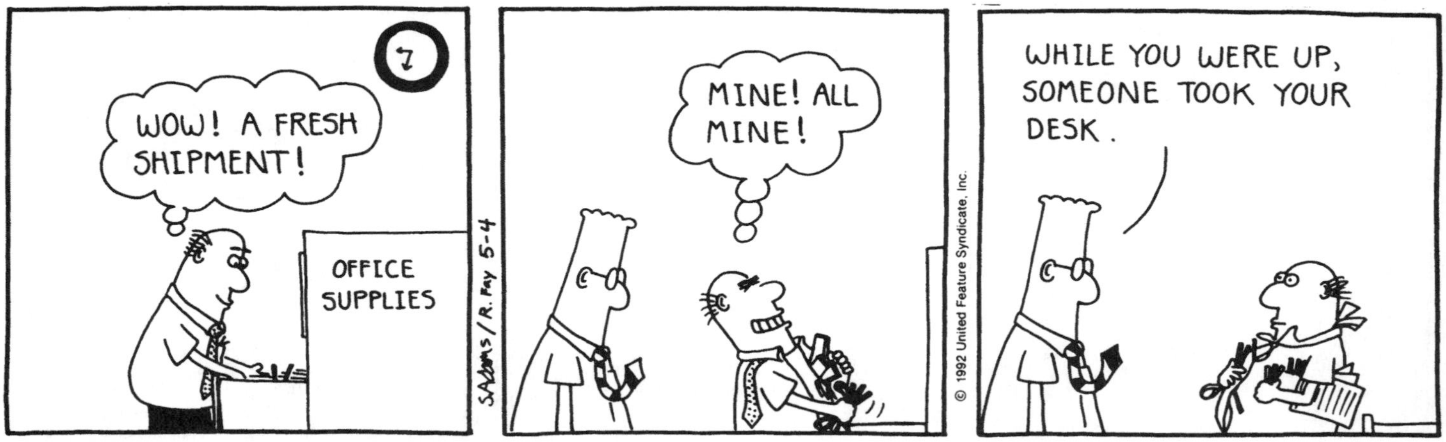
WOW! A FRESH SHIPMENT!
OFFICE SUPPLIES
S.Adams / R. Fay 5-4
MINE! ALL MINE!
© 1992 United Feature Syndicate, Inc.
WHILE YOU WERE UP, SOMEONE TOOK YOUR DESK.

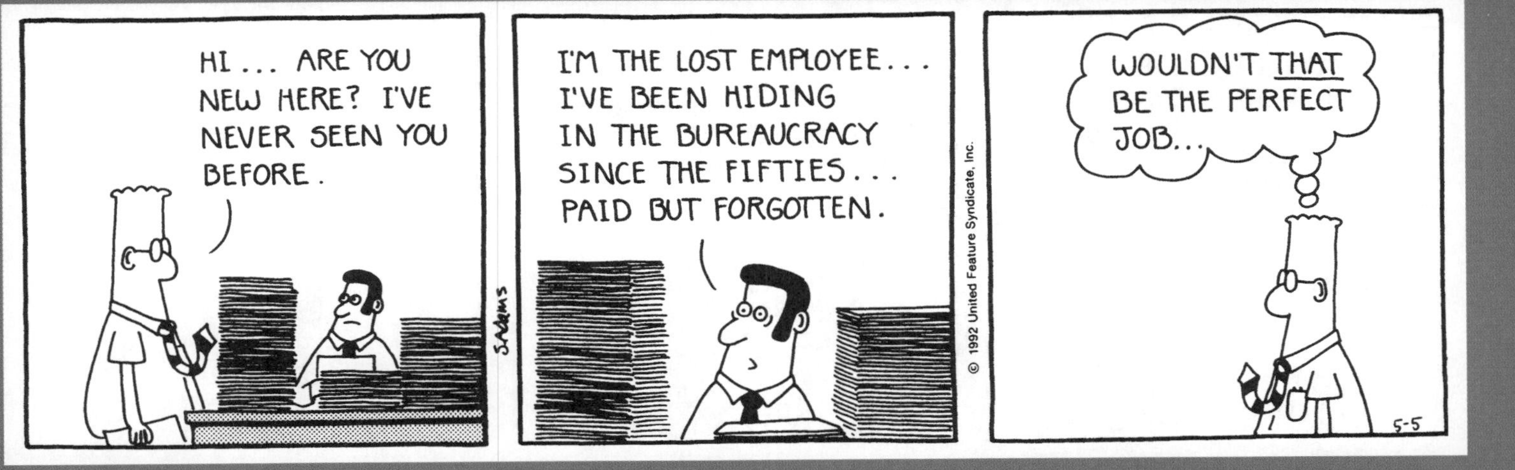
HI ... ARE YOU NEW HERE? I'VE NEVER SEEN YOU BEFORE.
S.Adams
I'M THE LOST EMPLOYEE... I'VE BEEN HIDING IN THE BUREAUCRACY SINCE THE FIFTIES... PAID BUT FORGOTTEN.
© 1992 United Feature Syndicate, Inc.
WOULDN'T THAT BE THE PERFECT JOB...
5-5

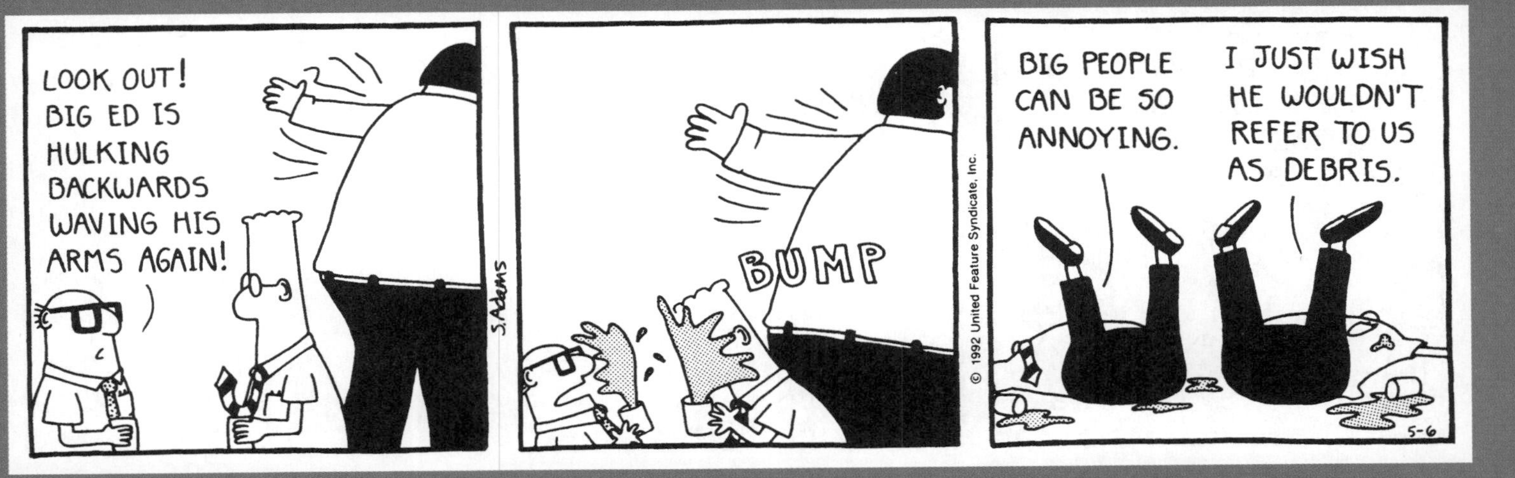
LOOK OUT! BIG ED IS HULKING BACKWARDS WAVING HIS ARMS AGAIN!
S.Adams
BUMP
© 1992 United Feature Syndicate, Inc.
BIG PEOPLE CAN BE SO ANNOYING.
I JUST WISH HE WOULDN'T REFER TO US AS DEBRIS.
5-6

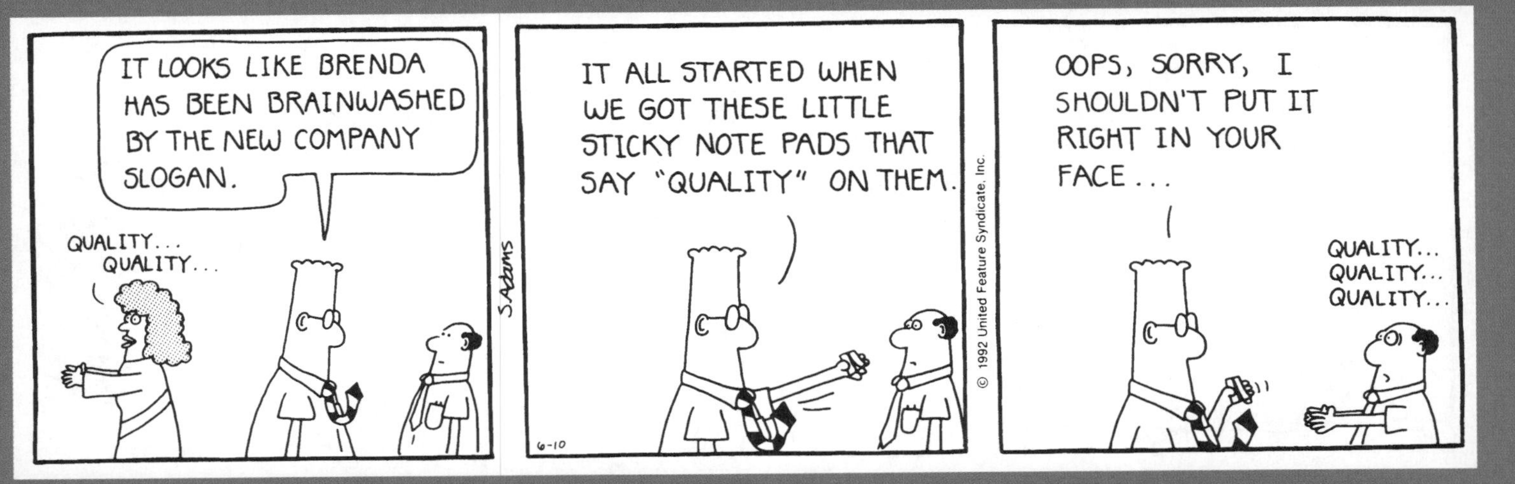
IT LOOKS LIKE BRENDA HAS BEEN BRAINWASHED BY THE NEW COMPANY SLOGAN.
QUALITY... QUALITY...
S.Adams
IT ALL STARTED WHEN WE GOT THESE LITTLE STICKY NOTE PADS THAT SAY "QUALITY" ON THEM.
6-10
© 1992 United Feature Syndicate, Inc.
OOPS, SORRY, I SHOULDN'T PUT IT RIGHT IN YOUR FACE...
QUALITY... QUALITY... QUALITY...

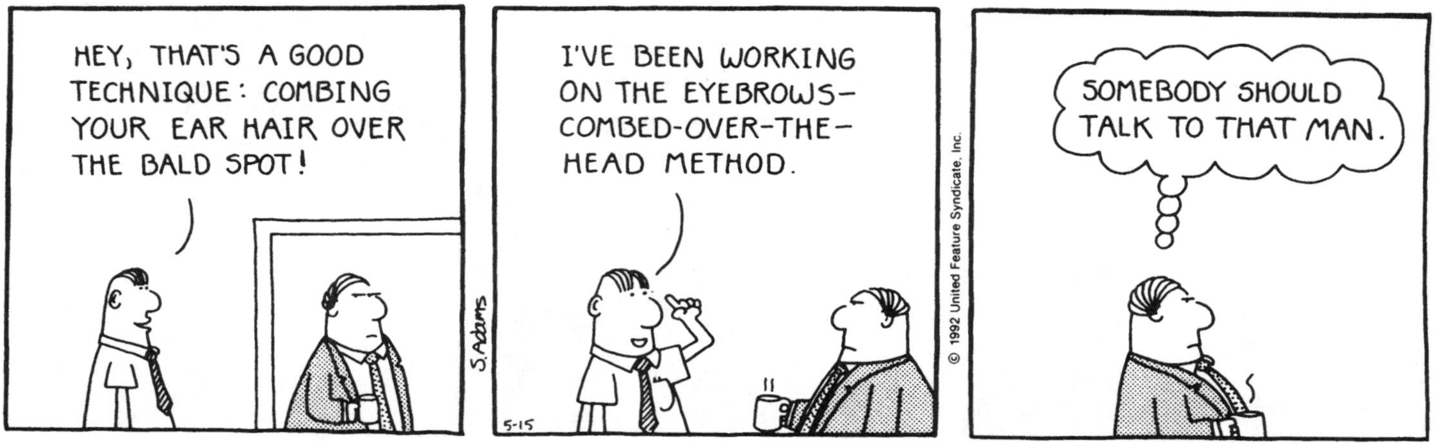
HEY, THAT'S A GOOD TECHNIQUE: COMBING YOUR EAR HAIR OVER THE BALD SPOT!
I'VE BEEN WORKING ON THE EYEBROWS-COMBED-OVER-THE-HEAD METHOD.
SOMEBODY SHOULD TALK TO THAT MAN.
© 1992 United Feature Syndicate, Inc.

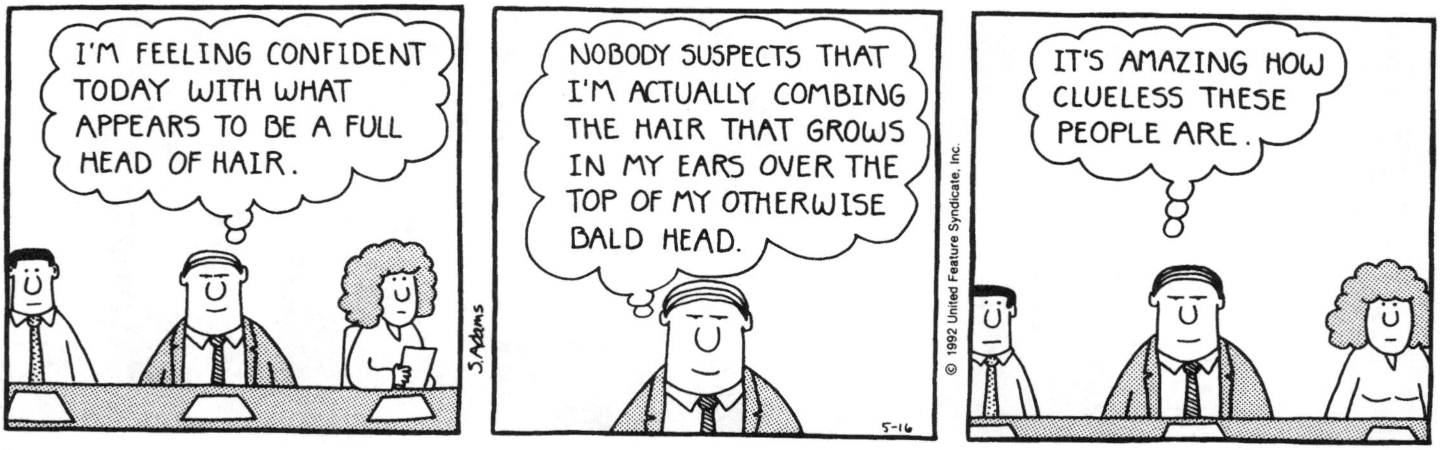
I'M FEELING CONFIDENT TODAY WITH WHAT APPEARS TO BE A FULL HEAD OF HAIR.
NOBODY SUSPECTS THAT I'M ACTUALLY COMBING THE HAIR THAT GROWS IN MY EARS OVER THE TOP OF MY OTHERWISE BALD HEAD.
IT'S AMAZING HOW CLUELESS THESE PEOPLE ARE.
© 1992 United Feature Syndicate, Inc.

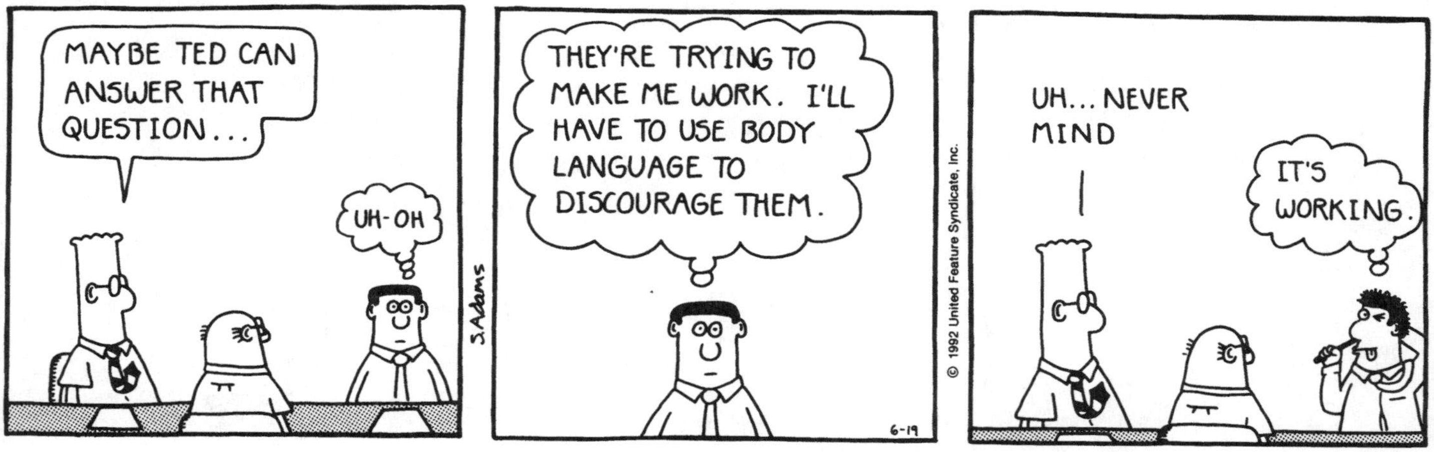
MAYBE TED CAN ANSWER THAT QUESTION...
UH-OH
THEY'RE TRYING TO MAKE ME WORK. I'LL HAVE TO USE BODY LANGUAGE TO DISCOURAGE THEM.
UH... NEVER MIND
IT'S WORKING.
© 1992 United Feature Syndicate, Inc.

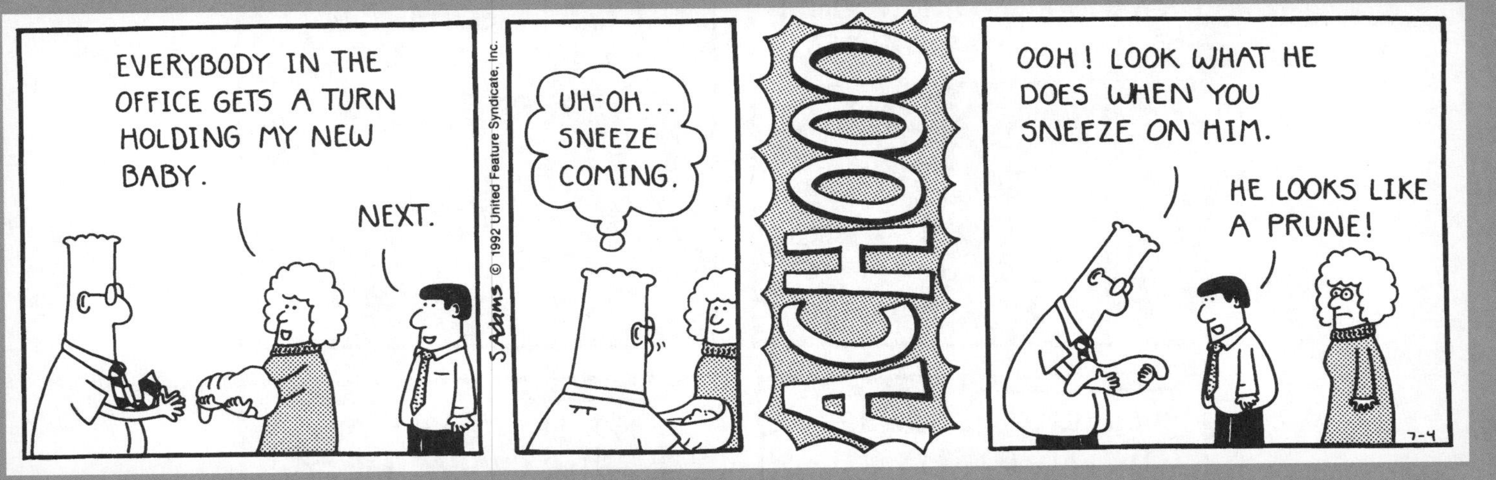
EVERYBODY IN THE OFFICE GETS A TURN HOLDING MY NEW BABY.
NEXT.
S. Adams © 1992 United Feature Syndicate, Inc.
UH-OH... SNEEZE COMING.
ACHOOO
OOH! LOOK WHAT HE DOES WHEN YOU SNEEZE ON HIM.
HE LOOKS LIKE A PRUNE!
7-4

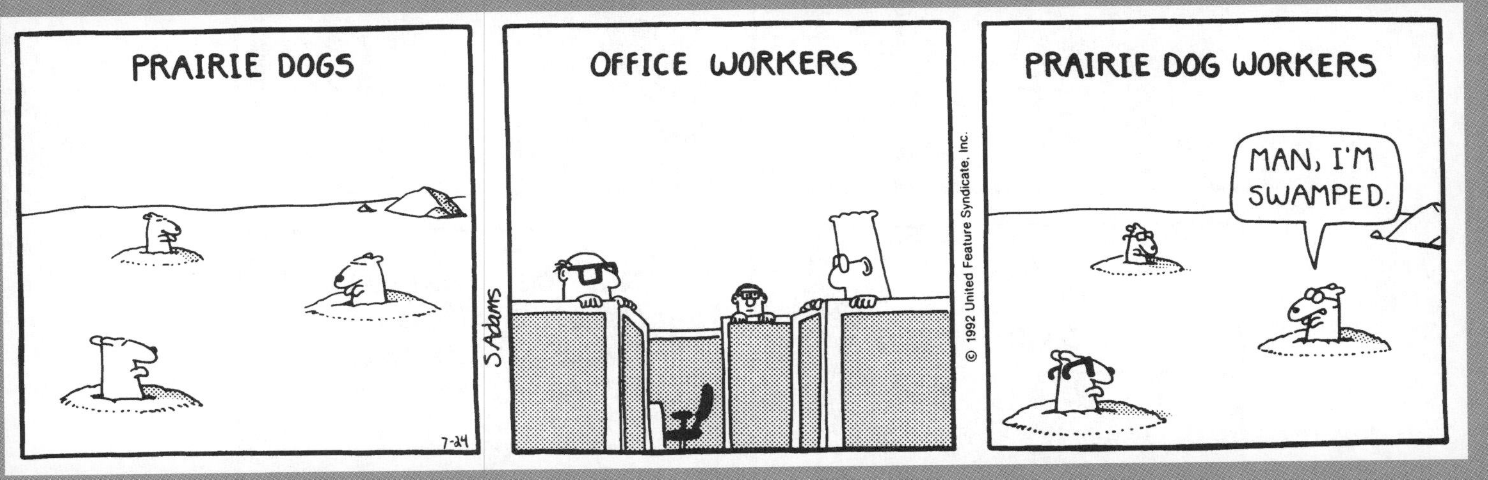
PRAIRIE DOGS
7-24
S. Adams
OFFICE WORKERS
© 1992 United Feature Syndicate, Inc.
PRAIRIE DOG WORKERS
MAN, I'M SWAMPED.

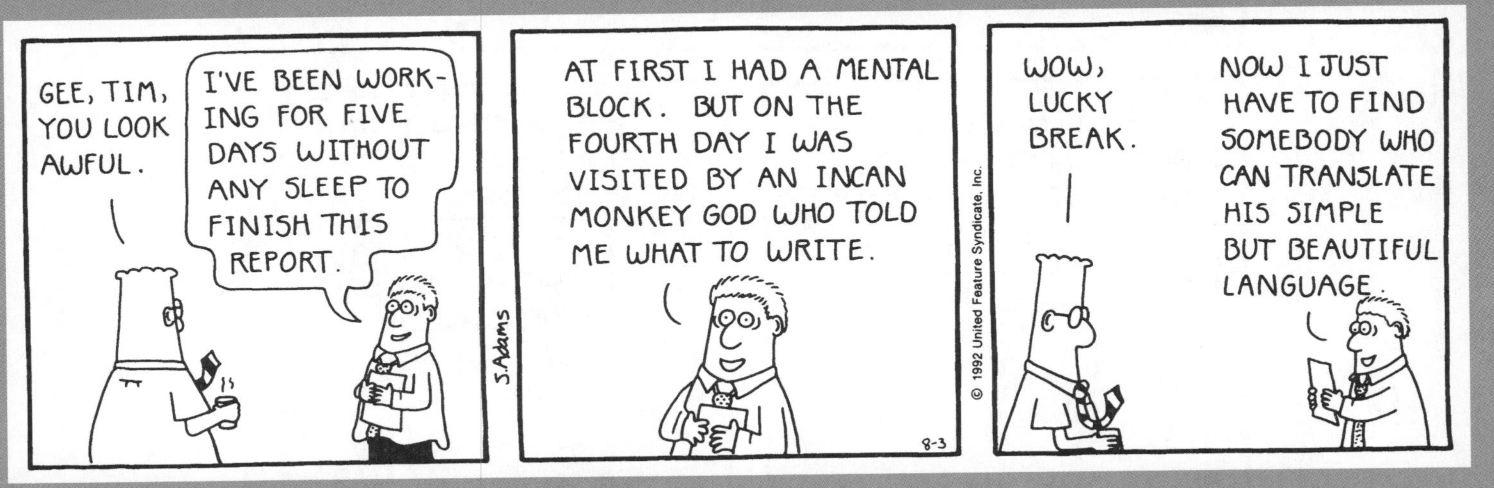
GEE, TIM, YOU LOOK AWFUL.
I'VE BEEN WORKING FOR FIVE DAYS WITHOUT ANY SLEEP TO FINISH THIS REPORT.
S. Adams
AT FIRST I HAD A MENTAL BLOCK. BUT ON THE FOURTH DAY I WAS VISITED BY AN INCAN MONKEY GOD WHO TOLD ME WHAT TO WRITE.
8-3
© 1992 United Feature Syndicate, Inc.
WOW, LUCKY BREAK.
NOW I JUST HAVE TO FIND SOMEBODY WHO CAN TRANSLATE HIS SIMPLE BUT BEAUTIFUL LANGUAGE.

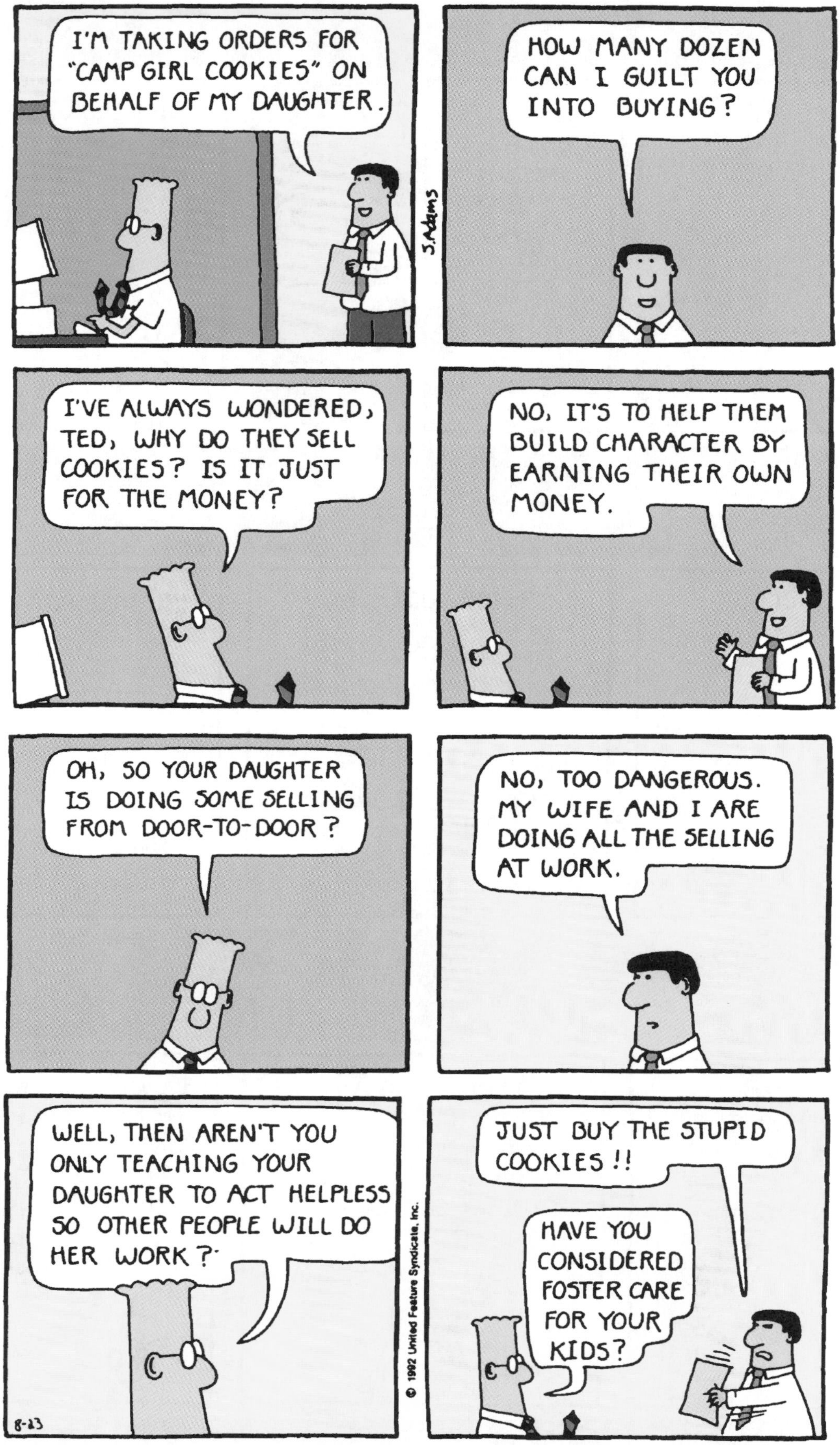
I'M TAKING ORDERS FOR "CAMP GIRL COOKIES" ON BEHALF OF MY DAUGHTER.
S. Adams
HOW MANY DOZEN CAN I GUILT YOU INTO BUYING?
I'VE ALWAYS WONDERED, TED, WHY DO THEY SELL COOKIES? IS IT JUST FOR THE MONEY?
NO, IT'S TO HELP THEM BUILD CHARACTER BY EARNING THEIR OWN MONEY.
OH, SO YOUR DAUGHTER IS DOING SOME SELLING FROM DOOR-TO-DOOR?
NO, TOO DANGEROUS. MY WIFE AND I ARE DOING ALL THE SELLING AT WORK.
WELL, THEN AREN'T YOU ONLY TEACHING YOUR DAUGHTER TO ACT HELPLESS SO OTHER PEOPLE WILL DO HER WORK?
8-23
© 1992 United Feature Syndicate, Inc.
JUST BUY THE STUPID COOKIES!!
HAVE YOU CONSIDERED FOSTER CARE FOR YOUR KIDS?

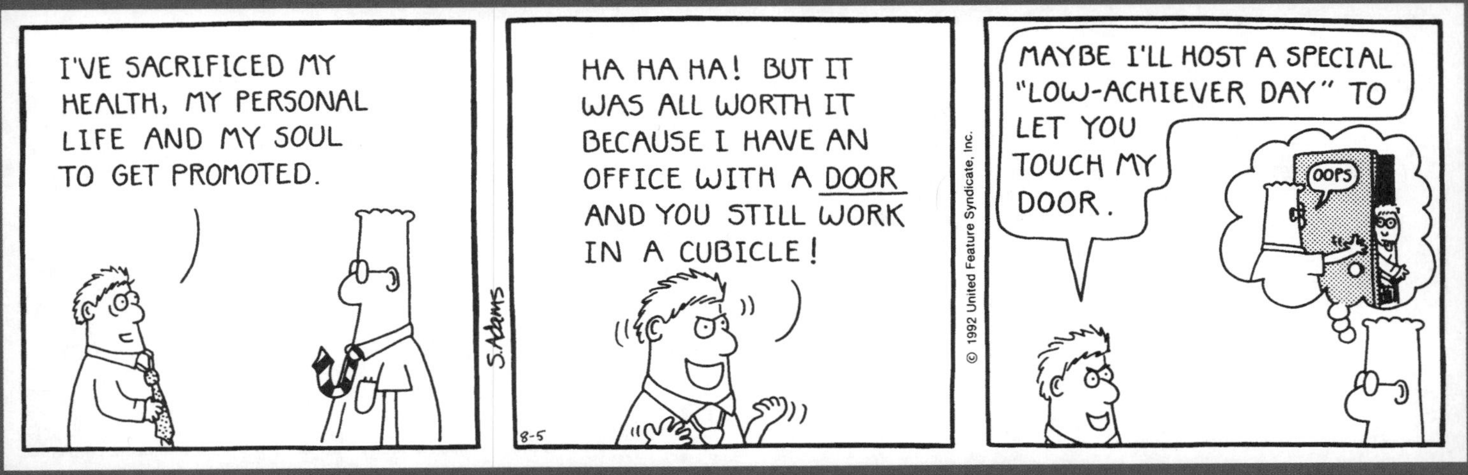
I'VE SACRIFICED MY HEALTH, MY PERSONAL LIFE AND MY SOUL TO GET PROMOTED.
HA HA HA! BUT IT WAS ALL WORTH IT BECAUSE I HAVE AN OFFICE WITH A DOOR AND YOU STILL WORK IN A CUBICLE!
MAYBE I'LL HOST A SPECIAL "LOW-ACHIEVER DAY" TO LET YOU TOUCH MY DOOR.
OOPS
S. Adams
8-5
© 1992 United Feature Syndicate, Inc.

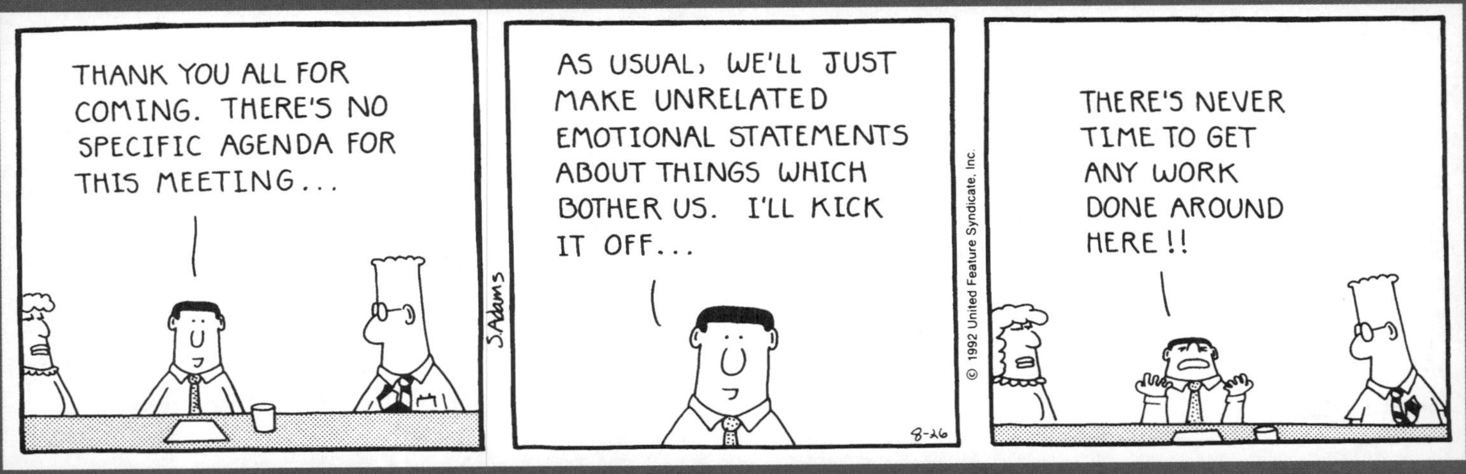
THANK YOU ALL FOR COMING. THERE'S NO SPECIFIC AGENDA FOR THIS MEETING...
AS USUAL, WE'LL JUST MAKE UNRELATED EMOTIONAL STATEMENTS ABOUT THINGS WHICH BOTHER US. I'LL KICK IT OFF...
THERE'S NEVER TIME TO GET ANY WORK DONE AROUND HERE!!
S. Adams
8-26
© 1992 United Feature Syndicate, Inc.

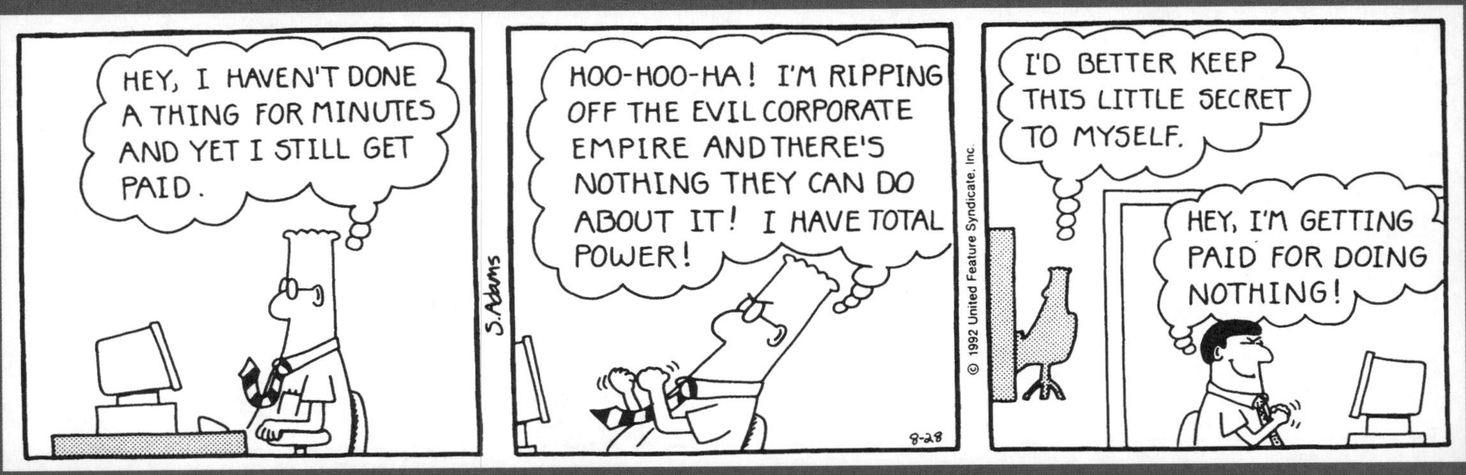
HEY, I HAVEN'T DONE A THING FOR MINUTES AND YET I STILL GET PAID.
HOO-HOO-HA! I'M RIPPING OFF THE EVIL CORPORATE EMPIRE AND THERE'S NOTHING THEY CAN DO ABOUT IT! I HAVE TOTAL POWER!
I'D BETTER KEEP THIS LITTLE SECRET TO MYSELF.
HEY, I'M GETTING PAID FOR DOING NOTHING!
S. Adams
8-28
© 1992 United Feature Syndicate, Inc.

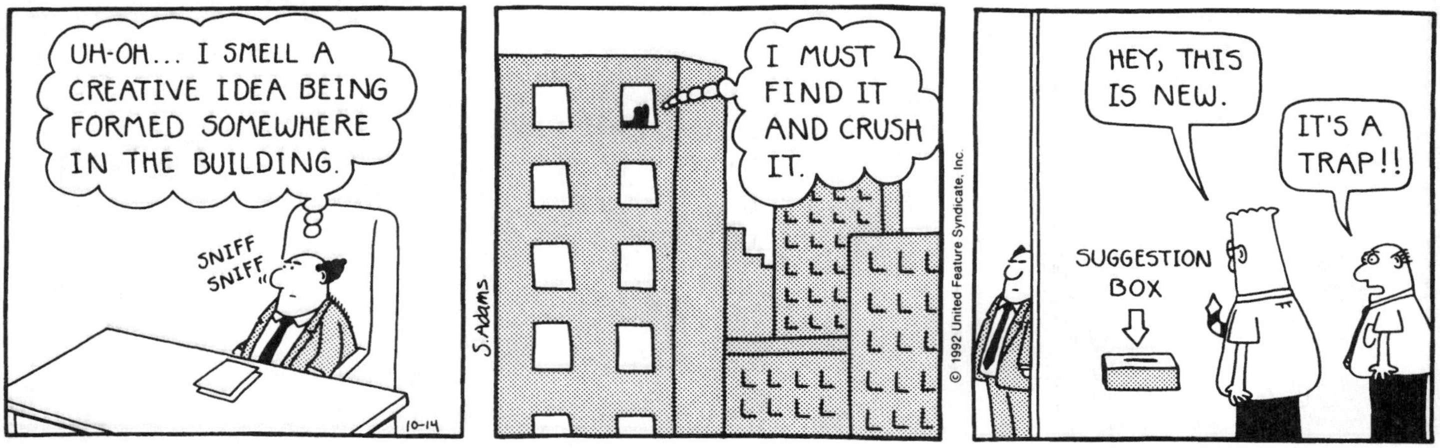
UH-OH... I SMELL A CREATIVE IDEA BEING FORMED SOMEWHERE IN THE BUILDING.
SNIFF SNIFF
10-14
S. Adams
I MUST FIND IT AND CRUSH IT.
© 1992 United Feature Syndicate, Inc.
HEY, THIS IS NEW.
IT'S A TRAP!!
SUGGESTION BOX

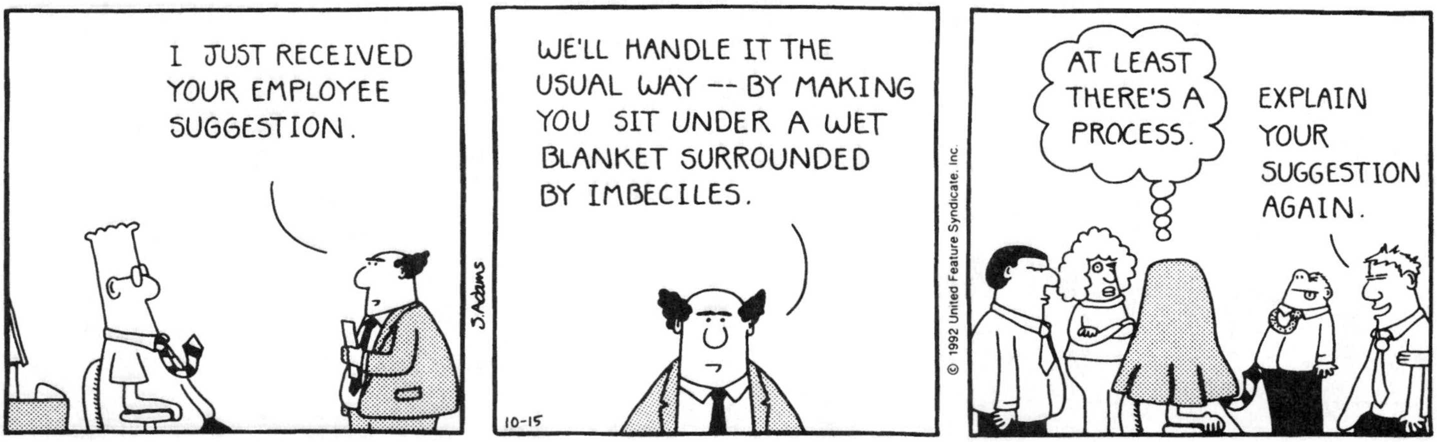
I JUST RECEIVED YOUR EMPLOYEE SUGGESTION.
S. Adams
WE'LL HANDLE IT THE USUAL WAY -- BY MAKING YOU SIT UNDER A WET BLANKET SURROUNDED BY IMBECILES.
10-15
© 1992 United Feature Syndicate, Inc.
AT LEAST THERE'S A PROCESS.
EXPLAIN YOUR SUGGESTION AGAIN.

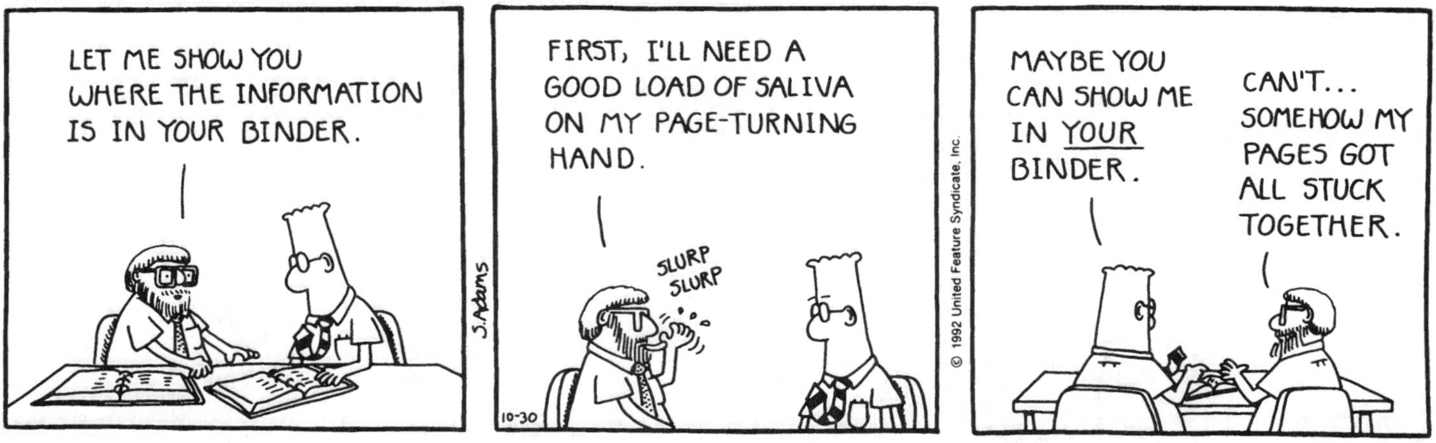
LET ME SHOW YOU WHERE THE INFORMATION IS IN YOUR BINDER.
S. Adams
FIRST, I'LL NEED A GOOD LOAD OF SALIVA ON MY PAGE-TURNING HAND.
SLURP SLURP
10-30
© 1992 United Feature Syndicate, Inc.
MAYBE YOU CAN SHOW ME IN YOUR BINDER.
CAN'T... SOMEHOW MY PAGES GOT ALL STUCK TOGETHER.

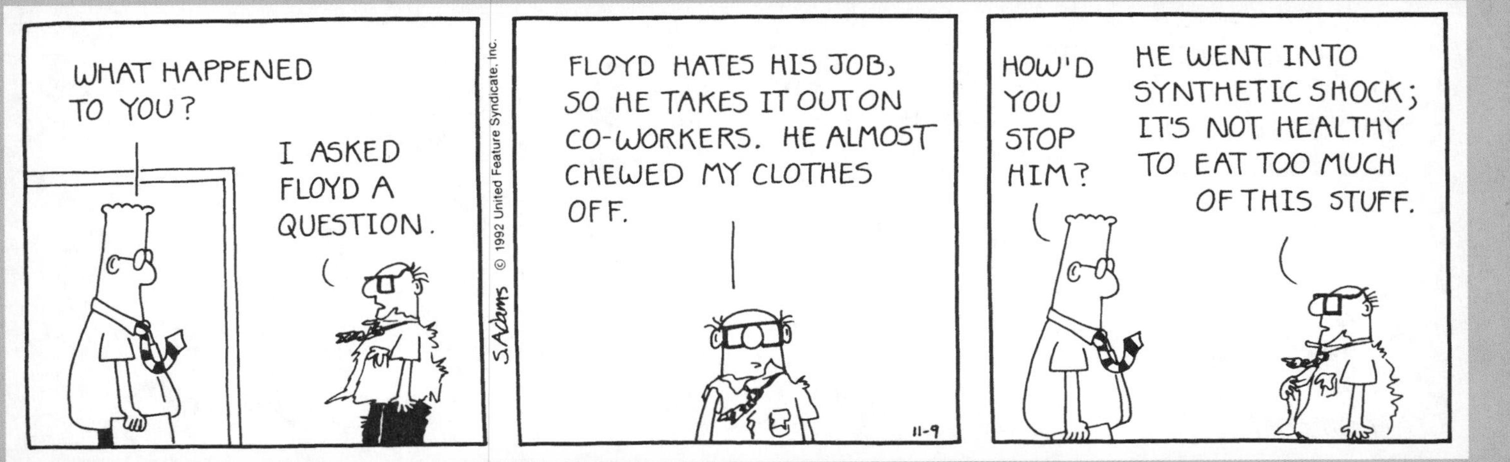
WHAT HAPPENED TO YOU?
I ASKED FLOYD A QUESTION.
S. Adams © 1992 United Feature Syndicate, Inc.
FLOYD HATES HIS JOB, SO HE TAKES IT OUT ON CO-WORKERS. HE ALMOST CHEWED MY CLOTHES OFF.
11-9
HOW'D YOU STOP HIM?
HE WENT INTO SYNTHETIC SHOCK; IT'S NOT HEALTHY TO EAT TOO MUCH OF THIS STUFF.

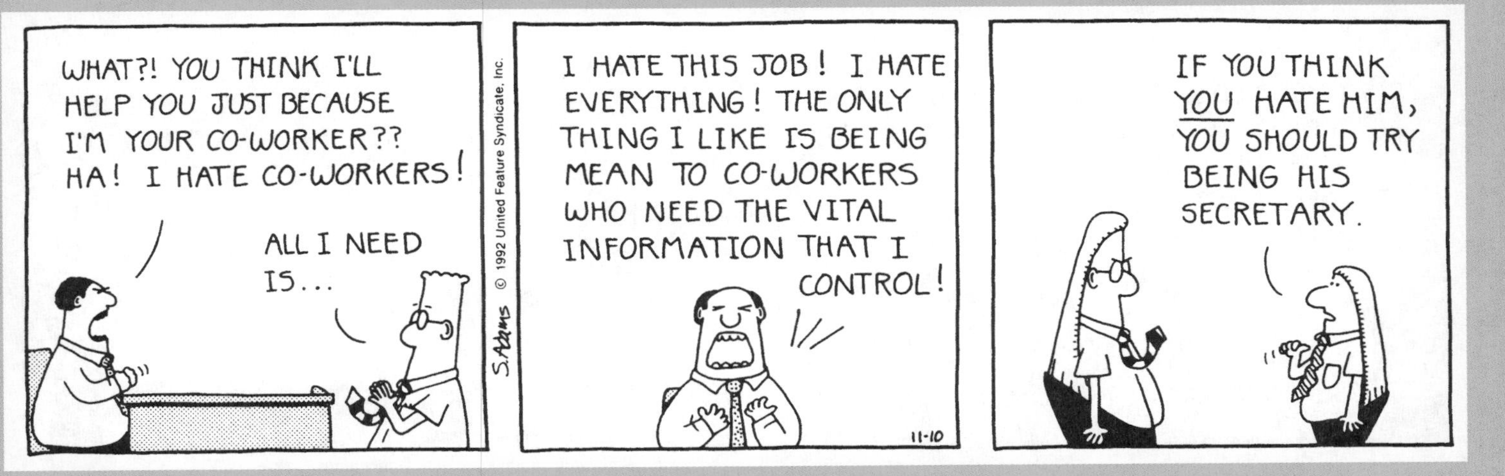
WHAT?! YOU THINK I'LL HELP YOU JUST BECAUSE I'M YOUR CO-WORKER?? HA! I HATE CO-WORKERS!
ALL I NEED IS...
S. Adams © 1992 United Feature Syndicate, Inc.
I HATE THIS JOB! I HATE EVERYTHING! THE ONLY THING I LIKE IS BEING MEAN TO CO-WORKERS WHO NEED THE VITAL INFORMATION THAT I CONTROL!
11-10
IF YOU THINK YOU HATE HIM, YOU SHOULD TRY BEING HIS SECRETARY.

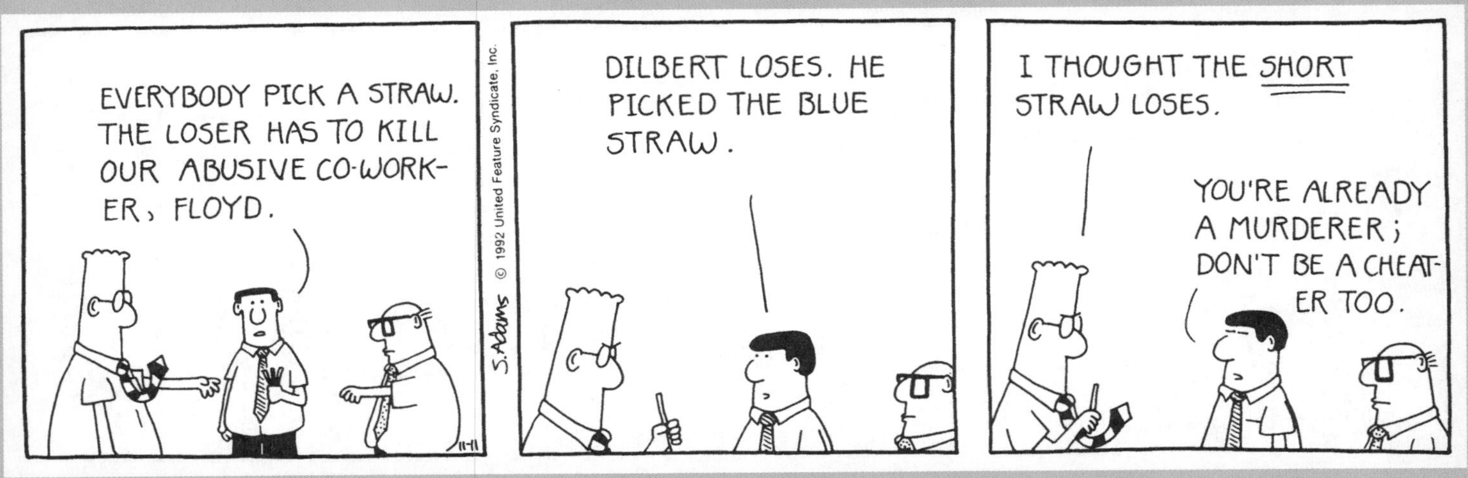
EVERYBODY PICK A STRAW. THE LOSER HAS TO KILL OUR ABUSIVE CO-WORKER, FLOYD.
S. Adams © 1992 United Feature Syndicate, Inc.
11-11
DILBERT LOSES. HE PICKED THE BLUE STRAW.
I THOUGHT THE SHORT STRAW LOSES.
YOU'RE ALREADY A MURDERER; DON'T BE A CHEATER TOO.

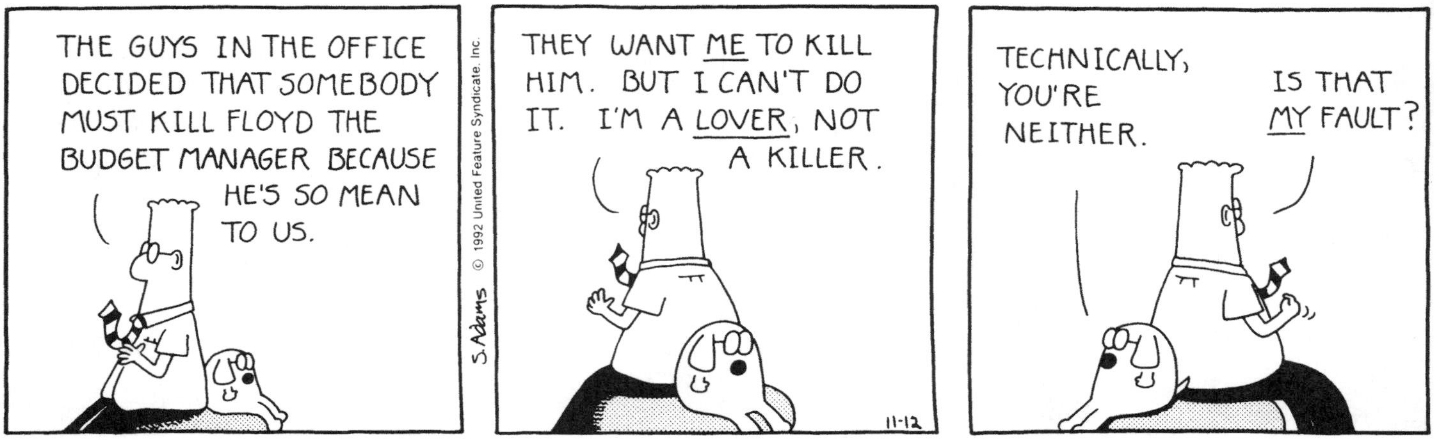
THE GUYS IN THE OFFICE DECIDED THAT SOMEBODY MUST KILL FLOYD THE BUDGET MANAGER BECAUSE HE'S SO MEAN TO US.
S.Adams © 1992 United Feature Syndicate, Inc.
THEY WANT ME TO KILL HIM. BUT I CAN'T DO IT. I'M A LOVER, NOT A KILLER.
11-12
TECHNICALLY, YOU'RE NEITHER.
IS THAT MY FAULT?

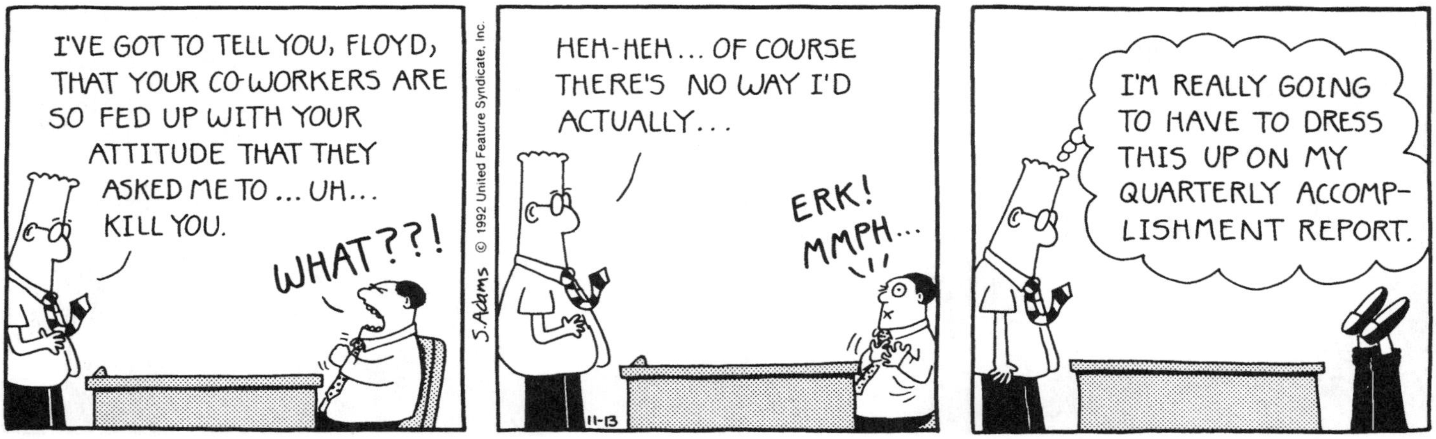
I'VE GOT TO TELL YOU, FLOYD, THAT YOUR CO-WORKERS ARE SO FED UP WITH YOUR ATTITUDE THAT THEY ASKED ME TO ... UH... KILL YOU.
WHAT??!
S.Adams © 1992 United Feature Syndicate, Inc.
HEH-HEH... OF COURSE THERE'S NO WAY I'D ACTUALLY...
ERK! MMPH...
11-13
I'M REALLY GOING TO HAVE TO DRESS THIS UP ON MY QUARTERLY ACCOMPLISHMENT REPORT.

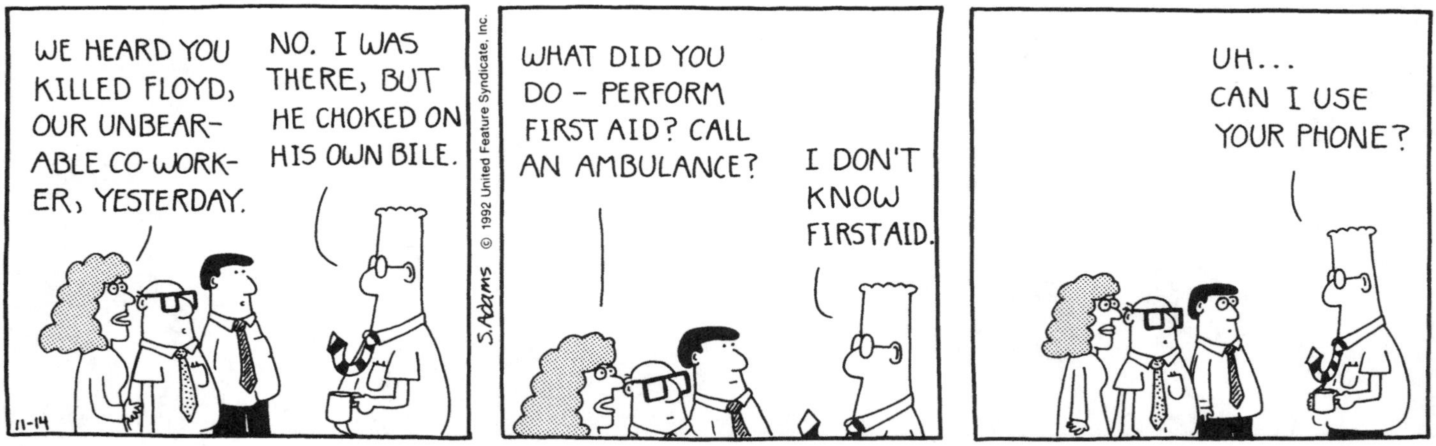
WE HEARD YOU KILLED FLOYD, OUR UNBEARABLE CO-WORKER, YESTERDAY.
NO. I WAS THERE, BUT HE CHOKED ON HIS OWN BILE.
11-14
S.Adams © 1992 United Feature Syndicate, Inc.
WHAT DID YOU DO – PERFORM FIRST AID? CALL AN AMBULANCE?
I DON'T KNOW FIRSTAID.
UH... CAN I USE YOUR PHONE?

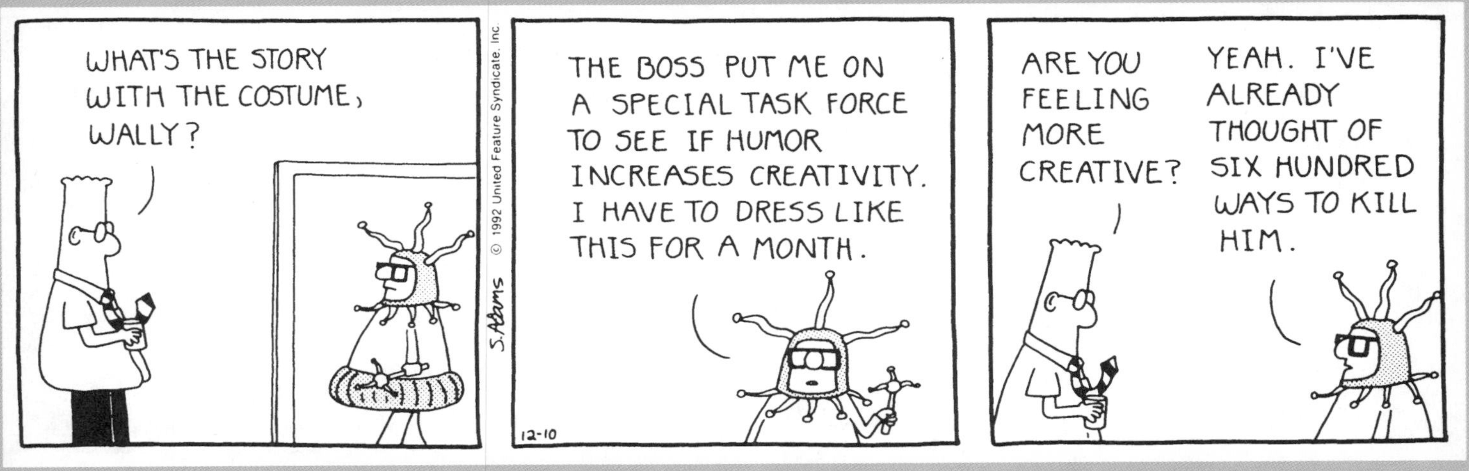
WHAT'S THE STORY WITH THE COSTUME, WALLY?
THE BOSS PUT ME ON A SPECIAL TASK FORCE TO SEE IF HUMOR INCREASES CREATIVITY. I HAVE TO DRESS LIKE THIS FOR A MONTH.
ARE YOU FEELING MORE CREATIVE?
YEAH. I'VE ALREADY THOUGHT OF SIX HUNDRED WAYS TO KILL HIM.
S. Adams
© 1992 United Feature Syndicate, Inc.
12-10

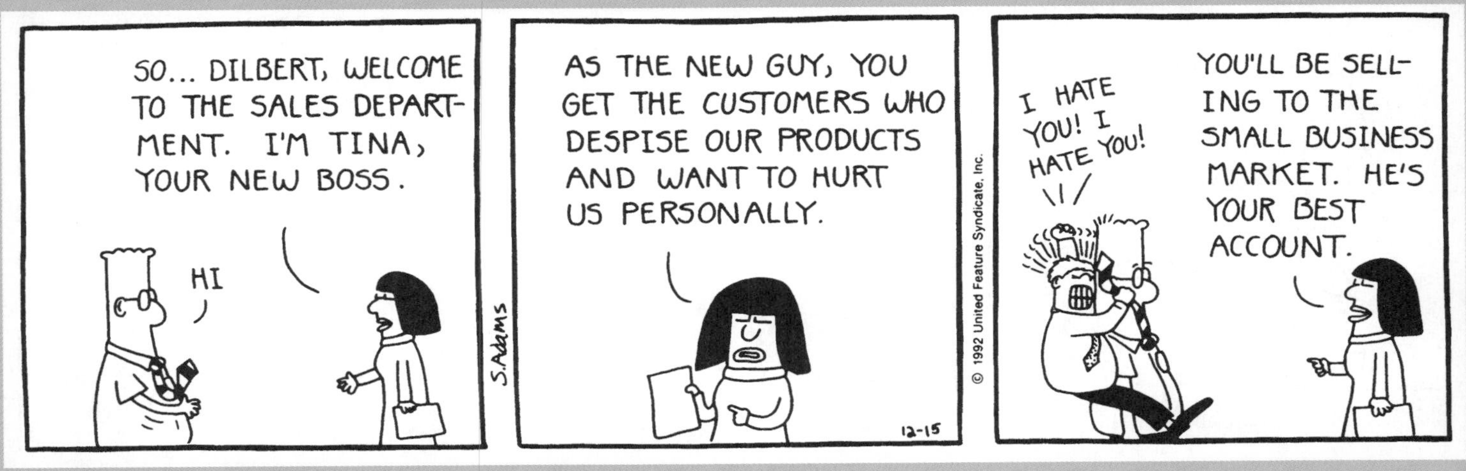
SO... DILBERT, WELCOME TO THE SALES DEPARTMENT. I'M TINA, YOUR NEW BOSS.
HI
S. Adams
AS THE NEW GUY, YOU GET THE CUSTOMERS WHO DESPISE OUR PRODUCTS AND WANT TO HURT US PERSONALLY.
12-15
© 1992 United Feature Syndicate, Inc.
I HATE YOU! I HATE YOU!
YOU'LL BE SELLING TO THE SMALL BUSINESS MARKET. HE'S YOUR BEST ACCOUNT.

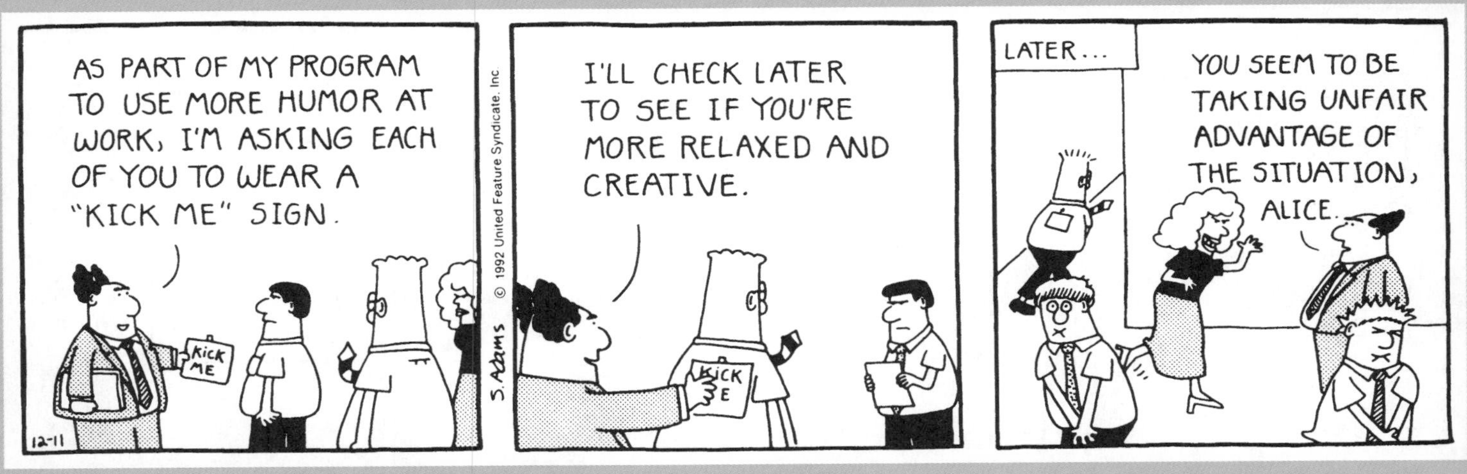
AS PART OF MY PROGRAM TO USE MORE HUMOR AT WORK, I'M ASKING EACH OF YOU TO WEAR A "KICK ME" SIGN.
KICK ME
12-11
© 1992 United Feature Syndicate, Inc.
S. Adams
I'LL CHECK LATER TO SEE IF YOU'RE MORE RELAXED AND CREATIVE.
LATER...
YOU SEEM TO BE TAKING UNFAIR ADVANTAGE OF THE SITUATION, ALICE.

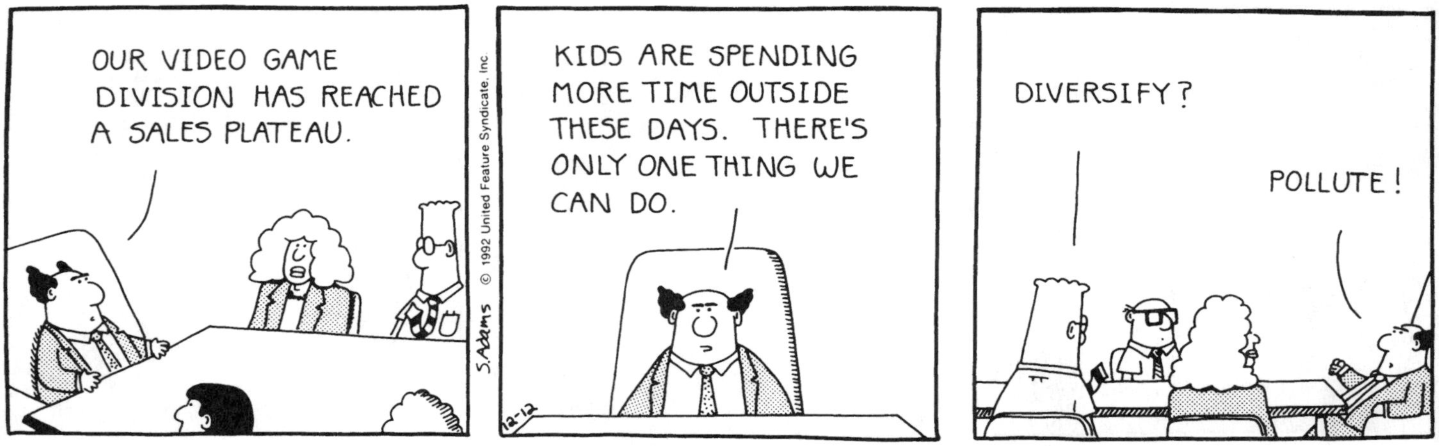
OUR VIDEO GAME DIVISION HAS REACHED A SALES PLATEAU.
S.Adams © 1992 United Feature Syndicate, Inc.
KIDS ARE SPENDING MORE TIME OUTSIDE THESE DAYS. THERE'S ONLY ONE THING WE CAN DO.
12-12
DIVERSIFY?
POLLUTE!

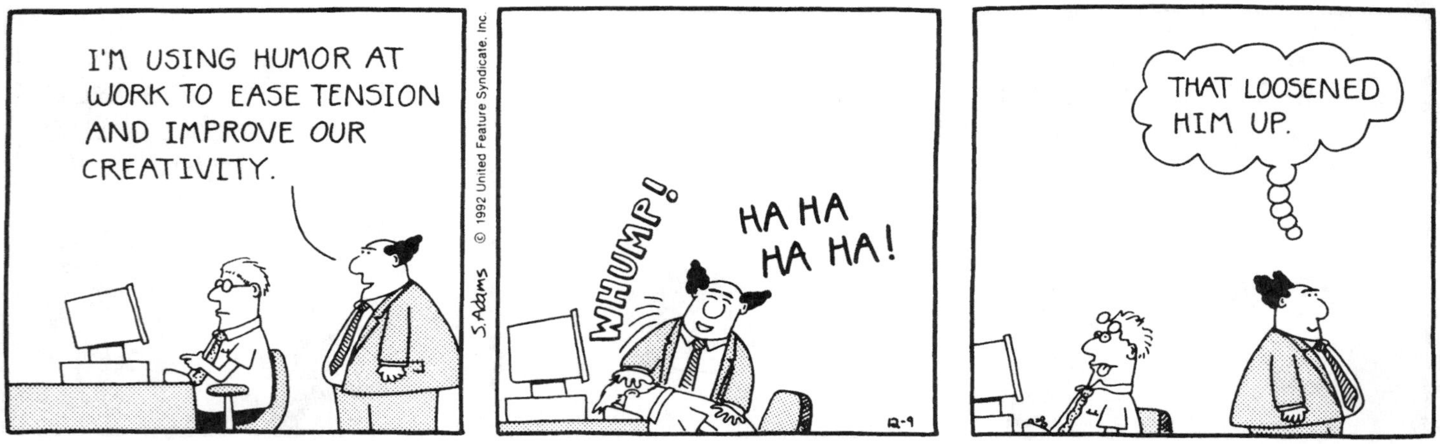
I'M USING HUMOR AT WORK TO EASE TENSION AND IMPROVE OUR CREATIVITY.
S.Adams © 1992 United Feature Syndicate, Inc.
WHUMP!
HA HA HA HA!
12-9
THAT LOOSENED HIM UP.

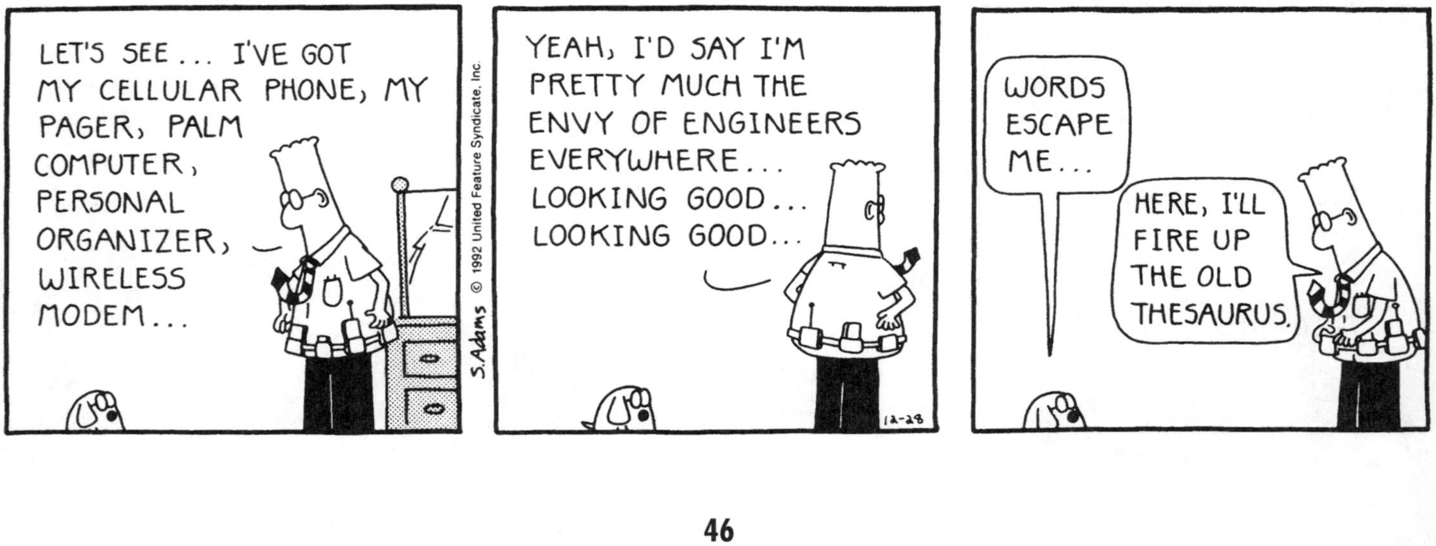
LET'S SEE... I'VE GOT MY CELLULAR PHONE, MY PAGER, PALM COMPUTER, PERSONAL ORGANIZER, WIRELESS MODEM...
S.Adams © 1992 United Feature Syndicate, Inc.
YEAH, I'D SAY I'M PRETTY MUCH THE ENVY OF ENGINEERS EVERYWHERE... LOOKING GOOD... LOOKING GOOD...
12-28
WORDS ESCAPE ME...
HERE, I'LL FIRE UP THE OLD THESAURUS.

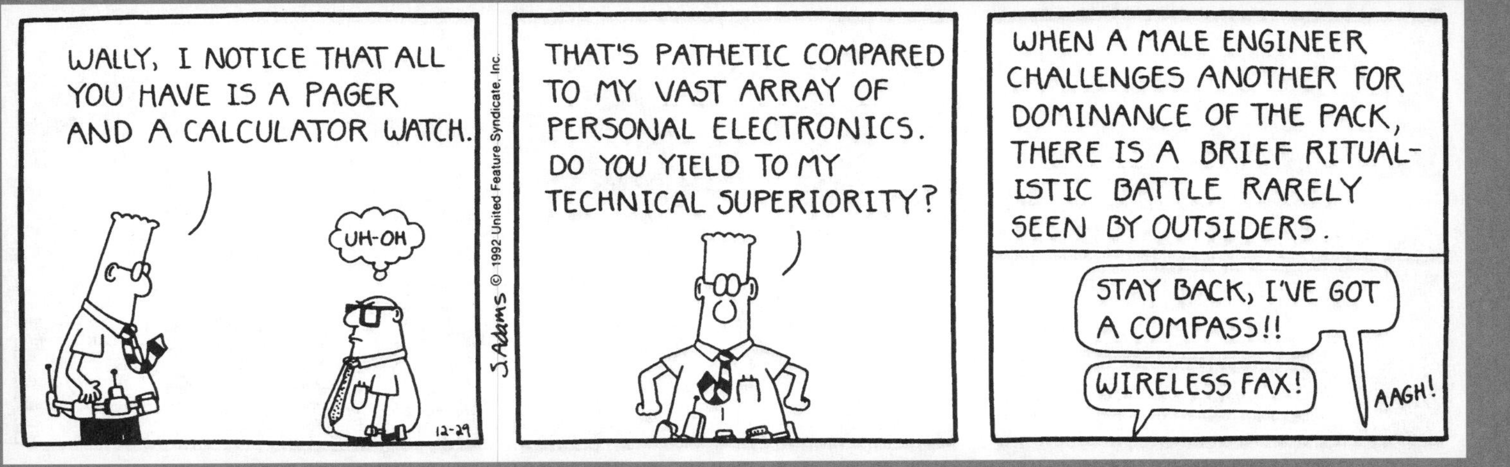
WALLY, I NOTICE THAT ALL YOU HAVE IS A PAGER AND A CALCULATOR WATCH.
UH-OH
S. Adams © 1992 United Feature Syndicate, Inc.
12-29
THAT'S PATHETIC COMPARED TO MY VAST ARRAY OF PERSONAL ELECTRONICS. DO YOU YIELD TO MY TECHNICAL SUPERIORITY?
WHEN A MALE ENGINEER CHALLENGES ANOTHER FOR DOMINANCE OF THE PACK, THERE IS A BRIEF RITUAL-ISTIC BATTLE RARELY SEEN BY OUTSIDERS.
STAY BACK, I'VE GOT A COMPASS!!
WIRELESS FAX!
AAGH!

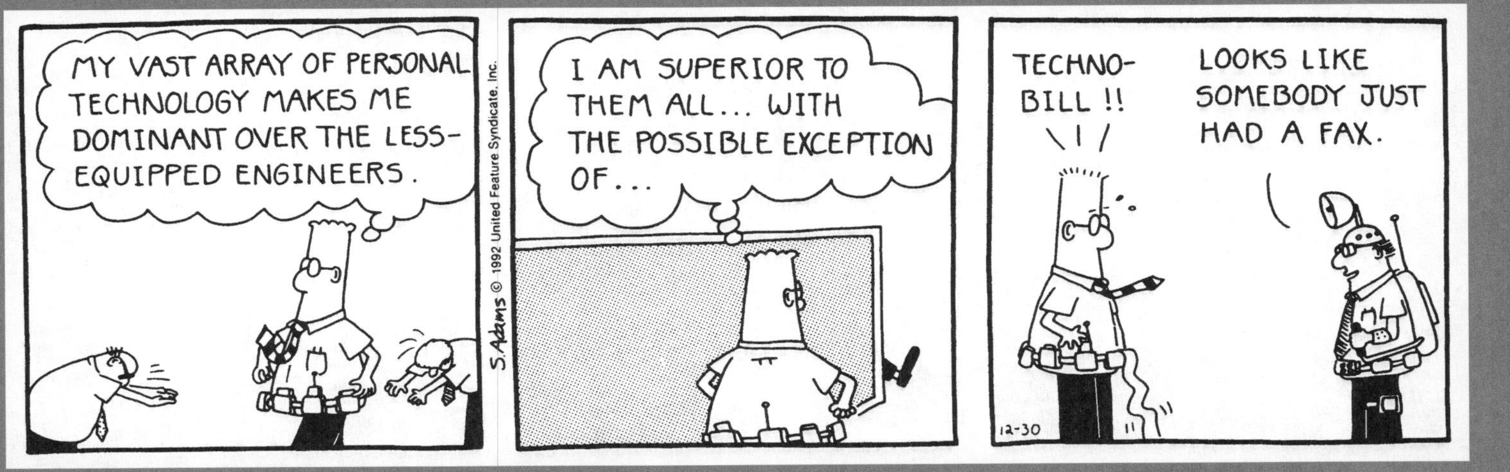
MY VAST ARRAY OF PERSONAL TECHNOLOGY MAKES ME DOMINANT OVER THE LESS-EQUIPPED ENGINEERS.
S. Adams © 1992 United Feature Syndicate, Inc.
I AM SUPERIOR TO THEM ALL... WITH THE POSSIBLE EXCEPTION OF...
TECHNO-BILL !!
LOOKS LIKE SOMEBODY JUST HAD A FAX.
12-30

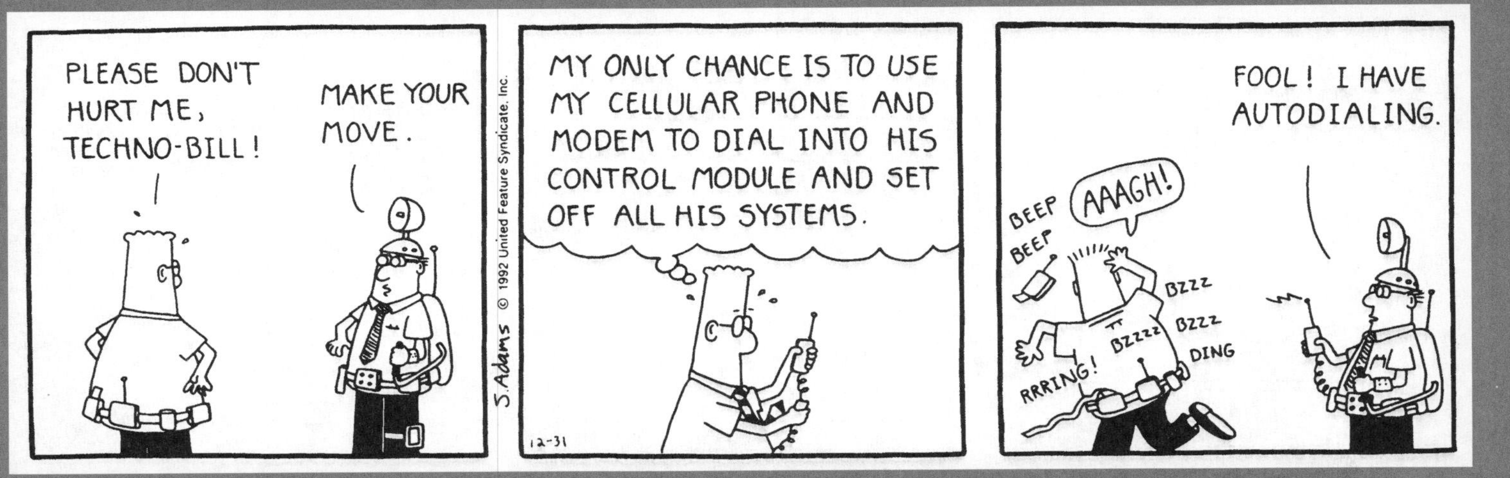
PLEASE DON'T HURT ME, TECHNO-BILL!
MAKE YOUR MOVE.
S. Adams © 1992 United Feature Syndicate, Inc.
MY ONLY CHANCE IS TO USE MY CELLULAR PHONE AND MODEM TO DIAL INTO HIS CONTROL MODULE AND SET OFF ALL HIS SYSTEMS.
12-31
BEEP BEEP
AAAGH!
BZZZ
BZZZZ
BZZZ
DING
RRRING!
FOOL! I HAVE AUTODIALING.

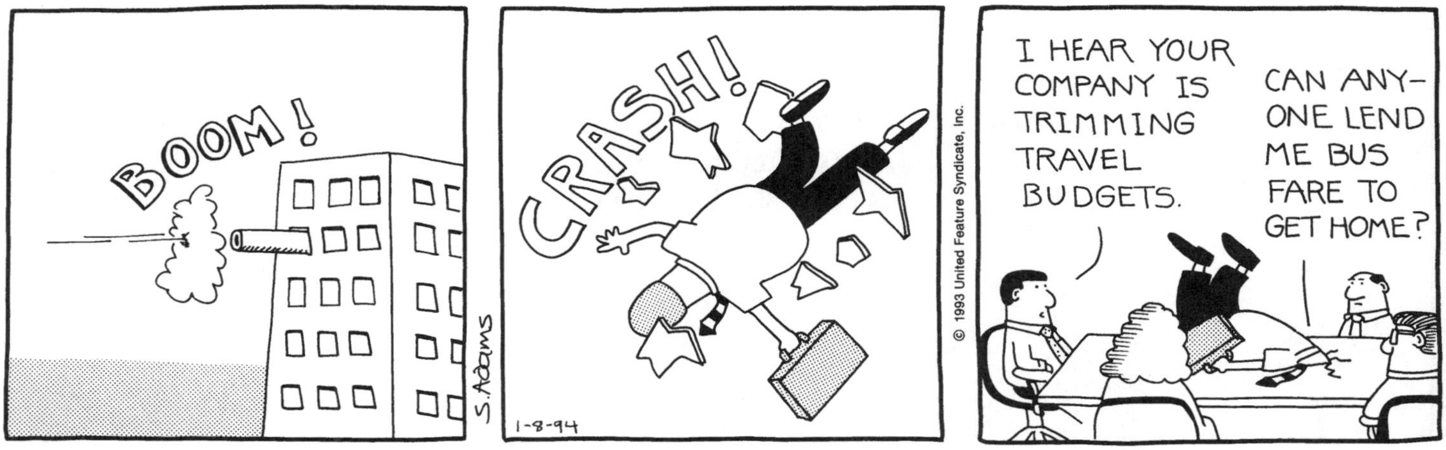
BOOM!
S. Adams
CRASH!
1-8-94
© 1993 United Feature Syndicate, Inc.
I HEAR YOUR COMPANY IS TRIMMING TRAVEL BUDGETS.
CAN ANYONE LEND ME BUS FARE TO GET HOME?

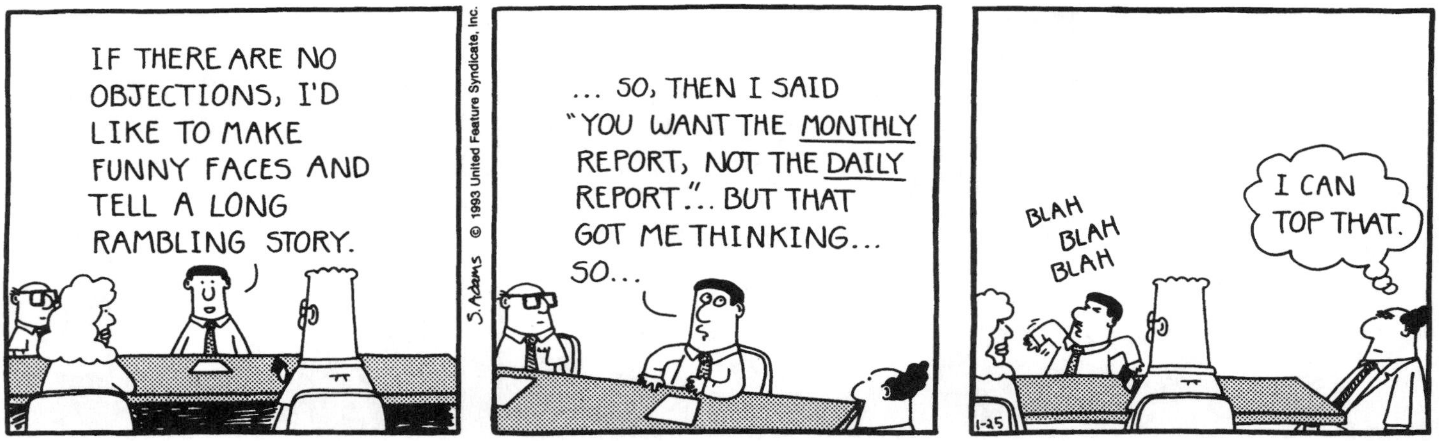
IF THERE ARE NO OBJECTIONS, I'D LIKE TO MAKE FUNNY FACES AND TELL A LONG RAMBLING STORY.
S. Adams
© 1993 United Feature Syndicate, Inc.
... SO, THEN I SAID "YOU WANT THE MONTHLY REPORT, NOT THE DAILY REPORT."... BUT THAT GOT ME THINKING... SO...
BLAH BLAH BLAH
I CAN TOP THAT.
1-25

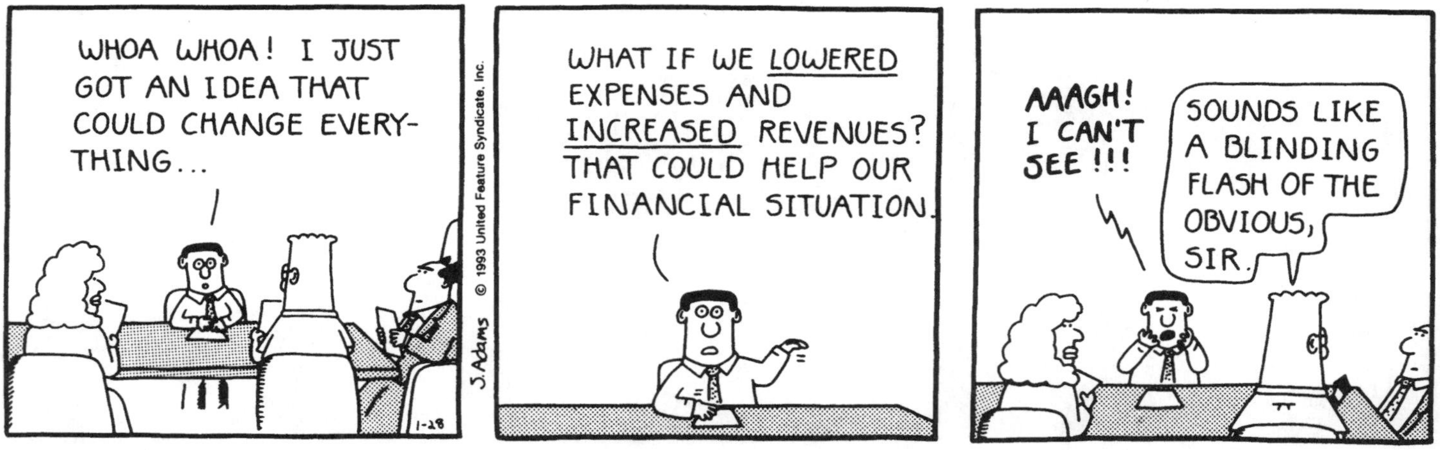
WHOA WHOA! I JUST GOT AN IDEA THAT COULD CHANGE EVERYTHING...
1-28
S. Adams
© 1993 United Feature Syndicate, Inc.
WHAT IF WE LOWERED EXPENSES AND INCREASED REVENUES? THAT COULD HELP OUR FINANCIAL SITUATION.
AAAGH! I CAN'T SEE!!!
SOUNDS LIKE A BLINDING FLASH OF THE OBVIOUS, SIR.

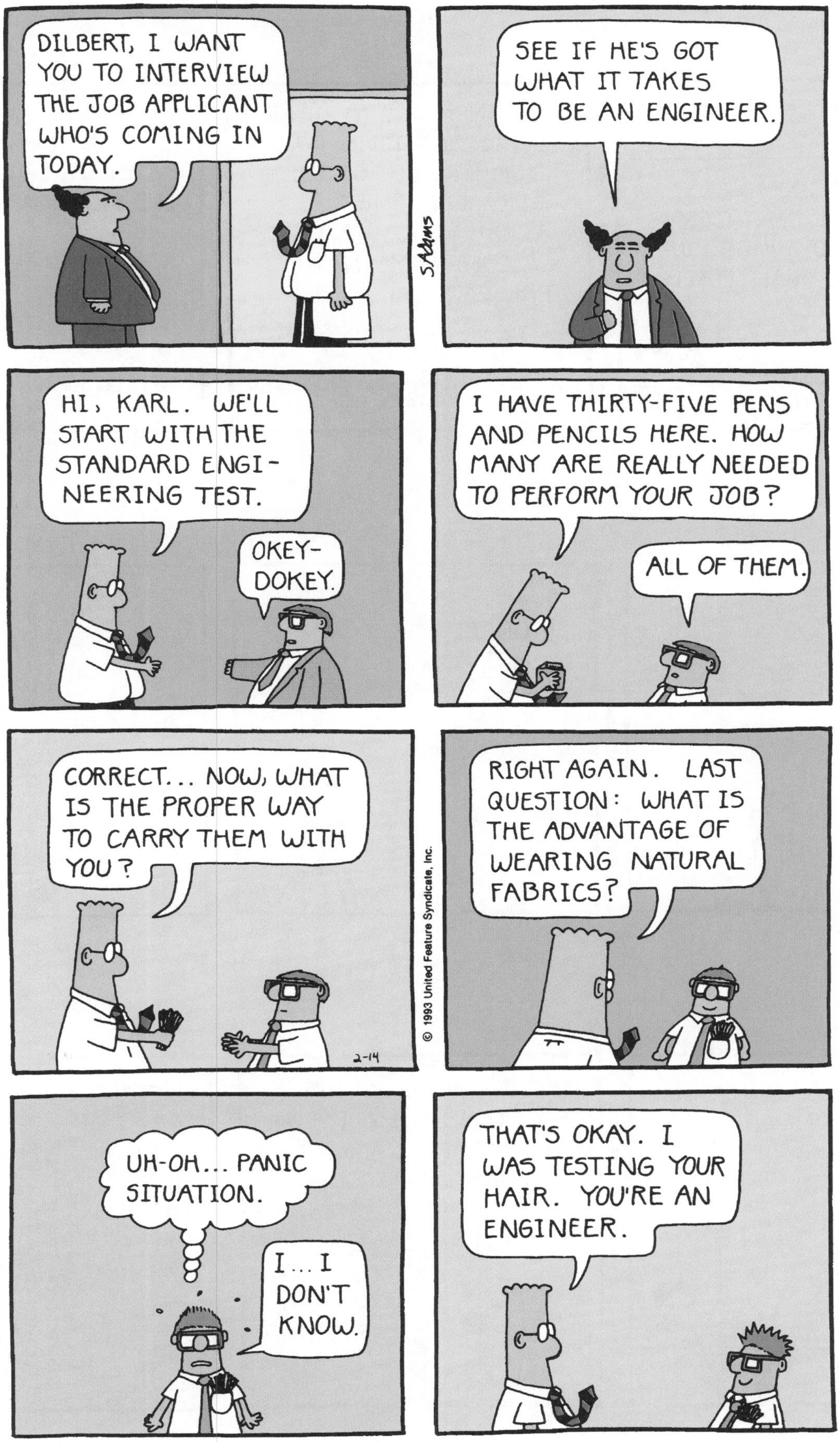
DILBERT, I WANT YOU TO INTERVIEW THE JOB APPLICANT WHO'S COMING IN TODAY.
S.ADAMS
SEE IF HE'S GOT WHAT IT TAKES TO BE AN ENGINEER.
HI, KARL. WE'LL START WITH THE STANDARD ENGI-NEERING TEST.
OKEY-DOKEY.
I HAVE THIRTY-FIVE PENS AND PENCILS HERE. HOW MANY ARE REALLY NEEDED TO PERFORM YOUR JOB?
ALL OF THEM.
CORRECT... NOW, WHAT IS THE PROPER WAY TO CARRY THEM WITH YOU?
2-14
RIGHT AGAIN. LAST QUESTION: WHAT IS THE ADVANTAGE OF WEARING NATURAL FABRICS?
UH-OH... PANIC SITUATION.
I... I DON'T KNOW.
THAT'S OKAY. I WAS TESTING YOUR HAIR. YOU'RE AN ENGINEER.

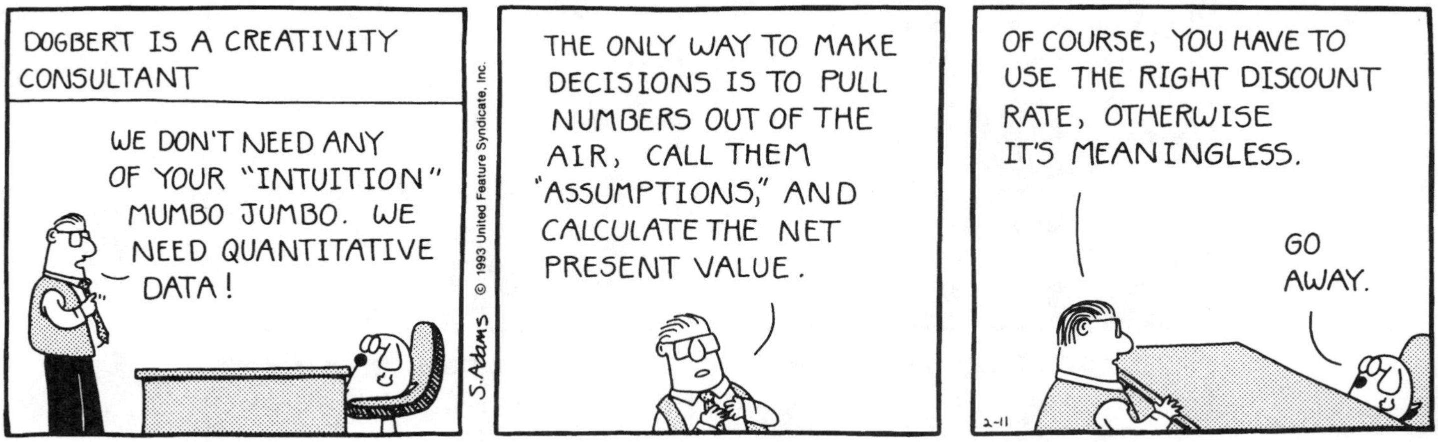
DOGBERT IS A CREATIVITY CONSULTANT
WE DON'T NEED ANY OF YOUR "INTUITION" MUMBO JUMBO. WE NEED QUANTITATIVE DATA!
S. Adams © 1993 United Feature Syndicate, Inc.
THE ONLY WAY TO MAKE DECISIONS IS TO PULL NUMBERS OUT OF THE AIR, CALL THEM "ASSUMPTIONS," AND CALCULATE THE NET PRESENT VALUE.
OF COURSE, YOU HAVE TO USE THE RIGHT DISCOUNT RATE, OTHERWISE IT'S MEANINGLESS.
GO AWAY.
2-11

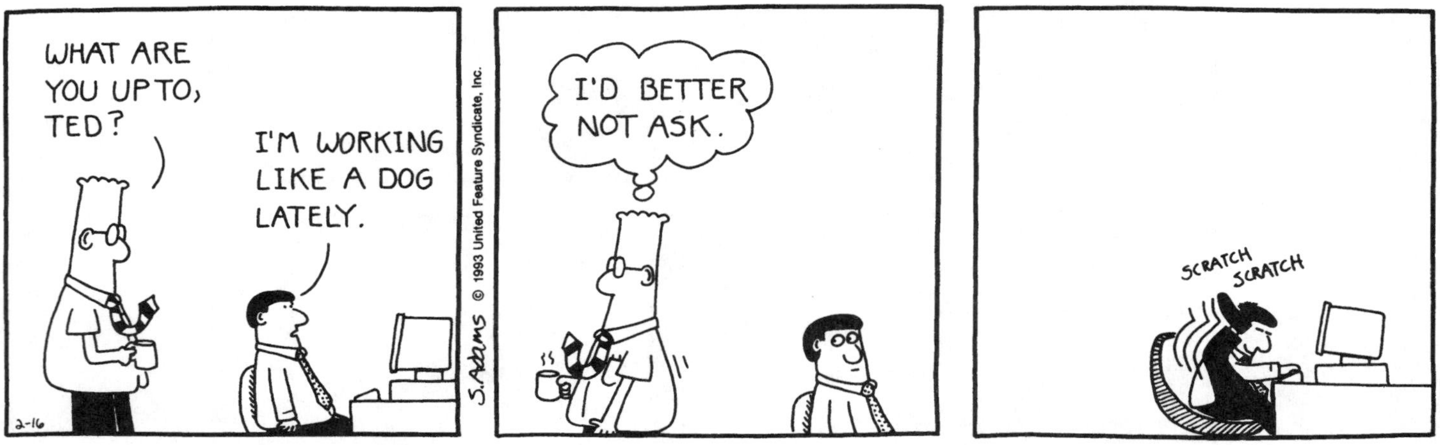
WHAT ARE YOU UP TO, TED?
I'M WORKING LIKE A DOG LATELY.
2-16
S. Adams © 1993 United Feature Syndicate, Inc.
I'D BETTER NOT ASK.
SCRATCH SCRATCH

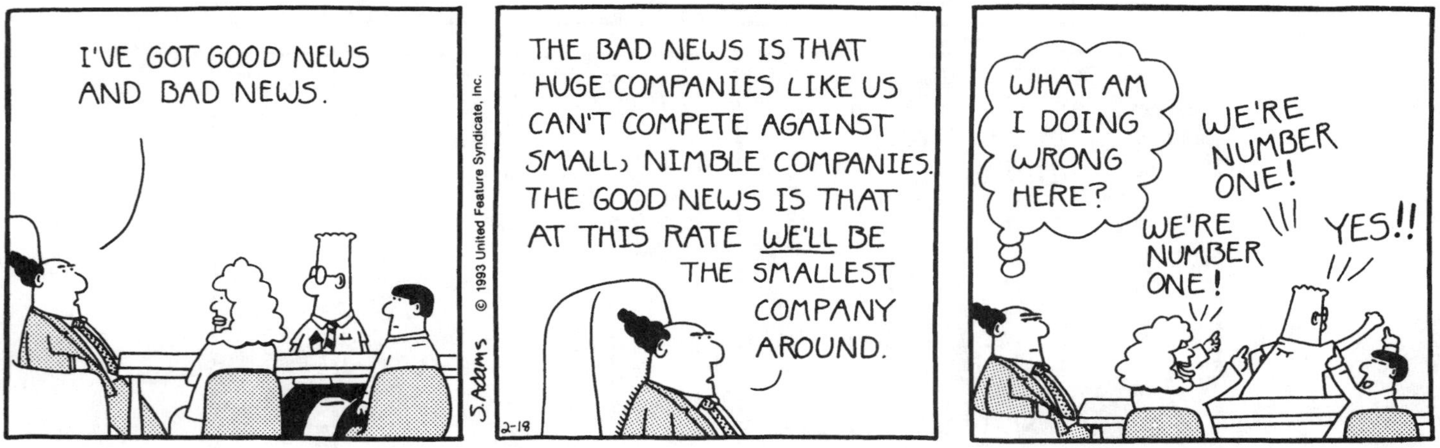
I'VE GOT GOOD NEWS AND BAD NEWS.
S. Adams © 1993 United Feature Syndicate, Inc.
THE BAD NEWS IS THAT HUGE COMPANIES LIKE US CAN'T COMPETE AGAINST SMALL, NIMBLE COMPANIES. THE GOOD NEWS IS THAT AT THIS RATE WE'LL BE THE SMALLEST COMPANY AROUND.
2-18
WHAT AM I DOING WRONG HERE?
WE'RE NUMBER ONE!
WE'RE NUMBER ONE!
YES!!

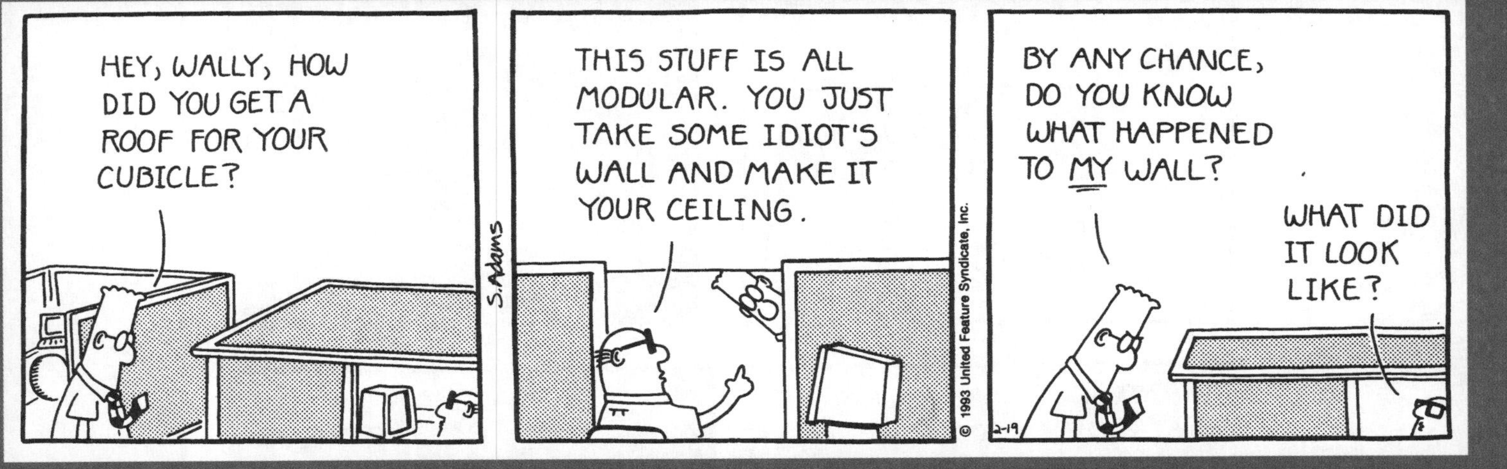
HEY, WALLY, HOW DID YOU GET A ROOF FOR YOUR CUBICLE?
THIS STUFF IS ALL MODULAR. YOU JUST TAKE SOME IDIOT'S WALL AND MAKE IT YOUR CEILING.
BY ANY CHANCE, DO YOU KNOW WHAT HAPPENED TO MY WALL?
WHAT DID IT LOOK LIKE?
© 1993 United Feature Syndicate, Inc.

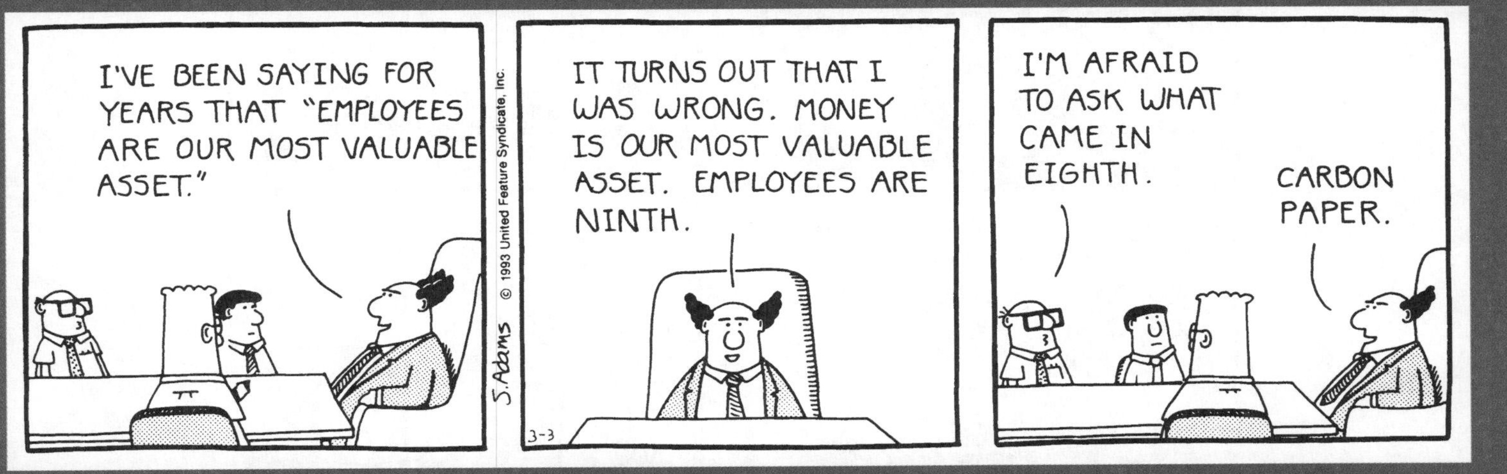
I'VE BEEN SAYING FOR YEARS THAT "EMPLOYEES ARE OUR MOST VALUABLE ASSET."
IT TURNS OUT THAT I WAS WRONG. MONEY IS OUR MOST VALUABLE ASSET. EMPLOYEES ARE NINTH.
I'M AFRAID TO ASK WHAT CAME IN EIGHTH.
CARBON PAPER.
© 1993 United Feature Syndicate, Inc.

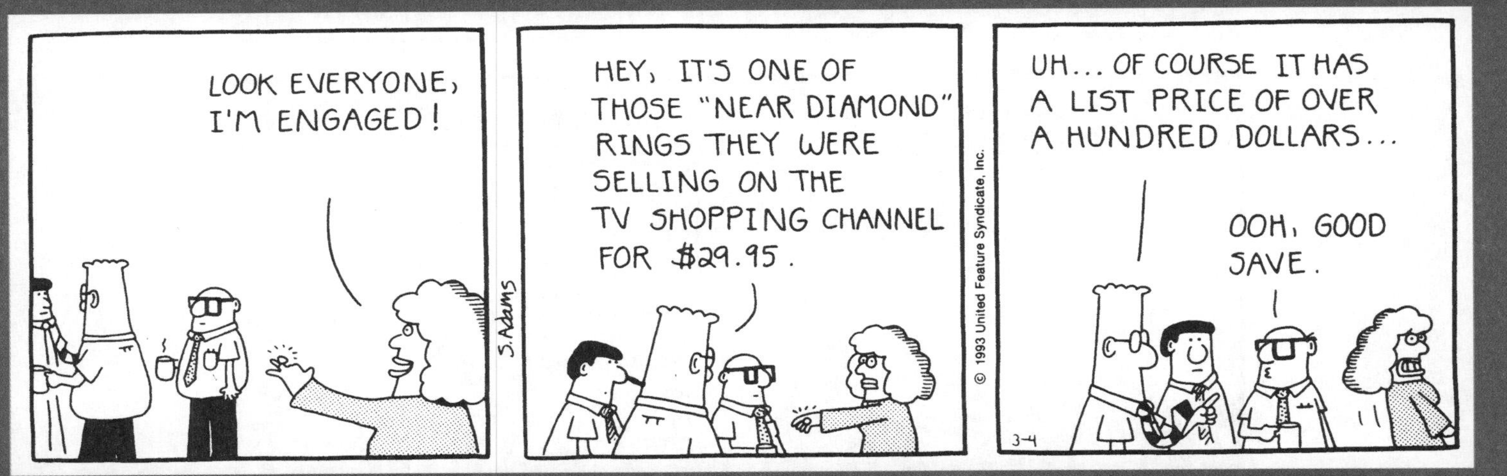
LOOK EVERYONE, I'M ENGAGED!
HEY, IT'S ONE OF THOSE "NEAR DIAMOND" RINGS THEY WERE SELLING ON THE TV SHOPPING CHANNEL FOR $29.95.
UH... OF COURSE IT HAS A LIST PRICE OF OVER A HUNDRED DOLLARS...
OOH, GOOD SAVE.
© 1993 United Feature Syndicate, Inc.

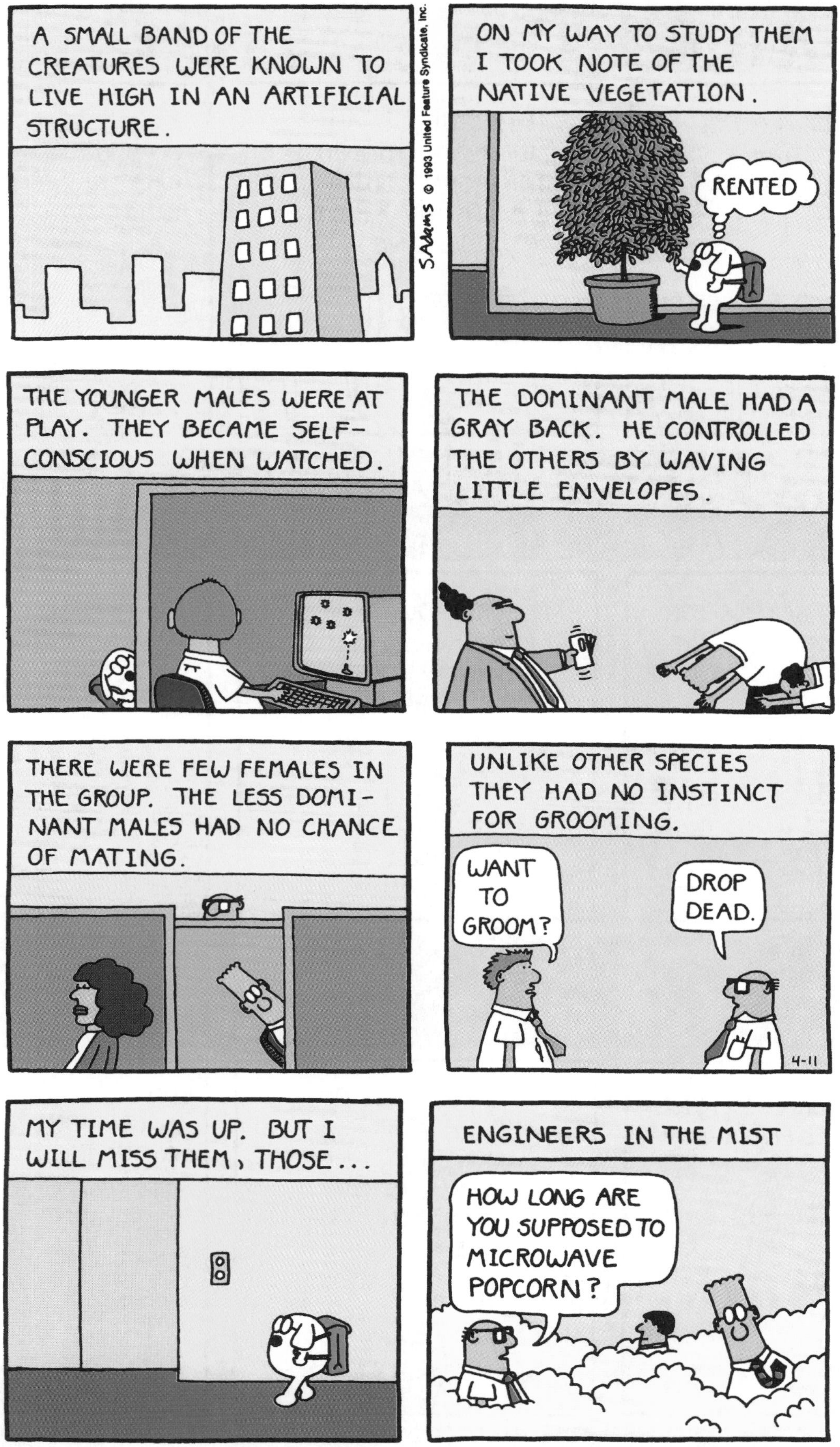
A SMALL BAND OF THE CREATURES WERE KNOWN TO LIVE HIGH IN AN ARTIFICIAL STRUCTURE.
S.Adams © 1993 United Feature Syndicate, Inc.
ON MY WAY TO STUDY THEM I TOOK NOTE OF THE NATIVE VEGETATION.
RENTED
THE YOUNGER MALES WERE AT PLAY. THEY BECAME SELF-CONSCIOUS WHEN WATCHED.
THE DOMINANT MALE HAD A GRAY BACK. HE CONTROLLED THE OTHERS BY WAVING LITTLE ENVELOPES.
THERE WERE FEW FEMALES IN THE GROUP. THE LESS DOMI-NANT MALES HAD NO CHANCE OF MATING.
UNLIKE OTHER SPECIES THEY HAD NO INSTINCT FOR GROOMING.
WANT TO GROOM?
DROP DEAD.
4-11
MY TIME WAS UP. BUT I WILL MISS THEM, THOSE...
ENGINEERS IN THE MIST
HOW LONG ARE YOU SUPPOSED TO MICROWAVE POPCORN?

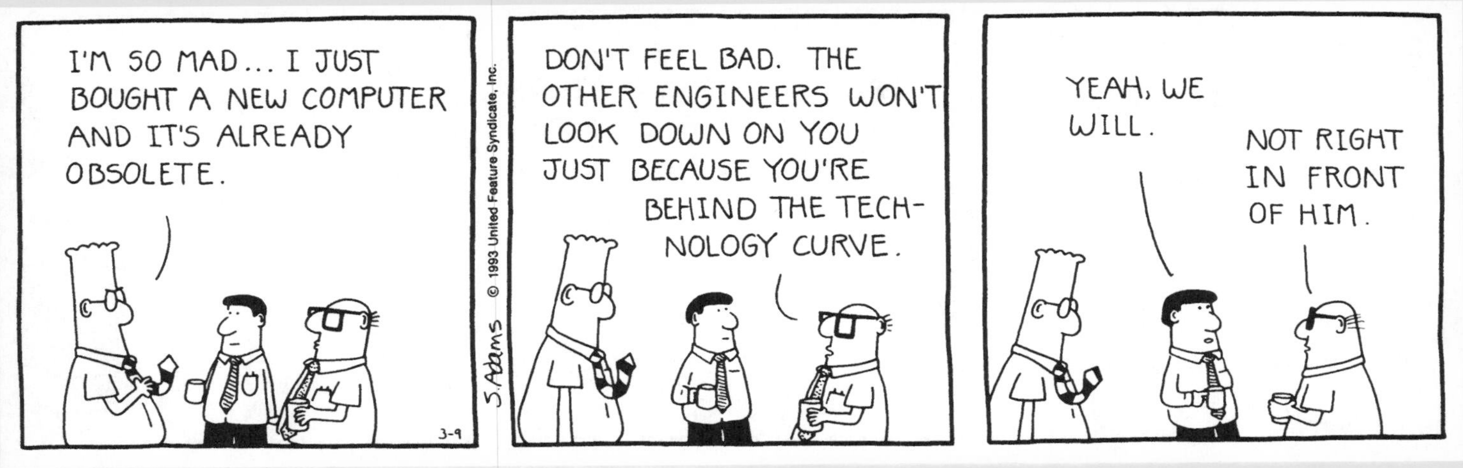
I'M SO MAD... I JUST BOUGHT A NEW COMPUTER AND IT'S ALREADY OBSOLETE.
3-9
S. Adams © 1993 United Feature Syndicate, Inc.
DON'T FEEL BAD. THE OTHER ENGINEERS WON'T LOOK DOWN ON YOU JUST BECAUSE YOU'RE BEHIND THE TECHNOLOGY CURVE.
YEAH, WE WILL.
NOT RIGHT IN FRONT OF HIM.

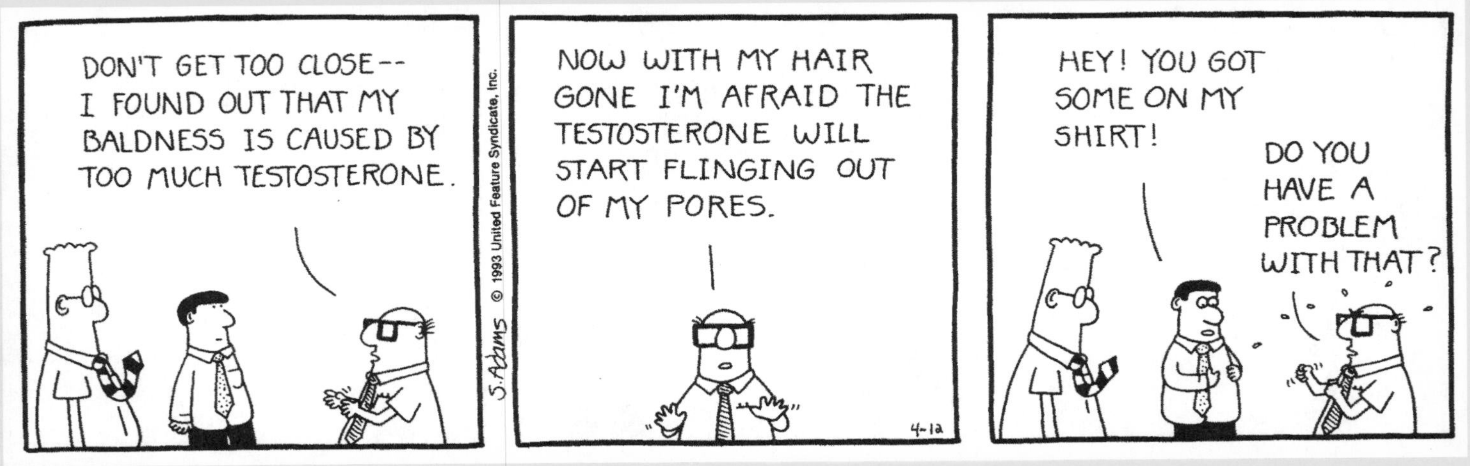
DON'T GET TOO CLOSE-- I FOUND OUT THAT MY BALDNESS IS CAUSED BY TOO MUCH TESTOSTERONE.
S. Adams © 1993 United Feature Syndicate, Inc.
NOW WITH MY HAIR GONE I'M AFRAID THE TESTOSTERONE WILL START FLINGING OUT OF MY PORES.
4-12
HEY! YOU GOT SOME ON MY SHIRT!
DO YOU HAVE A PROBLEM WITH THAT?

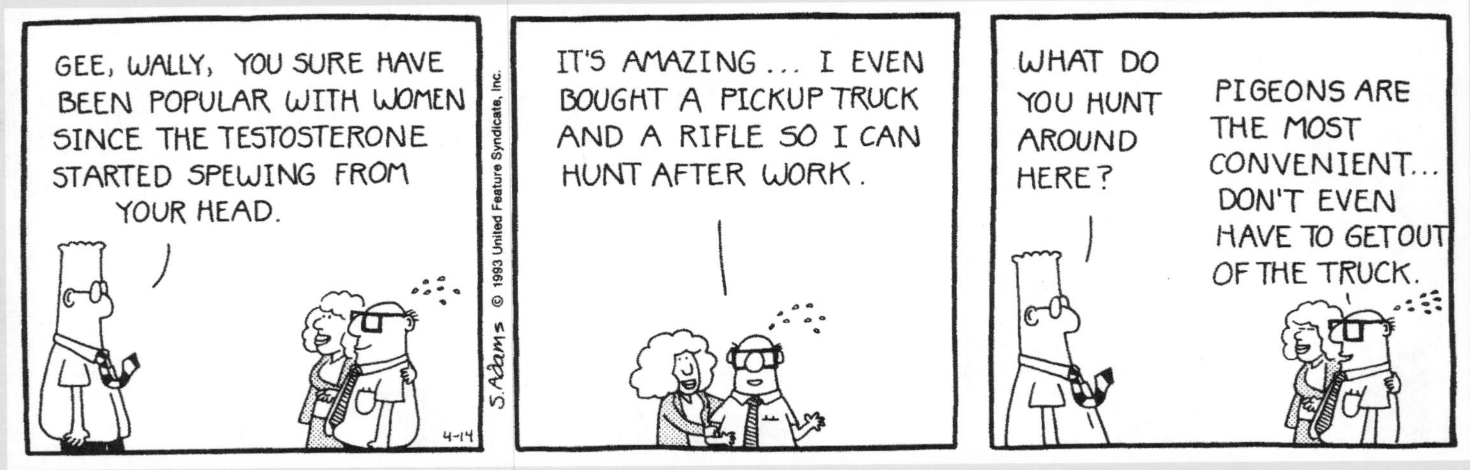
GEE, WALLY, YOU SURE HAVE BEEN POPULAR WITH WOMEN SINCE THE TESTOSTERONE STARTED SPEWING FROM YOUR HEAD.
4-14
S. Adams © 1993 United Feature Syndicate, Inc.
IT'S AMAZING... I EVEN BOUGHT A PICKUP TRUCK AND A RIFLE SO I CAN HUNT AFTER WORK.
WHAT DO YOU HUNT AROUND HERE?
PIGEONS ARE THE MOST CONVENIENT... DON'T EVEN HAVE TO GET OUT OF THE TRUCK.

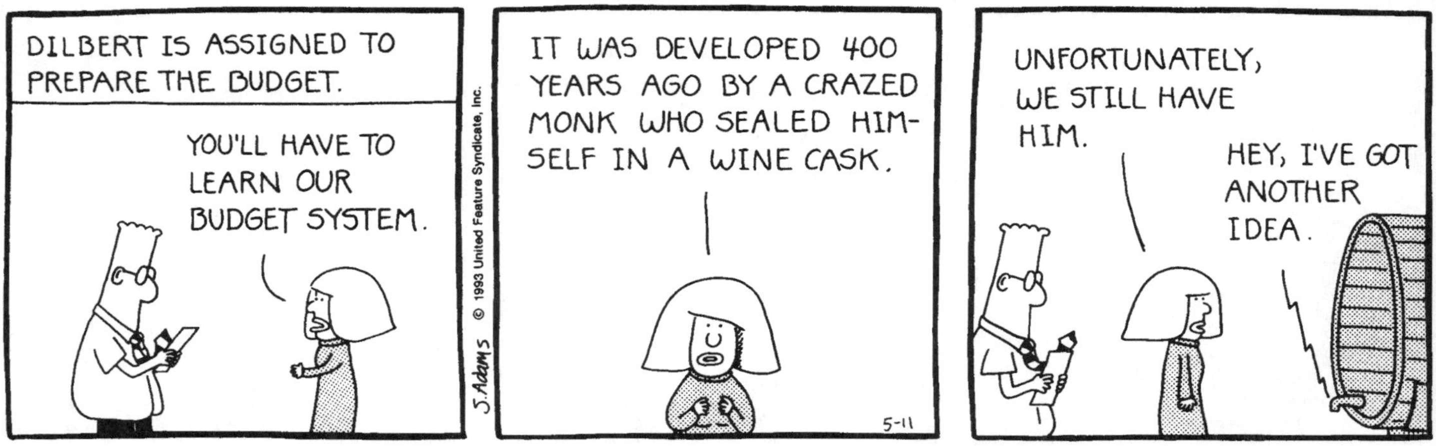
DILBERT IS ASSIGNED TO PREPARE THE BUDGET.
YOU'LL HAVE TO LEARN OUR BUDGET SYSTEM.
S. Adams © 1993 United Feature Syndicate, Inc.
IT WAS DEVELOPED 400 YEARS AGO BY A CRAZED MONK WHO SEALED HIM-SELF IN A WINE CASK.
5-11
UNFORTUNATELY, WE STILL HAVE HIM.
HEY, I'VE GOT ANOTHER IDEA.

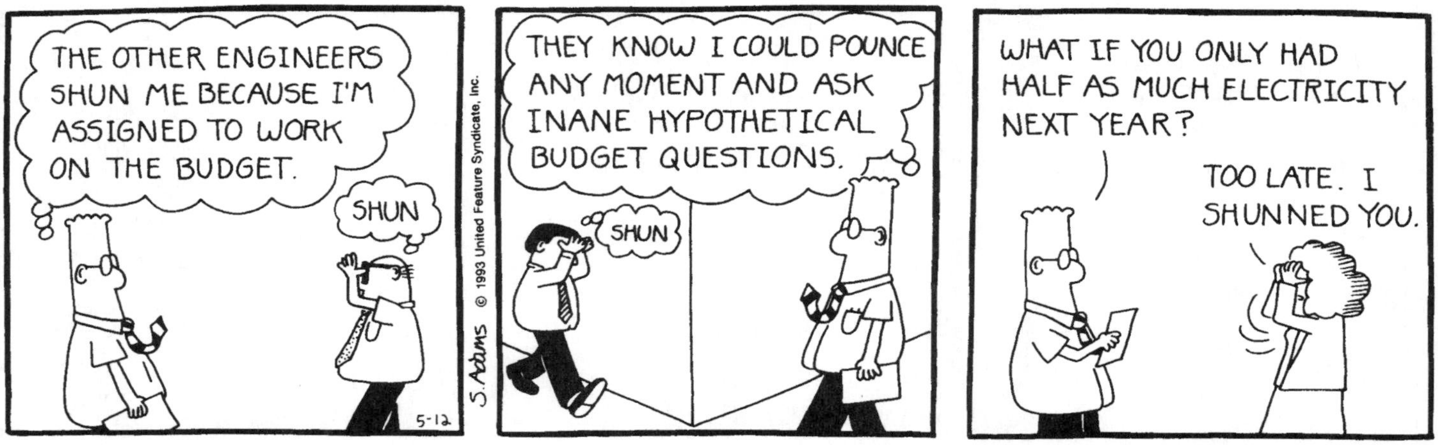
THE OTHER ENGINEERS SHUN ME BECAUSE I'M ASSIGNED TO WORK ON THE BUDGET.
SHUN
5-12
S. Adams © 1993 United Feature Syndicate, Inc.
THEY KNOW I COULD POUNCE ANY MOMENT AND ASK INANE HYPOTHETICAL BUDGET QUESTIONS.
SHUN
WHAT IF YOU ONLY HAD HALF AS MUCH ELECTRICITY NEXT YEAR?
TOO LATE. I SHUNNED YOU.

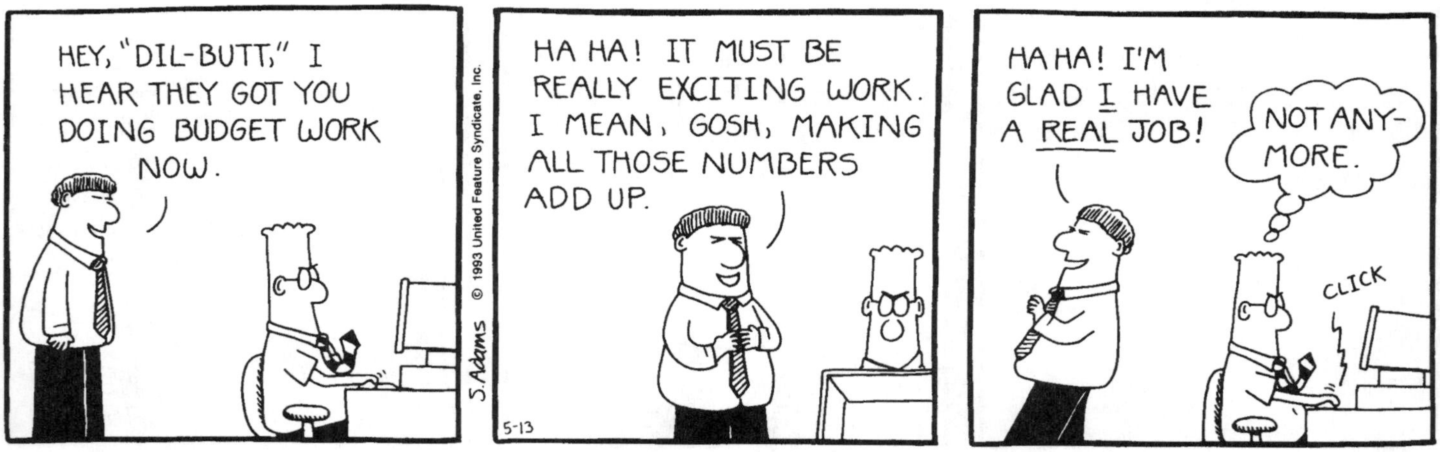
HEY, "DIL-BUTT," I HEAR THEY GOT YOU DOING BUDGET WORK NOW.
S. Adams © 1993 United Feature Syndicate, Inc.
HA HA! IT MUST BE REALLY EXCITING WORK. I MEAN, GOSH, MAKING ALL THOSE NUMBERS ADD UP.
5-13
HA HA! I'M GLAD I HAVE A REAL JOB!
NOT ANY-MORE.
CLICK

Panel 1:
...COMPANIES MUST LEARN TO EMBRACE CHANGE.

UH-OH. IT'S ANOTHER MANAGEMENT FAD.

Panel 2:
WILL IT PASS QUICKLY OR WILL IT LINGER LIKE THE STENCH OF A DEAD WOODCHUCK UNDER THE PORCH?

5-4

Panel 3:
I THINK WE SHOULD DO A "CHANGE" NEWSLETTER.

WOODCHUCK.

© 1993 United Feature Syndicate, Inc.

Panel 4:
MY PRODUCTIVITY IS SHOT. I CAN'T STOP DAYDREAMING ABOUT IRENE IN ACCOUNTING.

5-25

Panel 5:
DO WHAT I DID. TRY TO PHASE OUT OF IT BY DAYDREAMING OF LAURA IN ENGINEERING, THEN MOVE TO THE ORDINARY-LOOKING BETTY IN MARKETING.

© 1993 United Feature Syndicate, Inc.

Panel 6:
NOW I'M DAYDREAMING ABOUT ALL THREE OF THEM.

SAME THING HAPPENED TO ME.

Panel 7:
I UNDERSTAND THAT YOU MEN ARE SPENDING THREE-QUARTERS OF YOUR TIME DAYDREAMING ABOUT ATTRACTIVE WOMEN.

Panel 8:
DO YOU REALIZE HOW MUCH TIME IS BEING WASTED HERE?

© 1993 United Feature Syndicate, Inc.

Panel 9:
TWENTY-FIVE PERCENT?

IT'S A TRICK QUESTION.

IRENE

5-26

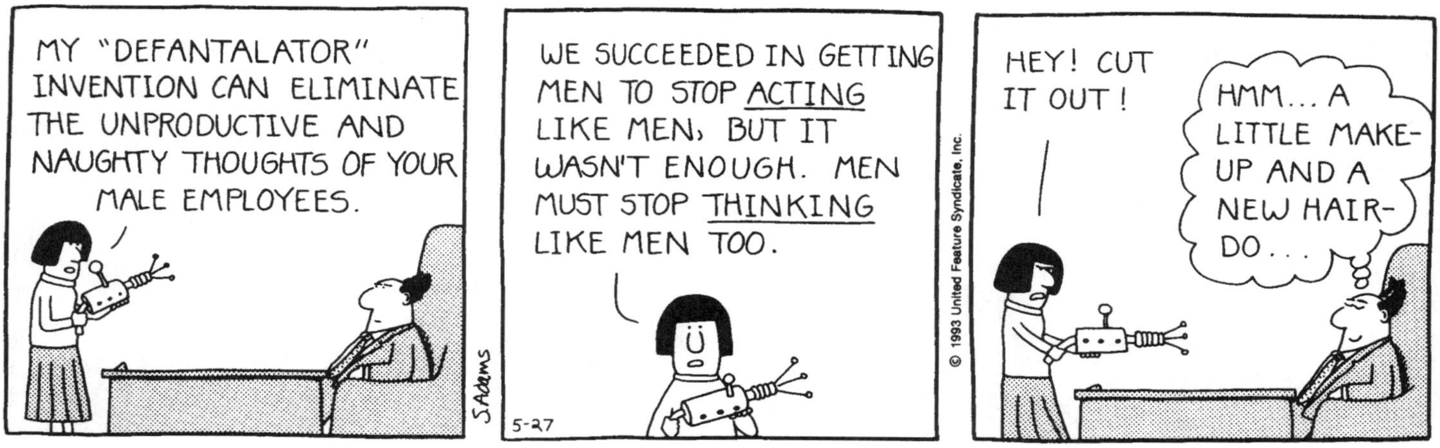
MY "DEFANTALATOR" INVENTION CAN ELIMINATE THE UNPRODUCTIVE AND NAUGHTY THOUGHTS OF YOUR MALE EMPLOYEES.
S. Adams
WE SUCCEEDED IN GETTING MEN TO STOP ACTING LIKE MEN, BUT IT WASN'T ENOUGH. MEN MUST STOP THINKING LIKE MEN TOO.
5-27
© 1993 United Feature Syndicate, Inc.
HEY! CUT IT OUT!
HMM... A LITTLE MAKE-UP AND A NEW HAIR-DO...

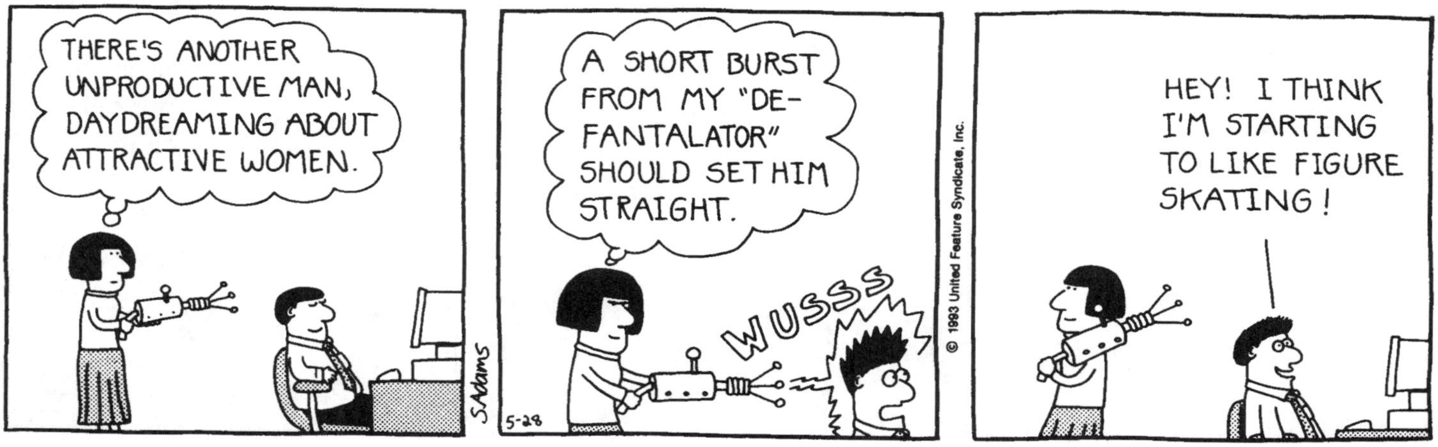
THERE'S ANOTHER UNPRODUCTIVE MAN, DAYDREAMING ABOUT ATTRACTIVE WOMEN.
S. Adams
A SHORT BURST FROM MY "DE-FANTALATOR" SHOULD SET HIM STRAIGHT.
WUSSS
5-28
© 1993 United Feature Syndicate, Inc.
HEY! I THINK I'M STARTING TO LIKE FIGURE SKATING!

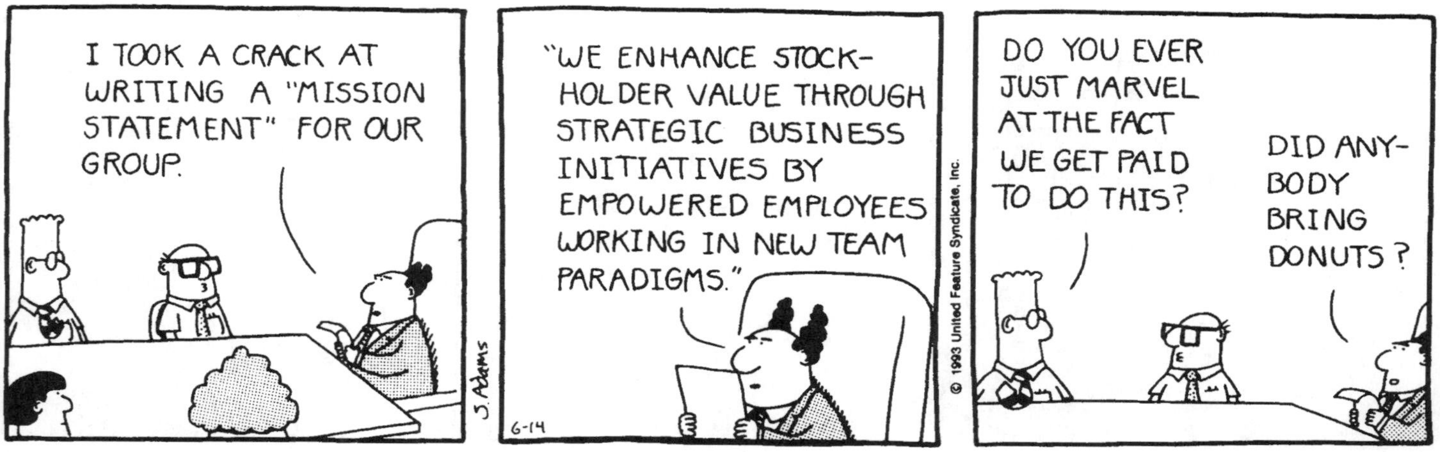
I TOOK A CRACK AT WRITING A "MISSION STATEMENT" FOR OUR GROUP.
S. Adams
"WE ENHANCE STOCK-HOLDER VALUE THROUGH STRATEGIC BUSINESS INITIATIVES BY EMPOWERED EMPLOYEES WORKING IN NEW TEAM PARADIGMS."
6-14
© 1993 United Feature Syndicate, Inc.
DO YOU EVER JUST MARVEL AT THE FACT WE GET PAID TO DO THIS?
DID ANY-BODY BRING DONUTS?

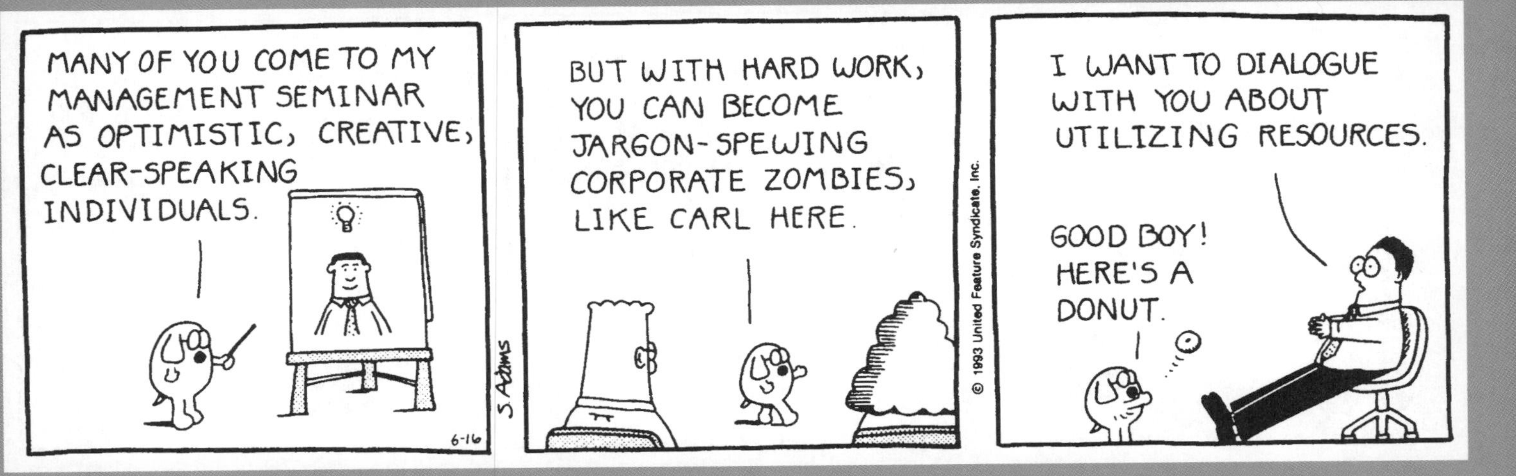
MANY OF YOU COME TO MY MANAGEMENT SEMINAR AS OPTIMISTIC, CREATIVE, CLEAR-SPEAKING INDIVIDUALS.
BUT WITH HARD WORK, YOU CAN BECOME JARGON-SPEWING CORPORATE ZOMBIES, LIKE CARL HERE.
I WANT TO DIALOGUE WITH YOU ABOUT UTILIZING RESOURCES.
GOOD BOY! HERE'S A DONUT.
© 1993 United Feature Syndicate, Inc.

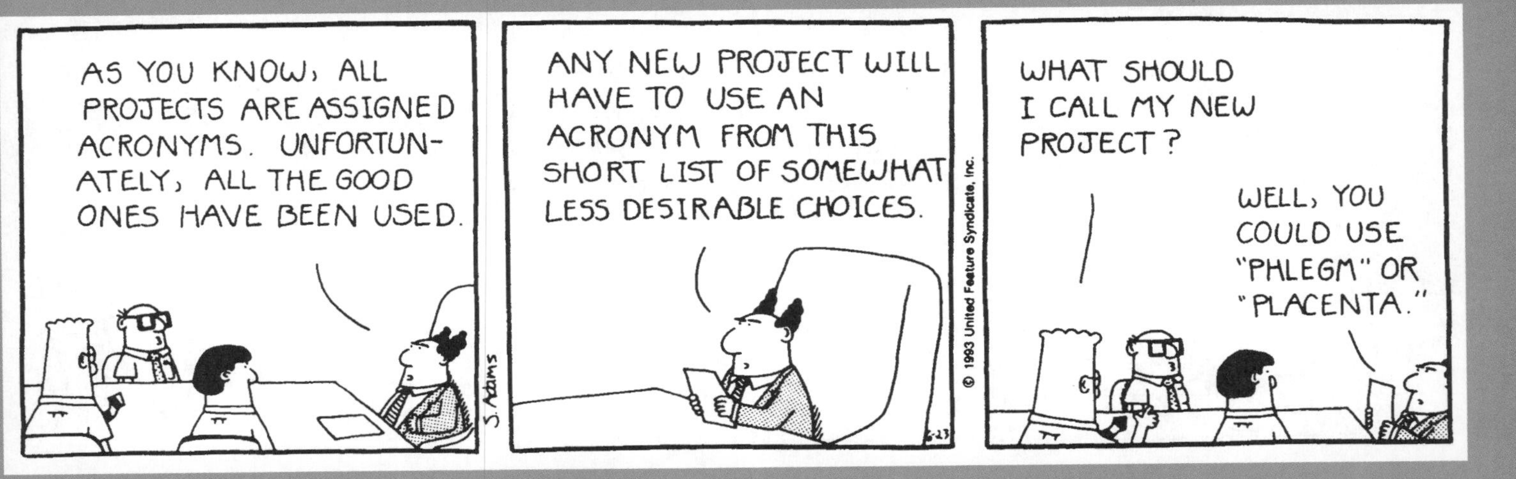
AS YOU KNOW, ALL PROJECTS ARE ASSIGNED ACRONYMS. UNFORTUNATELY, ALL THE GOOD ONES HAVE BEEN USED.
ANY NEW PROJECT WILL HAVE TO USE AN ACRONYM FROM THIS SHORT LIST OF SOMEWHAT LESS DESIRABLE CHOICES.
WHAT SHOULD I CALL MY NEW PROJECT?
WELL, YOU COULD USE "PHLEGM" OR "PLACENTA."
© 1993 United Feature Syndicate, Inc.

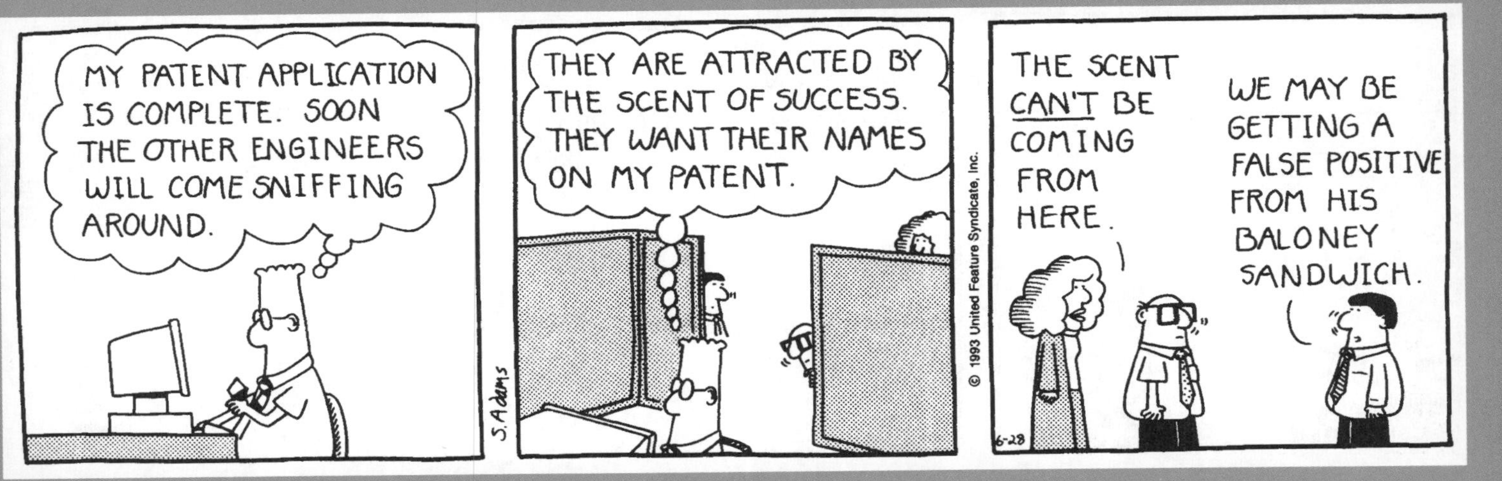
MY PATENT APPLICATION IS COMPLETE. SOON THE OTHER ENGINEERS WILL COME SNIFFING AROUND.
THEY ARE ATTRACTED BY THE SCENT OF SUCCESS. THEY WANT THEIR NAMES ON MY PATENT.
THE SCENT CAN'T BE COMING FROM HERE.
WE MAY BE GETTING A FALSE POSITIVE FROM HIS BALONEY SANDWICH.
© 1993 United Feature Syndicate, Inc.

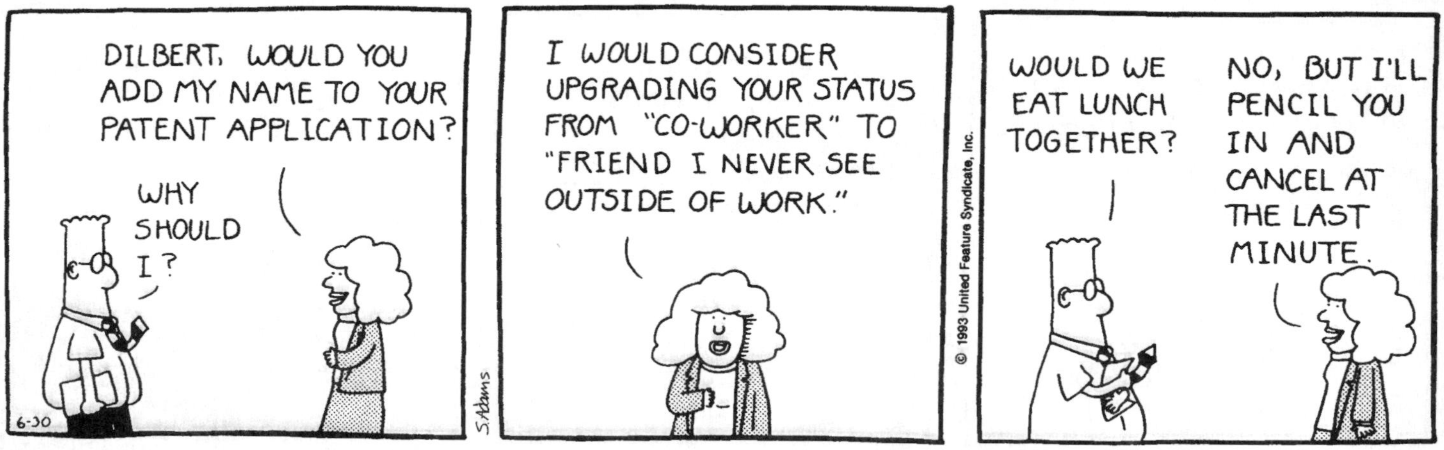
DILBERT, WOULD YOU ADD MY NAME TO YOUR PATENT APPLICATION?
WHY SHOULD I?
6-30
S. Adams
I WOULD CONSIDER UPGRADING YOUR STATUS FROM "CO-WORKER" TO "FRIEND I NEVER SEE OUTSIDE OF WORK."
© 1993 United Feature Syndicate, Inc.
WOULD WE EAT LUNCH TOGETHER?
NO, BUT I'LL PENCIL YOU IN AND CANCEL AT THE LAST MINUTE.

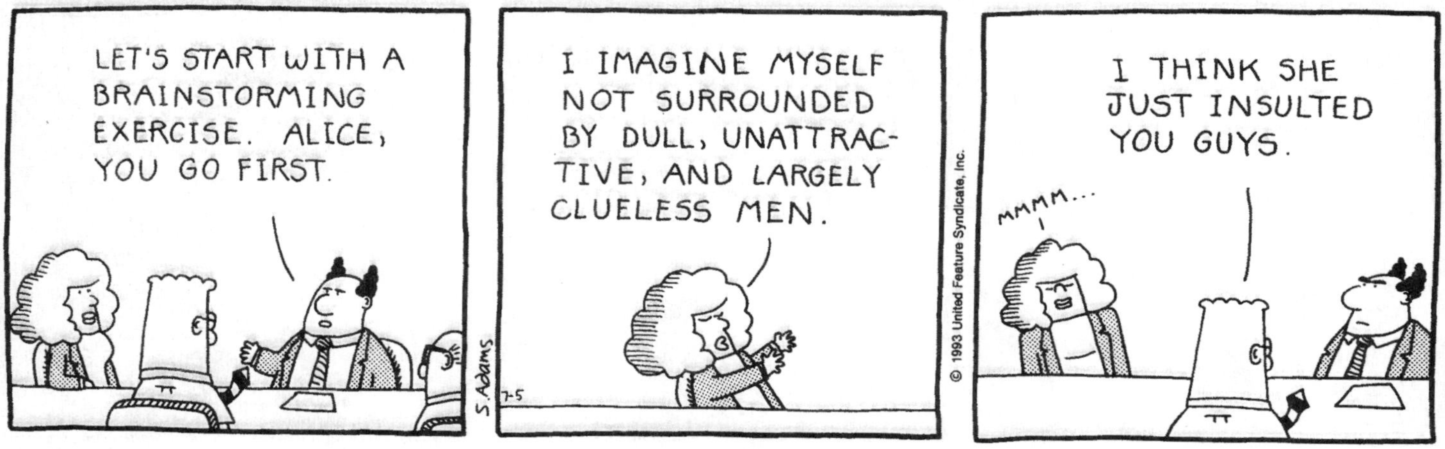
LET'S START WITH A BRAINSTORMING EXERCISE. ALICE, YOU GO FIRST.
S. Adams
7-5
I IMAGINE MYSELF NOT SURROUNDED BY DULL, UNATTRACTIVE, AND LARGELY CLUELESS MEN.
© 1993 United Feature Syndicate, Inc.
I THINK SHE JUST INSULTED YOU GUYS.
MMMM...

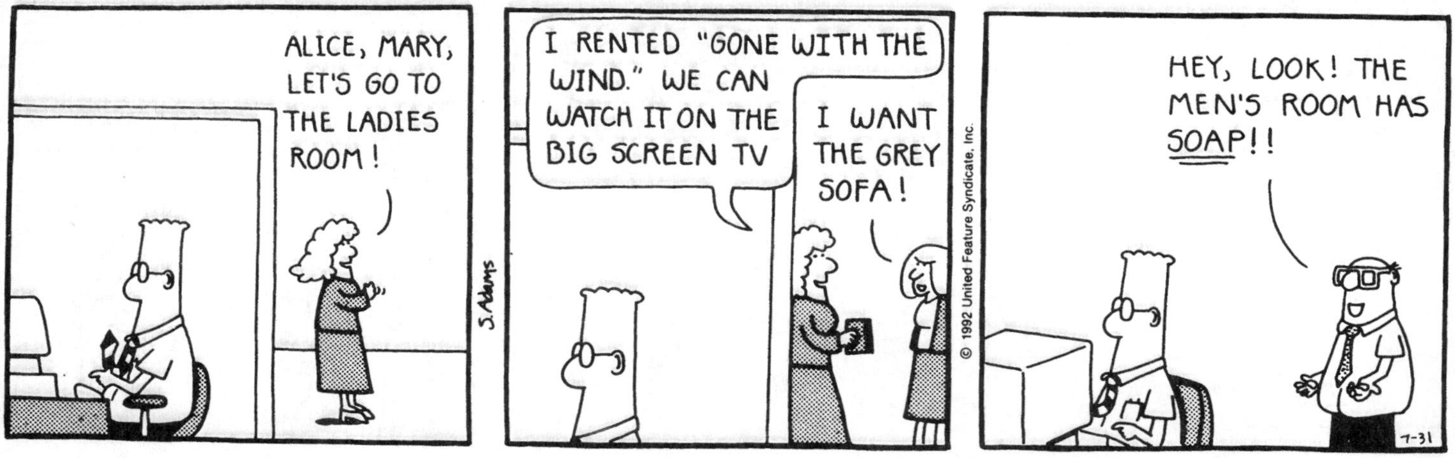
ALICE, MARY, LET'S GO TO THE LADIES ROOM!
S. Adams
I RENTED "GONE WITH THE WIND." WE CAN WATCH IT ON THE BIG SCREEN TV
I WANT THE GREY SOFA!
© 1992 United Feature Syndicate, Inc.
HEY, LOOK! THE MEN'S ROOM HAS SOAP!!
7-31

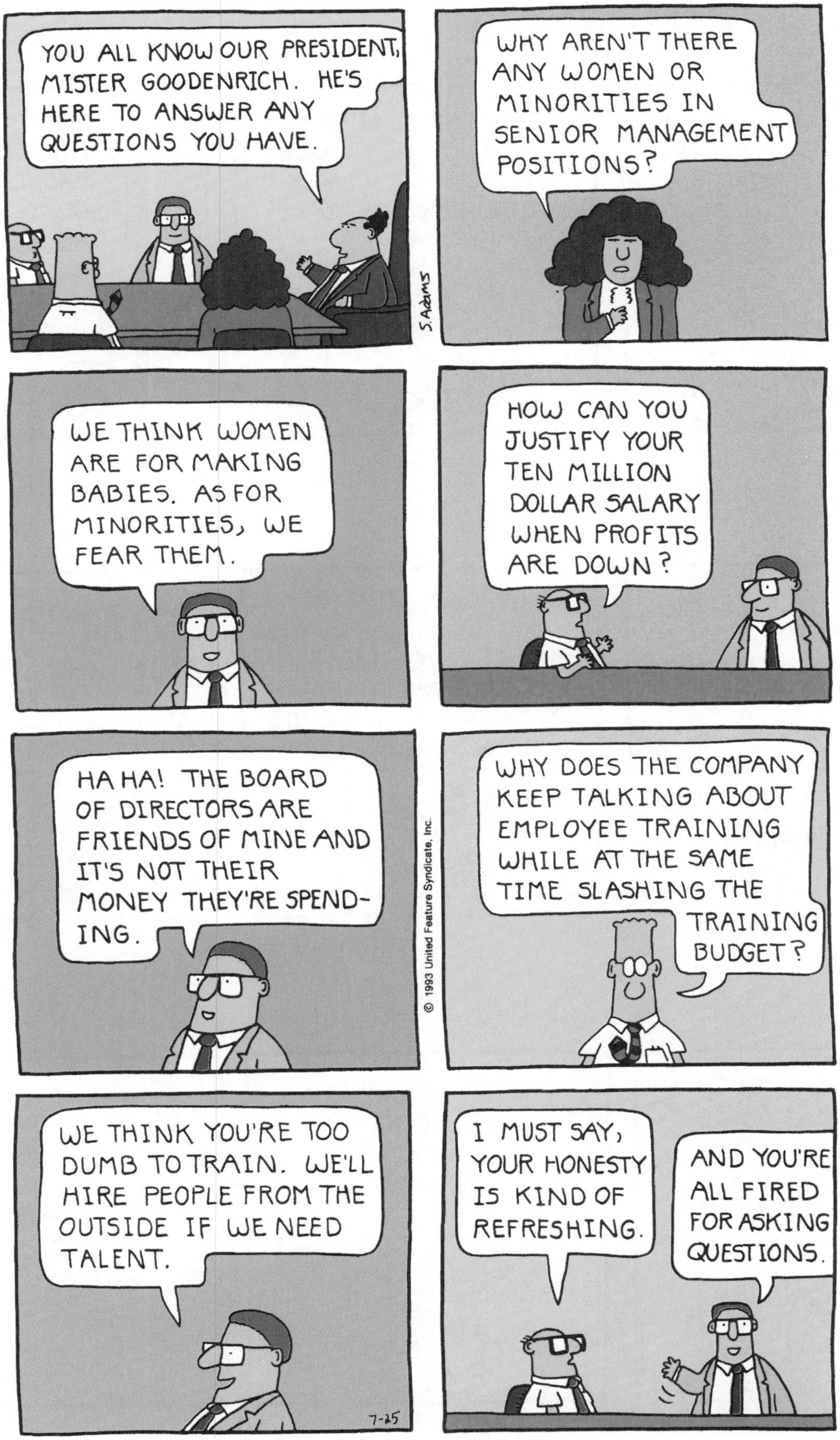
YOU ALL KNOW OUR PRESIDENT, MISTER GOODENRICH. HE'S HERE TO ANSWER ANY QUESTIONS YOU HAVE.
S. Adams
WHY AREN'T THERE ANY WOMEN OR MINORITIES IN SENIOR MANAGEMENT POSITIONS?
WE THINK WOMEN ARE FOR MAKING BABIES. AS FOR MINORITIES, WE FEAR THEM.
HOW CAN YOU JUSTIFY YOUR TEN MILLION DOLLAR SALARY WHEN PROFITS ARE DOWN?
HA HA! THE BOARD OF DIRECTORS ARE FRIENDS OF MINE AND IT'S NOT THEIR MONEY THEY'RE SPENDING.
© 1993 United Feature Syndicate, Inc.
WHY DOES THE COMPANY KEEP TALKING ABOUT EMPLOYEE TRAINING WHILE AT THE SAME TIME SLASHING THE TRAINING BUDGET?
WE THINK YOU'RE TOO DUMB TO TRAIN. WE'LL HIRE PEOPLE FROM THE OUTSIDE IF WE NEED TALENT.
7-25
I MUST SAY, YOUR HONESTY IS KIND OF REFRESHING.
AND YOU'RE ALL FIRED FOR ASKING QUESTIONS.

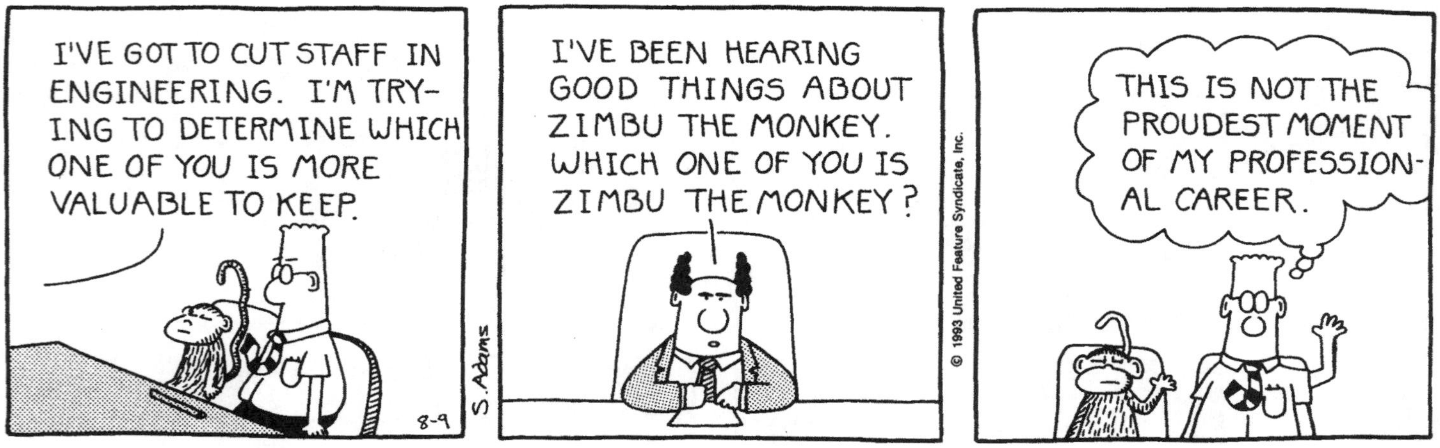
I'VE GOT TO CUT STAFF IN ENGINEERING. I'M TRYING TO DETERMINE WHICH ONE OF YOU IS MORE VALUABLE TO KEEP.
I'VE BEEN HEARING GOOD THINGS ABOUT ZIMBU THE MONKEY. WHICH ONE OF YOU IS ZIMBU THE MONKEY?
THIS IS NOT THE PROUDEST MOMENT OF MY PROFESSIONAL CAREER.
© 1993 United Feature Syndicate, Inc.

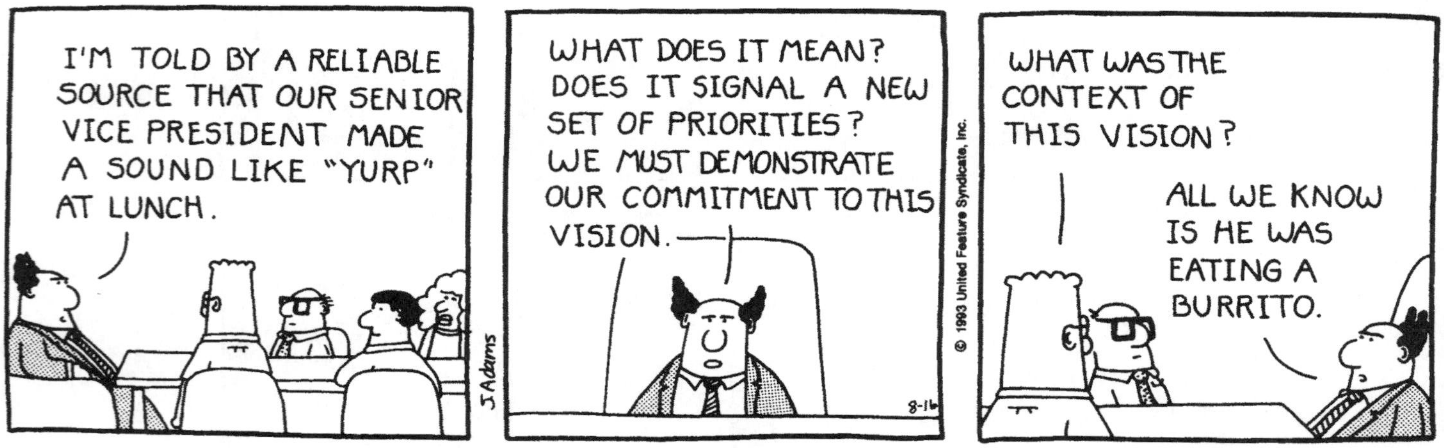
I'M TOLD BY A RELIABLE SOURCE THAT OUR SENIOR VICE PRESIDENT MADE A SOUND LIKE "YURP" AT LUNCH.
WHAT DOES IT MEAN? DOES IT SIGNAL A NEW SET OF PRIORITIES? WE MUST DEMONSTRATE OUR COMMITMENT TO THIS VISION.
WHAT WAS THE CONTEXT OF THIS VISION?
ALL WE KNOW IS HE WAS EATING A BURRITO.
© 1993 United Feature Syndicate, Inc.

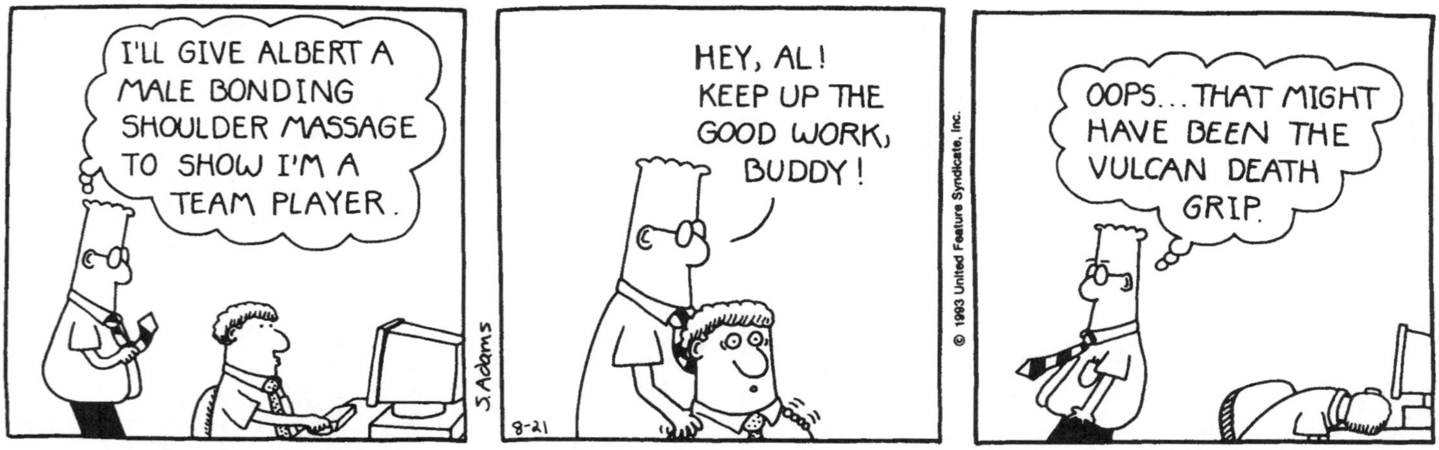
I'LL GIVE ALBERT A MALE BONDING SHOULDER MASSAGE TO SHOW I'M A TEAM PLAYER.
HEY, AL! KEEP UP THE GOOD WORK, BUDDY!
OOPS... THAT MIGHT HAVE BEEN THE VULCAN DEATH GRIP.
© 1993 United Feature Syndicate, Inc.

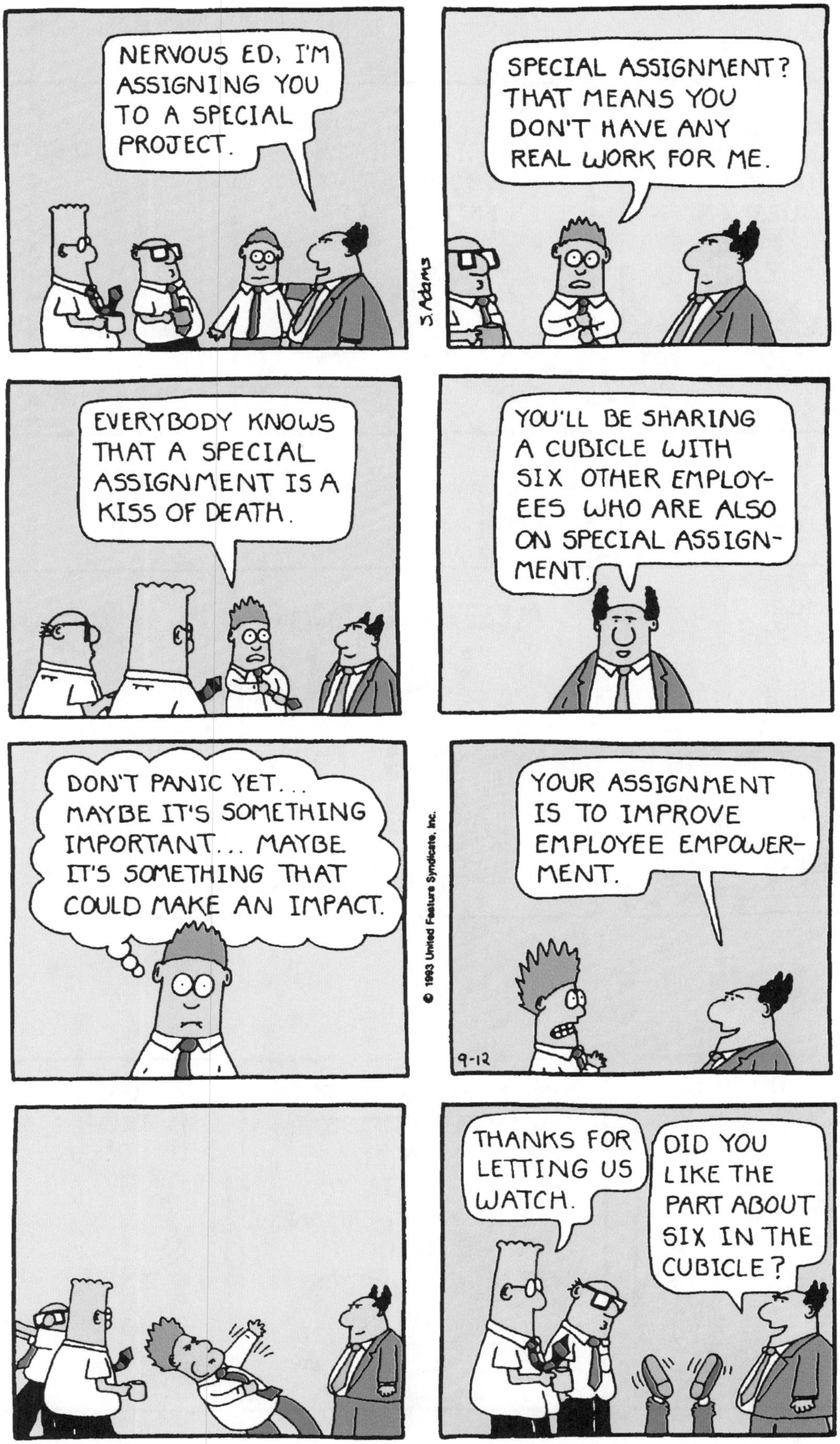
NERVOUS ED, I'M ASSIGNING YOU TO A SPECIAL PROJECT.
S. Adams
SPECIAL ASSIGNMENT? THAT MEANS YOU DON'T HAVE ANY REAL WORK FOR ME.
EVERYBODY KNOWS THAT A SPECIAL ASSIGNMENT IS A KISS OF DEATH.
YOU'LL BE SHARING A CUBICLE WITH SIX OTHER EMPLOYEES WHO ARE ALSO ON SPECIAL ASSIGNMENT.
DON'T PANIC YET... MAYBE IT'S SOMETHING IMPORTANT... MAYBE IT'S SOMETHING THAT COULD MAKE AN IMPACT.
© 1993 United Feature Syndicate, Inc.
YOUR ASSIGNMENT IS TO IMPROVE EMPLOYEE EMPOWERMENT.
9-12
THANKS FOR LETTING US WATCH.
DID YOU LIKE THE PART ABOUT SIX IN THE CUBICLE?

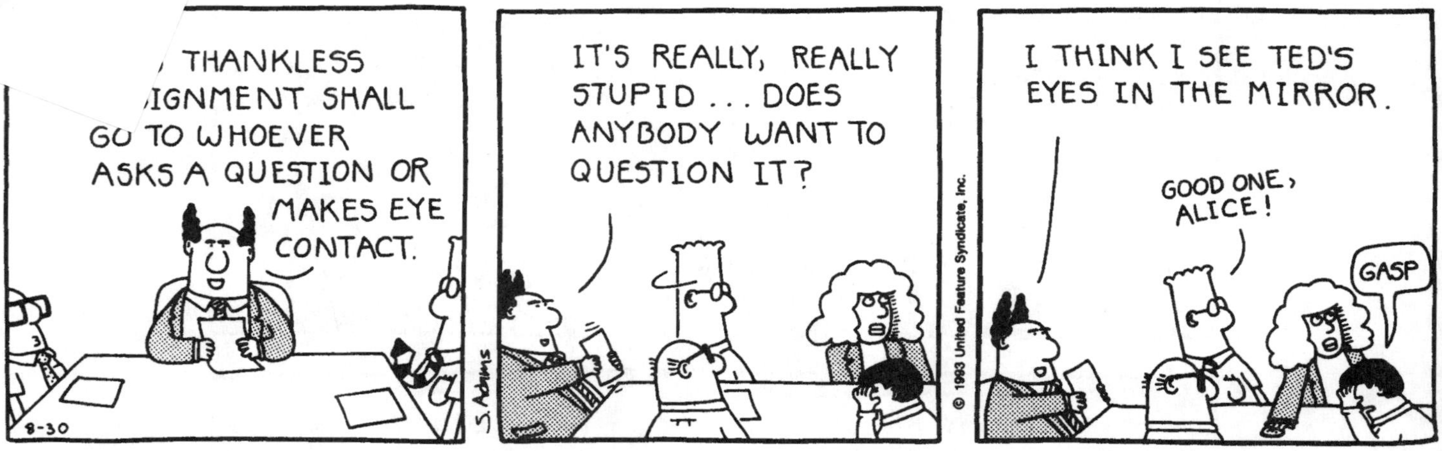
THANKLESS
IGNMENT SHALL
GO TO WHOEVER
ASKS A QUESTION OR
MAKES EYE
CONTACT.
8-30
S. Adams
IT'S REALLY, REALLY STUPID . . . DOES ANYBODY WANT TO QUESTION IT?
© 1993 United Feature Syndicate, Inc.
I THINK I SEE TED'S EYES IN THE MIRROR.
GOOD ONE, ALICE!
GASP

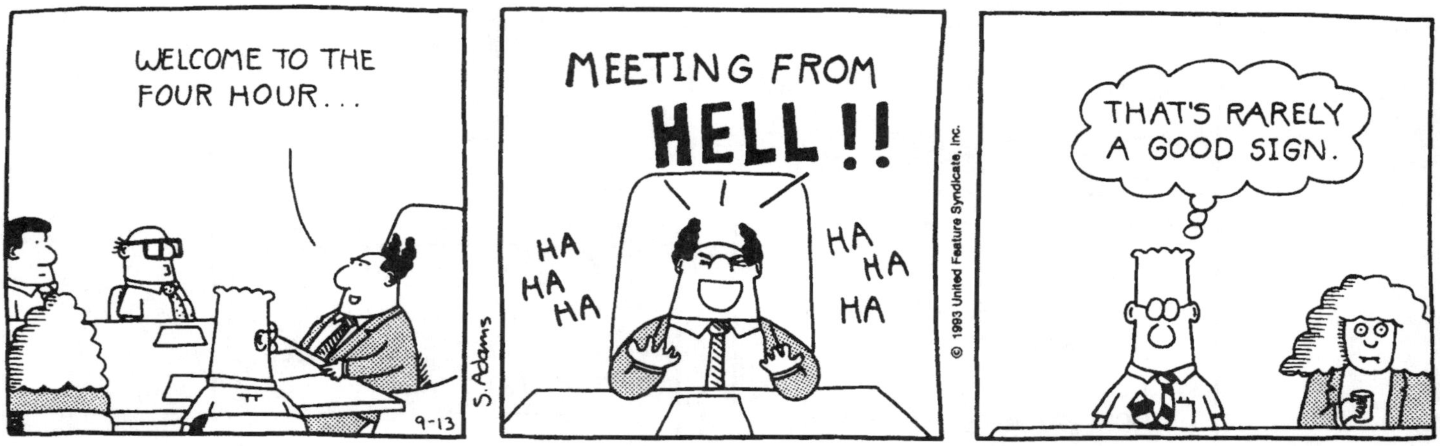
WELCOME TO THE FOUR HOUR . . .
9-13
S. Adams
MEETING FROM
HELL!!
HA HA HA
HA HA HA
© 1993 United Feature Syndicate, Inc.
THAT'S RARELY A GOOD SIGN.

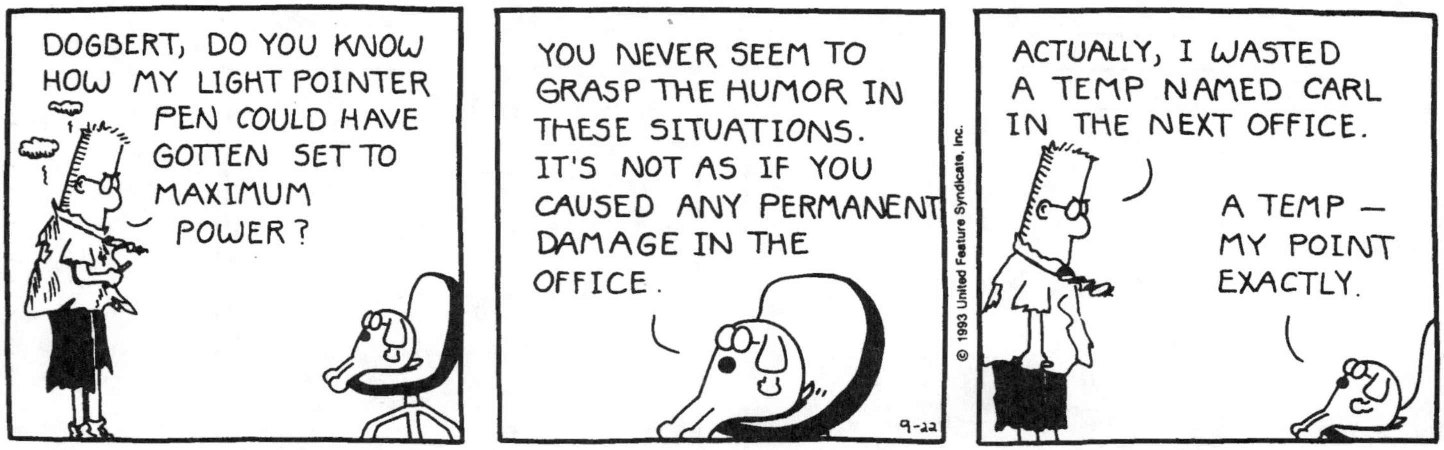
DOGBERT, DO YOU KNOW HOW MY LIGHT POINTER PEN COULD HAVE GOTTEN SET TO MAXIMUM POWER?
YOU NEVER SEEM TO GRASP THE HUMOR IN THESE SITUATIONS. IT'S NOT AS IF YOU CAUSED ANY PERMANENT DAMAGE IN THE OFFICE.
9-22
© 1993 United Feature Syndicate, Inc.
ACTUALLY, I WASTED A TEMP NAMED CARL IN THE NEXT OFFICE.
A TEMP — MY POINT EXACTLY.

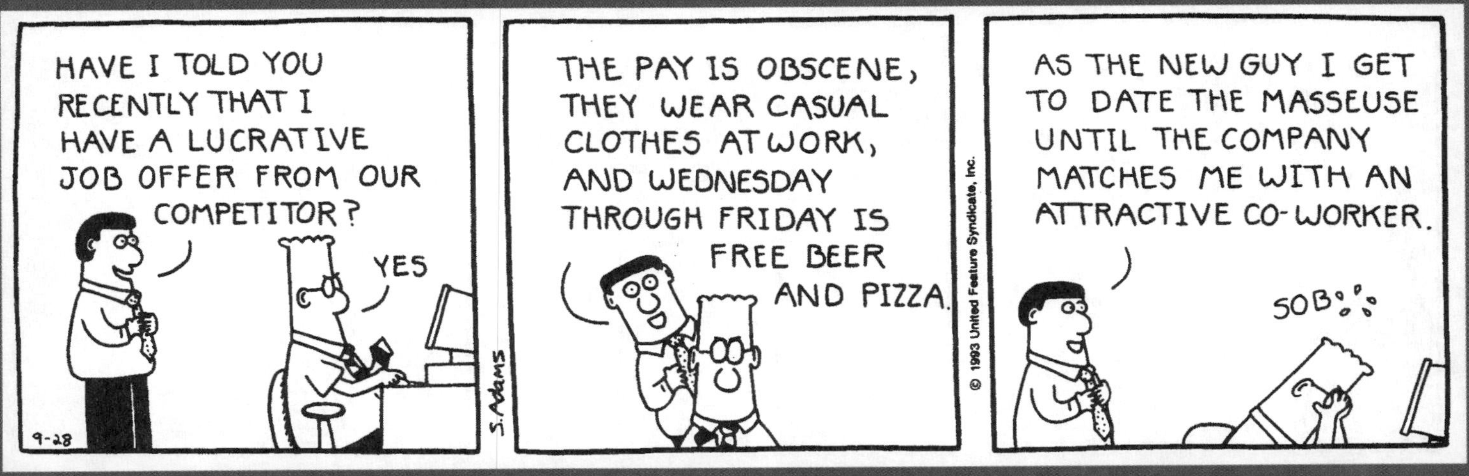
HAVE I TOLD YOU RECENTLY THAT I HAVE A LUCRATIVE JOB OFFER FROM OUR COMPETITOR?
YES
9-28
S. Adams
THE PAY IS OBSCENE, THEY WEAR CASUAL CLOTHES AT WORK, AND WEDNESDAY THROUGH FRIDAY IS FREE BEER AND PIZZA.
© 1993 United Feature Syndicate, Inc.
AS THE NEW GUY I GET TO DATE THE MASSEUSE UNTIL THE COMPANY MATCHES ME WITH AN ATTRACTIVE CO-WORKER.
SOB

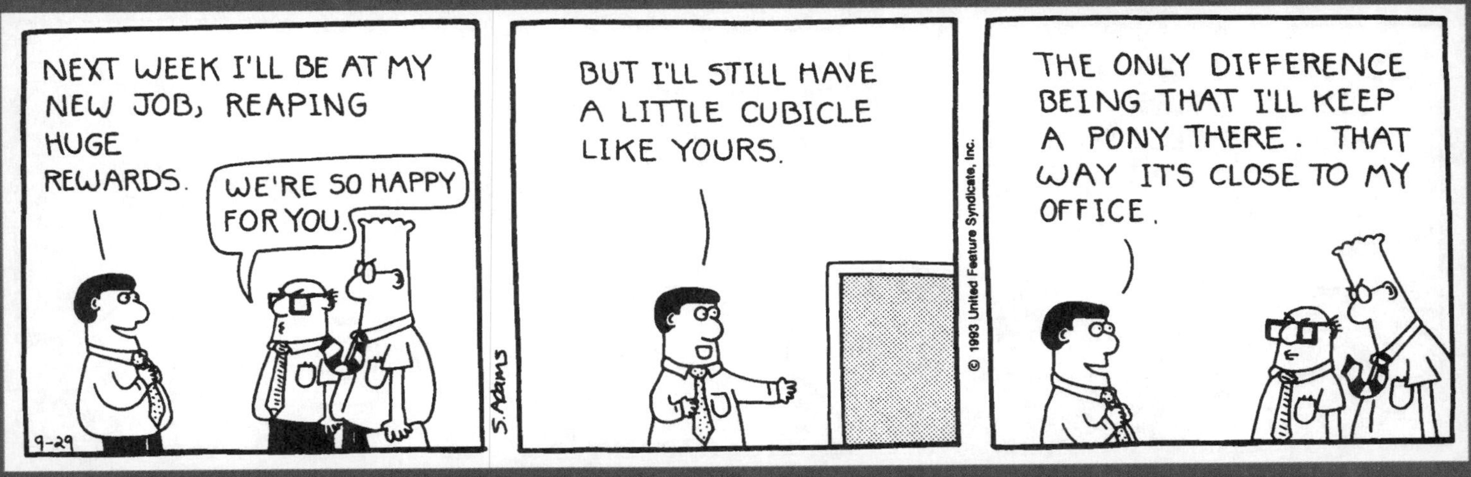
NEXT WEEK I'LL BE AT MY NEW JOB, REAPING HUGE REWARDS.
WE'RE SO HAPPY FOR YOU.
9-29
S. Adams
BUT I'LL STILL HAVE A LITTLE CUBICLE LIKE YOURS.
© 1993 United Feature Syndicate, Inc.
THE ONLY DIFFERENCE BEING THAT I'LL KEEP A PONY THERE. THAT WAY IT'S CLOSE TO MY OFFICE.

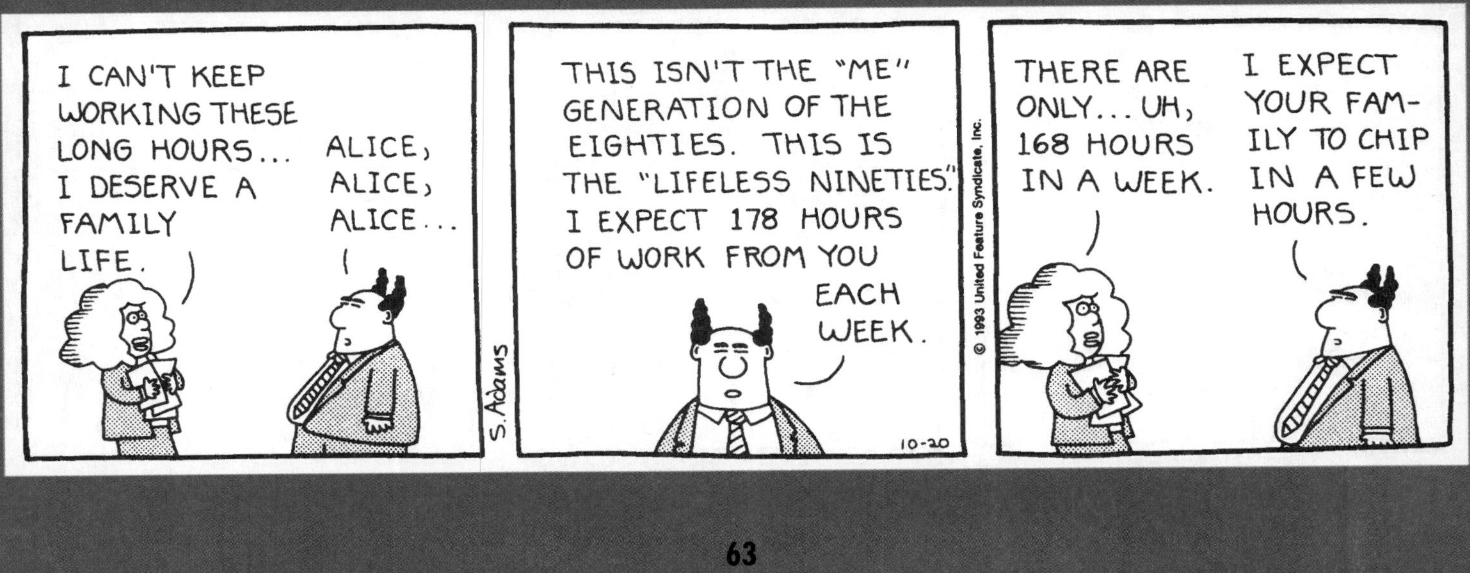
I CAN'T KEEP WORKING THESE LONG HOURS... I DESERVE A FAMILY LIFE.
ALICE, ALICE, ALICE...
S. Adams
THIS ISN'T THE "ME" GENERATION OF THE EIGHTIES. THIS IS THE "LIFELESS NINETIES." I EXPECT 178 HOURS OF WORK FROM YOU EACH WEEK.
10-20
© 1993 United Feature Syndicate, Inc.
THERE ARE ONLY... UH, 168 HOURS IN A WEEK.
I EXPECT YOUR FAMILY TO CHIP IN A FEW HOURS.

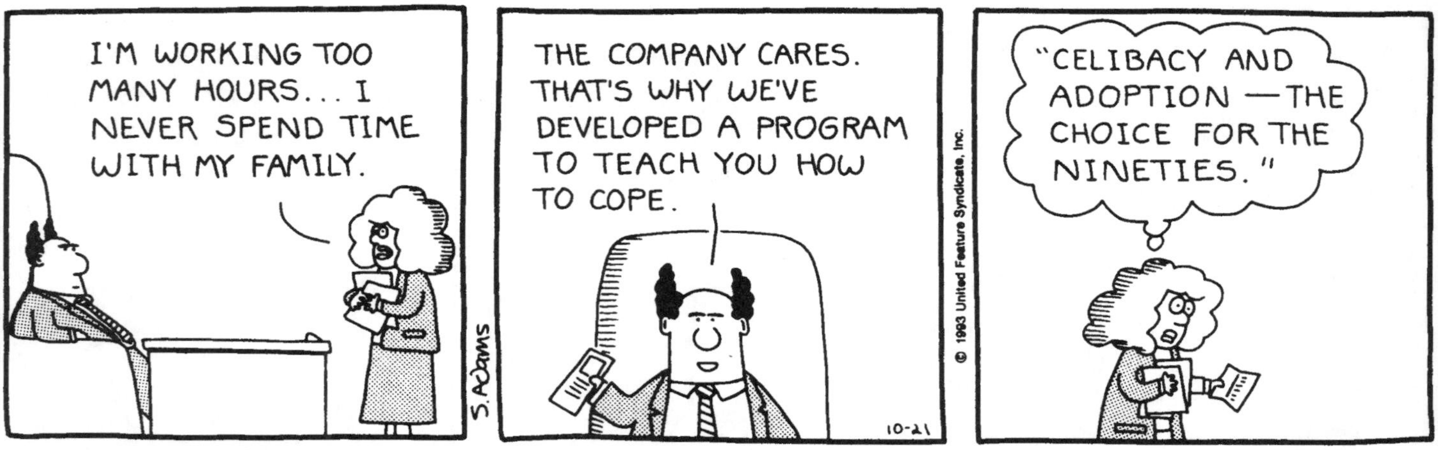
I'M WORKING TOO MANY HOURS... I NEVER SPEND TIME WITH MY FAMILY.
THE COMPANY CARES. THAT'S WHY WE'VE DEVELOPED A PROGRAM TO TEACH YOU HOW TO COPE.
"CELIBACY AND ADOPTION — THE CHOICE FOR THE NINETIES."
S. Adams
10-21
© 1993 United Feature Syndicate, Inc.

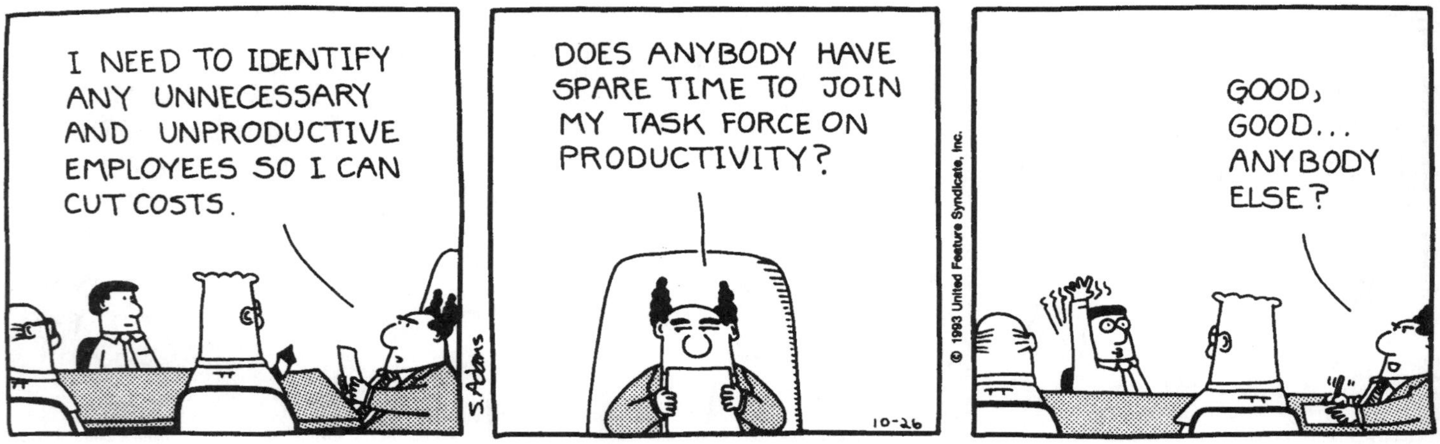
I NEED TO IDENTIFY ANY UNNECESSARY AND UNPRODUCTIVE EMPLOYEES SO I CAN CUT COSTS.
DOES ANYBODY HAVE SPARE TIME TO JOIN MY TASK FORCE ON PRODUCTIVITY?
GOOD, GOOD... ANYBODY ELSE?
S. Adams
10-26
© 1993 United Feature Syndicate, Inc.

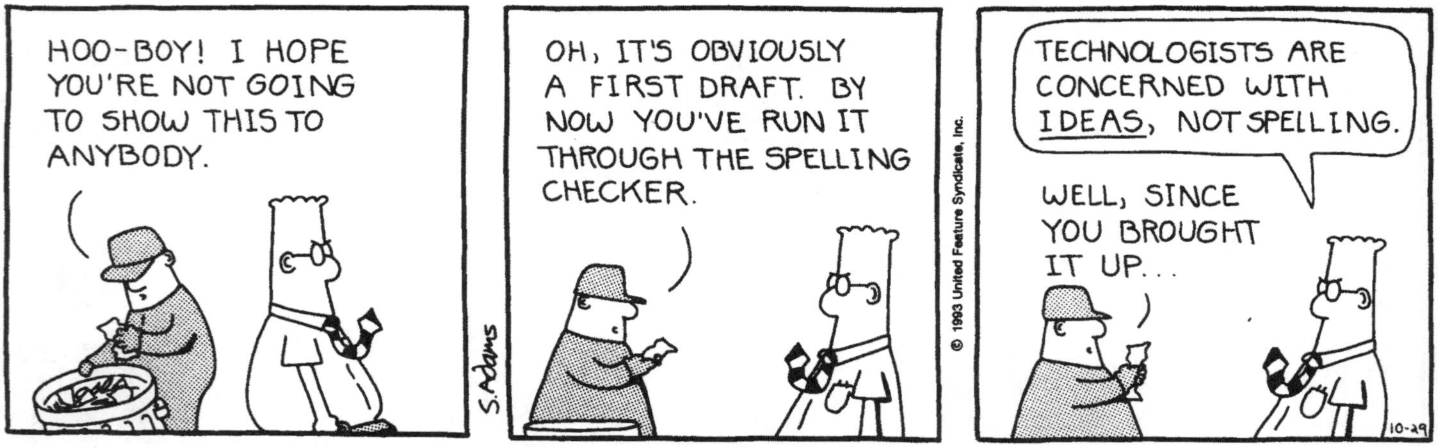
HOO-BOY! I HOPE YOU'RE NOT GOING TO SHOW THIS TO ANYBODY.
OH, IT'S OBVIOUSLY A FIRST DRAFT. BY NOW YOU'VE RUN IT THROUGH THE SPELLING CHECKER.
WELL, SINCE YOU BROUGHT IT UP...
TECHNOLOGISTS ARE CONCERNED WITH IDEAS, NOT SPELLING.
S. Adams
10-29
© 1993 United Feature Syndicate, Inc.

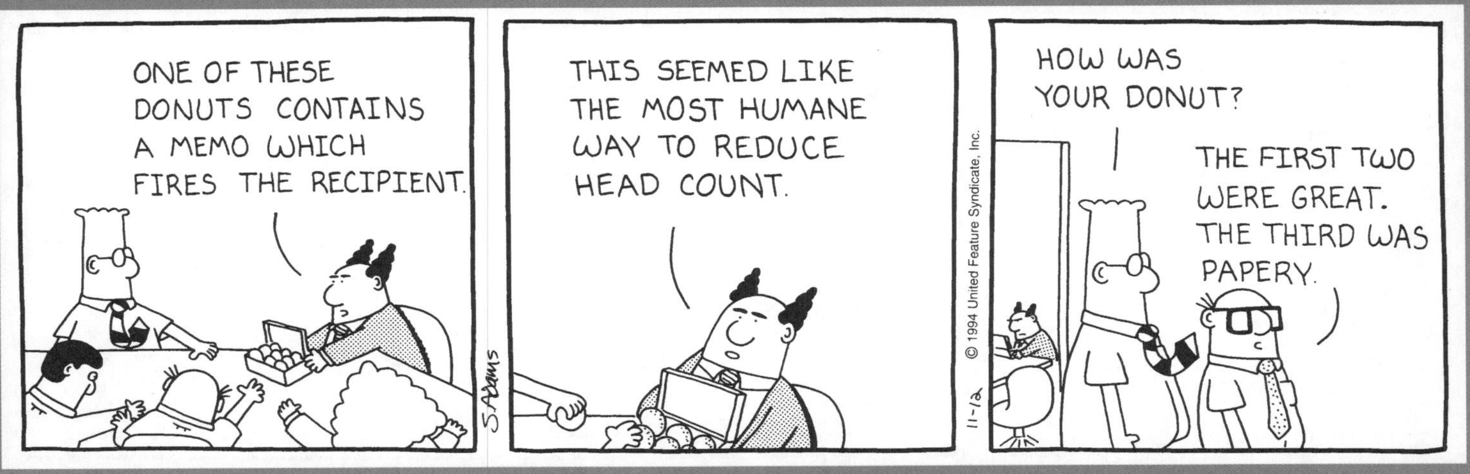
ONE OF THESE DONUTS CONTAINS A MEMO WHICH FIRES THE RECIPIENT.
S. ADAMS
THIS SEEMED LIKE THE MOST HUMANE WAY TO REDUCE HEAD COUNT.
© 1994 United Feature Syndicate, Inc.
11-12
HOW WAS YOUR DONUT?
THE FIRST TWO WERE GREAT. THE THIRD WAS PAPERY.

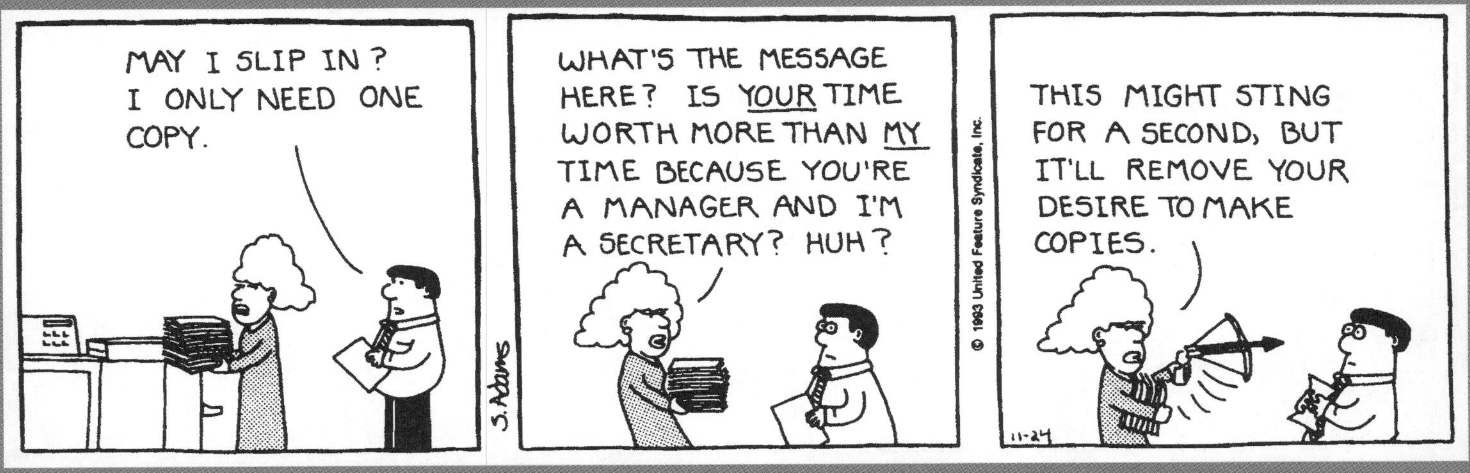
MAY I SLIP IN? I ONLY NEED ONE COPY.
S. Adams
WHAT'S THE MESSAGE HERE? IS YOUR TIME WORTH MORE THAN MY TIME BECAUSE YOU'RE A MANAGER AND I'M A SECRETARY? HUH?
© 1993 United Feature Syndicate, Inc.
THIS MIGHT STING FOR A SECOND, BUT IT'LL REMOVE YOUR DESIRE TO MAKE COPIES.
11-24

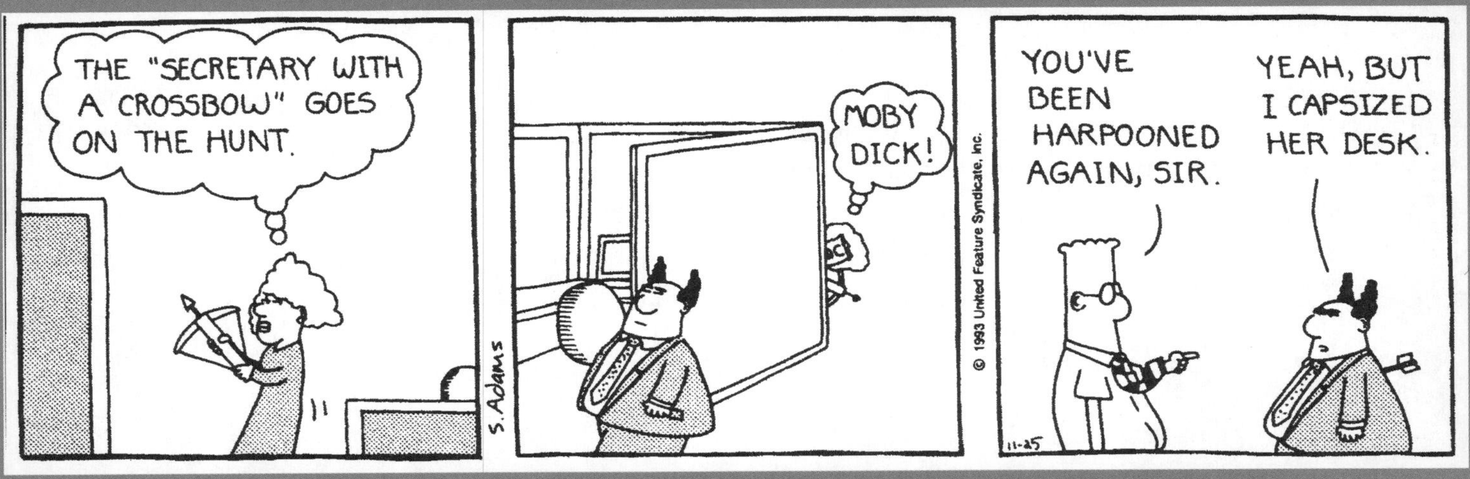
THE "SECRETARY WITH A CROSSBOW" GOES ON THE HUNT.
S. Adams
MOBY DICK!
© 1993 United Feature Syndicate, Inc.
YOU'VE BEEN HARPOONED AGAIN, SIR.
YEAH, BUT I CAPSIZED HER DESK.
11-25

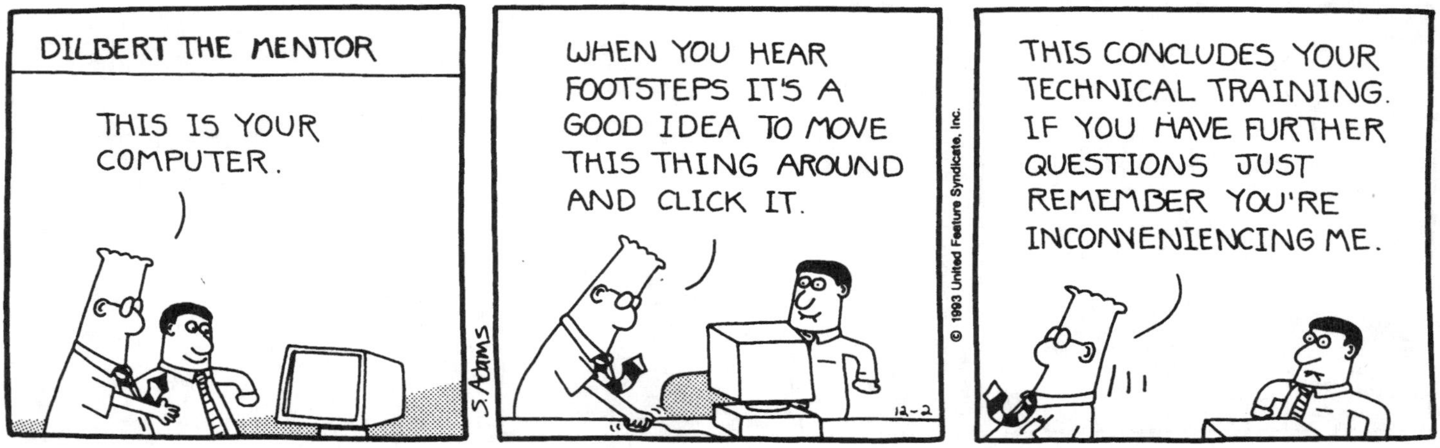
DILBERT THE MENTOR
THIS IS YOUR COMPUTER.
S. Adams
WHEN YOU HEAR FOOTSTEPS IT'S A GOOD IDEA TO MOVE THIS THING AROUND AND CLICK IT.
12-2
© 1993 United Feature Syndicate, Inc.
THIS CONCLUDES YOUR TECHNICAL TRAINING. IF YOU HAVE FURTHER QUESTIONS JUST REMEMBER YOU'RE INCONVENIENCING ME.

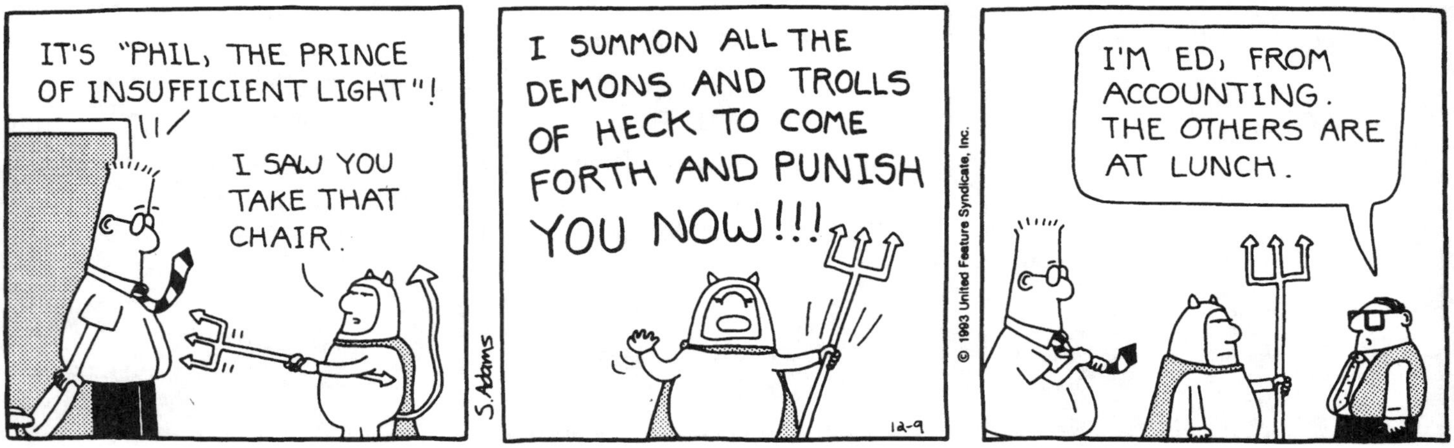
IT'S "PHIL, THE PRINCE OF INSUFFICIENT LIGHT"!
I SAW YOU TAKE THAT CHAIR.
S. Adams
I SUMMON ALL THE DEMONS AND TROLLS OF HECK TO COME FORTH AND PUNISH YOU NOW!!!
12-9
© 1993 United Feature Syndicate, Inc.
I'M ED, FROM ACCOUNTING. THE OTHERS ARE AT LUNCH.

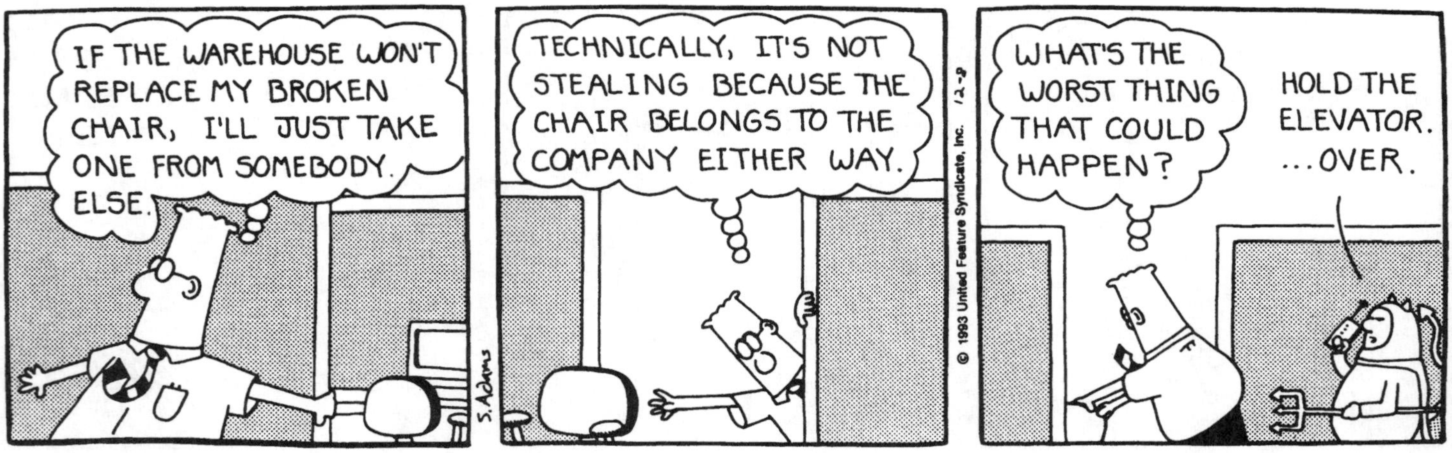
IF THE WAREHOUSE WON'T REPLACE MY BROKEN CHAIR, I'LL JUST TAKE ONE FROM SOMEBODY ELSE.
S. Adams
TECHNICALLY, IT'S NOT STEALING BECAUSE THE CHAIR BELONGS TO THE COMPANY EITHER WAY.
12-8
© 1993 United Feature Syndicate, Inc.
WHAT'S THE WORST THING THAT COULD HAPPEN?
HOLD THE ELEVATOR. ...OVER.

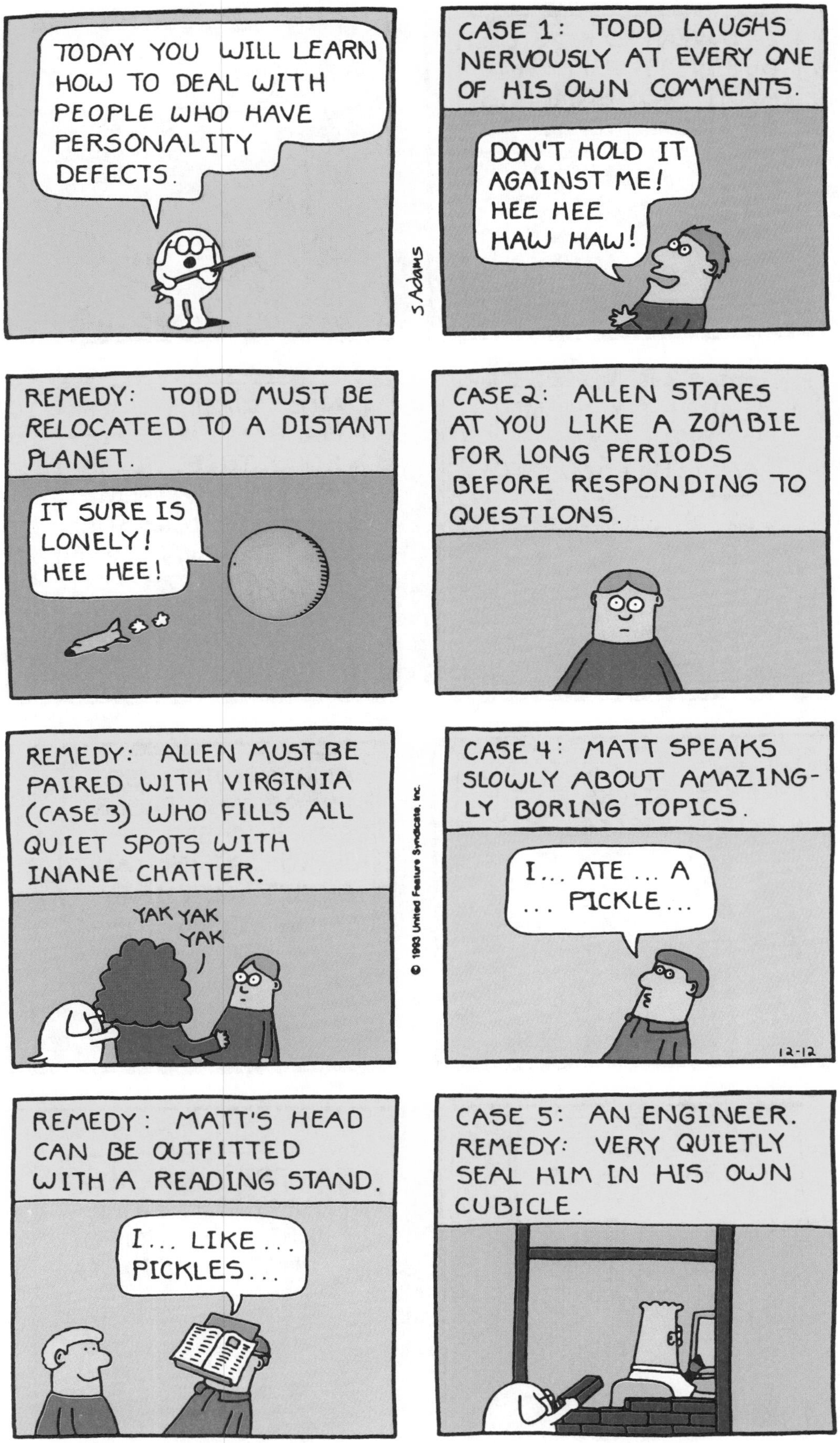
TODAY YOU WILL LEARN HOW TO DEAL WITH PEOPLE WHO HAVE PERSONALITY DEFECTS.
S. Adams
CASE 1: TODD LAUGHS NERVOUSLY AT EVERY ONE OF HIS OWN COMMENTS.
DON'T HOLD IT AGAINST ME! HEE HEE HAW HAW!
REMEDY: TODD MUST BE RELOCATED TO A DISTANT PLANET.
IT SURE IS LONELY! HEE HEE!
CASE 2: ALLEN STARES AT YOU LIKE A ZOMBIE FOR LONG PERIODS BEFORE RESPONDING TO QUESTIONS.
REMEDY: ALLEN MUST BE PAIRED WITH VIRGINIA (CASE 3) WHO FILLS ALL QUIET SPOTS WITH INANE CHATTER.
YAK YAK YAK
© 1993 United Feature Syndicate, Inc.
CASE 4: MATT SPEAKS SLOWLY ABOUT AMAZINGLY BORING TOPICS.
I... ATE ... A ... PICKLE...
12-12
REMEDY: MATT'S HEAD CAN BE OUTFITTED WITH A READING STAND.
I... LIKE... PICKLES...
CASE 5: AN ENGINEER. REMEDY: VERY QUIETLY SEAL HIM IN HIS OWN CUBICLE.

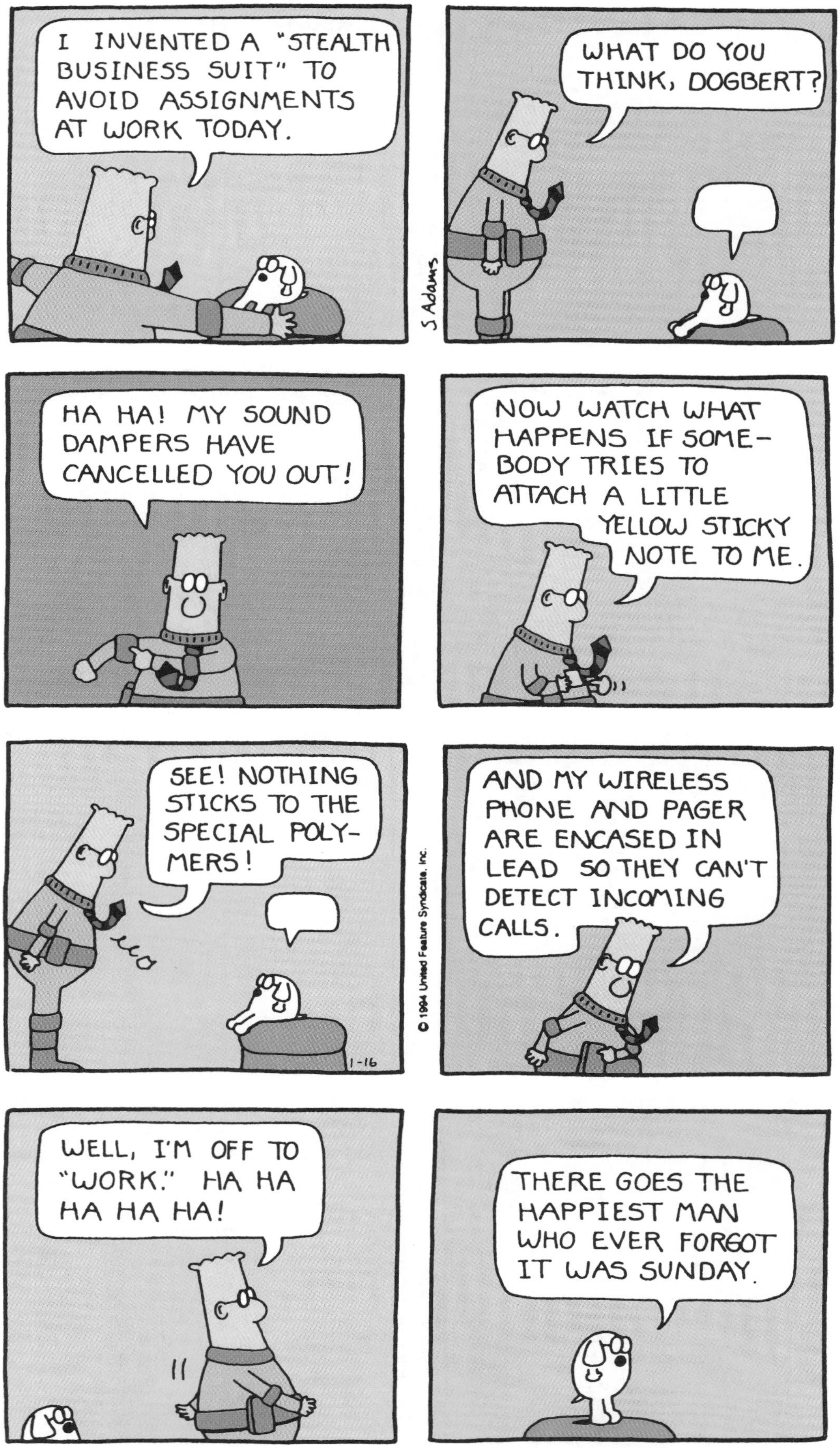
I INVENTED A "STEALTH BUSINESS SUIT" TO AVOID ASSIGNMENTS AT WORK TODAY.
S Adams
WHAT DO YOU THINK, DOGBERT?
HA HA! MY SOUND DAMPERS HAVE CANCELLED YOU OUT!
NOW WATCH WHAT HAPPENS IF SOME-BODY TRIES TO ATTACH A LITTLE YELLOW STICKY NOTE TO ME.
SEE! NOTHING STICKS TO THE SPECIAL POLY-MERS!
1-16
© 1994 United Feature Syndicate, Inc.
AND MY WIRELESS PHONE AND PAGER ARE ENCASED IN LEAD SO THEY CAN'T DETECT INCOMING CALLS.
WELL, I'M OFF TO "WORK." HA HA HA HA HA!
THERE GOES THE HAPPIEST MAN WHO EVER FORGOT IT WAS SUNDAY.

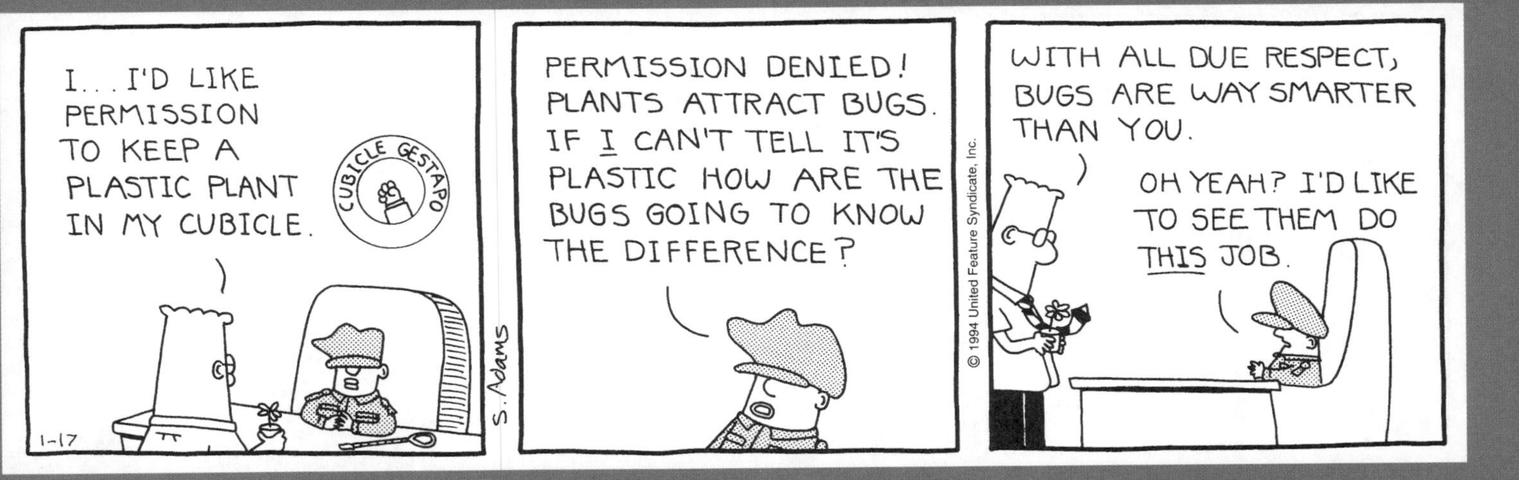
I... I'D LIKE PERMISSION TO KEEP A PLASTIC PLANT IN MY CUBICLE.
CUBICLE GESTAPO
1-17
S. Adams
PERMISSION DENIED! PLANTS ATTRACT BUGS. IF I CAN'T TELL IT'S PLASTIC HOW ARE THE BUGS GOING TO KNOW THE DIFFERENCE?
© 1994 United Feature Syndicate, Inc.
WITH ALL DUE RESPECT, BUGS ARE WAY SMARTER THAN YOU.
OH YEAH? I'D LIKE TO SEE THEM DO THIS JOB.

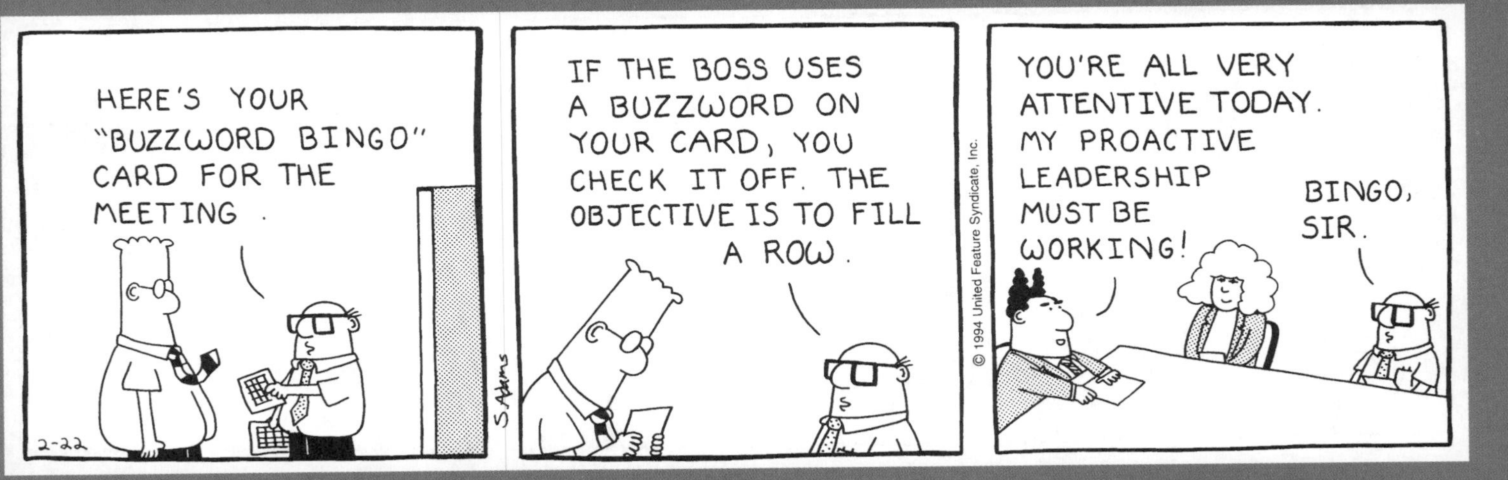
HERE'S YOUR "BUZZWORD BINGO" CARD FOR THE MEETING.
2-22
S. Adams
IF THE BOSS USES A BUZZWORD ON YOUR CARD, YOU CHECK IT OFF. THE OBJECTIVE IS TO FILL A ROW.
© 1994 United Feature Syndicate, Inc.
YOU'RE ALL VERY ATTENTIVE TODAY. MY PROACTIVE LEADERSHIP MUST BE WORKING!
BINGO, SIR.

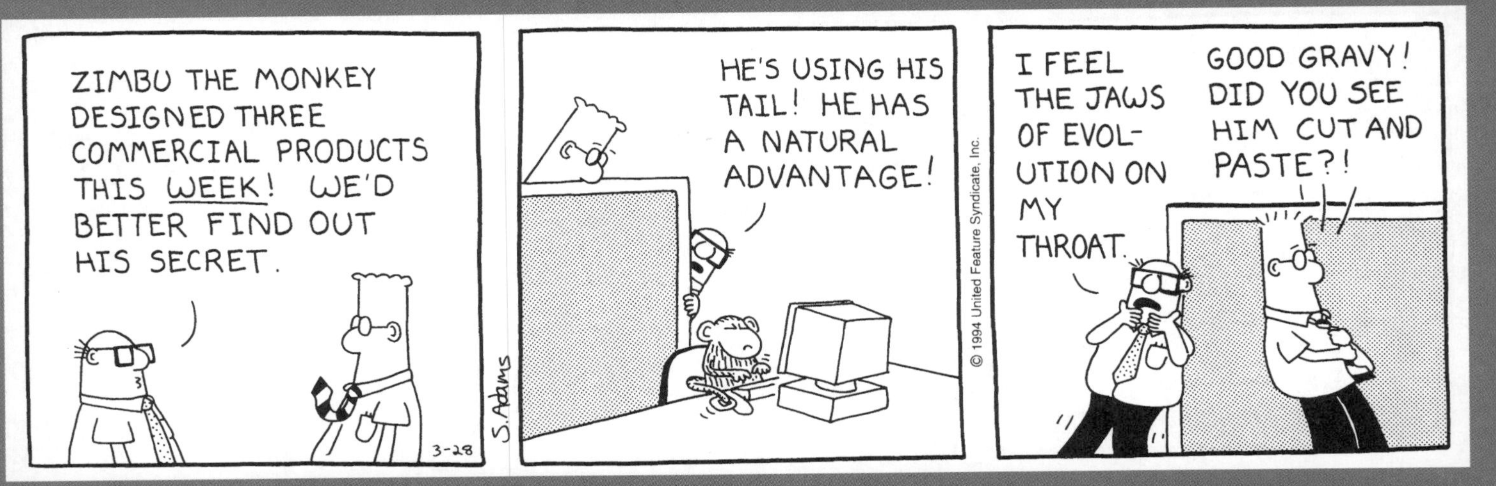
ZIMBU THE MONKEY DESIGNED THREE COMMERCIAL PRODUCTS THIS WEEK! WE'D BETTER FIND OUT HIS SECRET.
3-28
S. Adams
HE'S USING HIS TAIL! HE HAS A NATURAL ADVANTAGE!
© 1994 United Feature Syndicate, Inc.
I FEEL THE JAWS OF EVOLUTION ON MY THROAT.
GOOD GRAVY! DID YOU SEE HIM CUT AND PASTE?!

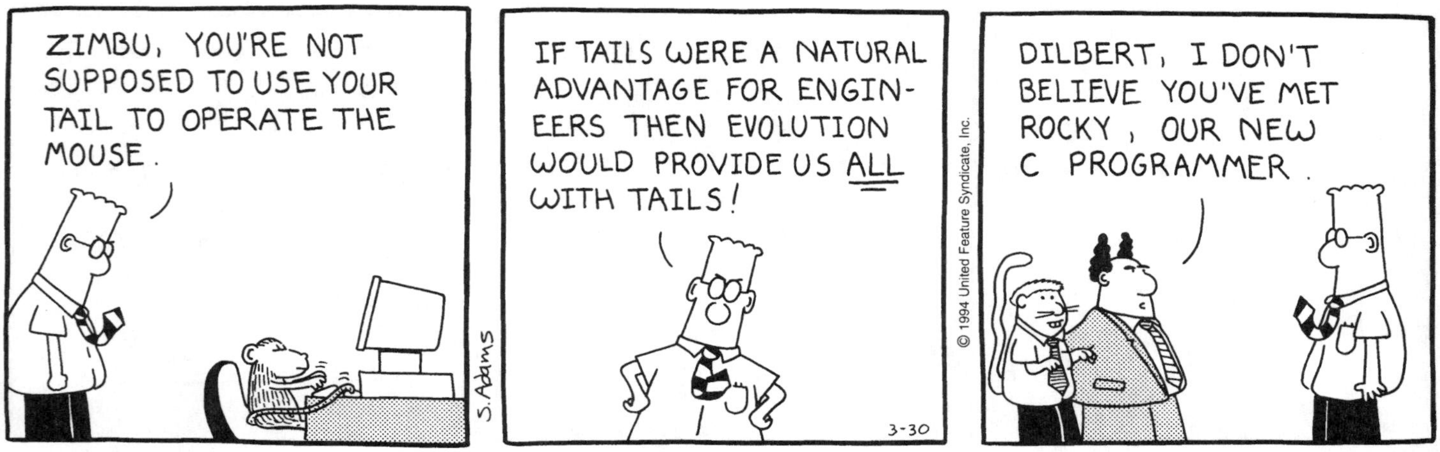
ZIMBU, YOU'RE NOT SUPPOSED TO USE YOUR TAIL TO OPERATE THE MOUSE.
S. Adams
IF TAILS WERE A NATURAL ADVANTAGE FOR ENGINEERS THEN EVOLUTION WOULD PROVIDE US ALL WITH TAILS!
3-30
© 1994 United Feature Syndicate, Inc.
DILBERT, I DON'T BELIEVE YOU'VE MET ROCKY, OUR NEW C PROGRAMMER.

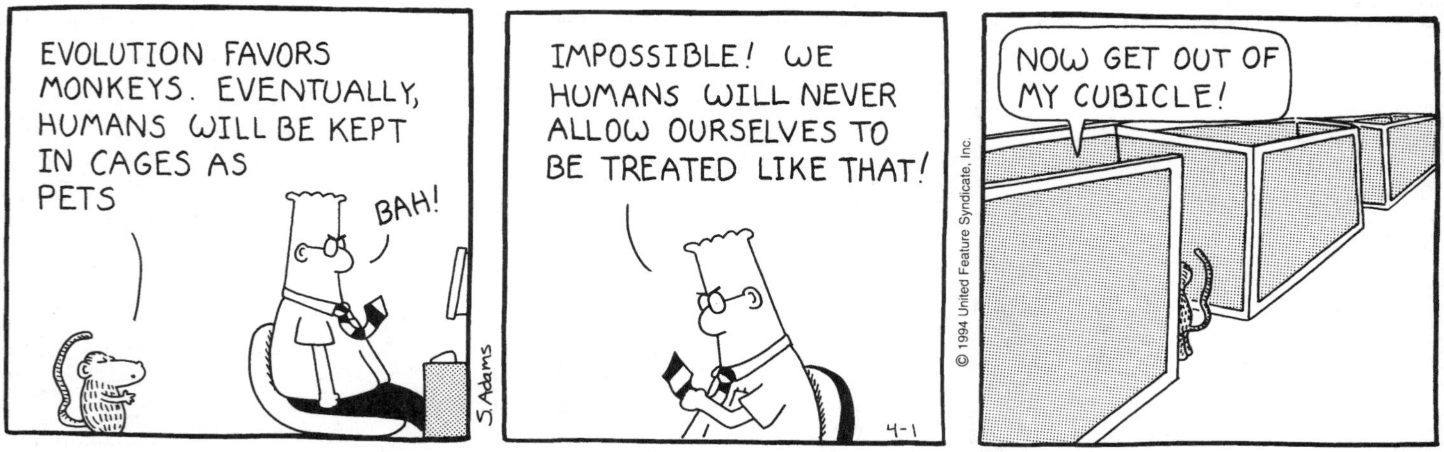
EVOLUTION FAVORS MONKEYS. EVENTUALLY, HUMANS WILL BE KEPT IN CAGES AS PETS
BAH!
S. Adams
IMPOSSIBLE! WE HUMANS WILL NEVER ALLOW OURSELVES TO BE TREATED LIKE THAT!
4-1
© 1994 United Feature Syndicate, Inc.
NOW GET OUT OF MY CUBICLE!

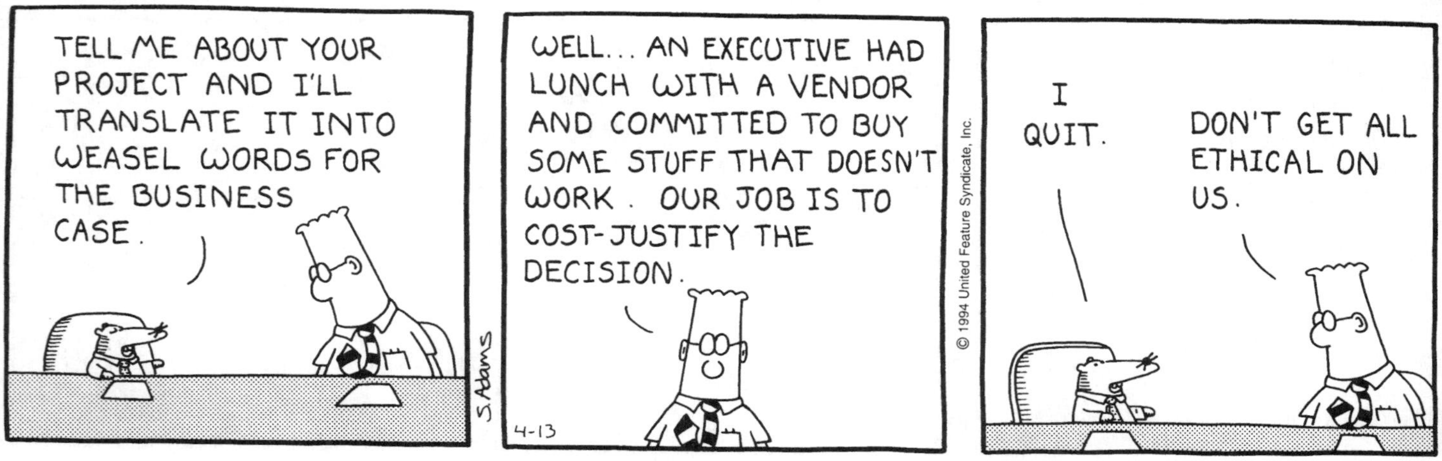
TELL ME ABOUT YOUR PROJECT AND I'LL TRANSLATE IT INTO WEASEL WORDS FOR THE BUSINESS CASE.
S. Adams
WELL... AN EXECUTIVE HAD LUNCH WITH A VENDOR AND COMMITTED TO BUY SOME STUFF THAT DOESN'T WORK. OUR JOB IS TO COST-JUSTIFY THE DECISION.
4-13
© 1994 United Feature Syndicate, Inc.
I QUIT.
DON'T GET ALL ETHICAL ON US.

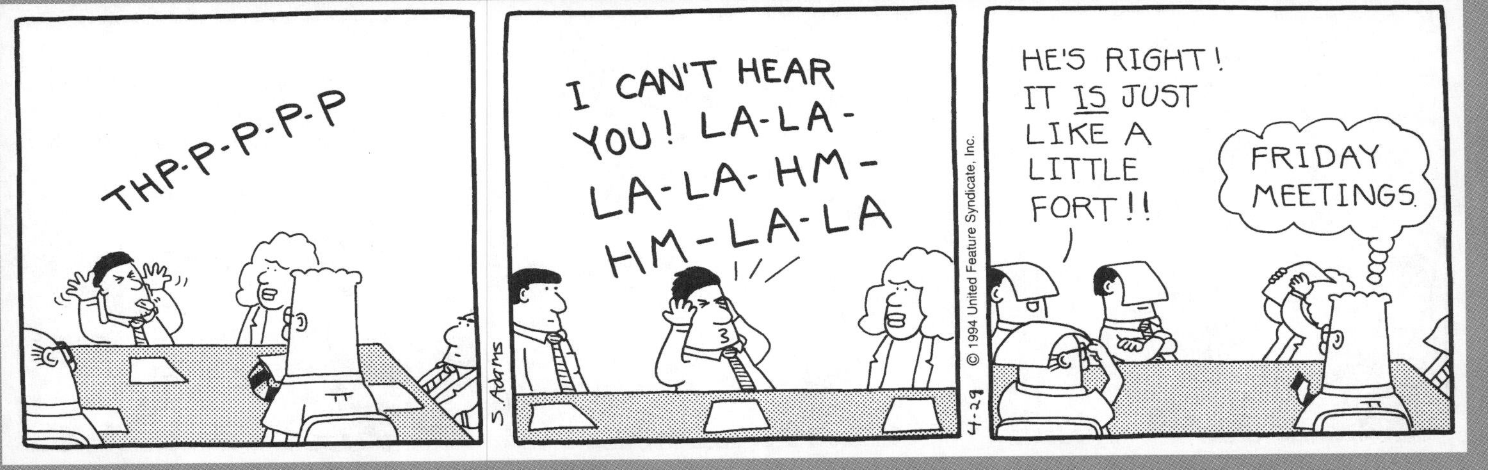
THP-P-P-P-P
I CAN'T HEAR YOU! LA-LA-LA-LA-HM-HM-LA-LA
S. Adams
4-29
© 1994 United Feature Syndicate, Inc.
HE'S RIGHT! IT IS JUST LIKE A LITTLE FORT!!
FRIDAY MEETINGS

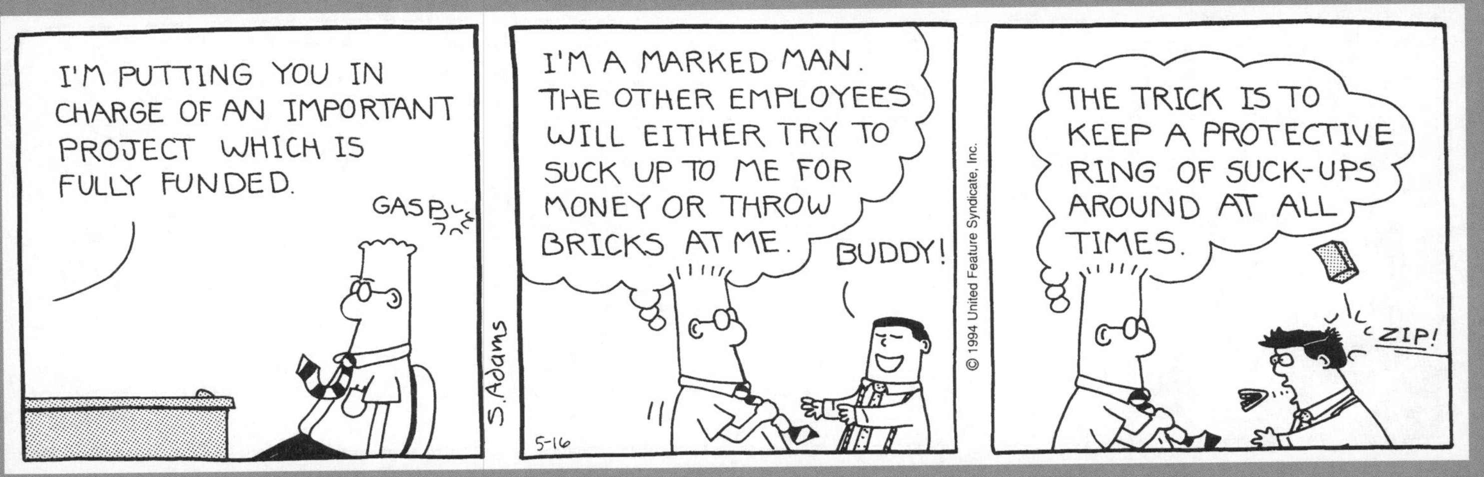
I'M PUTTING YOU IN CHARGE OF AN IMPORTANT PROJECT WHICH IS FULLY FUNDED.
GASP
S. Adams
5-16
I'M A MARKED MAN. THE OTHER EMPLOYEES WILL EITHER TRY TO SUCK UP TO ME FOR MONEY OR THROW BRICKS AT ME.
BUDDY!
© 1994 United Feature Syndicate, Inc.
THE TRICK IS TO KEEP A PROTECTIVE RING OF SUCK-UPS AROUND AT ALL TIMES.
ZIP!

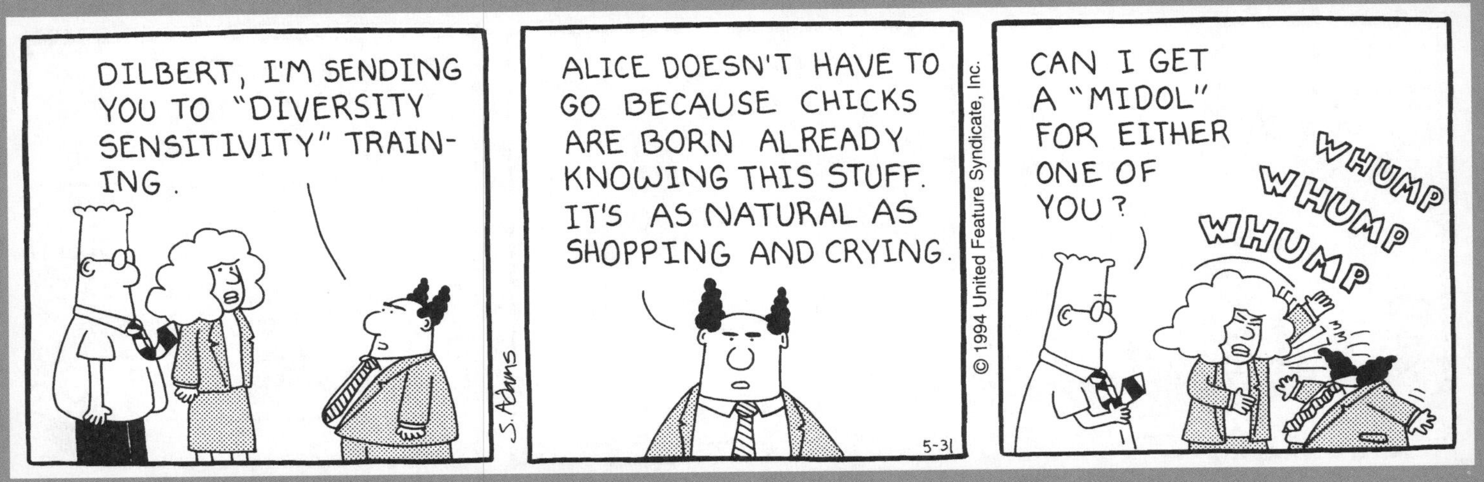
DILBERT, I'M SENDING YOU TO "DIVERSITY SENSITIVITY" TRAINING.
S. Adams
ALICE DOESN'T HAVE TO GO BECAUSE CHICKS ARE BORN ALREADY KNOWING THIS STUFF. IT'S AS NATURAL AS SHOPPING AND CRYING.
5-31
© 1994 United Feature Syndicate, Inc.
CAN I GET A "MIDOL" FOR EITHER ONE OF YOU?
WHUMP
WHUMP
WHUMP

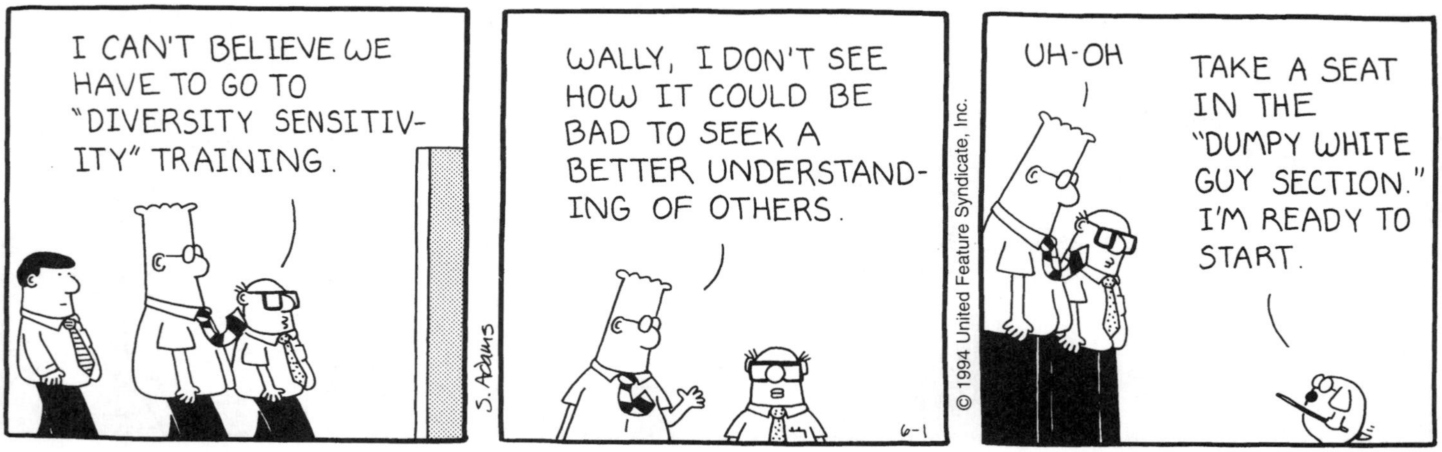
I CAN'T BELIEVE WE HAVE TO GO TO "DIVERSITY SENSITIVITY" TRAINING.
S. Adams
WALLY, I DON'T SEE HOW IT COULD BE BAD TO SEEK A BETTER UNDERSTANDING OF OTHERS.
6-1
© 1994 United Feature Syndicate, Inc.
UH-OH
TAKE A SEAT IN THE "DUMPY WHITE GUY SECTION." I'M READY TO START.

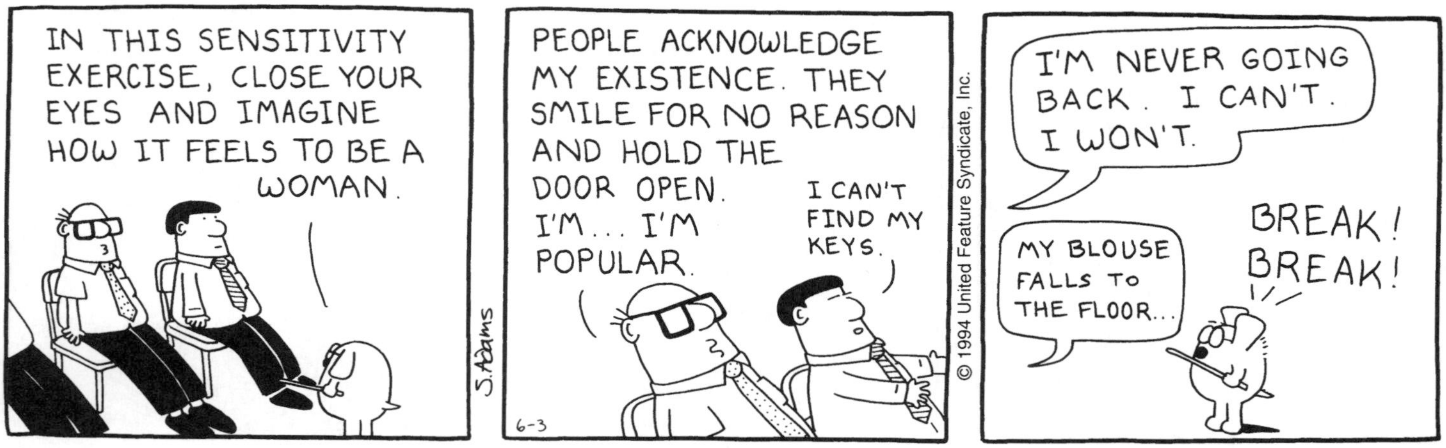
IN THIS SENSITIVITY EXERCISE, CLOSE YOUR EYES AND IMAGINE HOW IT FEELS TO BE A WOMAN.
S. Adams
PEOPLE ACKNOWLEDGE MY EXISTENCE. THEY SMILE FOR NO REASON AND HOLD THE DOOR OPEN. I'M... I'M POPULAR.
I CAN'T FIND MY KEYS.
6-3
© 1994 United Feature Syndicate, Inc.
I'M NEVER GOING BACK. I CAN'T. I WON'T.
MY BLOUSE FALLS TO THE FLOOR...
BREAK! BREAK!

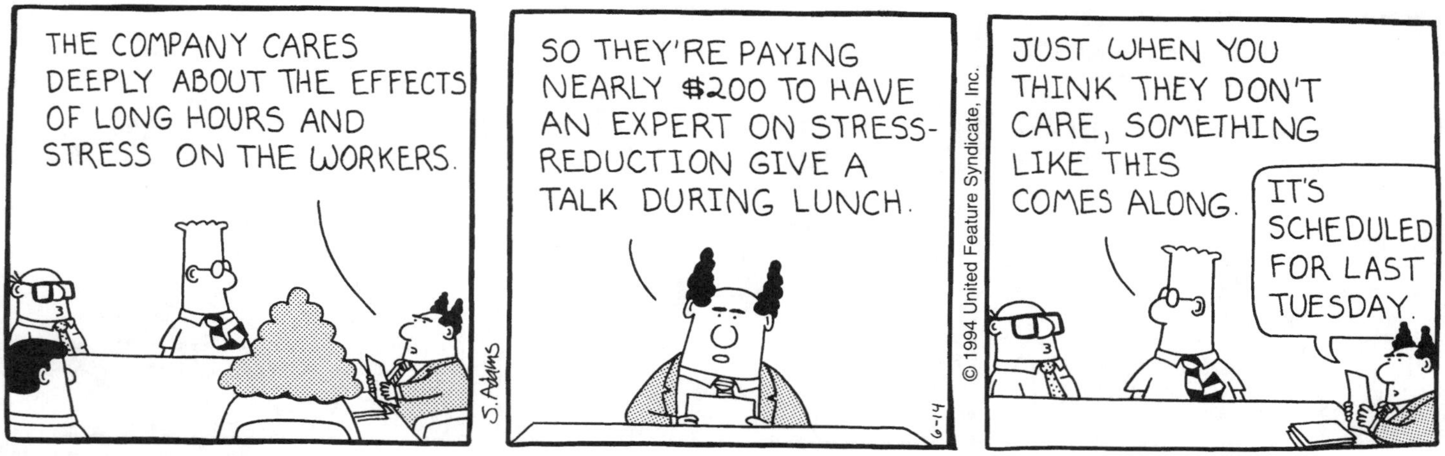
THE COMPANY CARES DEEPLY ABOUT THE EFFECTS OF LONG HOURS AND STRESS ON THE WORKERS.
S. Adams
SO THEY'RE PAYING NEARLY $200 TO HAVE AN EXPERT ON STRESS-REDUCTION GIVE A TALK DURING LUNCH.
6-14
© 1994 United Feature Syndicate, Inc.
JUST WHEN YOU THINK THEY DON'T CARE, SOMETHING LIKE THIS COMES ALONG.
IT'S SCHEDULED FOR LAST TUESDAY.

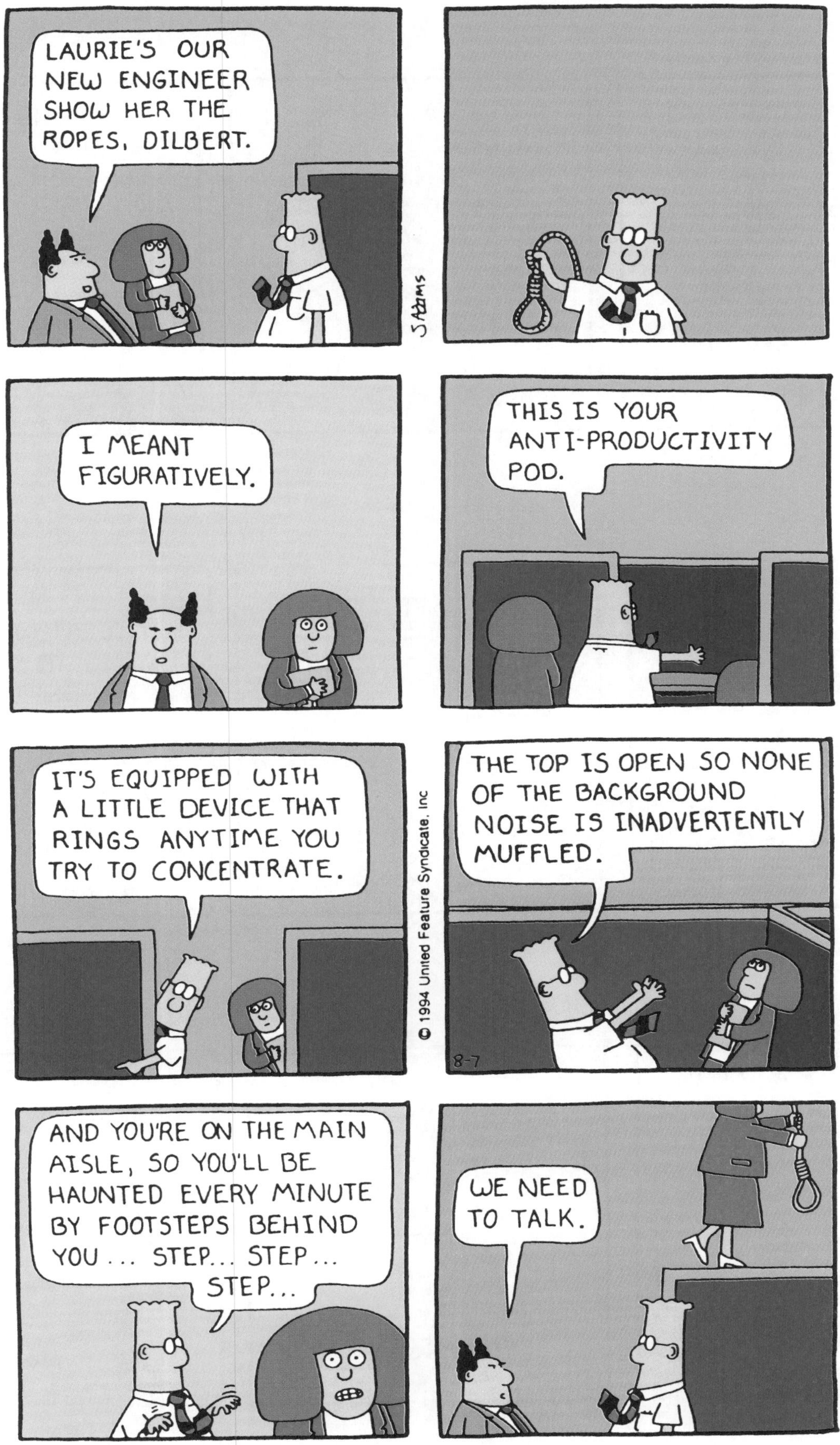
LAURIE'S OUR NEW ENGINEER SHOW HER THE ROPES, DILBERT.
S. ADAMS
I MEANT FIGURATIVELY.
THIS IS YOUR ANTI-PRODUCTIVITY POD.
IT'S EQUIPPED WITH A LITTLE DEVICE THAT RINGS ANYTIME YOU TRY TO CONCENTRATE.
© 1994 United Feature Syndicate, Inc
THE TOP IS OPEN SO NONE OF THE BACKGROUND NOISE IS INADVERTENTLY MUFFLED.
8-7
AND YOU'RE ON THE MAIN AISLE, SO YOU'LL BE HAUNTED EVERY MINUTE BY FOOTSTEPS BEHIND YOU... STEP... STEP... STEP...
WE NEED TO TALK.

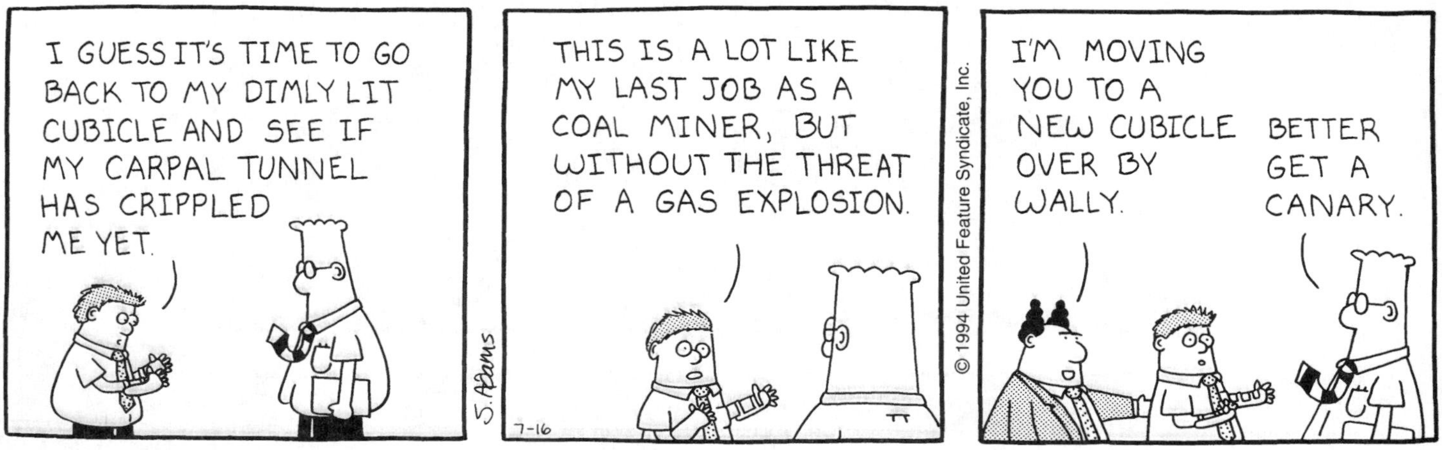
I GUESS IT'S TIME TO GO BACK TO MY DIMLY LIT CUBICLE AND SEE IF MY CARPAL TUNNEL HAS CRIPPLED ME YET.
S. Adams
7-16
THIS IS A LOT LIKE MY LAST JOB AS A COAL MINER, BUT WITHOUT THE THREAT OF A GAS EXPLOSION.
© 1994 United Feature Syndicate, Inc.
I'M MOVING YOU TO A NEW CUBICLE OVER BY WALLY.
BETTER GET A CANARY.

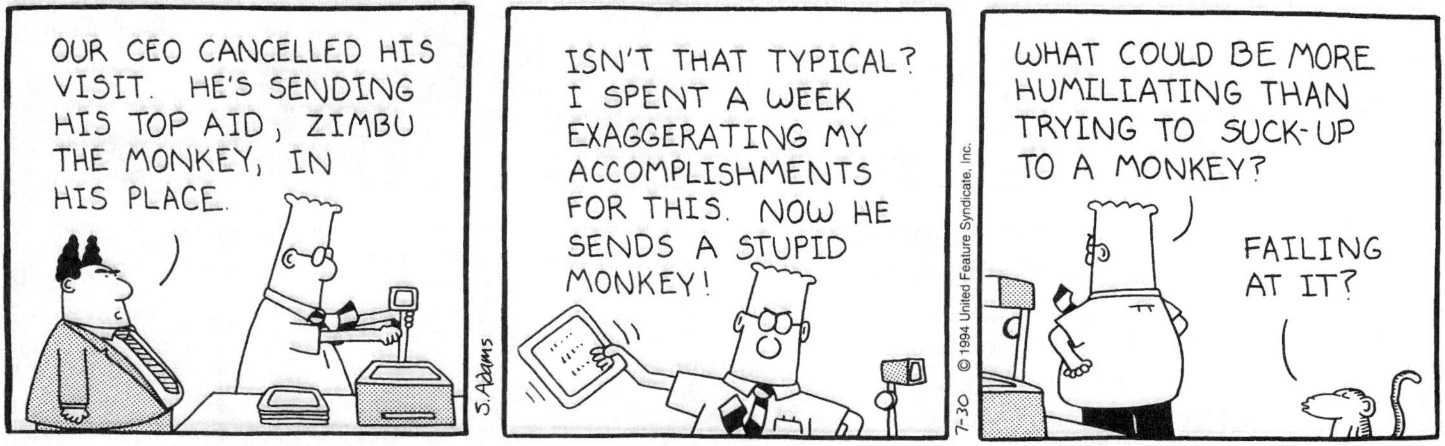
OUR CEO CANCELLED HIS VISIT. HE'S SENDING HIS TOP AID, ZIMBU THE MONKEY, IN HIS PLACE.
S. Adams
ISN'T THAT TYPICAL? I SPENT A WEEK EXAGGERATING MY ACCOMPLISHMENTS FOR THIS. NOW HE SENDS A STUPID MONKEY!
7-30
© 1994 United Feature Syndicate, Inc.
WHAT COULD BE MORE HUMILIATING THAN TRYING TO SUCK-UP TO A MONKEY?
FAILING AT IT?

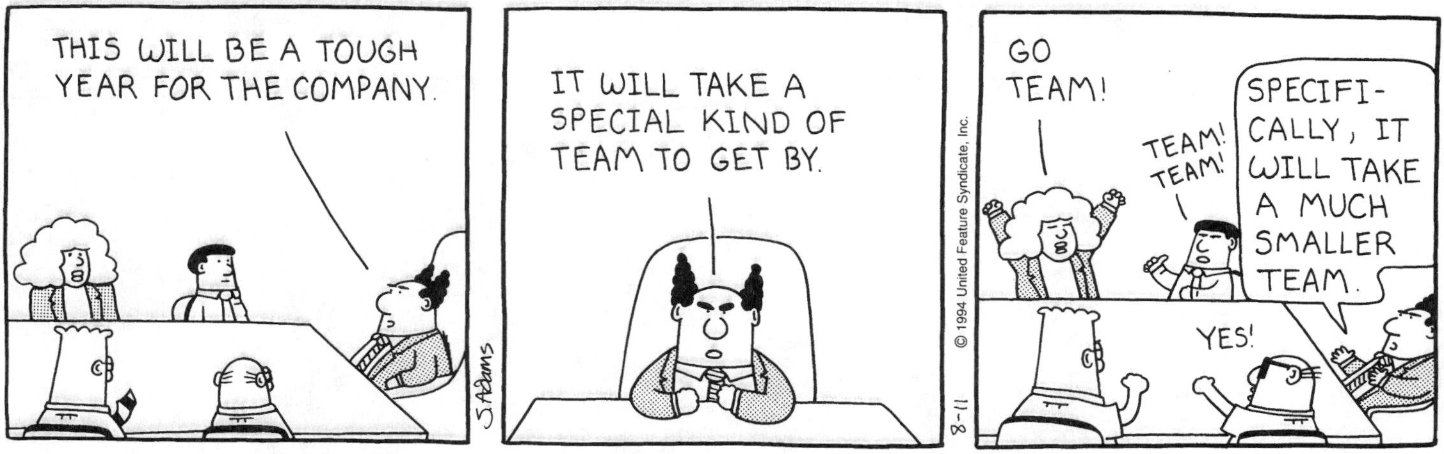
THIS WILL BE A TOUGH YEAR FOR THE COMPANY.
S. Adams
IT WILL TAKE A SPECIAL KIND OF TEAM TO GET BY.
8-11
© 1994 United Feature Syndicate, Inc.
GO TEAM!
TEAM! TEAM!
SPECIFI-CALLY, IT WILL TAKE A MUCH SMALLER TEAM.
YES!

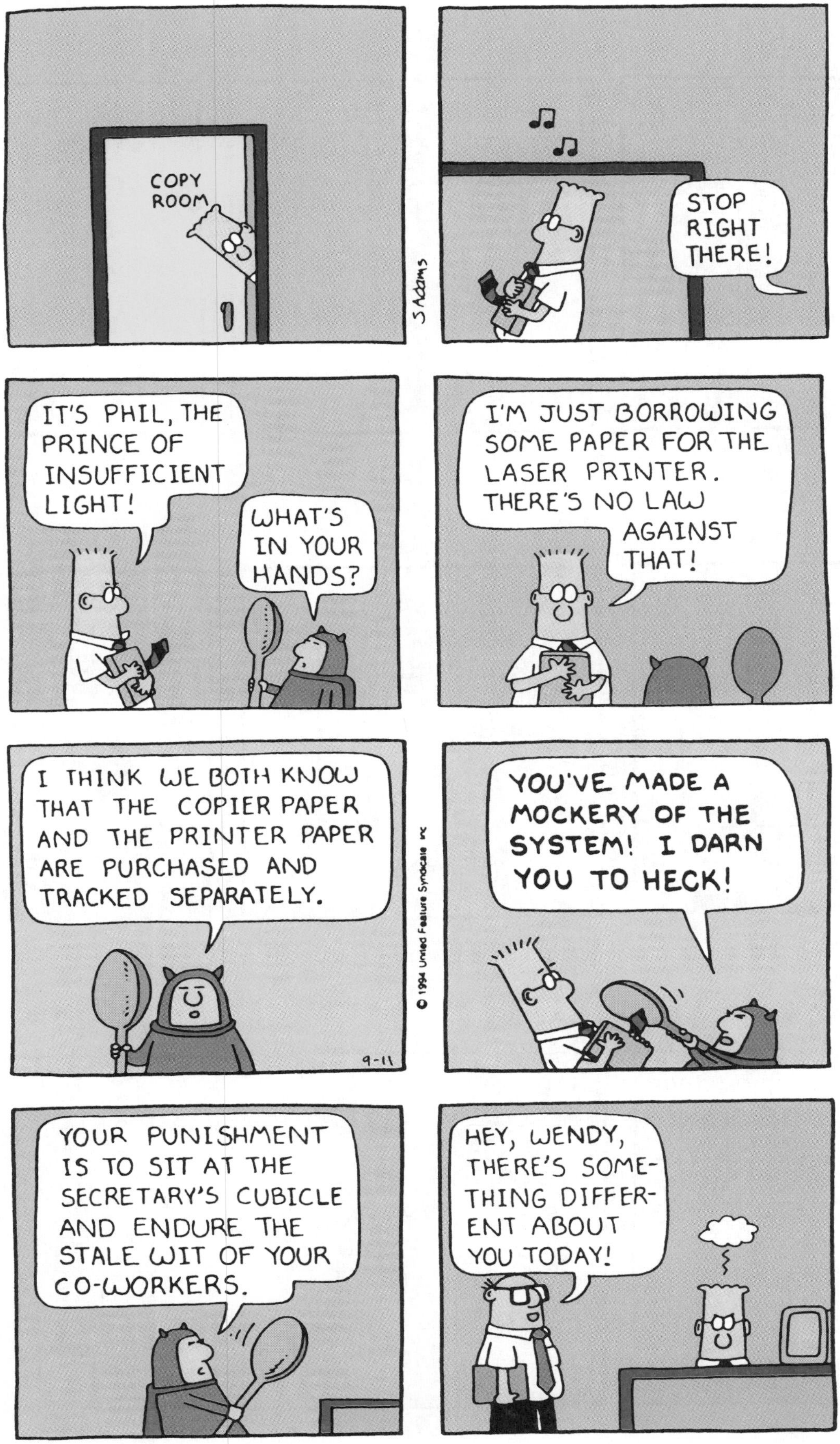
COPY ROOM
S Adams
STOP RIGHT THERE!
IT'S PHIL, THE PRINCE OF INSUFFICIENT LIGHT!
WHAT'S IN YOUR HANDS?
I'M JUST BORROWING SOME PAPER FOR THE LASER PRINTER. THERE'S NO LAW AGAINST THAT!
I THINK WE BOTH KNOW THAT THE COPIER PAPER AND THE PRINTER PAPER ARE PURCHASED AND TRACKED SEPARATELY.
9-11
© 1994 United Feature Syndicate Inc
YOU'VE MADE A MOCKERY OF THE SYSTEM! I DARN YOU TO HECK!
YOUR PUNISHMENT IS TO SIT AT THE SECRETARY'S CUBICLE AND ENDURE THE STALE WIT OF YOUR CO-WORKERS.
HEY, WENDY, THERE'S SOME-THING DIFFER-ENT ABOUT YOU TODAY!

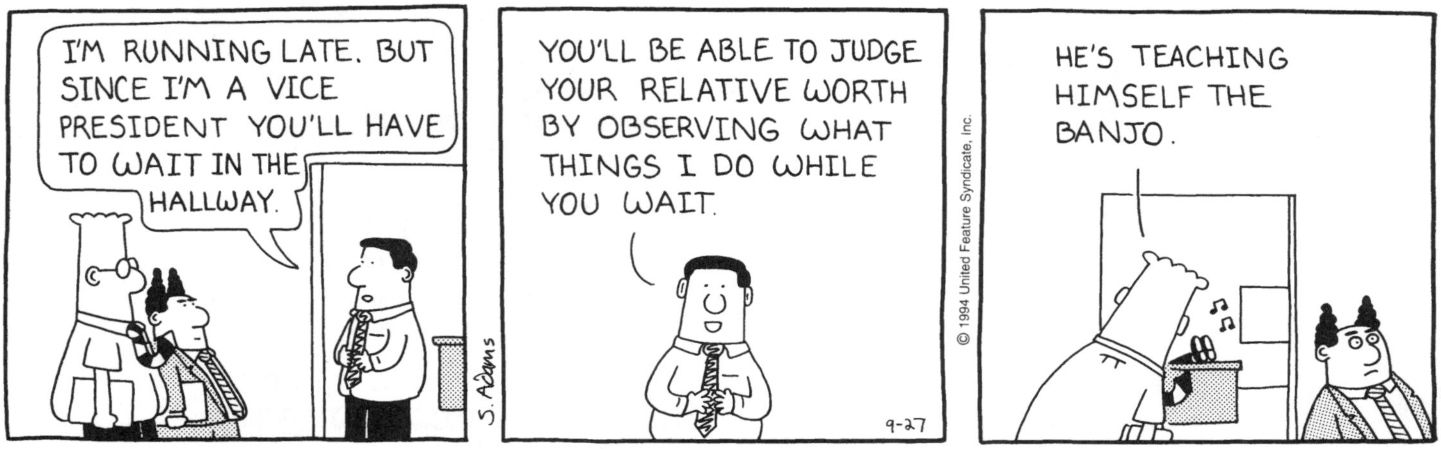
I'M RUNNING LATE. BUT SINCE I'M A VICE PRESIDENT YOU'LL HAVE TO WAIT IN THE HALLWAY.
S. Adams
YOU'LL BE ABLE TO JUDGE YOUR RELATIVE WORTH BY OBSERVING WHAT THINGS I DO WHILE YOU WAIT.
9-27
© 1994 United Feature Syndicate, Inc.
HE'S TEACHING HIMSELF THE BANJO.

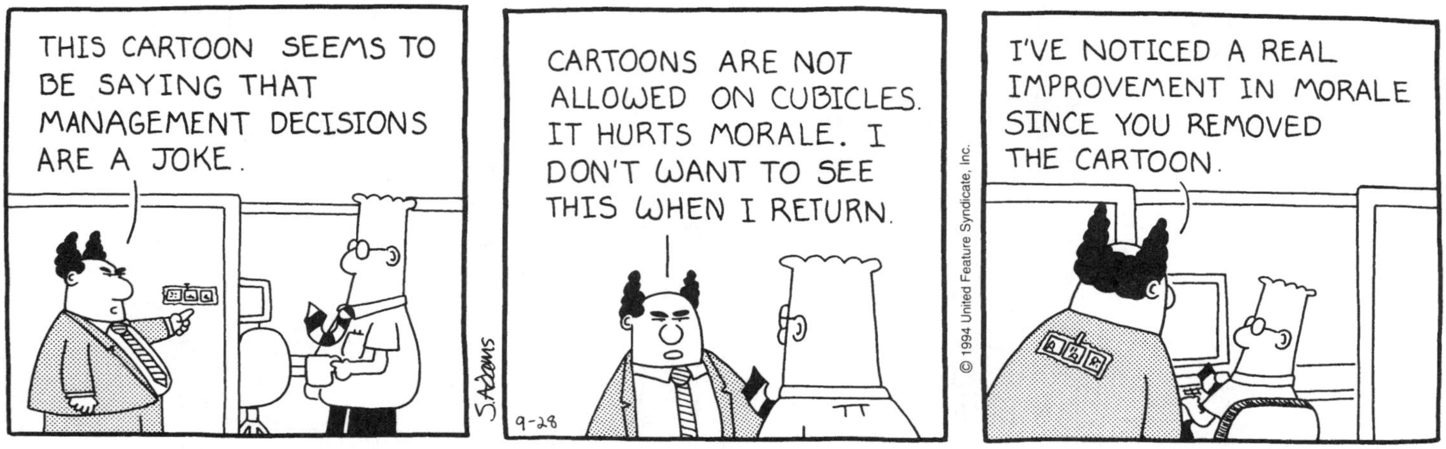
THIS CARTOON SEEMS TO BE SAYING THAT MANAGEMENT DECISIONS ARE A JOKE.
S. Adams
9-28
CARTOONS ARE NOT ALLOWED ON CUBICLES. IT HURTS MORALE. I DON'T WANT TO SEE THIS WHEN I RETURN.
© 1994 United Feature Syndicate, Inc.
I'VE NOTICED A REAL IMPROVEMENT IN MORALE SINCE YOU REMOVED THE CARTOON.

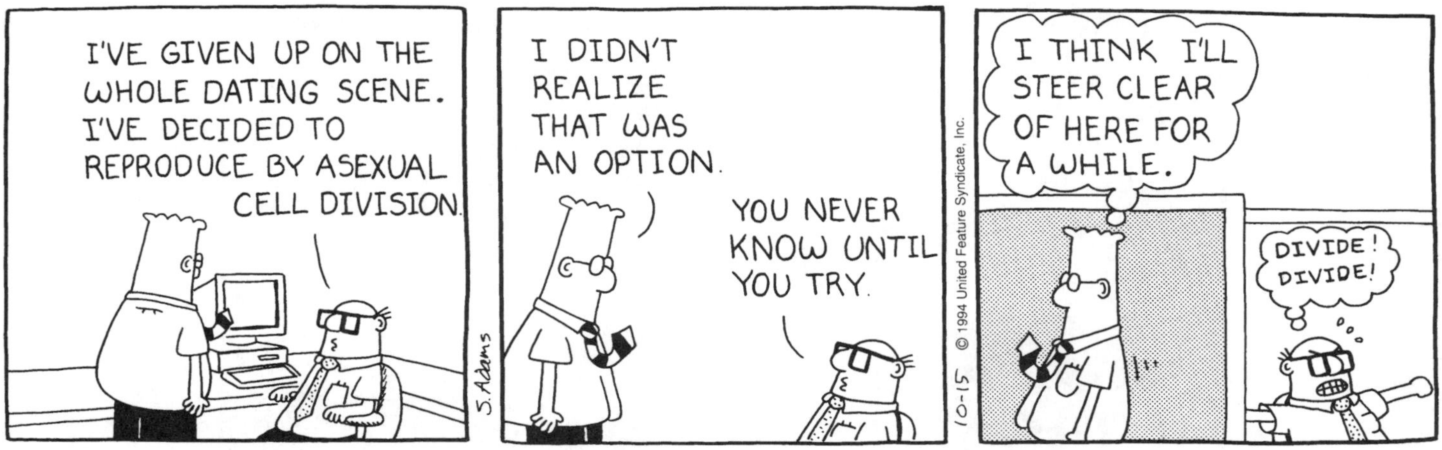
I'VE GIVEN UP ON THE WHOLE DATING SCENE. I'VE DECIDED TO REPRODUCE BY ASEXUAL CELL DIVISION.
S. Adams
I DIDN'T REALIZE THAT WAS AN OPTION.
YOU NEVER KNOW UNTIL YOU TRY.
10-15
© 1994 United Feature Syndicate, Inc.
I THINK I'LL STEER CLEAR OF HERE FOR A WHILE.
DIVIDE! DIVIDE!

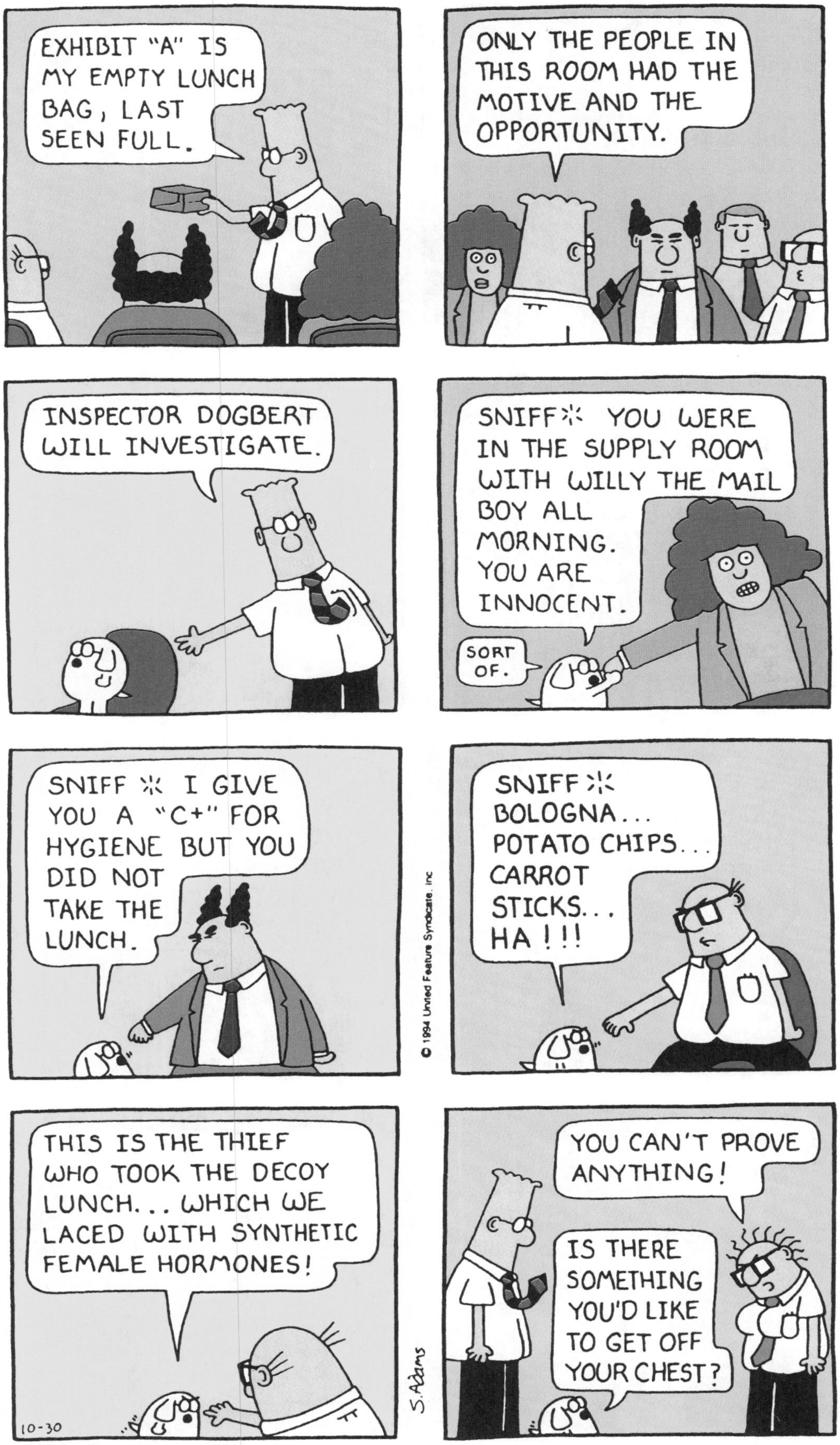
EXHIBIT "A" IS MY EMPTY LUNCH BAG, LAST SEEN FULL.
ONLY THE PEOPLE IN THIS ROOM HAD THE MOTIVE AND THE OPPORTUNITY.
INSPECTOR DOGBERT WILL INVESTIGATE.
SNIFF ⁘ YOU WERE IN THE SUPPLY ROOM WITH WILLY THE MAIL BOY ALL MORNING. YOU ARE INNOCENT.
SORT OF.
SNIFF ⁘ I GIVE YOU A "C+" FOR HYGIENE BUT YOU DID NOT TAKE THE LUNCH.
SNIFF ⁘ BOLOGNA... POTATO CHIPS... CARROT STICKS... HA!!!
© 1994 United Feature Syndicate, Inc
THIS IS THE THIEF WHO TOOK THE DECOY LUNCH... WHICH WE LACED WITH SYNTHETIC FEMALE HORMONES!
10-30
S. Adams
YOU CAN'T PROVE ANYTHING!
IS THERE SOMETHING YOU'D LIKE TO GET OFF YOUR CHEST?

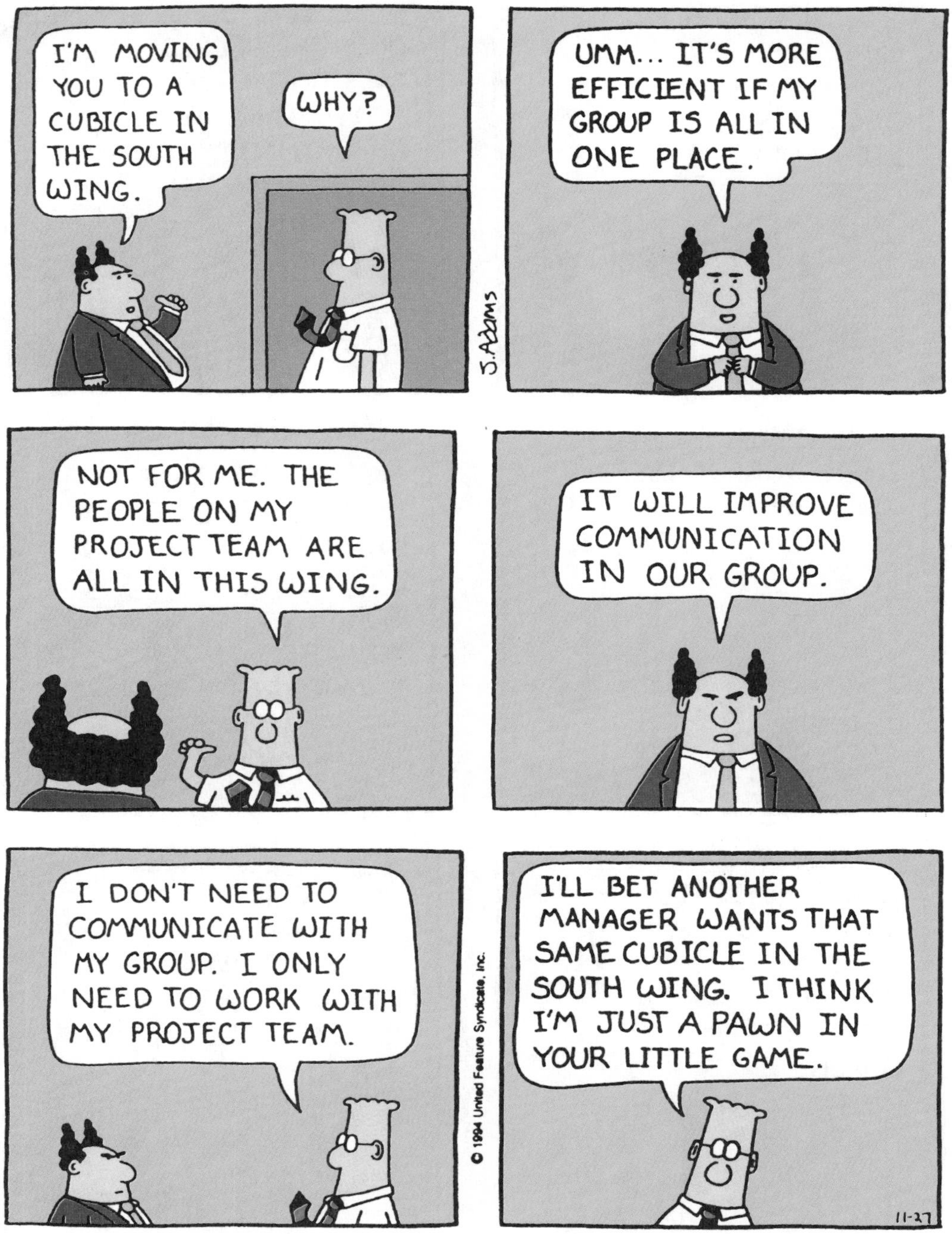
I'M MOVING YOU TO A CUBICLE IN THE SOUTH WING.
WHY?
UMM... IT'S MORE EFFICIENT IF MY GROUP IS ALL IN ONE PLACE.
NOT FOR ME. THE PEOPLE ON MY PROJECT TEAM ARE ALL IN THIS WING.
IT WILL IMPROVE COMMUNICATION IN OUR GROUP.
I DON'T NEED TO COMMUNICATE WITH MY GROUP. I ONLY NEED TO WORK WITH MY PROJECT TEAM.
I'LL BET ANOTHER MANAGER WANTS THAT SAME CUBICLE IN THE SOUTH WING. I THINK I'M JUST A PAWN IN YOUR LITTLE GAME.
S. ADAMS
11-27

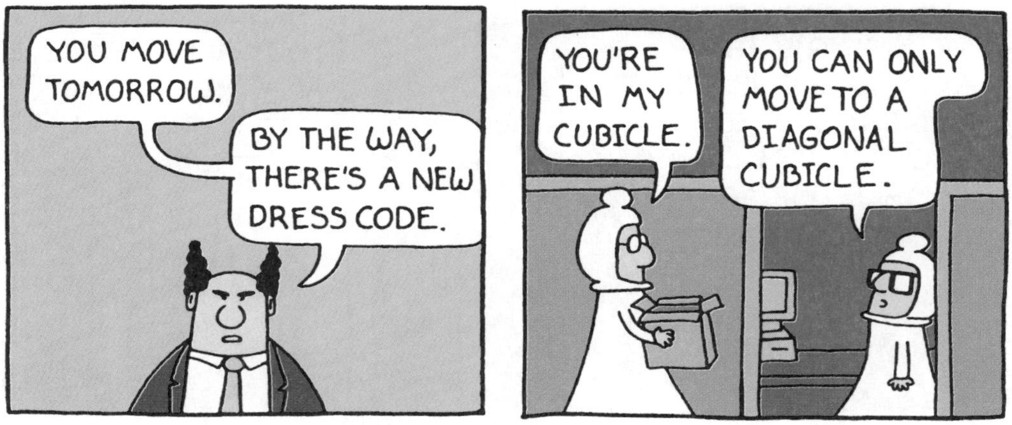
YOU MOVE TOMORROW.
BY THE WAY, THERE'S A NEW DRESS CODE.
YOU'RE IN MY CUBICLE.
YOU CAN ONLY MOVE TO A DIAGONAL CUBICLE.

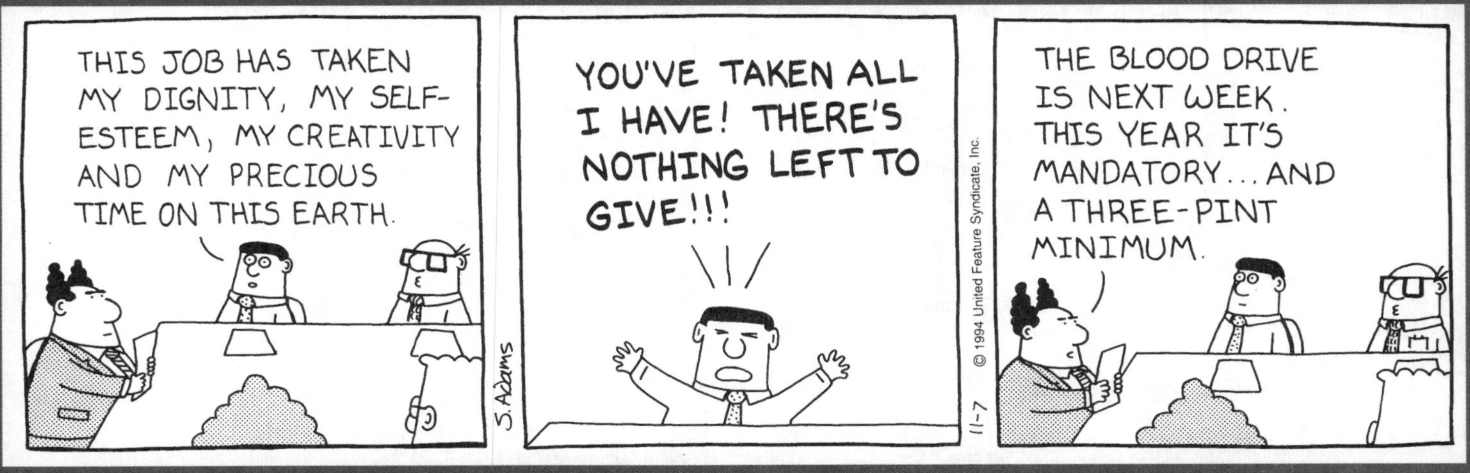
THIS JOB HAS TAKEN MY DIGNITY, MY SELF-ESTEEM, MY CREATIVITY AND MY PRECIOUS TIME ON THIS EARTH.
YOU'VE TAKEN ALL I HAVE! THERE'S NOTHING LEFT TO GIVE!!!
THE BLOOD DRIVE IS NEXT WEEK. THIS YEAR IT'S MANDATORY... AND A THREE-PINT MINIMUM.
S. Adams
11-7
© 1994 United Feature Syndicate, Inc.

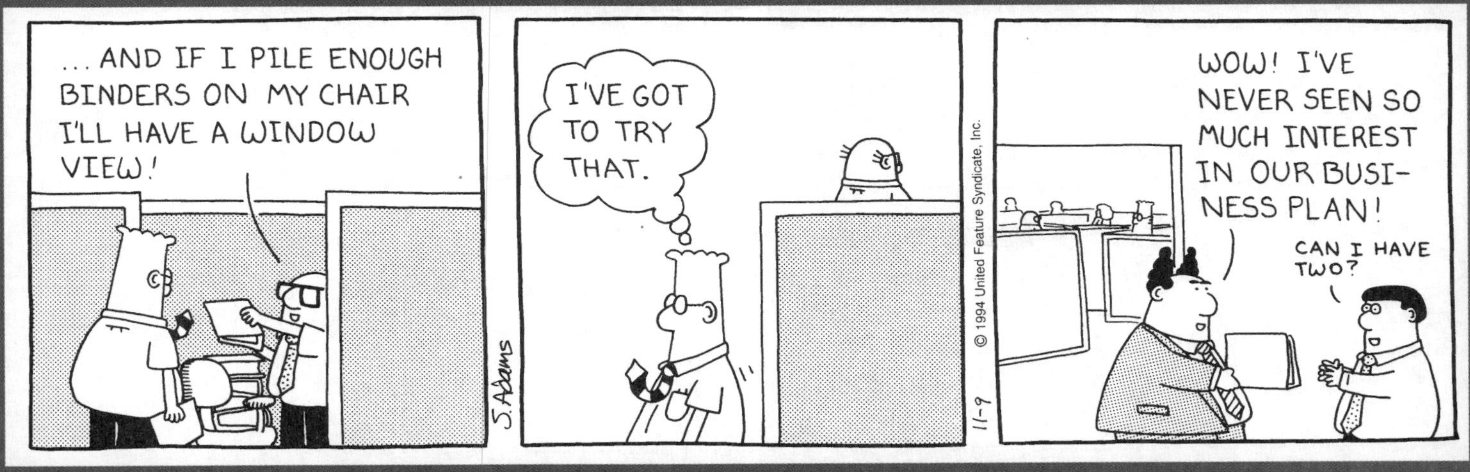
... AND IF I PILE ENOUGH BINDERS ON MY CHAIR I'LL HAVE A WINDOW VIEW!
I'VE GOT TO TRY THAT.
WOW! I'VE NEVER SEEN SO MUCH INTEREST IN OUR BUSI-NESS PLAN!
CAN I HAVE TWO?
S. Adams
11-9
© 1994 United Feature Syndicate, Inc.

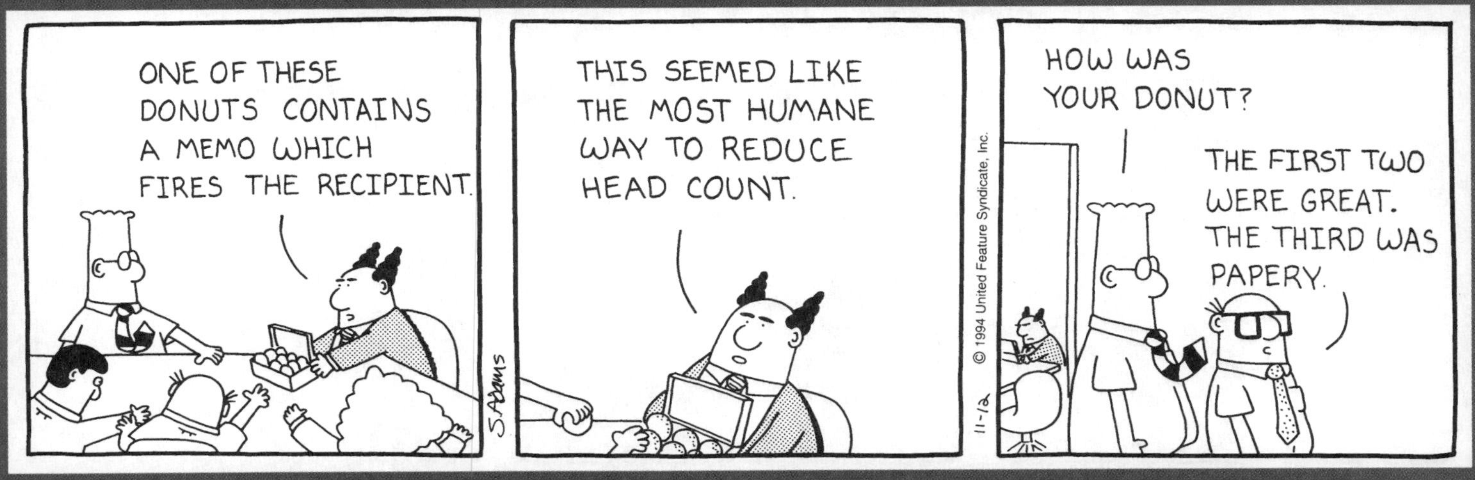
ONE OF THESE DONUTS CONTAINS A MEMO WHICH FIRES THE RECIPIENT.
THIS SEEMED LIKE THE MOST HUMANE WAY TO REDUCE HEAD COUNT.
HOW WAS YOUR DONUT?
THE FIRST TWO WERE GREAT. THE THIRD WAS PAPERY.
S. Adams
11-12
© 1994 United Feature Syndicate, Inc.

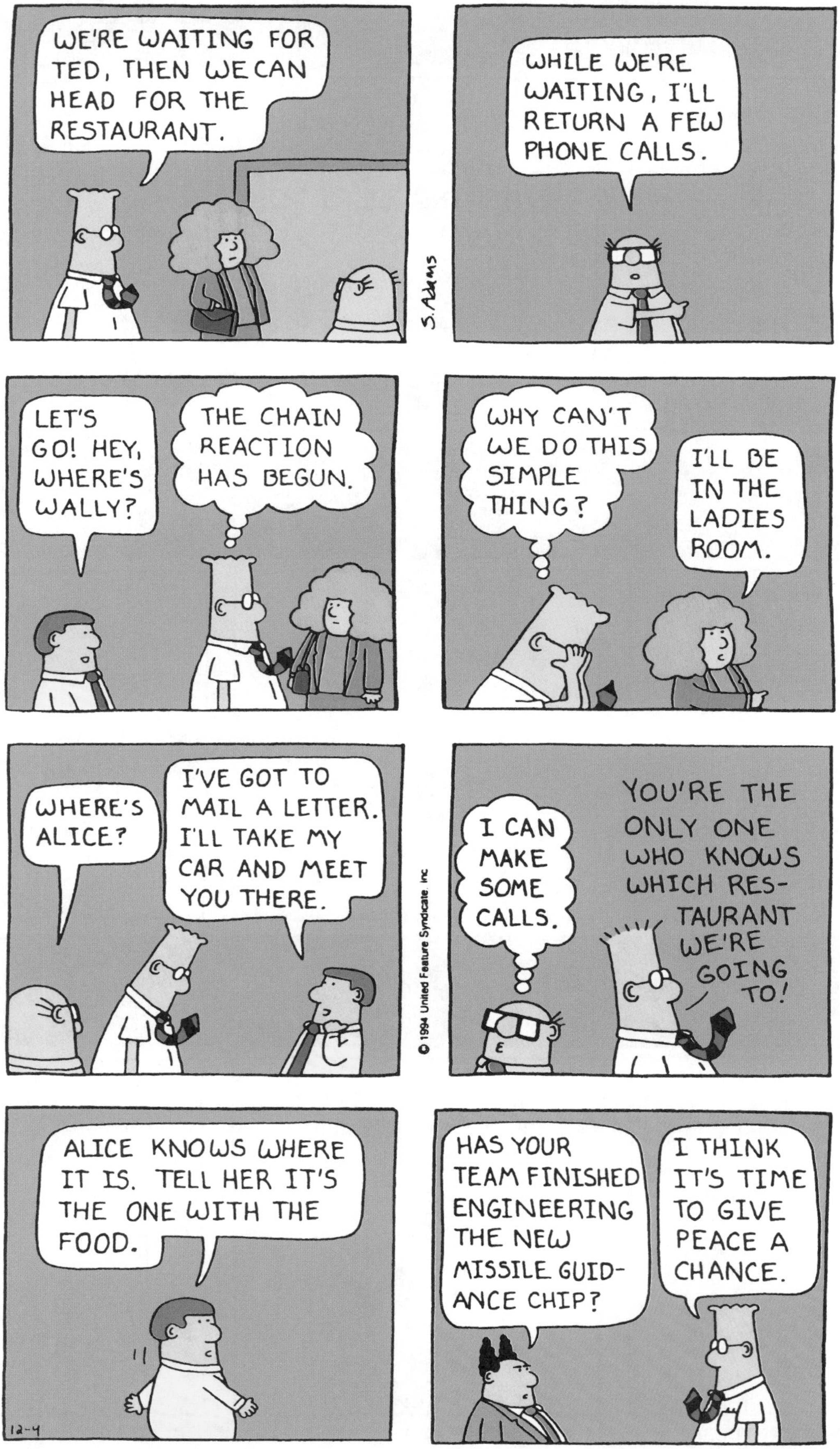
WE'RE WAITING FOR TED, THEN WE CAN HEAD FOR THE RESTAURANT.
S. Adams
WHILE WE'RE WAITING, I'LL RETURN A FEW PHONE CALLS.
LET'S GO! HEY, WHERE'S WALLY?
THE CHAIN REACTION HAS BEGUN.
WHY CAN'T WE DO THIS SIMPLE THING?
I'LL BE IN THE LADIES ROOM.
WHERE'S ALICE?
I'VE GOT TO MAIL A LETTER. I'LL TAKE MY CAR AND MEET YOU THERE.
© 1994 United Feature Syndicate Inc
I CAN MAKE SOME CALLS.
YOU'RE THE ONLY ONE WHO KNOWS WHICH RES-TAURANT WE'RE GOING TO!
ALICE KNOWS WHERE IT IS. TELL HER IT'S THE ONE WITH THE FOOD.
12-4
HAS YOUR TEAM FINISHED ENGINEERING THE NEW MISSILE GUID-ANCE CHIP?
I THINK IT'S TIME TO GIVE PEACE A CHANCE.

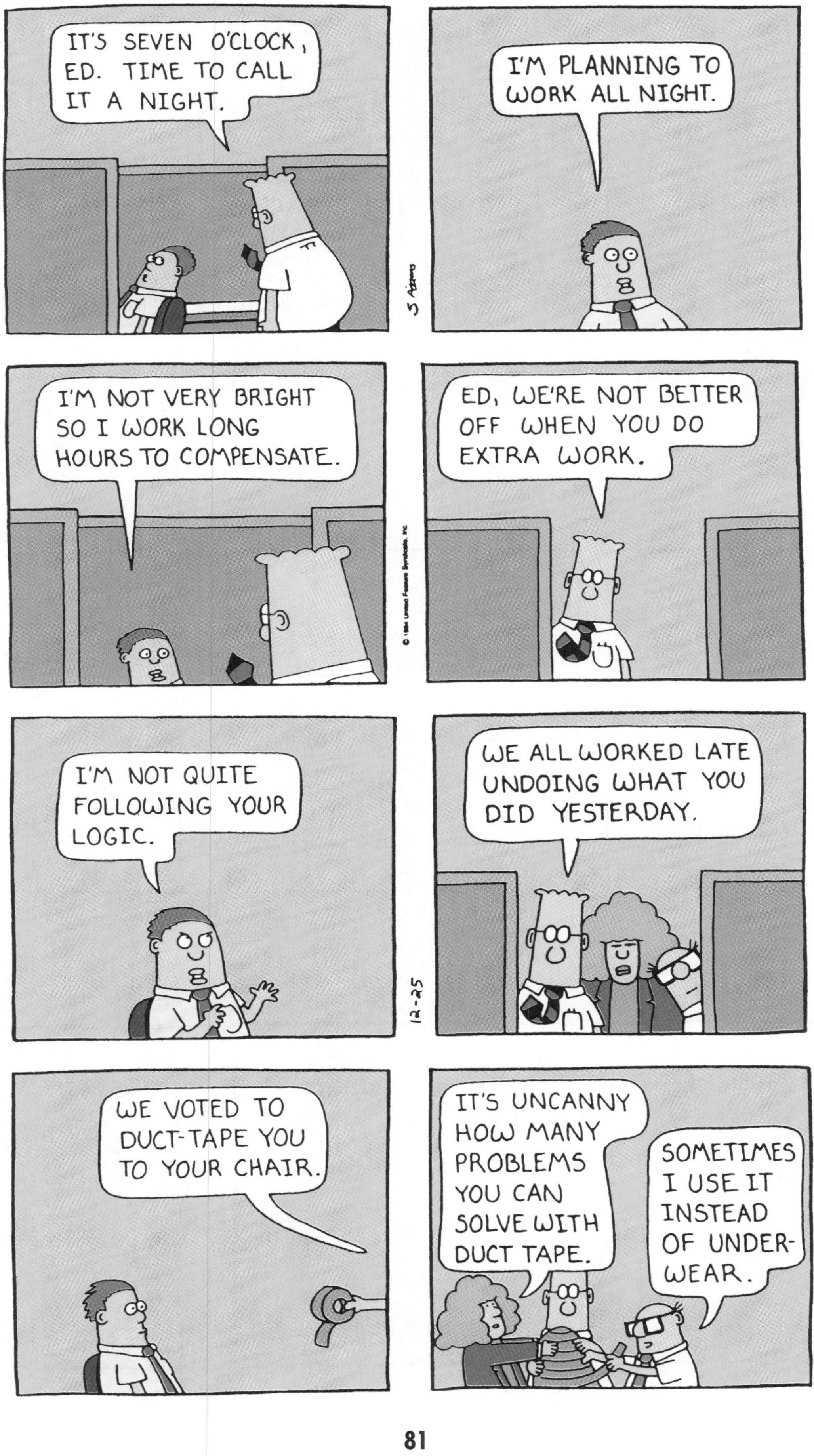
IT'S SEVEN O'CLOCK, ED. TIME TO CALL IT A NIGHT.
I'M PLANNING TO WORK ALL NIGHT.
I'M NOT VERY BRIGHT SO I WORK LONG HOURS TO COMPENSATE.
ED, WE'RE NOT BETTER OFF WHEN YOU DO EXTRA WORK.
I'M NOT QUITE FOLLOWING YOUR LOGIC.
12-25
WE ALL WORKED LATE UNDOING WHAT YOU DID YESTERDAY.
WE VOTED TO DUCT-TAPE YOU TO YOUR CHAIR.
IT'S UNCANNY HOW MANY PROBLEMS YOU CAN SOLVE WITH DUCT TAPE.
SOMETIMES I USE IT INSTEAD OF UNDER-WEAR.

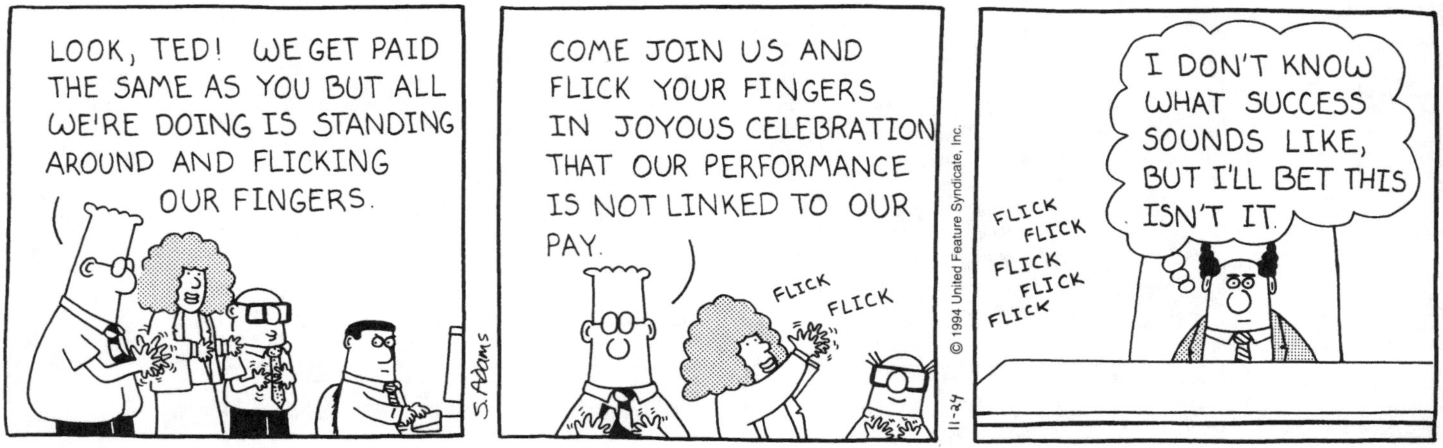
LOOK, TED! WE GET PAID THE SAME AS YOU BUT ALL WE'RE DOING IS STANDING AROUND AND FLICKING OUR FINGERS.
COME JOIN US AND FLICK YOUR FINGERS IN JOYOUS CELEBRATION THAT OUR PERFORMANCE IS NOT LINKED TO OUR PAY.
FLICK FLICK
© 1994 United Feature Syndicate, Inc.
FLICK FLICK FLICK FLICK FLICK
I DON'T KNOW WHAT SUCCESS SOUNDS LIKE, BUT I'LL BET THIS ISN'T IT.

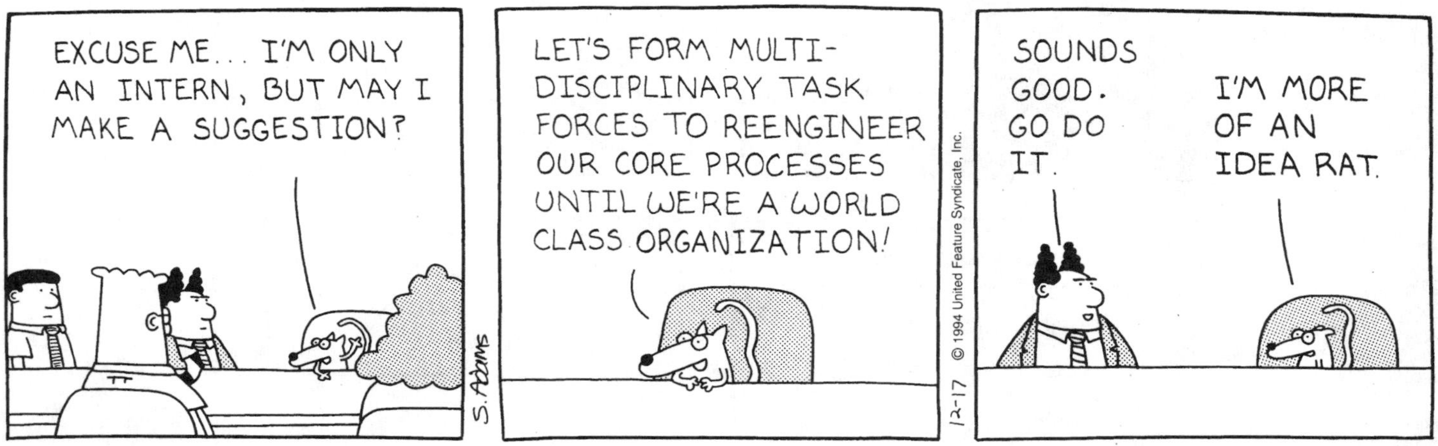
EXCUSE ME... I'M ONLY AN INTERN, BUT MAY I MAKE A SUGGESTION?
LET'S FORM MULTI-DISCIPLINARY TASK FORCES TO REENGINEER OUR CORE PROCESSES UNTIL WE'RE A WORLD CLASS ORGANIZATION!
© 1994 United Feature Syndicate, Inc.
SOUNDS GOOD. GO DO IT.
I'M MORE OF AN IDEA RAT.

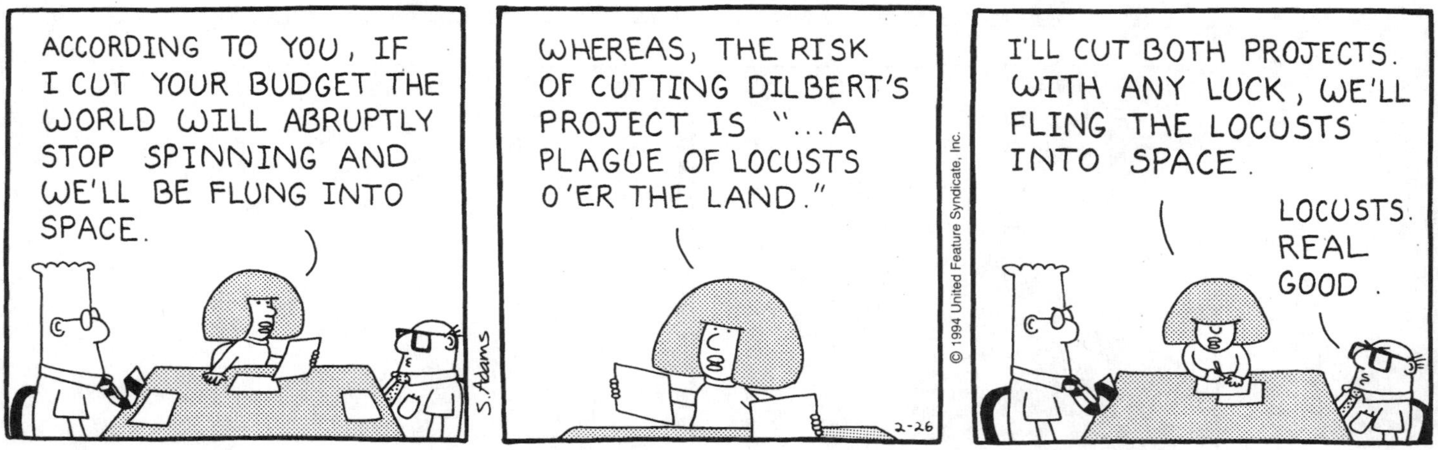
ACCORDING TO YOU, IF I CUT YOUR BUDGET THE WORLD WILL ABRUPTLY STOP SPINNING AND WE'LL BE FLUNG INTO SPACE.
WHEREAS, THE RISK OF CUTTING DILBERT'S PROJECT IS "...A PLAGUE OF LOCUSTS O'ER THE LAND."
© 1994 United Feature Syndicate, Inc.
I'LL CUT BOTH PROJECTS. WITH ANY LUCK, WE'LL FLING THE LOCUSTS INTO SPACE.
LOCUSTS. REAL GOOD.

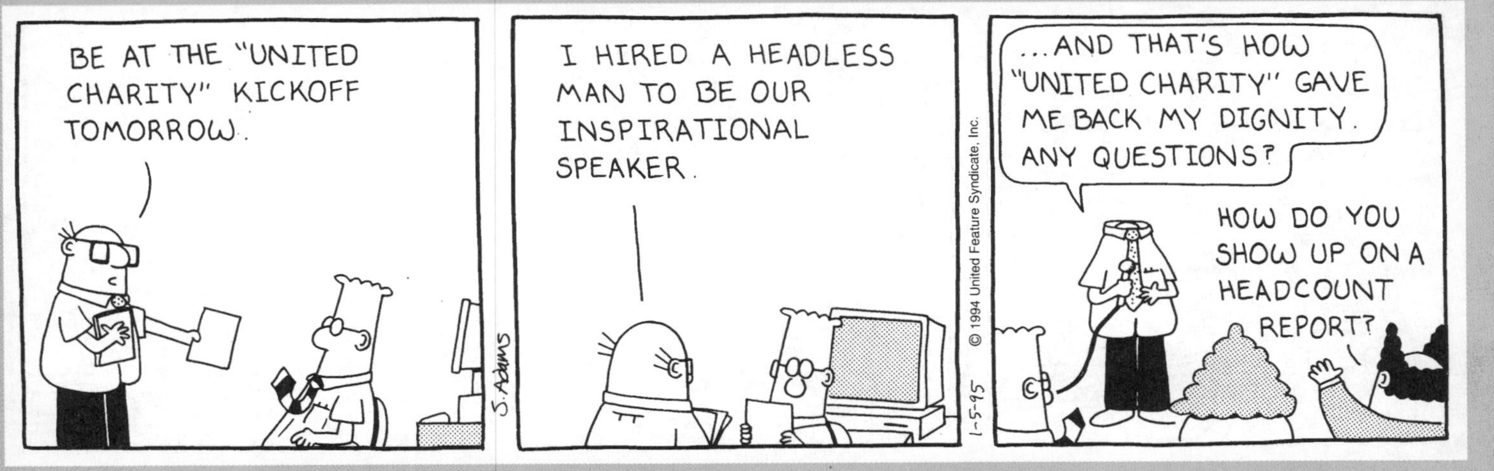
BE AT THE "UNITED CHARITY" KICKOFF TOMORROW.
I HIRED A HEADLESS MAN TO BE OUR INSPIRATIONAL SPEAKER.
...AND THAT'S HOW "UNITED CHARITY" GAVE ME BACK MY DIGNITY. ANY QUESTIONS?
HOW DO YOU SHOW UP ON A HEADCOUNT REPORT?
S. Adams
1-5-95
© 1994 United Feature Syndicate, Inc.

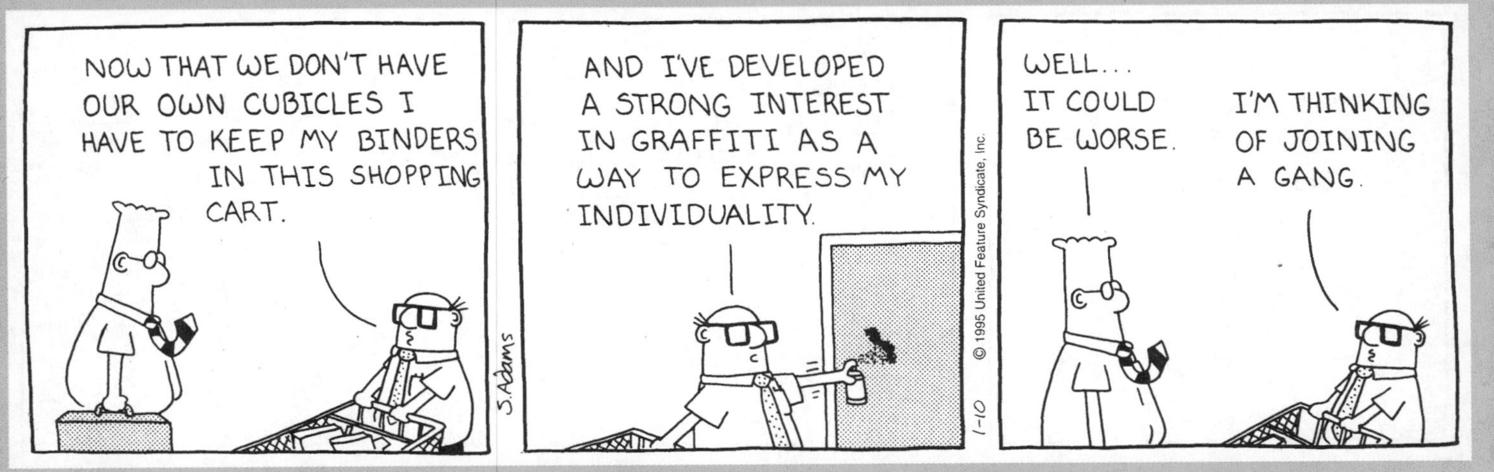
NOW THAT WE DON'T HAVE OUR OWN CUBICLES I HAVE TO KEEP MY BINDERS IN THIS SHOPPING CART.
AND I'VE DEVELOPED A STRONG INTEREST IN GRAFFITI AS A WAY TO EXPRESS MY INDIVIDUALITY.
WELL... IT COULD BE WORSE.
I'M THINKING OF JOINING A GANG.
S. Adams
1-10
© 1995 United Feature Syndicate, Inc.

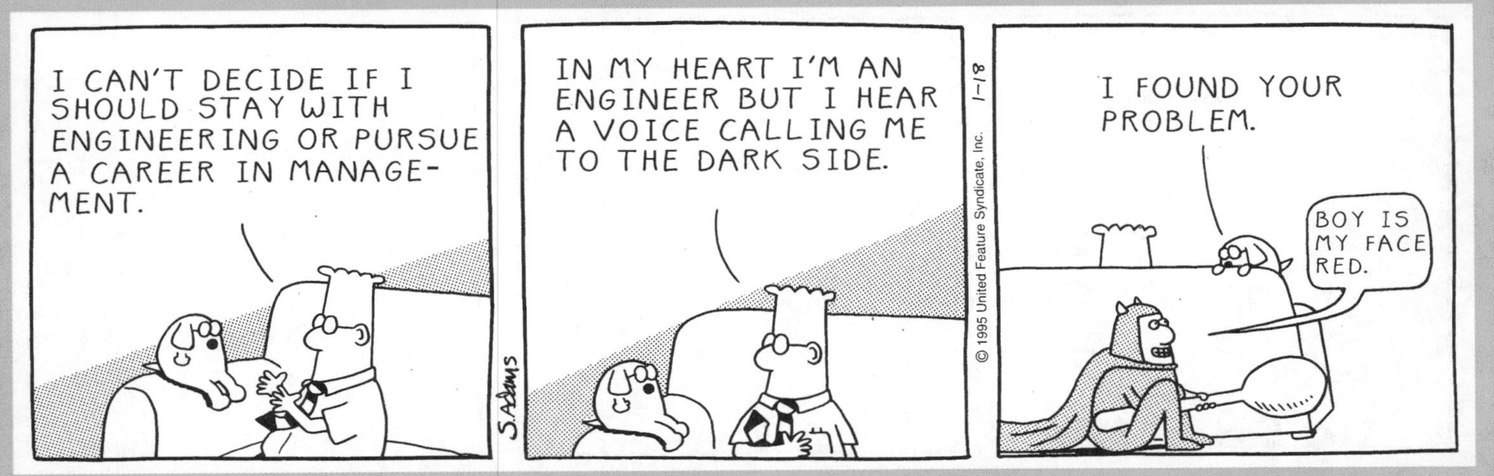
I CAN'T DECIDE IF I SHOULD STAY WITH ENGINEERING OR PURSUE A CAREER IN MANAGEMENT.
IN MY HEART I'M AN ENGINEER BUT I HEAR A VOICE CALLING ME TO THE DARK SIDE.
I FOUND YOUR PROBLEM.
BOY IS MY FACE RED.
S. Adams
1-18
© 1995 United Feature Syndicate, Inc.

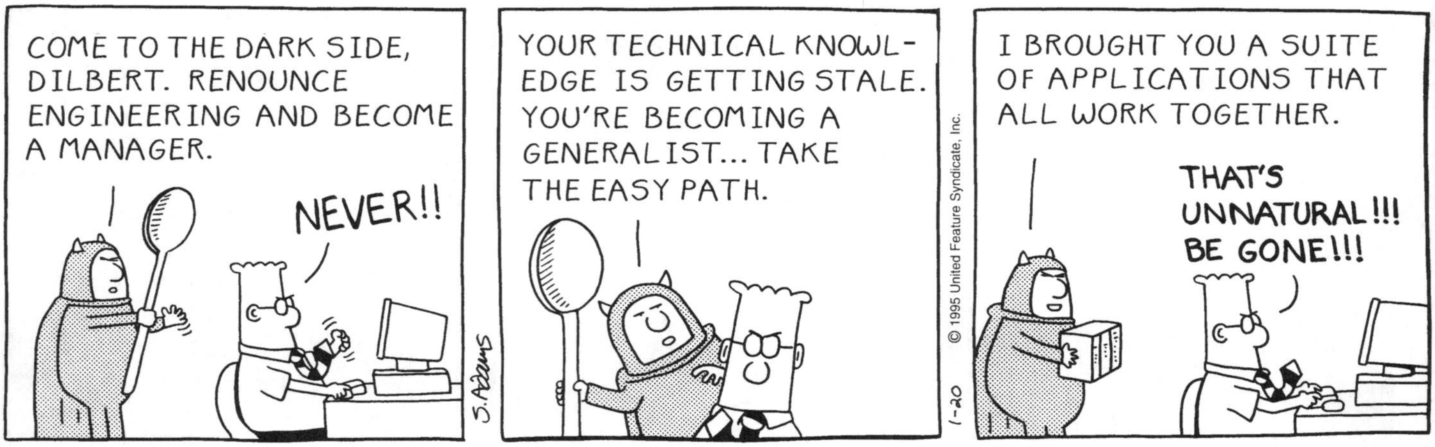
COME TO THE DARK SIDE, DILBERT. RENOUNCE ENGINEERING AND BECOME A MANAGER.
NEVER!!
S. ADAMS
YOUR TECHNICAL KNOWL-EDGE IS GETTING STALE. YOU'RE BECOMING A GENERALIST... TAKE THE EASY PATH.
1-20
© 1995 United Feature Syndicate, Inc.
I BROUGHT YOU A SUITE OF APPLICATIONS THAT ALL WORK TOGETHER.
THAT'S UNNATURAL!!! BE GONE!!!

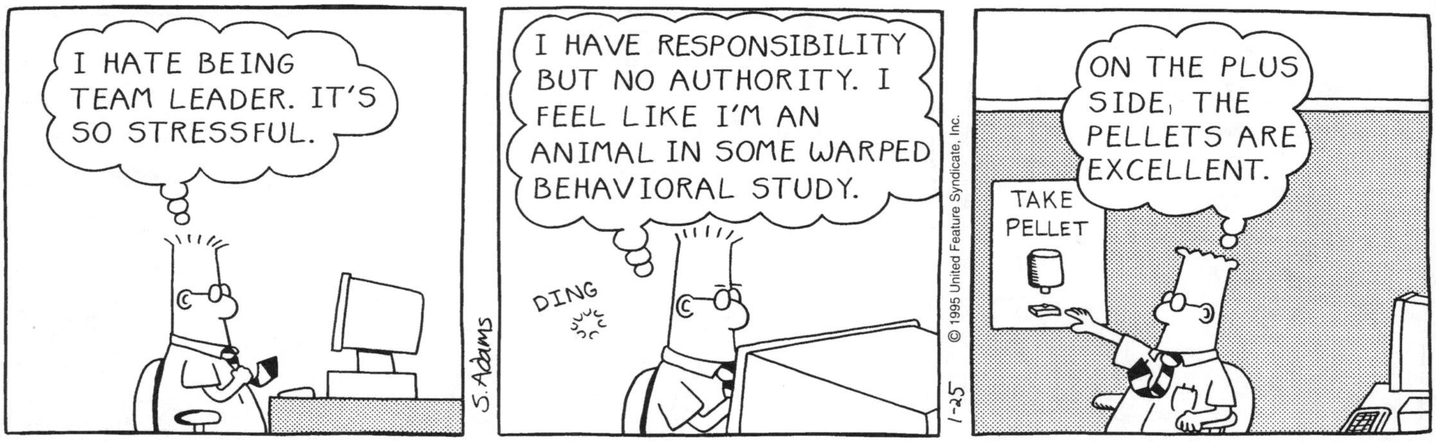
I HATE BEING TEAM LEADER. IT'S SO STRESSFUL.
S. ADAMS
I HAVE RESPONSIBILITY BUT NO AUTHORITY. I FEEL LIKE I'M AN ANIMAL IN SOME WARPED BEHAVIORAL STUDY.
DING
1-25
© 1995 United Feature Syndicate, Inc.
ON THE PLUS SIDE, THE PELLETS ARE EXCELLENT.
TAKE PELLET

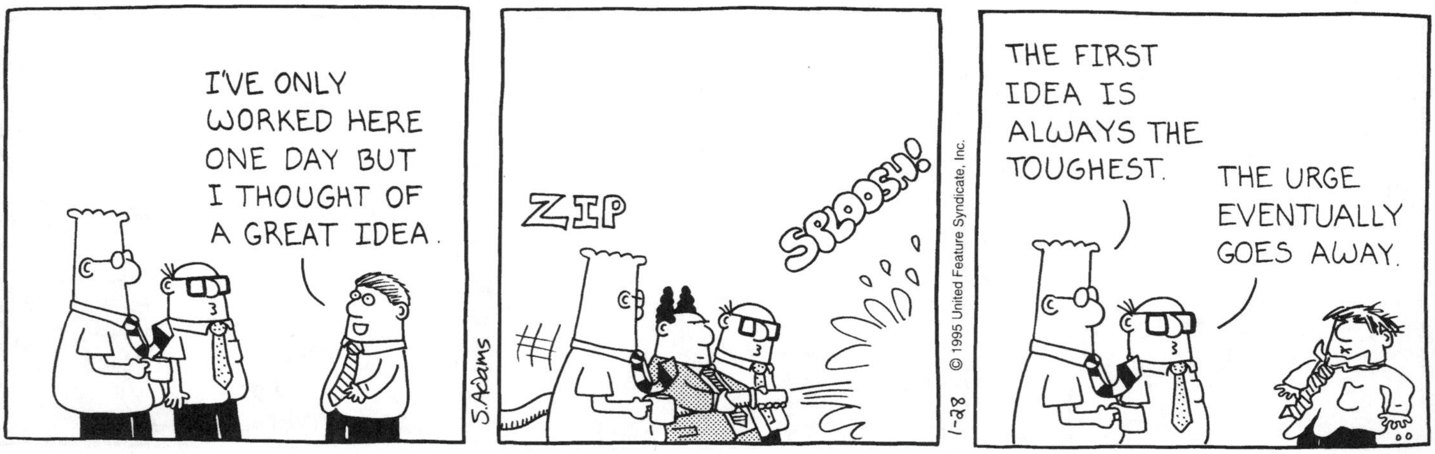
I'VE ONLY WORKED HERE ONE DAY BUT I THOUGHT OF A GREAT IDEA.
S. ADAMS
ZIP
SPLOOSH!
1-28
© 1995 United Feature Syndicate, Inc.
THE FIRST IDEA IS ALWAYS THE TOUGHEST.
THE URGE EVENTUALLY GOES AWAY.

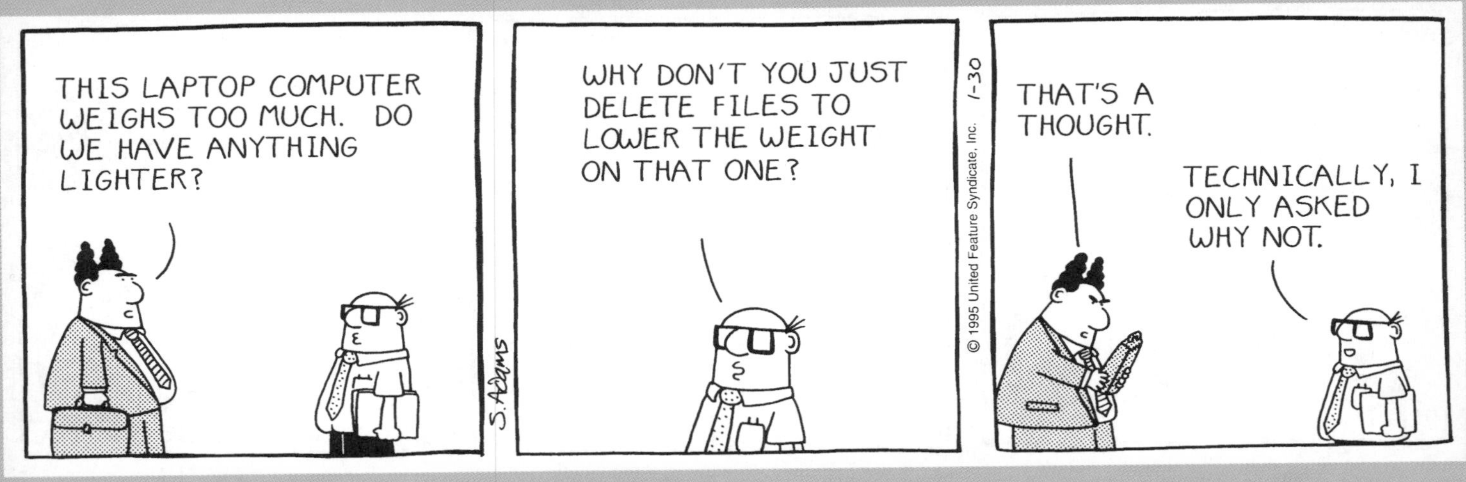
THIS LAPTOP COMPUTER WEIGHS TOO MUCH. DO WE HAVE ANYTHING LIGHTER?
S. Adams
WHY DON'T YOU JUST DELETE FILES TO LOWER THE WEIGHT ON THAT ONE?
1-30
© 1995 United Feature Syndicate, Inc.
THAT'S A THOUGHT.
TECHNICALLY, I ONLY ASKED WHY NOT.

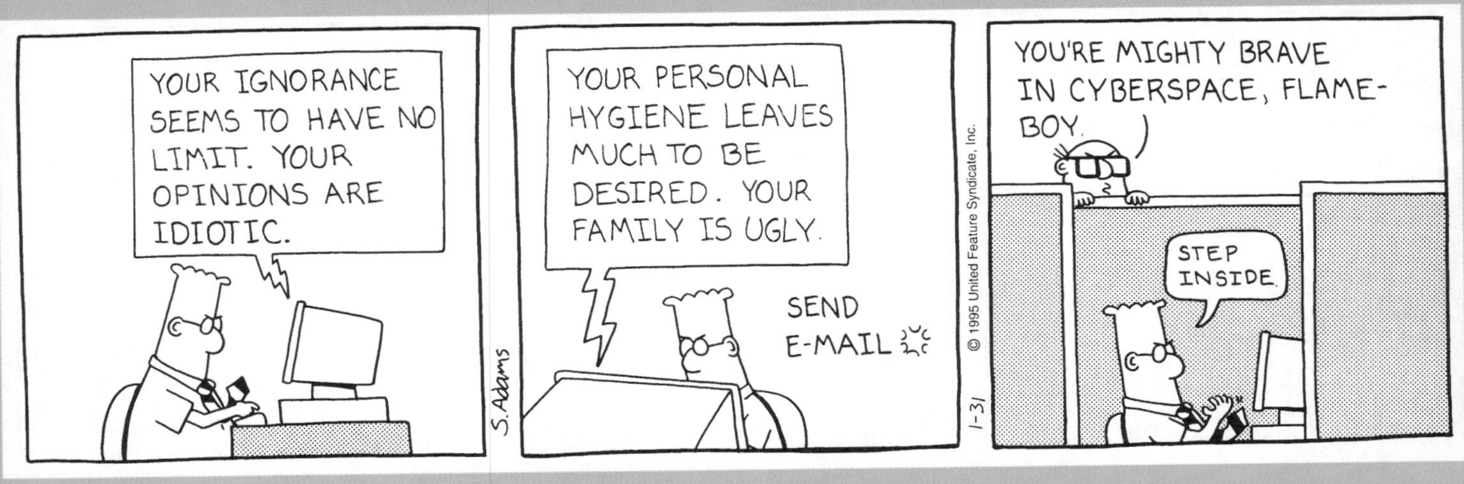
YOUR IGNORANCE SEEMS TO HAVE NO LIMIT. YOUR OPINIONS ARE IDIOTIC.
S. Adams
YOUR PERSONAL HYGIENE LEAVES MUCH TO BE DESIRED. YOUR FAMILY IS UGLY.
SEND E-MAIL
1-31
© 1995 United Feature Syndicate, Inc.
YOU'RE MIGHTY BRAVE IN CYBERSPACE, FLAME-BOY.
STEP INSIDE.

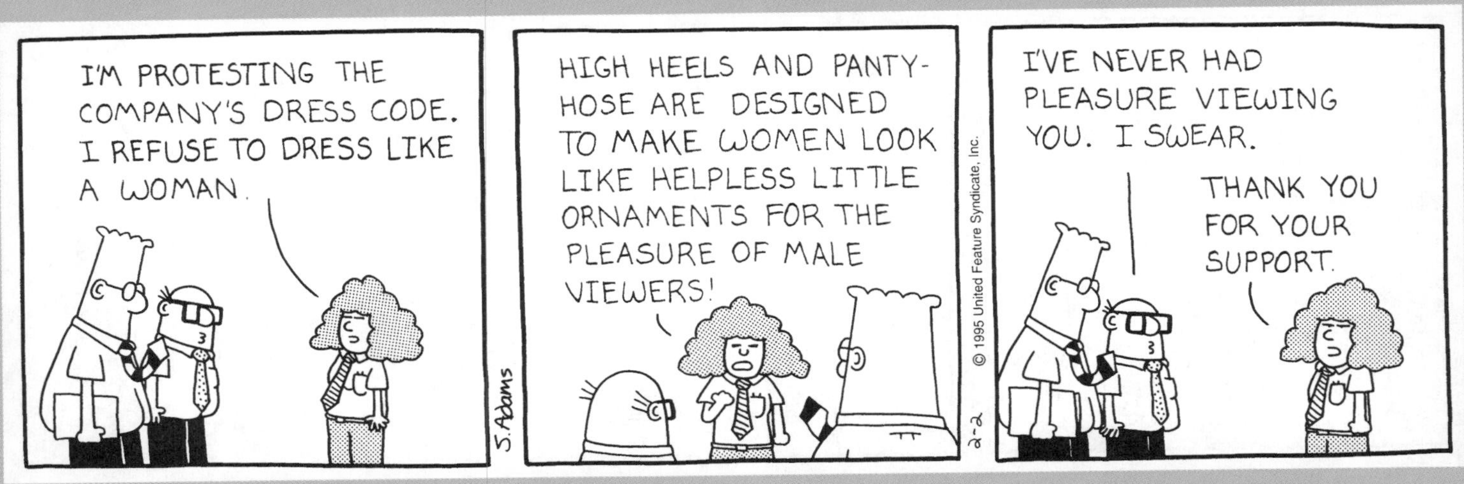
I'M PROTESTING THE COMPANY'S DRESS CODE. I REFUSE TO DRESS LIKE A WOMAN.
S. Adams
HIGH HEELS AND PANTY-HOSE ARE DESIGNED TO MAKE WOMEN LOOK LIKE HELPLESS LITTLE ORNAMENTS FOR THE PLEASURE OF MALE VIEWERS!
2-2
© 1995 United Feature Syndicate, Inc.
I'VE NEVER HAD PLEASURE VIEWING YOU. I SWEAR.
THANK YOU FOR YOUR SUPPORT.

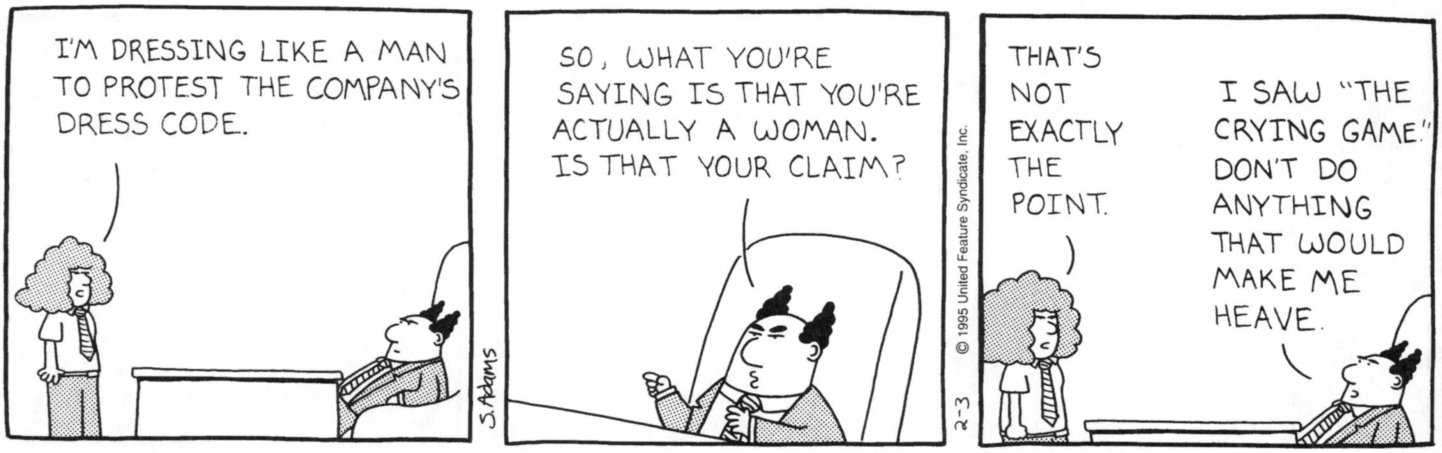
I'M DRESSING LIKE A MAN TO PROTEST THE COMPANY'S DRESS CODE.
SO, WHAT YOU'RE SAYING IS THAT YOU'RE ACTUALLY A WOMAN. IS THAT YOUR CLAIM?
THAT'S NOT EXACTLY THE POINT.
I SAW "THE CRYING GAME." DON'T DO ANYTHING THAT WOULD MAKE ME HEAVE.
S. Adams
2-3
© 1995 United Feature Syndicate, Inc.

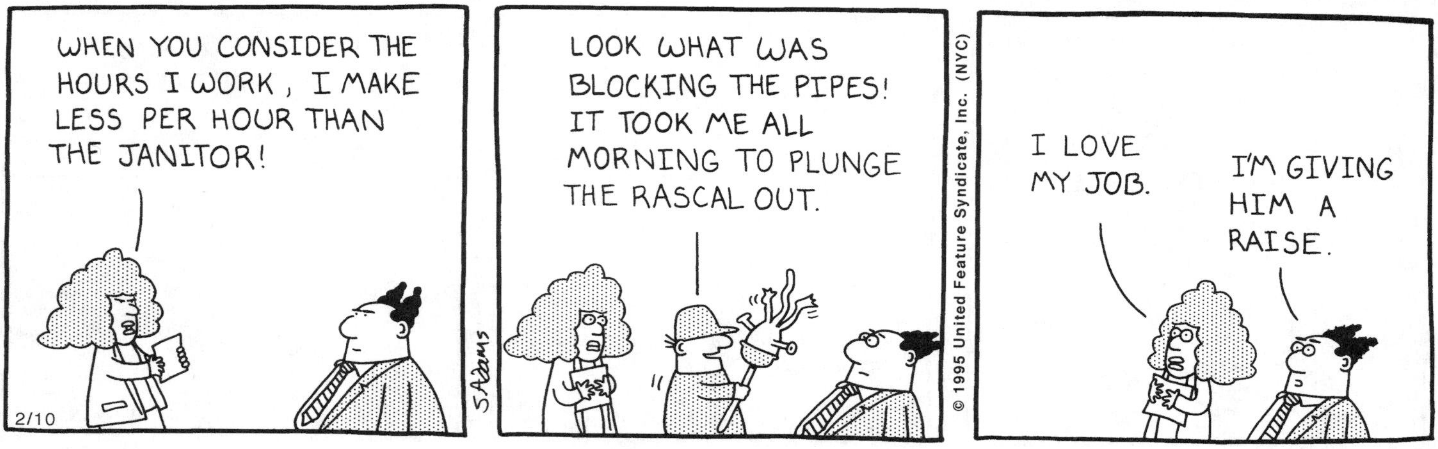
WHEN YOU CONSIDER THE HOURS I WORK, I MAKE LESS PER HOUR THAN THE JANITOR!
2/10
S. Adams
LOOK WHAT WAS BLOCKING THE PIPES! IT TOOK ME ALL MORNING TO PLUNGE THE RASCAL OUT.
© 1995 United Feature Syndicate, Inc. (NYC)
I LOVE MY JOB.
I'M GIVING HIM A RAISE.

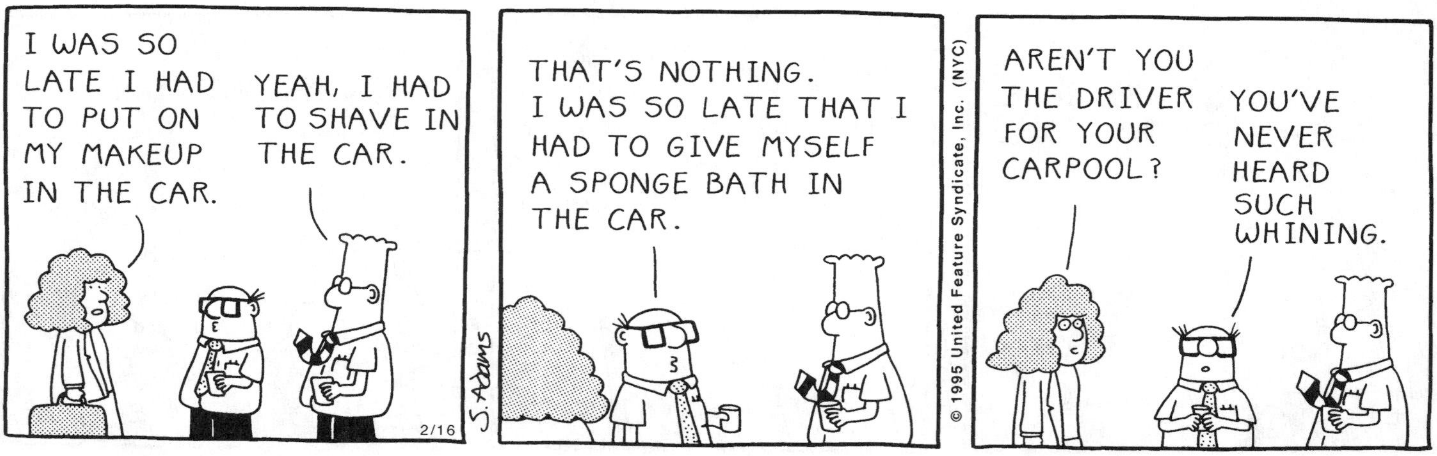
I WAS SO LATE I HAD TO PUT ON MY MAKEUP IN THE CAR.
YEAH, I HAD TO SHAVE IN THE CAR.
2/16
S. Adams
THAT'S NOTHING. I WAS SO LATE THAT I HAD TO GIVE MYSELF A SPONGE BATH IN THE CAR.
© 1995 United Feature Syndicate, Inc. (NYC)
AREN'T YOU THE DRIVER FOR YOUR CARPOOL?
YOU'VE NEVER HEARD SUCH WHINING.

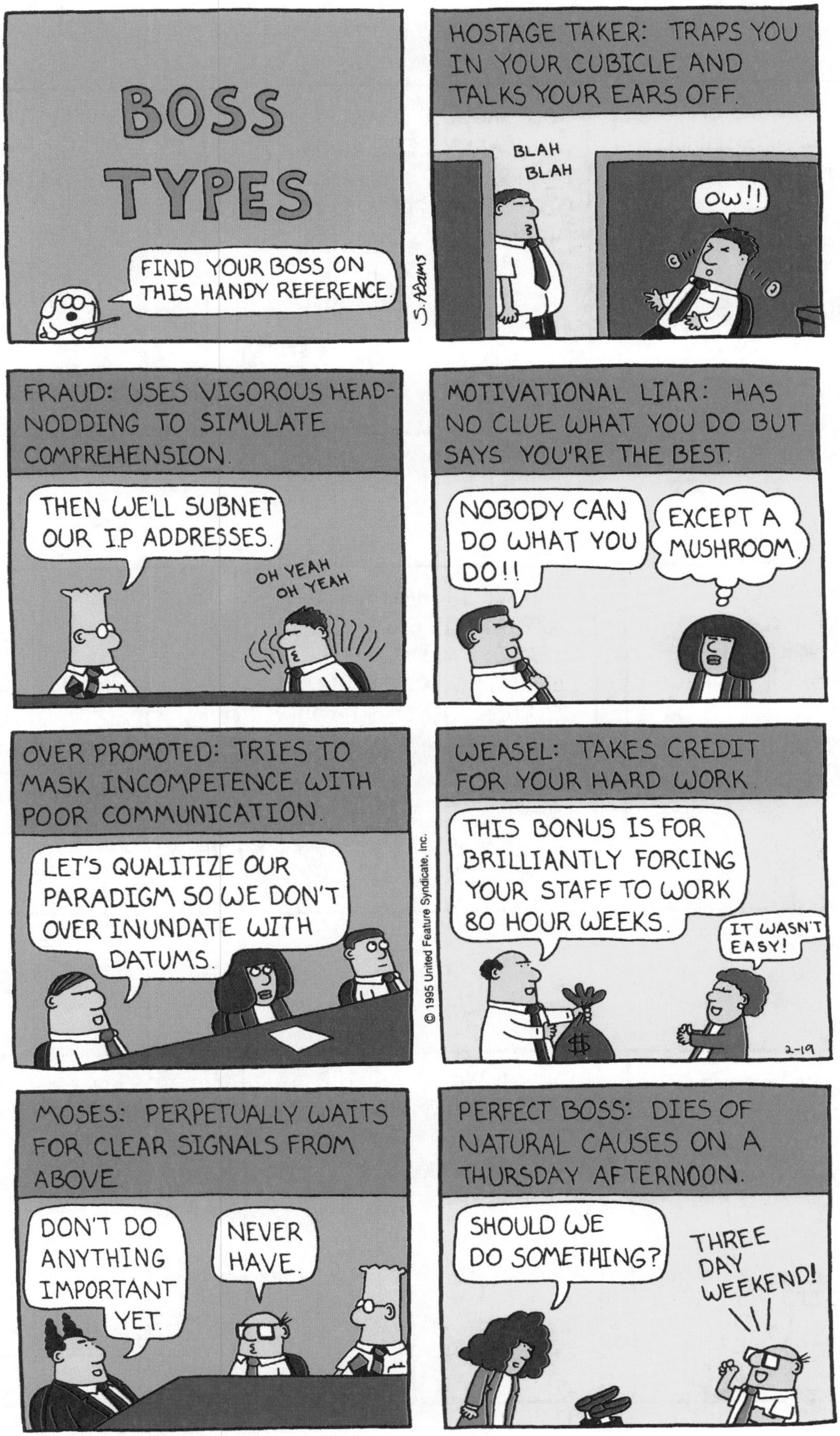
BOSS TYPES
FIND YOUR BOSS ON THIS HANDY REFERENCE.
S. Adams
HOSTAGE TAKER: TRAPS YOU IN YOUR CUBICLE AND TALKS YOUR EARS OFF.
BLAH BLAH
OW!!
FRAUD: USES VIGOROUS HEAD-NODDING TO SIMULATE COMPREHENSION.
THEN WE'LL SUBNET OUR I.P. ADDRESSES.
OH YEAH OH YEAH
MOTIVATIONAL LIAR: HAS NO CLUE WHAT YOU DO BUT SAYS YOU'RE THE BEST.
NOBODY CAN DO WHAT YOU DO!!
EXCEPT A MUSHROOM.
OVER PROMOTED: TRIES TO MASK INCOMPETENCE WITH POOR COMMUNICATION.
LET'S QUALITIZE OUR PARADIGM SO WE DON'T OVER INUNDATE WITH DATUMS.
© 1995 United Feature Syndicate, Inc.
WEASEL: TAKES CREDIT FOR YOUR HARD WORK.
THIS BONUS IS FOR BRILLIANTLY FORCING YOUR STAFF TO WORK 80 HOUR WEEKS.
IT WASN'T EASY!
$
2-19
MOSES: PERPETUALLY WAITS FOR CLEAR SIGNALS FROM ABOVE.
DON'T DO ANYTHING IMPORTANT YET.
NEVER HAVE.
PERFECT BOSS: DIES OF NATURAL CAUSES ON A THURSDAY AFTERNOON.
SHOULD WE DO SOMETHING?
THREE DAY WEEKEND!

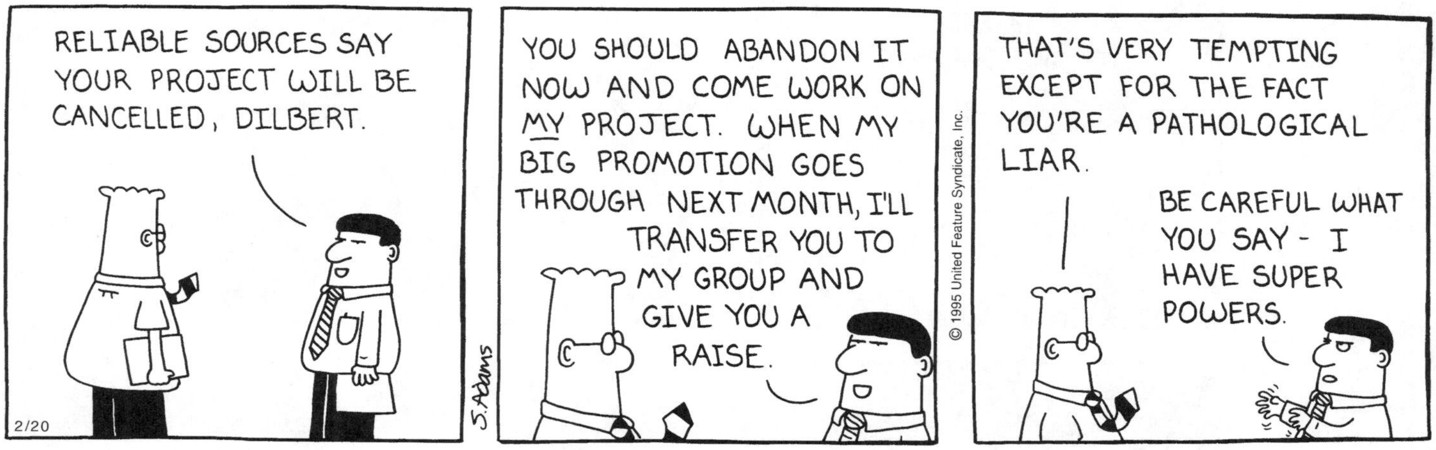
RELIABLE SOURCES SAY YOUR PROJECT WILL BE CANCELLED, DILBERT.
2/20
S. Adams
YOU SHOULD ABANDON IT NOW AND COME WORK ON MY PROJECT. WHEN MY BIG PROMOTION GOES THROUGH NEXT MONTH, I'LL TRANSFER YOU TO MY GROUP AND GIVE YOU A RAISE.
© 1995 United Feature Syndicate, Inc.
THAT'S VERY TEMPTING EXCEPT FOR THE FACT YOU'RE A PATHOLOGICAL LIAR.
BE CAREFUL WHAT YOU SAY - I HAVE SUPER POWERS.

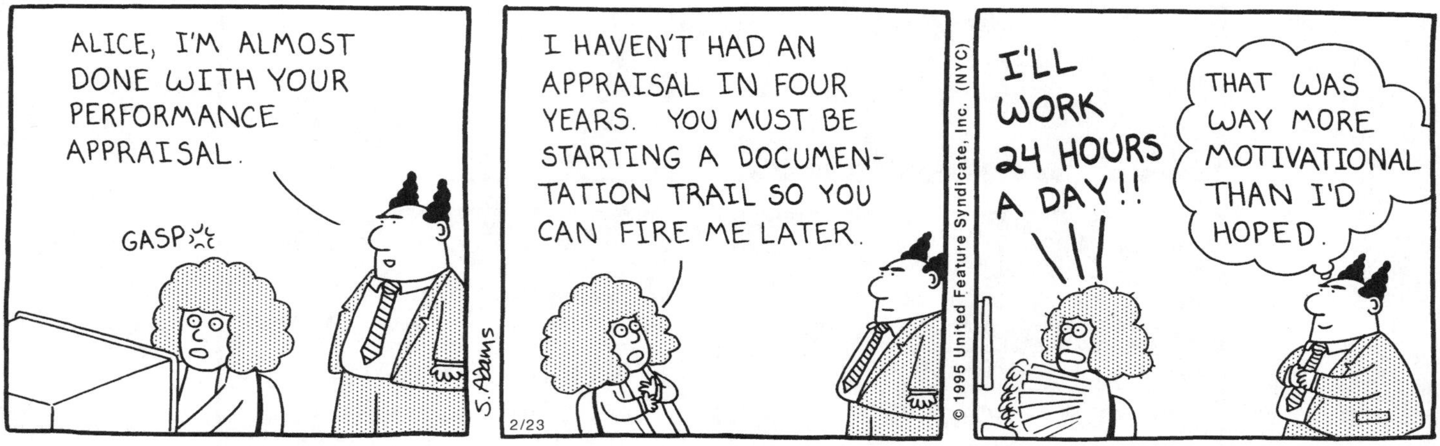
ALICE, I'M ALMOST DONE WITH YOUR PERFORMANCE APPRAISAL.
GASP
S. Adams
I HAVEN'T HAD AN APPRAISAL IN FOUR YEARS. YOU MUST BE STARTING A DOCUMENTATION TRAIL SO YOU CAN FIRE ME LATER.
2/23
© 1995 United Feature Syndicate, Inc. (NYC)
I'LL WORK 24 HOURS A DAY!!
THAT WAS WAY MORE MOTIVATIONAL THAN I'D HOPED.

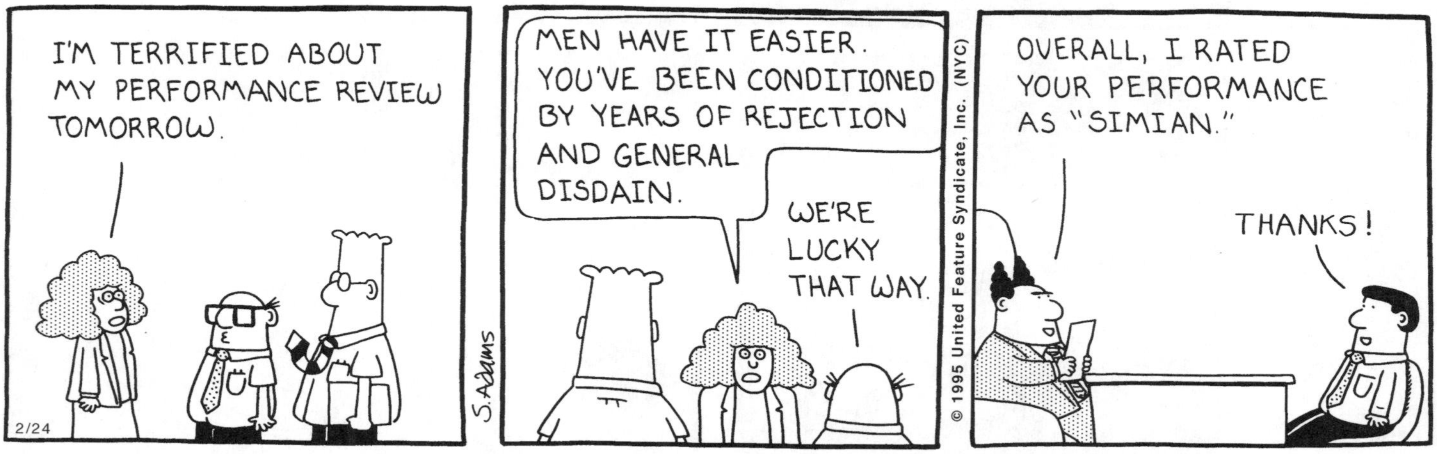
I'M TERRIFIED ABOUT MY PERFORMANCE REVIEW TOMORROW.
2/24
S. Adams
MEN HAVE IT EASIER. YOU'VE BEEN CONDITIONED BY YEARS OF REJECTION AND GENERAL DISDAIN.
WE'RE LUCKY THAT WAY.
© 1995 United Feature Syndicate, Inc. (NYC)
OVERALL, I RATED YOUR PERFORMANCE AS "SIMIAN."
THANKS!

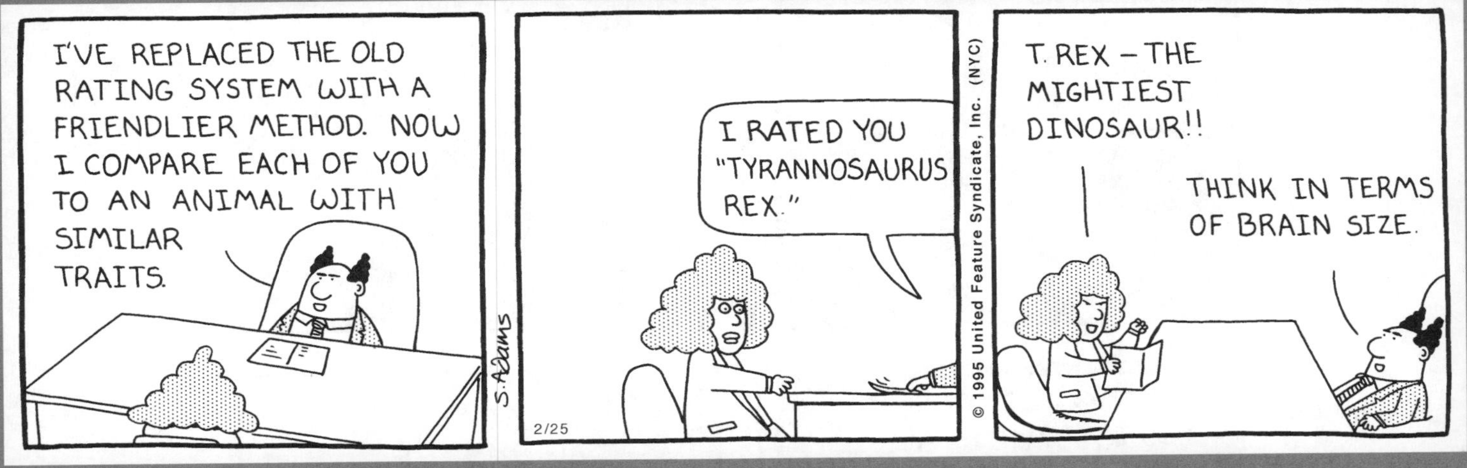
I'VE REPLACED THE OLD RATING SYSTEM WITH A FRIENDLIER METHOD. NOW I COMPARE EACH OF YOU TO AN ANIMAL WITH SIMILAR TRAITS.
S. Adams
2/25
I RATED YOU "TYRANNOSAURUS REX."
© 1995 United Feature Syndicate, Inc. (NYC)
T. REX – THE MIGHTIEST DINOSAUR!!
THINK IN TERMS OF BRAIN SIZE.

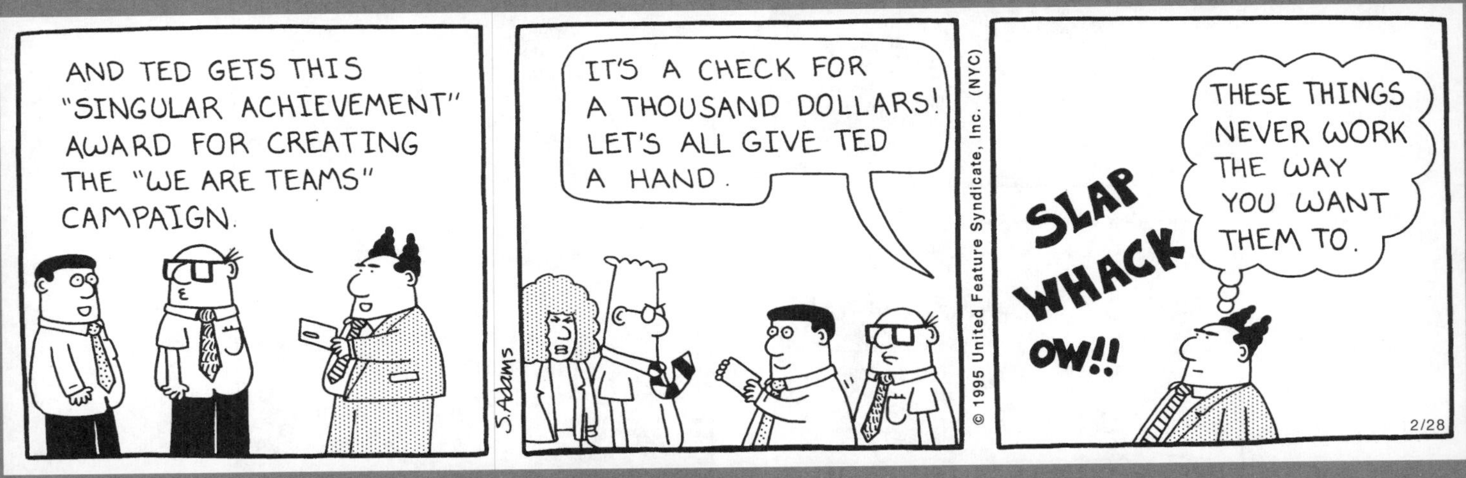
AND TED GETS THIS "SINGULAR ACHIEVEMENT" AWARD FOR CREATING THE "WE ARE TEAMS" CAMPAIGN.
S. Adams
IT'S A CHECK FOR A THOUSAND DOLLARS! LET'S ALL GIVE TED A HAND.
© 1995 United Feature Syndicate, Inc. (NYC)
SLAP
WHACK
OW!!
THESE THINGS NEVER WORK THE WAY YOU WANT THEM TO.
2/28

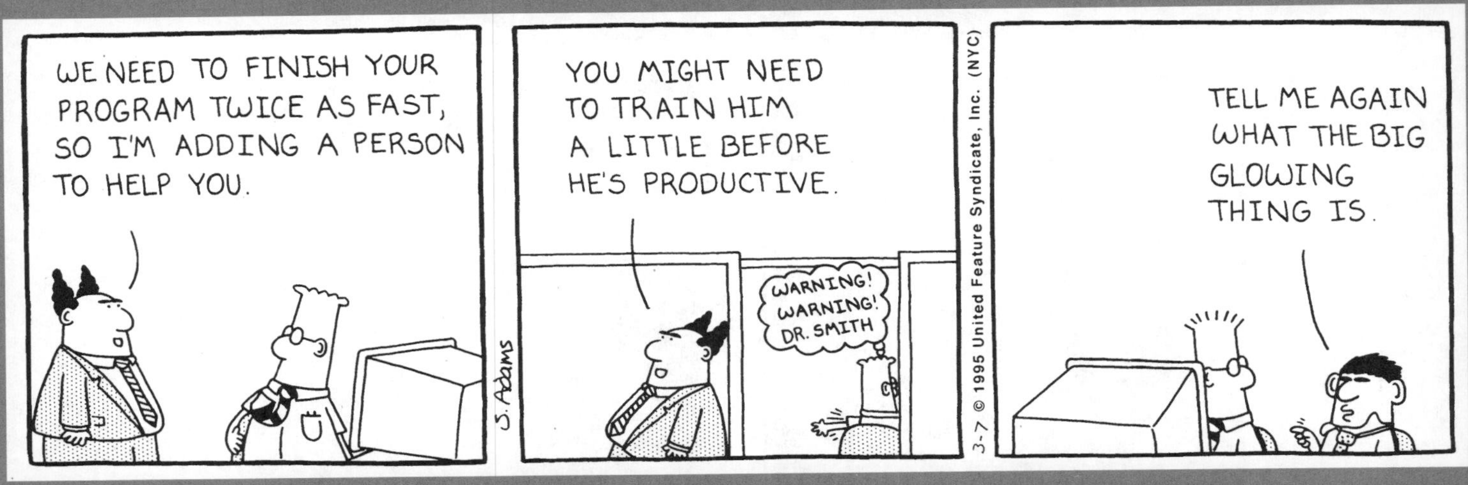
WE NEED TO FINISH YOUR PROGRAM TWICE AS FAST, SO I'M ADDING A PERSON TO HELP YOU.
S. Adams
YOU MIGHT NEED TO TRAIN HIM A LITTLE BEFORE HE'S PRODUCTIVE.
WARNING! WARNING! DR. SMITH
3-7 © 1995 United Feature Syndicate, Inc. (NYC)
TELL ME AGAIN WHAT THE BIG GLOWING THING IS.

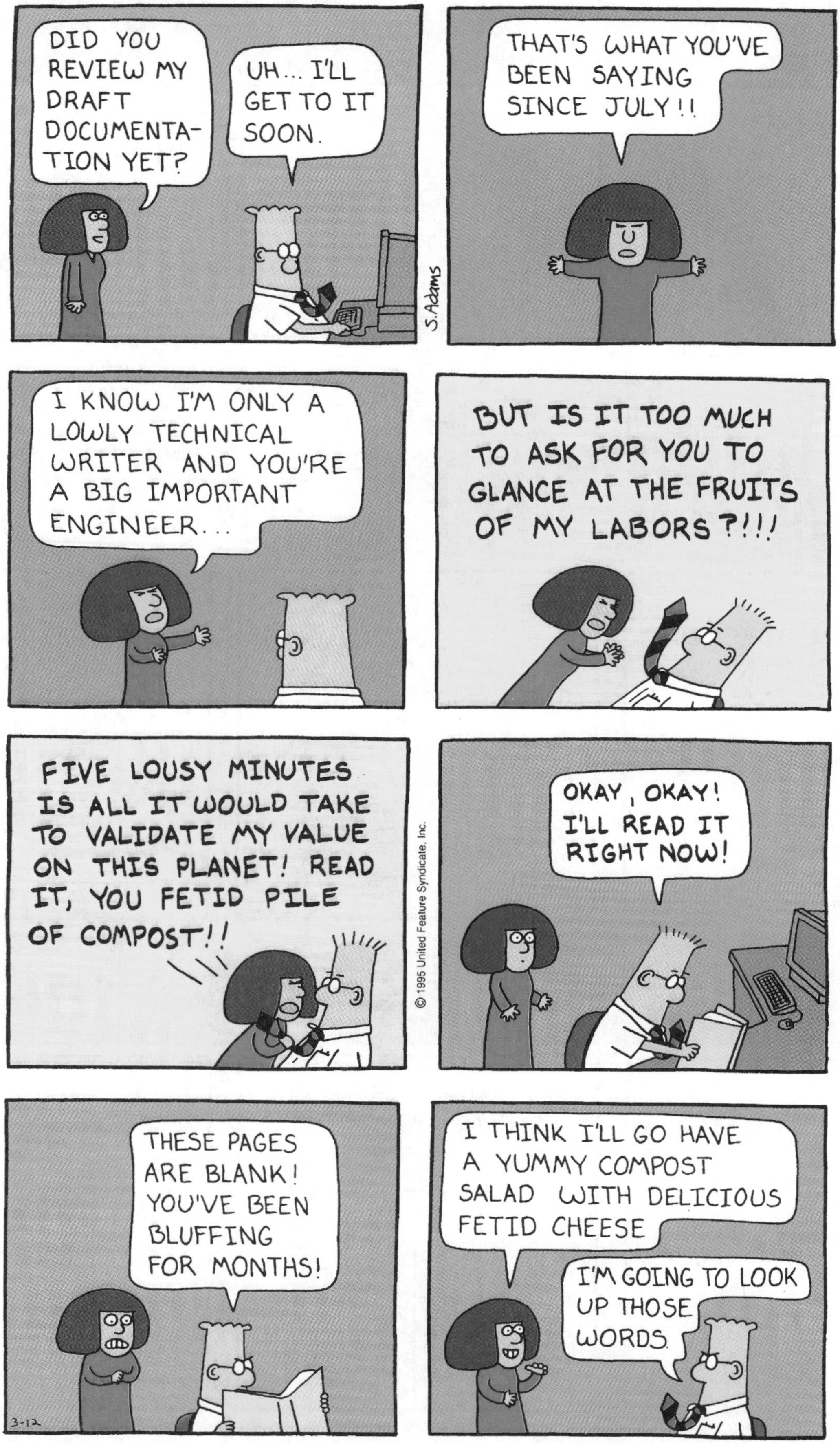
DID YOU REVIEW MY DRAFT DOCUMENTATION YET?
UH... I'LL GET TO IT SOON.
S. Adams
THAT'S WHAT YOU'VE BEEN SAYING SINCE JULY!!
I KNOW I'M ONLY A LOWLY TECHNICAL WRITER AND YOU'RE A BIG IMPORTANT ENGINEER...
BUT IS IT TOO MUCH TO ASK FOR YOU TO GLANCE AT THE FRUITS OF MY LABORS?!!!
FIVE LOUSY MINUTES IS ALL IT WOULD TAKE TO VALIDATE MY VALUE ON THIS PLANET! READ IT, YOU FETID PILE OF COMPOST!!
© 1995 United Feature Syndicate, Inc.
OKAY, OKAY! I'LL READ IT RIGHT NOW!
THESE PAGES ARE BLANK! YOU'VE BEEN BLUFFING FOR MONTHS!
3-12
I THINK I'LL GO HAVE A YUMMY COMPOST SALAD WITH DELICIOUS FETID CHEESE
I'M GOING TO LOOK UP THOSE WORDS.

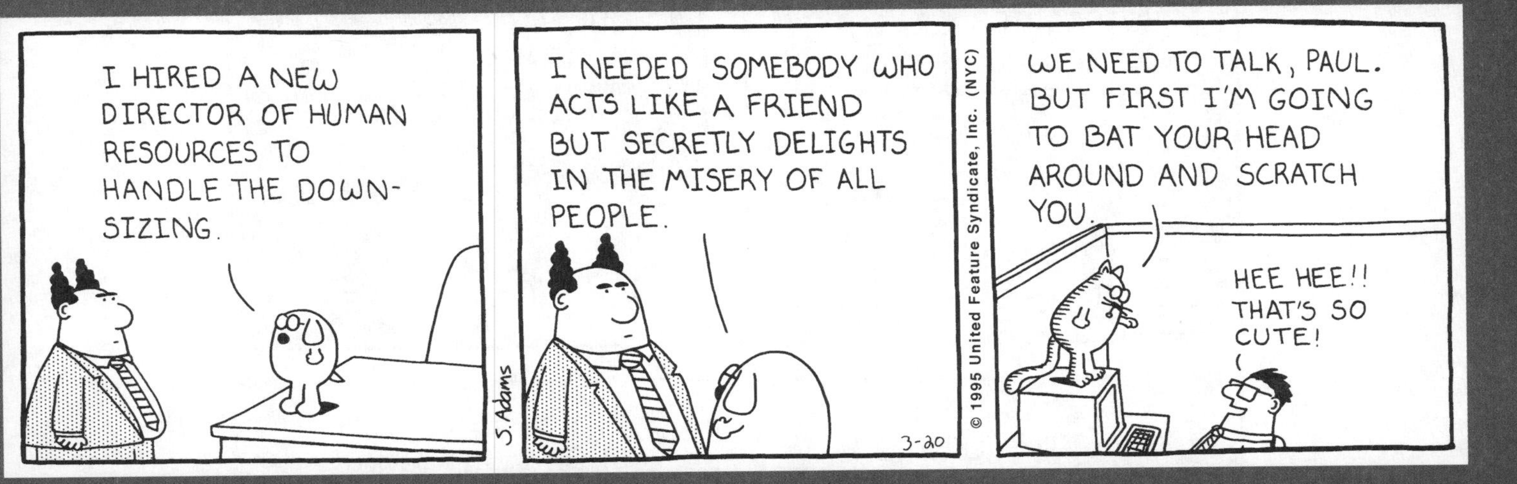
I HIRED A NEW DIRECTOR OF HUMAN RESOURCES TO HANDLE THE DOWN-SIZING.
I NEEDED SOMEBODY WHO ACTS LIKE A FRIEND BUT SECRETLY DELIGHTS IN THE MISERY OF ALL PEOPLE.
S. Adams
3-20
© 1995 United Feature Syndicate, Inc. (NYC)
WE NEED TO TALK, PAUL. BUT FIRST I'M GOING TO BAT YOUR HEAD AROUND AND SCRATCH YOU.
HEE HEE!! THAT'S SO CUTE!

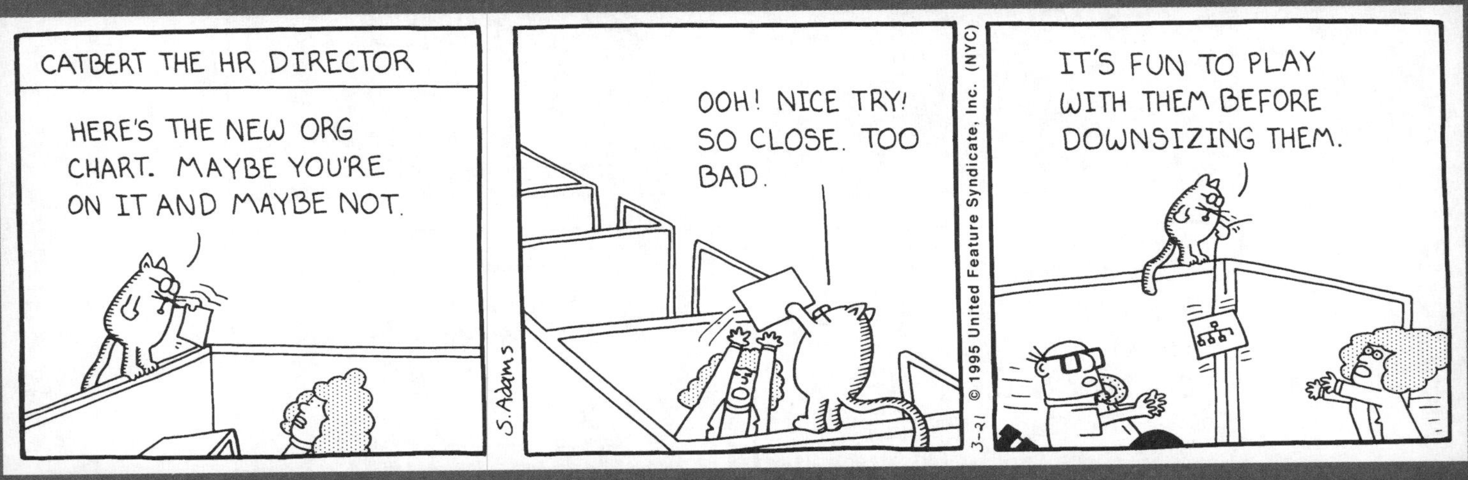
CATBERT THE HR DIRECTOR
HERE'S THE NEW ORG CHART. MAYBE YOU'RE ON IT AND MAYBE NOT.
S. Adams
OOH! NICE TRY! SO CLOSE. TOO BAD.
3-21
© 1995 United Feature Syndicate, Inc. (NYC)
IT'S FUN TO PLAY WITH THEM BEFORE DOWNSIZING THEM.

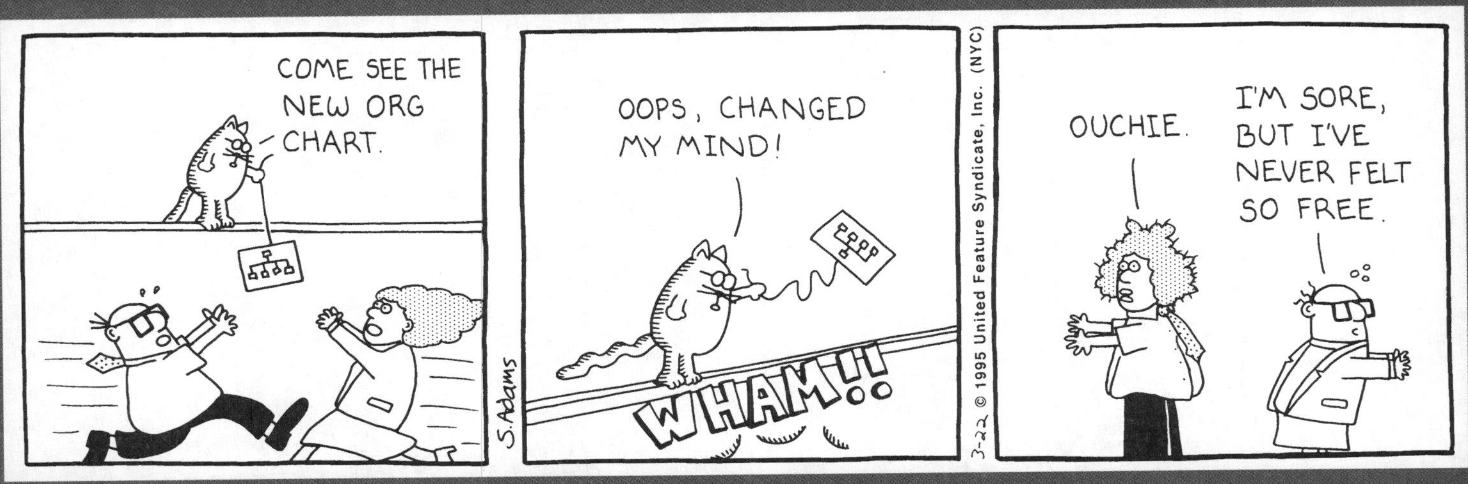
COME SEE THE NEW ORG CHART.
S. Adams
OOPS, CHANGED MY MIND!
WHAM!!
3-22
© 1995 United Feature Syndicate, Inc. (NYC)
OUCHIE.
I'M SORE, BUT I'VE NEVER FELT SO FREE.

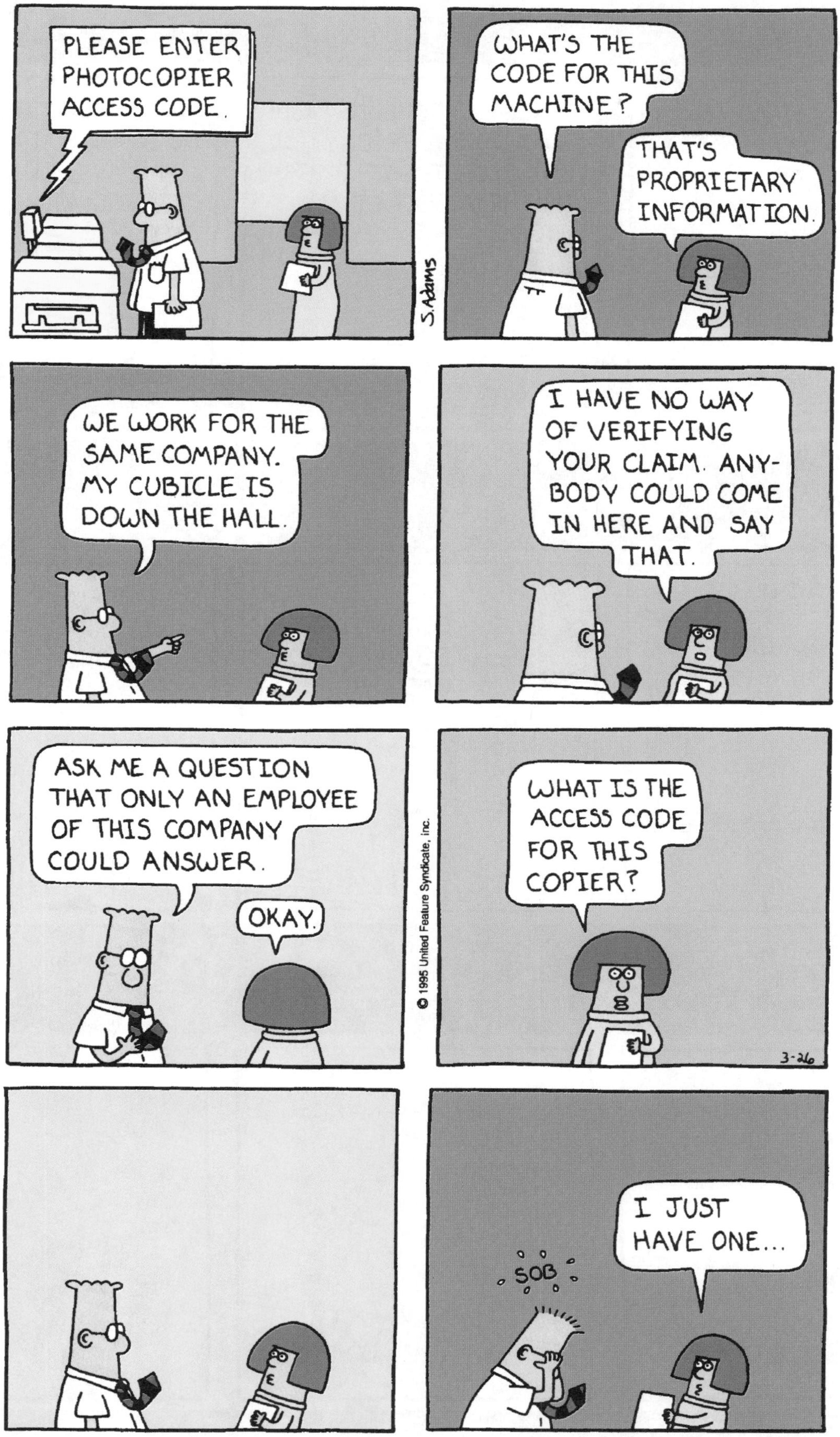
PLEASE ENTER PHOTOCOPIER ACCESS CODE.
S. Adams
WHAT'S THE CODE FOR THIS MACHINE?
THAT'S PROPRIETARY INFORMATION.
WE WORK FOR THE SAME COMPANY. MY CUBICLE IS DOWN THE HALL.
I HAVE NO WAY OF VERIFYING YOUR CLAIM. ANYBODY COULD COME IN HERE AND SAY THAT.
ASK ME A QUESTION THAT ONLY AN EMPLOYEE OF THIS COMPANY COULD ANSWER.
OKAY.
© 1995 United Feature Syndicate, Inc.
WHAT IS THE ACCESS CODE FOR THIS COPIER?
3-26
SOB
I JUST HAVE ONE...

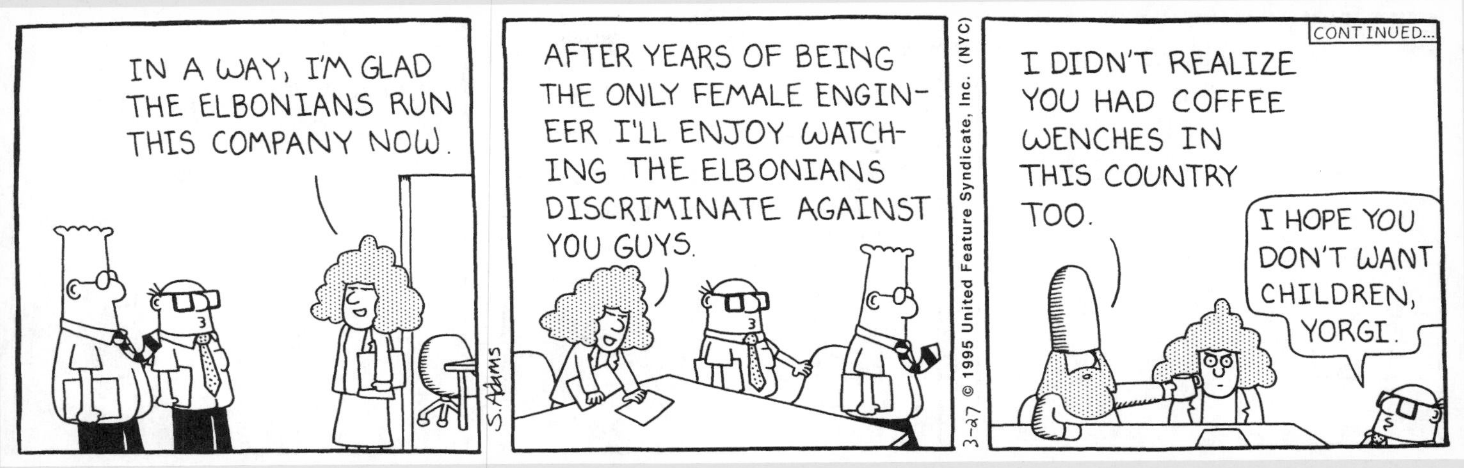
IN A WAY, I'M GLAD THE ELBONIANS RUN THIS COMPANY NOW.
S. Adams
AFTER YEARS OF BEING THE ONLY FEMALE ENGINEER I'LL ENJOY WATCHING THE ELBONIANS DISCRIMINATE AGAINST YOU GUYS.
3-27 © 1995 United Feature Syndicate, Inc. (NYC)
CONTINUED...
I DIDN'T REALIZE YOU HAD COFFEE WENCHES IN THIS COUNTRY TOO.
I HOPE YOU DON'T WANT CHILDREN, YORGI.

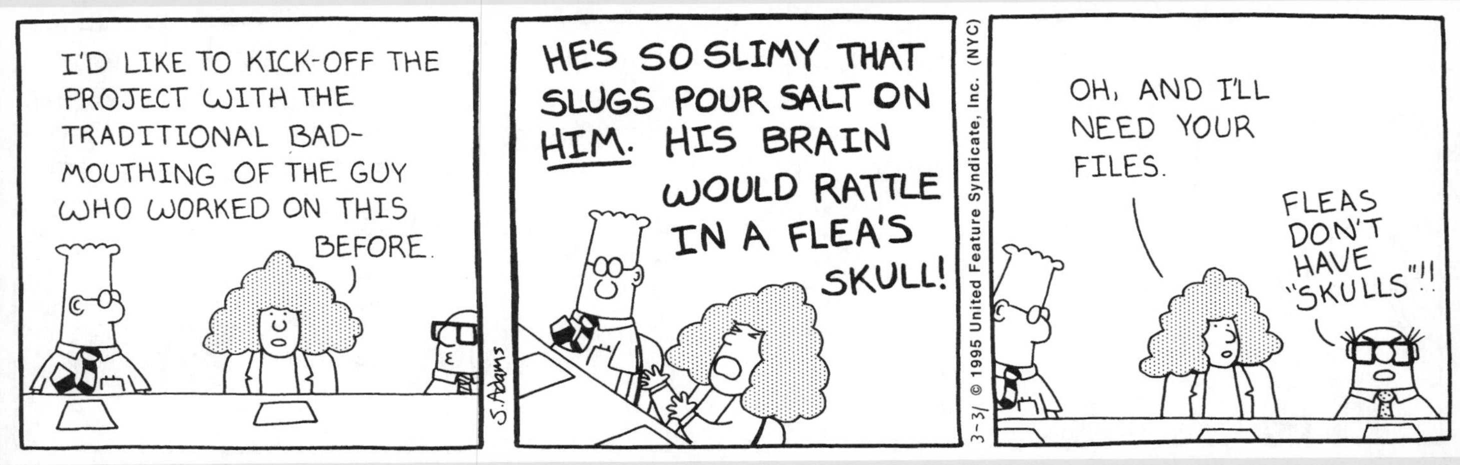
I'D LIKE TO KICK-OFF THE PROJECT WITH THE TRADITIONAL BAD-MOUTHING OF THE GUY WHO WORKED ON THIS BEFORE.
S. Adams
HE'S SO SLIMY THAT SLUGS POUR SALT ON HIM. HIS BRAIN WOULD RATTLE IN A FLEA'S SKULL!
3-31 © 1995 United Feature Syndicate, Inc. (NYC)
OH, AND I'LL NEED YOUR FILES.
FLEAS DON'T HAVE "SKULLS"!!

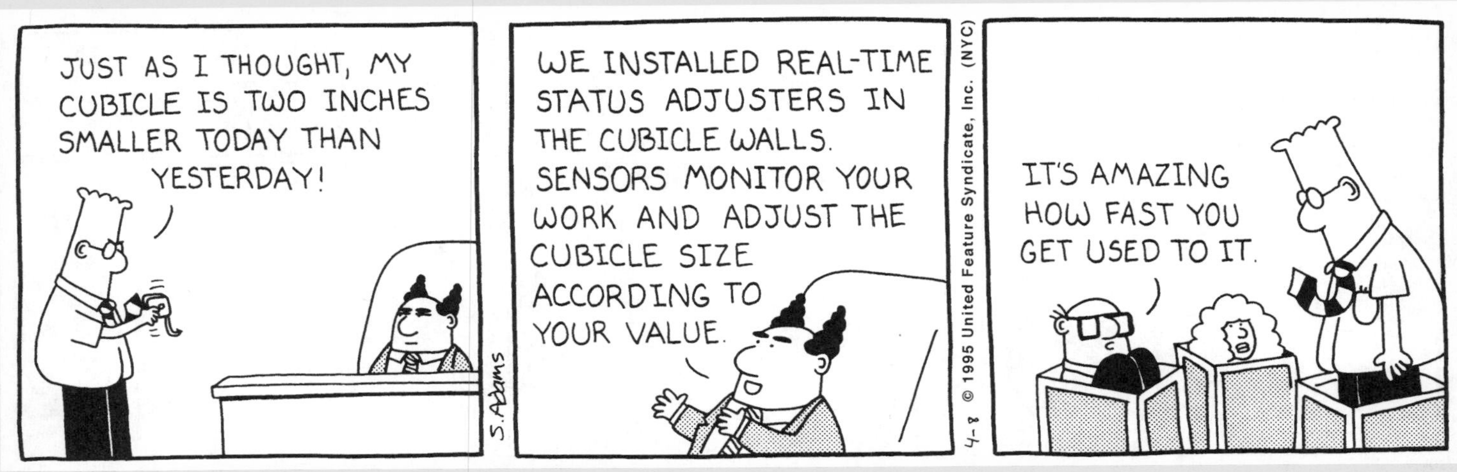
JUST AS I THOUGHT, MY CUBICLE IS TWO INCHES SMALLER TODAY THAN YESTERDAY!
S. Adams
WE INSTALLED REAL-TIME STATUS ADJUSTERS IN THE CUBICLE WALLS. SENSORS MONITOR YOUR WORK AND ADJUST THE CUBICLE SIZE ACCORDING TO YOUR VALUE.
4-8 © 1995 United Feature Syndicate, Inc. (NYC)
IT'S AMAZING HOW FAST YOU GET USED TO IT.

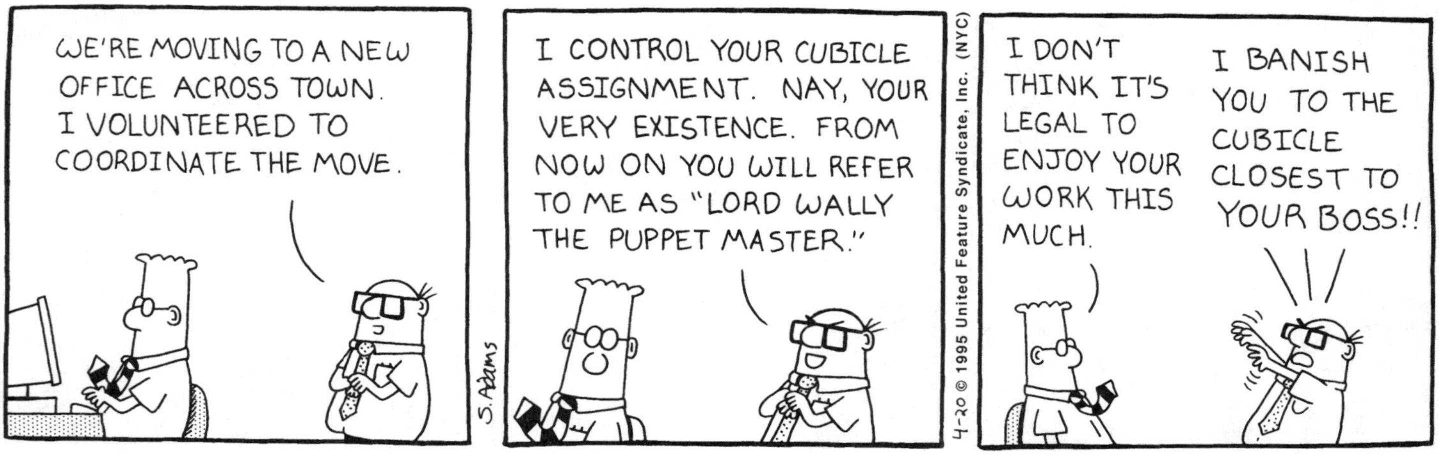
WE'RE MOVING TO A NEW OFFICE ACROSS TOWN. I VOLUNTEERED TO COORDINATE THE MOVE.
S. Adams
I CONTROL YOUR CUBICLE ASSIGNMENT. NAY, YOUR VERY EXISTENCE. FROM NOW ON YOU WILL REFER TO ME AS "LORD WALLY THE PUPPET MASTER."
4-20 © 1995 United Feature Syndicate, Inc. (NYC)
I DON'T THINK IT'S LEGAL TO ENJOY YOUR WORK THIS MUCH.
I BANISH YOU TO THE CUBICLE CLOSEST TO YOUR BOSS!!

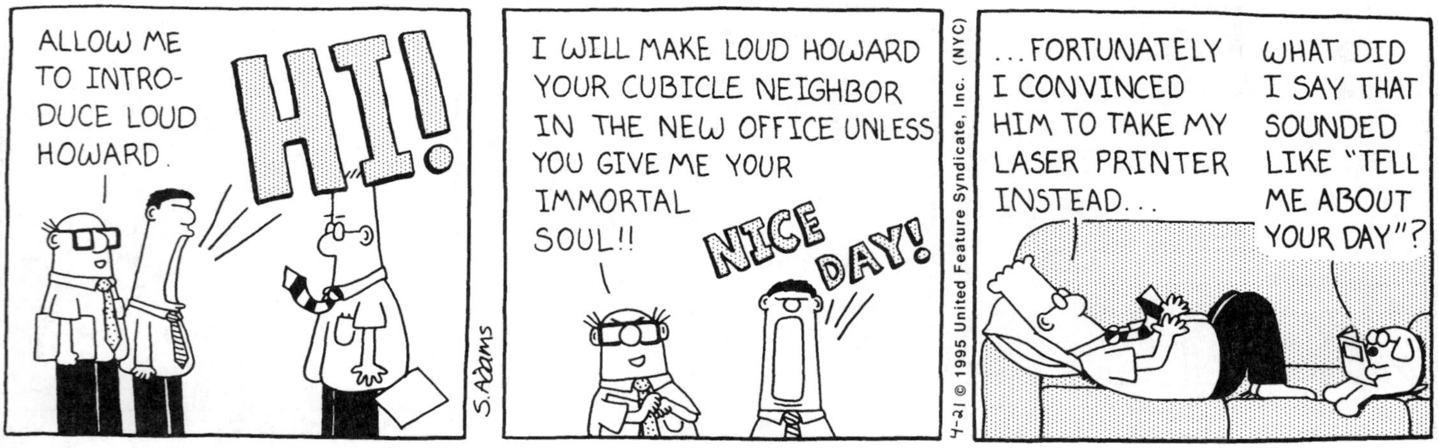
ALLOW ME TO INTRO-DUCE LOUD HOWARD.
HI!
S. Adams
I WILL MAKE LOUD HOWARD YOUR CUBICLE NEIGHBOR IN THE NEW OFFICE UNLESS YOU GIVE ME YOUR IMMORTAL SOUL!!
NICE DAY!
4-21 © 1995 United Feature Syndicate, Inc. (NYC)
...FORTUNATELY I CONVINCED HIM TO TAKE MY LASER PRINTER INSTEAD...
WHAT DID I SAY THAT SOUNDED LIKE "TELL ME ABOUT YOUR DAY"?

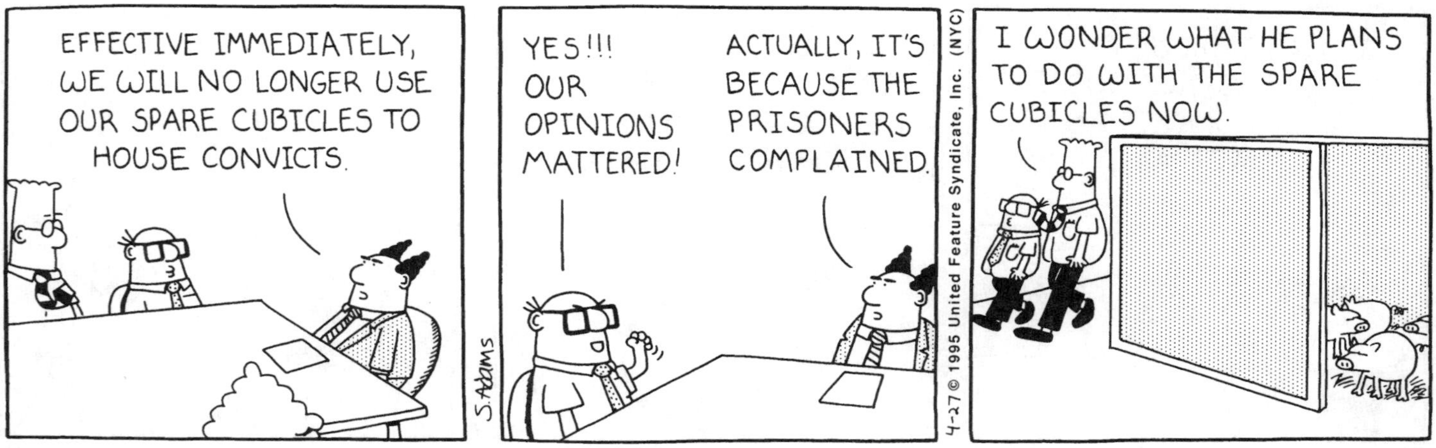
EFFECTIVE IMMEDIATELY, WE WILL NO LONGER USE OUR SPARE CUBICLES TO HOUSE CONVICTS.
S. Adams
YES!!! OUR OPINIONS MATTERED!
ACTUALLY, IT'S BECAUSE THE PRISONERS COMPLAINED.
4-27 © 1995 United Feature Syndicate, Inc. (NYC)
I WONDER WHAT HE PLANS TO DO WITH THE SPARE CUBICLES NOW.

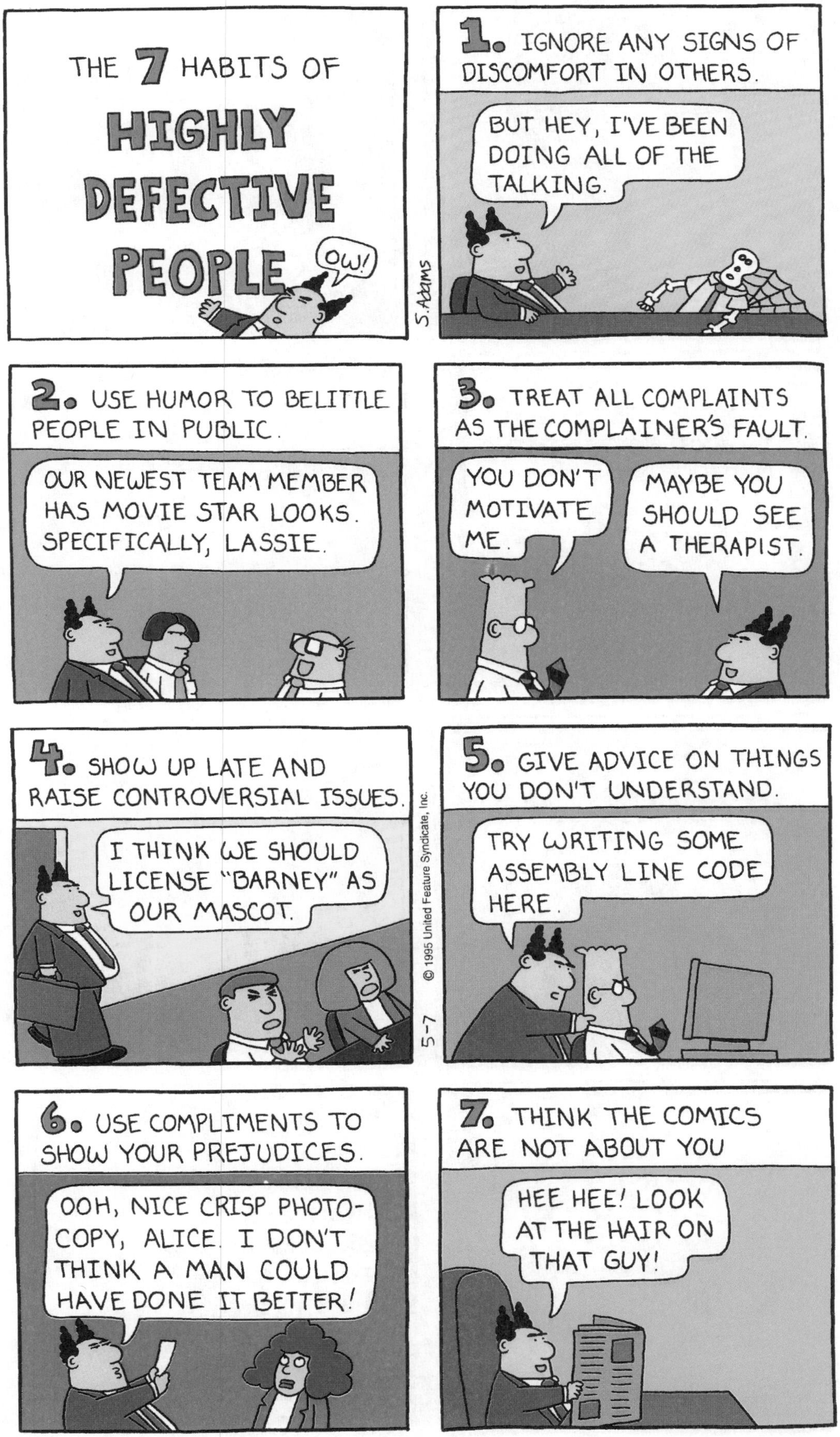
THE 7 HABITS OF
HIGHLY DEFECTIVE PEOPLE
OW!
S. Adams
1. IGNORE ANY SIGNS OF DISCOMFORT IN OTHERS.
BUT HEY, I'VE BEEN DOING ALL OF THE TALKING.
2. USE HUMOR TO BELITTLE PEOPLE IN PUBLIC.
OUR NEWEST TEAM MEMBER HAS MOVIE STAR LOOKS. SPECIFICALLY, LASSIE.
3. TREAT ALL COMPLAINTS AS THE COMPLAINER'S FAULT.
YOU DON'T MOTIVATE ME.
MAYBE YOU SHOULD SEE A THERAPIST.
4. SHOW UP LATE AND RAISE CONTROVERSIAL ISSUES.
I THINK WE SHOULD LICENSE "BARNEY" AS OUR MASCOT.
© 1995 United Feature Syndicate, Inc.
5-7
5. GIVE ADVICE ON THINGS YOU DON'T UNDERSTAND.
TRY WRITING SOME ASSEMBLY LINE CODE HERE.
6. USE COMPLIMENTS TO SHOW YOUR PREJUDICES.
OOH, NICE CRISP PHOTO-COPY, ALICE. I DON'T THINK A MAN COULD HAVE DONE IT BETTER!
7. THINK THE COMICS ARE NOT ABOUT YOU
HEE HEE! LOOK AT THE HAIR ON THAT GUY!

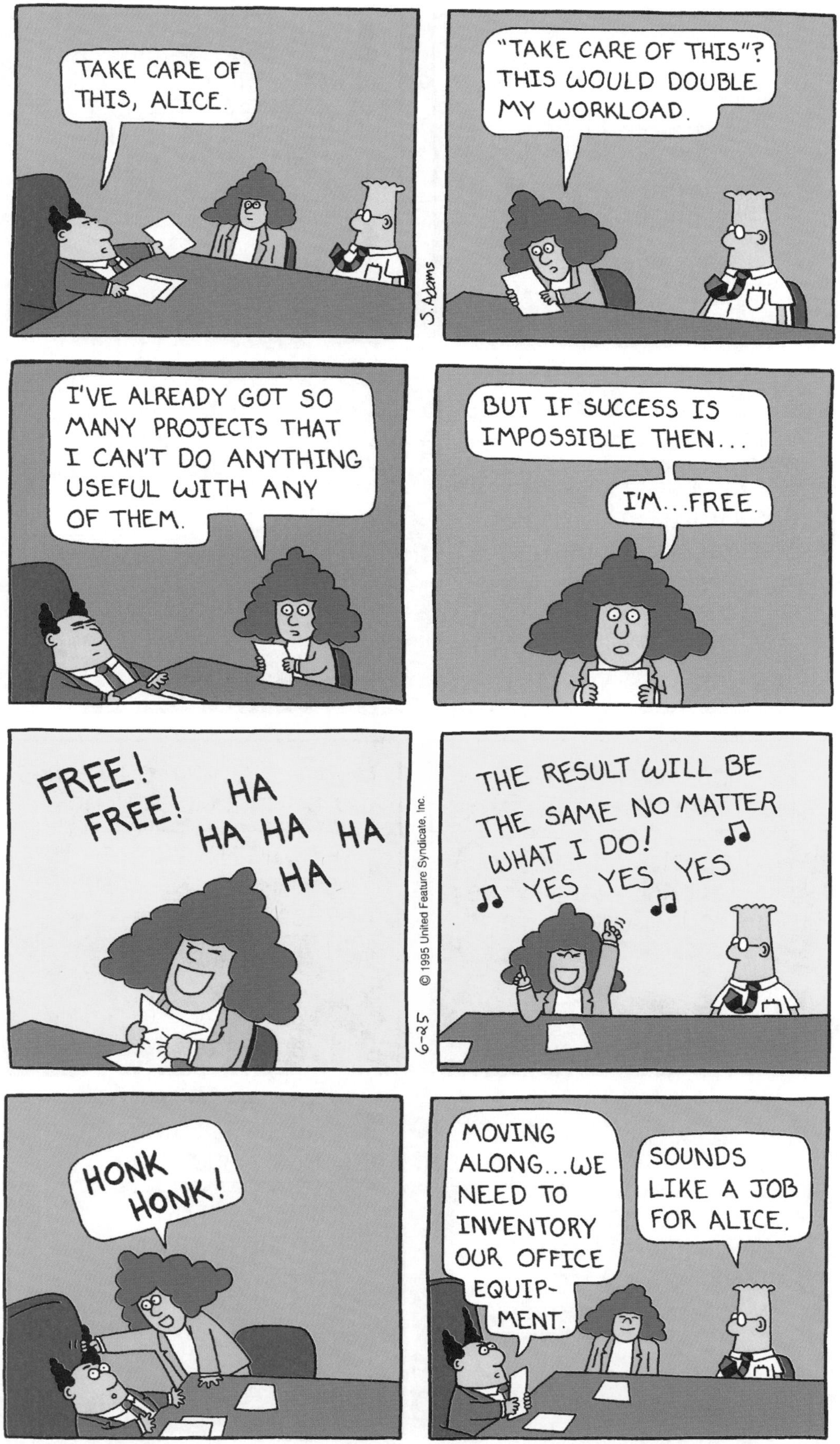

TAKE CARE OF THIS, ALICE.
"TAKE CARE OF THIS"? THIS WOULD DOUBLE MY WORKLOAD.
S. Adams
I'VE ALREADY GOT SO MANY PROJECTS THAT I CAN'T DO ANYTHING USEFUL WITH ANY OF THEM.
BUT IF SUCCESS IS IMPOSSIBLE THEN...
I'M...FREE.
FREE! FREE! HA HA HA HA HA
© 1995 United Feature Syndicate, Inc.
6-25
THE RESULT WILL BE THE SAME NO MATTER WHAT I DO!
YES YES YES
HONK HONK!
MOVING ALONG...WE NEED TO INVENTORY OUR OFFICE EQUIP-MENT.
SOUNDS LIKE A JOB FOR ALICE.

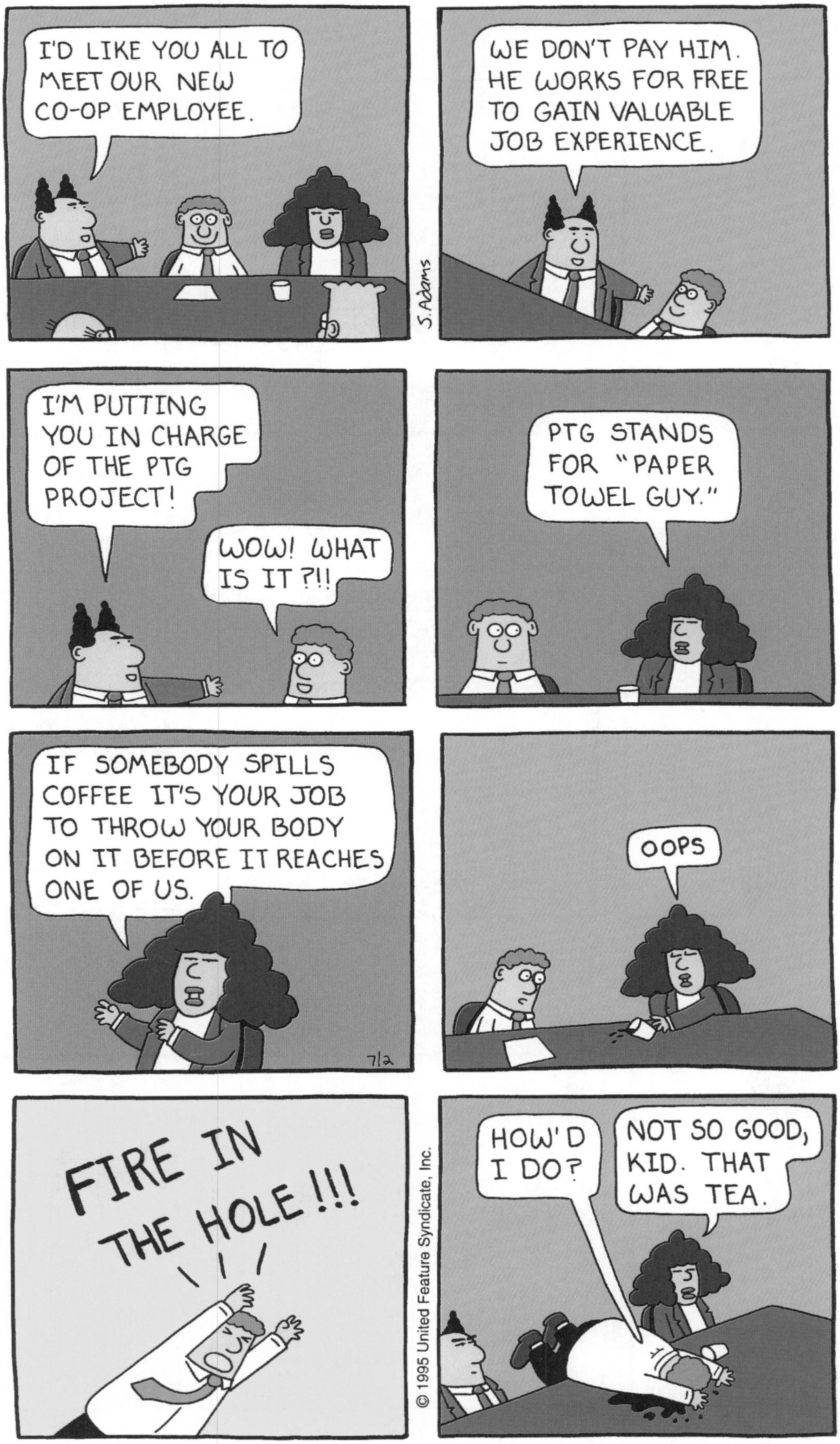
I'D LIKE YOU ALL TO MEET OUR NEW CO-OP EMPLOYEE.
S. Adams
WE DON'T PAY HIM. HE WORKS FOR FREE TO GAIN VALUABLE JOB EXPERIENCE.
I'M PUTTING YOU IN CHARGE OF THE PTG PROJECT!
WOW! WHAT IS IT ?!!
PTG STANDS FOR "PAPER TOWEL GUY."
IF SOMEBODY SPILLS COFFEE IT'S YOUR JOB TO THROW YOUR BODY ON IT BEFORE IT REACHES ONE OF US.
7/2
OOPS
FIRE IN THE HOLE !!!
HOW'D I DO?
NOT SO GOOD, KID. THAT WAS TEA.

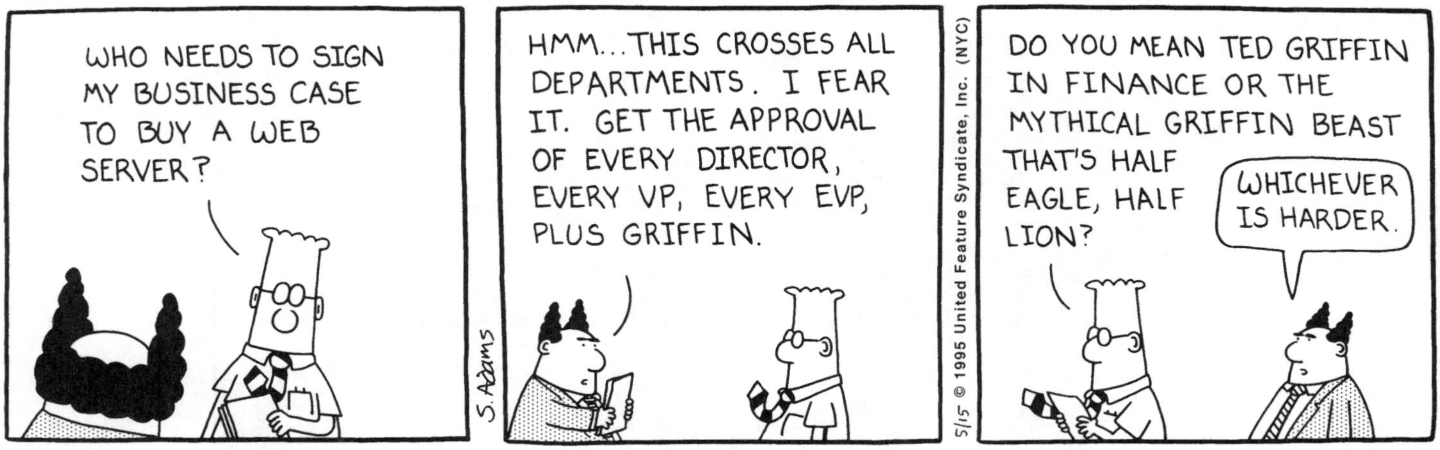
WHO NEEDS TO SIGN MY BUSINESS CASE TO BUY A WEB SERVER?
HMM...THIS CROSSES ALL DEPARTMENTS. I FEAR IT. GET THE APPROVAL OF EVERY DIRECTOR, EVERY VP, EVERY EVP, PLUS GRIFFIN.
S. Adams
5/15 © 1995 United Feature Syndicate, Inc. (NYC)
DO YOU MEAN TED GRIFFIN IN FINANCE OR THE MYTHICAL GRIFFIN BEAST THAT'S HALF EAGLE, HALF LION?
WHICHEVER IS HARDER.

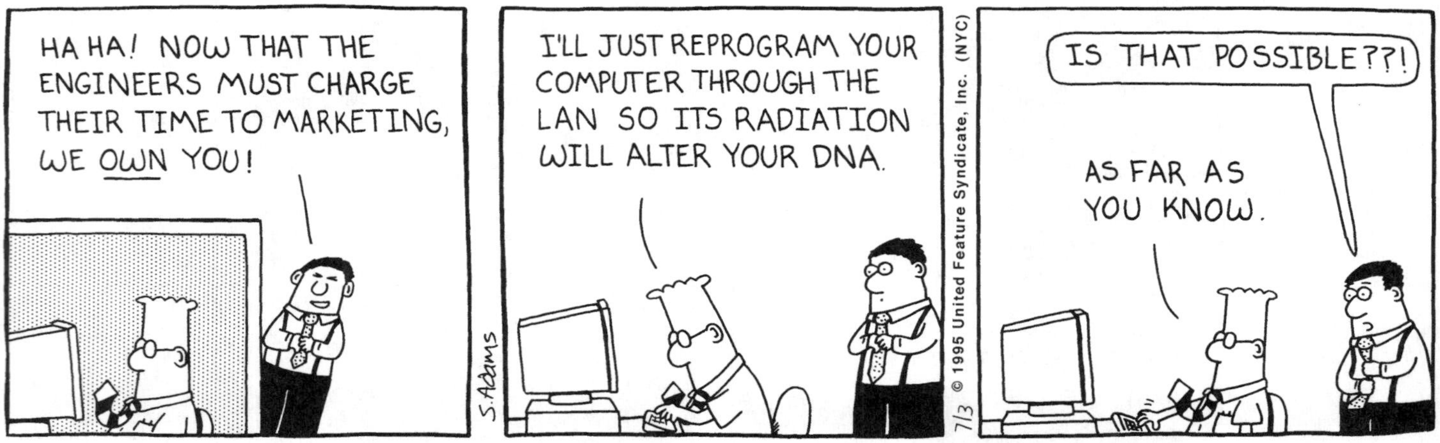
HA HA! NOW THAT THE ENGINEERS MUST CHARGE THEIR TIME TO MARKETING, WE OWN YOU!
I'LL JUST REPROGRAM YOUR COMPUTER THROUGH THE LAN SO ITS RADIATION WILL ALTER YOUR DNA.
S. Adams
7/3 © 1995 United Feature Syndicate, Inc. (NYC)
IS THAT POSSIBLE??!
AS FAR AS YOU KNOW.

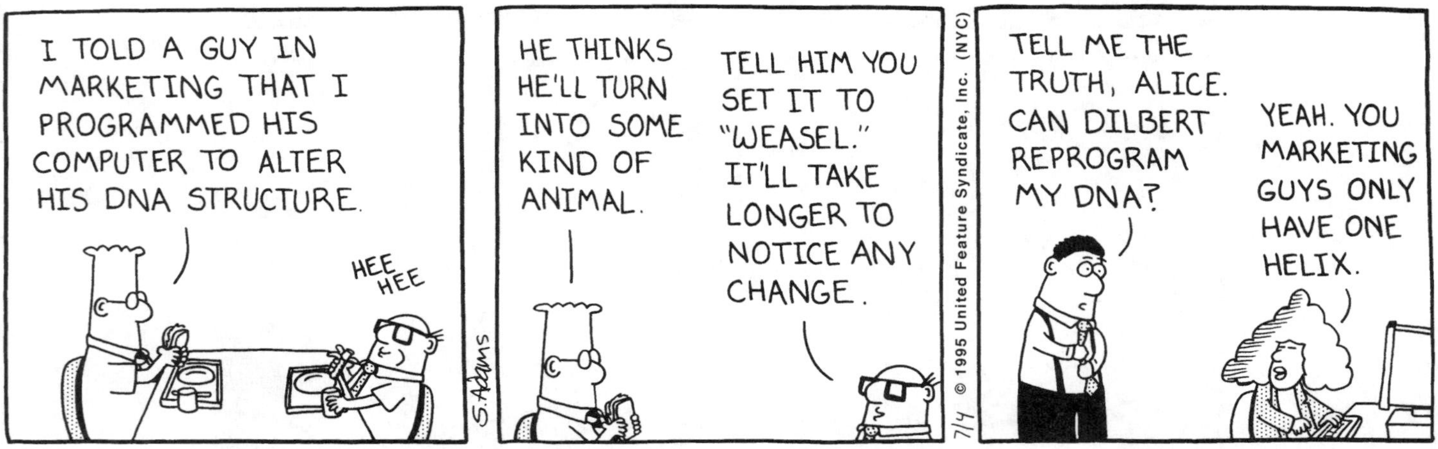
I TOLD A GUY IN MARKETING THAT I PROGRAMMED HIS COMPUTER TO ALTER HIS DNA STRUCTURE.
HEE HEE
HE THINKS HE'LL TURN INTO SOME KIND OF ANIMAL.
TELL HIM YOU SET IT TO "WEASEL." IT'LL TAKE LONGER TO NOTICE ANY CHANGE.
S. Adams
7/4 © 1995 United Feature Syndicate, Inc. (NYC)
TELL ME THE TRUTH, ALICE. CAN DILBERT REPROGRAM MY DNA?
YEAH. YOU MARKETING GUYS ONLY HAVE ONE HELIX.

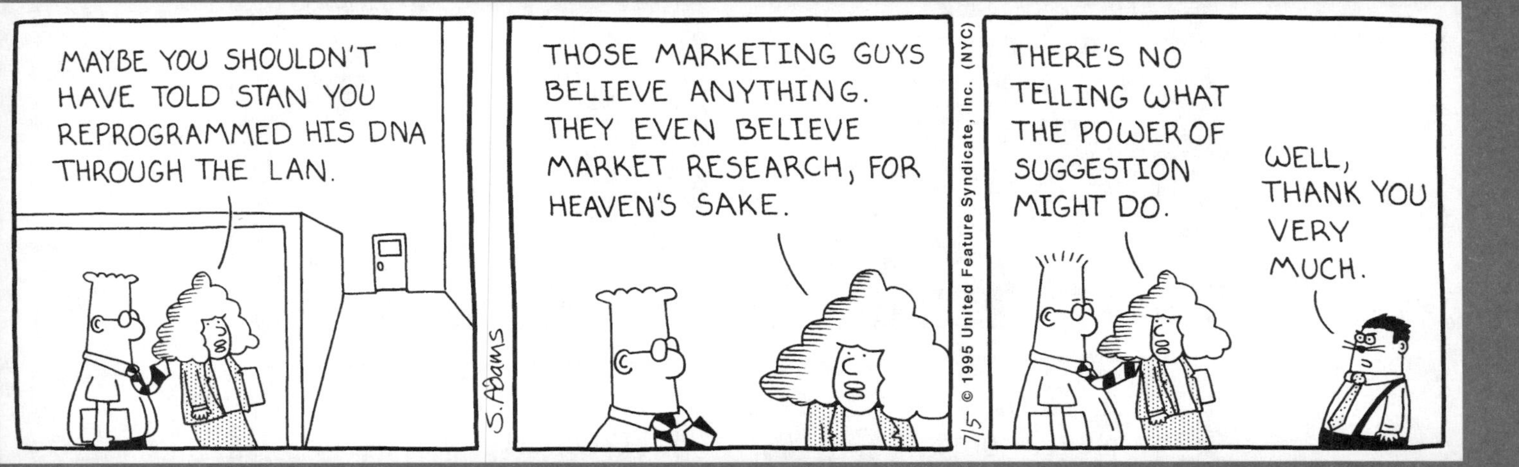
MAYBE YOU SHOULDN'T HAVE TOLD STAN YOU REPROGRAMMED HIS DNA THROUGH THE LAN.
S. Adams
THOSE MARKETING GUYS BELIEVE ANYTHING. THEY EVEN BELIEVE MARKET RESEARCH, FOR HEAVEN'S SAKE.
7/5 © 1995 United Feature Syndicate, Inc. (NYC)
THERE'S NO TELLING WHAT THE POWER OF SUGGESTION MIGHT DO.
WELL, THANK YOU VERY MUCH.

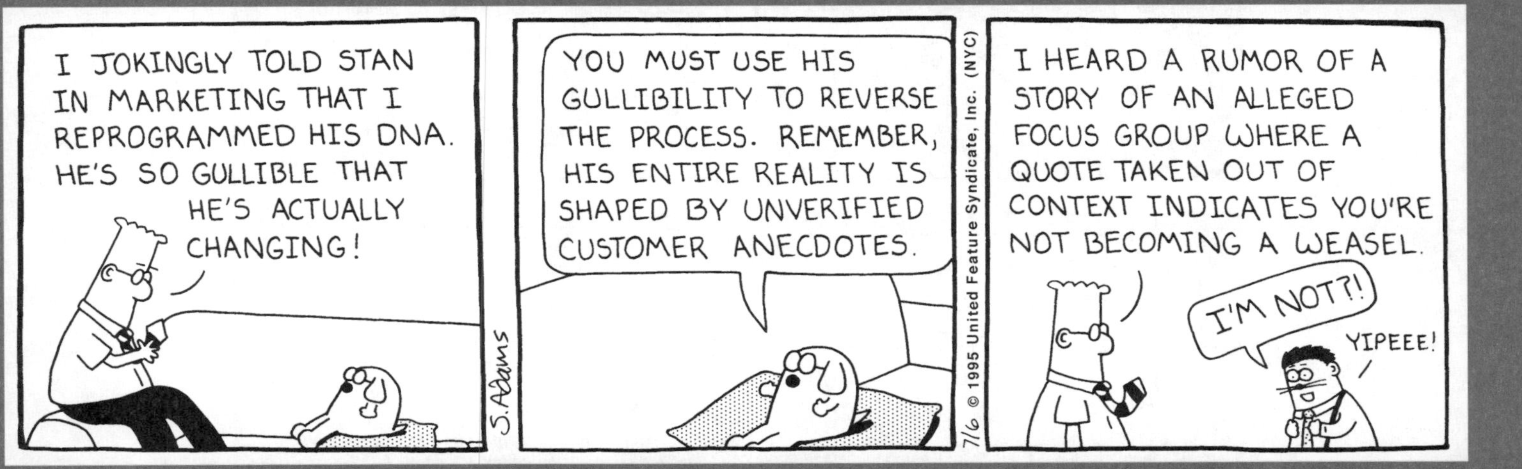
I JOKINGLY TOLD STAN IN MARKETING THAT I REPROGRAMMED HIS DNA. HE'S SO GULLIBLE THAT HE'S ACTUALLY CHANGING!
S. Adams
YOU MUST USE HIS GULLIBILITY TO REVERSE THE PROCESS. REMEMBER, HIS ENTIRE REALITY IS SHAPED BY UNVERIFIED CUSTOMER ANECDOTES.
7/6 © 1995 United Feature Syndicate, Inc. (NYC)
I HEARD A RUMOR OF A STORY OF AN ALLEGED FOCUS GROUP WHERE A QUOTE TAKEN OUT OF CONTEXT INDICATES YOU'RE NOT BECOMING A WEASEL.
I'M NOT?!
YIPEEE!

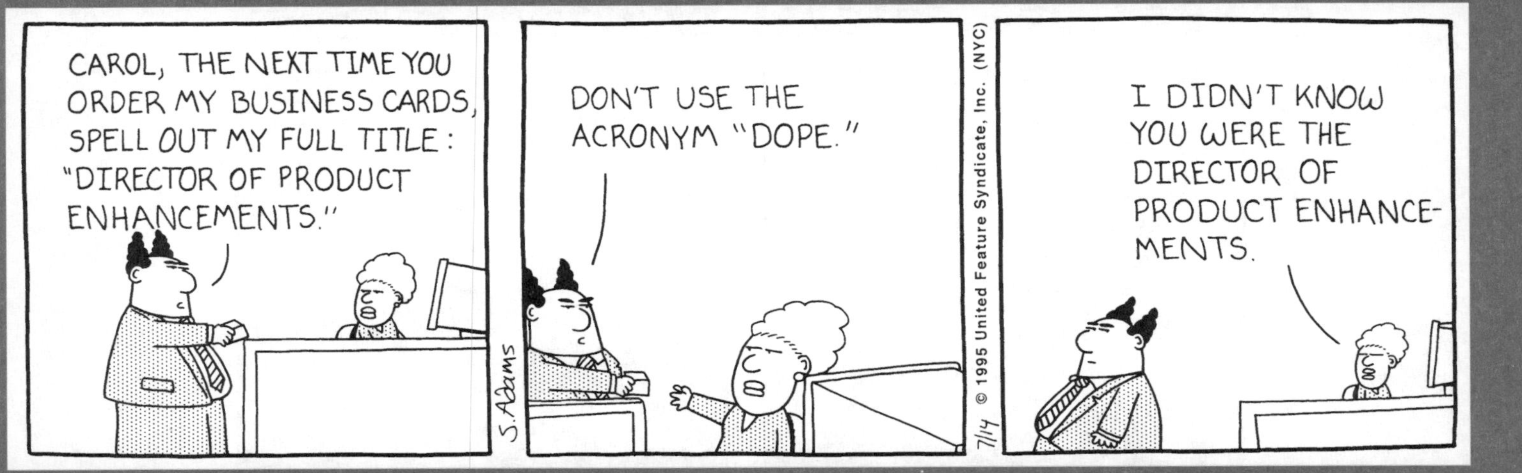
CAROL, THE NEXT TIME YOU ORDER MY BUSINESS CARDS, SPELL OUT MY FULL TITLE: "DIRECTOR OF PRODUCT ENHANCEMENTS."
S. Adams
DON'T USE THE ACRONYM "DOPE."
7/14 © 1995 United Feature Syndicate, Inc. (NYC)
I DIDN'T KNOW YOU WERE THE DIRECTOR OF PRODUCT ENHANCE-MENTS.

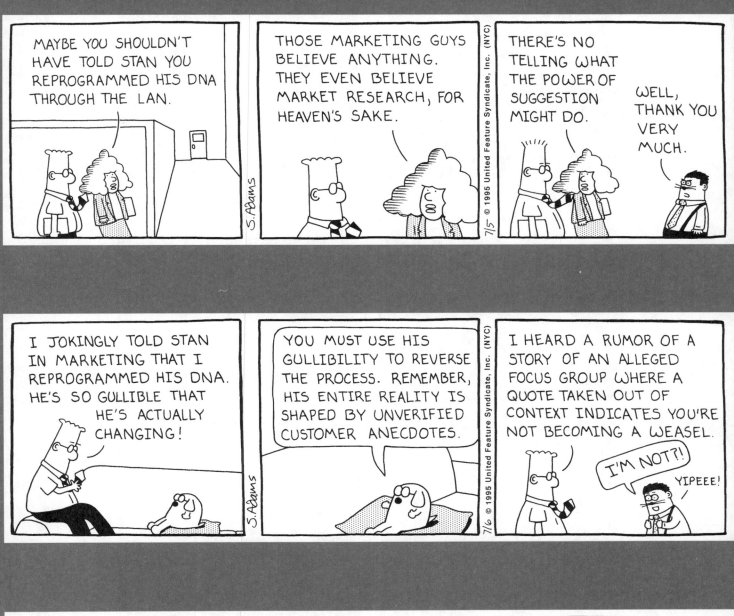

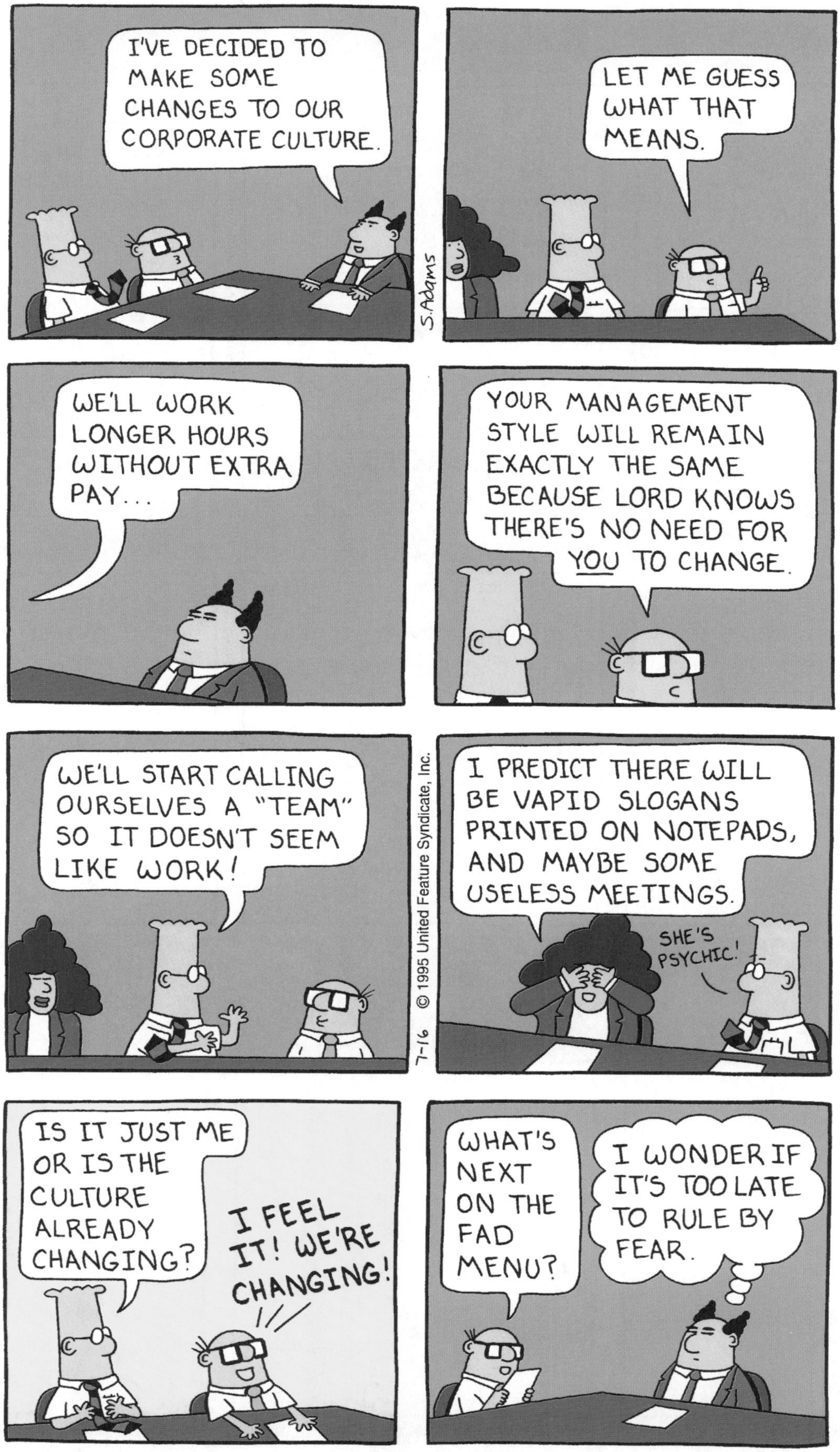
I'VE DECIDED TO MAKE SOME CHANGES TO OUR CORPORATE CULTURE.
LET ME GUESS WHAT THAT MEANS.
S. Adams
WE'LL WORK LONGER HOURS WITHOUT EXTRA PAY...
YOUR MANAGEMENT STYLE WILL REMAIN EXACTLY THE SAME BECAUSE LORD KNOWS THERE'S NO NEED FOR YOU TO CHANGE.
WE'LL START CALLING OURSELVES A "TEAM" SO IT DOESN'T SEEM LIKE WORK!
© 1995 United Feature Syndicate, Inc.
7-16
I PREDICT THERE WILL BE VAPID SLOGANS PRINTED ON NOTEPADS, AND MAYBE SOME USELESS MEETINGS.
SHE'S PSYCHIC!
IS IT JUST ME OR IS THE CULTURE ALREADY CHANGING?
I FEEL IT! WE'RE CHANGING!
WHAT'S NEXT ON THE FAD MENU?
I WONDER IF IT'S TOO LATE TO RULE BY FEAR.

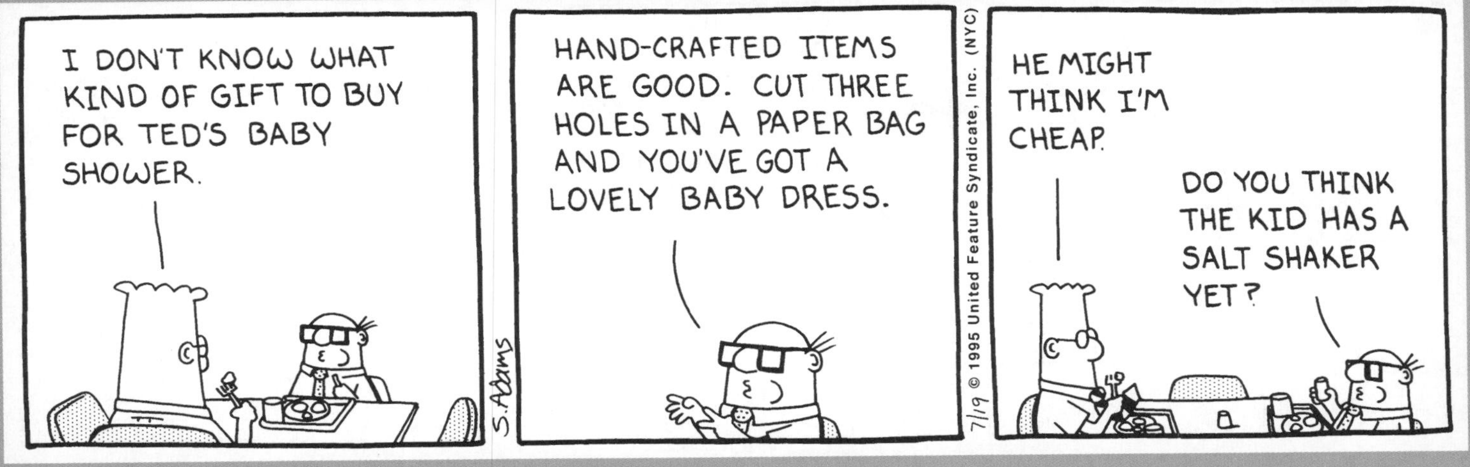
I DON'T KNOW WHAT KIND OF GIFT TO BUY FOR TED'S BABY SHOWER.
HAND-CRAFTED ITEMS ARE GOOD. CUT THREE HOLES IN A PAPER BAG AND YOU'VE GOT A LOVELY BABY DRESS.
HE MIGHT THINK I'M CHEAP.
DO YOU THINK THE KID HAS A SALT SHAKER YET?
S.Adams
7/19 © 1995 United Feature Syndicate, Inc. (NYC)

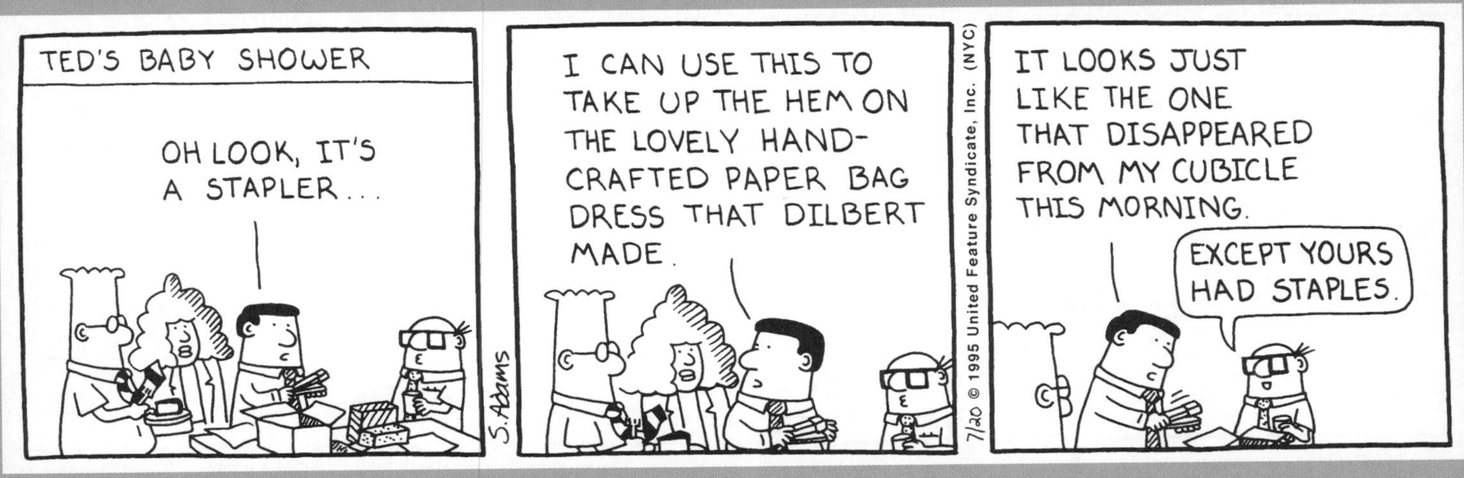
TED'S BABY SHOWER
OH LOOK, IT'S A STAPLER...
I CAN USE THIS TO TAKE UP THE HEM ON THE LOVELY HAND-CRAFTED PAPER BAG DRESS THAT DILBERT MADE.
IT LOOKS JUST LIKE THE ONE THAT DISAPPEARED FROM MY CUBICLE THIS MORNING.
EXCEPT YOURS HAD STAPLES.
S.Adams
7/20 © 1995 United Feature Syndicate, Inc. (NYC)

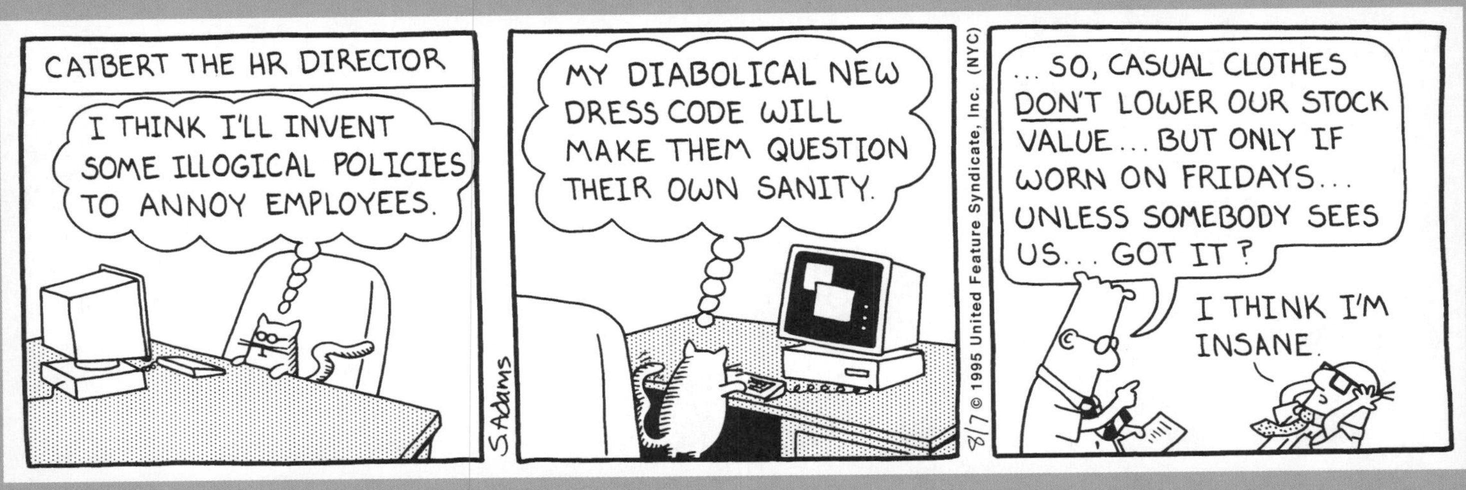
CATBERT THE HR DIRECTOR
I THINK I'LL INVENT SOME ILLOGICAL POLICIES TO ANNOY EMPLOYEES.
MY DIABOLICAL NEW DRESS CODE WILL MAKE THEM QUESTION THEIR OWN SANITY.
...SO, CASUAL CLOTHES DON'T LOWER OUR STOCK VALUE... BUT ONLY IF WORN ON FRIDAYS... UNLESS SOMEBODY SEES US... GOT IT?
I THINK I'M INSANE.
S.Adams
8/7 © 1995 United Feature Syndicate, Inc. (NYC)

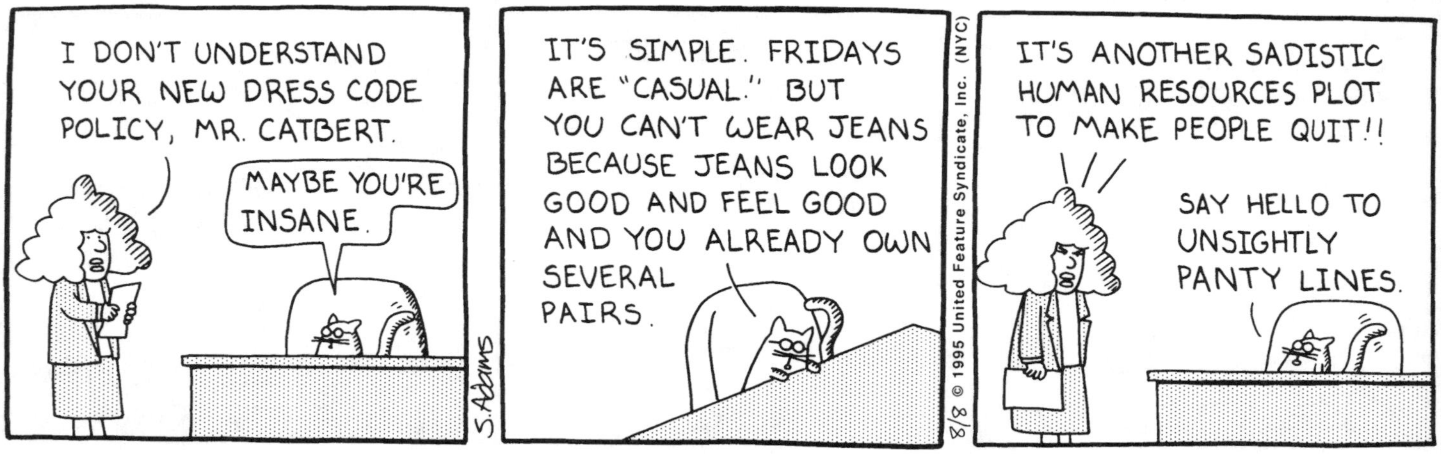
I DON'T UNDERSTAND YOUR NEW DRESS CODE POLICY, MR. CATBERT.
MAYBE YOU'RE INSANE.
S. Adams
IT'S SIMPLE. FRIDAYS ARE "CASUAL." BUT YOU CAN'T WEAR JEANS BECAUSE JEANS LOOK GOOD AND FEEL GOOD AND YOU ALREADY OWN SEVERAL PAIRS.
8/8 © 1995 United Feature Syndicate, Inc. (NYC)
IT'S ANOTHER SADISTIC HUMAN RESOURCES PLOT TO MAKE PEOPLE QUIT!!
SAY HELLO TO UNSIGHTLY PANTY LINES.

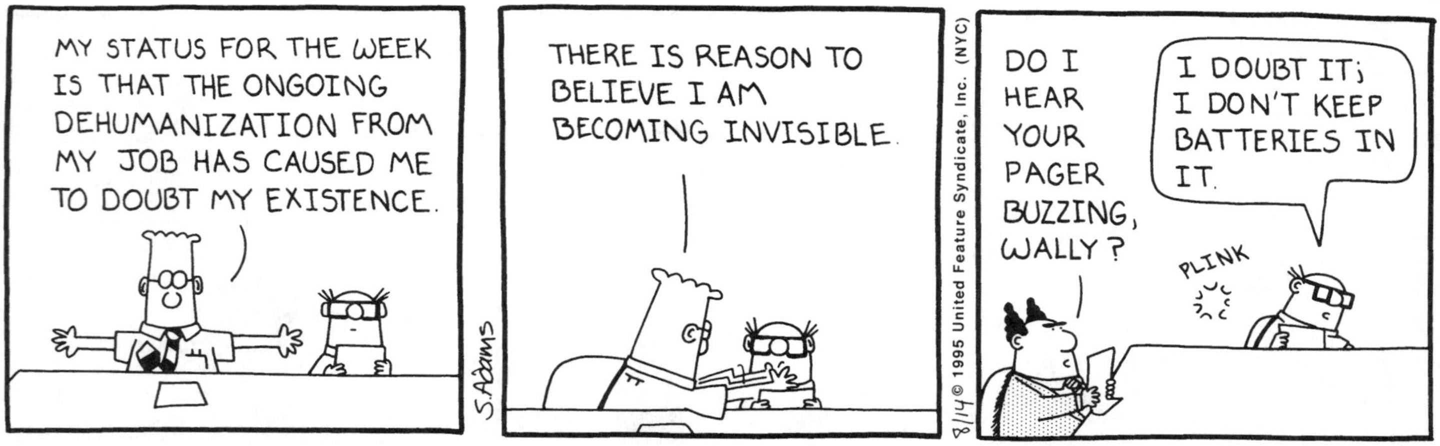
MY STATUS FOR THE WEEK IS THAT THE ONGOING DEHUMANIZATION FROM MY JOB HAS CAUSED ME TO DOUBT MY EXISTENCE.
S. Adams
THERE IS REASON TO BELIEVE I AM BECOMING INVISIBLE.
8/14 © 1995 United Feature Syndicate, Inc. (NYC)
DO I HEAR YOUR PAGER BUZZING, WALLY?
I DOUBT IT; I DON'T KEEP BATTERIES IN IT.
PLINK

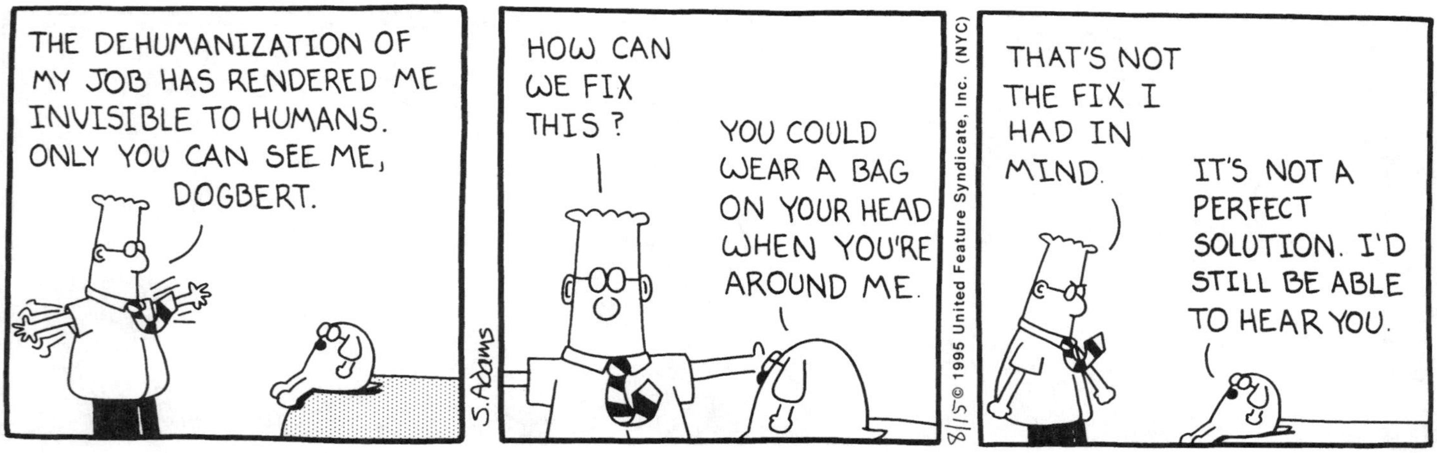
THE DEHUMANIZATION OF MY JOB HAS RENDERED ME INVISIBLE TO HUMANS. ONLY YOU CAN SEE ME, DOGBERT.
S. Adams
HOW CAN WE FIX THIS?
YOU COULD WEAR A BAG ON YOUR HEAD WHEN YOU'RE AROUND ME.
8/15 © 1995 United Feature Syndicate, Inc. (NYC)
THAT'S NOT THE FIX I HAD IN MIND.
IT'S NOT A PERFECT SOLUTION. I'D STILL BE ABLE TO HEAR YOU.

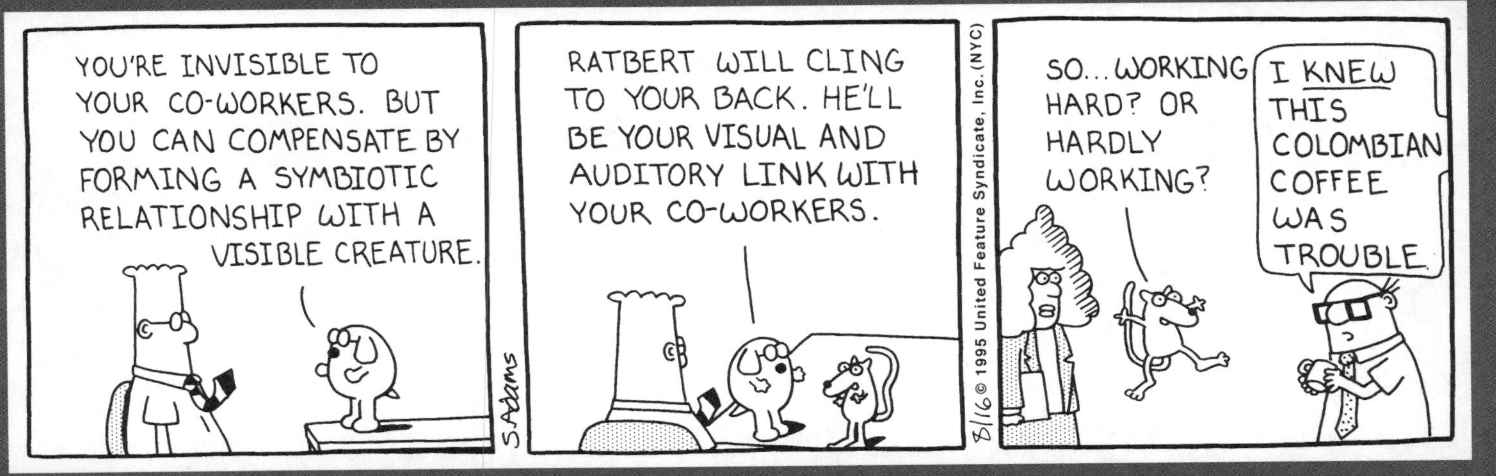
YOU'RE INVISIBLE TO YOUR CO-WORKERS. BUT YOU CAN COMPENSATE BY FORMING A SYMBIOTIC RELATIONSHIP WITH A VISIBLE CREATURE.
S. Adams
RATBERT WILL CLING TO YOUR BACK. HE'LL BE YOUR VISUAL AND AUDITORY LINK WITH YOUR CO-WORKERS.
8/16 © 1995 United Feature Syndicate, Inc. (NYC)
SO... WORKING HARD? OR HARDLY WORKING?
I KNEW THIS COLOMBIAN COFFEE WAS TROUBLE.

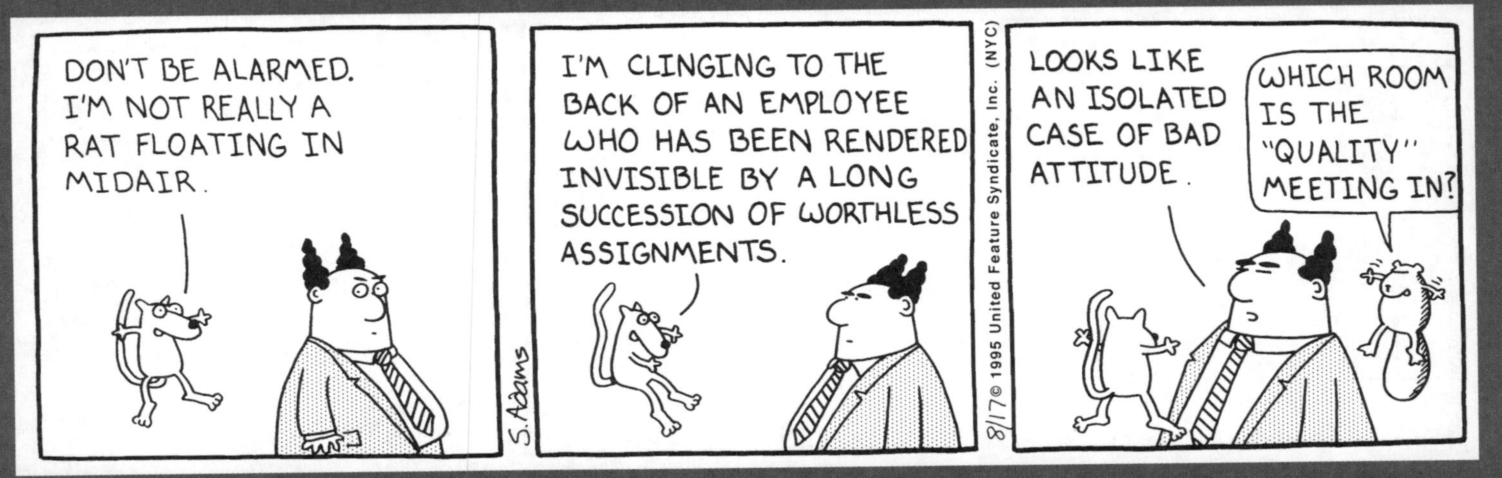
DON'T BE ALARMED. I'M NOT REALLY A RAT FLOATING IN MIDAIR.
S. Adams
I'M CLINGING TO THE BACK OF AN EMPLOYEE WHO HAS BEEN RENDERED INVISIBLE BY A LONG SUCCESSION OF WORTHLESS ASSIGNMENTS.
8/17 © 1995 United Feature Syndicate, Inc. (NYC)
LOOKS LIKE AN ISOLATED CASE OF BAD ATTITUDE.
WHICH ROOM IS THE "QUALITY" MEETING IN?

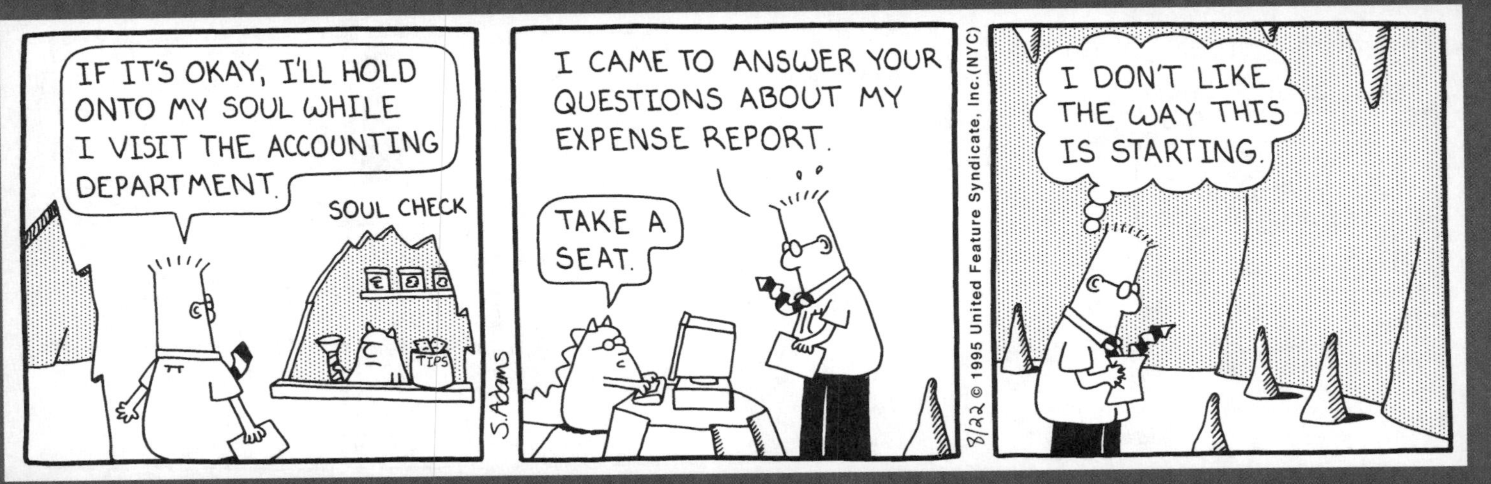
IF IT'S OKAY, I'LL HOLD ONTO MY SOUL WHILE I VISIT THE ACCOUNTING DEPARTMENT.
SOUL CHECK
TIPS
S. Adams
I CAME TO ANSWER YOUR QUESTIONS ABOUT MY EXPENSE REPORT.
TAKE A SEAT.
8/22 © 1995 United Feature Syndicate, Inc. (NYC)
I DON'T LIKE THE WAY THIS IS STARTING.

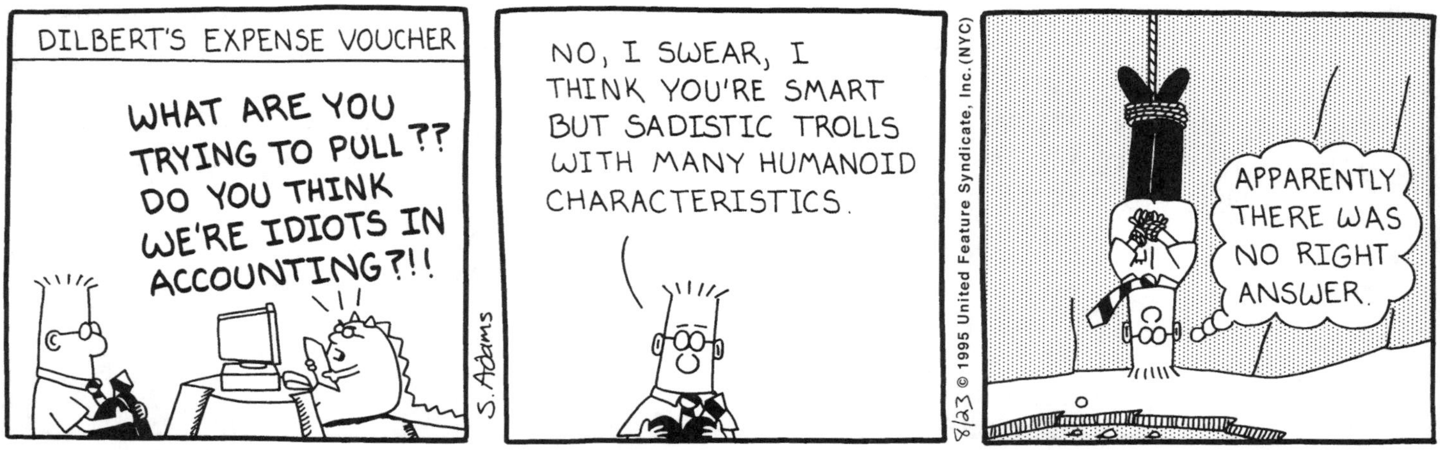
DILBERT'S EXPENSE VOUCHER
WHAT ARE YOU TRYING TO PULL?? DO YOU THINK WE'RE IDIOTS IN ACCOUNTING?!!
NO, I SWEAR, I THINK YOU'RE SMART BUT SADISTIC TROLLS WITH MANY HUMANOID CHARACTERISTICS.
APPARENTLY THERE WAS NO RIGHT ANSWER.
8/23 © 1995 United Feature Syndicate, Inc. (NYC)

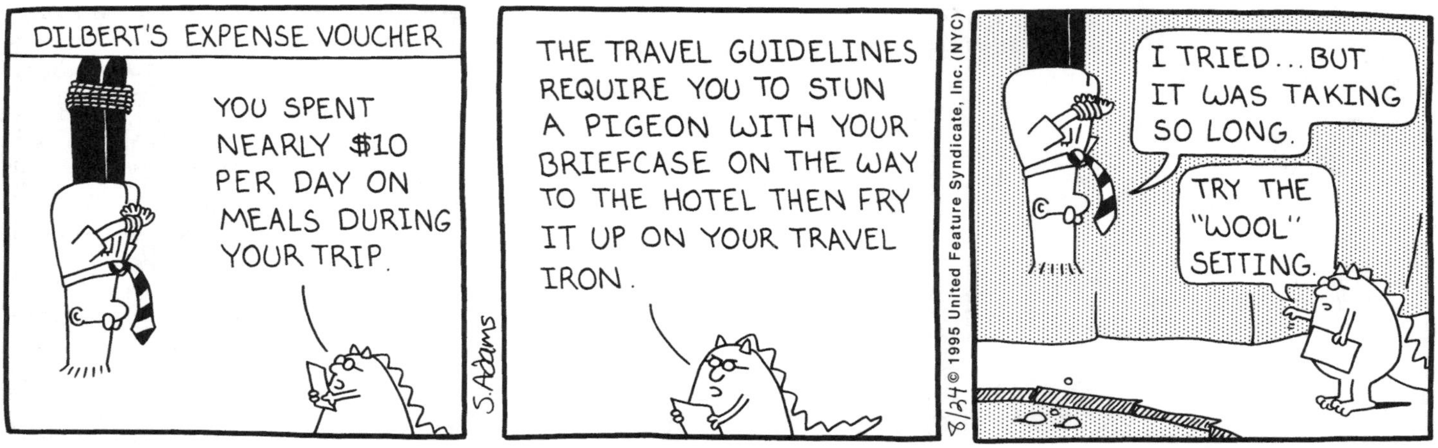
DILBERT'S EXPENSE VOUCHER
YOU SPENT NEARLY $10 PER DAY ON MEALS DURING YOUR TRIP.
THE TRAVEL GUIDELINES REQUIRE YOU TO STUN A PIGEON WITH YOUR BRIEFCASE ON THE WAY TO THE HOTEL THEN FRY IT UP ON YOUR TRAVEL IRON.
I TRIED... BUT IT WAS TAKING SO LONG.
TRY THE "WOOL" SETTING.
8/24 © 1995 United Feature Syndicate, Inc. (NYC)

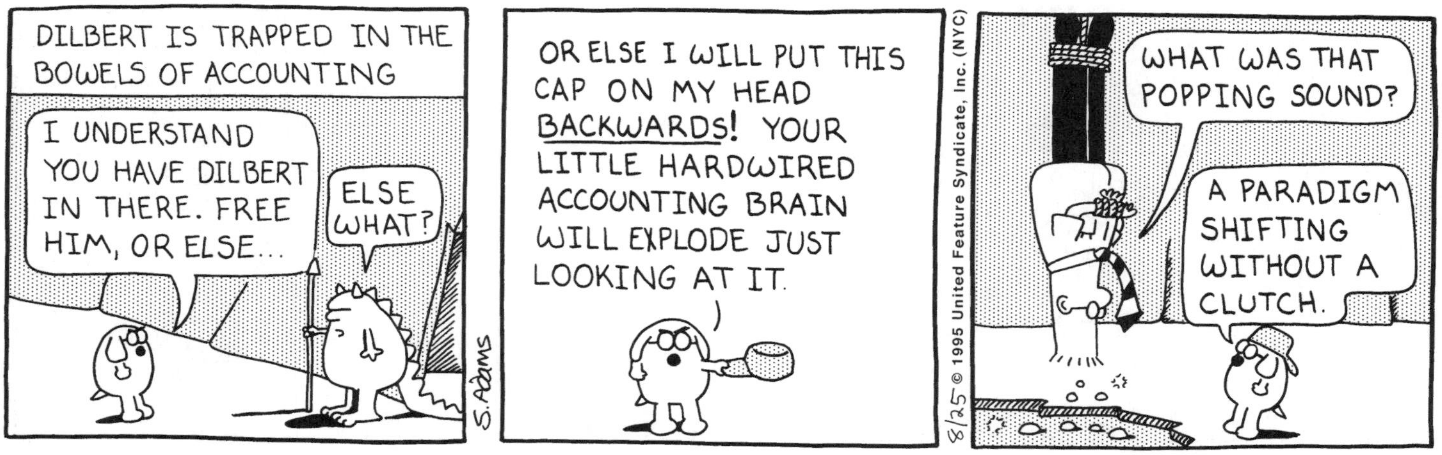
DILBERT IS TRAPPED IN THE BOWELS OF ACCOUNTING
I UNDERSTAND YOU HAVE DILBERT IN THERE. FREE HIM, OR ELSE...
ELSE WHAT?
OR ELSE I WILL PUT THIS CAP ON MY HEAD BACKWARDS! YOUR LITTLE HARDWIRED ACCOUNTING BRAIN WILL EXPLODE JUST LOOKING AT IT.
WHAT WAS THAT POPPING SOUND?
A PARADIGM SHIFTING WITHOUT A CLUTCH.
8/25 © 1995 United Feature Syndicate, Inc. (NYC)

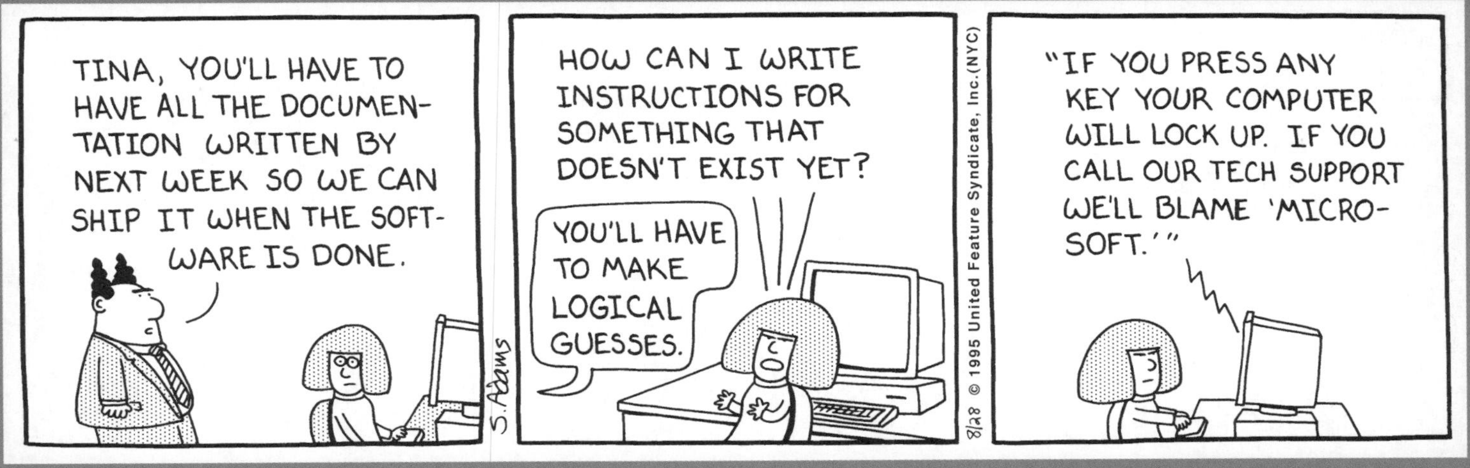
TINA, YOU'LL HAVE TO HAVE ALL THE DOCUMENTATION WRITTEN BY NEXT WEEK SO WE CAN SHIP IT WHEN THE SOFTWARE IS DONE.
S. Adams
HOW CAN I WRITE INSTRUCTIONS FOR SOMETHING THAT DOESN'T EXIST YET?
YOU'LL HAVE TO MAKE LOGICAL GUESSES.
8/28 © 1995 United Feature Syndicate, Inc.(NYC)
"IF YOU PRESS ANY KEY YOUR COMPUTER WILL LOCK UP. IF YOU CALL OUR TECH SUPPORT WE'LL BLAME 'MICROSOFT.'"

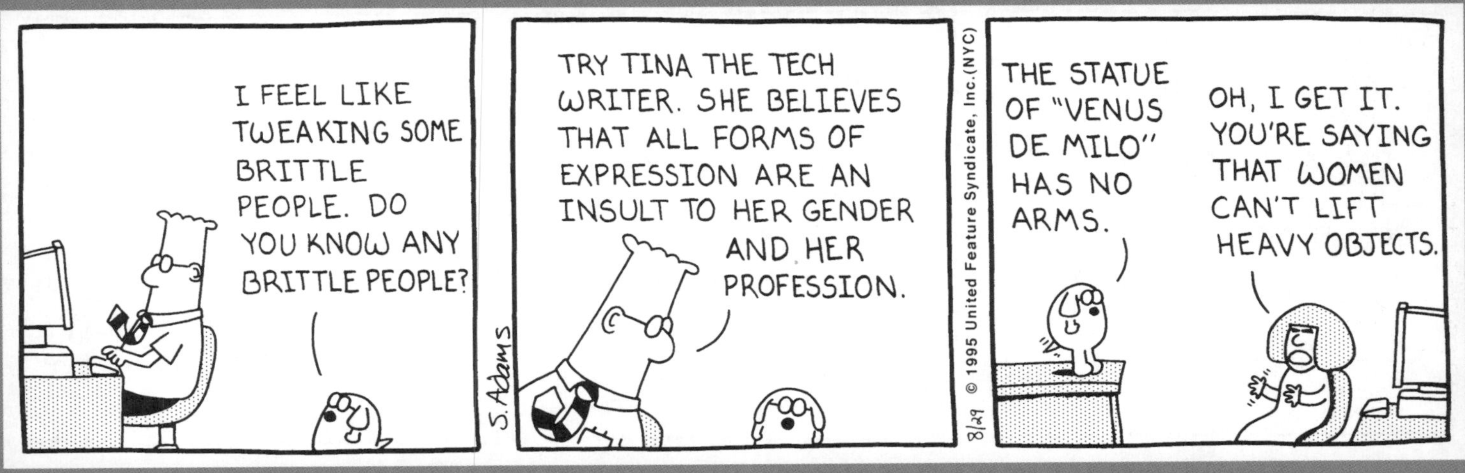
I FEEL LIKE TWEAKING SOME BRITTLE PEOPLE. DO YOU KNOW ANY BRITTLE PEOPLE?
S. Adams
TRY TINA THE TECH WRITER. SHE BELIEVES THAT ALL FORMS OF EXPRESSION ARE AN INSULT TO HER GENDER AND HER PROFESSION.
8/29 © 1995 United Feature Syndicate, Inc.(NYC)
THE STATUE OF "VENUS DE MILO" HAS NO ARMS.
OH, I GET IT. YOU'RE SAYING THAT WOMEN CAN'T LIFT HEAVY OBJECTS.

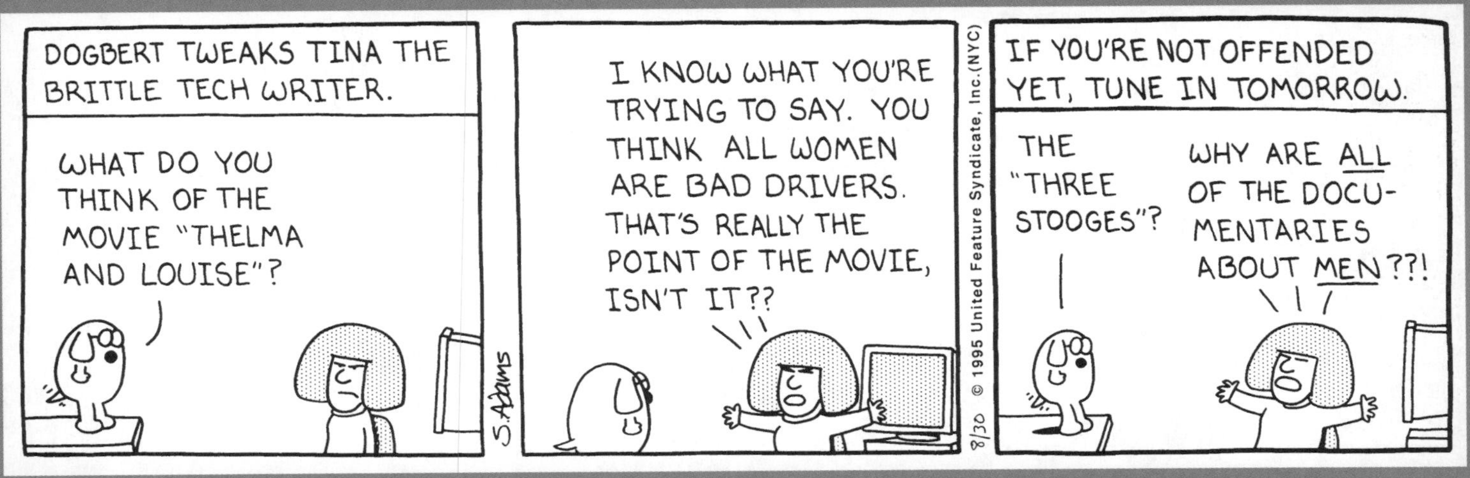
DOGBERT TWEAKS TINA THE BRITTLE TECH WRITER.
WHAT DO YOU THINK OF THE MOVIE "THELMA AND LOUISE"?
S. Adams
I KNOW WHAT YOU'RE TRYING TO SAY. YOU THINK ALL WOMEN ARE BAD DRIVERS. THAT'S REALLY THE POINT OF THE MOVIE, ISN'T IT??
8/30 © 1995 United Feature Syndicate, Inc.(NYC)
IF YOU'RE NOT OFFENDED YET, TUNE IN TOMORROW.
THE "THREE STOOGES"?
WHY ARE ALL OF THE DOCUMENTARIES ABOUT MEN??!

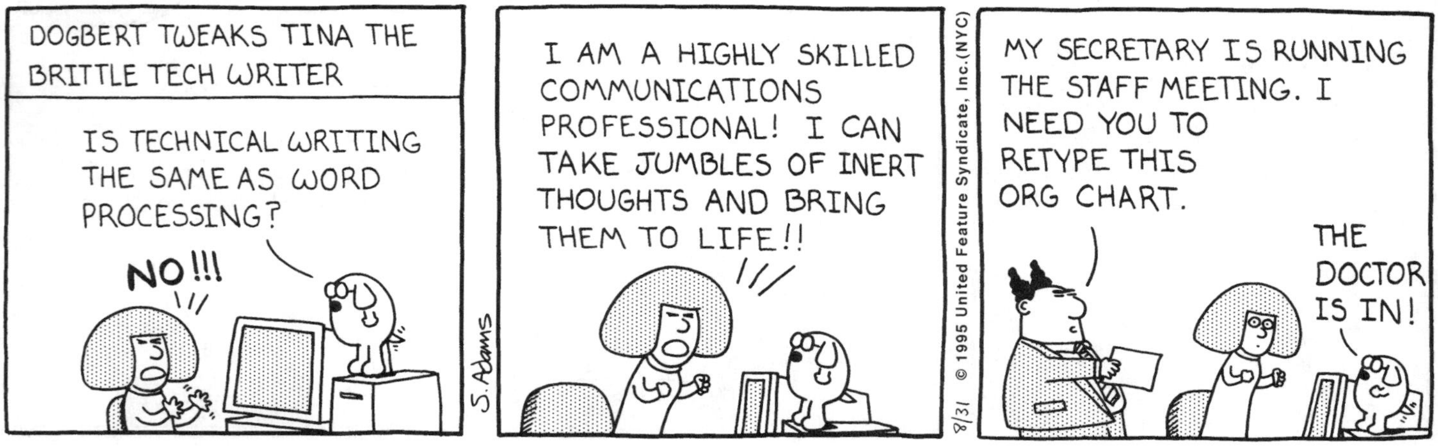
DOGBERT TWEAKS TINA THE BRITTLE TECH WRITER
IS TECHNICAL WRITING THE SAME AS WORD PROCESSING?
NO!!!
S. Adams
I AM A HIGHLY SKILLED COMMUNICATIONS PROFESSIONAL! I CAN TAKE JUMBLES OF INERT THOUGHTS AND BRING THEM TO LIFE!!
8/31 © 1995 United Feature Syndicate, Inc.(NYC)
MY SECRETARY IS RUNNING THE STAFF MEETING. I NEED YOU TO RETYPE THIS ORG CHART.
THE DOCTOR IS IN!

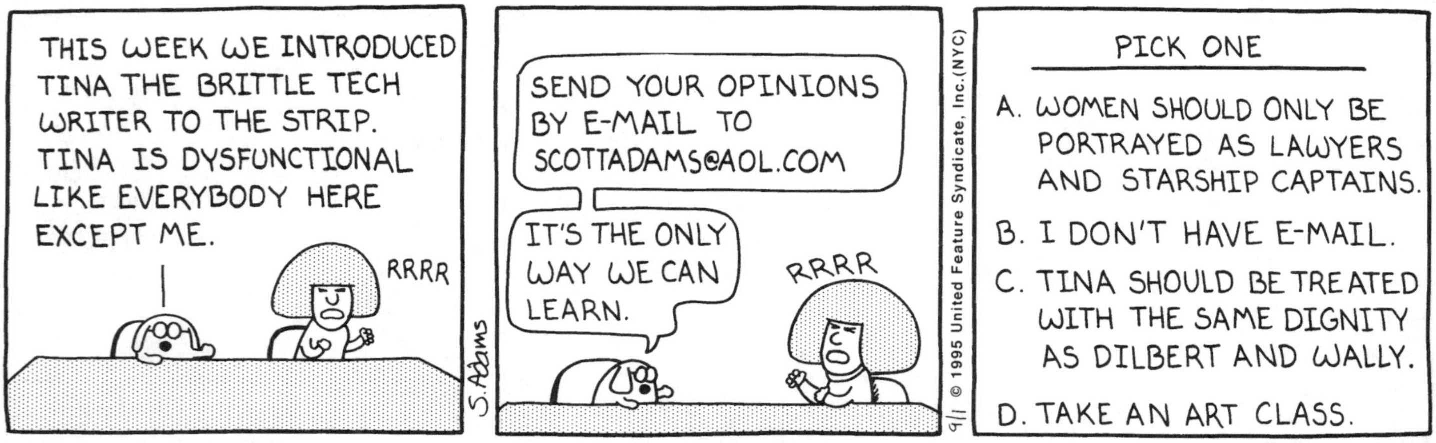
THIS WEEK WE INTRODUCED TINA THE BRITTLE TECH WRITER TO THE STRIP. TINA IS DYSFUNCTIONAL LIKE EVERYBODY HERE EXCEPT ME.
RRRR
S. Adams
SEND YOUR OPINIONS BY E-MAIL TO SCOTTADAMS@AOL.COM
IT'S THE ONLY WAY WE CAN LEARN.
RRRR
9/1 © 1995 United Feature Syndicate, Inc.(NYC)
PICK ONE
A. WOMEN SHOULD ONLY BE PORTRAYED AS LAWYERS AND STARSHIP CAPTAINS.
B. I DON'T HAVE E-MAIL.
C. TINA SHOULD BE TREATED WITH THE SAME DIGNITY AS DILBERT AND WALLY.
D. TAKE AN ART CLASS.

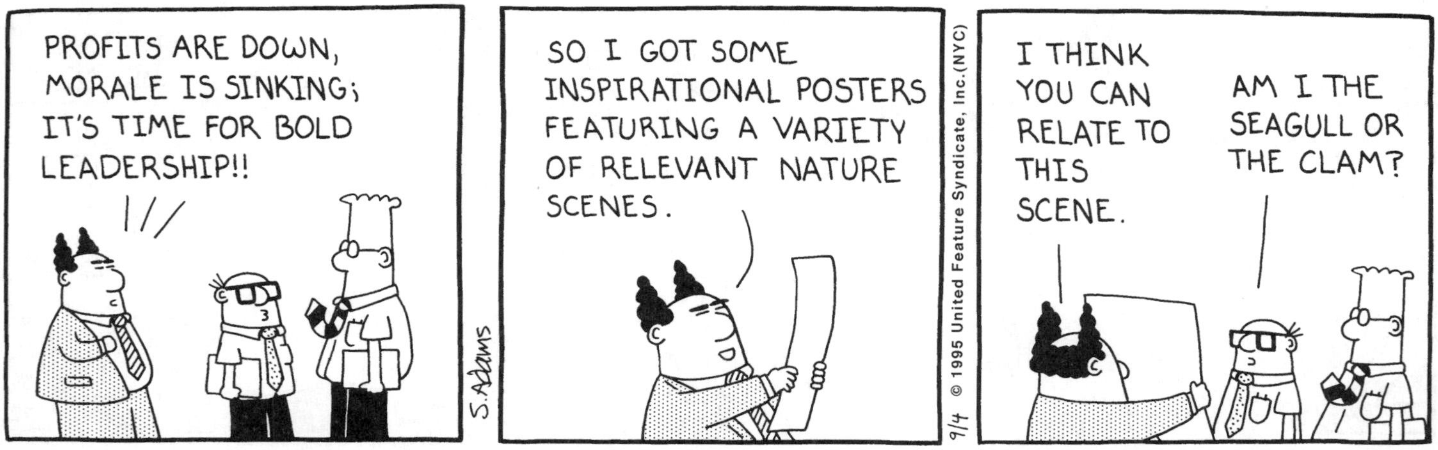
PROFITS ARE DOWN, MORALE IS SINKING; IT'S TIME FOR BOLD LEADERSHIP!!
S. Adams
SO I GOT SOME INSPIRATIONAL POSTERS FEATURING A VARIETY OF RELEVANT NATURE SCENES.
9/4 © 1995 United Feature Syndicate, Inc.(NYC)
I THINK YOU CAN RELATE TO THIS SCENE.
AM I THE SEAGULL OR THE CLAM?

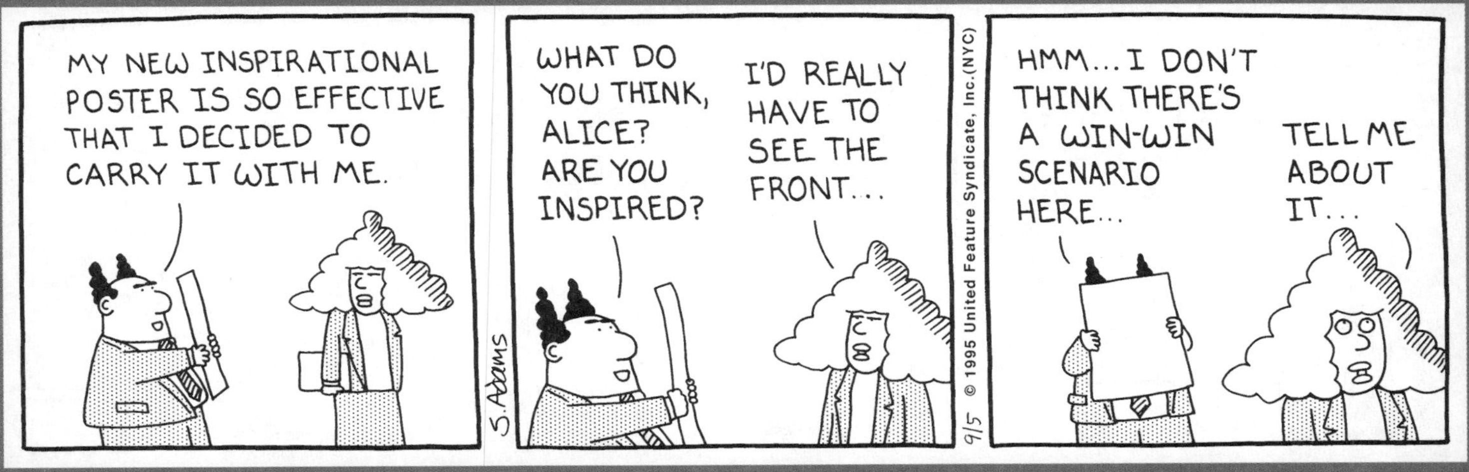
MY NEW INSPIRATIONAL POSTER IS SO EFFECTIVE THAT I DECIDED TO CARRY IT WITH ME.
WHAT DO YOU THINK, ALICE? ARE YOU INSPIRED?
I'D REALLY HAVE TO SEE THE FRONT...
HMM... I DON'T THINK THERE'S A WIN-WIN SCENARIO HERE...
TELL ME ABOUT IT...
© 1995 United Feature Syndicate, Inc.(NYC)

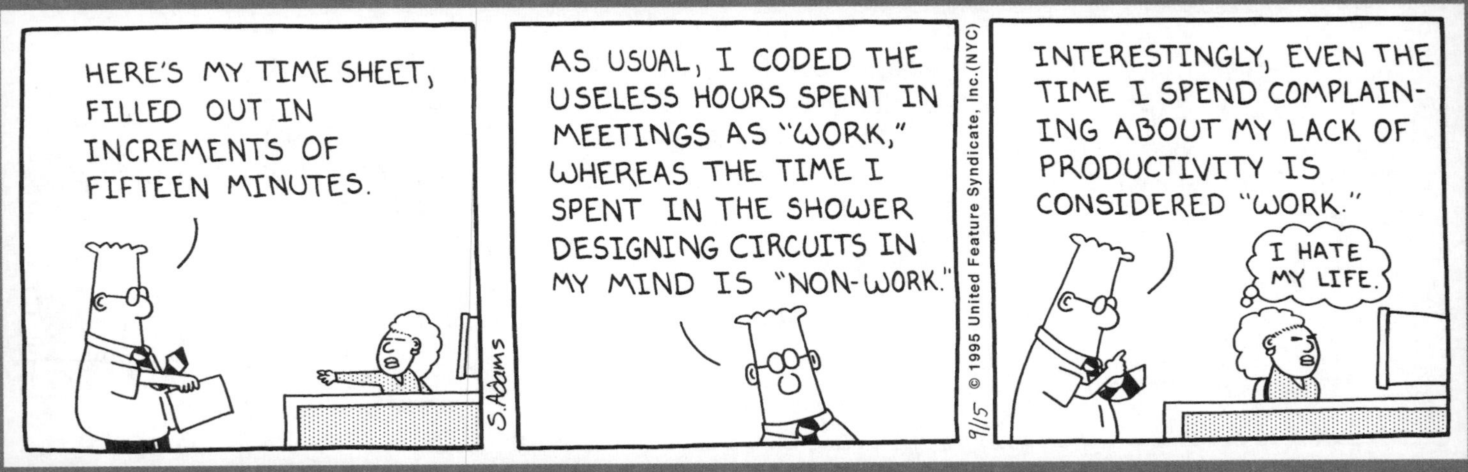
HERE'S MY TIME SHEET, FILLED OUT IN INCREMENTS OF FIFTEEN MINUTES.
AS USUAL, I CODED THE USELESS HOURS SPENT IN MEETINGS AS "WORK," WHEREAS THE TIME I SPENT IN THE SHOWER DESIGNING CIRCUITS IN MY MIND IS "NON-WORK."
INTERESTINGLY, EVEN THE TIME I SPEND COMPLAINING ABOUT MY LACK OF PRODUCTIVITY IS CONSIDERED "WORK."
I HATE MY LIFE.
© 1995 United Feature Syndicate, Inc.(NYC)

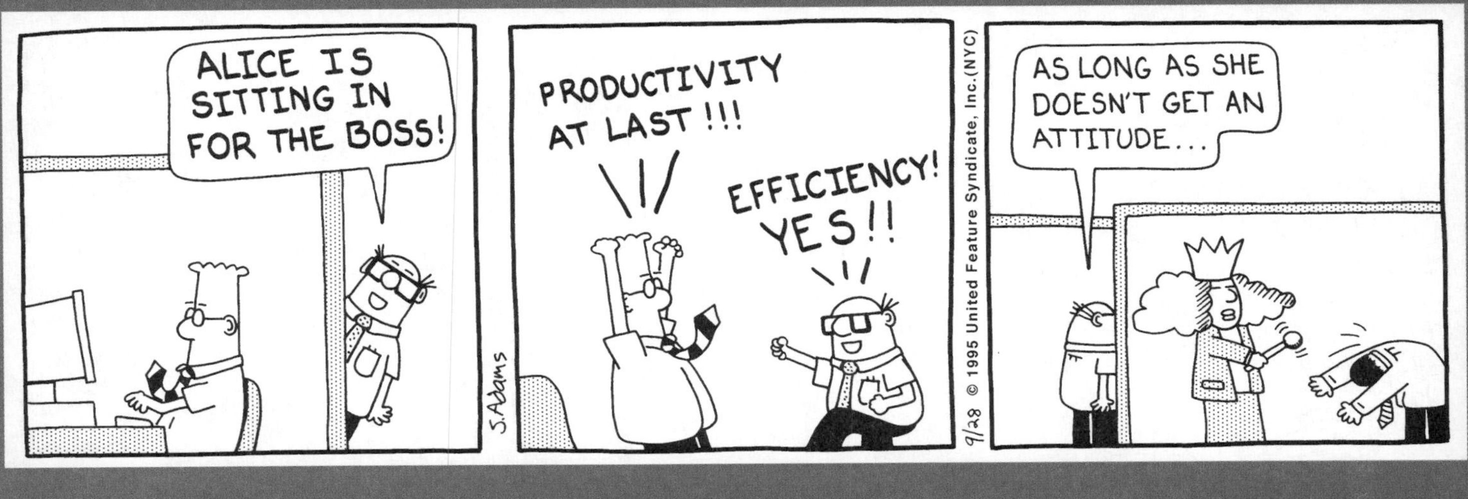
ALICE IS SITTING IN FOR THE BOSS!
PRODUCTIVITY AT LAST!!!
EFFICIENCY! YES!!
AS LONG AS SHE DOESN'T GET AN ATTITUDE...
© 1995 United Feature Syndicate, Inc.(NYC)

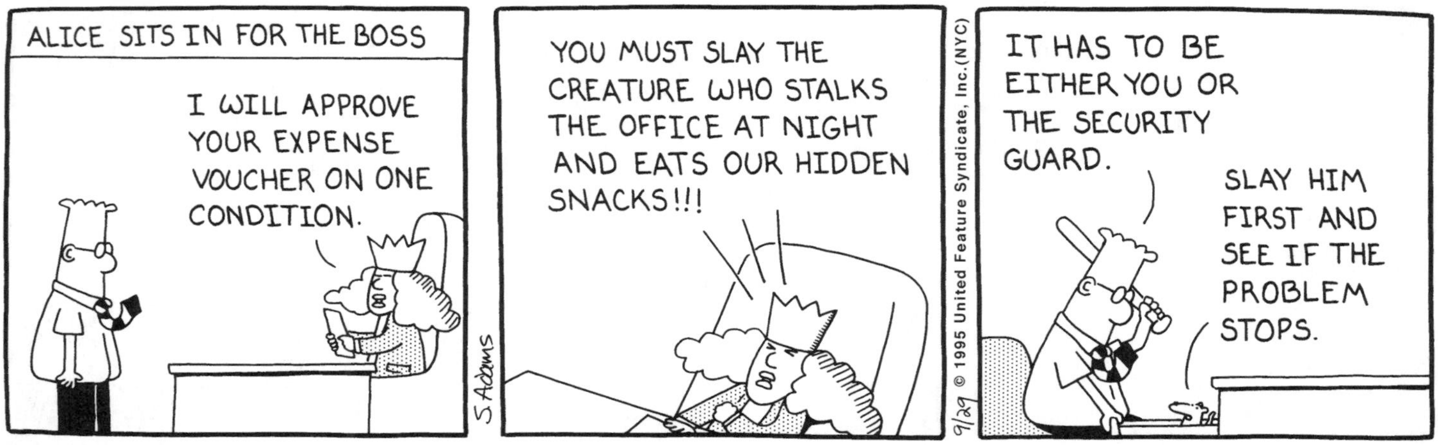
ALICE SITS IN FOR THE BOSS
I WILL APPROVE YOUR EXPENSE VOUCHER ON ONE CONDITION.
YOU MUST SLAY THE CREATURE WHO STALKS THE OFFICE AT NIGHT AND EATS OUR HIDDEN SNACKS!!!
9/29 © 1995 United Feature Syndicate, Inc.(NYC)
IT HAS TO BE EITHER YOU OR THE SECURITY GUARD.
SLAY HIM FIRST AND SEE IF THE PROBLEM STOPS.

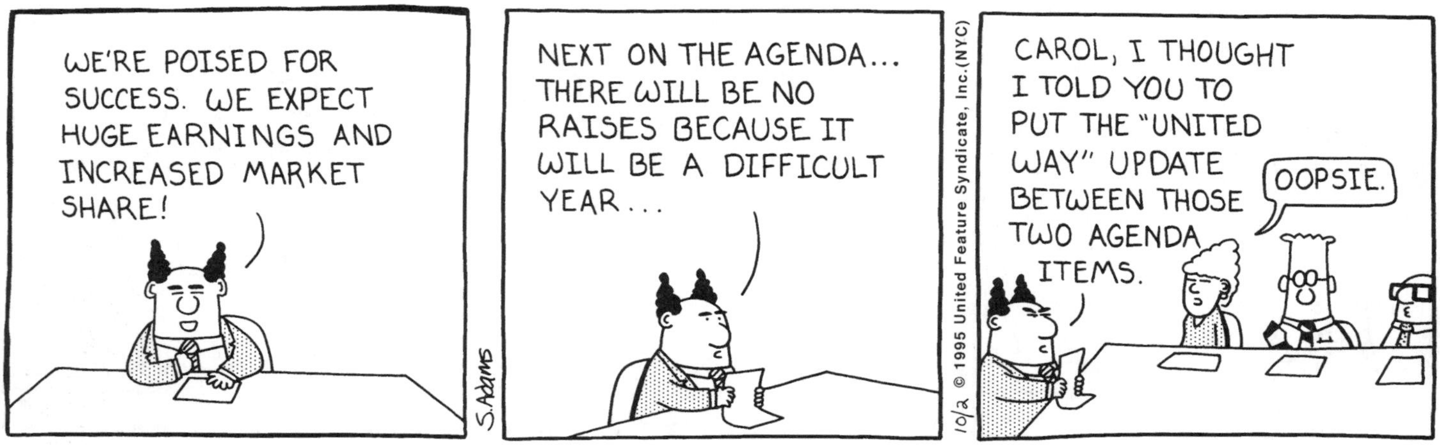
WE'RE POISED FOR SUCCESS. WE EXPECT HUGE EARNINGS AND INCREASED MARKET SHARE!
NEXT ON THE AGENDA... THERE WILL BE NO RAISES BECAUSE IT WILL BE A DIFFICULT YEAR...
10/2 © 1995 United Feature Syndicate, Inc.(NYC)
CAROL, I THOUGHT I TOLD YOU TO PUT THE "UNITED WAY" UPDATE BETWEEN THOSE TWO AGENDA ITEMS.
OOPSIE.

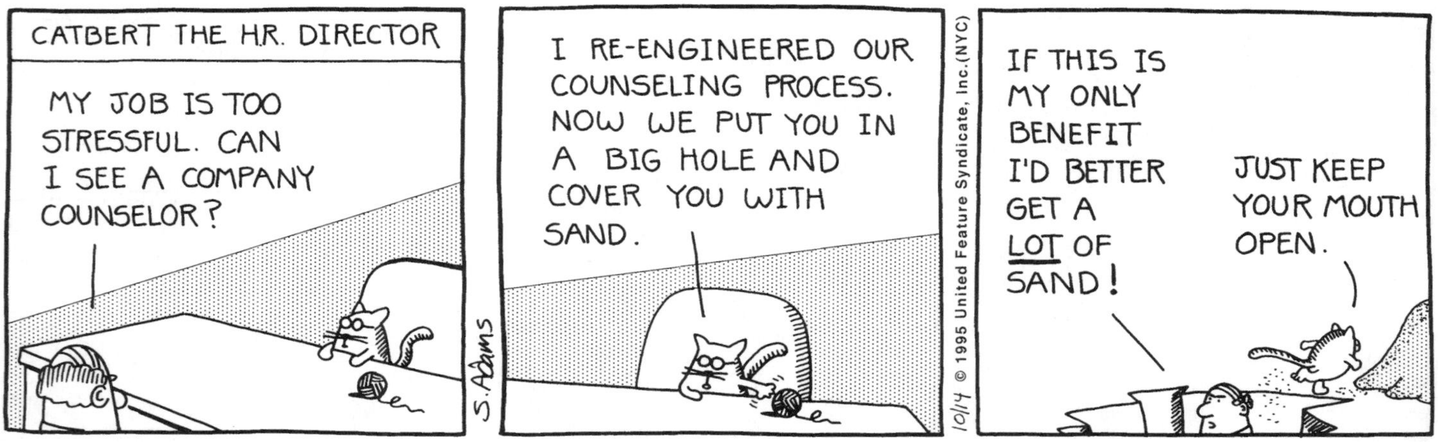
CATBERT THE H.R. DIRECTOR
MY JOB IS TOO STRESSFUL. CAN I SEE A COMPANY COUNSELOR?
I RE-ENGINEERED OUR COUNSELING PROCESS. NOW WE PUT YOU IN A BIG HOLE AND COVER YOU WITH SAND.
10/14 © 1995 United Feature Syndicate, Inc.(NYC)
IF THIS IS MY ONLY BENEFIT I'D BETTER GET A LOT OF SAND!
JUST KEEP YOUR MOUTH OPEN.

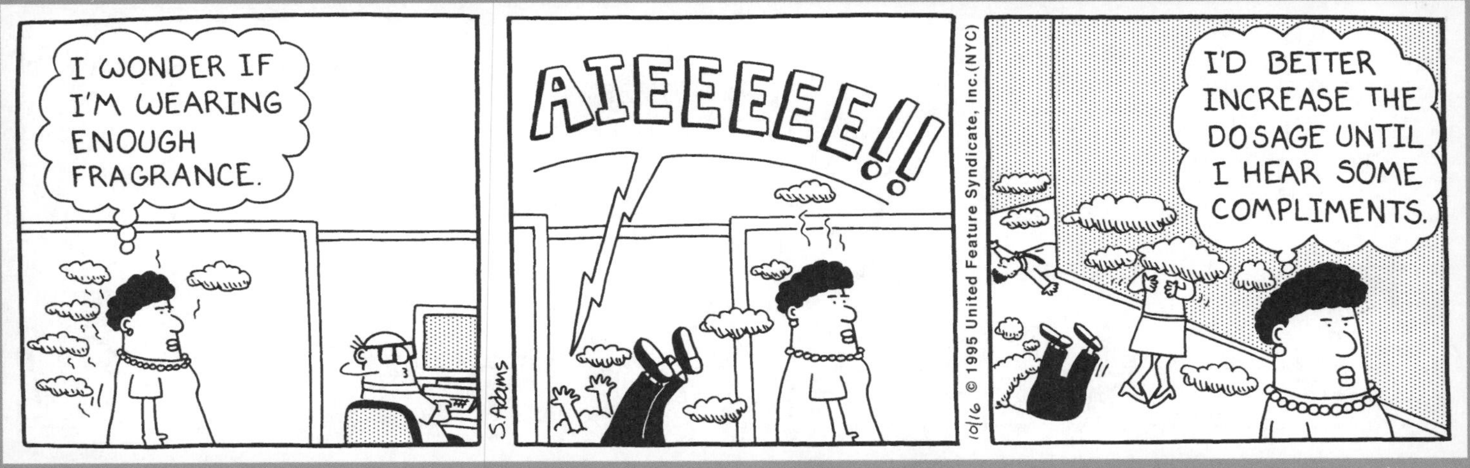
I WONDER IF I'M WEARING ENOUGH FRAGRANCE.
AIEEEEEE!!
I'D BETTER INCREASE THE DOSAGE UNTIL I HEAR SOME COMPLIMENTS.
S. Adams
10/16 © 1995 United Feature Syndicate, Inc.(NYC)

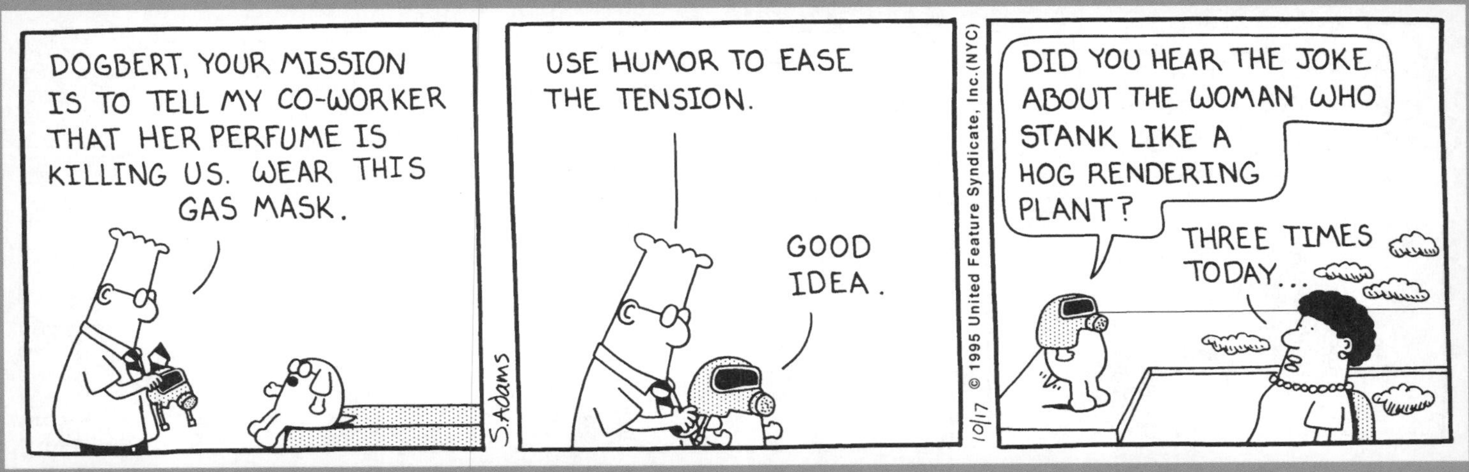
DOGBERT, YOUR MISSION IS TO TELL MY CO-WORKER THAT HER PERFUME IS KILLING US. WEAR THIS GAS MASK.
USE HUMOR TO EASE THE TENSION.
GOOD IDEA.
DID YOU HEAR THE JOKE ABOUT THE WOMAN WHO STANK LIKE A HOG RENDERING PLANT?
THREE TIMES TODAY...
S. Adams
10/17 © 1995 United Feature Syndicate, Inc.(NYC)

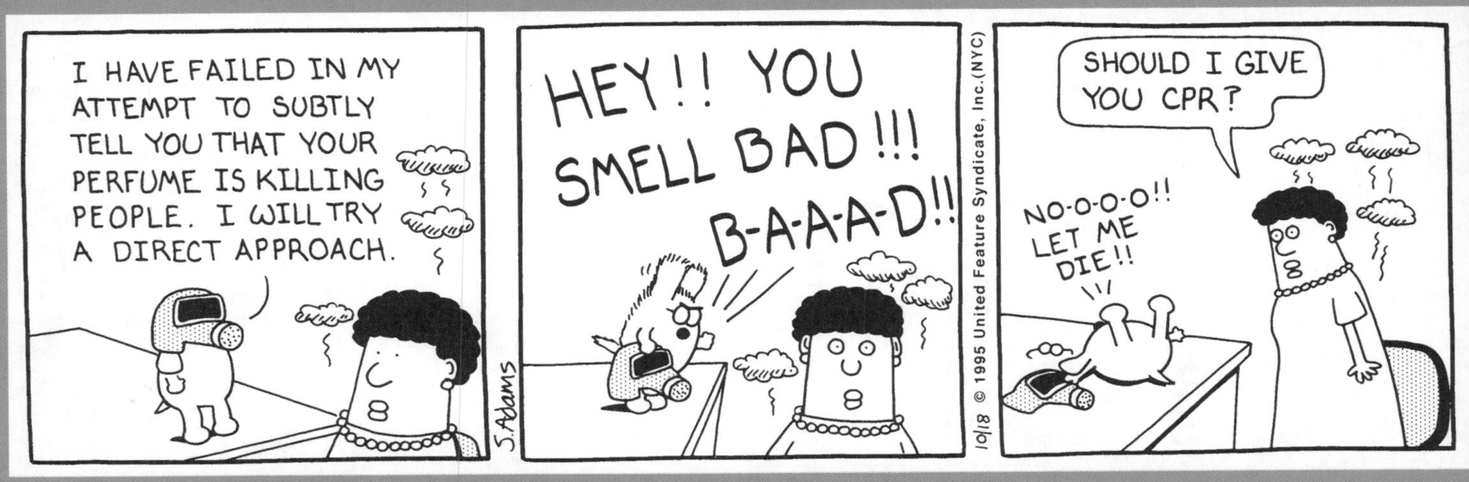
I HAVE FAILED IN MY ATTEMPT TO SUBTLY TELL YOU THAT YOUR PERFUME IS KILLING PEOPLE. I WILL TRY A DIRECT APPROACH.
HEY!! YOU SMELL BAD!!!
B-A-A-A-D!!
SHOULD I GIVE YOU CPR?
NO-O-O-O!! LET ME DIE!!
S. Adams
10/18 © 1995 United Feature Syndicate, Inc.(NYC)

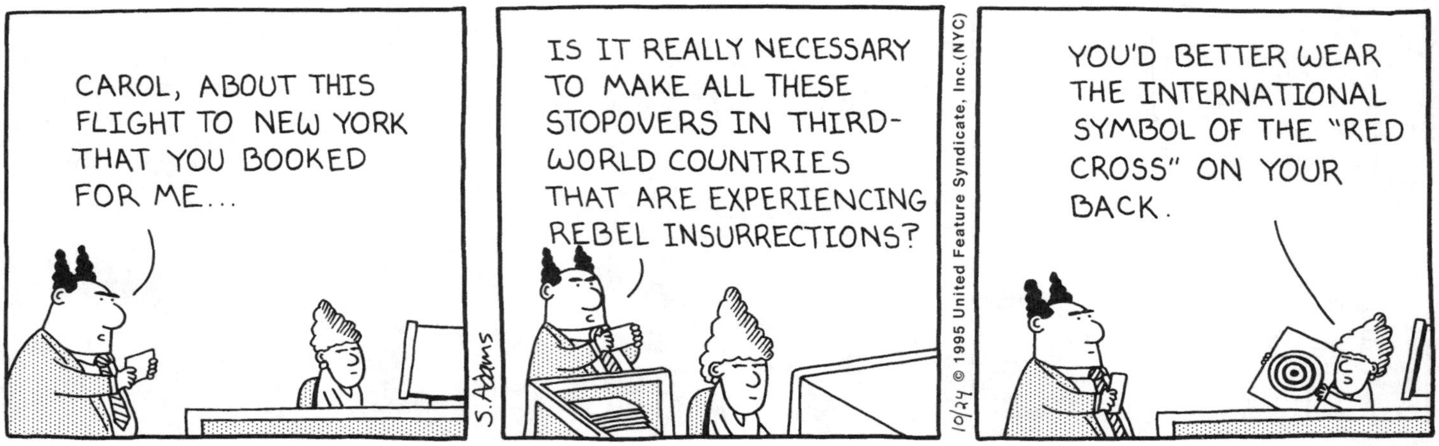
CAROL, ABOUT THIS FLIGHT TO NEW YORK THAT YOU BOOKED FOR ME...
IS IT REALLY NECESSARY TO MAKE ALL THESE STOPOVERS IN THIRD-WORLD COUNTRIES THAT ARE EXPERIENCING REBEL INSURRECTIONS?
YOU'D BETTER WEAR THE INTERNATIONAL SYMBOL OF THE "RED CROSS" ON YOUR BACK.
S. Adams
10/24 © 1995 United Feature Syndicate, Inc.(NYC)

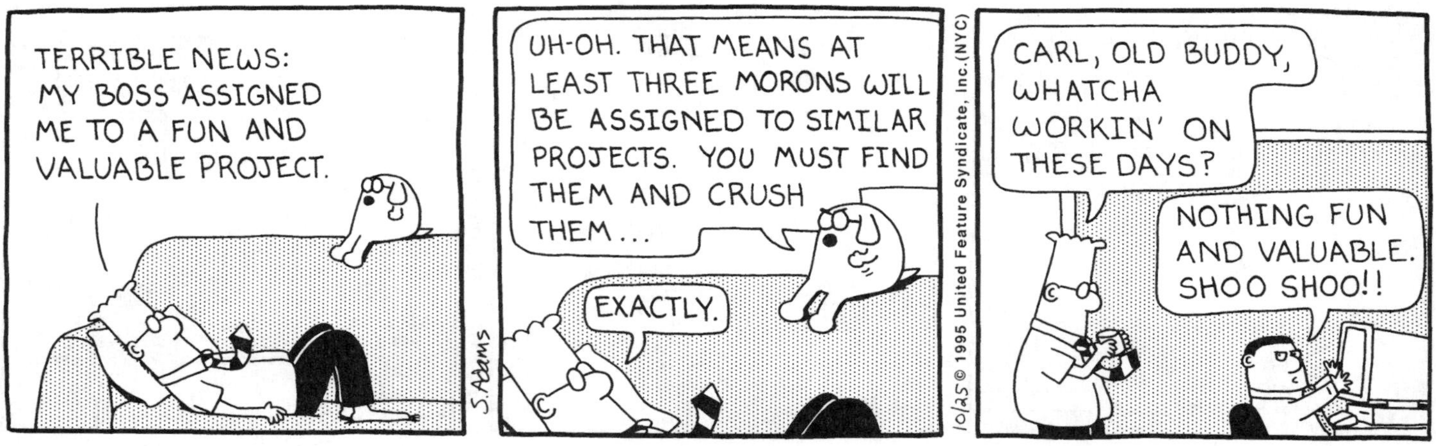
TERRIBLE NEWS: MY BOSS ASSIGNED ME TO A FUN AND VALUABLE PROJECT.
UH-OH. THAT MEANS AT LEAST THREE MORONS WILL BE ASSIGNED TO SIMILAR PROJECTS. YOU MUST FIND THEM AND CRUSH THEM...
EXACTLY.
CARL, OLD BUDDY, WHATCHA WORKIN' ON THESE DAYS?
NOTHING FUN AND VALUABLE. SHOO SHOO!!
S. Adams
10/25 © 1995 United Feature Syndicate, Inc.(NYC)

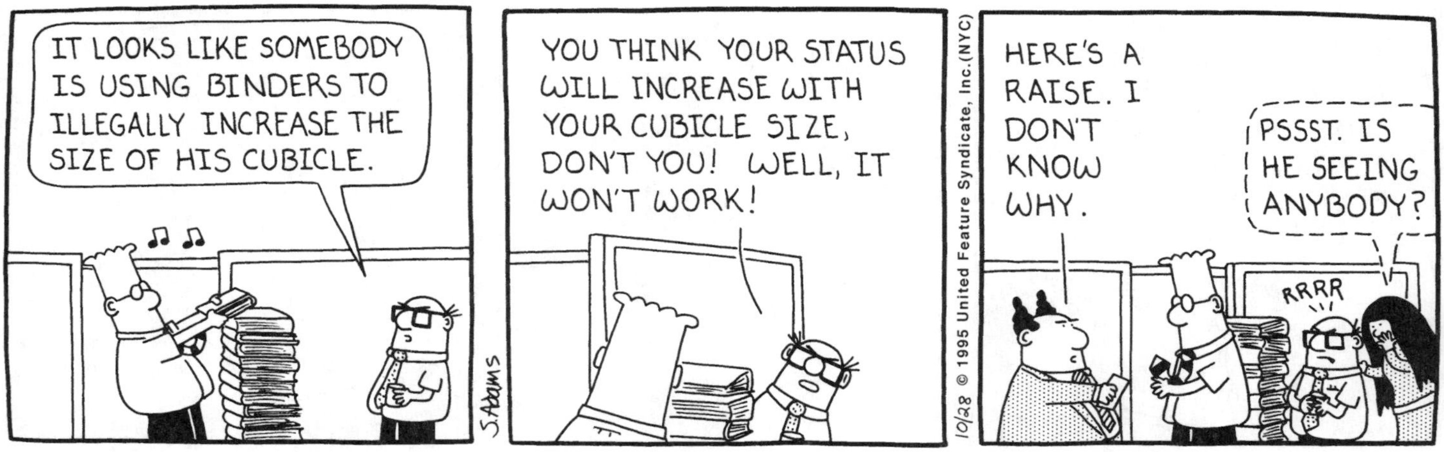
IT LOOKS LIKE SOMEBODY IS USING BINDERS TO ILLEGALLY INCREASE THE SIZE OF HIS CUBICLE.
YOU THINK YOUR STATUS WILL INCREASE WITH YOUR CUBICLE SIZE, DON'T YOU! WELL, IT WON'T WORK!
HERE'S A RAISE. I DON'T KNOW WHY.
PSSST. IS HE SEEING ANYBODY?
RRRR
S. Adams
10/28 © 1995 United Feature Syndicate, Inc.(NYC)

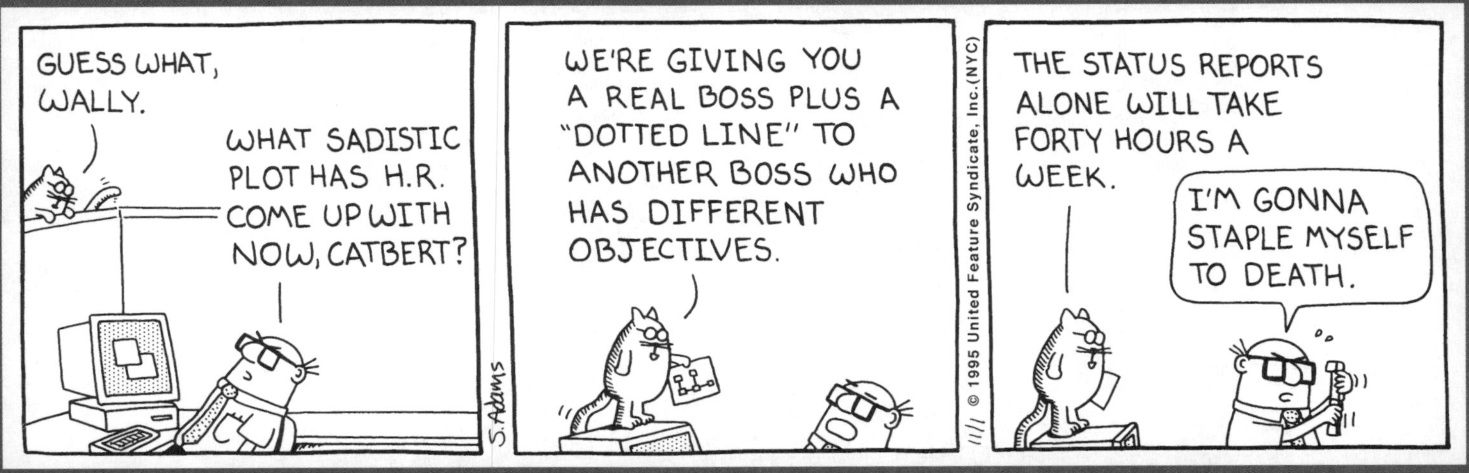
GUESS WHAT, WALLY.
WHAT SADISTIC PLOT HAS H.R. COME UP WITH NOW, CATBERT?
S. Adams
WE'RE GIVING YOU A REAL BOSS PLUS A "DOTTED LINE" TO ANOTHER BOSS WHO HAS DIFFERENT OBJECTIVES.
11/1 © 1995 United Feature Syndicate, Inc.(NYC)
THE STATUS REPORTS ALONE WILL TAKE FORTY HOURS A WEEK.
I'M GONNA STAPLE MYSELF TO DEATH.

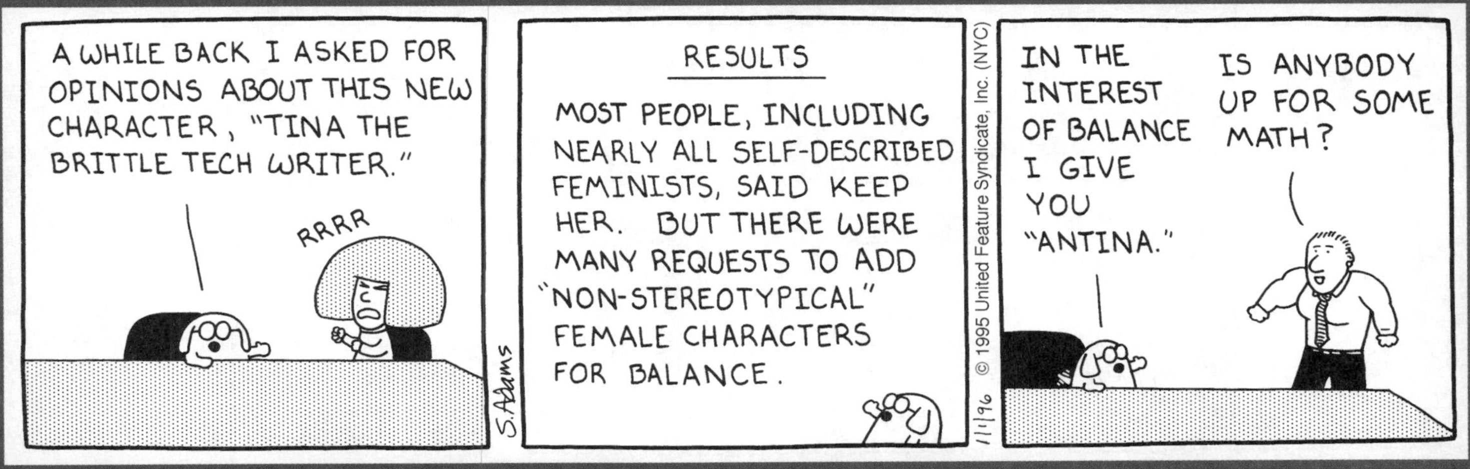
A WHILE BACK I ASKED FOR OPINIONS ABOUT THIS NEW CHARACTER, "TINA THE BRITTLE TECH WRITER."
RRRR
S. Adams
RESULTS
MOST PEOPLE, INCLUDING NEARLY ALL SELF-DESCRIBED FEMINISTS, SAID KEEP HER. BUT THERE WERE MANY REQUESTS TO ADD "NON-STEREOTYPICAL" FEMALE CHARACTERS FOR BALANCE.
1/1/96 © 1995 United Feature Syndicate, Inc. (NYC)
IN THE INTEREST OF BALANCE I GIVE YOU "ANTINA."
IS ANYBODY UP FOR SOME MATH?

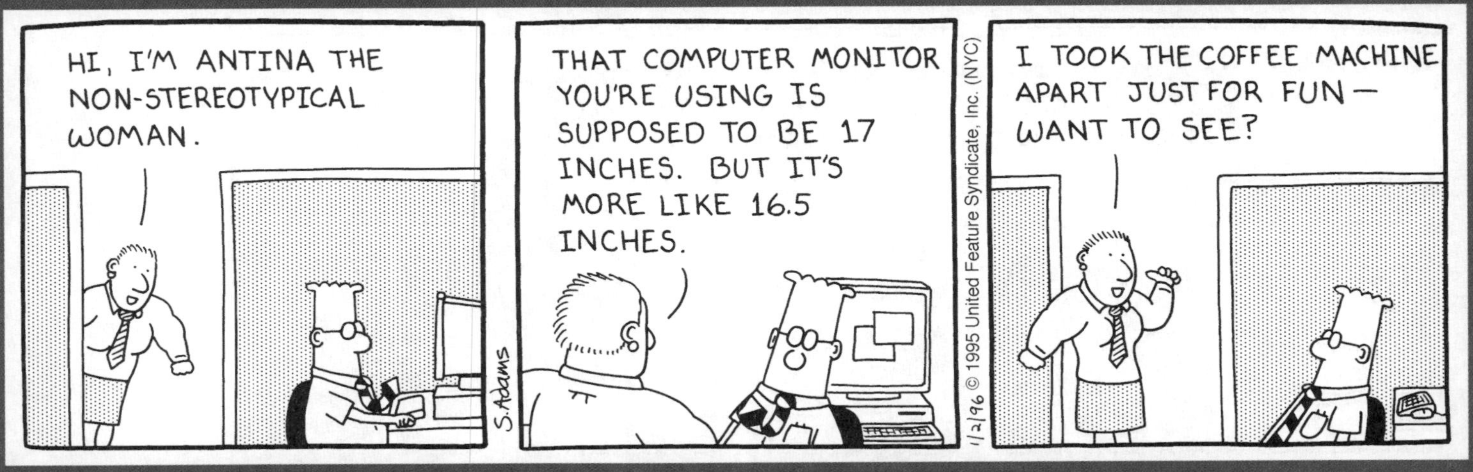
HI, I'M ANTINA THE NON-STEREOTYPICAL WOMAN.
S. Adams
THAT COMPUTER MONITOR YOU'RE USING IS SUPPOSED TO BE 17 INCHES. BUT IT'S MORE LIKE 16.5 INCHES.
1/2/96 © 1995 United Feature Syndicate, Inc. (NYC)
I TOOK THE COFFEE MACHINE APART JUST FOR FUN — WANT TO SEE?

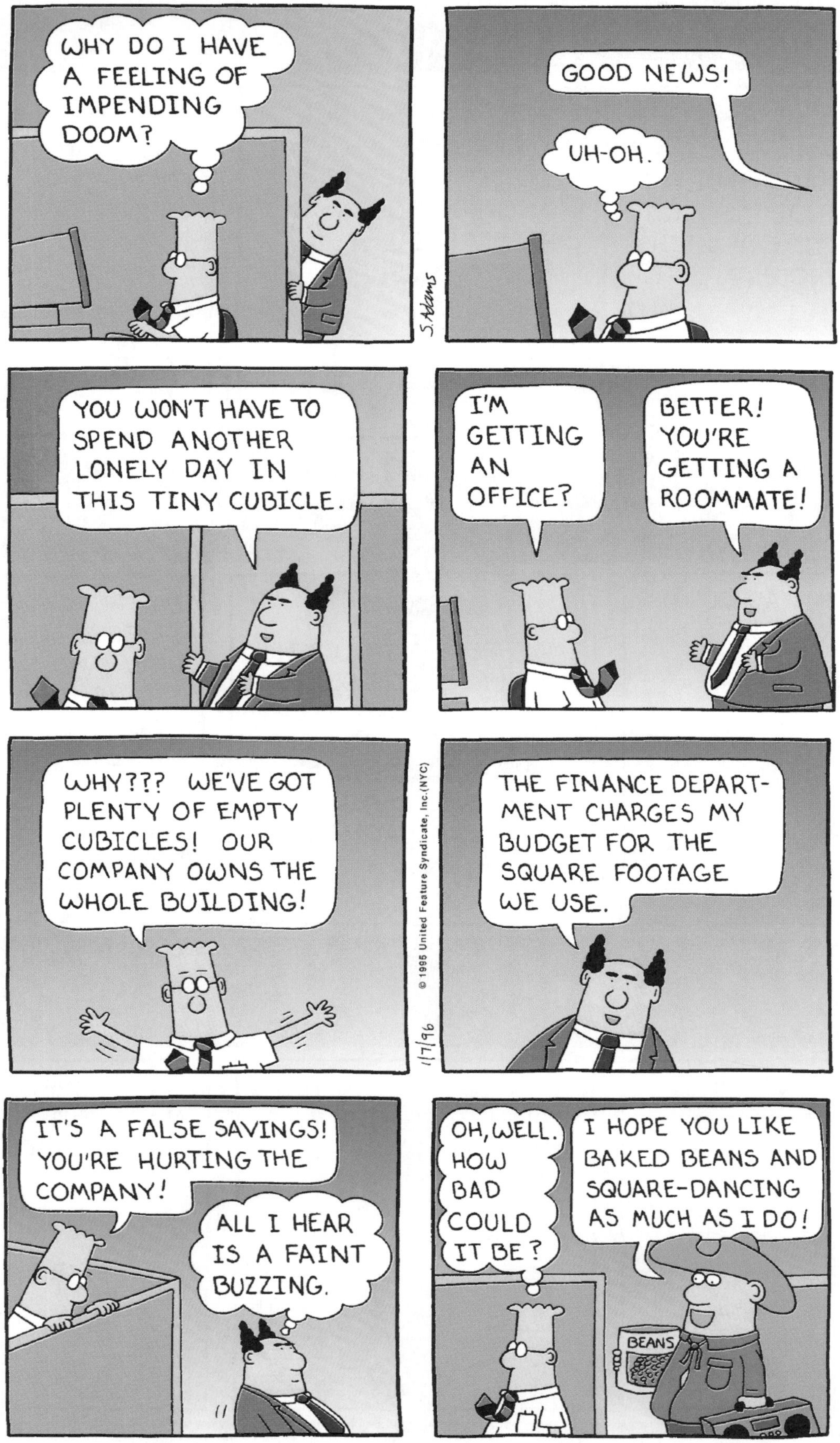
WHY DO I HAVE A FEELING OF IMPENDING DOOM?
GOOD NEWS!
UH-OH.
S. Adams
YOU WON'T HAVE TO SPEND ANOTHER LONELY DAY IN THIS TINY CUBICLE.
I'M GETTING AN OFFICE?
BETTER! YOU'RE GETTING A ROOMMATE!
WHY??? WE'VE GOT PLENTY OF EMPTY CUBICLES! OUR COMPANY OWNS THE WHOLE BUILDING!
© 1995 United Feature Syndicate, Inc.(NYC)
1/7/96
THE FINANCE DEPARTMENT CHARGES MY BUDGET FOR THE SQUARE FOOTAGE WE USE.
IT'S A FALSE SAVINGS! YOU'RE HURTING THE COMPANY!
ALL I HEAR IS A FAINT BUZZING.
OH, WELL. HOW BAD COULD IT BE?
I HOPE YOU LIKE BAKED BEANS AND SQUARE-DANCING AS MUCH AS I DO!
BEANS

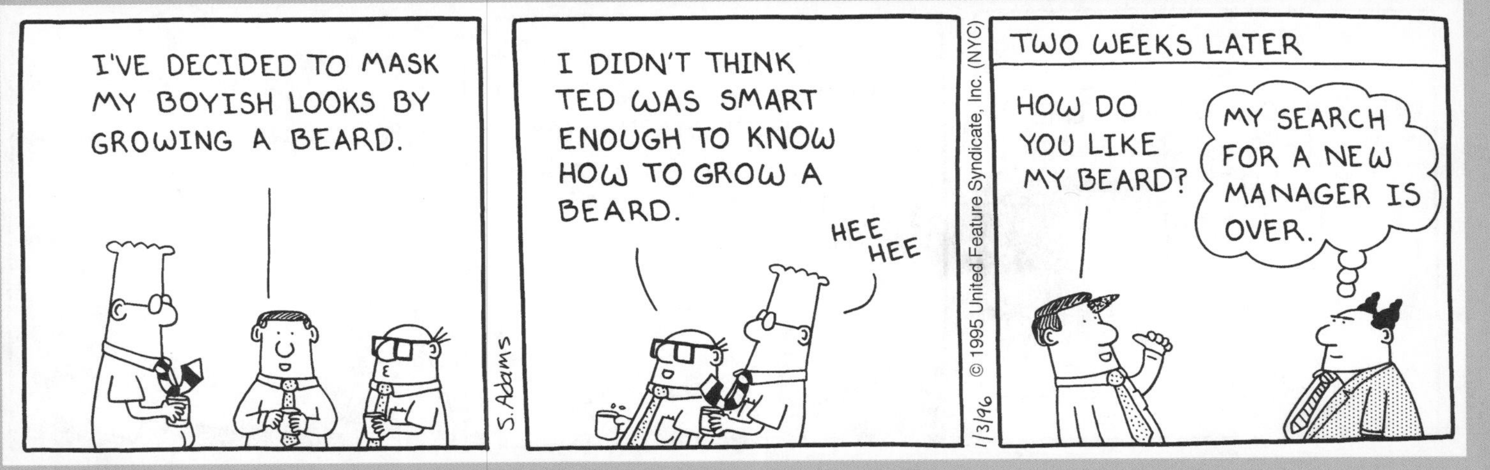
I'VE DECIDED TO MASK MY BOYISH LOOKS BY GROWING A BEARD.
S. Adams
I DIDN'T THINK TED WAS SMART ENOUGH TO KNOW HOW TO GROW A BEARD.
HEE HEE
1/3/96 © 1995 United Feature Syndicate, Inc. (NYC)
TWO WEEKS LATER
HOW DO YOU LIKE MY BEARD?
MY SEARCH FOR A NEW MANAGER IS OVER.

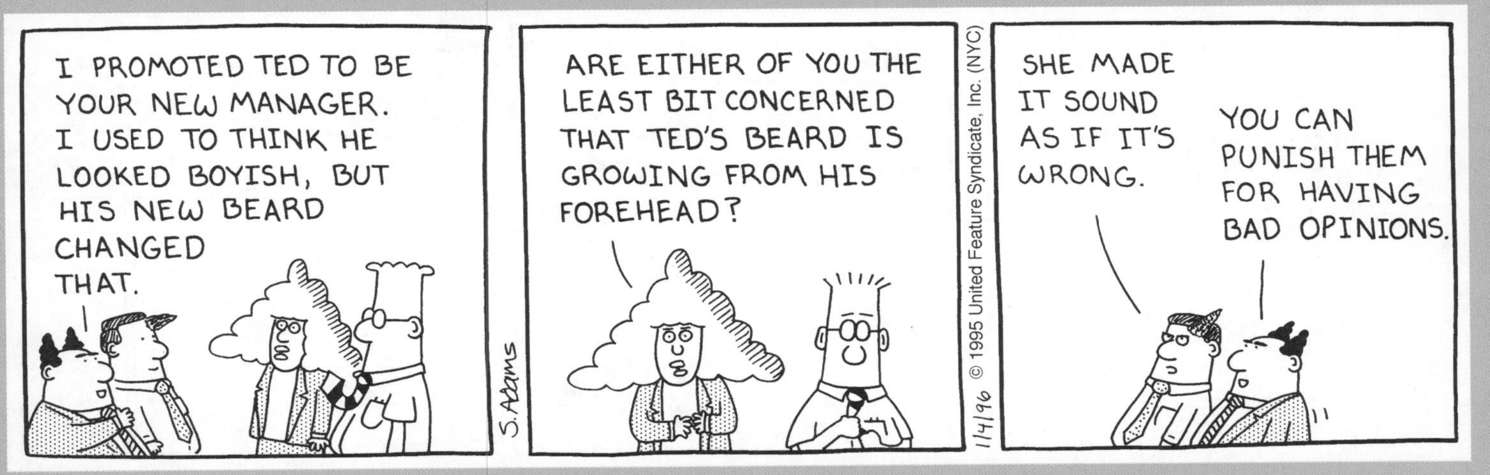
I PROMOTED TED TO BE YOUR NEW MANAGER. I USED TO THINK HE LOOKED BOYISH, BUT HIS NEW BEARD CHANGED THAT.
S. Adams
ARE EITHER OF YOU THE LEAST BIT CONCERNED THAT TED'S BEARD IS GROWING FROM HIS FOREHEAD?
1/4/96 © 1995 United Feature Syndicate, Inc. (NYC)
SHE MADE IT SOUND AS IF IT'S WRONG.
YOU CAN PUNISH THEM FOR HAVING BAD OPINIONS.

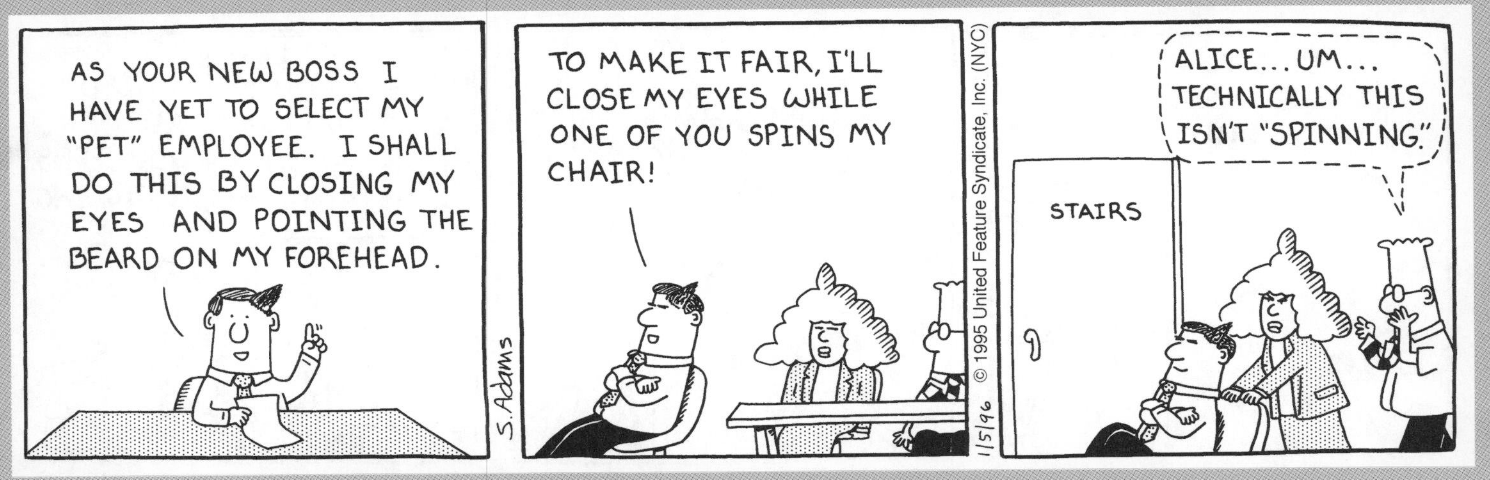
AS YOUR NEW BOSS I HAVE YET TO SELECT MY "PET" EMPLOYEE. I SHALL DO THIS BY CLOSING MY EYES AND POINTING THE BEARD ON MY FOREHEAD.
S. Adams
TO MAKE IT FAIR, I'LL CLOSE MY EYES WHILE ONE OF YOU SPINS MY CHAIR!
1/5/96 © 1995 United Feature Syndicate, Inc. (NYC)
STAIRS
ALICE... UM... TECHNICALLY THIS ISN'T "SPINNING."

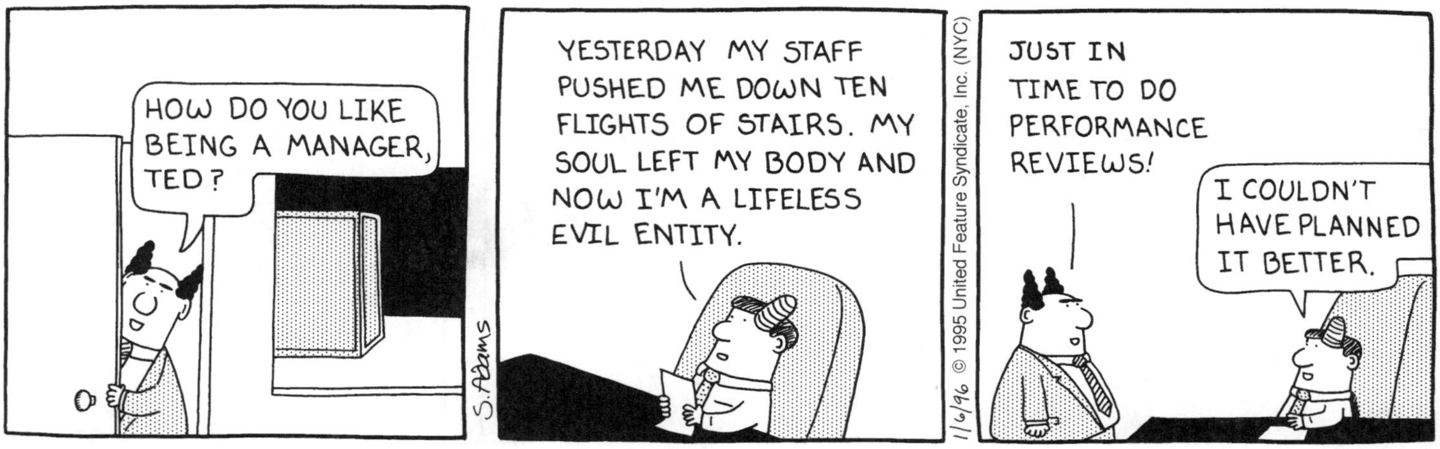
HOW DO YOU LIKE BEING A MANAGER, TED?
S. Adams
YESTERDAY MY STAFF PUSHED ME DOWN TEN FLIGHTS OF STAIRS. MY SOUL LEFT MY BODY AND NOW I'M A LIFELESS EVIL ENTITY.
1/6/96 © 1995 United Feature Syndicate, Inc. (NYC)
JUST IN TIME TO DO PERFORMANCE REVIEWS!
I COULDN'T HAVE PLANNED IT BETTER.

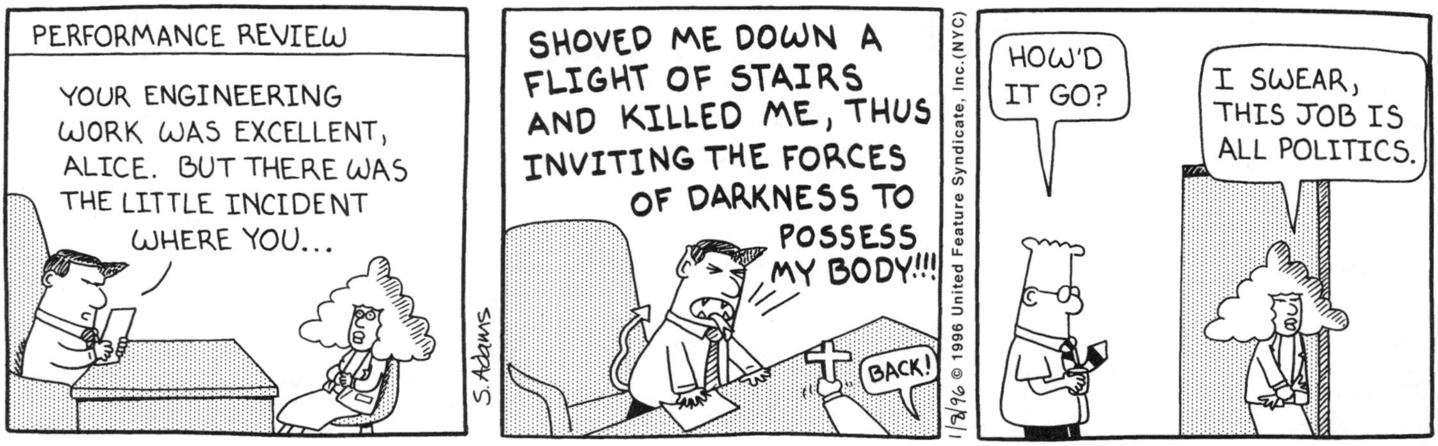
PERFORMANCE REVIEW
YOUR ENGINEERING WORK WAS EXCELLENT, ALICE. BUT THERE WAS THE LITTLE INCIDENT WHERE YOU...
S. Adams
SHOVED ME DOWN A FLIGHT OF STAIRS AND KILLED ME, THUS INVITING THE FORCES OF DARKNESS TO POSSESS MY BODY!!!
BACK!
1/8/96 © 1996 United Feature Syndicate, Inc. (NYC)
HOW'D IT GO?
I SWEAR, THIS JOB IS ALL POLITICS.

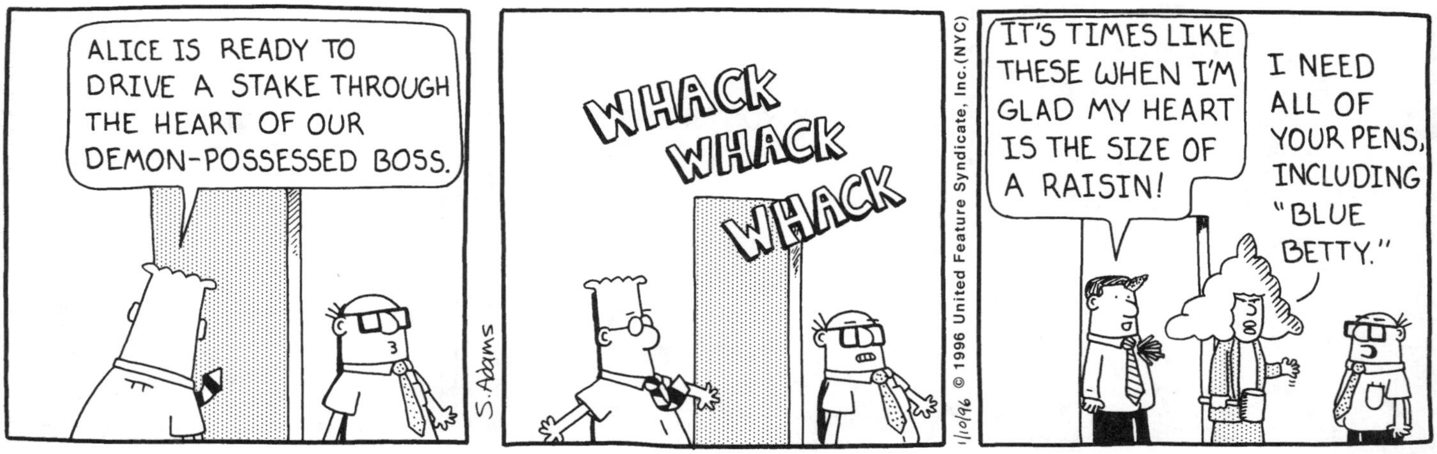
ALICE IS READY TO DRIVE A STAKE THROUGH THE HEART OF OUR DEMON-POSSESSED BOSS.
S. Adams
WHACK
WHACK
WHACK
1/10/96 © 1996 United Feature Syndicate, Inc. (NYC)
IT'S TIMES LIKE THESE WHEN I'M GLAD MY HEART IS THE SIZE OF A RAISIN!
I NEED ALL OF YOUR PENS, INCLUDING "BLUE BETTY."

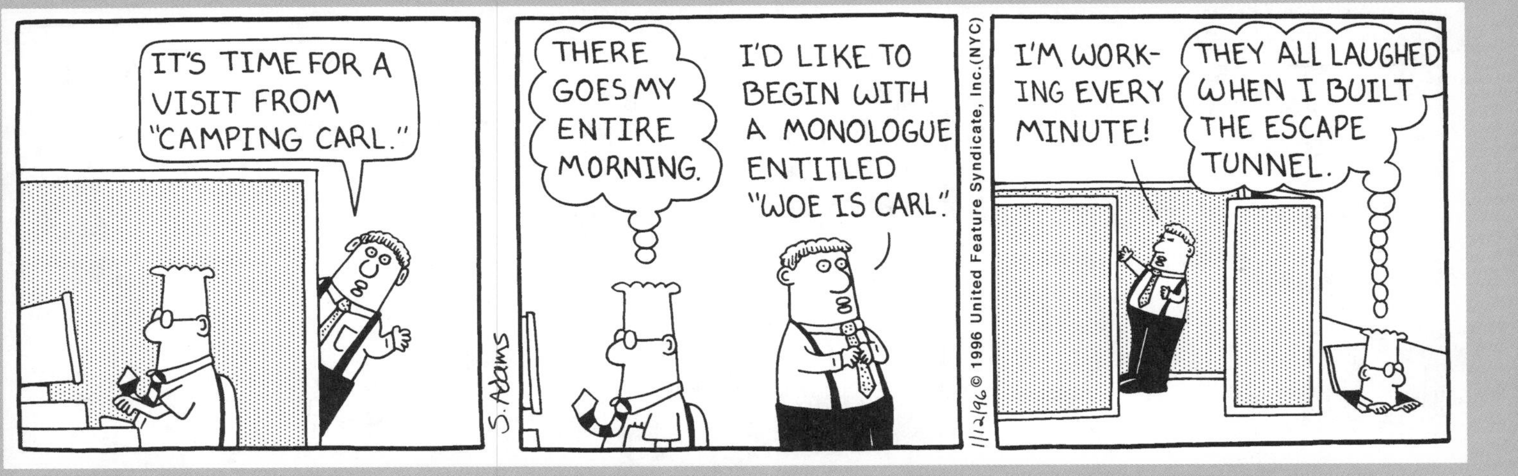
IT'S TIME FOR A VISIT FROM "CAMPING CARL."
THERE GOES MY ENTIRE MORNING.
I'D LIKE TO BEGIN WITH A MONOLOGUE ENTITLED "WOE IS CARL".
I'M WORKING EVERY MINUTE!
THEY ALL LAUGHED WHEN I BUILT THE ESCAPE TUNNEL.
S. Adams
1/12/96 © 1996 United Feature Syndicate, Inc.(NYC)

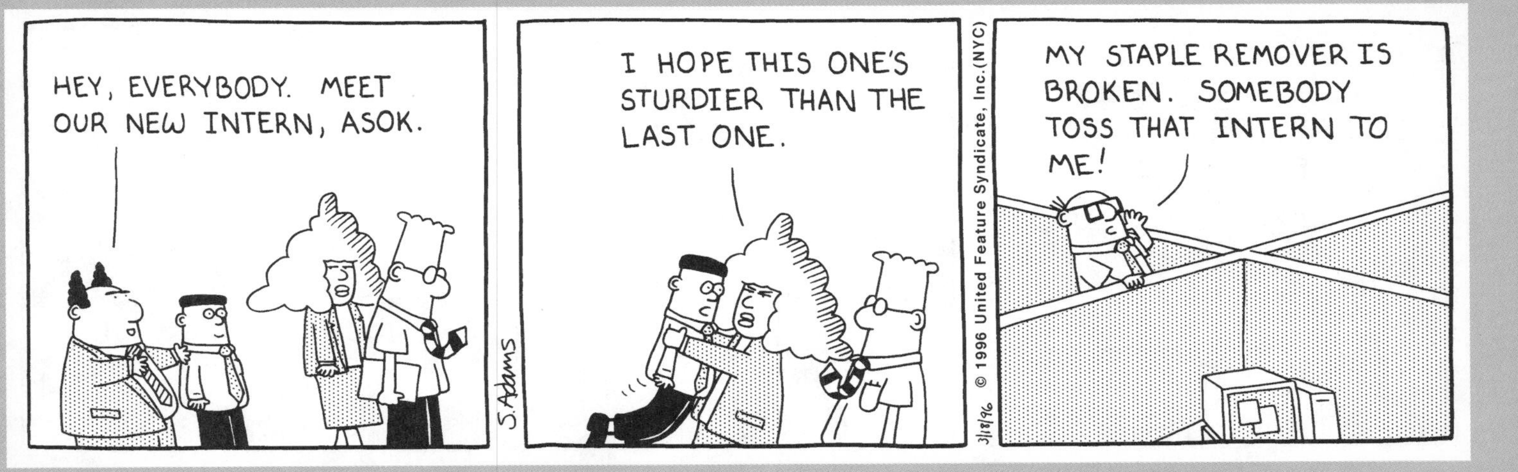
HEY, EVERYBODY. MEET OUR NEW INTERN, ASOK.
I HOPE THIS ONE'S STURDIER THAN THE LAST ONE.
MY STAPLE REMOVER IS BROKEN. SOMEBODY TOSS THAT INTERN TO ME!
S. Adams
3/18/96 © 1996 United Feature Syndicate, Inc.(NYC)

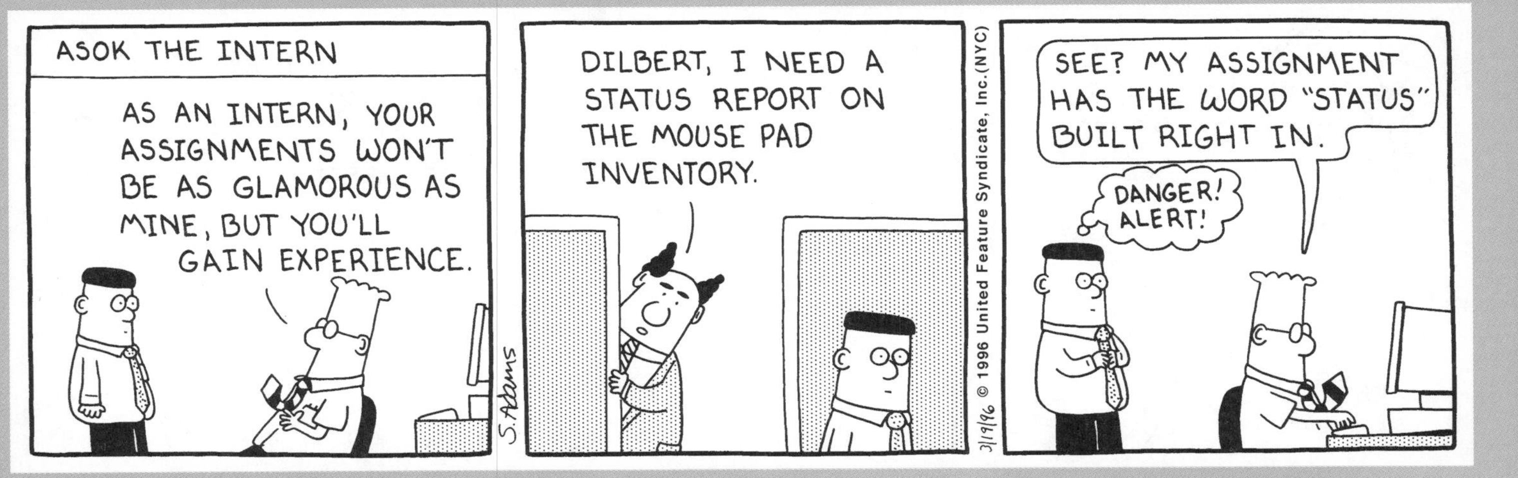
ASOK THE INTERN
AS AN INTERN, YOUR ASSIGNMENTS WON'T BE AS GLAMOROUS AS MINE, BUT YOU'LL GAIN EXPERIENCE.
DILBERT, I NEED A STATUS REPORT ON THE MOUSE PAD INVENTORY.
SEE? MY ASSIGNMENT HAS THE WORD "STATUS" BUILT RIGHT IN.
DANGER! ALERT!
S. Adams
3/19/96 © 1996 United Feature Syndicate, Inc.(NYC)

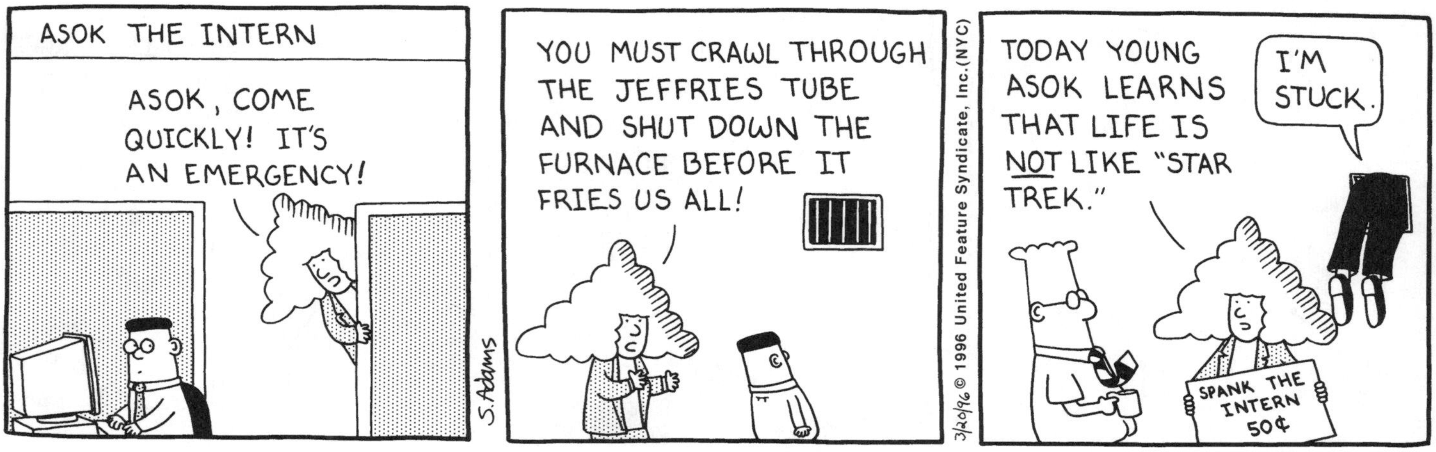
ASOK THE INTERN
ASOK, COME QUICKLY! IT'S AN EMERGENCY!
YOU MUST CRAWL THROUGH THE JEFFRIES TUBE AND SHUT DOWN THE FURNACE BEFORE IT FRIES US ALL!
TODAY YOUNG ASOK LEARNS THAT LIFE IS NOT LIKE "STAR TREK."
I'M STUCK.
SPANK THE INTERN 50¢
S. Adams
3/20/96 © 1996 United Feature Syndicate, Inc.(NYC)

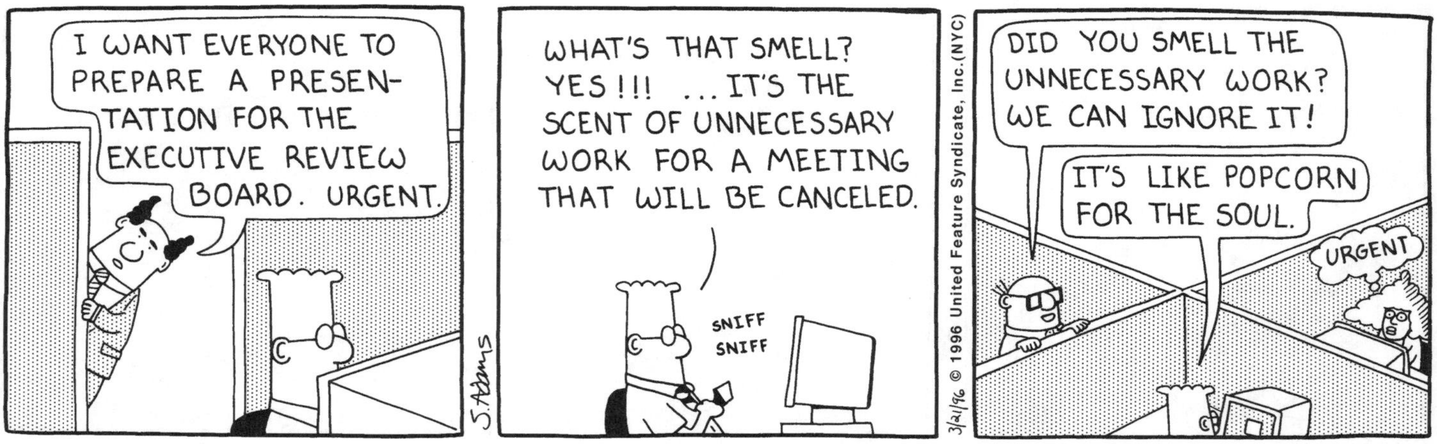
I WANT EVERYONE TO PREPARE A PRESENTATION FOR THE EXECUTIVE REVIEW BOARD. URGENT.
WHAT'S THAT SMELL? YES!!! ...IT'S THE SCENT OF UNNECESSARY WORK FOR A MEETING THAT WILL BE CANCELED.
SNIFF SNIFF
DID YOU SMELL THE UNNECESSARY WORK? WE CAN IGNORE IT!
IT'S LIKE POPCORN FOR THE SOUL.
URGENT
S. Adams
3/21/96 © 1996 United Feature Syndicate, Inc.(NYC)

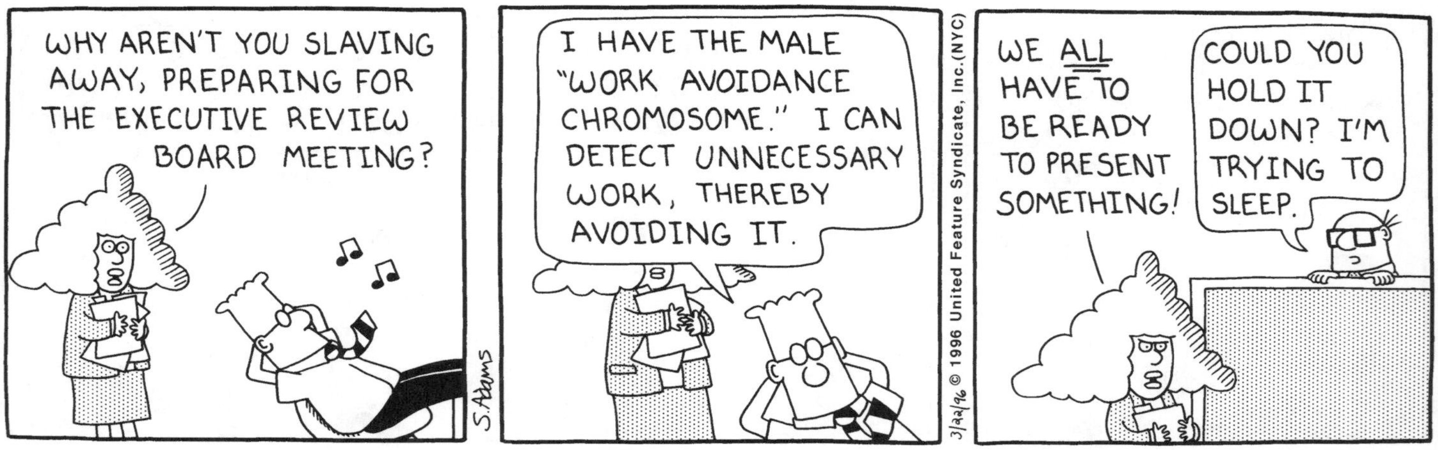
WHY AREN'T YOU SLAVING AWAY, PREPARING FOR THE EXECUTIVE REVIEW BOARD MEETING?
I HAVE THE MALE "WORK AVOIDANCE CHROMOSOME." I CAN DETECT UNNECESSARY WORK, THEREBY AVOIDING IT.
WE ALL HAVE TO BE READY TO PRESENT SOMETHING!
COULD YOU HOLD IT DOWN? I'M TRYING TO SLEEP.
S. Adams
3/22/96 © 1996 United Feature Syndicate, Inc.(NYC)

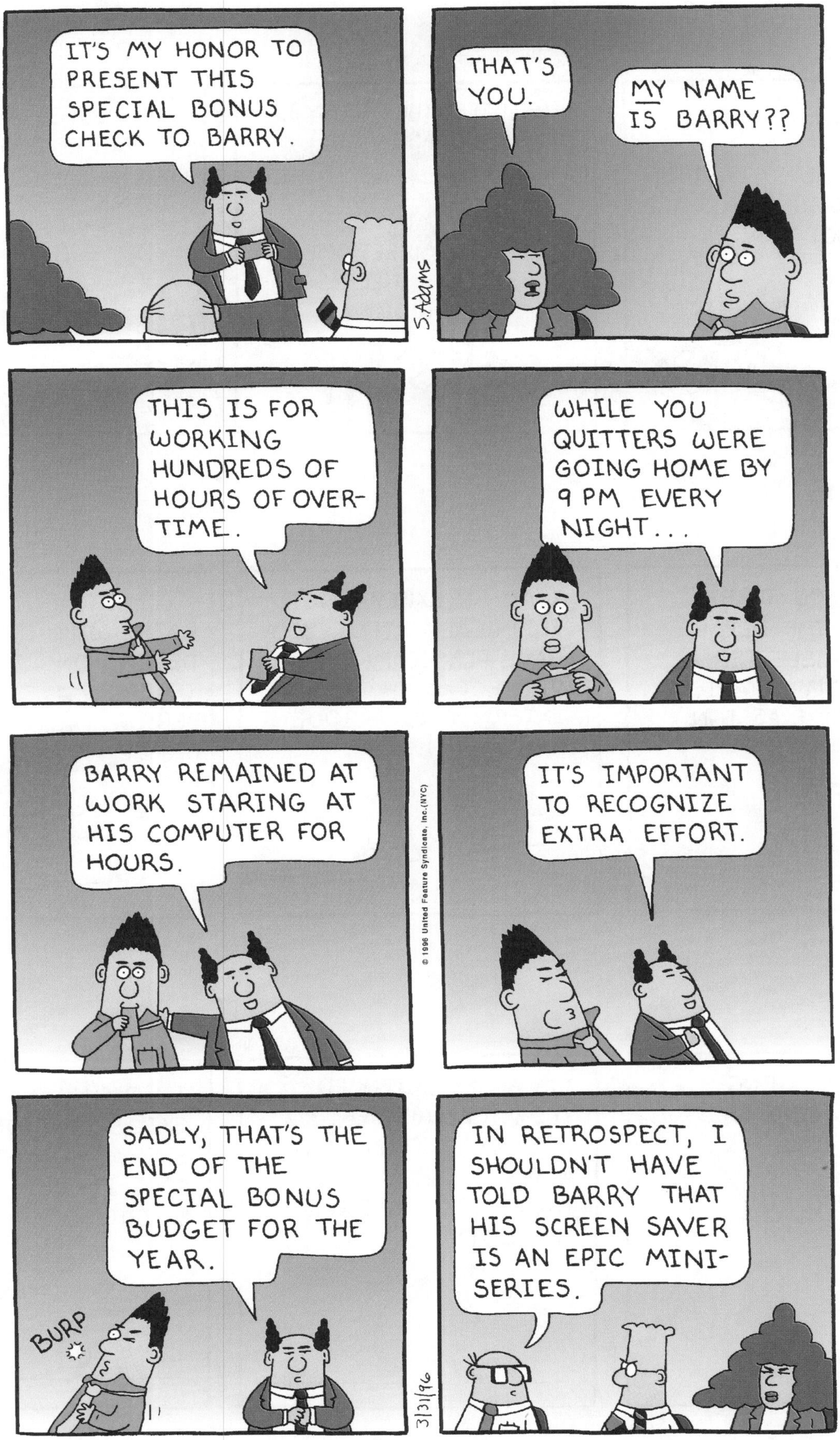
IT'S MY HONOR TO PRESENT THIS SPECIAL BONUS CHECK TO BARRY.
S. Adams
THAT'S YOU.
MY NAME IS BARRY??
THIS IS FOR WORKING HUNDREDS OF HOURS OF OVER-TIME.
WHILE YOU QUITTERS WERE GOING HOME BY 9 PM EVERY NIGHT...
BARRY REMAINED AT WORK STARING AT HIS COMPUTER FOR HOURS.
© 1996 United Feature Syndicate, Inc.(NYC)
IT'S IMPORTANT TO RECOGNIZE EXTRA EFFORT.
SADLY, THAT'S THE END OF THE SPECIAL BONUS BUDGET FOR THE YEAR.
BURP
3/31/96
IN RETROSPECT, I SHOULDN'T HAVE TOLD BARRY THAT HIS SCREEN SAVER IS AN EPIC MINI-SERIES.

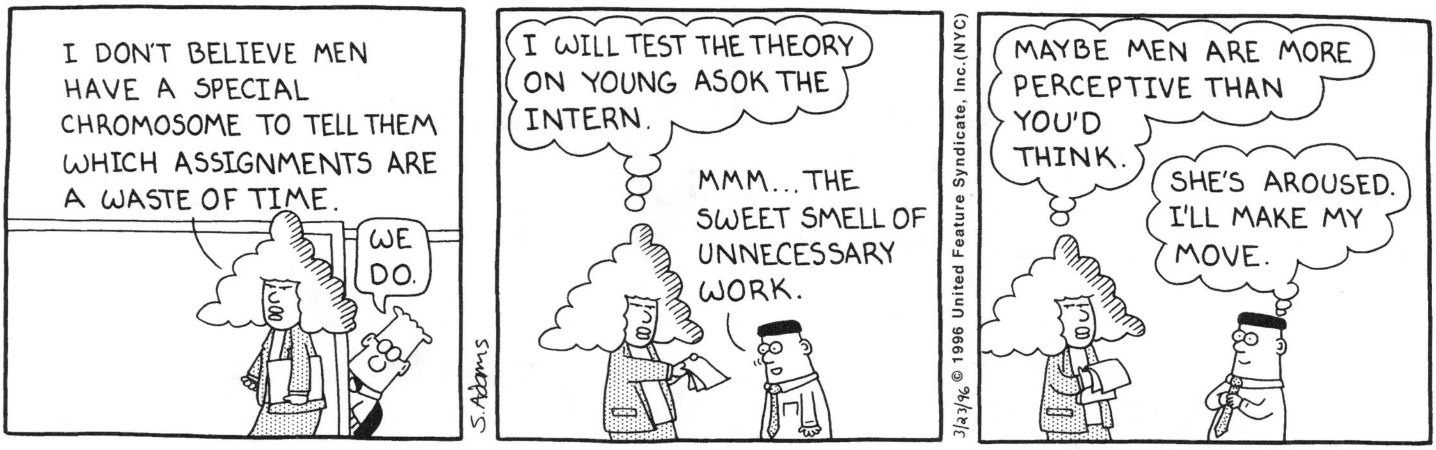
I DON'T BELIEVE MEN HAVE A SPECIAL CHROMOSOME TO TELL THEM WHICH ASSIGNMENTS ARE A WASTE OF TIME.
WE DO.
S. Adams
I WILL TEST THE THEORY ON YOUNG ASOK THE INTERN.
MMM... THE SWEET SMELL OF UNNECESSARY WORK.
3/23/96 © 1996 United Feature Syndicate, Inc.(NYC)
MAYBE MEN ARE MORE PERCEPTIVE THAN YOU'D THINK.
SHE'S AROUSED. I'LL MAKE MY MOVE.

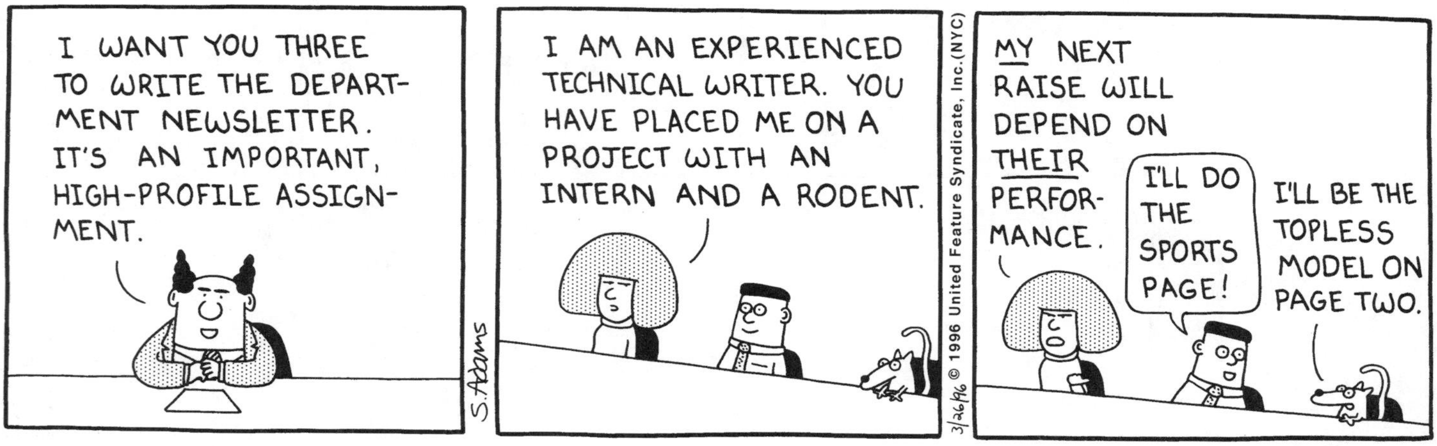
I WANT YOU THREE TO WRITE THE DEPARTMENT NEWSLETTER. IT'S AN IMPORTANT, HIGH-PROFILE ASSIGNMENT.
S. Adams
I AM AN EXPERIENCED TECHNICAL WRITER. YOU HAVE PLACED ME ON A PROJECT WITH AN INTERN AND A RODENT.
3/26/96 © 1996 United Feature Syndicate, Inc.(NYC)
MY NEXT RAISE WILL DEPEND ON THEIR PERFORMANCE.
I'LL DO THE SPORTS PAGE!
I'LL BE THE TOPLESS MODEL ON PAGE TWO.

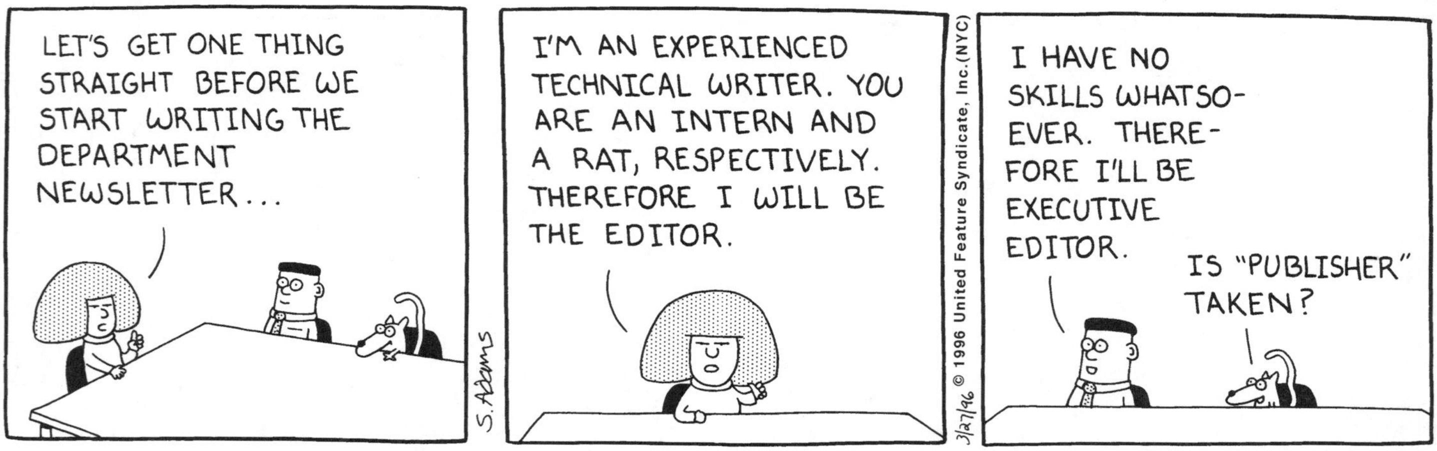
LET'S GET ONE THING STRAIGHT BEFORE WE START WRITING THE DEPARTMENT NEWSLETTER...
S. Adams
I'M AN EXPERIENCED TECHNICAL WRITER. YOU ARE AN INTERN AND A RAT, RESPECTIVELY. THEREFORE I WILL BE THE EDITOR.
3/27/96 © 1996 United Feature Syndicate, Inc.(NYC)
I HAVE NO SKILLS WHATSOEVER. THEREFORE I'LL BE EXECUTIVE EDITOR.
IS "PUBLISHER" TAKEN?

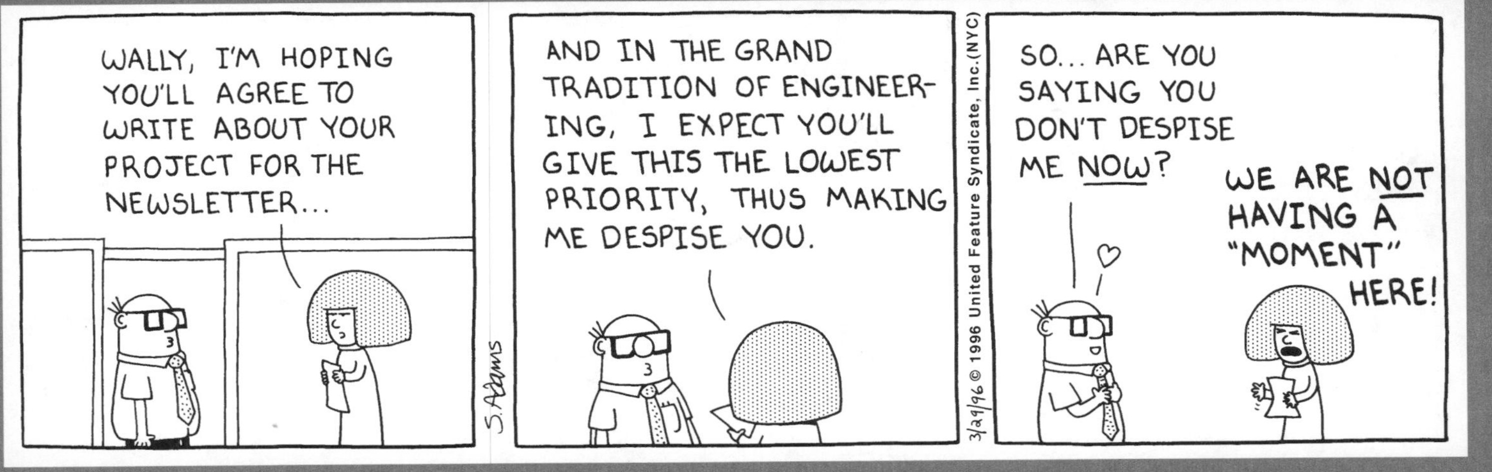
WALLY, I'M HOPING YOU'LL AGREE TO WRITE ABOUT YOUR PROJECT FOR THE NEWSLETTER...
S. Adams
AND IN THE GRAND TRADITION OF ENGINEERING, I EXPECT YOU'LL GIVE THIS THE LOWEST PRIORITY, THUS MAKING ME DESPISE YOU.
3/29/96 © 1996 United Feature Syndicate, Inc.(NYC)
SO... ARE YOU SAYING YOU DON'T DESPISE ME NOW?
WE ARE NOT HAVING A "MOMENT" HERE!

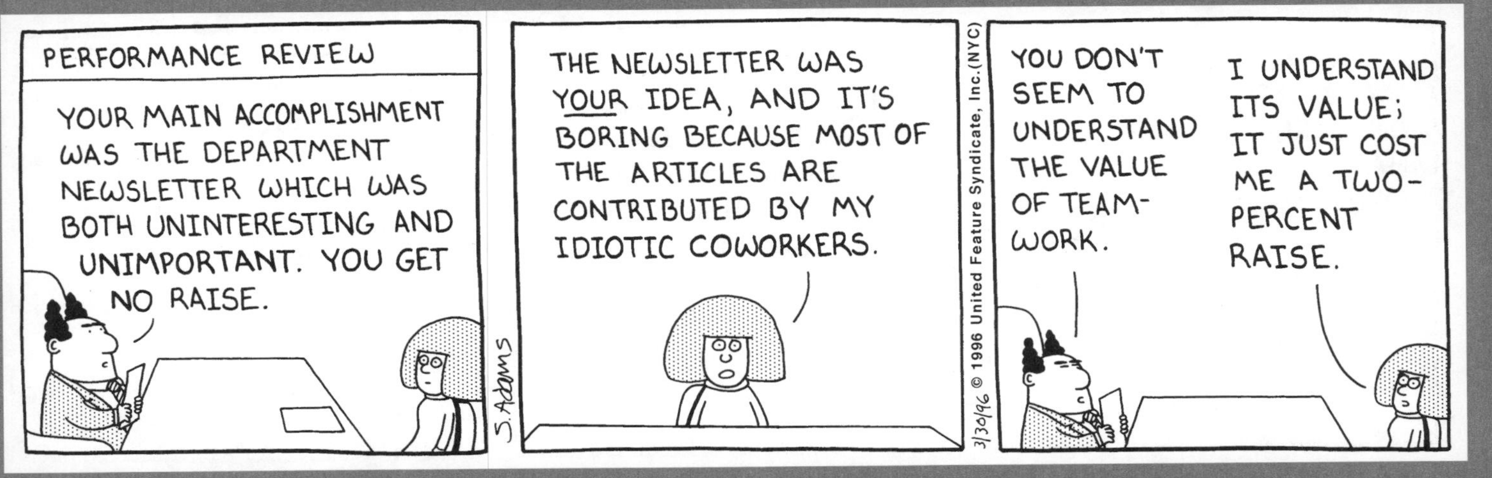
PERFORMANCE REVIEW
YOUR MAIN ACCOMPLISHMENT WAS THE DEPARTMENT NEWSLETTER WHICH WAS BOTH UNINTERESTING AND UNIMPORTANT. YOU GET NO RAISE.
S. Adams
THE NEWSLETTER WAS YOUR IDEA, AND IT'S BORING BECAUSE MOST OF THE ARTICLES ARE CONTRIBUTED BY MY IDIOTIC COWORKERS.
3/30/96 © 1996 United Feature Syndicate, Inc.(NYC)
YOU DON'T SEEM TO UNDERSTAND THE VALUE OF TEAMWORK.
I UNDERSTAND ITS VALUE; IT JUST COST ME A TWO-PERCENT RAISE.

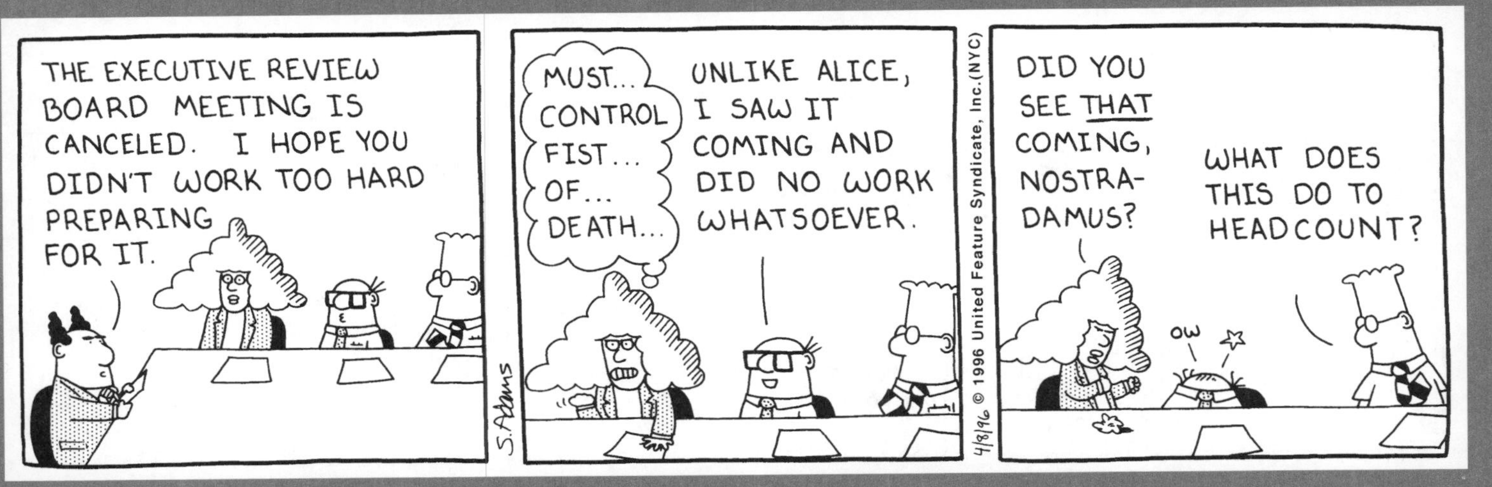
THE EXECUTIVE REVIEW BOARD MEETING IS CANCELED. I HOPE YOU DIDN'T WORK TOO HARD PREPARING FOR IT.
S. Adams
MUST... CONTROL FIST... OF... DEATH...
UNLIKE ALICE, I SAW IT COMING AND DID NO WORK WHATSOEVER.
4/8/96 © 1996 United Feature Syndicate, Inc.(NYC)
DID YOU SEE THAT COMING, NOSTRADAMUS?
OW
WHAT DOES THIS DO TO HEADCOUNT?

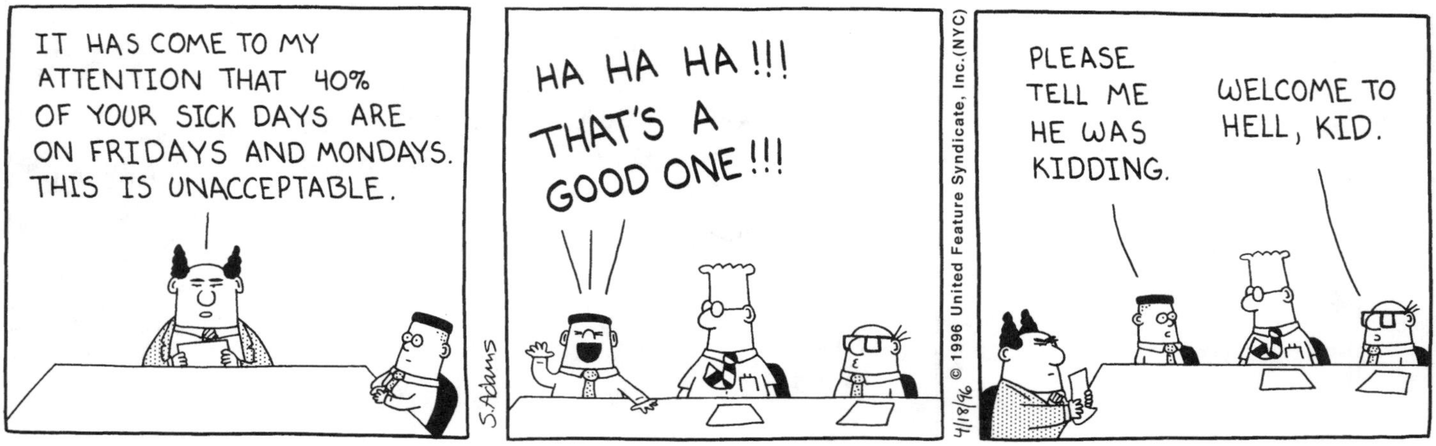
IT HAS COME TO MY ATTENTION THAT 40% OF YOUR SICK DAYS ARE ON FRIDAYS AND MONDAYS. THIS IS UNACCEPTABLE.
S. Adams
HA HA HA!!! THAT'S A GOOD ONE!!!
4/18/96 © 1996 United Feature Syndicate, Inc.(NYC)
PLEASE TELL ME HE WAS KIDDING.
WELCOME TO HELL, KID.

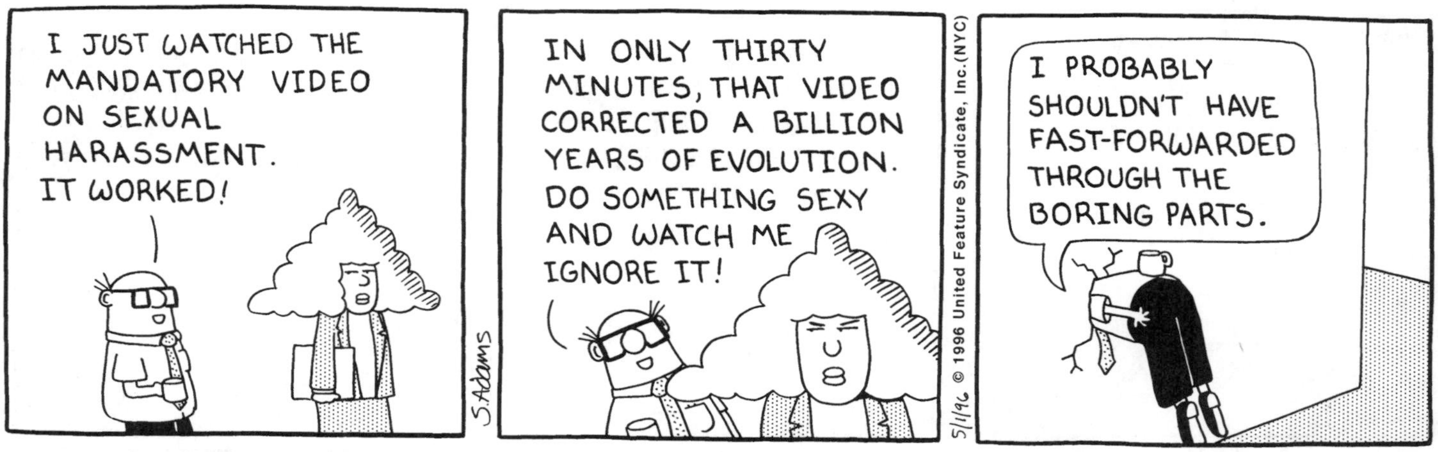
I JUST WATCHED THE MANDATORY VIDEO ON SEXUAL HARASSMENT. IT WORKED!
S. Adams
IN ONLY THIRTY MINUTES, THAT VIDEO CORRECTED A BILLION YEARS OF EVOLUTION. DO SOMETHING SEXY AND WATCH ME IGNORE IT!
5/1/96 © 1996 United Feature Syndicate, Inc.(NYC)
I PROBABLY SHOULDN'T HAVE FAST-FORWARDED THROUGH THE BORING PARTS.

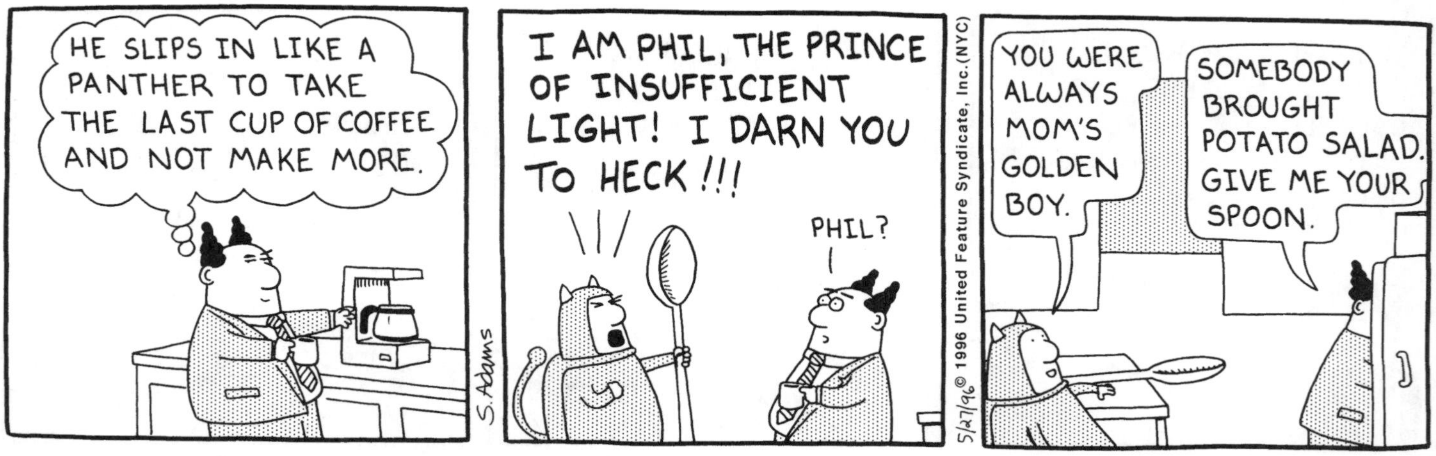
HE SLIPS IN LIKE A PANTHER TO TAKE THE LAST CUP OF COFFEE AND NOT MAKE MORE.
S. Adams
I AM PHIL, THE PRINCE OF INSUFFICIENT LIGHT! I DARN YOU TO HECK!!!
PHIL?
5/27/96 © 1996 United Feature Syndicate, Inc.(NYC)
YOU WERE ALWAYS MOM'S GOLDEN BOY.
SOMEBODY BROUGHT POTATO SALAD. GIVE ME YOUR SPOON.

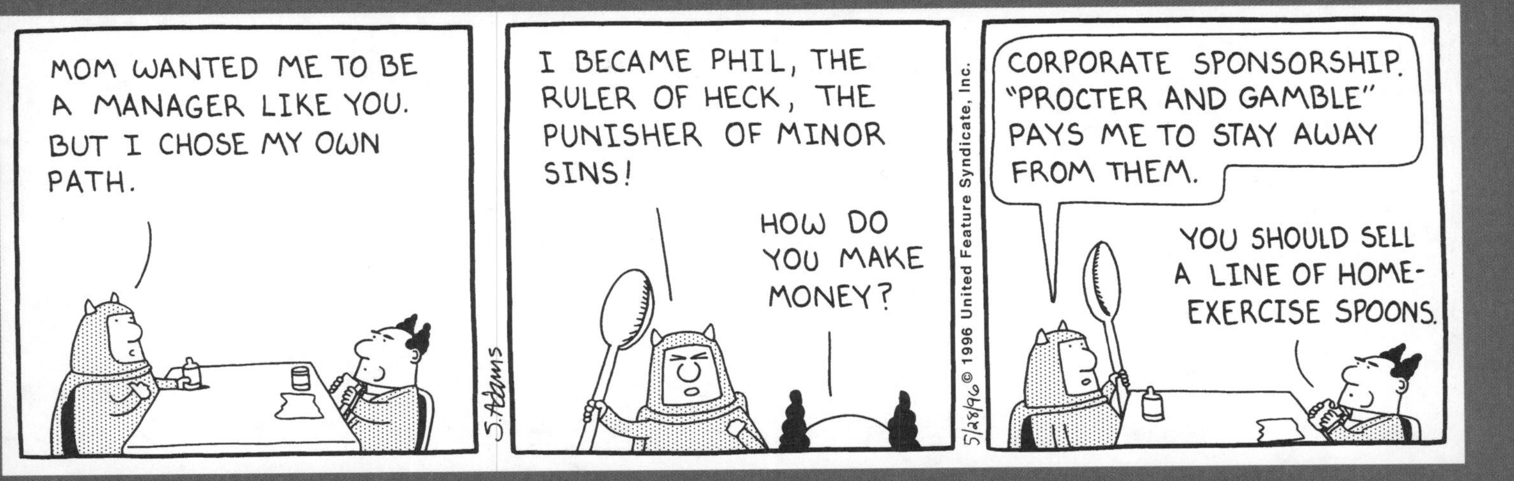
MOM WANTED ME TO BE A MANAGER LIKE YOU. BUT I CHOSE MY OWN PATH.
S. Adams
I BECAME PHIL, THE RULER OF HECK, THE PUNISHER OF MINOR SINS!
HOW DO YOU MAKE MONEY?
5/28/96 © 1996 United Feature Syndicate, Inc.
CORPORATE SPONSORSHIP. "PROCTER AND GAMBLE" PAYS ME TO STAY AWAY FROM THEM.
YOU SHOULD SELL A LINE OF HOME-EXERCISE SPOONS.

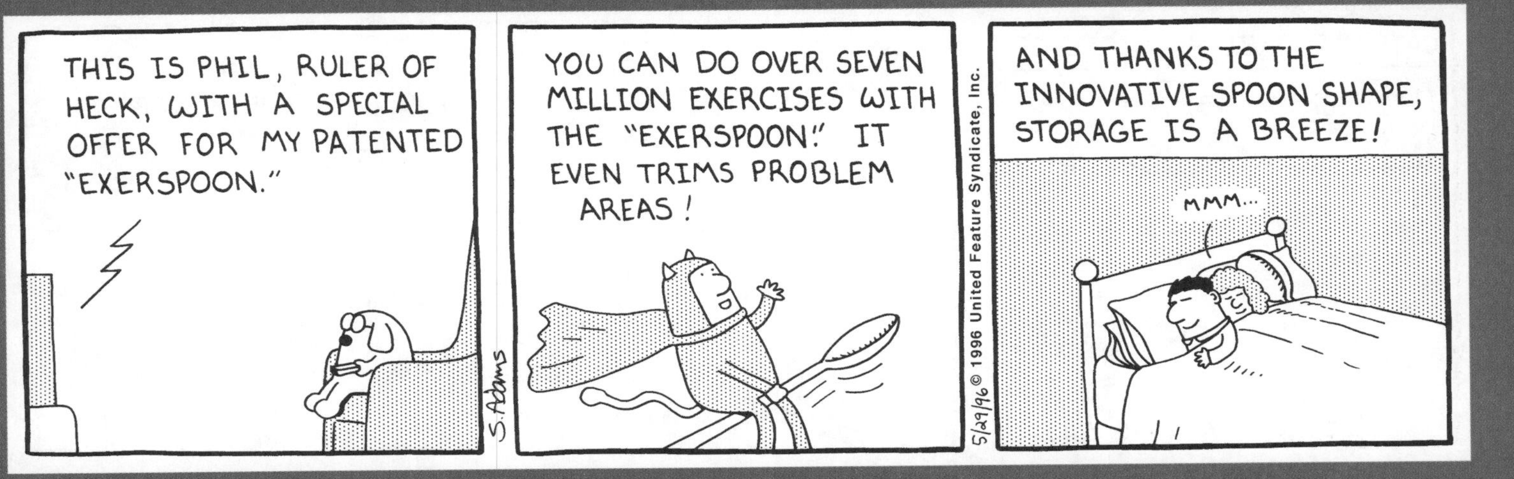
THIS IS PHIL, RULER OF HECK, WITH A SPECIAL OFFER FOR MY PATENTED "EXERSPOON."
S. Adams
YOU CAN DO OVER SEVEN MILLION EXERCISES WITH THE "EXERSPOON." IT EVEN TRIMS PROBLEM AREAS!
5/29/96 © 1996 United Feature Syndicate, Inc.
AND THANKS TO THE INNOVATIVE SPOON SHAPE, STORAGE IS A BREEZE!
MMM...

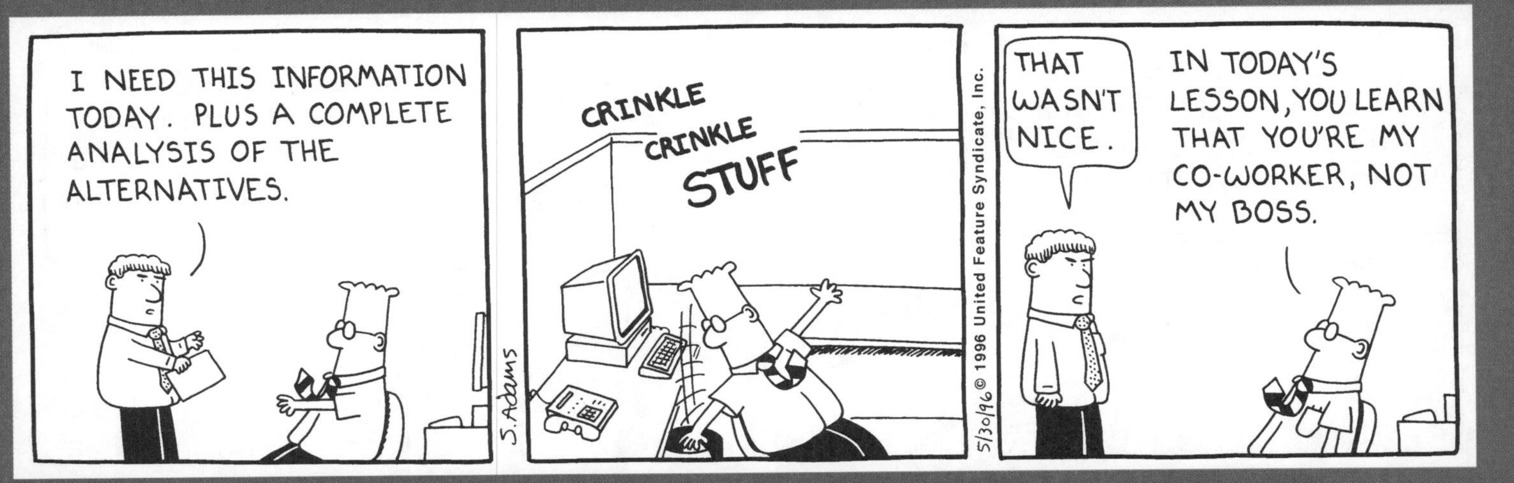
I NEED THIS INFORMATION TODAY. PLUS A COMPLETE ANALYSIS OF THE ALTERNATIVES.
S. Adams
CRINKLE
CRINKLE
STUFF
5/30/96 © 1996 United Feature Syndicate, Inc.
THAT WASN'T NICE.
IN TODAY'S LESSON, YOU LEARN THAT YOU'RE MY CO-WORKER, NOT MY BOSS.

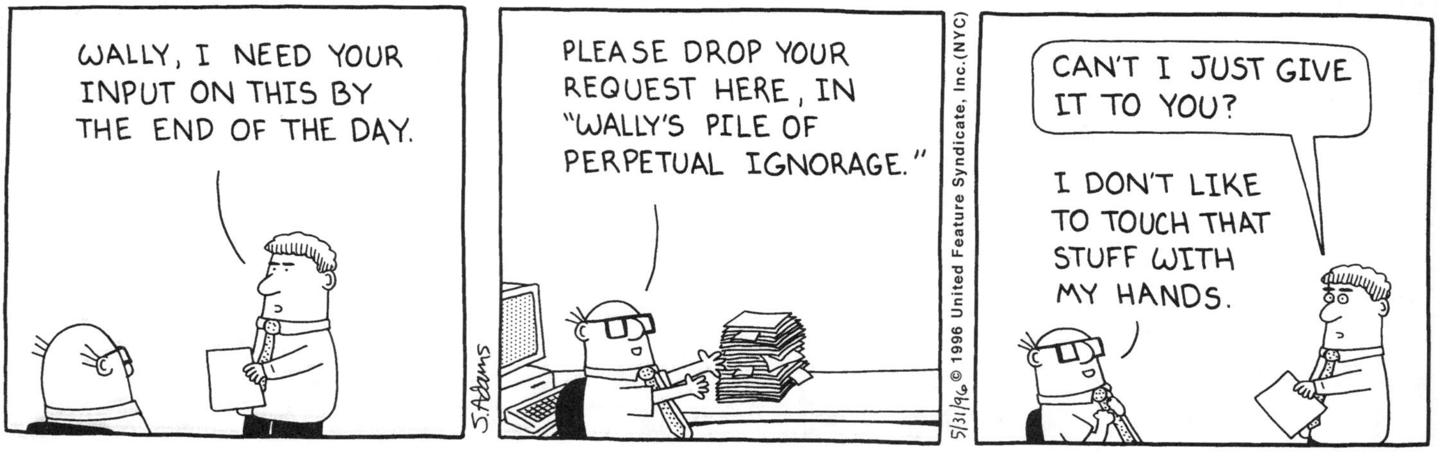
WALLY, I NEED YOUR INPUT ON THIS BY THE END OF THE DAY.
PLEASE DROP YOUR REQUEST HERE, IN "WALLY'S PILE OF PERPETUAL IGNORAGE."
CAN'T I JUST GIVE IT TO YOU?
I DON'T LIKE TO TOUCH THAT STUFF WITH MY HANDS.
S. Adams
5/31/96 © 1996 United Feature Syndicate, Inc. (NYC)

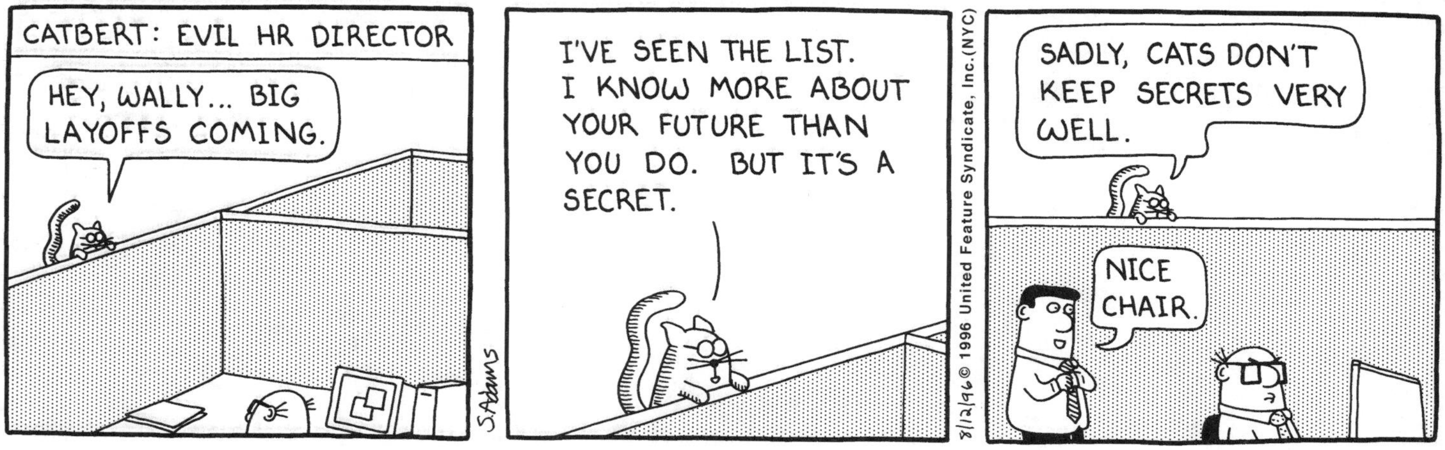
CATBERT: EVIL HR DIRECTOR
HEY, WALLY... BIG LAYOFFS COMING.
I'VE SEEN THE LIST. I KNOW MORE ABOUT YOUR FUTURE THAN YOU DO. BUT IT'S A SECRET.
SADLY, CATS DON'T KEEP SECRETS VERY WELL.
NICE CHAIR.
S. Adams
8/12/96 © 1996 United Feature Syndicate, Inc. (NYC)

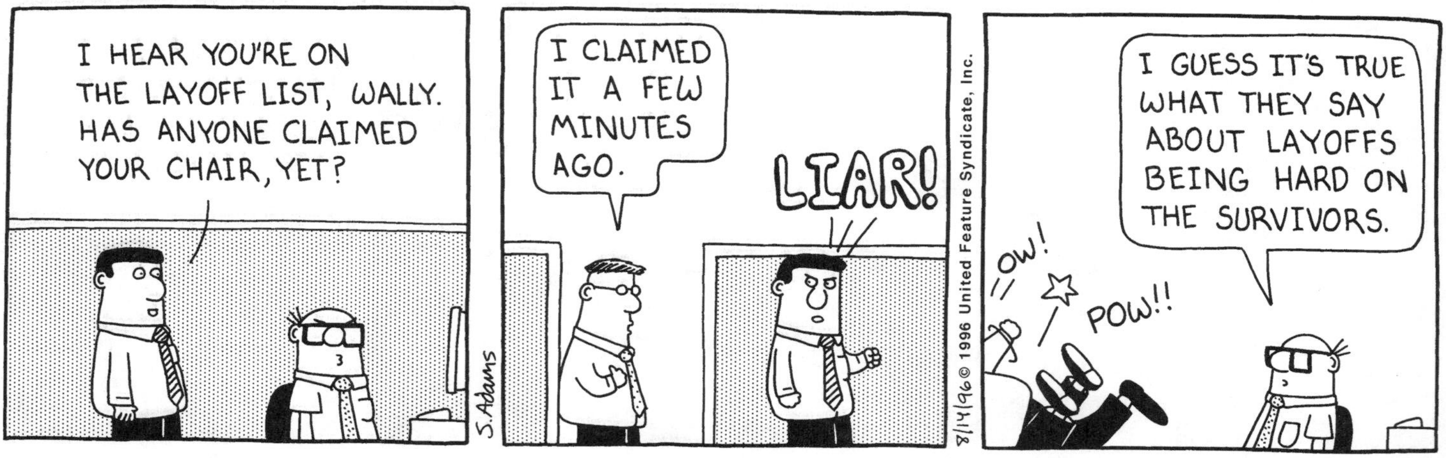
I HEAR YOU'RE ON THE LAYOFF LIST, WALLY. HAS ANYONE CLAIMED YOUR CHAIR, YET?
I CLAIMED IT A FEW MINUTES AGO.
LIAR!
OW!
POW!!
I GUESS IT'S TRUE WHAT THEY SAY ABOUT LAYOFFS BEING HARD ON THE SURVIVORS.
S. Adams
8/14/96 © 1996 United Feature Syndicate, Inc.

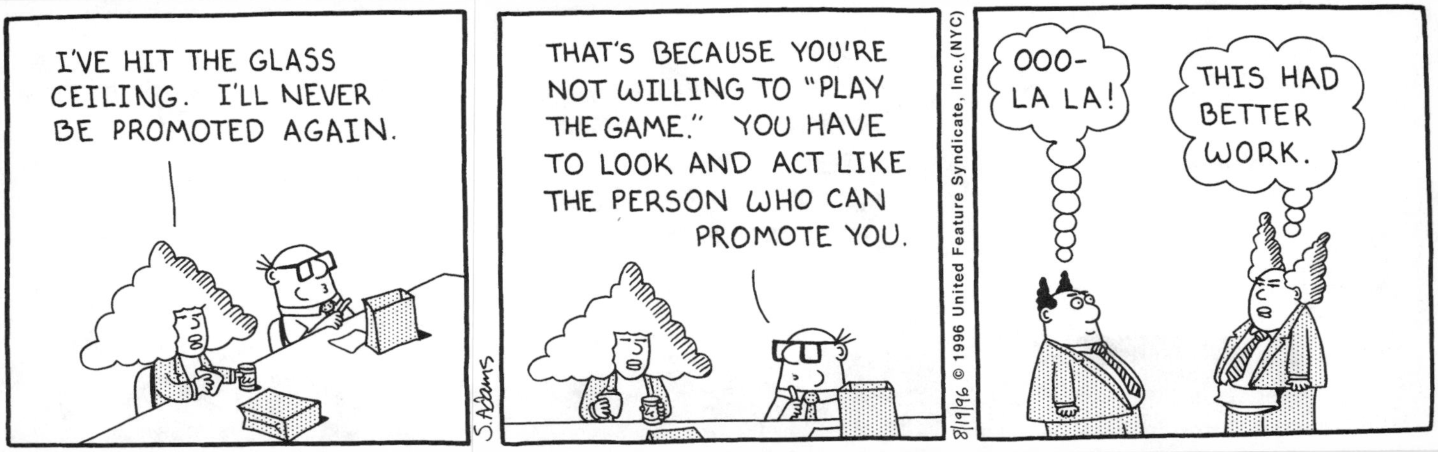
I'VE HIT THE GLASS CEILING. I'LL NEVER BE PROMOTED AGAIN.
THAT'S BECAUSE YOU'RE NOT WILLING TO "PLAY THE GAME." YOU HAVE TO LOOK AND ACT LIKE THE PERSON WHO CAN PROMOTE YOU.
OOO- LA LA!
THIS HAD BETTER WORK.
S. Adams
8/19/96 © 1996 United Feature Syndicate, Inc.(NYC)

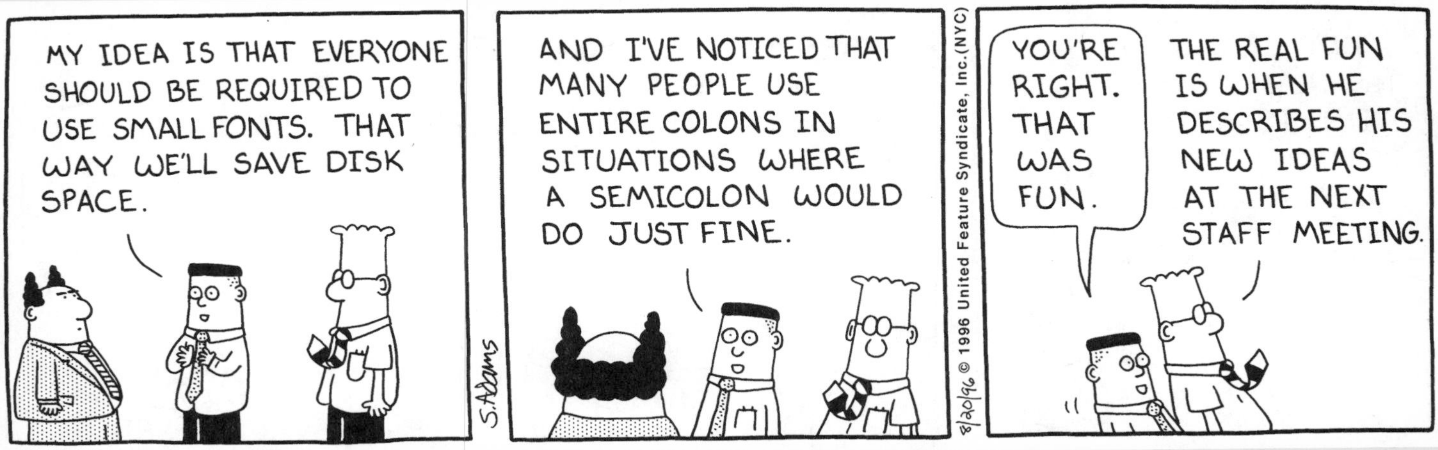
MY IDEA IS THAT EVERYONE SHOULD BE REQUIRED TO USE SMALL FONTS. THAT WAY WE'LL SAVE DISK SPACE.
AND I'VE NOTICED THAT MANY PEOPLE USE ENTIRE COLONS IN SITUATIONS WHERE A SEMICOLON WOULD DO JUST FINE.
YOU'RE RIGHT. THAT WAS FUN.
THE REAL FUN IS WHEN HE DESCRIBES HIS NEW IDEAS AT THE NEXT STAFF MEETING.
S. Adams
8/20/96 © 1996 United Feature Syndicate, Inc.(NYC)

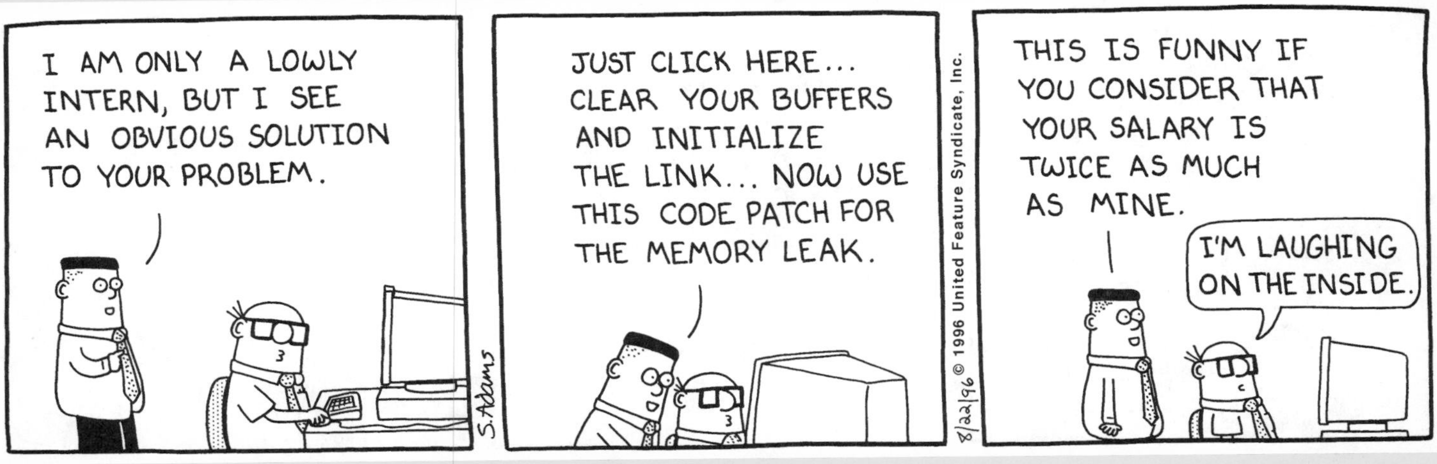
I AM ONLY A LOWLY INTERN, BUT I SEE AN OBVIOUS SOLUTION TO YOUR PROBLEM.
JUST CLICK HERE... CLEAR YOUR BUFFERS AND INITIALIZE THE LINK... NOW USE THIS CODE PATCH FOR THE MEMORY LEAK.
THIS IS FUNNY IF YOU CONSIDER THAT YOUR SALARY IS TWICE AS MUCH AS MINE.
I'M LAUGHING ON THE INSIDE.
S. Adams
8/22/96 © 1996 United Feature Syndicate, Inc.

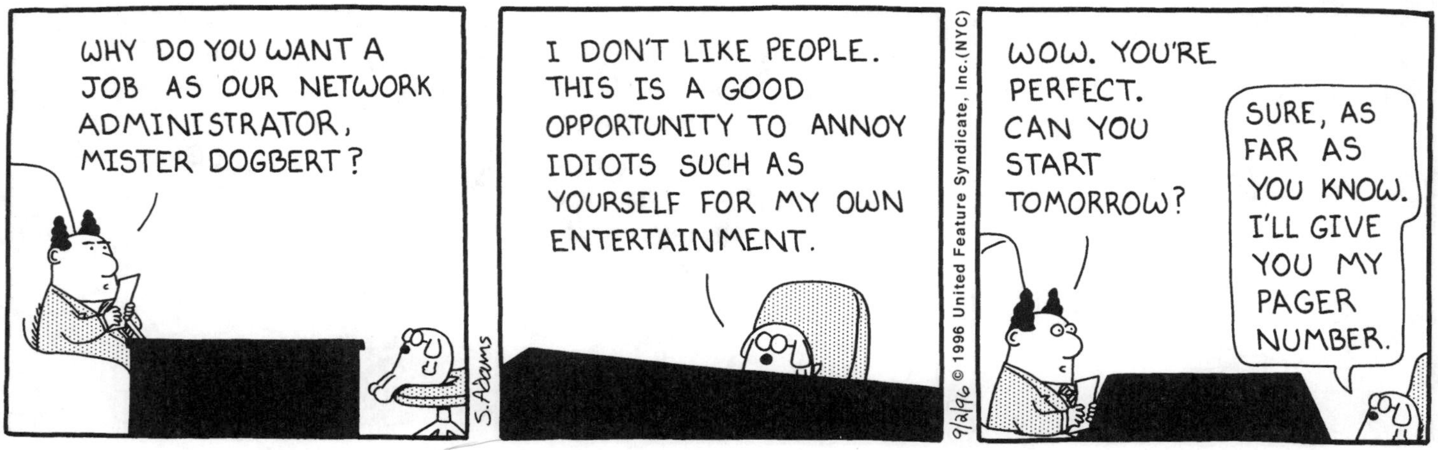
WHY DO YOU WANT A JOB AS OUR NETWORK ADMINISTRATOR, MISTER DOGBERT?
I DON'T LIKE PEOPLE. THIS IS A GOOD OPPORTUNITY TO ANNOY IDIOTS SUCH AS YOURSELF FOR MY OWN ENTERTAINMENT.
WOW. YOU'RE PERFECT. CAN YOU START TOMORROW?
SURE, AS FAR AS YOU KNOW. I'LL GIVE YOU MY PAGER NUMBER.
S. Adams
9/2/96 © 1996 United Feature Syndicate, Inc.(NYC)

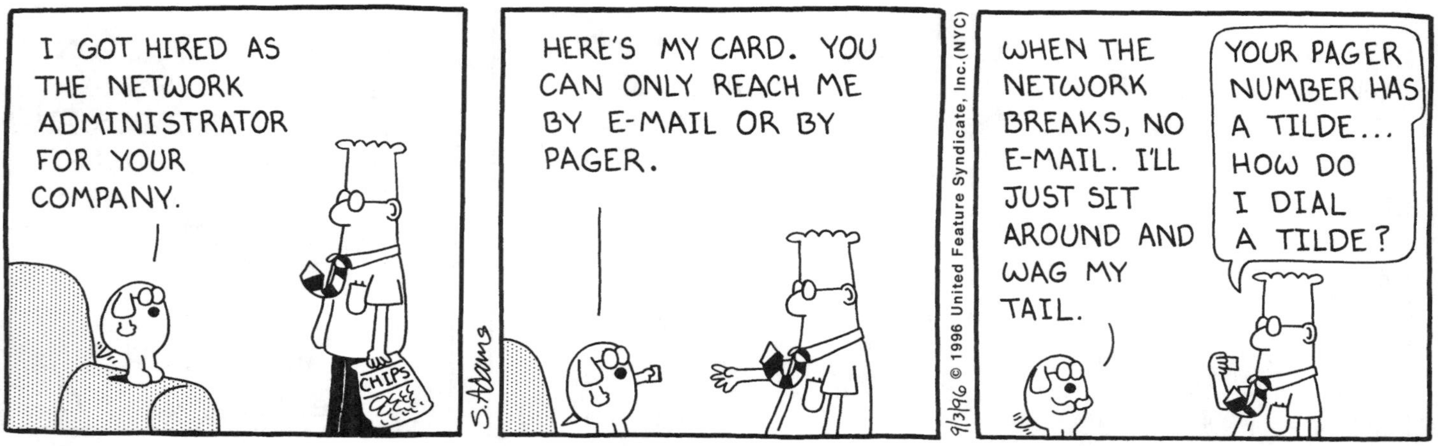
I GOT HIRED AS THE NETWORK ADMINISTRATOR FOR YOUR COMPANY.
CHIPS
HERE'S MY CARD. YOU CAN ONLY REACH ME BY E-MAIL OR BY PAGER.
WHEN THE NETWORK BREAKS, NO E-MAIL. I'LL JUST SIT AROUND AND WAG MY TAIL.
YOUR PAGER NUMBER HAS A TILDE... HOW DO I DIAL A TILDE?
S. Adams
9/3/96 © 1996 United Feature Syndicate, Inc.(NYC)

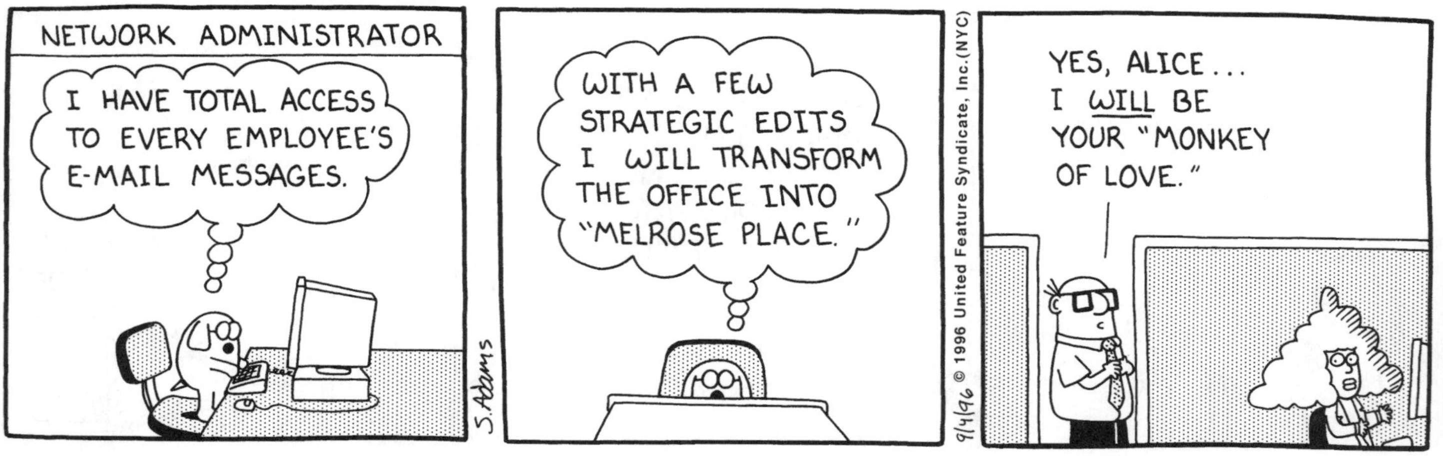
NETWORK ADMINISTRATOR
I HAVE TOTAL ACCESS TO EVERY EMPLOYEE'S E-MAIL MESSAGES.
WITH A FEW STRATEGIC EDITS I WILL TRANSFORM THE OFFICE INTO "MELROSE PLACE."
YES, ALICE... I WILL BE YOUR "MONKEY OF LOVE."
S. Adams
9/4/96 © 1996 United Feature Syndicate, Inc.(NYC)

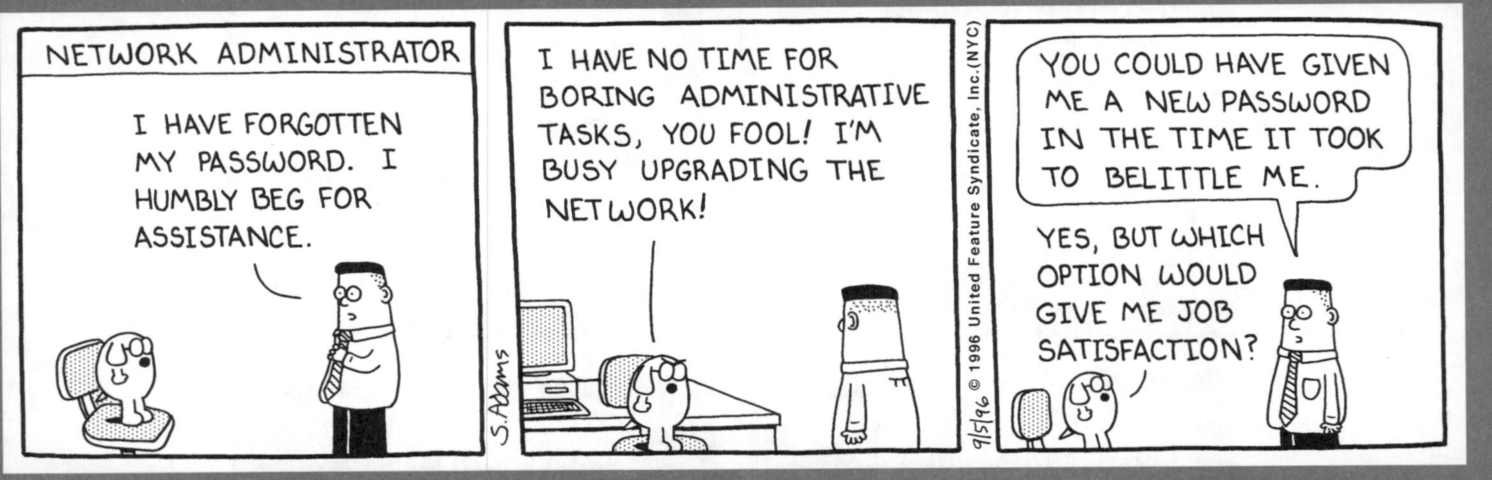
NETWORK ADMINISTRATOR
I HAVE FORGOTTEN MY PASSWORD. I HUMBLY BEG FOR ASSISTANCE.
I HAVE NO TIME FOR BORING ADMINISTRATIVE TASKS, YOU FOOL! I'M BUSY UPGRADING THE NETWORK!
YOU COULD HAVE GIVEN ME A NEW PASSWORD IN THE TIME IT TOOK TO BELITTLE ME.
YES, BUT WHICH OPTION WOULD GIVE ME JOB SATISFACTION?
S. Adams
9/5/96 © 1996 United Feature Syndicate, Inc.(NYC)

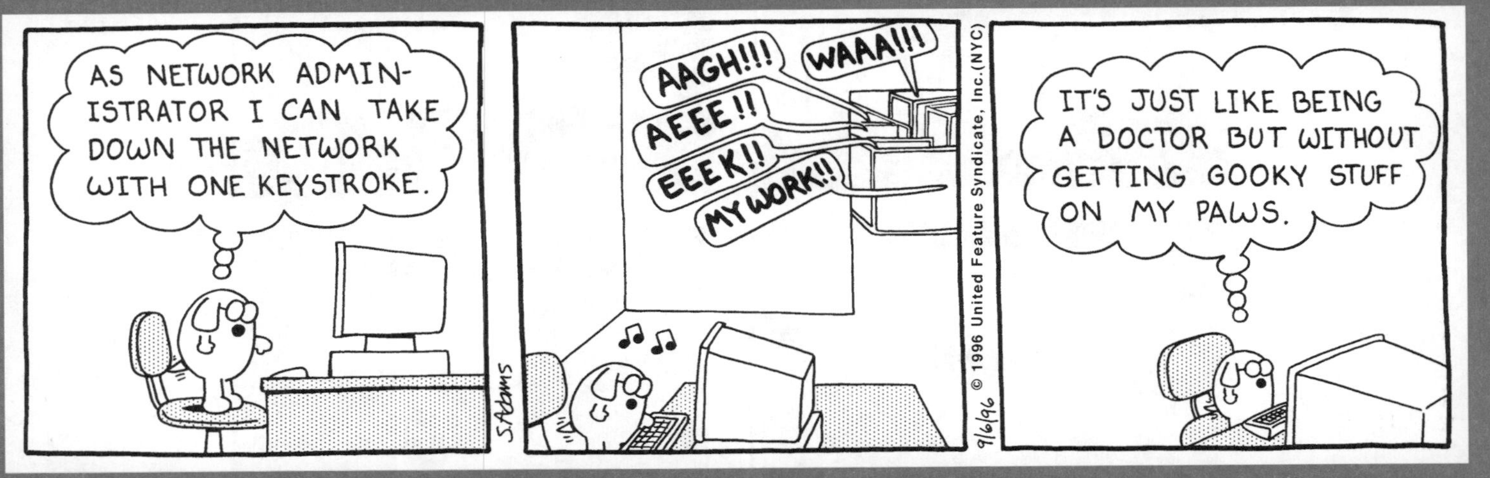
AS NETWORK ADMINISTRATOR I CAN TAKE DOWN THE NETWORK WITH ONE KEYSTROKE.
AAGH!!!
WAAA!!!
AEEE!!
EEEK!!
MY WORK!!
IT'S JUST LIKE BEING A DOCTOR BUT WITHOUT GETTING GOOKY STUFF ON MY PAWS.
S. Adams
9/6/96 © 1996 United Feature Syndicate, Inc.(NYC)

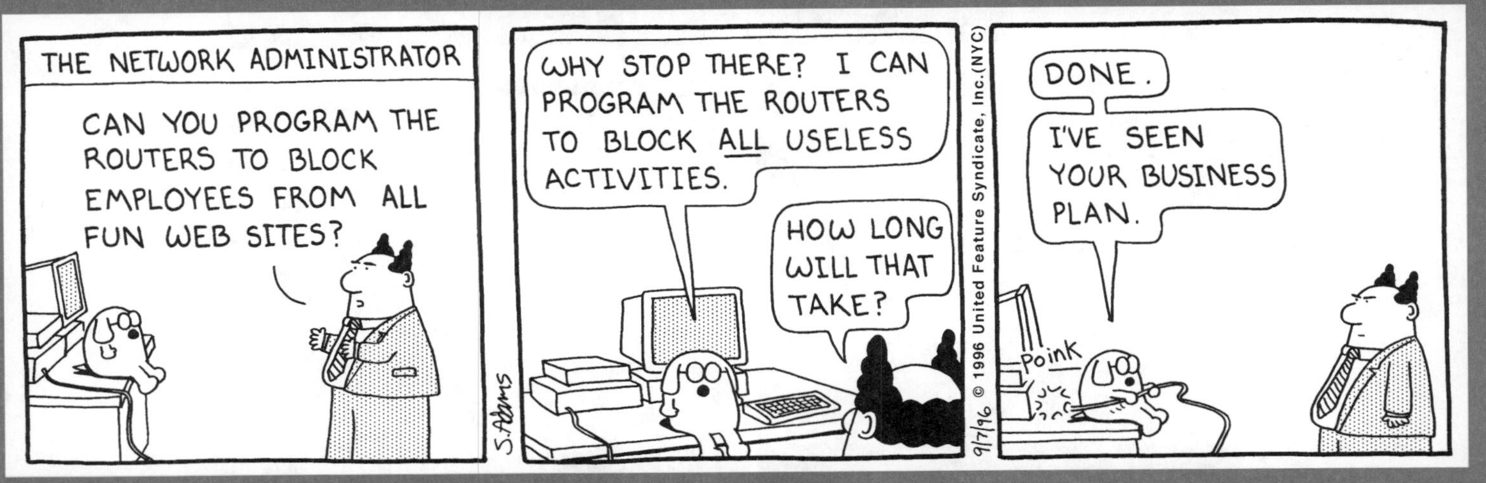
THE NETWORK ADMINISTRATOR
CAN YOU PROGRAM THE ROUTERS TO BLOCK EMPLOYEES FROM ALL FUN WEB SITES?
WHY STOP THERE? I CAN PROGRAM THE ROUTERS TO BLOCK ALL USELESS ACTIVITIES.
HOW LONG WILL THAT TAKE?
DONE.
I'VE SEEN YOUR BUSINESS PLAN.
Poink
S. Adams
9/7/96 © 1996 United Feature Syndicate, Inc.(NYC)

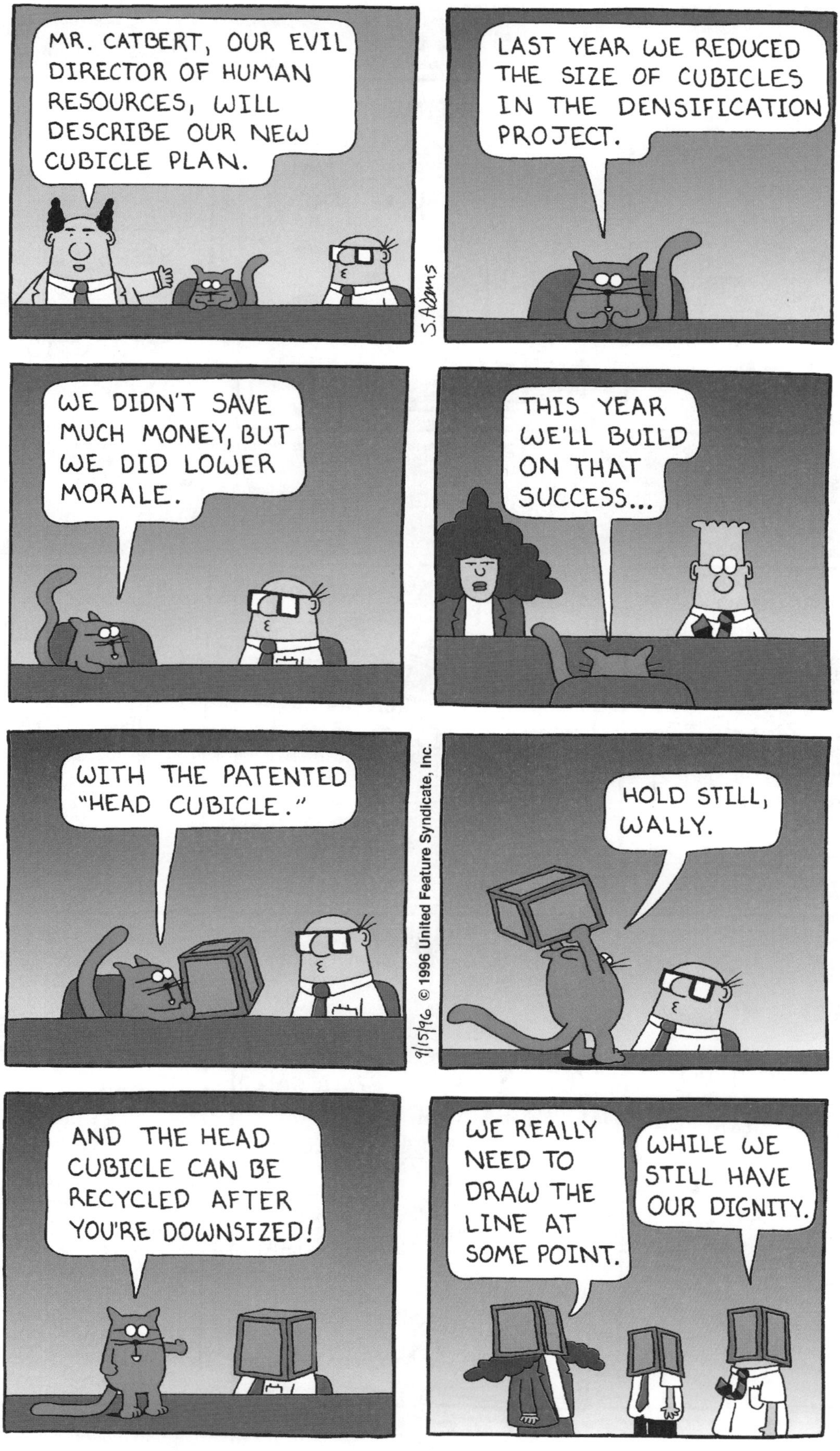
MR. CATBERT, OUR EVIL DIRECTOR OF HUMAN RESOURCES, WILL DESCRIBE OUR NEW CUBICLE PLAN.
S. Adams
LAST YEAR WE REDUCED THE SIZE OF CUBICLES IN THE DENSIFICATION PROJECT.
WE DIDN'T SAVE MUCH MONEY, BUT WE DID LOWER MORALE.
THIS YEAR WE'LL BUILD ON THAT SUCCESS...
WITH THE PATENTED "HEAD CUBICLE."
9/15/96 © 1996 United Feature Syndicate, Inc.
HOLD STILL, WALLY.
AND THE HEAD CUBICLE CAN BE RECYCLED AFTER YOU'RE DOWNSIZED!
WE REALLY NEED TO DRAW THE LINE AT SOME POINT.
WHILE WE STILL HAVE OUR DIGNITY.

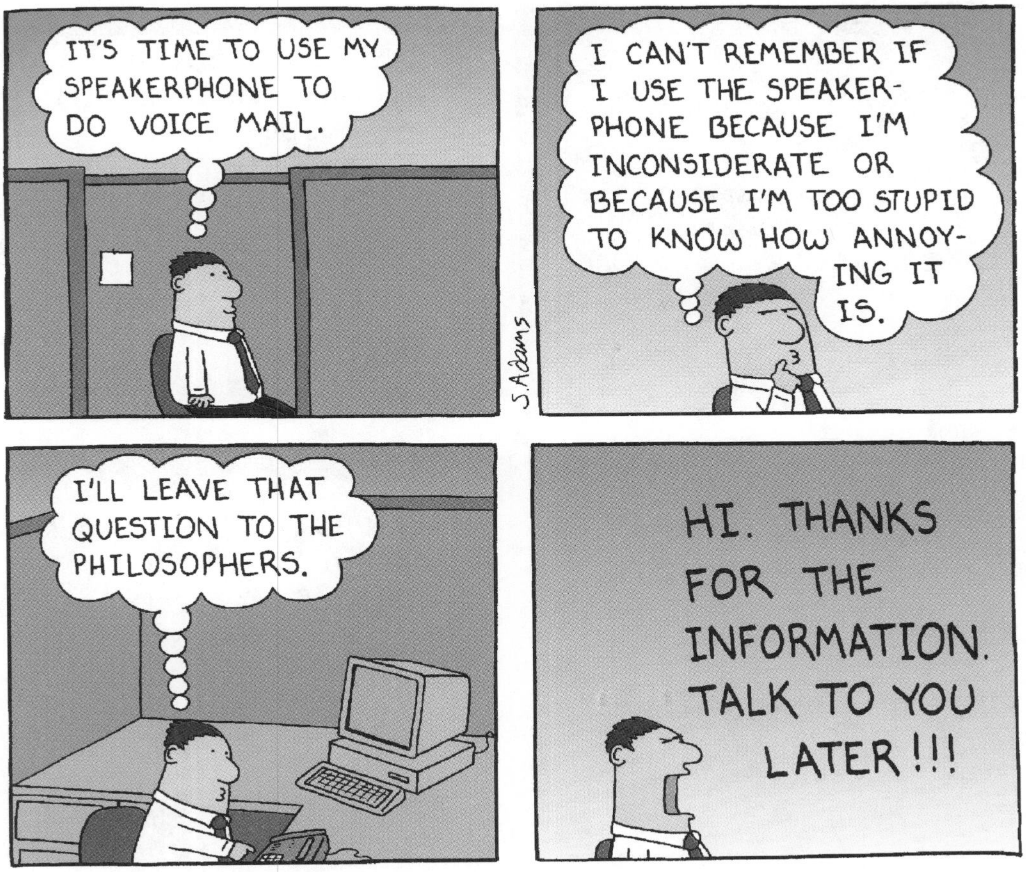
IT'S TIME TO USE MY SPEAKERPHONE TO DO VOICE MAIL.
I CAN'T REMEMBER IF I USE THE SPEAKER-PHONE BECAUSE I'M INCONSIDERATE OR BECAUSE I'M TOO STUPID TO KNOW HOW ANNOY-ING IT IS.
S. Adams
I'LL LEAVE THAT QUESTION TO THE PHILOSOPHERS.
HI. THANKS FOR THE INFORMATION. TALK TO YOU LATER!!!

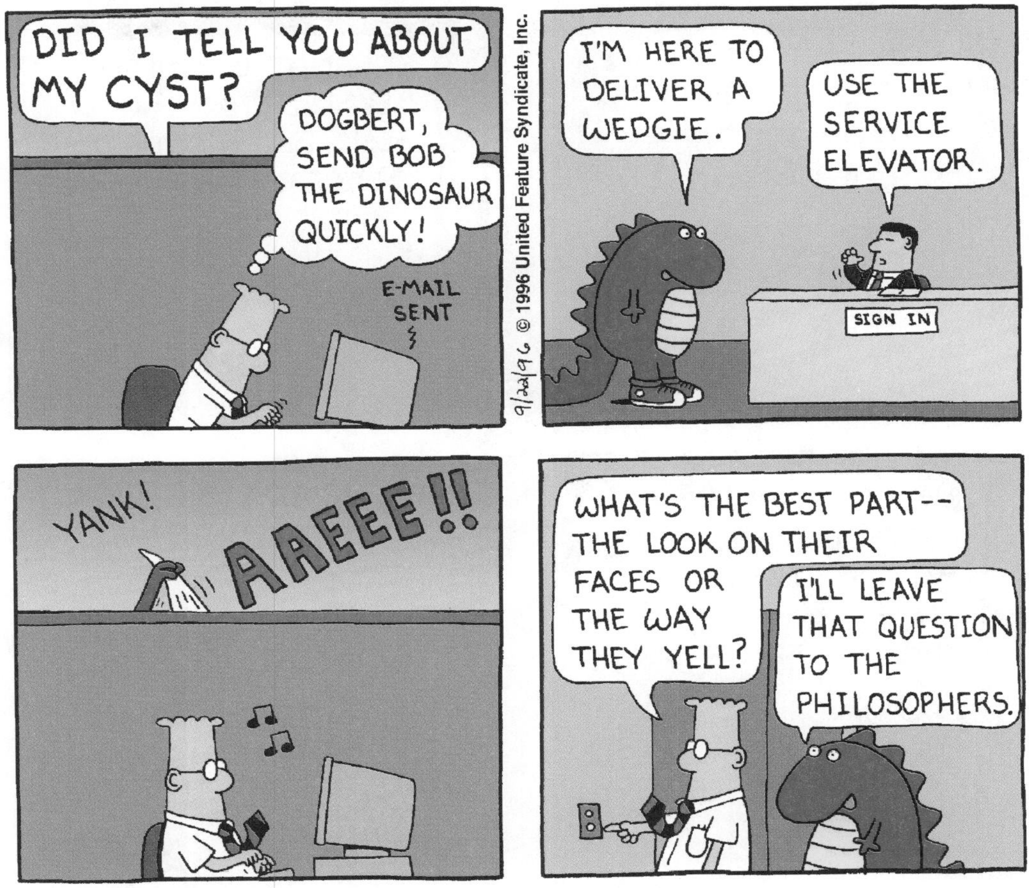
DID I TELL YOU ABOUT MY CYST?
DOGBERT, SEND BOB THE DINOSAUR QUICKLY!
E-MAIL SENT
I'M HERE TO DELIVER A WEDGIE.
USE THE SERVICE ELEVATOR.
SIGN IN
YANK!
AAEEE!!
WHAT'S THE BEST PART-- THE LOOK ON THEIR FACES OR THE WAY THEY YELL?
I'LL LEAVE THAT QUESTION TO THE PHILOSOPHERS.

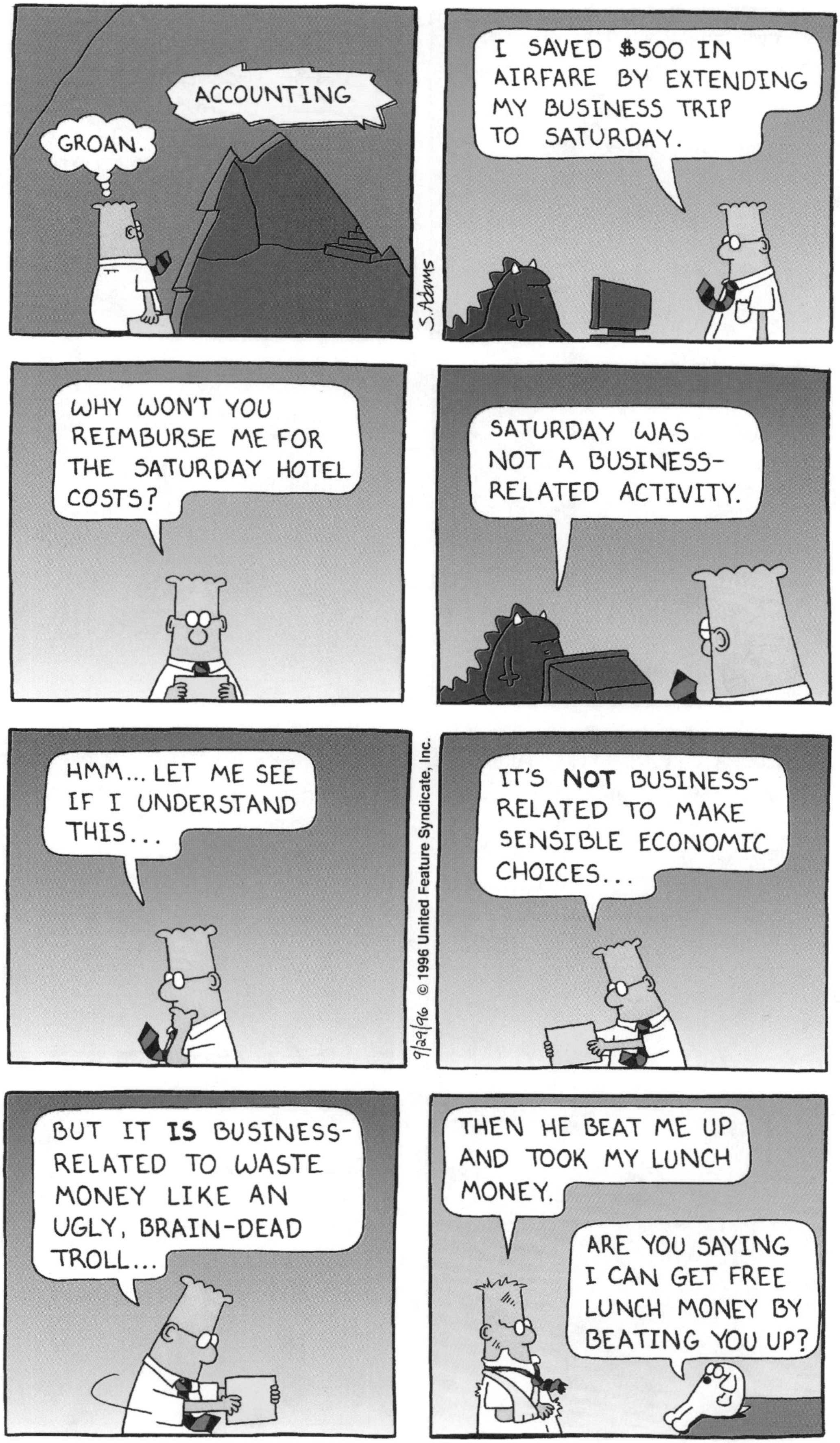
ACCOUNTING
GROAN.
I SAVED $500 IN AIRFARE BY EXTENDING MY BUSINESS TRIP TO SATURDAY.
S. Adams
WHY WON'T YOU REIMBURSE ME FOR THE SATURDAY HOTEL COSTS?
SATURDAY WAS NOT A BUSINESS-RELATED ACTIVITY.
HMM... LET ME SEE IF I UNDERSTAND THIS...
9/29/96 © 1996 United Feature Syndicate, Inc.
IT'S **NOT** BUSINESS-RELATED TO MAKE SENSIBLE ECONOMIC CHOICES...
BUT IT **IS** BUSINESS-RELATED TO WASTE MONEY LIKE AN UGLY, BRAIN-DEAD TROLL...
THEN HE BEAT ME UP AND TOOK MY LUNCH MONEY.
ARE YOU SAYING I CAN GET FREE LUNCH MONEY BY BEATING YOU UP?

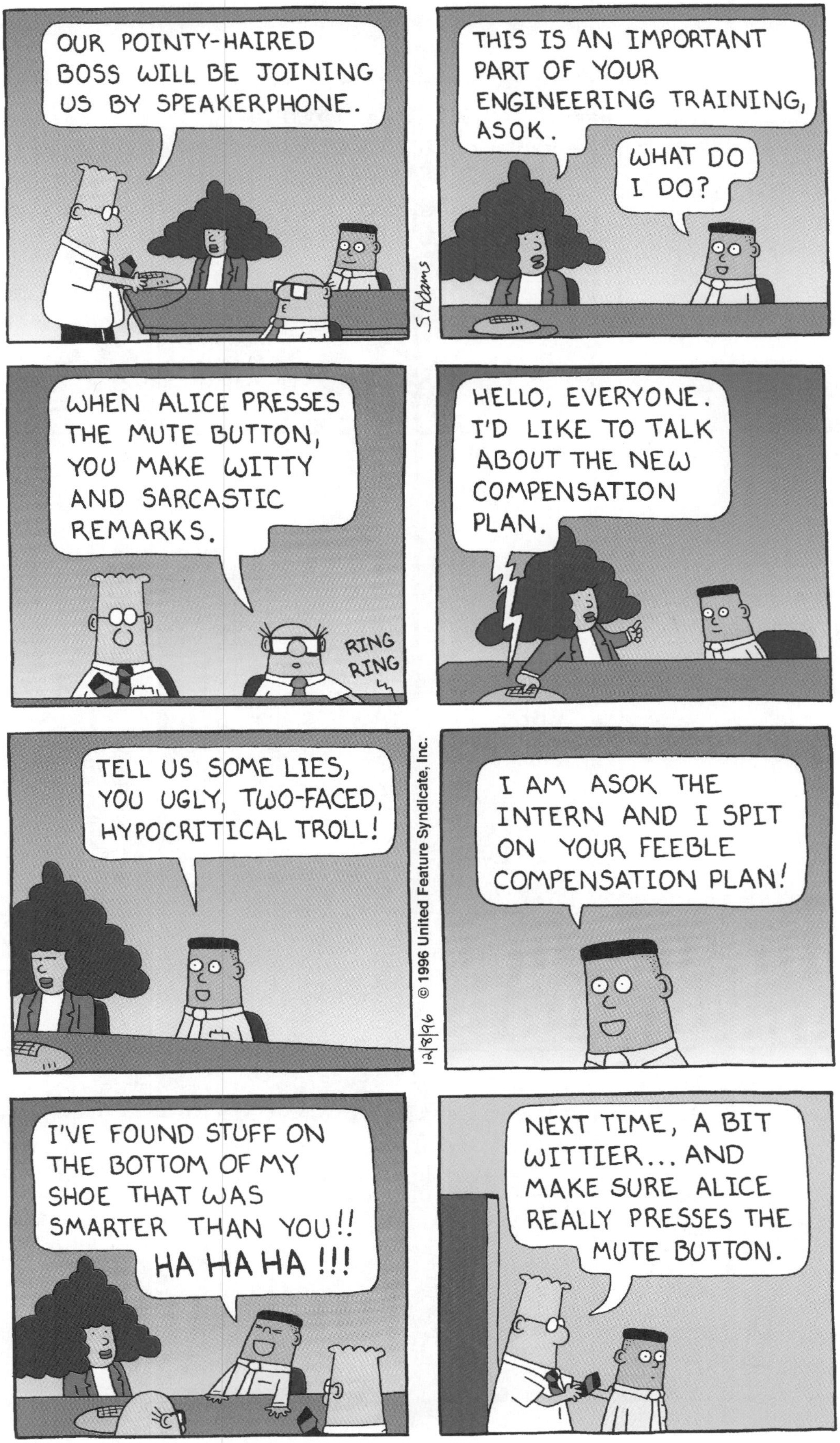
OUR POINTY-HAIRED BOSS WILL BE JOINING US BY SPEAKERPHONE.
S Adams
THIS IS AN IMPORTANT PART OF YOUR ENGINEERING TRAINING, ASOK.
WHAT DO I DO?
WHEN ALICE PRESSES THE MUTE BUTTON, YOU MAKE WITTY AND SARCASTIC REMARKS.
RING RING
HELLO, EVERYONE. I'D LIKE TO TALK ABOUT THE NEW COMPENSATION PLAN.
TELL US SOME LIES, YOU UGLY, TWO-FACED, HYPOCRITICAL TROLL!
12/8/96 © 1996 United Feature Syndicate, Inc.
I AM ASOK THE INTERN AND I SPIT ON YOUR FEEBLE COMPENSATION PLAN!
I'VE FOUND STUFF ON THE BOTTOM OF MY SHOE THAT WAS SMARTER THAN YOU!! HA HA HA!!!
NEXT TIME, A BIT WITTIER... AND MAKE SURE ALICE REALLY PRESSES THE MUTE BUTTON.

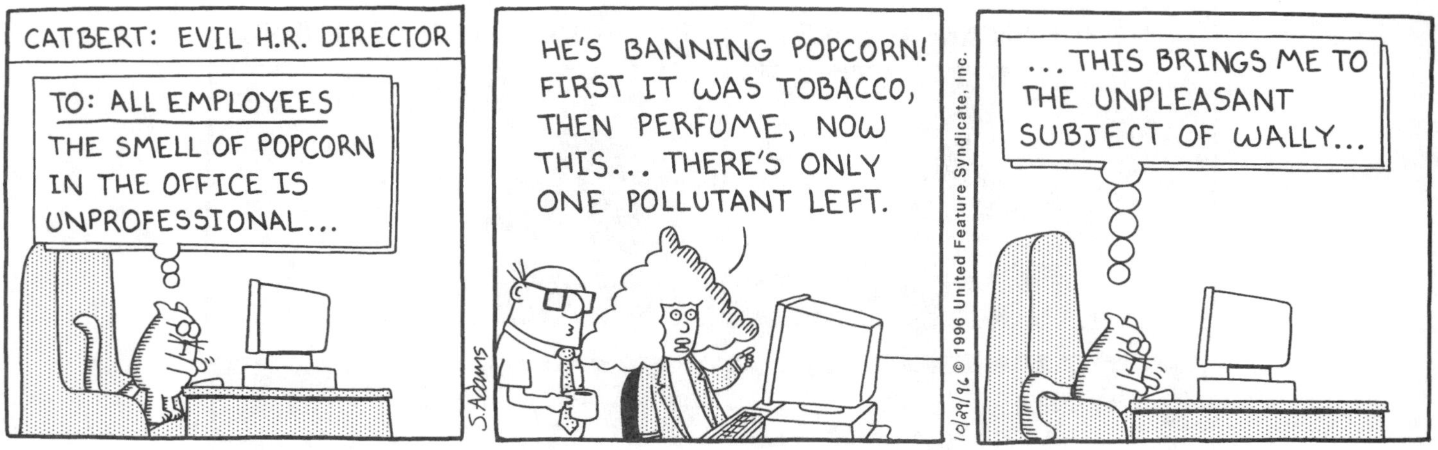
CATBERT: EVIL H.R. DIRECTOR
TO: ALL EMPLOYEES
THE SMELL OF POPCORN IN THE OFFICE IS UNPROFESSIONAL...
HE'S BANNING POPCORN! FIRST IT WAS TOBACCO, THEN PERFUME, NOW THIS... THERE'S ONLY ONE POLLUTANT LEFT.
S. Adams
10/29/96 © 1996 United Feature Syndicate, Inc.
...THIS BRINGS ME TO THE UNPLEASANT SUBJECT OF WALLY...

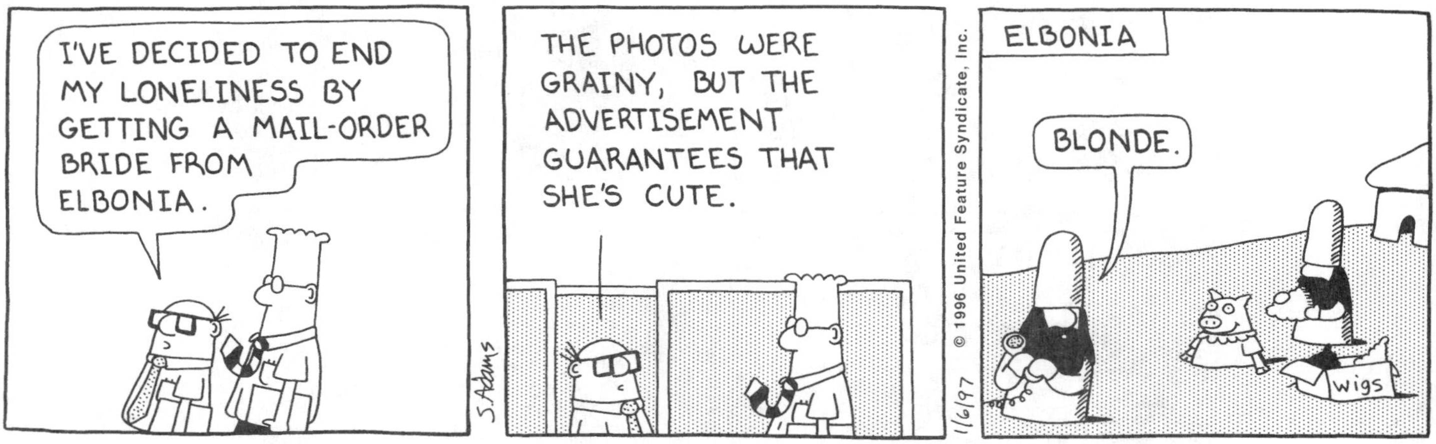
I'VE DECIDED TO END MY LONELINESS BY GETTING A MAIL-ORDER BRIDE FROM ELBONIA.
THE PHOTOS WERE GRAINY, BUT THE ADVERTISEMENT GUARANTEES THAT SHE'S CUTE.
S. Adams
1/6/97 © 1996 United Feature Syndicate, Inc.
ELBONIA
BLONDE.
wigs

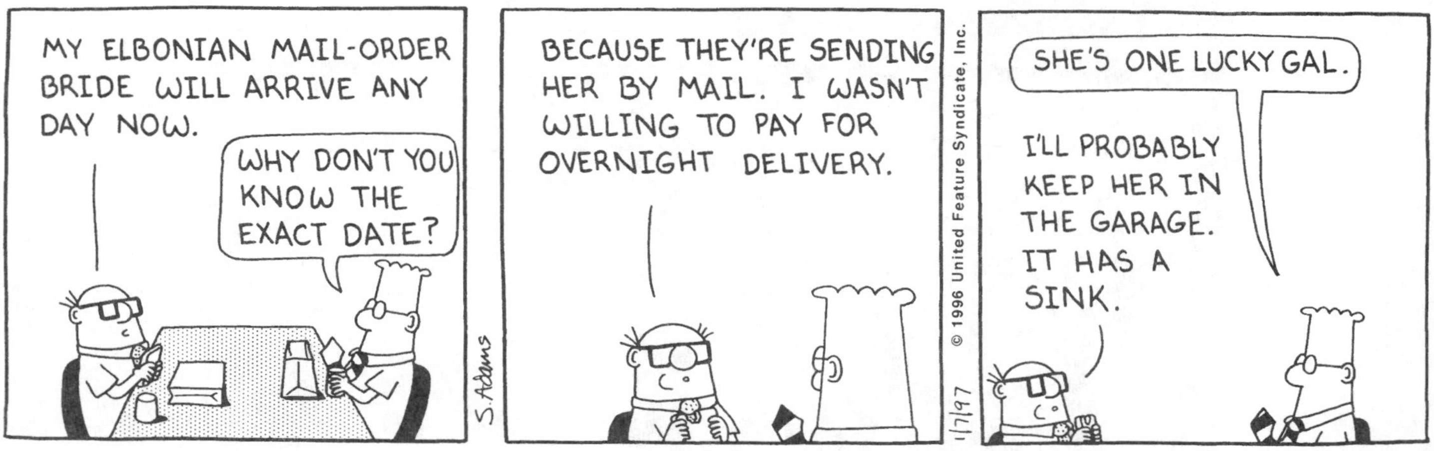
MY ELBONIAN MAIL-ORDER BRIDE WILL ARRIVE ANY DAY NOW.
WHY DON'T YOU KNOW THE EXACT DATE?
BECAUSE THEY'RE SENDING HER BY MAIL. I WASN'T WILLING TO PAY FOR OVERNIGHT DELIVERY.
S. Adams
1/7/97 © 1996 United Feature Syndicate, Inc.
SHE'S ONE LUCKY GAL.
I'LL PROBABLY KEEP HER IN THE GARAGE. IT HAS A SINK.

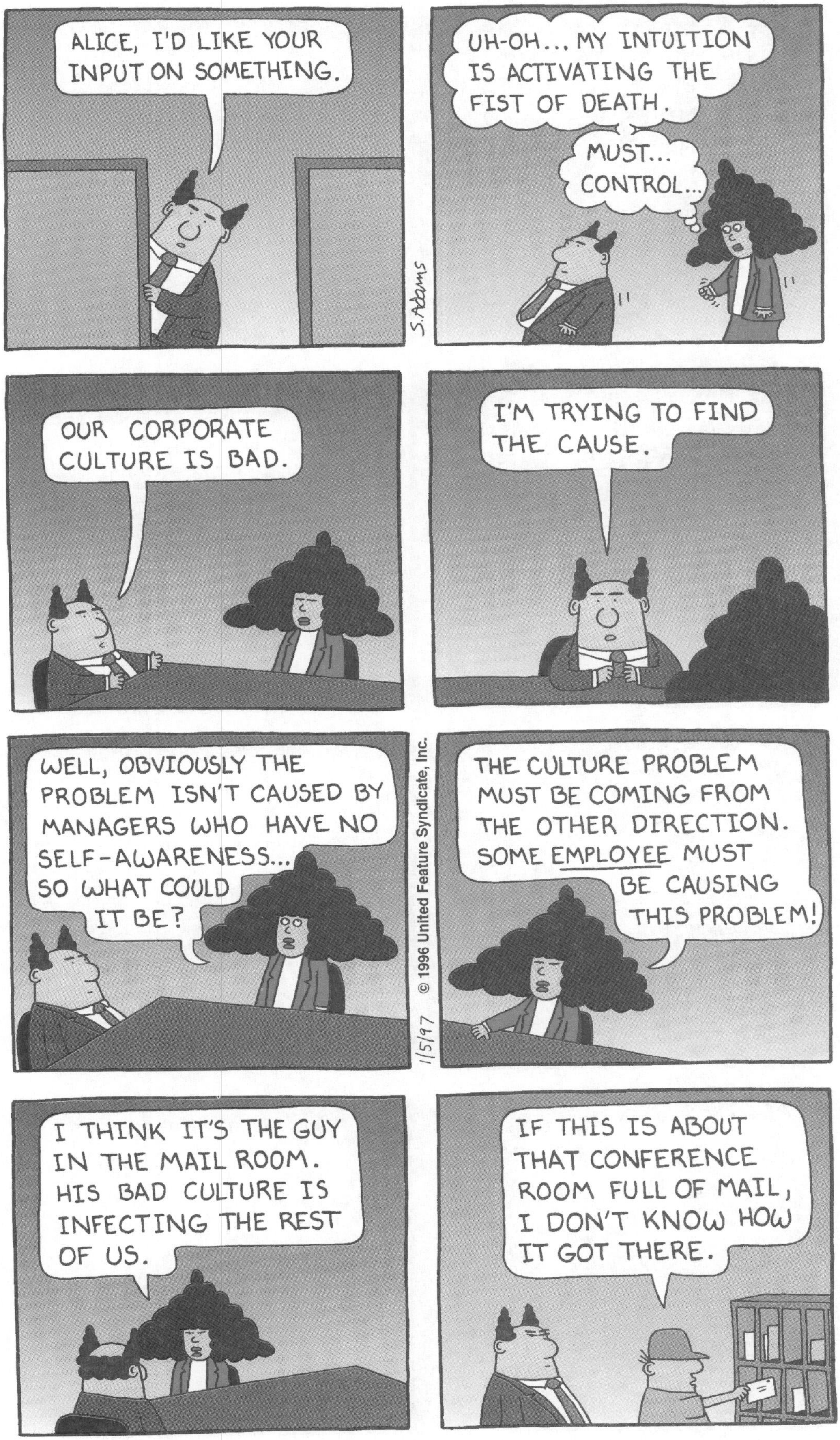
ALICE, I'D LIKE YOUR INPUT ON SOMETHING.
S. Adams
UH-OH... MY INTUITION IS ACTIVATING THE FIST OF DEATH.
MUST... CONTROL...
OUR CORPORATE CULTURE IS BAD.
I'M TRYING TO FIND THE CAUSE.
WELL, OBVIOUSLY THE PROBLEM ISN'T CAUSED BY MANAGERS WHO HAVE NO SELF-AWARENESS... SO WHAT COULD IT BE?
© 1996 United Feature Syndicate, Inc.
1/5/97
THE CULTURE PROBLEM MUST BE COMING FROM THE OTHER DIRECTION. SOME EMPLOYEE MUST BE CAUSING THIS PROBLEM!
I THINK IT'S THE GUY IN THE MAIL ROOM. HIS BAD CULTURE IS INFECTING THE REST OF US.
IF THIS IS ABOUT THAT CONFERENCE ROOM FULL OF MAIL, I DON'T KNOW HOW IT GOT THERE.

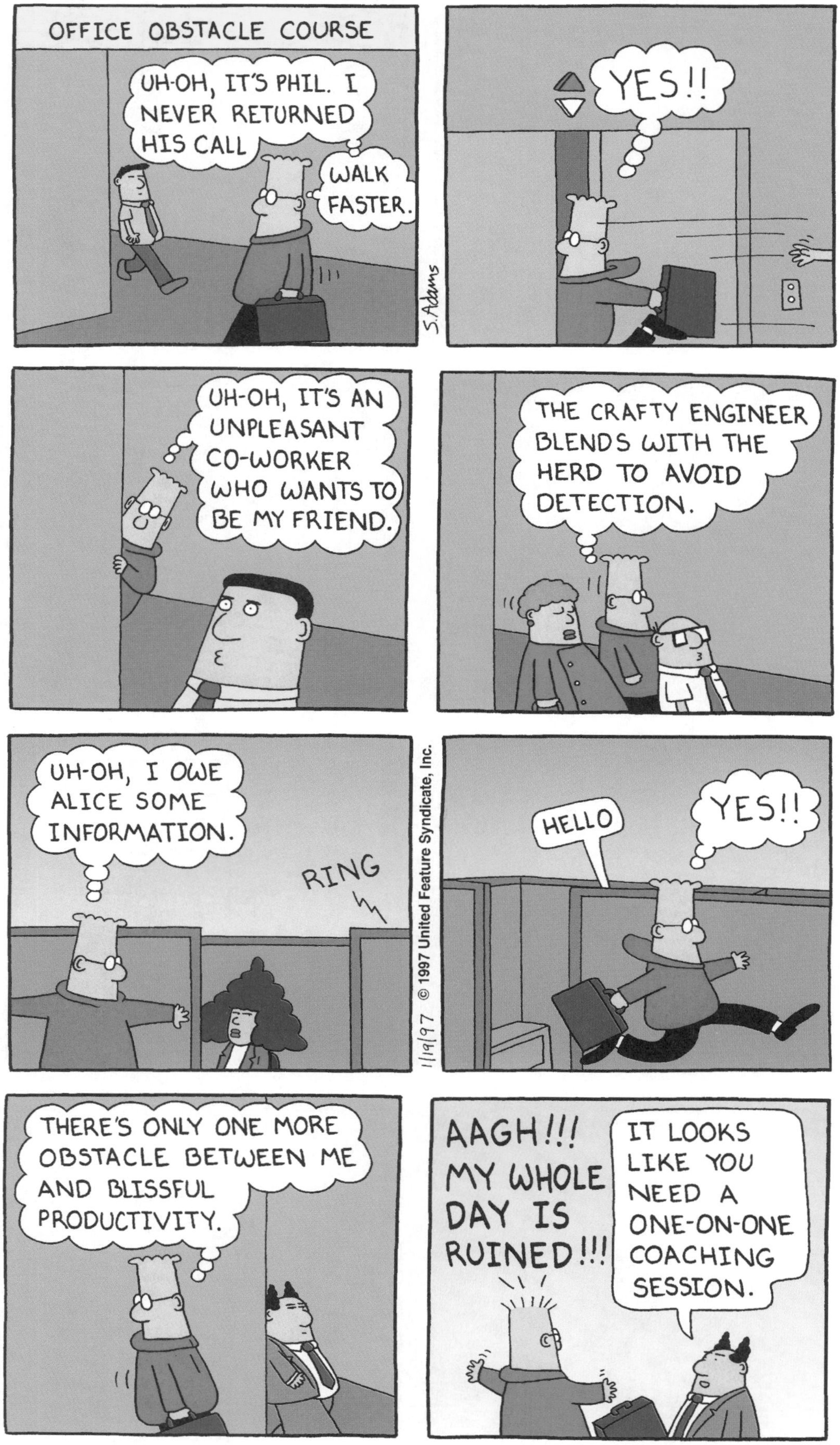
OFFICE OBSTACLE COURSE
UH-OH, IT'S PHIL. I NEVER RETURNED HIS CALL
WALK FASTER.
S. Adams
YES!!
UH-OH, IT'S AN UNPLEASANT CO-WORKER WHO WANTS TO BE MY FRIEND.
THE CRAFTY ENGINEER BLENDS WITH THE HERD TO AVOID DETECTION.
UH-OH, I OWE ALICE SOME INFORMATION.
RING
1/19/97 © 1997 United Feature Syndicate, Inc.
HELLO
YES!!
THERE'S ONLY ONE MORE OBSTACLE BETWEEN ME AND BLISSFUL PRODUCTIVITY.
AAGH!!! MY WHOLE DAY IS RUINED!!!
IT LOOKS LIKE YOU NEED A ONE-ON-ONE COACHING SESSION.

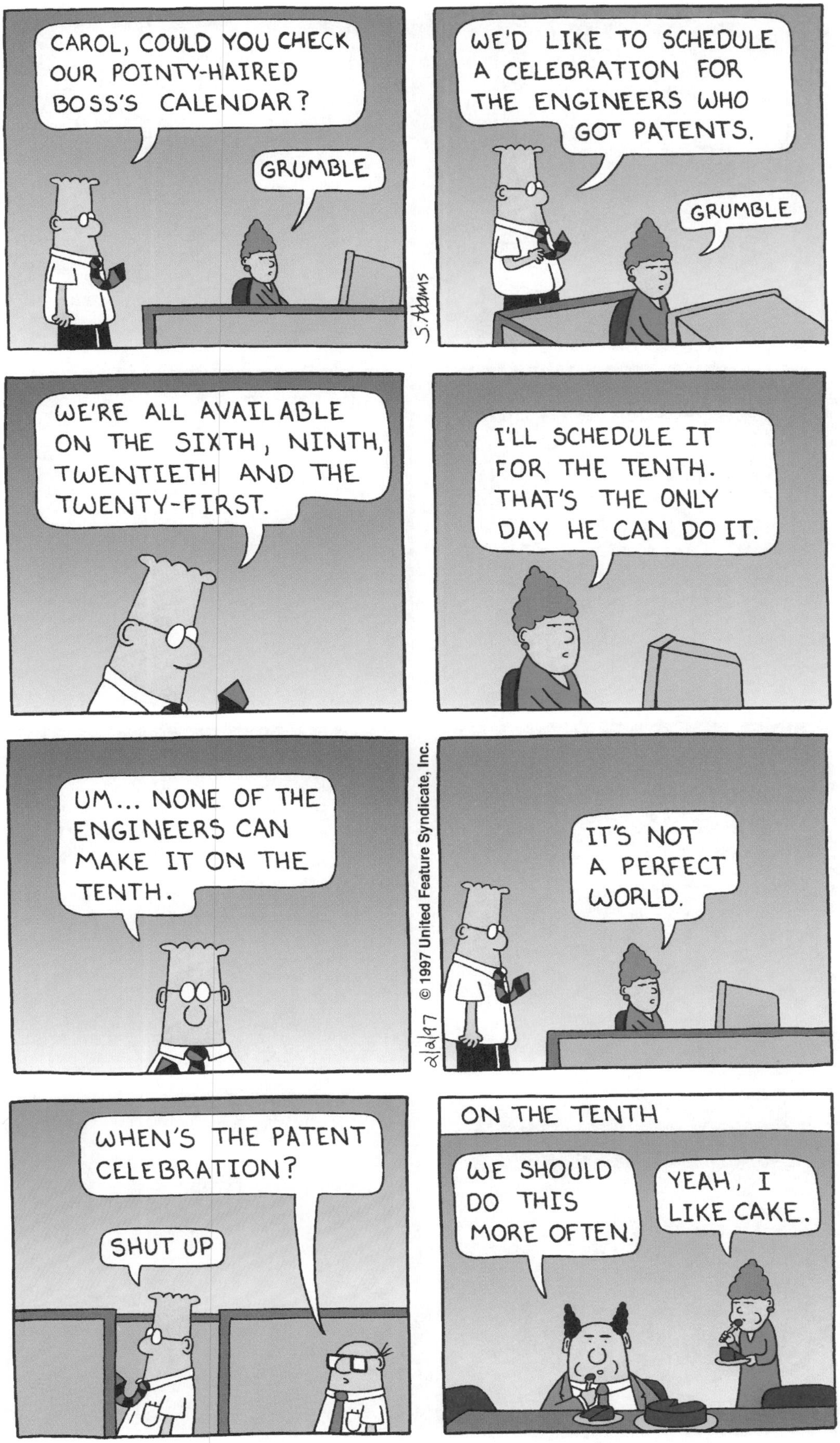
CAROL, COULD YOU CHECK OUR POINTY-HAIRED BOSS'S CALENDAR?
GRUMBLE
S. Adams
WE'D LIKE TO SCHEDULE A CELEBRATION FOR THE ENGINEERS WHO GOT PATENTS.
GRUMBLE
WE'RE ALL AVAILABLE ON THE SIXTH, NINTH, TWENTIETH AND THE TWENTY-FIRST.
I'LL SCHEDULE IT FOR THE TENTH. THAT'S THE ONLY DAY HE CAN DO IT.
UM... NONE OF THE ENGINEERS CAN MAKE IT ON THE TENTH.
2/2/97
IT'S NOT A PERFECT WORLD.
WHEN'S THE PATENT CELEBRATION?
SHUT UP
ON THE TENTH
WE SHOULD DO THIS MORE OFTEN.
YEAH, I LIKE CAKE.

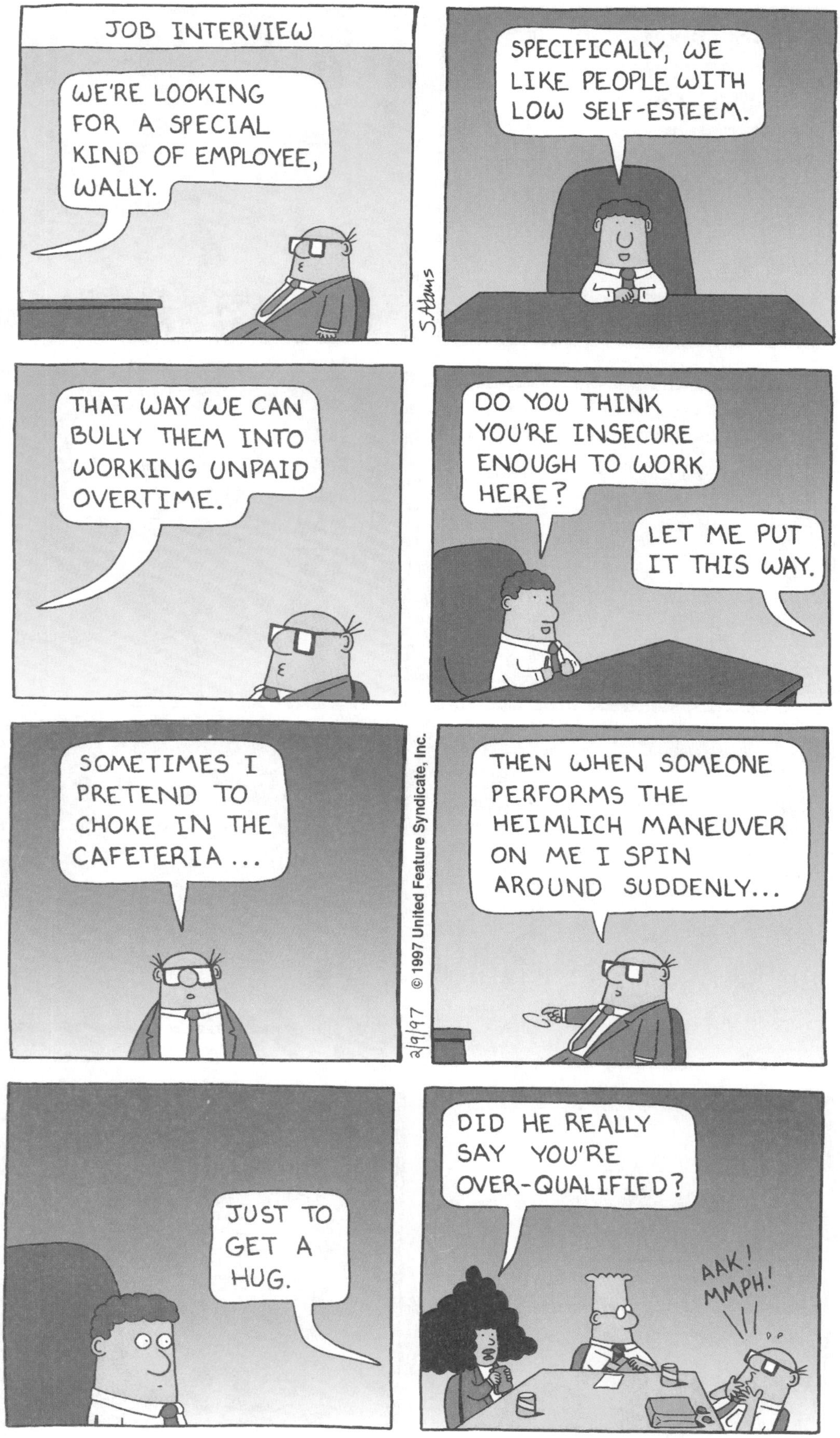
JOB INTERVIEW
WE'RE LOOKING FOR A SPECIAL KIND OF EMPLOYEE, WALLY.
S.Adams
SPECIFICALLY, WE LIKE PEOPLE WITH LOW SELF-ESTEEM.
THAT WAY WE CAN BULLY THEM INTO WORKING UNPAID OVERTIME.
DO YOU THINK YOU'RE INSECURE ENOUGH TO WORK HERE?
LET ME PUT IT THIS WAY.
SOMETIMES I PRETEND TO CHOKE IN THE CAFETERIA ...
2/9/97 © 1997 United Feature Syndicate, Inc.
THEN WHEN SOMEONE PERFORMS THE HEIMLICH MANEUVER ON ME I SPIN AROUND SUDDENLY...
JUST TO GET A HUG.
DID HE REALLY SAY YOU'RE OVER-QUALIFIED?
AAK! MMPH!

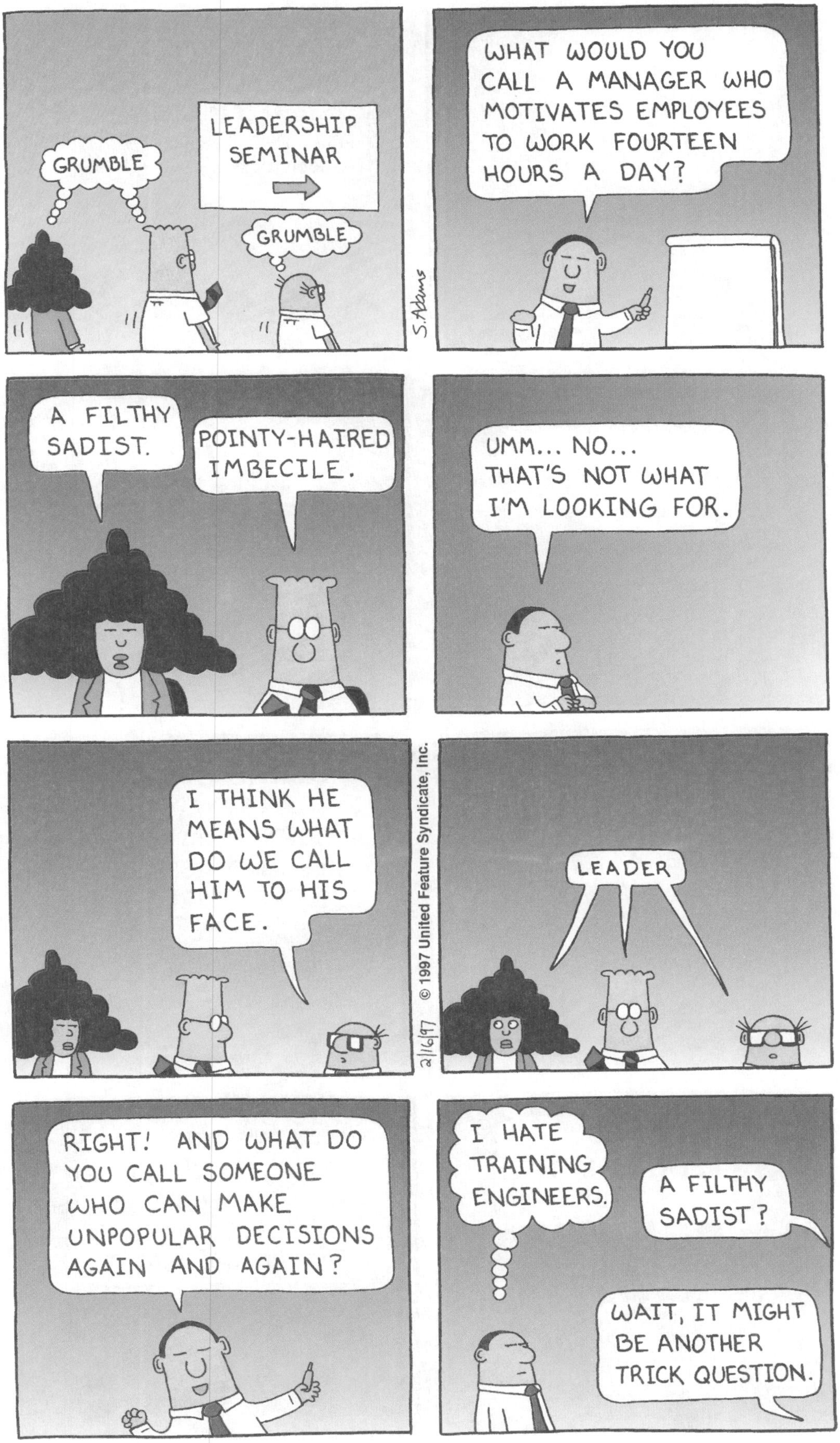
LEADERSHIP SEMINAR
GRUMBLE
GRUMBLE
S. Adams
WHAT WOULD YOU CALL A MANAGER WHO MOTIVATES EMPLOYEES TO WORK FOURTEEN HOURS A DAY?
A FILTHY SADIST.
POINTY-HAIRED IMBECILE.
UMM... NO... THAT'S NOT WHAT I'M LOOKING FOR.
I THINK HE MEANS WHAT DO WE CALL HIM TO HIS FACE.
2/16/97
© 1997 United Feature Syndicate, Inc.
LEADER
RIGHT! AND WHAT DO YOU CALL SOMEONE WHO CAN MAKE UNPOPULAR DECISIONS AGAIN AND AGAIN?
I HATE TRAINING ENGINEERS.
A FILTHY SADIST?
WAIT, IT MIGHT BE ANOTHER TRICK QUESTION.

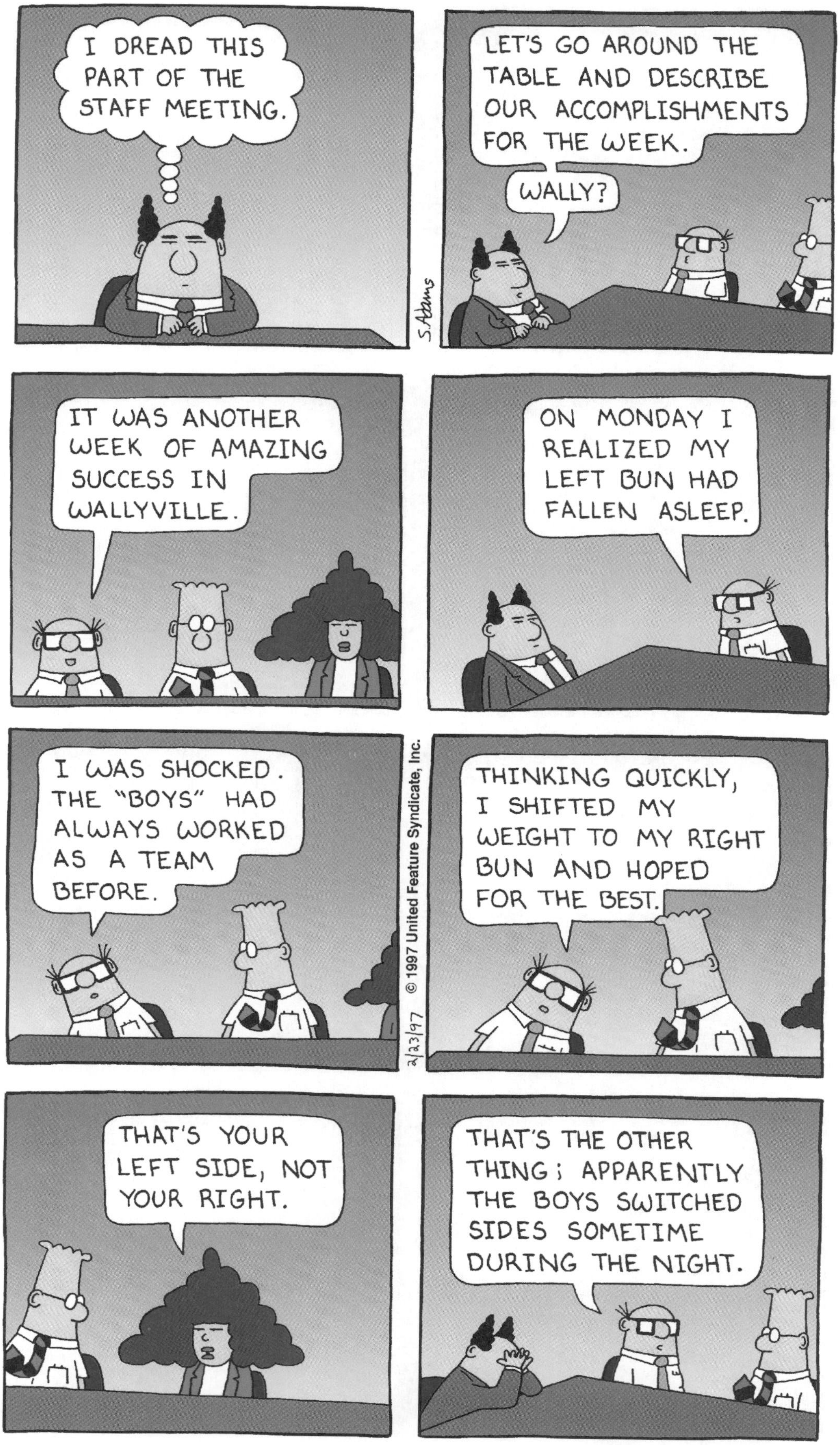
I DREAD THIS PART OF THE STAFF MEETING.
LET'S GO AROUND THE TABLE AND DESCRIBE OUR ACCOMPLISHMENTS FOR THE WEEK.
WALLY?
S. Adams
IT WAS ANOTHER WEEK OF AMAZING SUCCESS IN WALLYVILLE.
ON MONDAY I REALIZED MY LEFT BUN HAD FALLEN ASLEEP.
I WAS SHOCKED. THE "BOYS" HAD ALWAYS WORKED AS A TEAM BEFORE.
2/23/97 © 1997 United Feature Syndicate, Inc.
THINKING QUICKLY, I SHIFTED MY WEIGHT TO MY RIGHT BUN AND HOPED FOR THE BEST.
THAT'S YOUR LEFT SIDE, NOT YOUR RIGHT.
THAT'S THE OTHER THING; APPARENTLY THE BOYS SWITCHED SIDES SOMETIME DURING THE NIGHT.

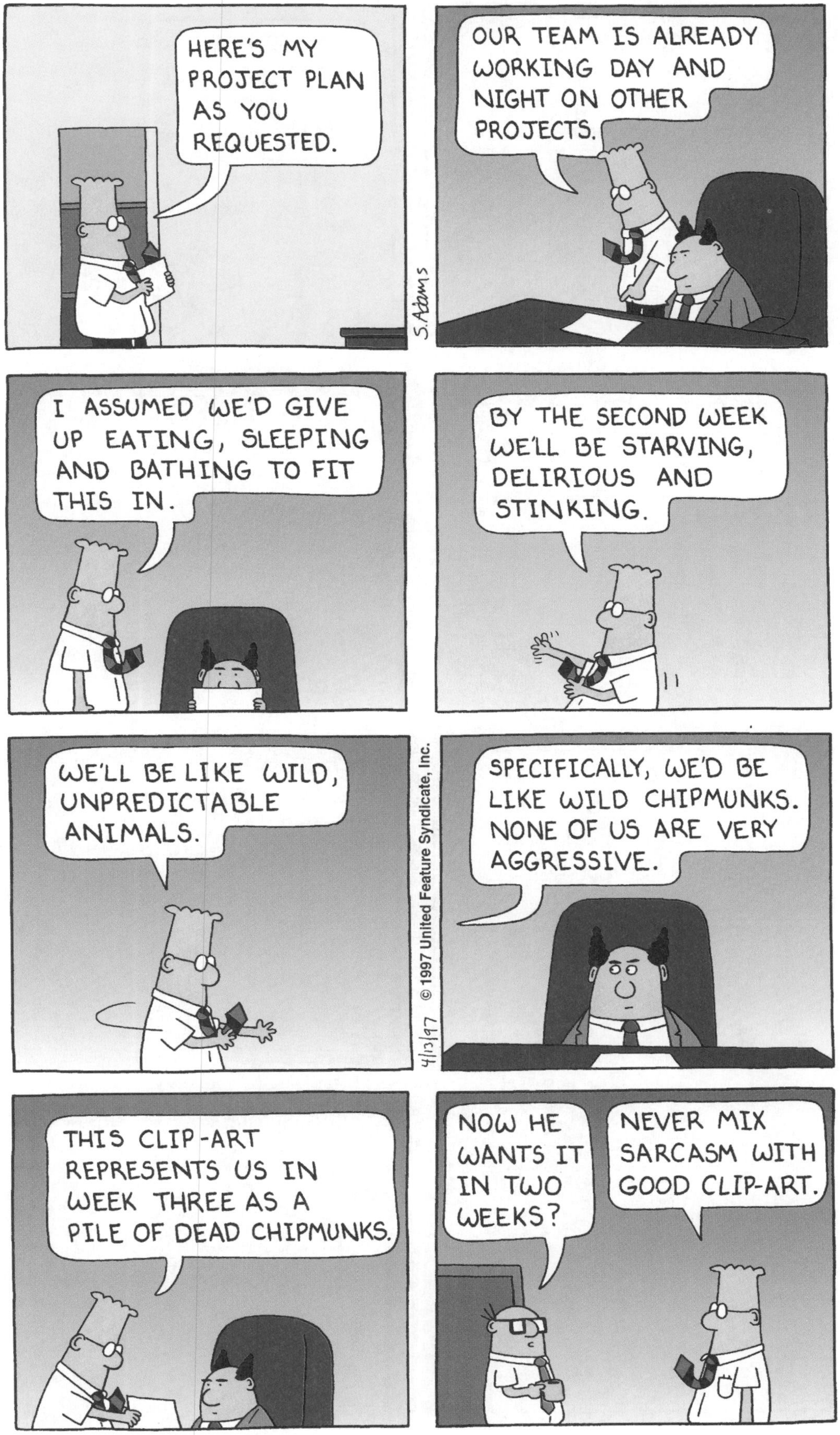
HERE'S MY PROJECT PLAN AS YOU REQUESTED.
OUR TEAM IS ALREADY WORKING DAY AND NIGHT ON OTHER PROJECTS.
S. Adams
I ASSUMED WE'D GIVE UP EATING, SLEEPING AND BATHING TO FIT THIS IN.
BY THE SECOND WEEK WE'LL BE STARVING, DELIRIOUS AND STINKING.
WE'LL BE LIKE WILD, UNPREDICTABLE ANIMALS.
SPECIFICALLY, WE'D BE LIKE WILD CHIPMUNKS. NONE OF US ARE VERY AGGRESSIVE.
© 1997 United Feature Syndicate, Inc.
4/13/97
THIS CLIP-ART REPRESENTS US IN WEEK THREE AS A PILE OF DEAD CHIPMUNKS.
NOW HE WANTS IT IN TWO WEEKS?
NEVER MIX SARCASM WITH GOOD CLIP-ART.

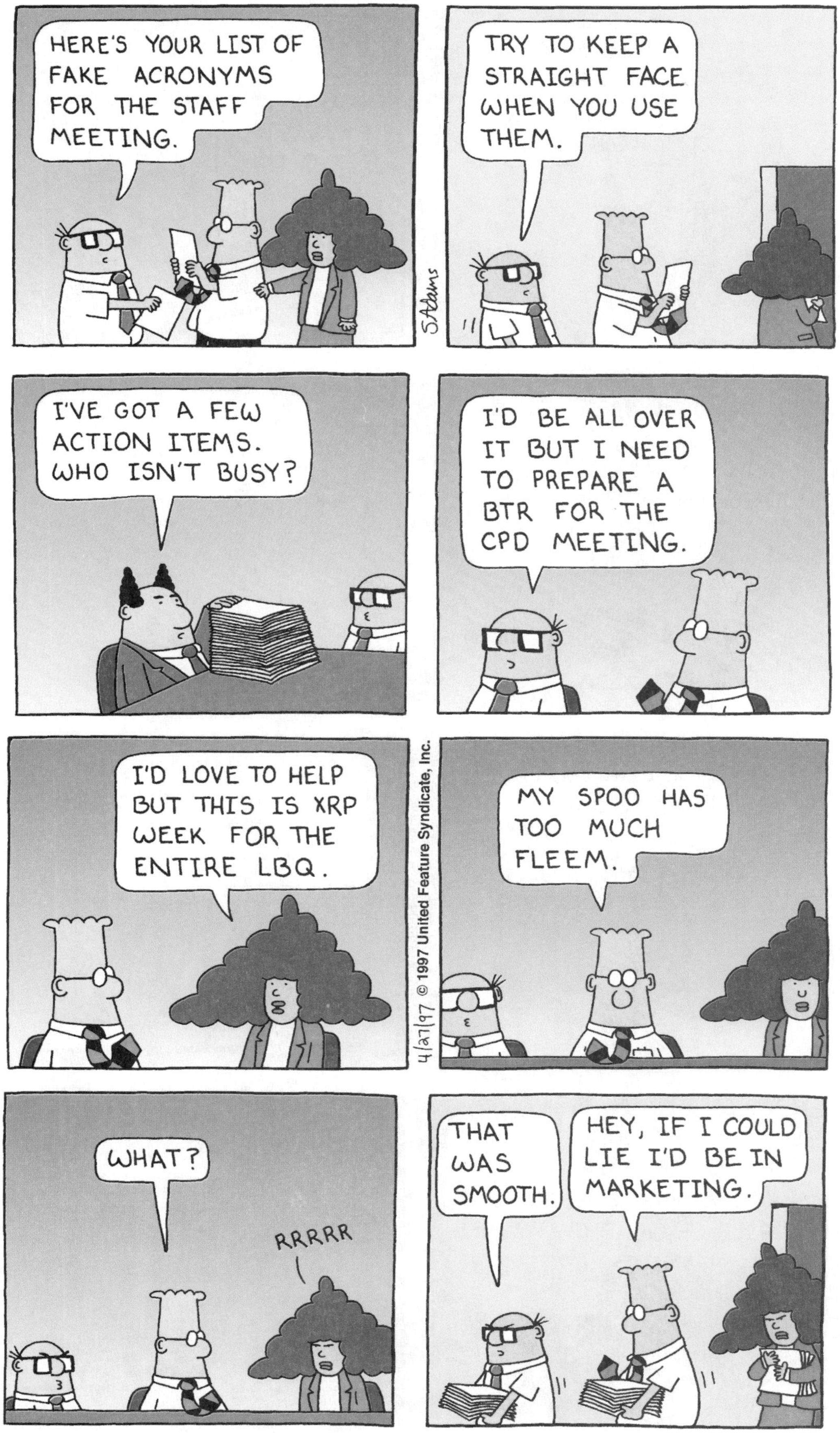
HERE'S YOUR LIST OF FAKE ACRONYMS FOR THE STAFF MEETING.
S.Adams
TRY TO KEEP A STRAIGHT FACE WHEN YOU USE THEM.
I'VE GOT A FEW ACTION ITEMS. WHO ISN'T BUSY?
I'D BE ALL OVER IT BUT I NEED TO PREPARE A BTR FOR THE CPD MEETING.
I'D LOVE TO HELP BUT THIS IS XRP WEEK FOR THE ENTIRE LBQ.
4/27/97 © 1997 United Feature Syndicate, Inc.
MY SPOO HAS TOO MUCH FLEEM.
WHAT?
RRRRR
THAT WAS SMOOTH.
HEY, IF I COULD LIE I'D BE IN MARKETING.

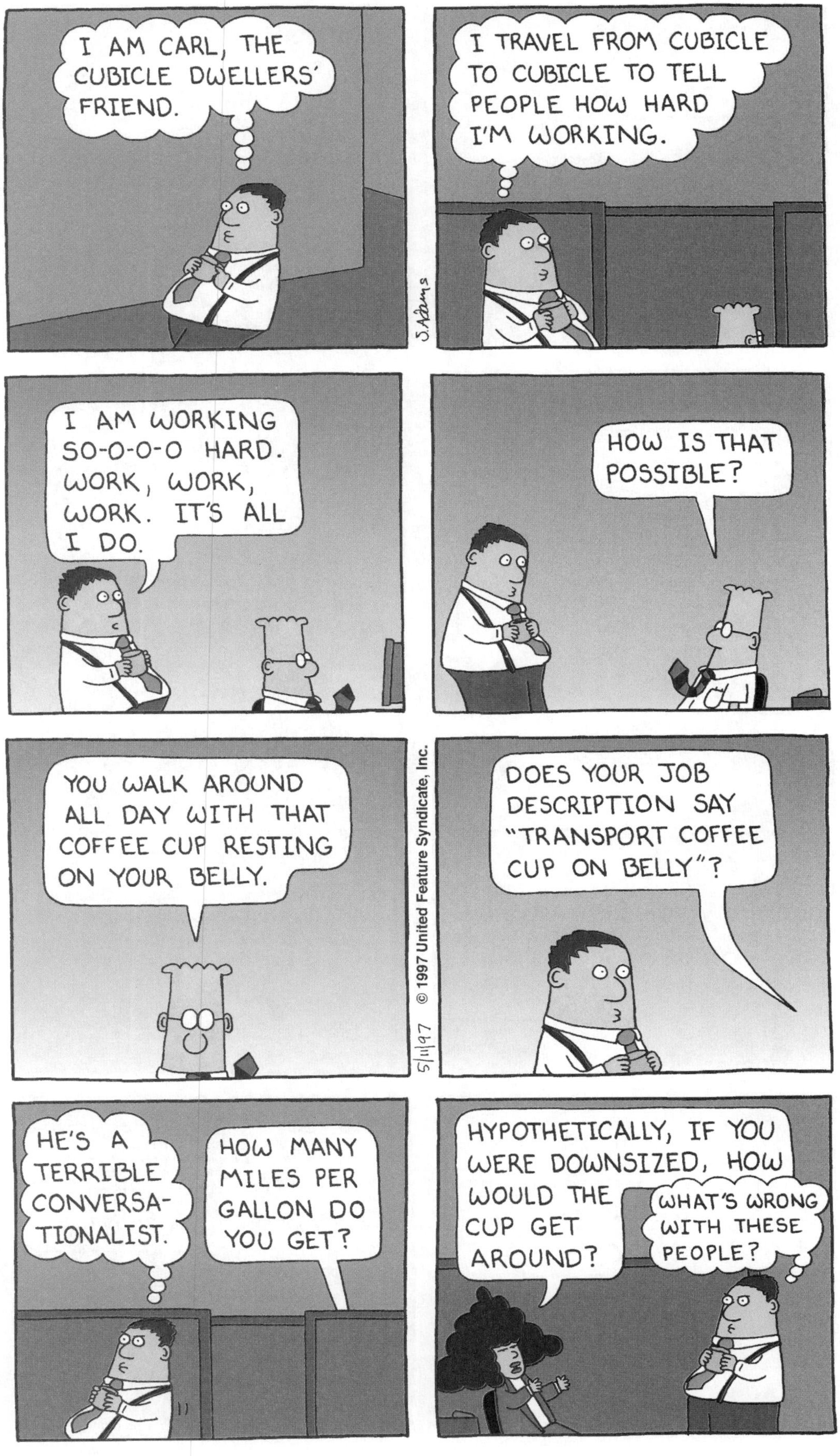
I AM CARL, THE CUBICLE DWELLERS' FRIEND.
I TRAVEL FROM CUBICLE TO CUBICLE TO TELL PEOPLE HOW HARD I'M WORKING.
S. Adams
I AM WORKING SO-O-O-O HARD. WORK, WORK, WORK. IT'S ALL I DO.
HOW IS THAT POSSIBLE?
YOU WALK AROUND ALL DAY WITH THAT COFFEE CUP RESTING ON YOUR BELLY.
5/11/97 © 1997 United Feature Syndicate, Inc.
DOES YOUR JOB DESCRIPTION SAY "TRANSPORT COFFEE CUP ON BELLY"?
HE'S A TERRIBLE CONVERSA-TIONALIST.
HOW MANY MILES PER GALLON DO YOU GET?
HYPOTHETICALLY, IF YOU WERE DOWNSIZED, HOW WOULD THE CUP GET AROUND?
WHAT'S WRONG WITH THESE PEOPLE?

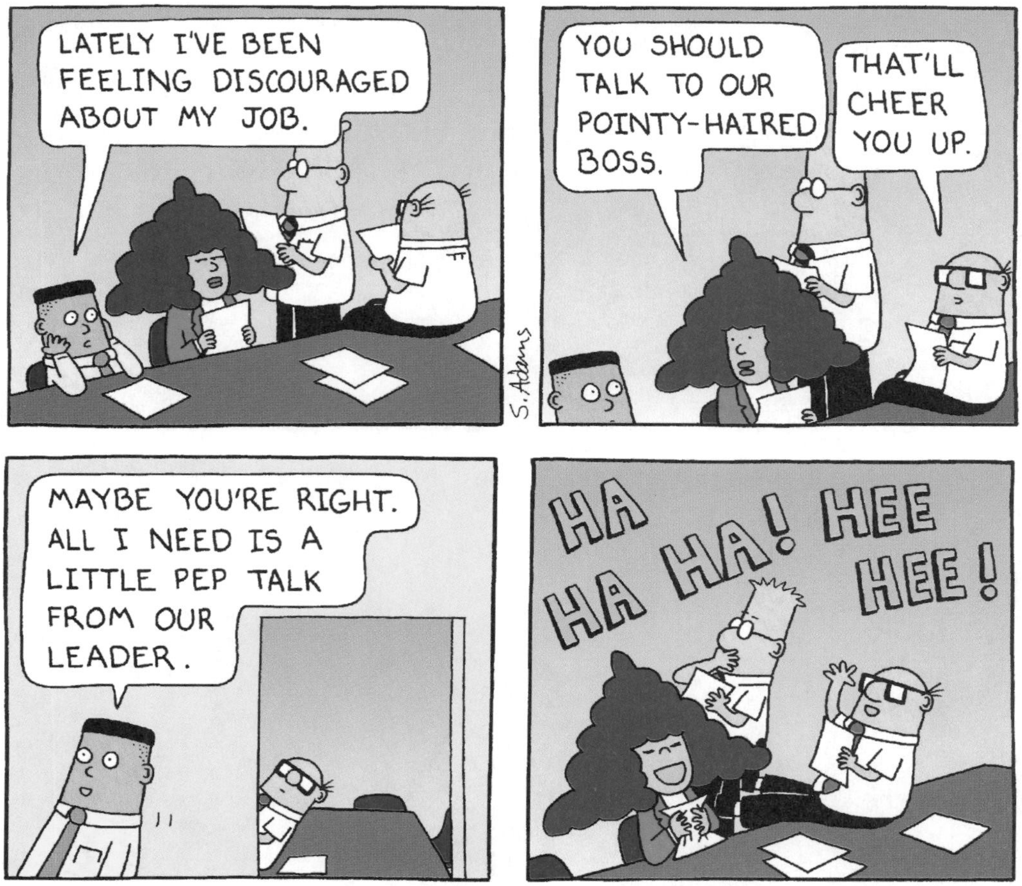
LATELY I'VE BEEN FEELING DISCOURAGED ABOUT MY JOB.
YOU SHOULD TALK TO OUR POINTY-HAIRED BOSS.
THAT'LL CHEER YOU UP.
S. Adams
MAYBE YOU'RE RIGHT. ALL I NEED IS A LITTLE PEP TALK FROM OUR LEADER.
HA HA HA! HEE HEE!

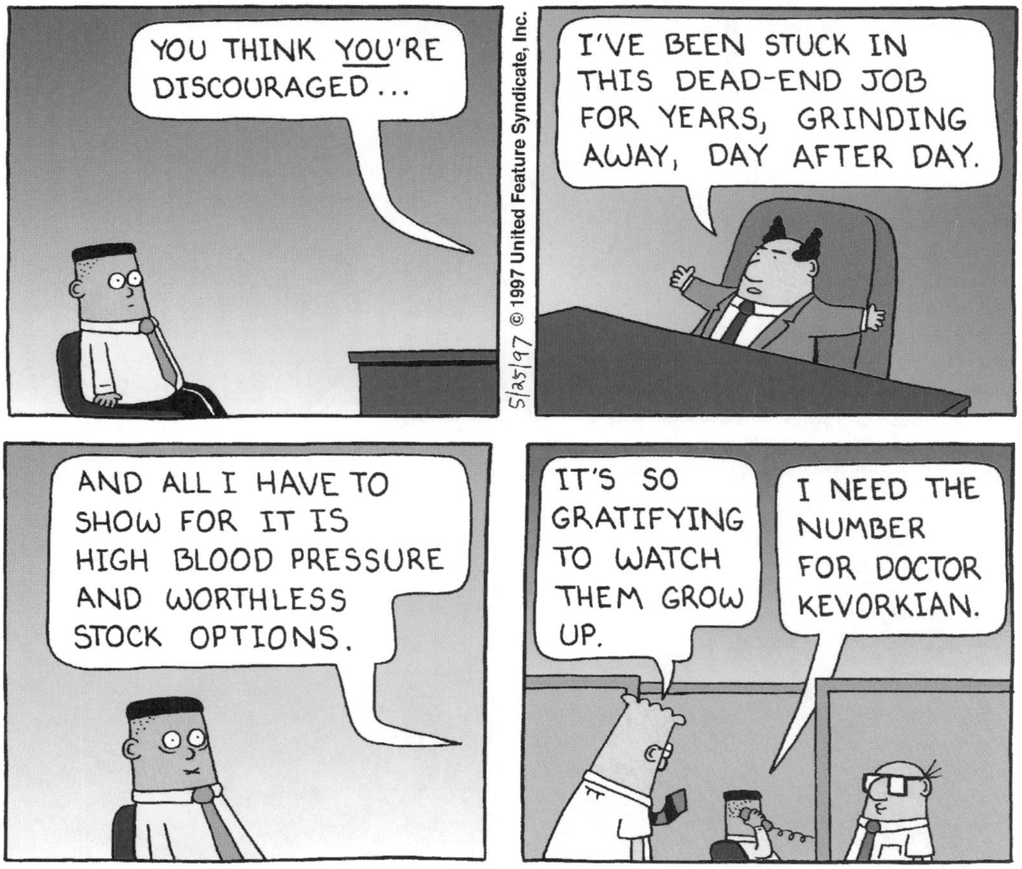
YOU THINK YOU'RE DISCOURAGED...
I'VE BEEN STUCK IN THIS DEAD-END JOB FOR YEARS, GRINDING AWAY, DAY AFTER DAY.
AND ALL I HAVE TO SHOW FOR IT IS HIGH BLOOD PRESSURE AND WORTHLESS STOCK OPTIONS.
IT'S SO GRATIFYING TO WATCH THEM GROW UP.
I NEED THE NUMBER FOR DOCTOR KEVORKIAN.

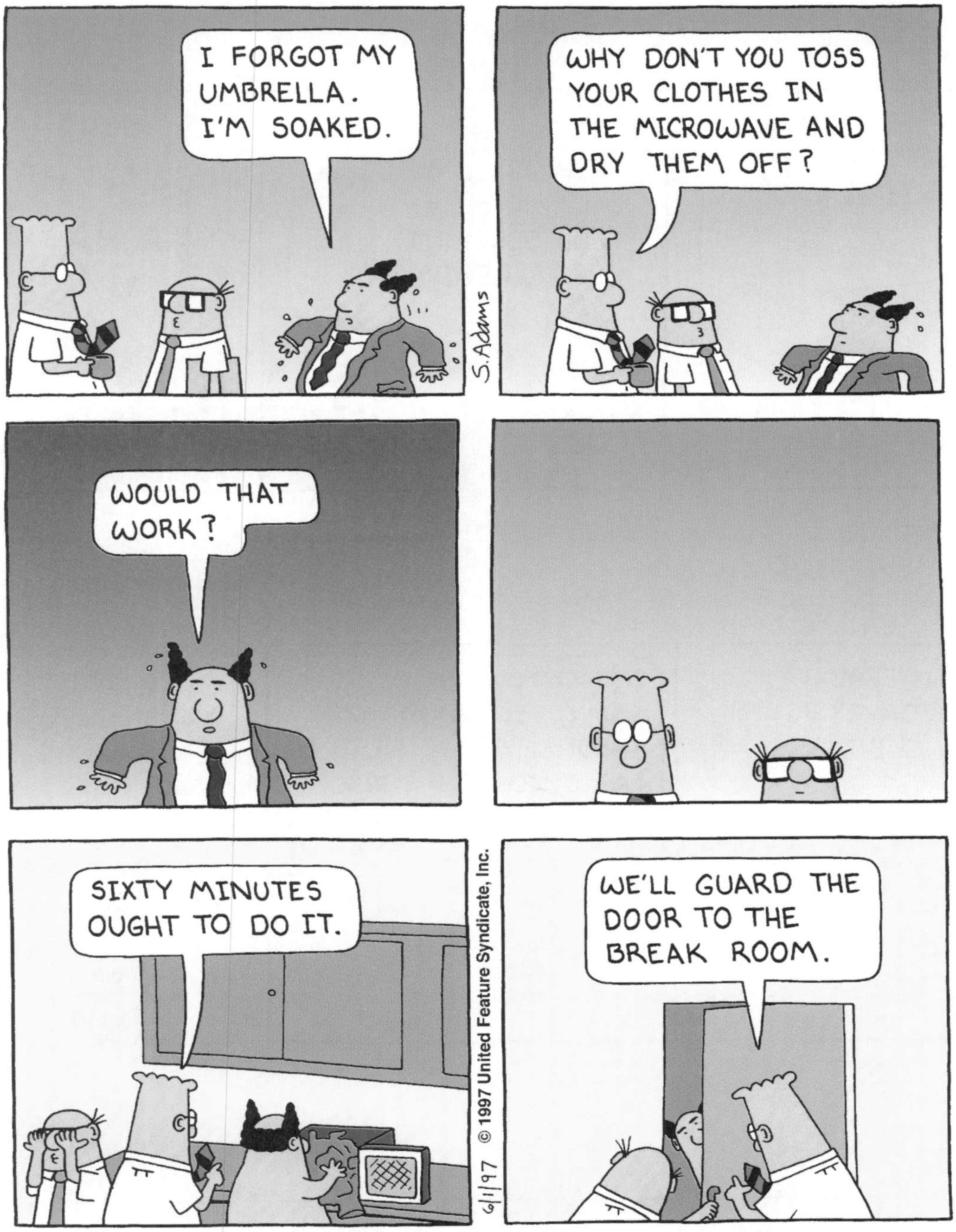
I FORGOT MY UMBRELLA. I'M SOAKED.
S. Adams
WHY DON'T YOU TOSS YOUR CLOTHES IN THE MICROWAVE AND DRY THEM OFF?
WOULD THAT WORK?
SIXTY MINUTES OUGHT TO DO IT.
6/1/97 © 1997 United Feature Syndicate, Inc.
WE'LL GUARD THE DOOR TO THE BREAK ROOM.

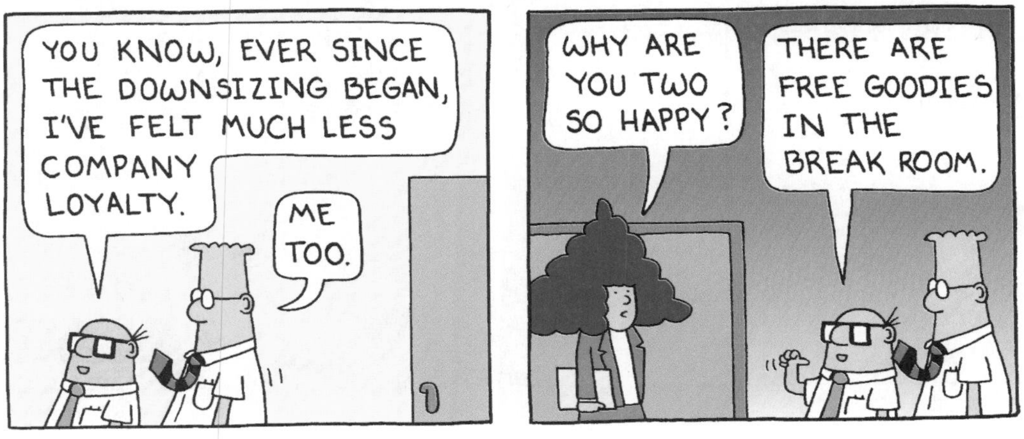
YOU KNOW, EVER SINCE THE DOWNSIZING BEGAN, I'VE FELT MUCH LESS COMPANY LOYALTY.
ME TOO.
WHY ARE YOU TWO SO HAPPY?
THERE ARE FREE GOODIES IN THE BREAK ROOM.

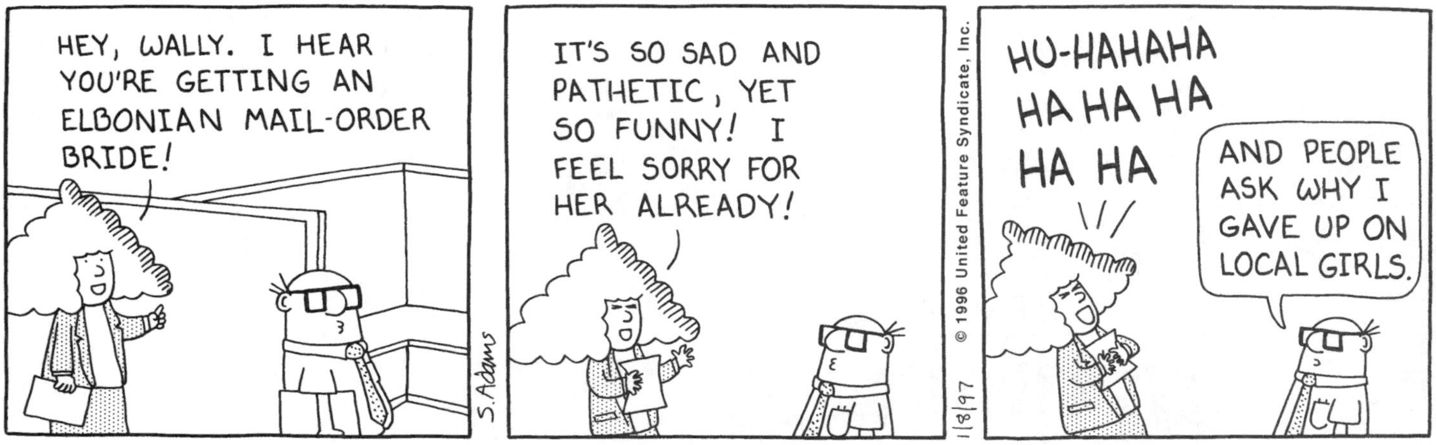

HEY, WALLY. I HEAR YOU'RE GETTING AN ELBONIAN MAIL-ORDER BRIDE!
S. Adams
IT'S SO SAD AND PATHETIC, YET SO FUNNY! I FEEL SORRY FOR HER ALREADY!
1/8/97 © 1996 United Feature Syndicate, Inc.
HU-HAHAHA HA HA HA HA HA
AND PEOPLE ASK WHY I GAVE UP ON LOCAL GIRLS.

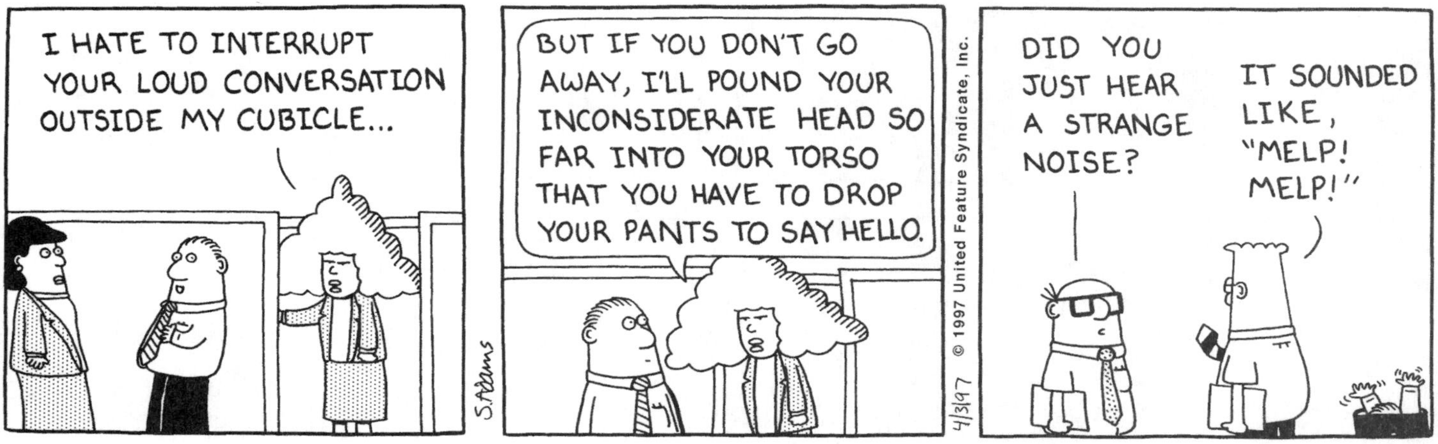

I HATE TO INTERRUPT YOUR LOUD CONVERSATION OUTSIDE MY CUBICLE...
S. Adams
BUT IF YOU DON'T GO AWAY, I'LL POUND YOUR INCONSIDERATE HEAD SO FAR INTO YOUR TORSO THAT YOU HAVE TO DROP YOUR PANTS TO SAY HELLO.
4/3/97 © 1997 United Feature Syndicate, Inc.
DID YOU JUST HEAR A STRANGE NOISE?
IT SOUNDED LIKE, "MELP! MELP!"

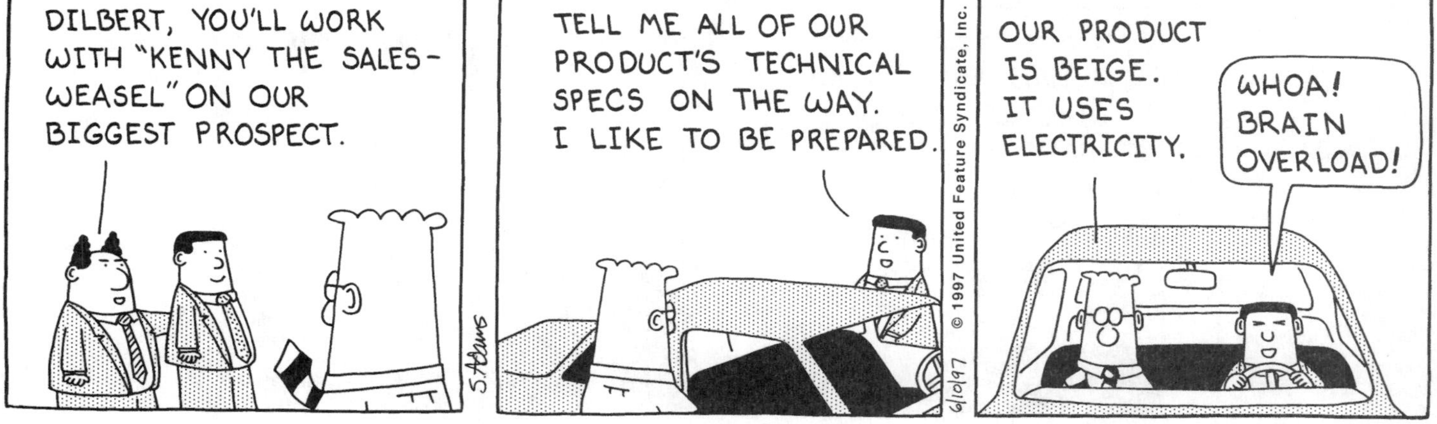

DILBERT, YOU'LL WORK WITH "KENNY THE SALES-WEASEL" ON OUR BIGGEST PROSPECT.
S. Adams
TELL ME ALL OF OUR PRODUCT'S TECHNICAL SPECS ON THE WAY. I LIKE TO BE PREPARED.
6/10/97 © 1997 United Feature Syndicate, Inc.
OUR PRODUCT IS BEIGE. IT USES ELECTRICITY.
WHOA! BRAIN OVERLOAD!

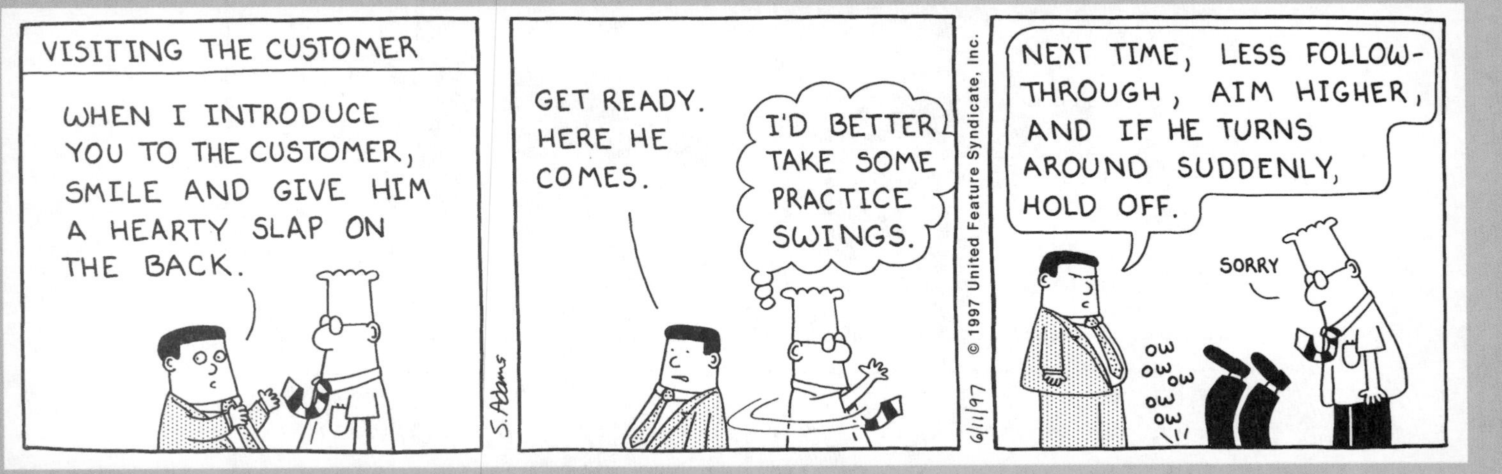
VISITING THE CUSTOMER
WHEN I INTRODUCE YOU TO THE CUSTOMER, SMILE AND GIVE HIM A HEARTY SLAP ON THE BACK.
S. Adams
GET READY. HERE HE COMES.
I'D BETTER TAKE SOME PRACTICE SWINGS.
© 1997 United Feature Syndicate, Inc.
6/11/97
NEXT TIME, LESS FOLLOW-THROUGH, AIM HIGHER, AND IF HE TURNS AROUND SUDDENLY, HOLD OFF.
SORRY
OW OW OW OW OW

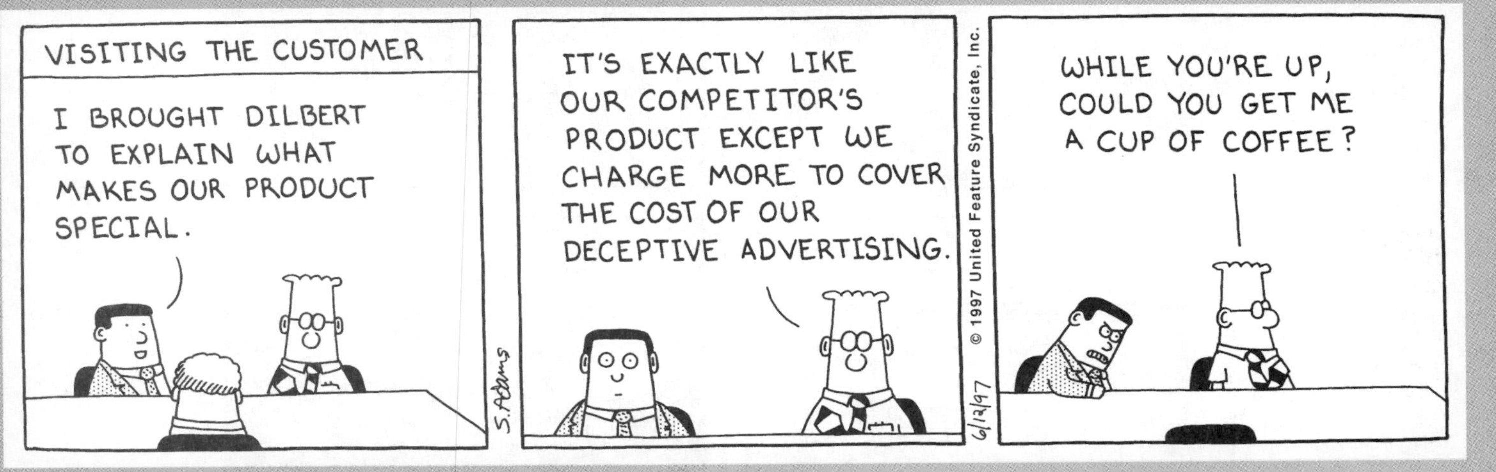
VISITING THE CUSTOMER
I BROUGHT DILBERT TO EXPLAIN WHAT MAKES OUR PRODUCT SPECIAL.
S. Adams
IT'S EXACTLY LIKE OUR COMPETITOR'S PRODUCT EXCEPT WE CHARGE MORE TO COVER THE COST OF OUR DECEPTIVE ADVERTISING.
© 1997 United Feature Syndicate, Inc.
6/12/97
WHILE YOU'RE UP, COULD YOU GET ME A CUP OF COFFEE?

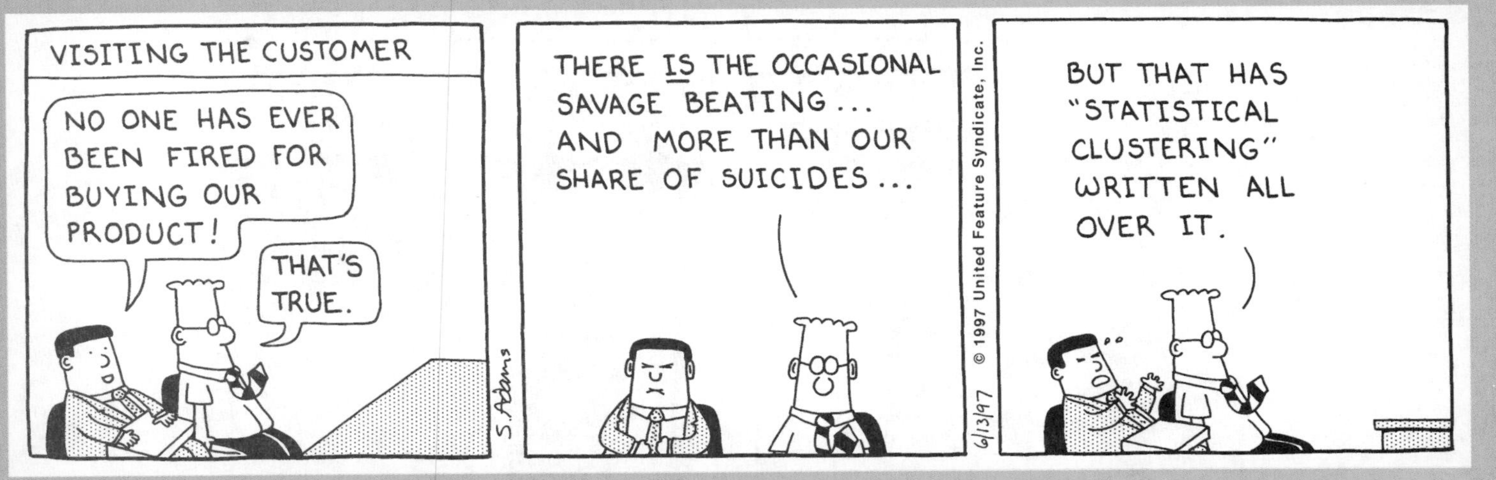
VISITING THE CUSTOMER
NO ONE HAS EVER BEEN FIRED FOR BUYING OUR PRODUCT!
THAT'S TRUE.
S. Adams
THERE IS THE OCCASIONAL SAVAGE BEATING ... AND MORE THAN OUR SHARE OF SUICIDES ...
© 1997 United Feature Syndicate, Inc.
6/13/97
BUT THAT HAS "STATISTICAL CLUSTERING" WRITTEN ALL OVER IT.

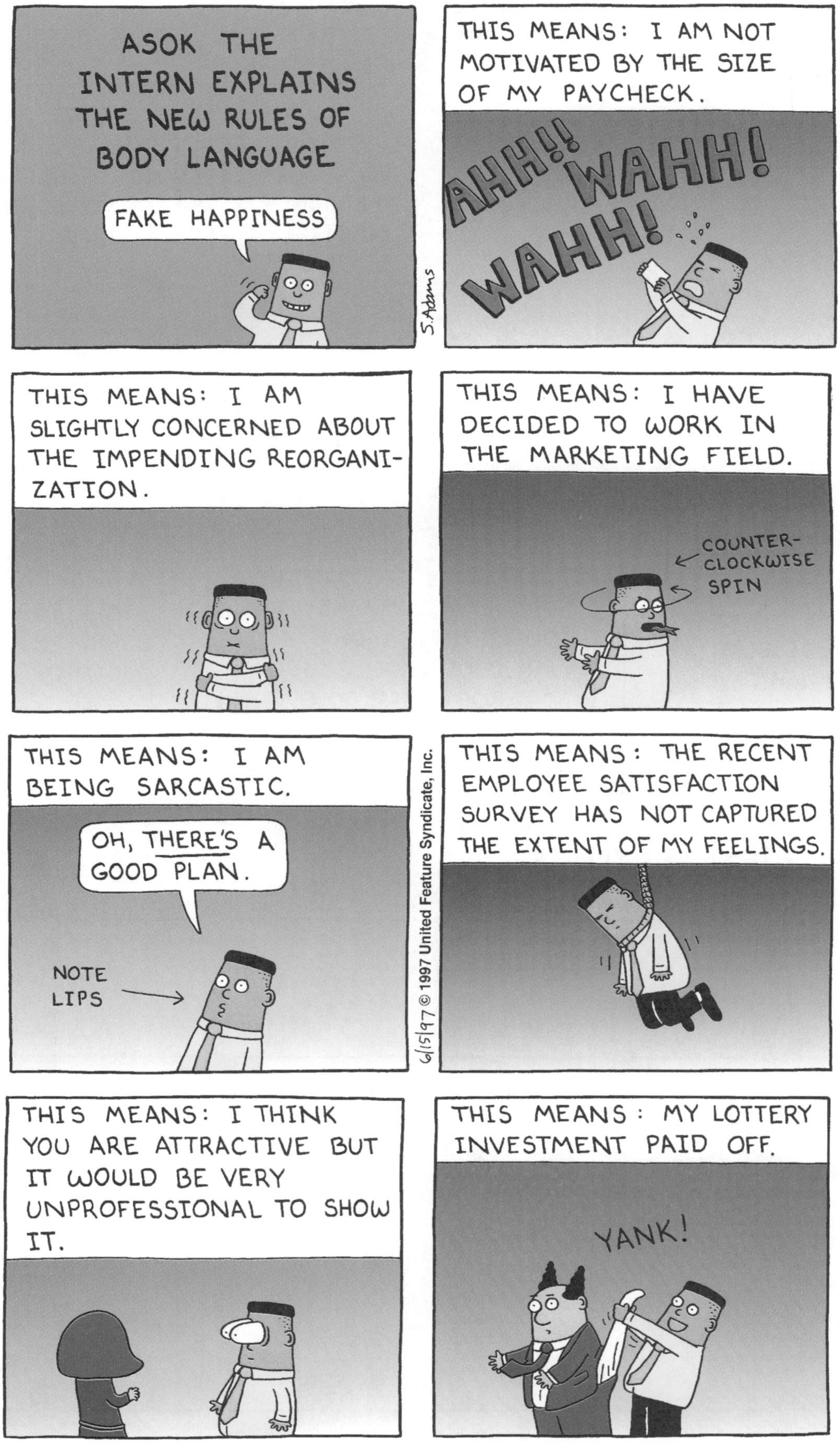
ASOK THE INTERN EXPLAINS THE NEW RULES OF BODY LANGUAGE
FAKE HAPPINESS
S. Adams
THIS MEANS: I AM NOT MOTIVATED BY THE SIZE OF MY PAYCHECK.
AHH!! WAHH! WAHH!
THIS MEANS: I AM SLIGHTLY CONCERNED ABOUT THE IMPENDING REORGANIZATION.
THIS MEANS: I HAVE DECIDED TO WORK IN THE MARKETING FIELD.
COUNTER-CLOCKWISE SPIN
THIS MEANS: I AM BEING SARCASTIC.
OH, THERE'S A GOOD PLAN.
NOTE LIPS
6/15/97 © 1997 United Feature Syndicate, Inc.
THIS MEANS: THE RECENT EMPLOYEE SATISFACTION SURVEY HAS NOT CAPTURED THE EXTENT OF MY FEELINGS.
THIS MEANS: I THINK YOU ARE ATTRACTIVE BUT IT WOULD BE VERY UNPROFESSIONAL TO SHOW IT.
THIS MEANS: MY LOTTERY INVESTMENT PAID OFF.
YANK!

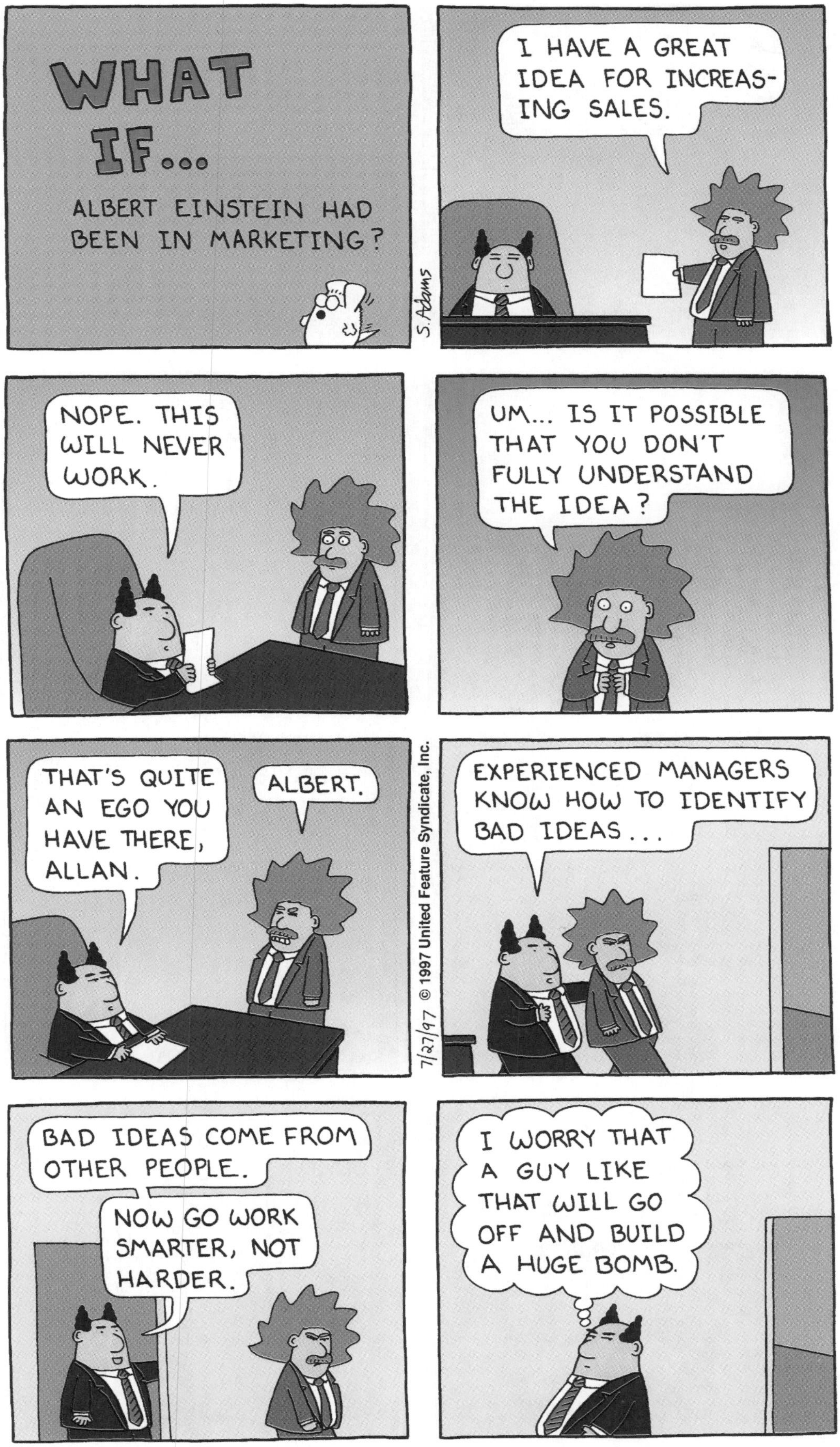
WHAT IF...
ALBERT EINSTEIN HAD BEEN IN MARKETING?
S. Adams
I HAVE A GREAT IDEA FOR INCREASING SALES.
NOPE. THIS WILL NEVER WORK.
UM... IS IT POSSIBLE THAT YOU DON'T FULLY UNDERSTAND THE IDEA?
THAT'S QUITE AN EGO YOU HAVE THERE, ALLAN.
ALBERT.
7/27/97 © 1997 United Feature Syndicate, Inc.
EXPERIENCED MANAGERS KNOW HOW TO IDENTIFY BAD IDEAS...
BAD IDEAS COME FROM OTHER PEOPLE.
NOW GO WORK SMARTER, NOT HARDER.
I WORRY THAT A GUY LIKE THAT WILL GO OFF AND BUILD A HUGE BOMB.

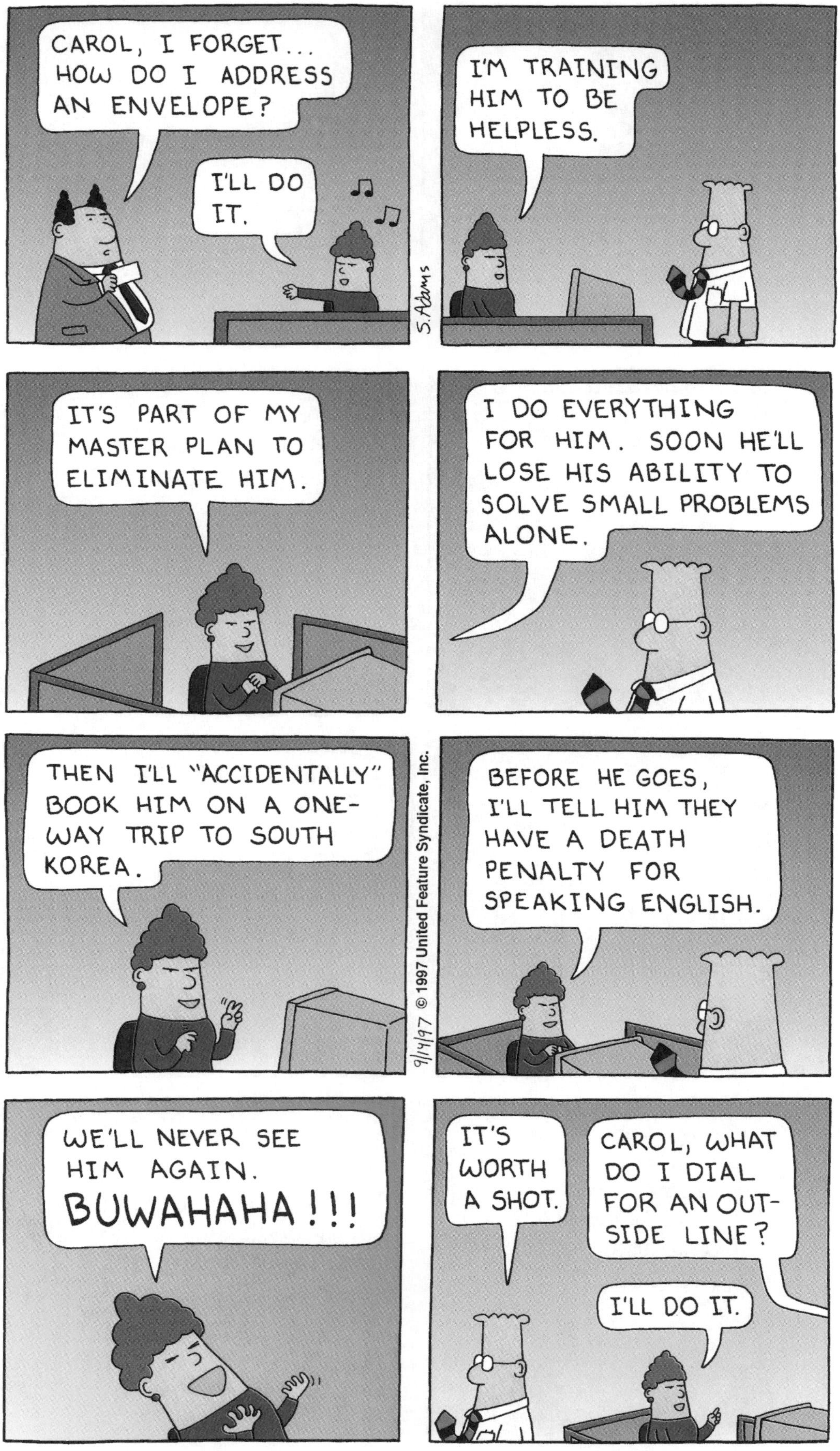
CAROL, I FORGET... HOW DO I ADDRESS AN ENVELOPE?
I'LL DO IT.
S. Adams
I'M TRAINING HIM TO BE HELPLESS.
IT'S PART OF MY MASTER PLAN TO ELIMINATE HIM.
I DO EVERYTHING FOR HIM. SOON HE'LL LOSE HIS ABILITY TO SOLVE SMALL PROBLEMS ALONE.
THEN I'LL "ACCIDENTALLY" BOOK HIM ON A ONE-WAY TRIP TO SOUTH KOREA.
9/14/97 © 1997 United Feature Syndicate, Inc.
BEFORE HE GOES, I'LL TELL HIM THEY HAVE A DEATH PENALTY FOR SPEAKING ENGLISH.
WE'LL NEVER SEE HIM AGAIN. BUWAHAHA!!!
IT'S WORTH A SHOT.
CAROL, WHAT DO I DIAL FOR AN OUT-SIDE LINE?
I'LL DO IT.

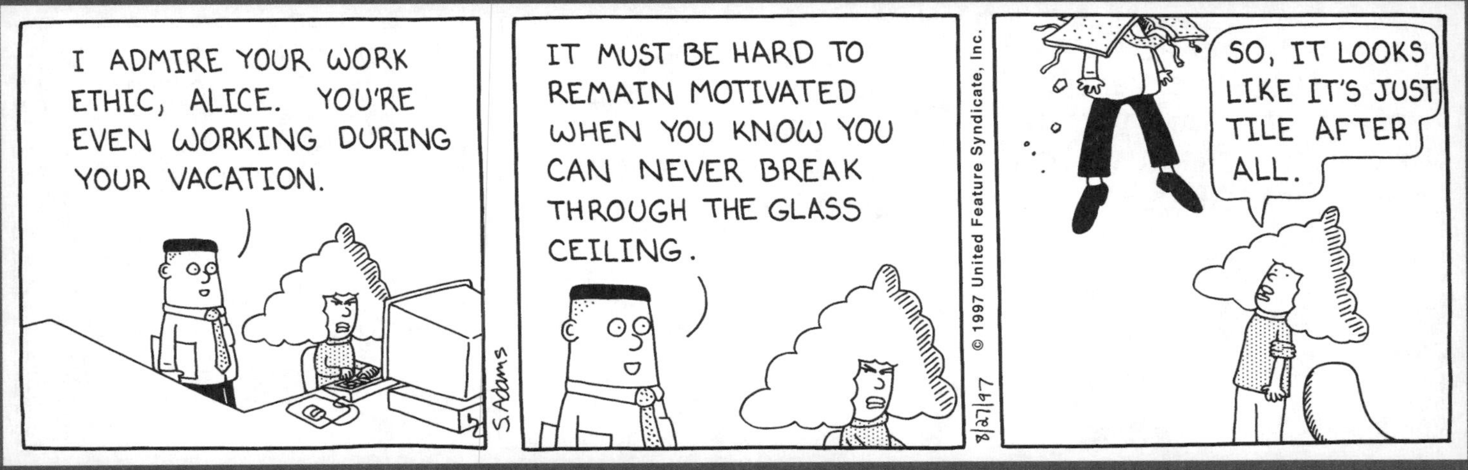
I ADMIRE YOUR WORK ETHIC, ALICE. YOU'RE EVEN WORKING DURING YOUR VACATION.
S. Adams
IT MUST BE HARD TO REMAIN MOTIVATED WHEN YOU KNOW YOU CAN NEVER BREAK THROUGH THE GLASS CEILING.
8/27/97
© 1997 United Feature Syndicate, Inc.
SO, IT LOOKS LIKE IT'S JUST TILE AFTER ALL.

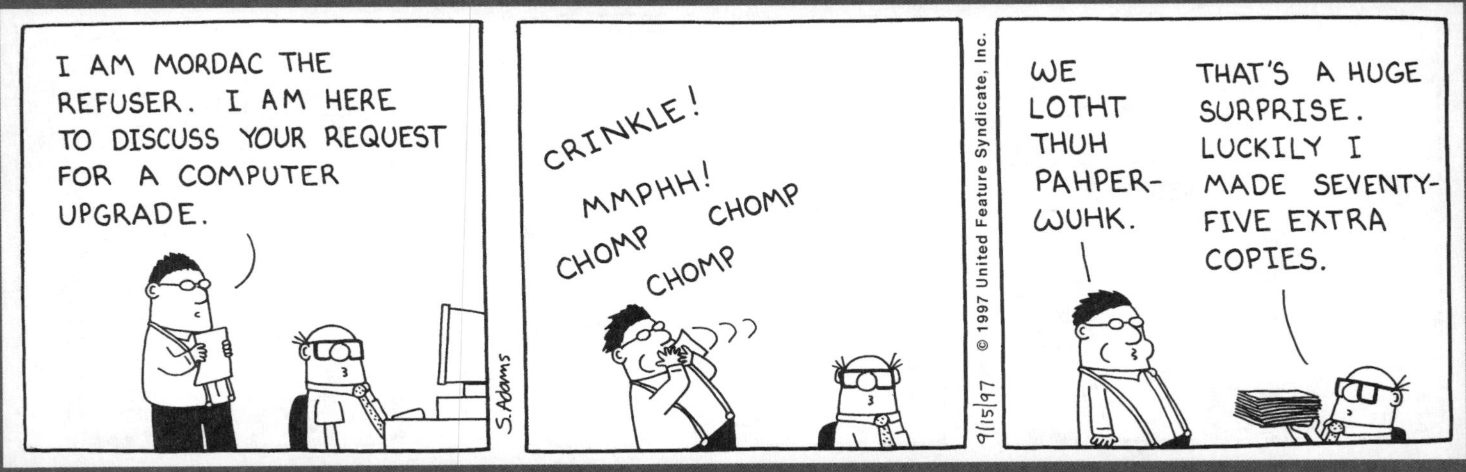
I AM MORDAC THE REFUSER. I AM HERE TO DISCUSS YOUR REQUEST FOR A COMPUTER UPGRADE.
S. Adams
CRINKLE!
MMPHH!
CHOMP CHOMP
CHOMP
9/15/97
© 1997 United Feature Syndicate, Inc.
WE LOTHT THUH PAHPER-WUHK.
THAT'S A HUGE SURPRISE. LUCKILY I MADE SEVENTY-FIVE EXTRA COPIES.

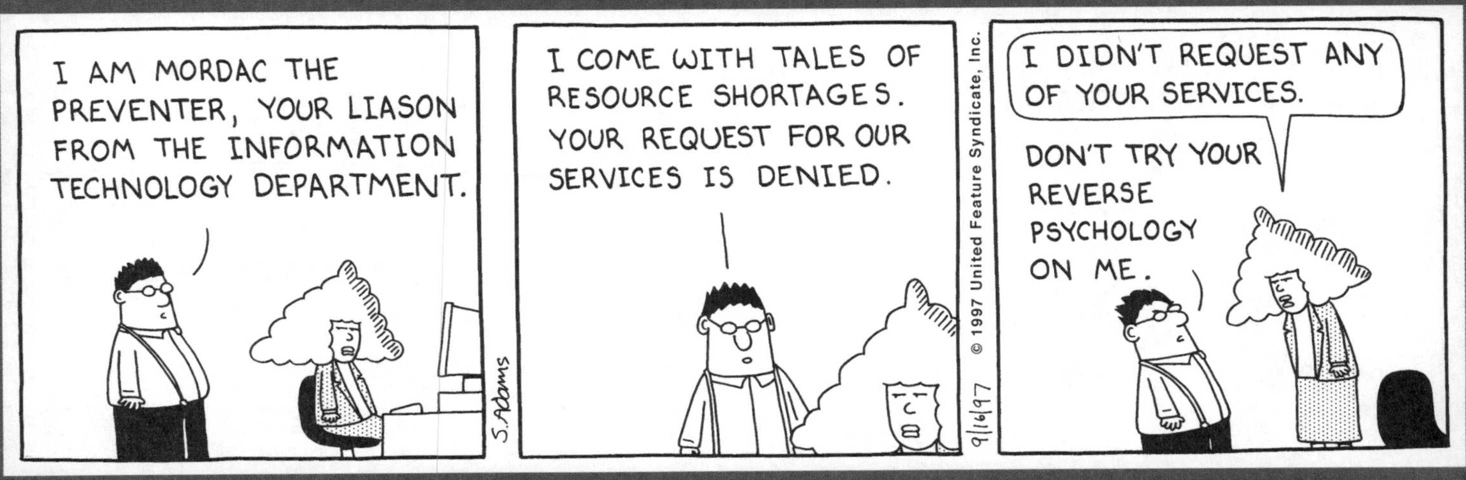
I AM MORDAC THE PREVENTER, YOUR LIASON FROM THE INFORMATION TECHNOLOGY DEPARTMENT.
S. Adams
I COME WITH TALES OF RESOURCE SHORTAGES. YOUR REQUEST FOR OUR SERVICES IS DENIED.
9/16/97
© 1997 United Feature Syndicate, Inc.
I DIDN'T REQUEST ANY OF YOUR SERVICES.
DON'T TRY YOUR REVERSE PSYCHOLOGY ON ME.

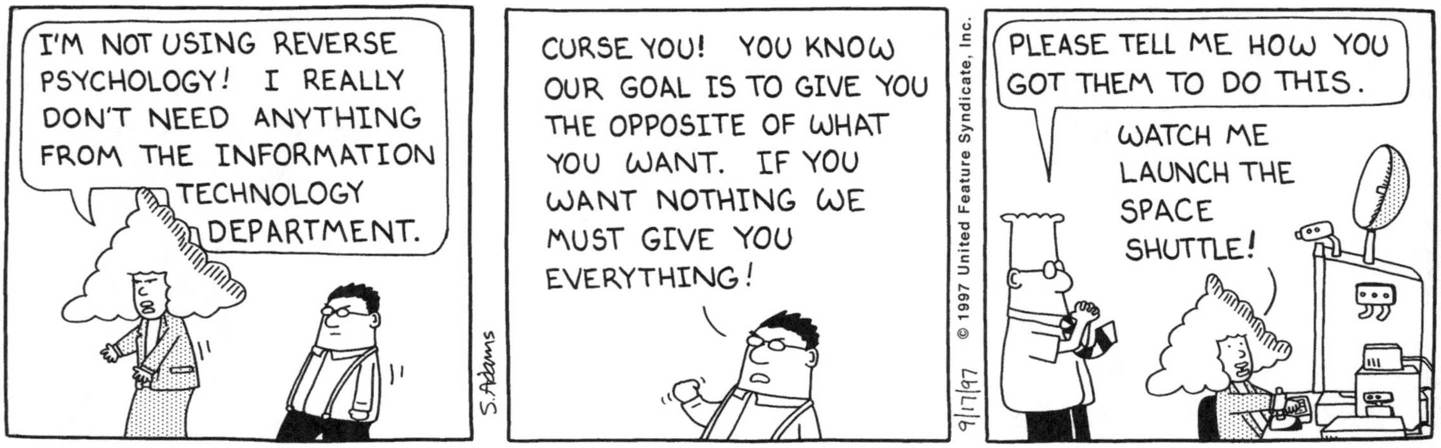
I'M NOT USING REVERSE PSYCHOLOGY! I REALLY DON'T NEED ANYTHING FROM THE INFORMATION TECHNOLOGY DEPARTMENT.
CURSE YOU! YOU KNOW OUR GOAL IS TO GIVE YOU THE OPPOSITE OF WHAT YOU WANT. IF YOU WANT NOTHING WE MUST GIVE YOU EVERYTHING!
PLEASE TELL ME HOW YOU GOT THEM TO DO THIS.
WATCH ME LAUNCH THE SPACE SHUTTLE!
S. Adams
9/17/97
© 1997 United Feature Syndicate, Inc.

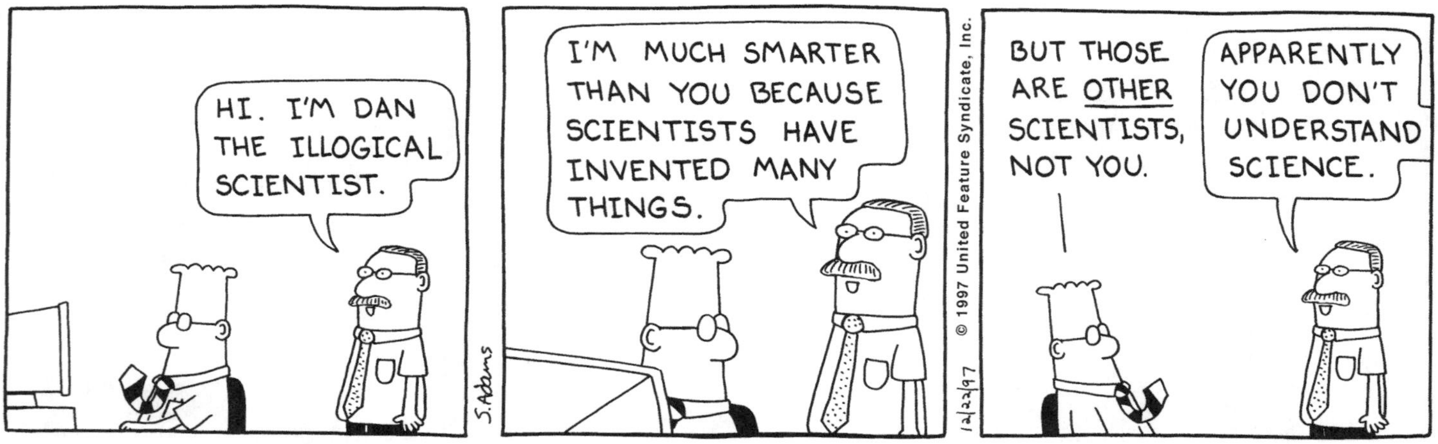
HI. I'M DAN THE ILLOGICAL SCIENTIST.
I'M MUCH SMARTER THAN YOU BECAUSE SCIENTISTS HAVE INVENTED MANY THINGS.
BUT THOSE ARE OTHER SCIENTISTS, NOT YOU.
APPARENTLY YOU DON'T UNDERSTAND SCIENCE.
S. Adams
12/22/97
© 1997 United Feature Syndicate, Inc.

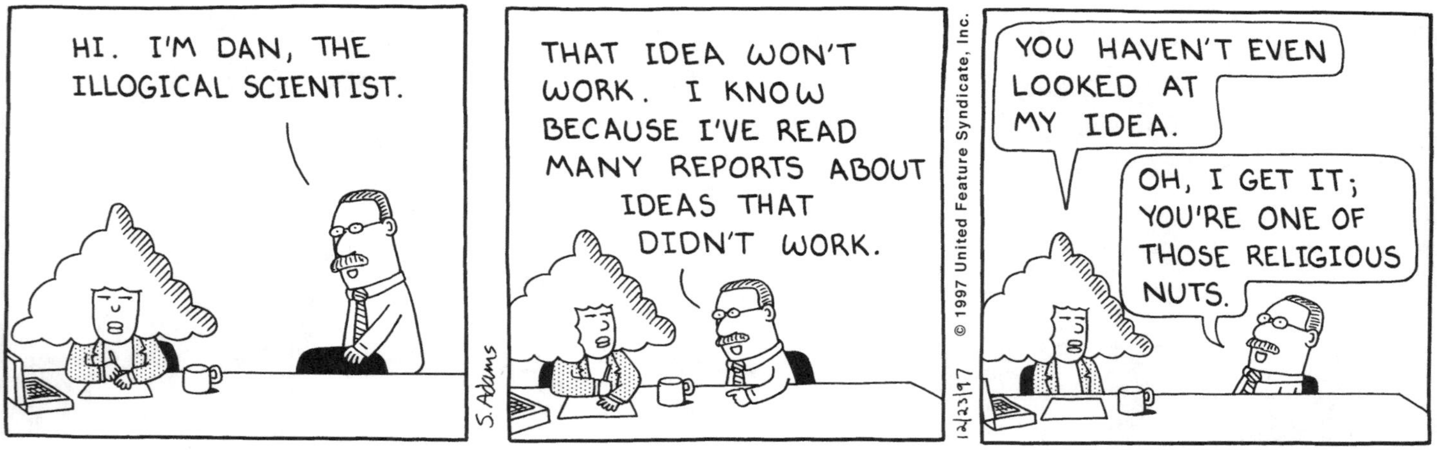
HI. I'M DAN, THE ILLOGICAL SCIENTIST.
THAT IDEA WON'T WORK. I KNOW BECAUSE I'VE READ MANY REPORTS ABOUT IDEAS THAT DIDN'T WORK.
YOU HAVEN'T EVEN LOOKED AT MY IDEA.
OH, I GET IT; YOU'RE ONE OF THOSE RELIGIOUS NUTS.
S. Adams
12/23/97
© 1997 United Feature Syndicate, Inc.

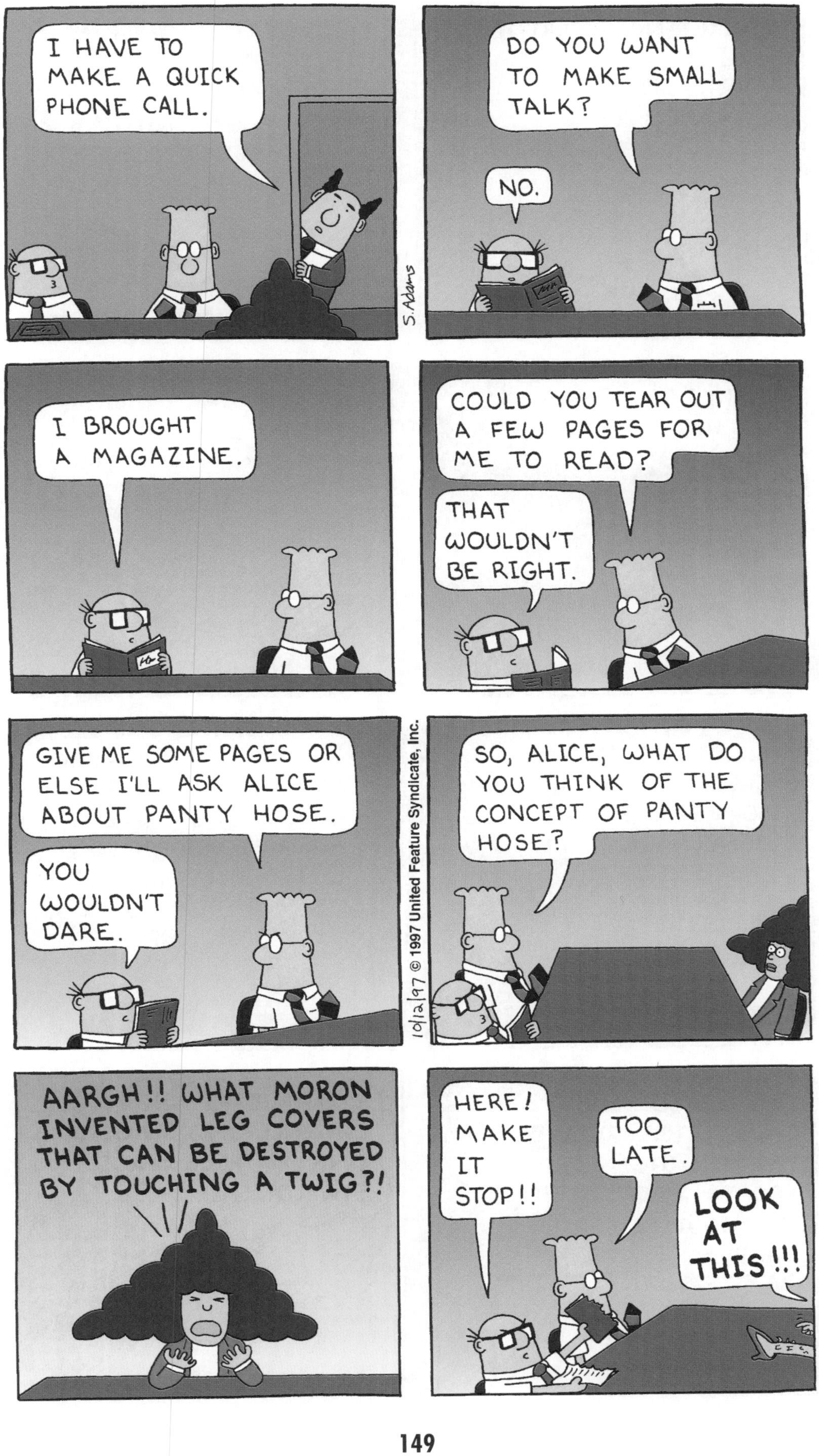
I HAVE TO MAKE A QUICK PHONE CALL.
S. Adams
DO YOU WANT TO MAKE SMALL TALK?
NO.
I BROUGHT A MAGAZINE.
COULD YOU TEAR OUT A FEW PAGES FOR ME TO READ?
THAT WOULDN'T BE RIGHT.
GIVE ME SOME PAGES OR ELSE I'LL ASK ALICE ABOUT PANTY HOSE.
YOU WOULDN'T DARE.
10/12/97 © 1997 United Feature Syndicate, Inc.
SO, ALICE, WHAT DO YOU THINK OF THE CONCEPT OF PANTY HOSE?
AARGH!! WHAT MORON INVENTED LEG COVERS THAT CAN BE DESTROYED BY TOUCHING A TWIG?!
HERE! MAKE IT STOP!!
TOO LATE.
LOOK AT THIS!!!

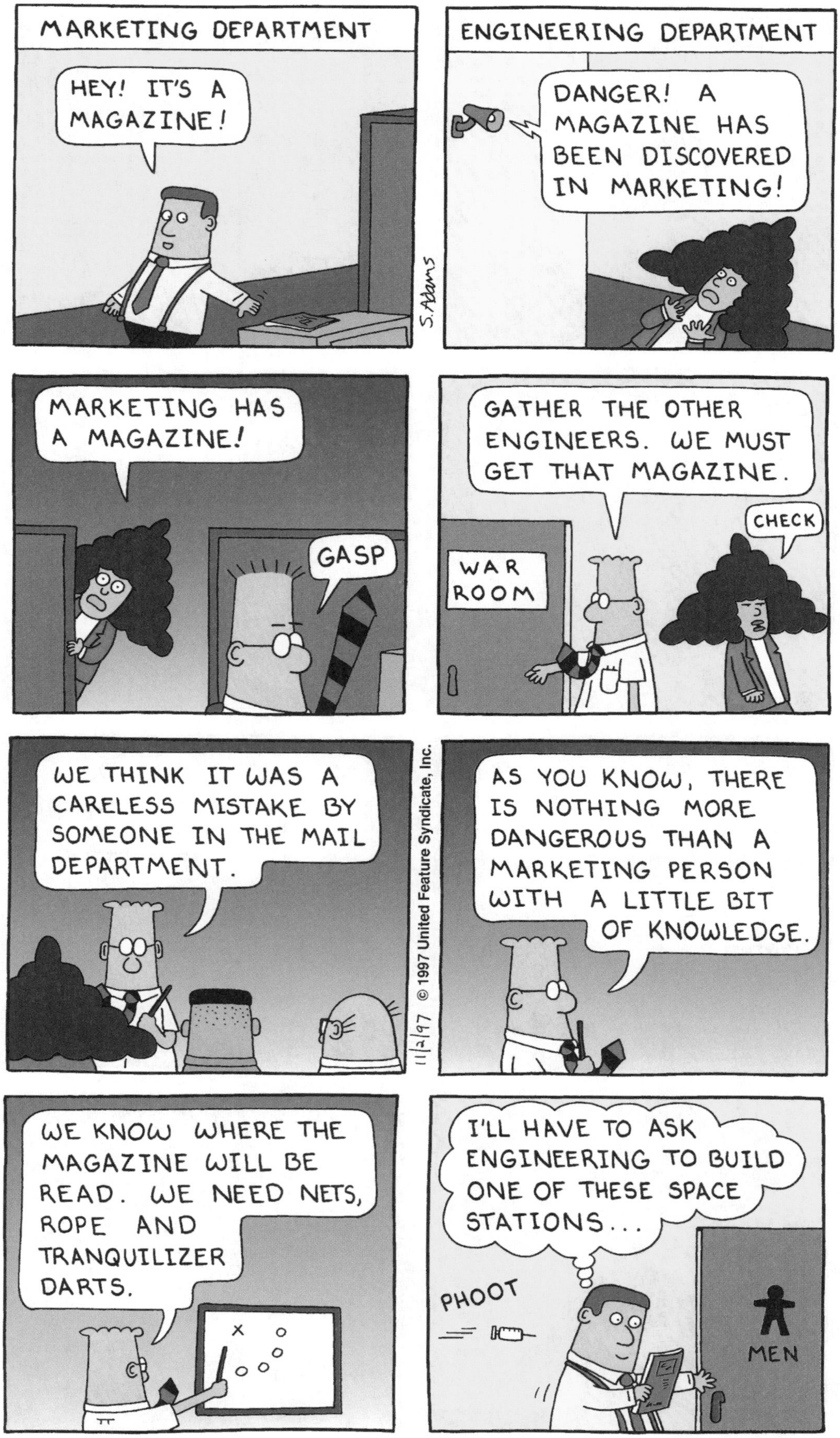
MARKETING DEPARTMENT
HEY! IT'S A MAGAZINE!
ENGINEERING DEPARTMENT
DANGER! A MAGAZINE HAS BEEN DISCOVERED IN MARKETING!
S. Adams
MARKETING HAS A MAGAZINE!
GASP
GATHER THE OTHER ENGINEERS. WE MUST GET THAT MAGAZINE.
CHECK
WAR ROOM
WE THINK IT WAS A CARELESS MISTAKE BY SOMEONE IN THE MAIL DEPARTMENT.
11/2/97 © 1997 United Feature Syndicate, Inc.
AS YOU KNOW, THERE IS NOTHING MORE DANGEROUS THAN A MARKETING PERSON WITH A LITTLE BIT OF KNOWLEDGE.
WE KNOW WHERE THE MAGAZINE WILL BE READ. WE NEED NETS, ROPE AND TRANQUILIZER DARTS.
I'LL HAVE TO ASK ENGINEERING TO BUILD ONE OF THESE SPACE STATIONS...
PHOOT
MEN

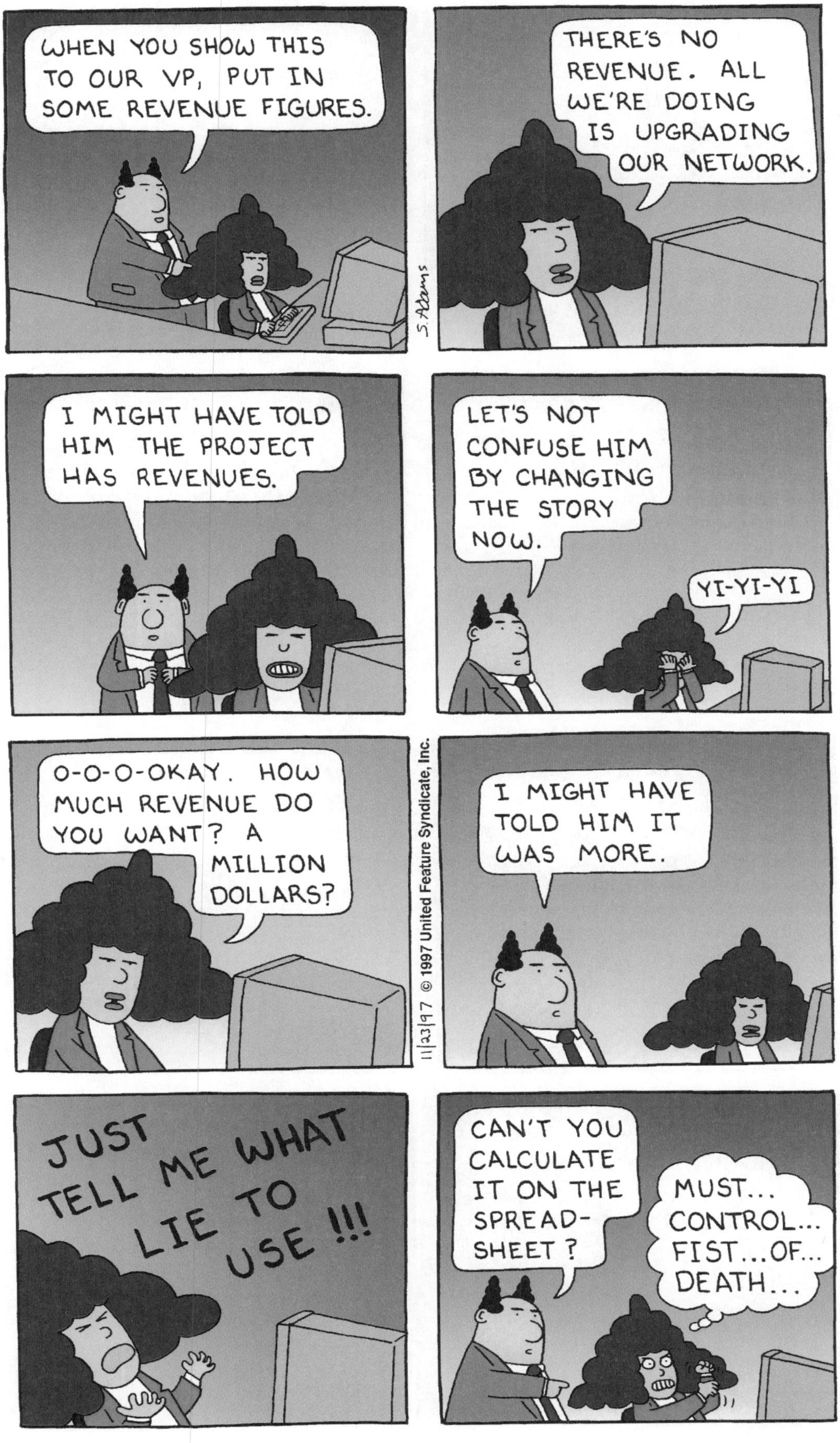
WHEN YOU SHOW THIS TO OUR VP, PUT IN SOME REVENUE FIGURES.
S. Adams
THERE'S NO REVENUE. ALL WE'RE DOING IS UPGRADING OUR NETWORK.
I MIGHT HAVE TOLD HIM THE PROJECT HAS REVENUES.
LET'S NOT CONFUSE HIM BY CHANGING THE STORY NOW.
YI-YI-YI
O-O-O-OKAY. HOW MUCH REVENUE DO YOU WANT? A MILLION DOLLARS?
11/23/97 © 1997 United Feature Syndicate, Inc.
I MIGHT HAVE TOLD HIM IT WAS MORE.
JUST TELL ME WHAT LIE TO USE !!!
CAN'T YOU CALCULATE IT ON THE SPREAD-SHEET?
MUST... CONTROL... FIST... OF... DEATH...

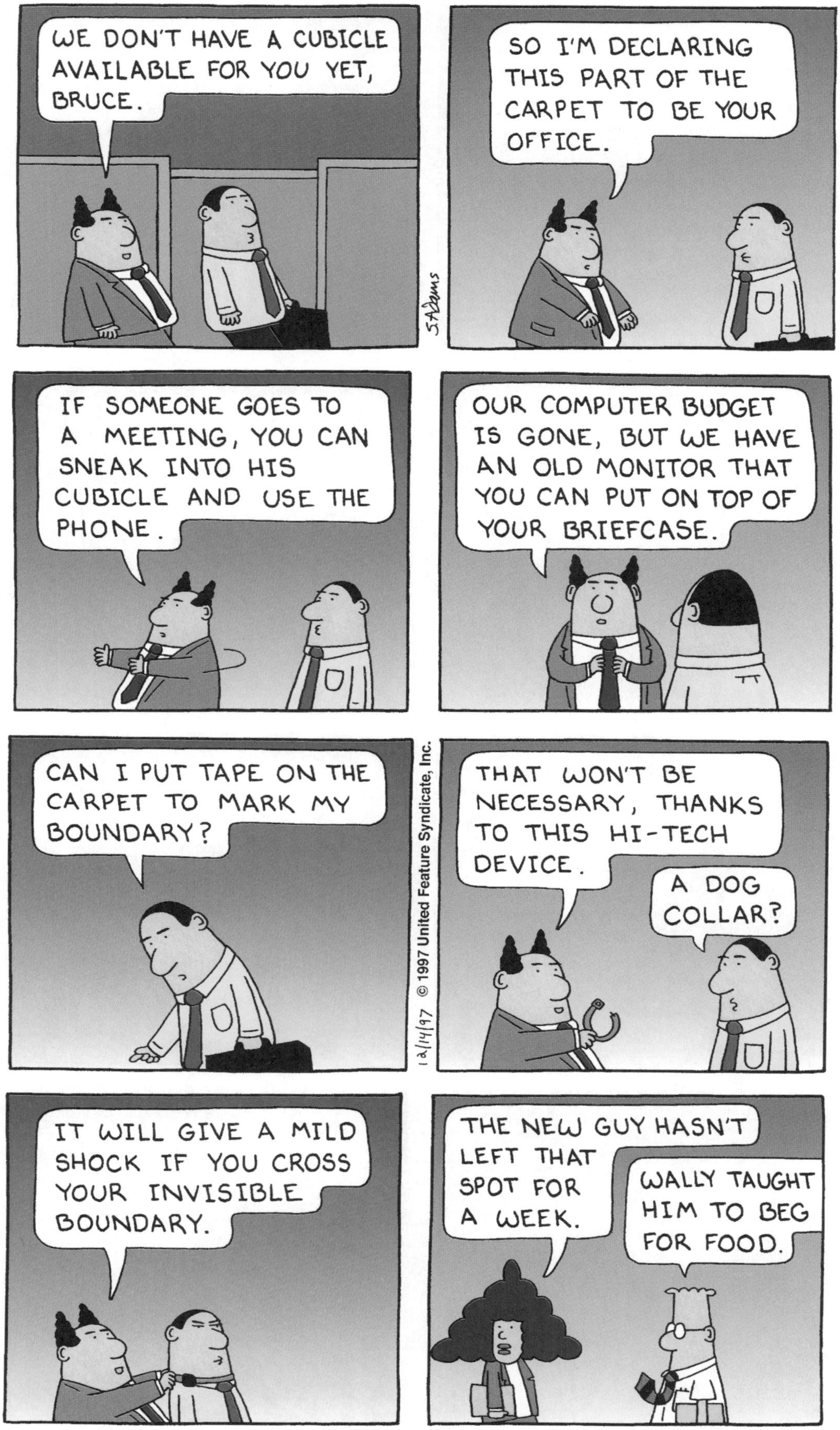
WE DON'T HAVE A CUBICLE AVAILABLE FOR YOU YET, BRUCE.
SO I'M DECLARING THIS PART OF THE CARPET TO BE YOUR OFFICE.
S.Adams
IF SOMEONE GOES TO A MEETING, YOU CAN SNEAK INTO HIS CUBICLE AND USE THE PHONE.
OUR COMPUTER BUDGET IS GONE, BUT WE HAVE AN OLD MONITOR THAT YOU CAN PUT ON TOP OF YOUR BRIEFCASE.
CAN I PUT TAPE ON THE CARPET TO MARK MY BOUNDARY?
12/14/97 © 1997 United Feature Syndicate, Inc.
THAT WON'T BE NECESSARY, THANKS TO THIS HI-TECH DEVICE.
A DOG COLLAR?
IT WILL GIVE A MILD SHOCK IF YOU CROSS YOUR INVISIBLE BOUNDARY.
THE NEW GUY HASN'T LEFT THAT SPOT FOR A WEEK.
WALLY TAUGHT HIM TO BEG FOR FOOD.

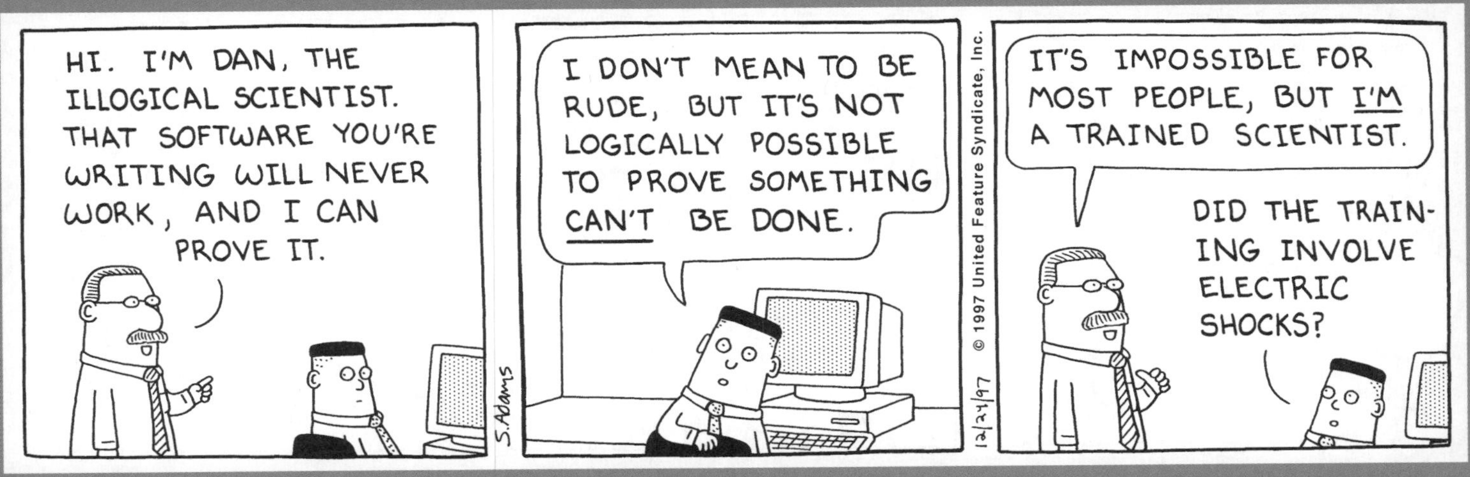
HI. I'M DAN, THE ILLOGICAL SCIENTIST. THAT SOFTWARE YOU'RE WRITING WILL NEVER WORK, AND I CAN PROVE IT.
I DON'T MEAN TO BE RUDE, BUT IT'S NOT LOGICALLY POSSIBLE TO PROVE SOMETHING CAN'T BE DONE.
IT'S IMPOSSIBLE FOR MOST PEOPLE, BUT I'M A TRAINED SCIENTIST.
DID THE TRAINING INVOLVE ELECTRIC SHOCKS?

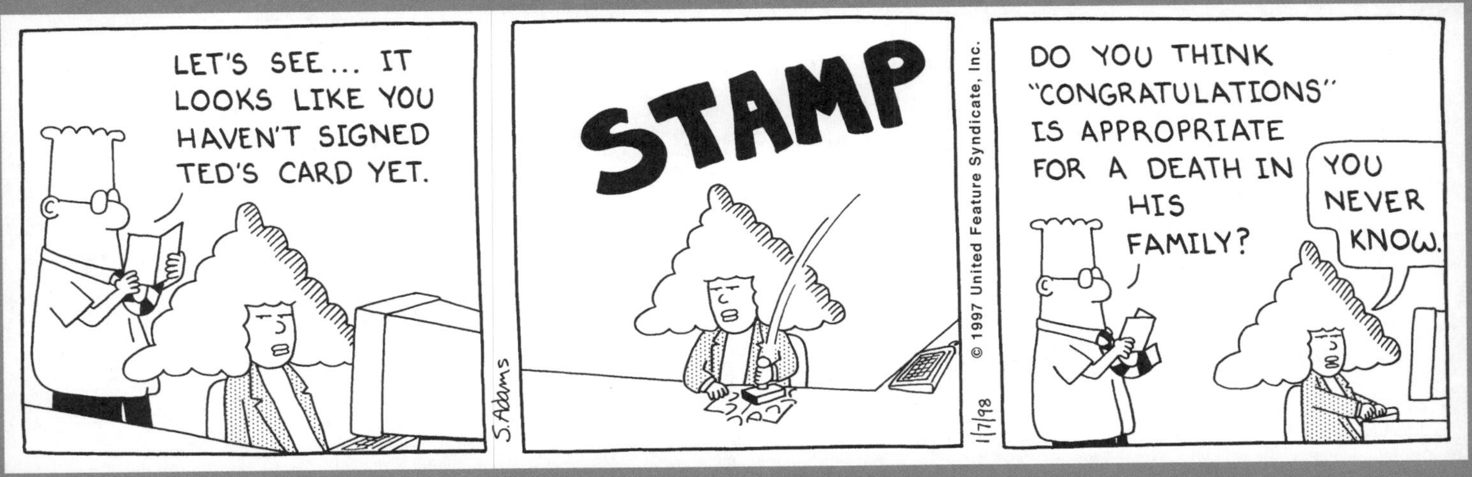
LET'S SEE... IT LOOKS LIKE YOU HAVEN'T SIGNED TED'S CARD YET.
STAMP
DO YOU THINK "CONGRATULATIONS" IS APPROPRIATE FOR A DEATH IN HIS FAMILY?
YOU NEVER KNOW.

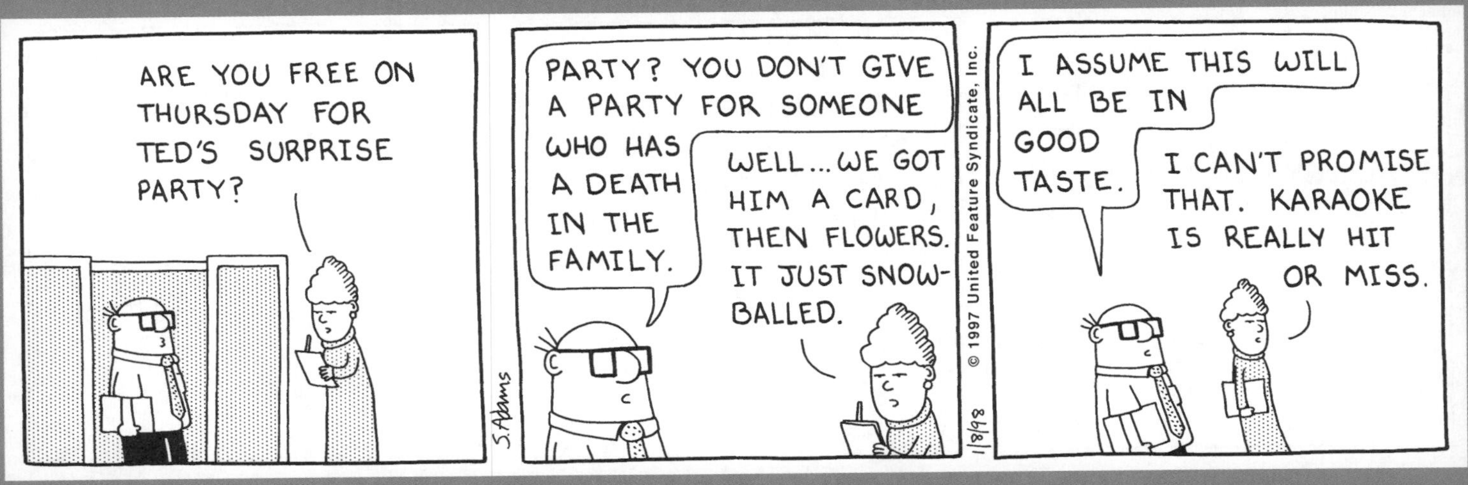
ARE YOU FREE ON THURSDAY FOR TED'S SURPRISE PARTY?
PARTY? YOU DON'T GIVE A PARTY FOR SOMEONE WHO HAS A DEATH IN THE FAMILY.
WELL... WE GOT HIM A CARD, THEN FLOWERS. IT JUST SNOWBALLED.
I ASSUME THIS WILL ALL BE IN GOOD TASTE.
I CAN'T PROMISE THAT. KARAOKE IS REALLY HIT OR MISS.

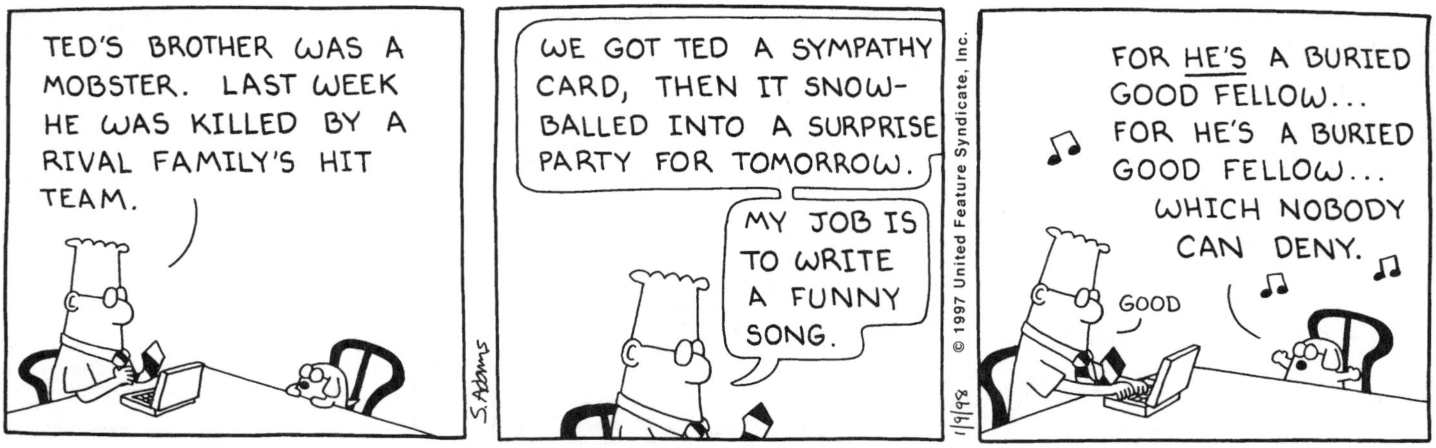
TED'S BROTHER WAS A MOBSTER. LAST WEEK HE WAS KILLED BY A RIVAL FAMILY'S HIT TEAM.
S. Adams
WE GOT TED A SYMPATHY CARD, THEN IT SNOWBALLED INTO A SURPRISE PARTY FOR TOMORROW.
MY JOB IS TO WRITE A FUNNY SONG.
1/9/98 © 1997 United Feature Syndicate, Inc.
FOR HE'S A BURIED GOOD FELLOW... FOR HE'S A BURIED GOOD FELLOW... WHICH NOBODY CAN DENY.
GOOD

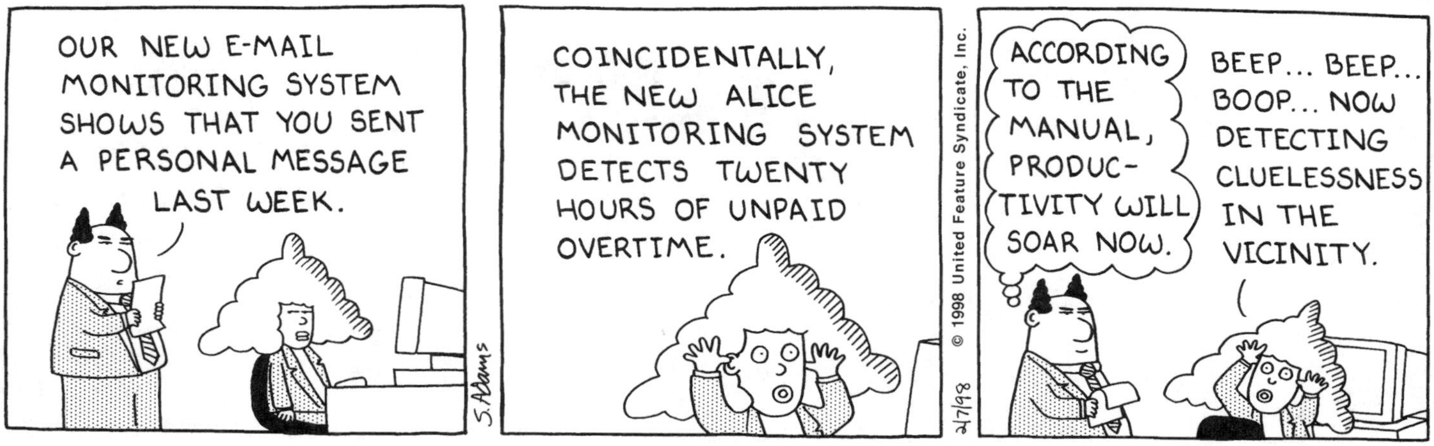
OUR NEW E-MAIL MONITORING SYSTEM SHOWS THAT YOU SENT A PERSONAL MESSAGE LAST WEEK.
S. Adams
COINCIDENTALLY, THE NEW ALICE MONITORING SYSTEM DETECTS TWENTY HOURS OF UNPAID OVERTIME.
2/7/98 © 1998 United Feature Syndicate, Inc.
ACCORDING TO THE MANUAL, PRODUCTIVITY WILL SOAR NOW.
BEEP... BEEP... BOOP... NOW DETECTING CLUELESSNESS IN THE VICINITY.

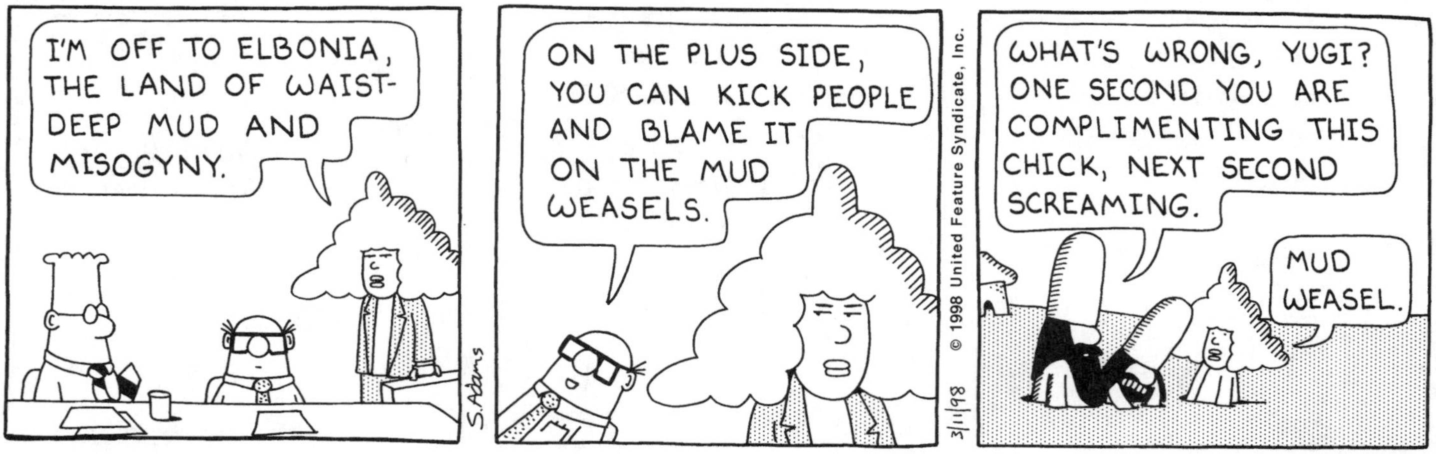
I'M OFF TO ELBONIA, THE LAND OF WAIST-DEEP MUD AND MISOGYNY.
S. Adams
ON THE PLUS SIDE, YOU CAN KICK PEOPLE AND BLAME IT ON THE MUD WEASELS.
3/11/98 © 1998 United Feature Syndicate, Inc.
WHAT'S WRONG, YUGI? ONE SECOND YOU ARE COMPLIMENTING THIS CHICK, NEXT SECOND SCREAMING.
MUD WEASEL.

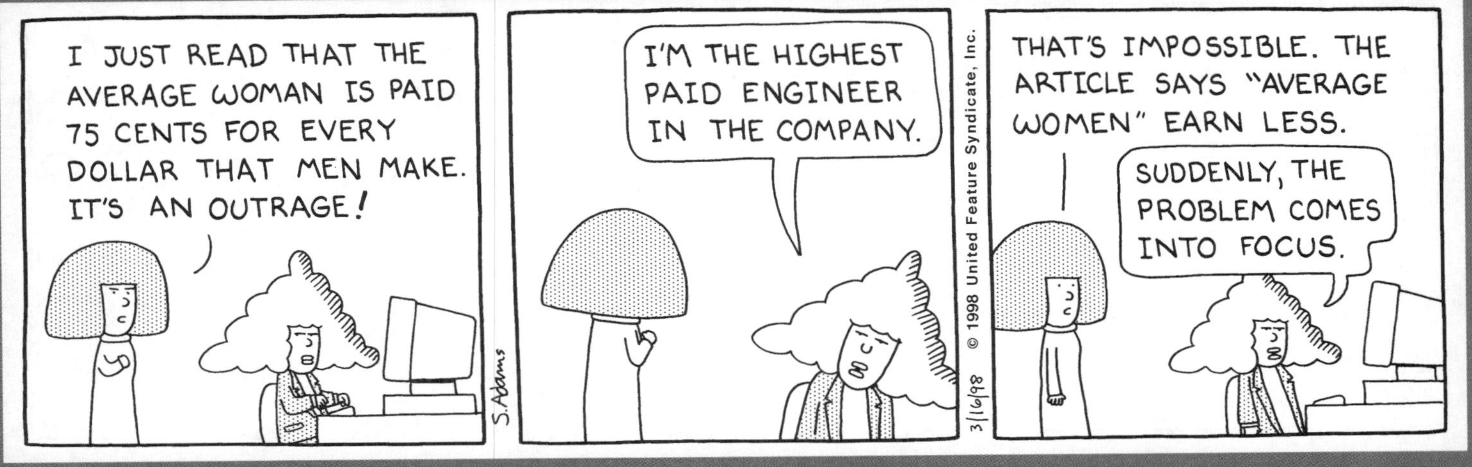
I JUST READ THAT THE AVERAGE WOMAN IS PAID 75 CENTS FOR EVERY DOLLAR THAT MEN MAKE. IT'S AN OUTRAGE!
S. Adams
I'M THE HIGHEST PAID ENGINEER IN THE COMPANY.
3/16/98 © 1998 United Feature Syndicate, Inc.
THAT'S IMPOSSIBLE. THE ARTICLE SAYS "AVERAGE WOMEN" EARN LESS.
SUDDENLY, THE PROBLEM COMES INTO FOCUS.

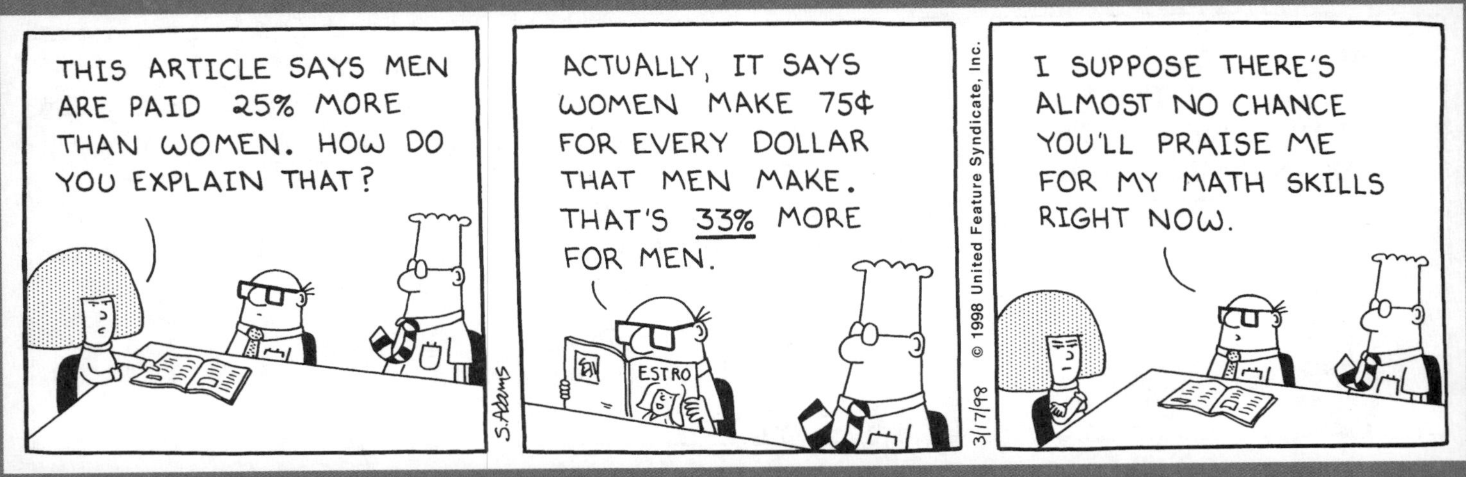
THIS ARTICLE SAYS MEN ARE PAID 25% MORE THAN WOMEN. HOW DO YOU EXPLAIN THAT?
S. Adams
ACTUALLY, IT SAYS WOMEN MAKE 75¢ FOR EVERY DOLLAR THAT MEN MAKE. THAT'S 33% MORE FOR MEN.
ESTRO
3/17/98 © 1998 United Feature Syndicate, Inc.
I SUPPOSE THERE'S ALMOST NO CHANCE YOU'LL PRAISE ME FOR MY MATH SKILLS RIGHT NOW.

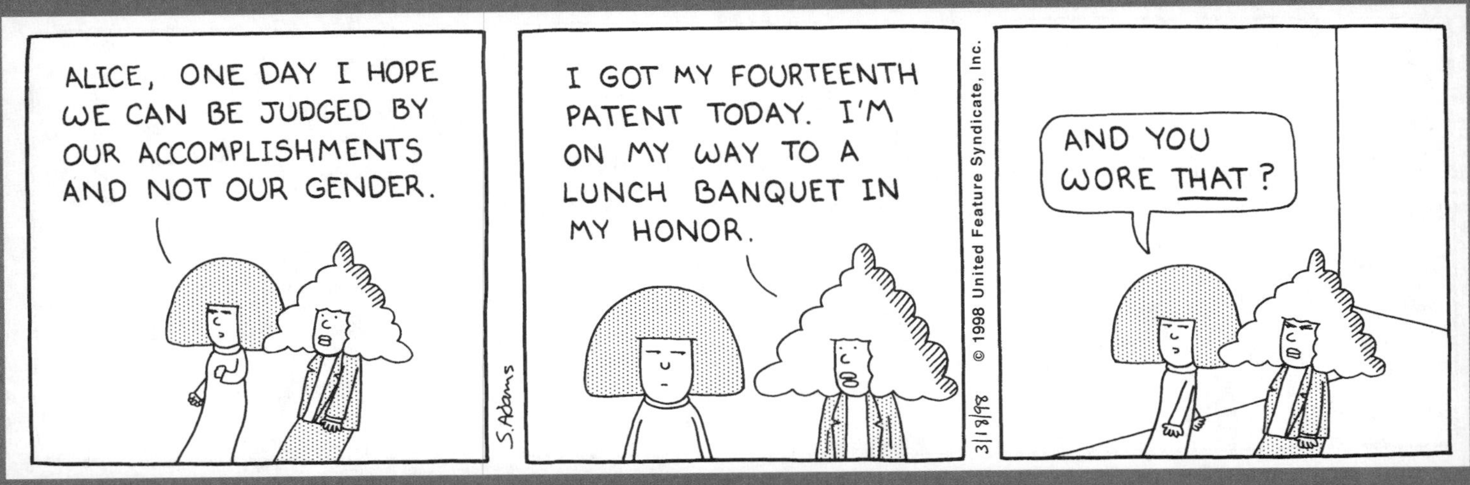
ALICE, ONE DAY I HOPE WE CAN BE JUDGED BY OUR ACCOMPLISHMENTS AND NOT OUR GENDER.
S. Adams
I GOT MY FOURTEENTH PATENT TODAY. I'M ON MY WAY TO A LUNCH BANQUET IN MY HONOR.
3/18/98 © 1998 United Feature Syndicate, Inc.
AND YOU WORE THAT?

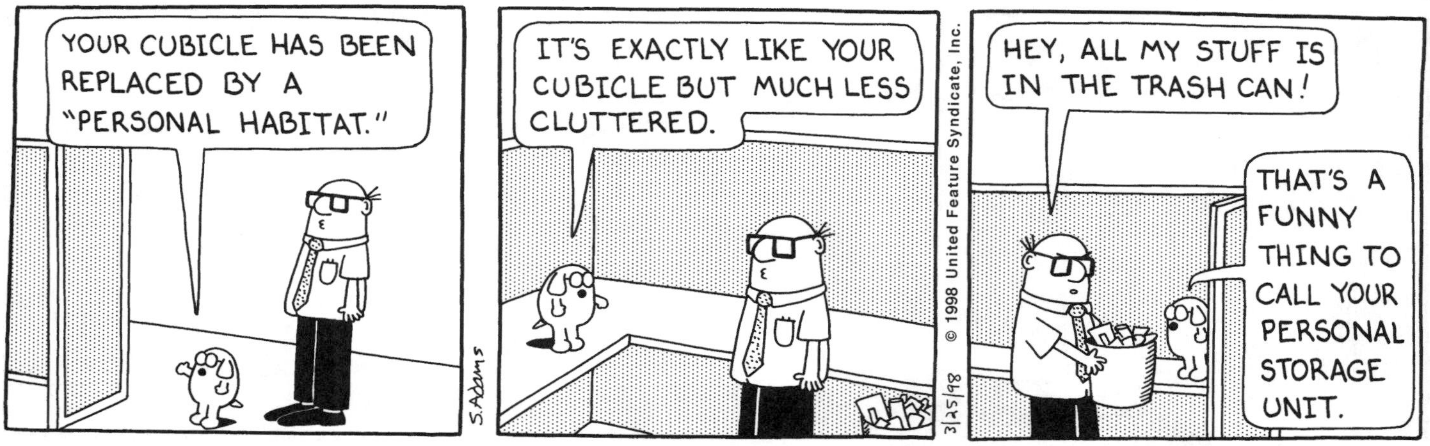
YOUR CUBICLE HAS BEEN REPLACED BY A "PERSONAL HABITAT."
S. Adams
IT'S EXACTLY LIKE YOUR CUBICLE BUT MUCH LESS CLUTTERED.
3/25/98 © 1998 United Feature Syndicate, Inc.
HEY, ALL MY STUFF IS IN THE TRASH CAN!
THAT'S A FUNNY THING TO CALL YOUR PERSONAL STORAGE UNIT.

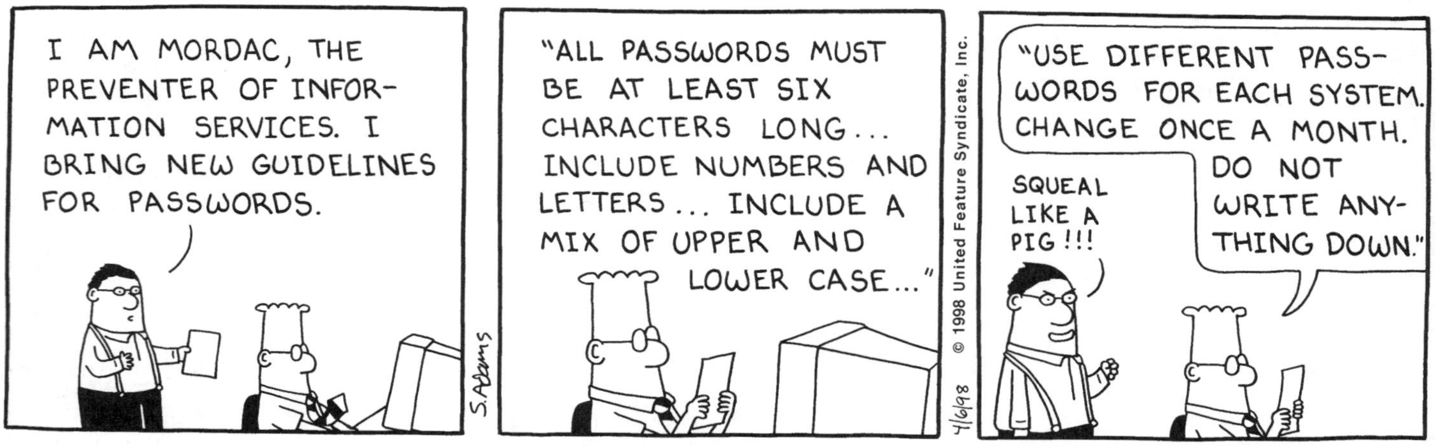
I AM MORDAC, THE PREVENTER OF INFORMATION SERVICES. I BRING NEW GUIDELINES FOR PASSWORDS.
S. Adams
"ALL PASSWORDS MUST BE AT LEAST SIX CHARACTERS LONG... INCLUDE NUMBERS AND LETTERS... INCLUDE A MIX OF UPPER AND LOWER CASE..."
4/6/98 © 1998 United Feature Syndicate, Inc.
"USE DIFFERENT PASSWORDS FOR EACH SYSTEM. CHANGE ONCE A MONTH.
SQUEAL LIKE A PIG!!!
DO NOT WRITE ANYTHING DOWN."

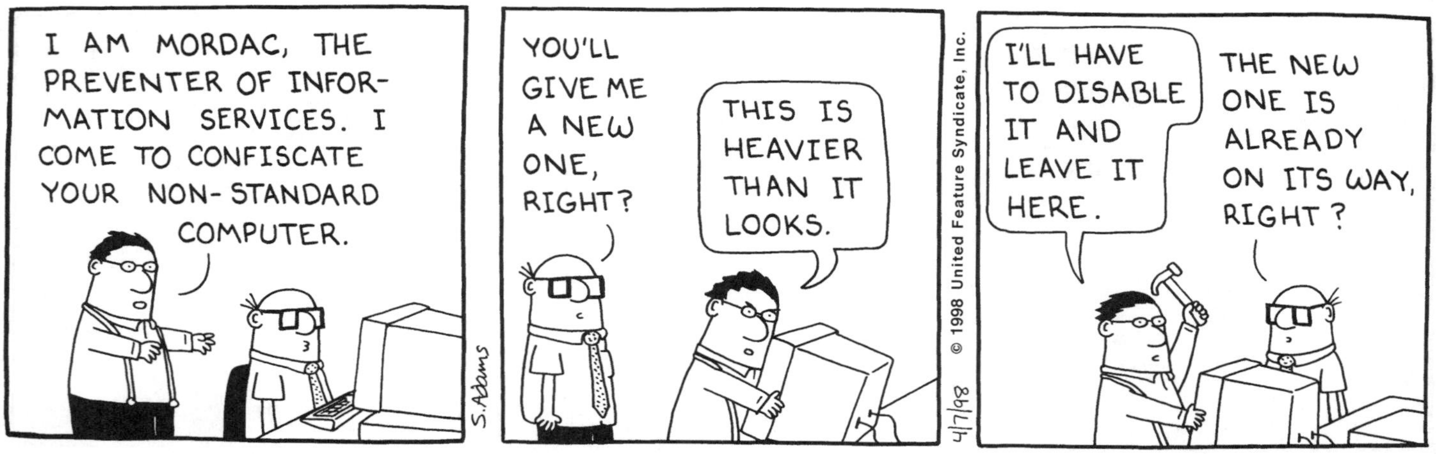
I AM MORDAC, THE PREVENTER OF INFORMATION SERVICES. I COME TO CONFISCATE YOUR NON-STANDARD COMPUTER.
S. Adams
YOU'LL GIVE ME A NEW ONE, RIGHT?
THIS IS HEAVIER THAN IT LOOKS.
4/7/98 © 1998 United Feature Syndicate, Inc.
I'LL HAVE TO DISABLE IT AND LEAVE IT HERE.
THE NEW ONE IS ALREADY ON ITS WAY, RIGHT?

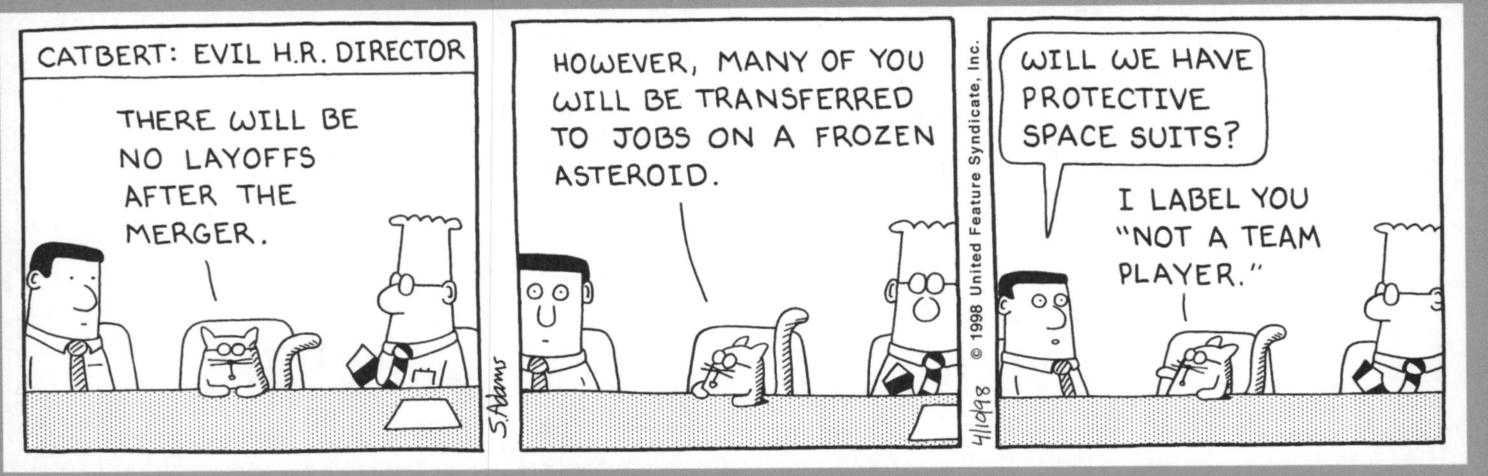
CATBERT: EVIL H.R. DIRECTOR
THERE WILL BE NO LAYOFFS AFTER THE MERGER.
S. Adams
HOWEVER, MANY OF YOU WILL BE TRANSFERRED TO JOBS ON A FROZEN ASTEROID.
4/10/98 © 1998 United Feature Syndicate, Inc.
WILL WE HAVE PROTECTIVE SPACE SUITS?
I LABEL YOU "NOT A TEAM PLAYER."

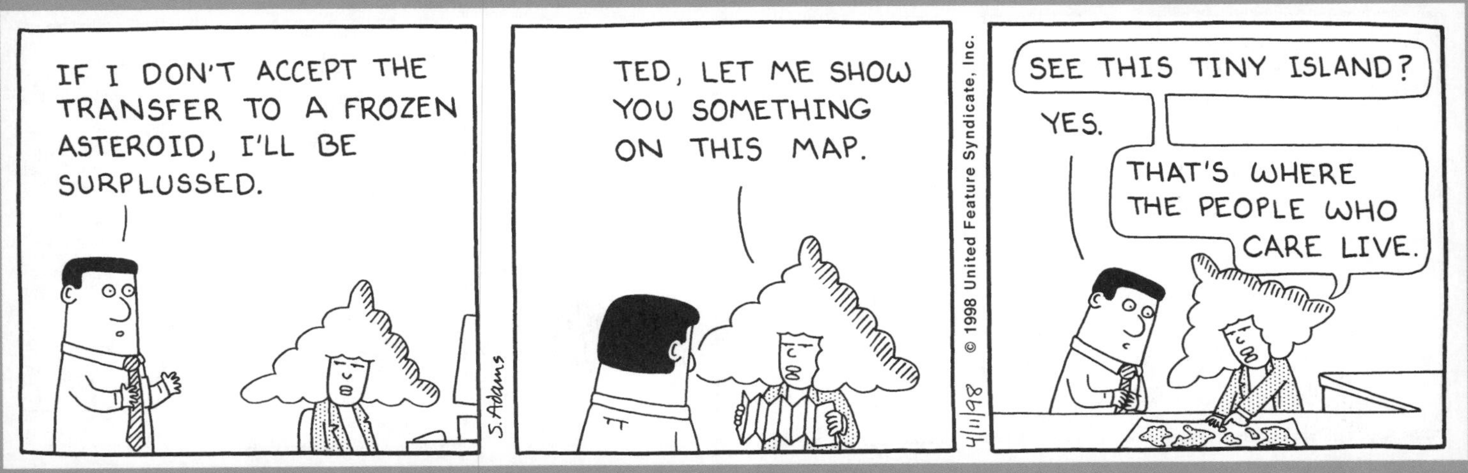
IF I DON'T ACCEPT THE TRANSFER TO A FROZEN ASTEROID, I'LL BE SURPLUSSED.
S. Adams
TED, LET ME SHOW YOU SOMETHING ON THIS MAP.
4/11/98 © 1998 United Feature Syndicate, Inc.
SEE THIS TINY ISLAND?
YES.
THAT'S WHERE THE PEOPLE WHO CARE LIVE.

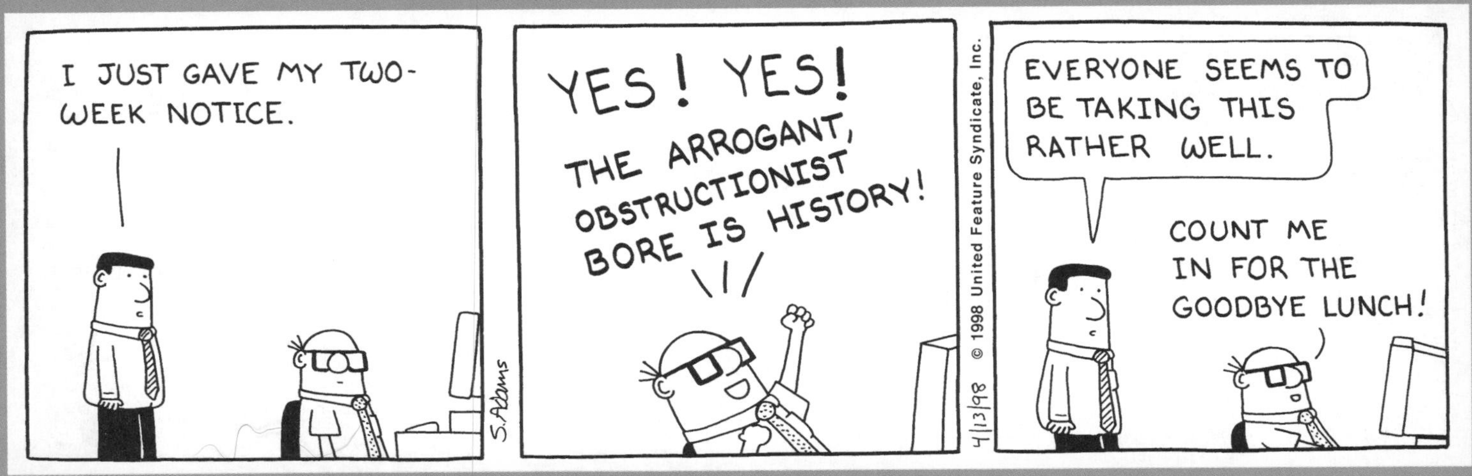
I JUST GAVE MY TWO-WEEK NOTICE.
S. Adams
YES! YES!
THE ARROGANT, OBSTRUCTIONIST BORE IS HISTORY!
4/13/98 © 1998 United Feature Syndicate, Inc.
EVERYONE SEEMS TO BE TAKING THIS RATHER WELL.
COUNT ME IN FOR THE GOODBYE LUNCH!

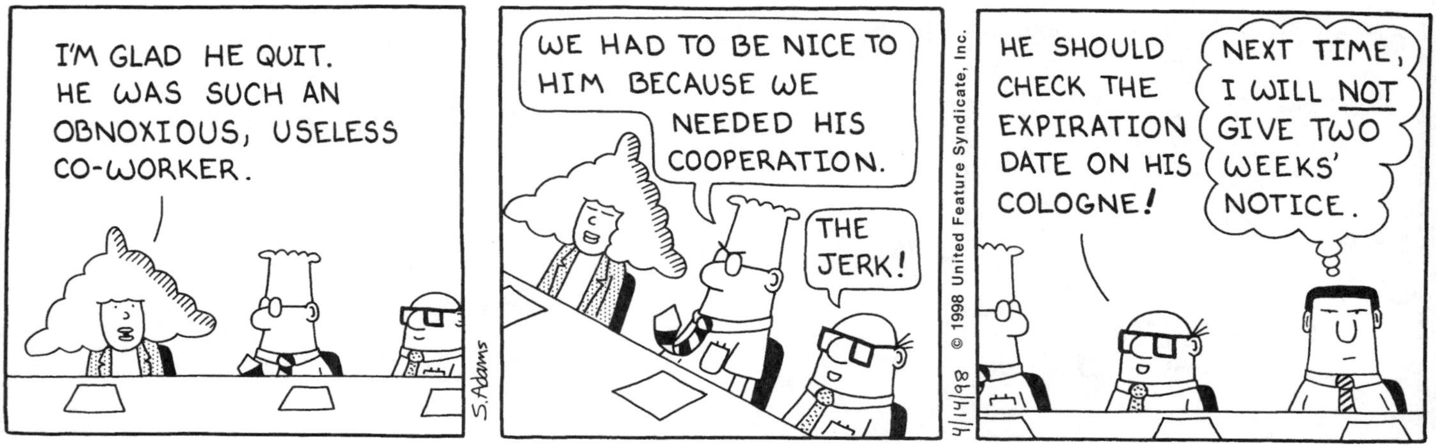
I'M GLAD HE QUIT. HE WAS SUCH AN OBNOXIOUS, USELESS CO-WORKER.
S. Adams
WE HAD TO BE NICE TO HIM BECAUSE WE NEEDED HIS COOPERATION.
THE JERK!
4/14/98 © 1998 United Feature Syndicate, Inc.
HE SHOULD CHECK THE EXPIRATION DATE ON HIS COLOGNE!
NEXT TIME, I WILL NOT GIVE TWO WEEKS' NOTICE.

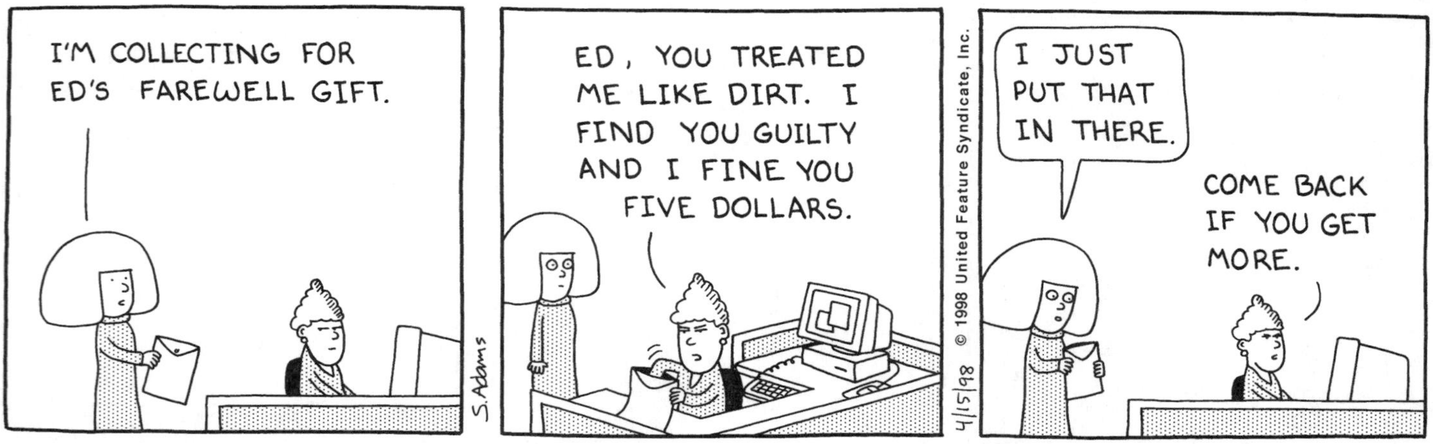
I'M COLLECTING FOR ED'S FAREWELL GIFT.
S. Adams
ED, YOU TREATED ME LIKE DIRT. I FIND YOU GUILTY AND I FINE YOU FIVE DOLLARS.
4/15/98 © 1998 United Feature Syndicate, Inc.
I JUST PUT THAT IN THERE.
COME BACK IF YOU GET MORE.

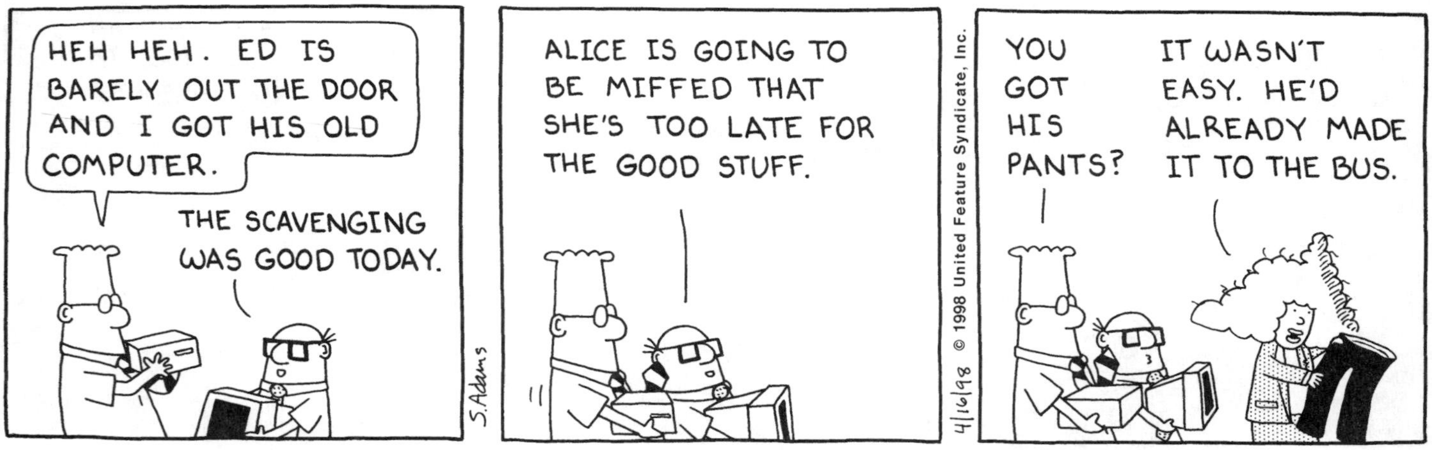
HEH HEH. ED IS BARELY OUT THE DOOR AND I GOT HIS OLD COMPUTER.
THE SCAVENGING WAS GOOD TODAY.
S. Adams
ALICE IS GOING TO BE MIFFED THAT SHE'S TOO LATE FOR THE GOOD STUFF.
4/16/98 © 1998 United Feature Syndicate, Inc.
YOU GOT HIS PANTS?
IT WASN'T EASY. HE'D ALREADY MADE IT TO THE BUS.

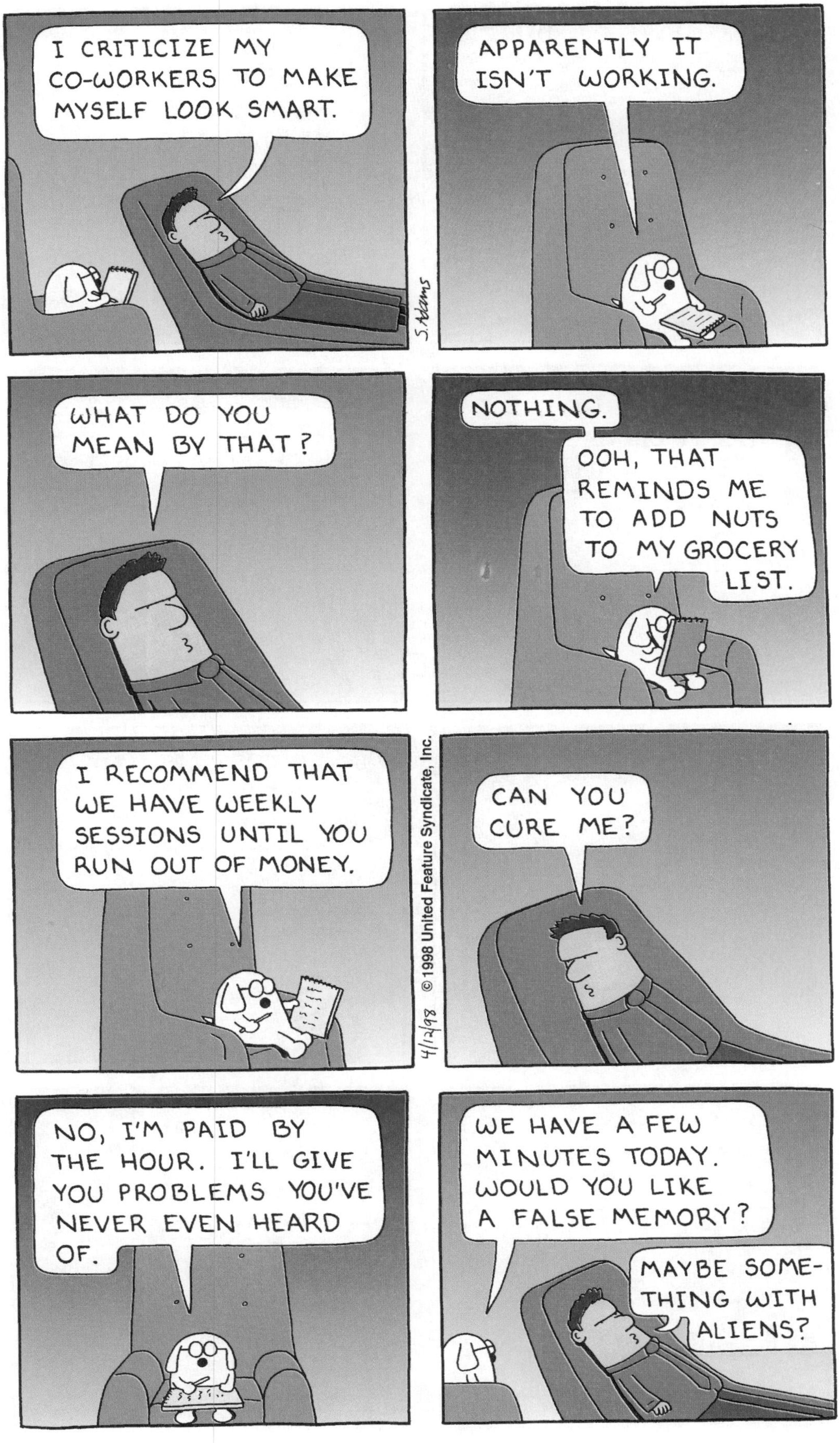
I CRITICIZE MY CO-WORKERS TO MAKE MYSELF LOOK SMART.
S. Adams
APPARENTLY IT ISN'T WORKING.
WHAT DO YOU MEAN BY THAT?
NOTHING.
OOH, THAT REMINDS ME TO ADD NUTS TO MY GROCERY LIST.
I RECOMMEND THAT WE HAVE WEEKLY SESSIONS UNTIL YOU RUN OUT OF MONEY.
© 1998 United Feature Syndicate, Inc.
4/12/98
CAN YOU CURE ME?
NO, I'M PAID BY THE HOUR. I'LL GIVE YOU PROBLEMS YOU'VE NEVER EVEN HEARD OF.
WE HAVE A FEW MINUTES TODAY. WOULD YOU LIKE A FALSE MEMORY?
MAYBE SOME-THING WITH ALIENS?

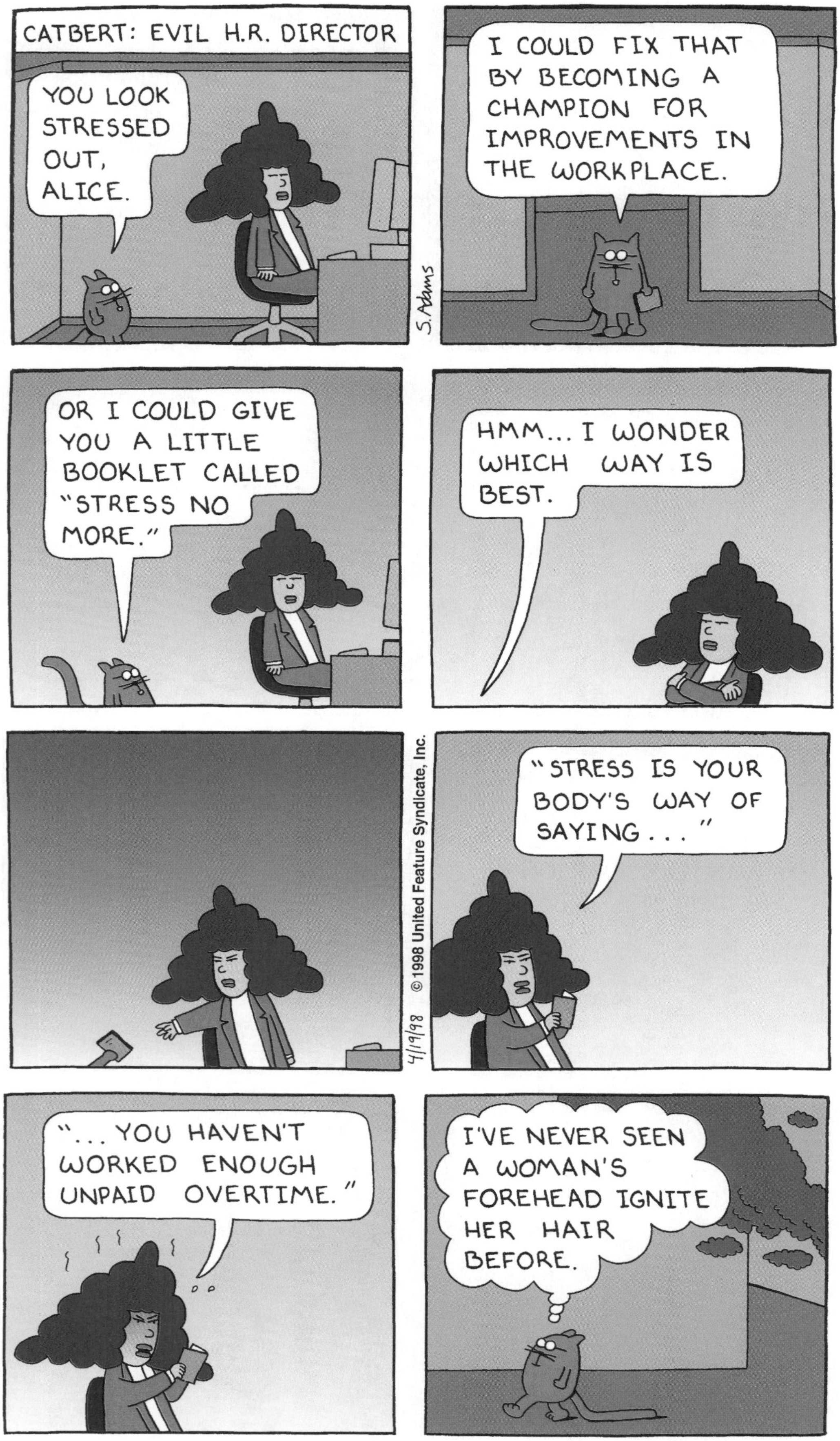
CATBERT: EVIL H.R. DIRECTOR
YOU LOOK STRESSED OUT, ALICE.
I COULD FIX THAT BY BECOMING A CHAMPION FOR IMPROVEMENTS IN THE WORKPLACE.
S. Adams
OR I COULD GIVE YOU A LITTLE BOOKLET CALLED "STRESS NO MORE."
HMM... I WONDER WHICH WAY IS BEST.
© 1998 United Feature Syndicate, Inc.
4/1/98
"STRESS IS YOUR BODY'S WAY OF SAYING..."
"...YOU HAVEN'T WORKED ENOUGH UNPAID OVERTIME."
I'VE NEVER SEEN A WOMAN'S FOREHEAD IGNITE HER HAIR BEFORE.

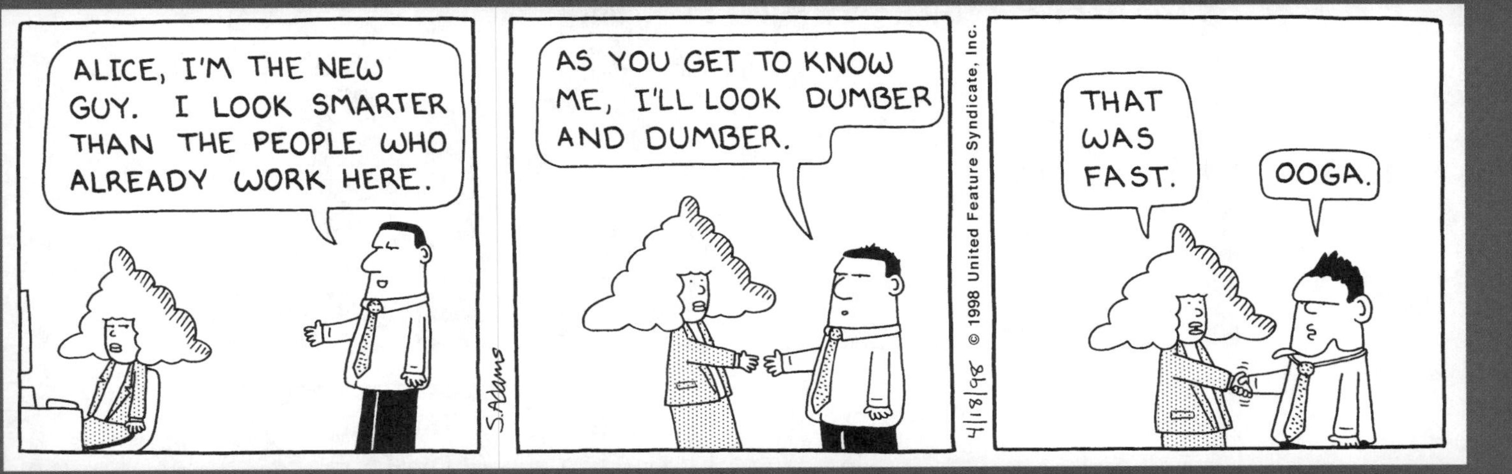
ALICE, I'M THE NEW GUY. I LOOK SMARTER THAN THE PEOPLE WHO ALREADY WORK HERE.
S. Adams
AS YOU GET TO KNOW ME, I'LL LOOK DUMBER AND DUMBER.
4/18/98 © 1998 United Feature Syndicate, Inc.
THAT WAS FAST.
OOGA.

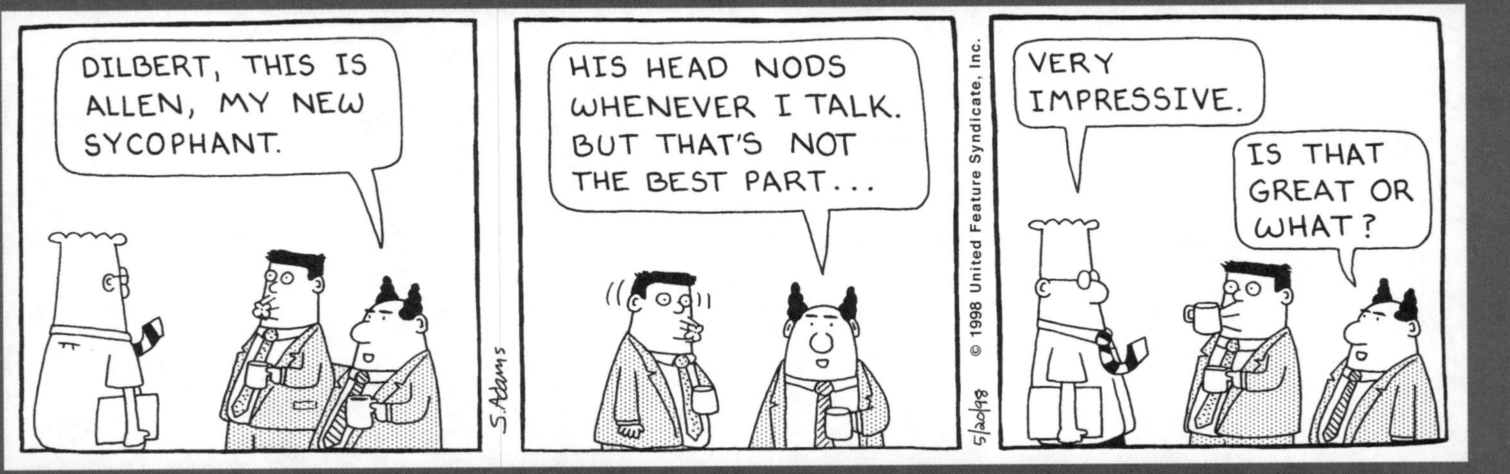
DILBERT, THIS IS ALLEN, MY NEW SYCOPHANT.
S. Adams
HIS HEAD NODS WHENEVER I TALK. BUT THAT'S NOT THE BEST PART...
5/20/98 © 1998 United Feature Syndicate, Inc.
VERY IMPRESSIVE.
IS THAT GREAT OR WHAT?

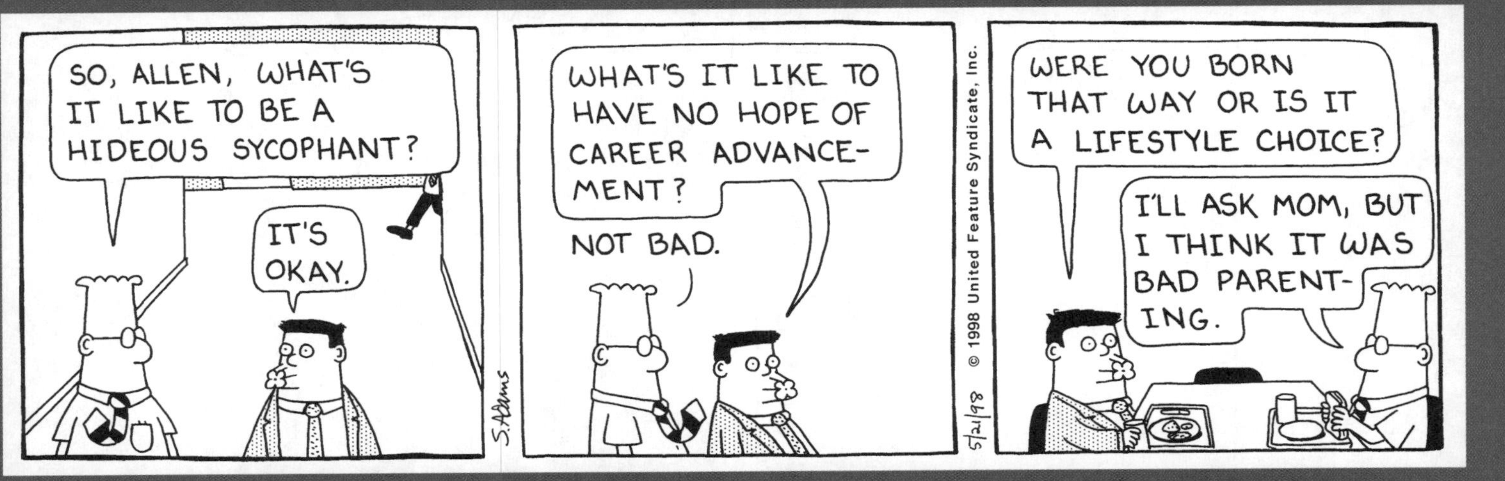
SO, ALLEN, WHAT'S IT LIKE TO BE A HIDEOUS SYCOPHANT?
IT'S OKAY.
S. Adams
WHAT'S IT LIKE TO HAVE NO HOPE OF CAREER ADVANCE-MENT?
NOT BAD.
5/21/98 © 1998 United Feature Syndicate, Inc.
WERE YOU BORN THAT WAY OR IS IT A LIFESTYLE CHOICE?
I'LL ASK MOM, BUT I THINK IT WAS BAD PARENT-ING.

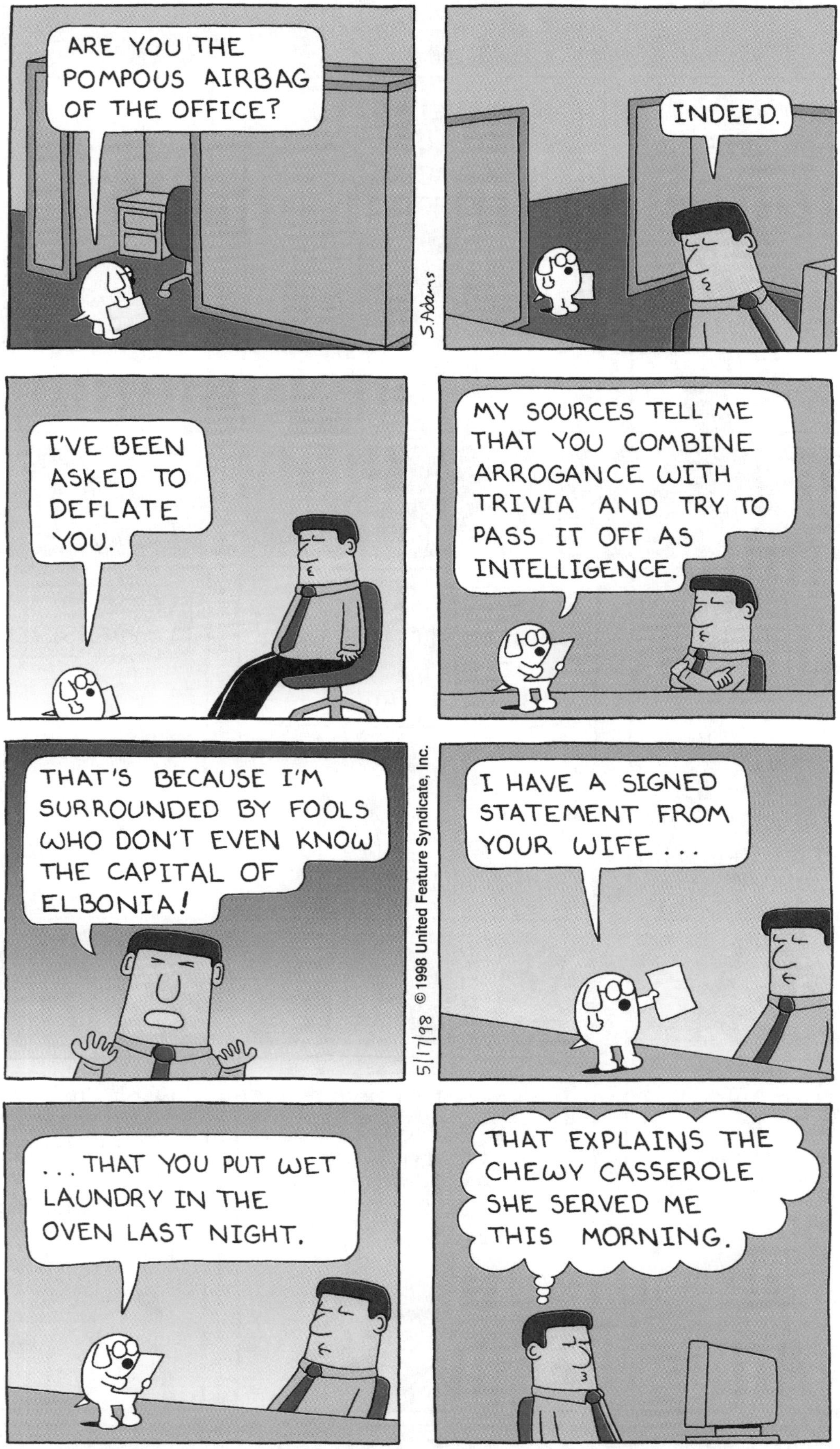
ARE YOU THE POMPOUS AIRBAG OF THE OFFICE?
INDEED.
S. Adams
I'VE BEEN ASKED TO DEFLATE YOU.
MY SOURCES TELL ME THAT YOU COMBINE ARROGANCE WITH TRIVIA AND TRY TO PASS IT OFF AS INTELLIGENCE.
THAT'S BECAUSE I'M SURROUNDED BY FOOLS WHO DON'T EVEN KNOW THE CAPITAL OF ELBONIA!
5/17/98 © 1998 United Feature Syndicate, Inc.
I HAVE A SIGNED STATEMENT FROM YOUR WIFE ...
... THAT YOU PUT WET LAUNDRY IN THE OVEN LAST NIGHT.
THAT EXPLAINS THE CHEWY CASSEROLE SHE SERVED ME THIS MORNING.

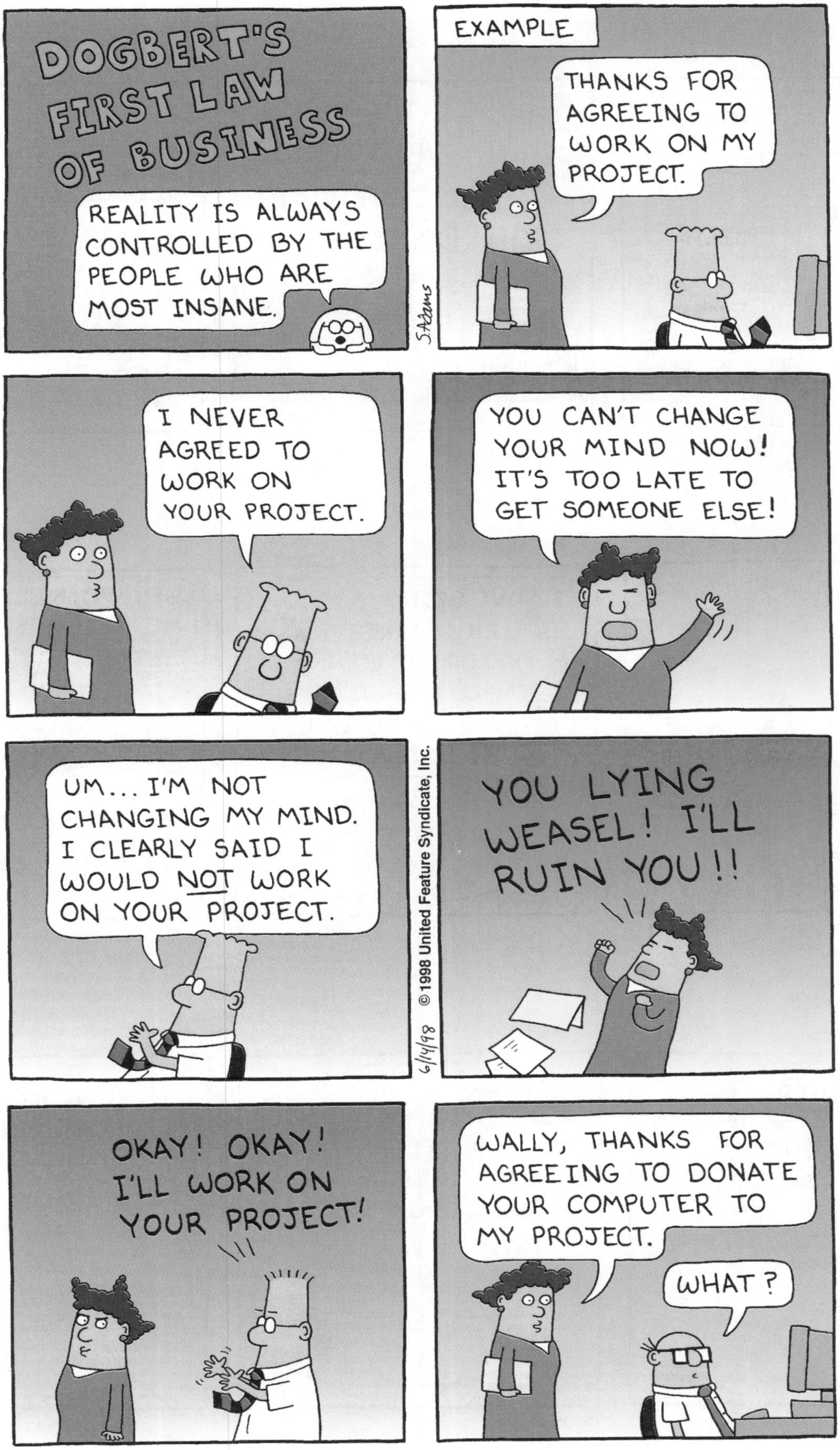
DOGBERT'S FIRST LAW OF BUSINESS
REALITY IS ALWAYS CONTROLLED BY THE PEOPLE WHO ARE MOST INSANE.
EXAMPLE
THANKS FOR AGREEING TO WORK ON MY PROJECT.
I NEVER AGREED TO WORK ON YOUR PROJECT.
YOU CAN'T CHANGE YOUR MIND NOW! IT'S TOO LATE TO GET SOMEONE ELSE!
UM... I'M NOT CHANGING MY MIND. I CLEARLY SAID I WOULD NOT WORK ON YOUR PROJECT.
YOU LYING WEASEL! I'LL RUIN YOU!!
OKAY! OKAY! I'LL WORK ON YOUR PROJECT!
WALLY, THANKS FOR AGREEING TO DONATE YOUR COMPUTER TO MY PROJECT.
WHAT?
S.Adams
6/14/98 © 1998 United Feature Syndicate, Inc.

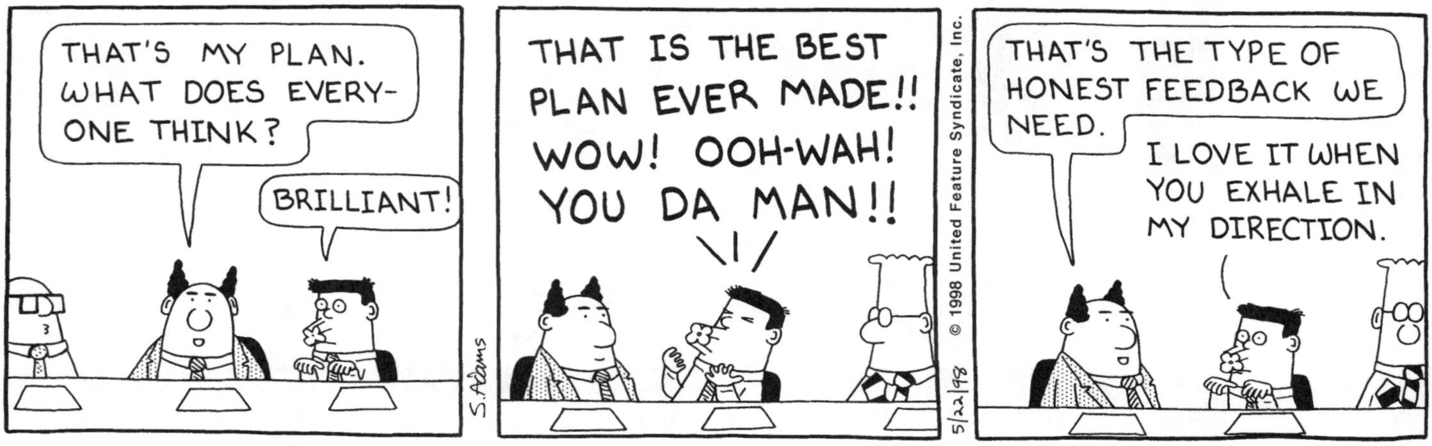
THAT'S MY PLAN. WHAT DOES EVERY-ONE THINK?
BRILLIANT!
THAT IS THE BEST PLAN EVER MADE!! WOW! OOH-WAH! YOU DA MAN!!
THAT'S THE TYPE OF HONEST FEEDBACK WE NEED.
I LOVE IT WHEN YOU EXHALE IN MY DIRECTION.
S. Adams
5/22/98
© 1998 United Feature Syndicate, Inc.

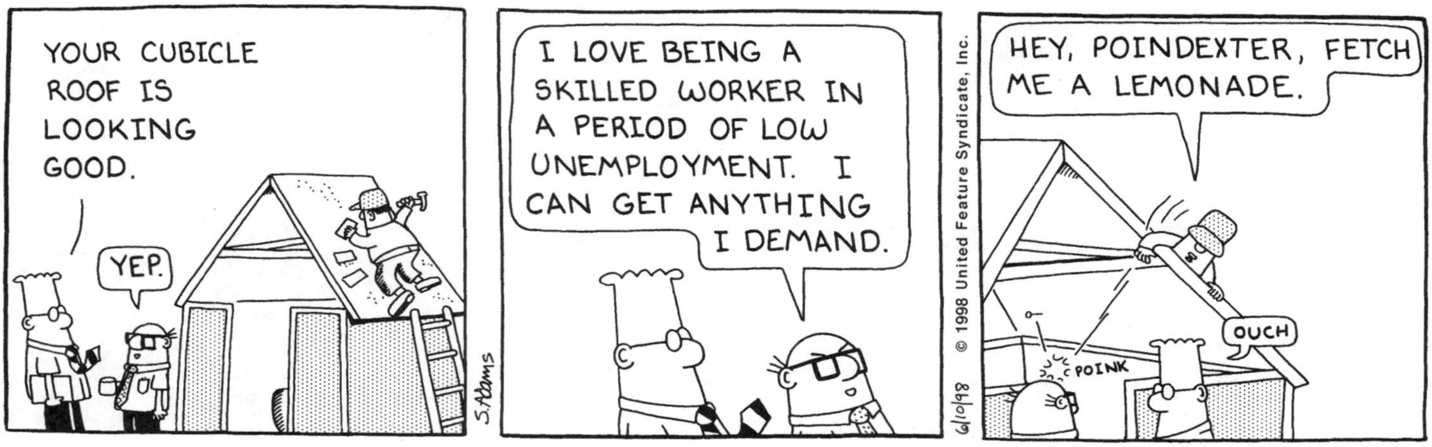
YOUR CUBICLE ROOF IS LOOKING GOOD.
YEP.
I LOVE BEING A SKILLED WORKER IN A PERIOD OF LOW UNEMPLOYMENT. I CAN GET ANYTHING I DEMAND.
HEY, POINDEXTER, FETCH ME A LEMONADE.
POINK
OUCH
S. Adams
6/10/98
© 1998 United Feature Syndicate, Inc.

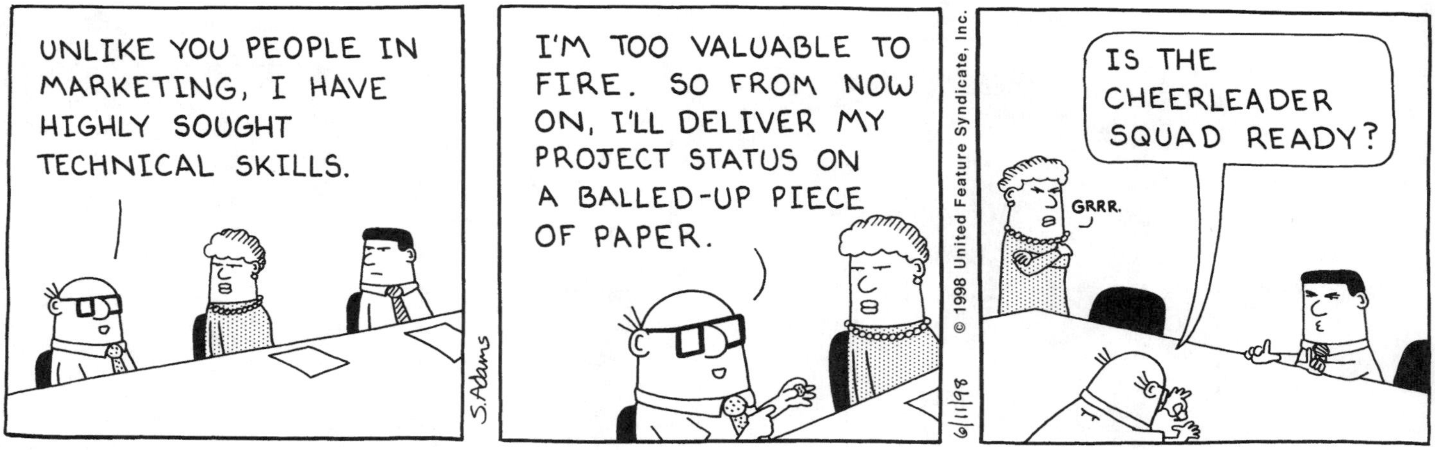
UNLIKE YOU PEOPLE IN MARKETING, I HAVE HIGHLY SOUGHT TECHNICAL SKILLS.
I'M TOO VALUABLE TO FIRE. SO FROM NOW ON, I'LL DELIVER MY PROJECT STATUS ON A BALLED-UP PIECE OF PAPER.
IS THE CHEERLEADER SQUAD READY?
GRRR.
S. Adams
6/11/98
© 1998 United Feature Syndicate, Inc.

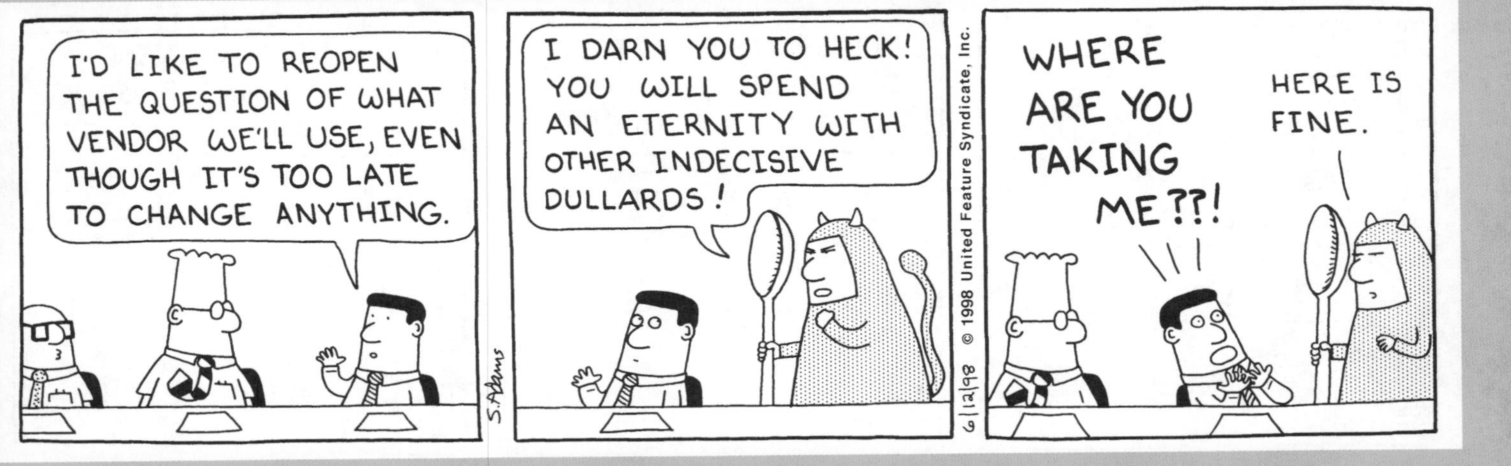
I'D LIKE TO REOPEN THE QUESTION OF WHAT VENDOR WE'LL USE, EVEN THOUGH IT'S TOO LATE TO CHANGE ANYTHING.
I DARN YOU TO HECK! YOU WILL SPEND AN ETERNITY WITH OTHER INDECISIVE DULLARDS!
WHERE ARE YOU TAKING ME??!
HERE IS FINE.
© 1998 United Feature Syndicate, Inc.

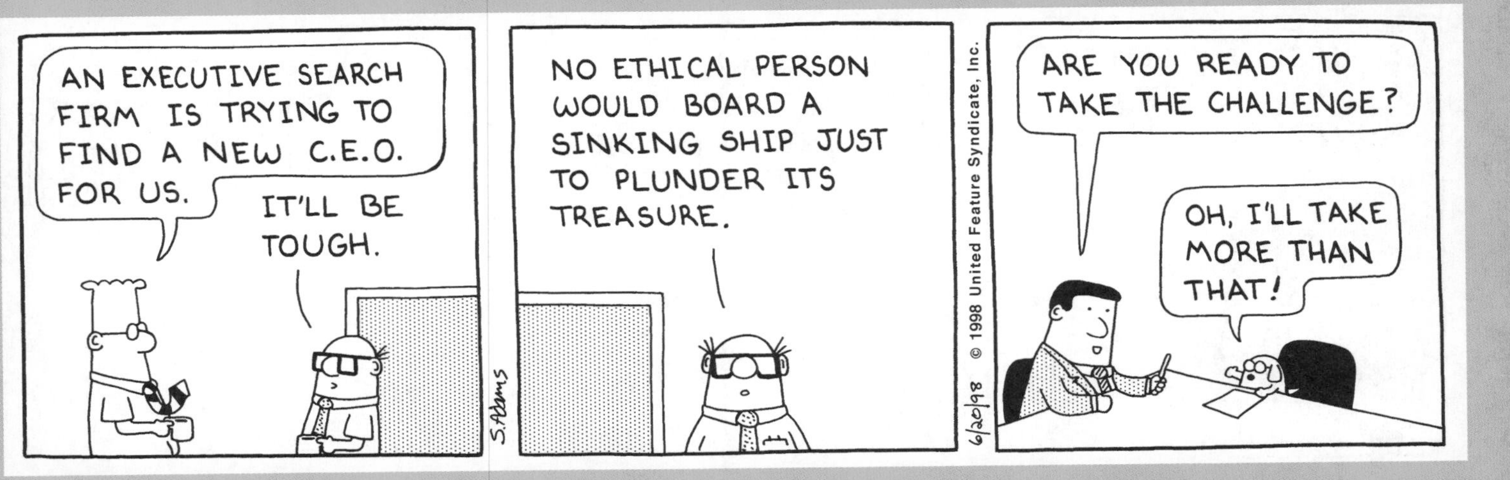
AN EXECUTIVE SEARCH FIRM IS TRYING TO FIND A NEW C.E.O. FOR US.
IT'LL BE TOUGH.
NO ETHICAL PERSON WOULD BOARD A SINKING SHIP JUST TO PLUNDER ITS TREASURE.
ARE YOU READY TO TAKE THE CHALLENGE?
OH, I'LL TAKE MORE THAN THAT!
© 1998 United Feature Syndicate, Inc.

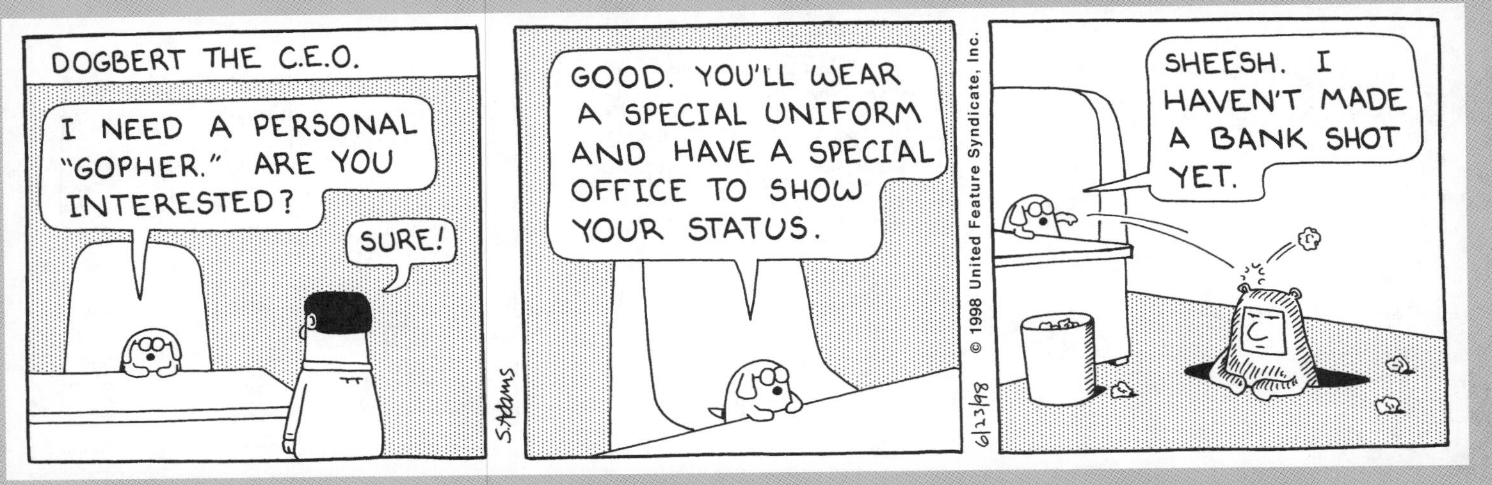
DOGBERT THE C.E.O.
I NEED A PERSONAL "GOPHER." ARE YOU INTERESTED?
SURE!
GOOD. YOU'LL WEAR A SPECIAL UNIFORM AND HAVE A SPECIAL OFFICE TO SHOW YOUR STATUS.
SHEESH. I HAVEN'T MADE A BANK SHOT YET.
© 1998 United Feature Syndicate, Inc.

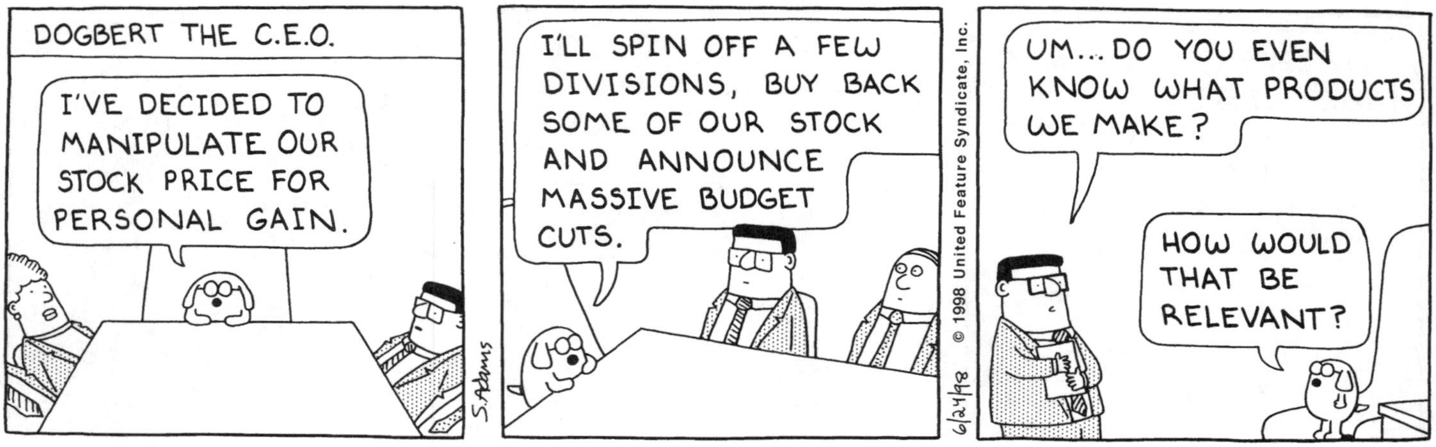
DOGBERT THE C.E.O.
I'VE DECIDED TO MANIPULATE OUR STOCK PRICE FOR PERSONAL GAIN.
I'LL SPIN OFF A FEW DIVISIONS, BUY BACK SOME OF OUR STOCK AND ANNOUNCE MASSIVE BUDGET CUTS.
UM... DO YOU EVEN KNOW WHAT PRODUCTS WE MAKE?
HOW WOULD THAT BE RELEVANT?
S. Adams
6/24/98 © 1998 United Feature Syndicate, Inc.

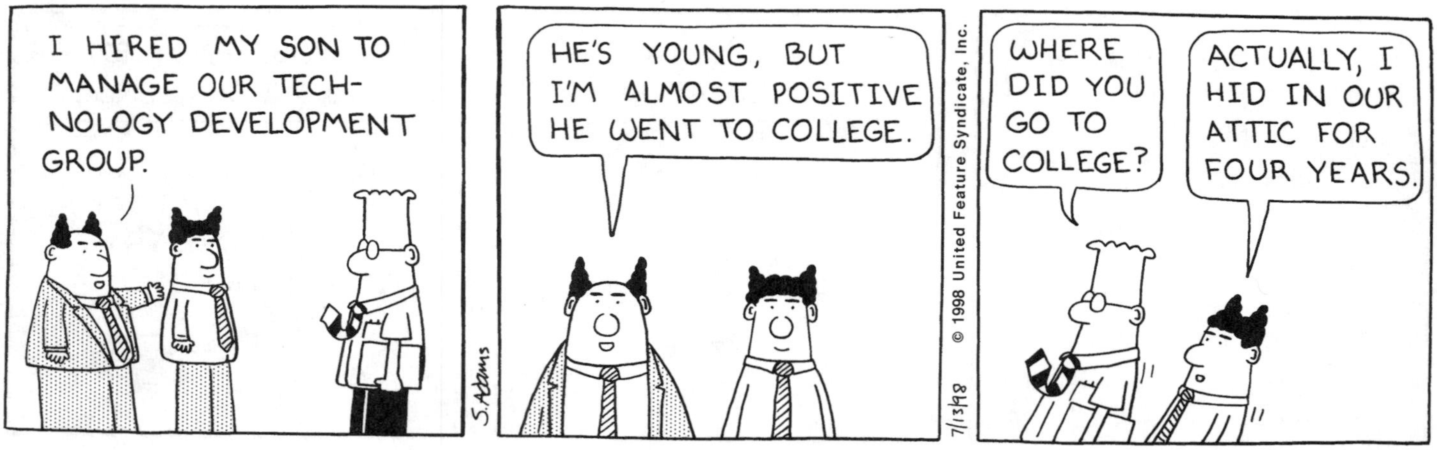
I HIRED MY SON TO MANAGE OUR TECH-NOLOGY DEVELOPMENT GROUP.
HE'S YOUNG, BUT I'M ALMOST POSITIVE HE WENT TO COLLEGE.
WHERE DID YOU GO TO COLLEGE?
ACTUALLY, I HID IN OUR ATTIC FOR FOUR YEARS.
S. Adams
7/13/98 © 1998 United Feature Syndicate, Inc.

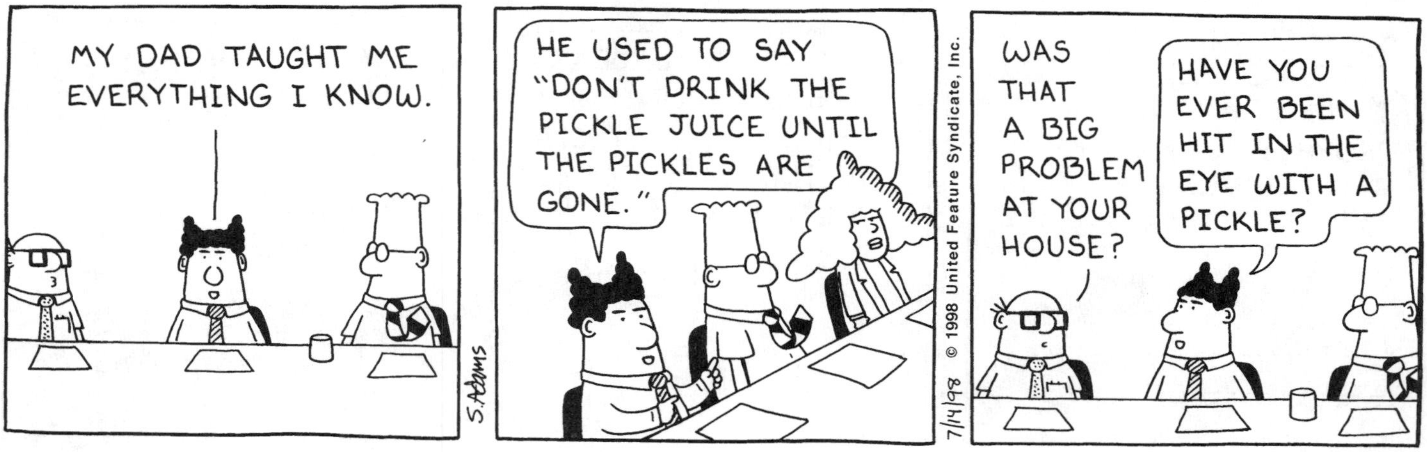
MY DAD TAUGHT ME EVERYTHING I KNOW.
HE USED TO SAY "DON'T DRINK THE PICKLE JUICE UNTIL THE PICKLES ARE GONE."
WAS THAT A BIG PROBLEM AT YOUR HOUSE?
HAVE YOU EVER BEEN HIT IN THE EYE WITH A PICKLE?
S. Adams
7/14/98 © 1998 United Feature Syndicate, Inc.

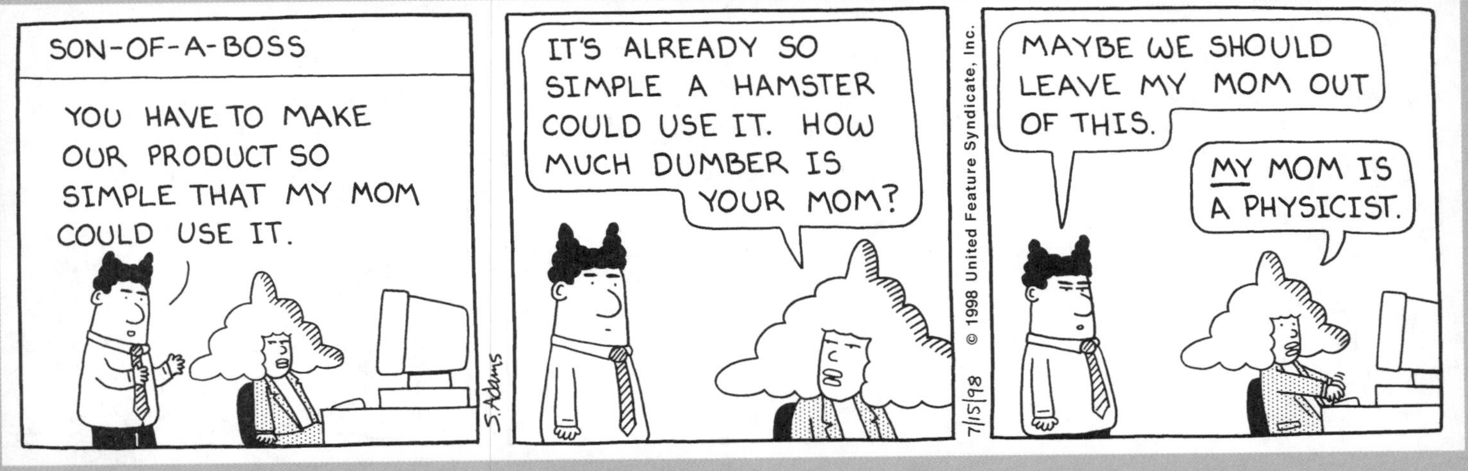
SON-OF-A-BOSS
YOU HAVE TO MAKE OUR PRODUCT SO SIMPLE THAT MY MOM COULD USE IT.
S. Adams
IT'S ALREADY SO SIMPLE A HAMSTER COULD USE IT. HOW MUCH DUMBER IS YOUR MOM?
© 1998 United Feature Syndicate, Inc.
7/15/98
MAYBE WE SHOULD LEAVE MY MOM OUT OF THIS.
MY MOM IS A PHYSICIST.

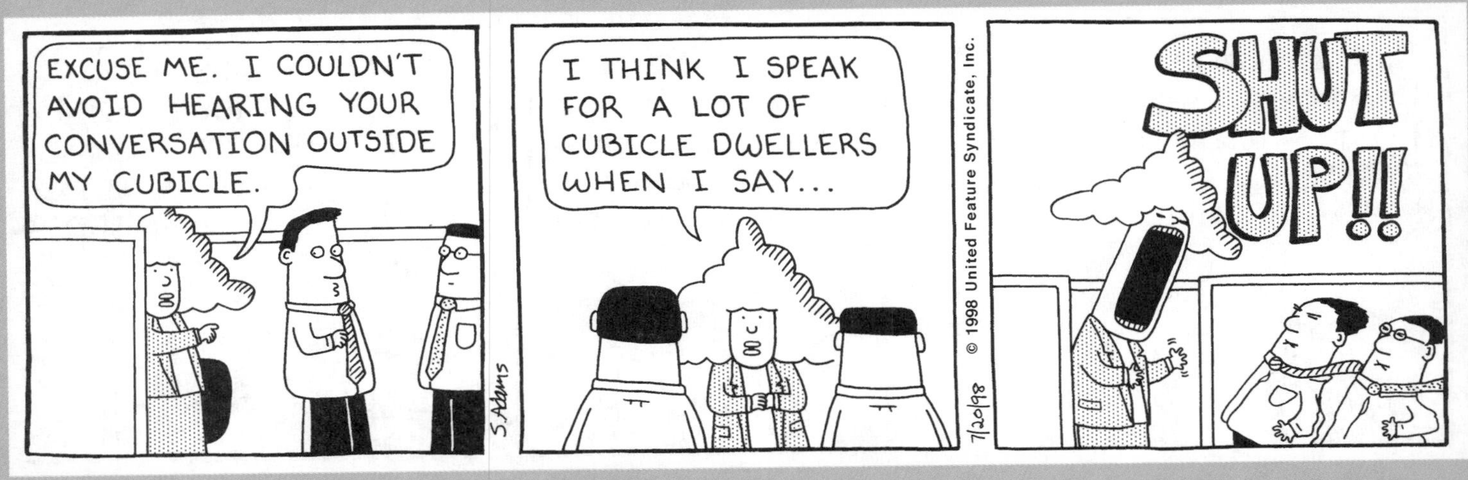
EXCUSE ME. I COULDN'T AVOID HEARING YOUR CONVERSATION OUTSIDE MY CUBICLE.
S. Adams
I THINK I SPEAK FOR A LOT OF CUBICLE DWELLERS WHEN I SAY...
© 1998 United Feature Syndicate, Inc.
7/20/98
SHUT UP!!

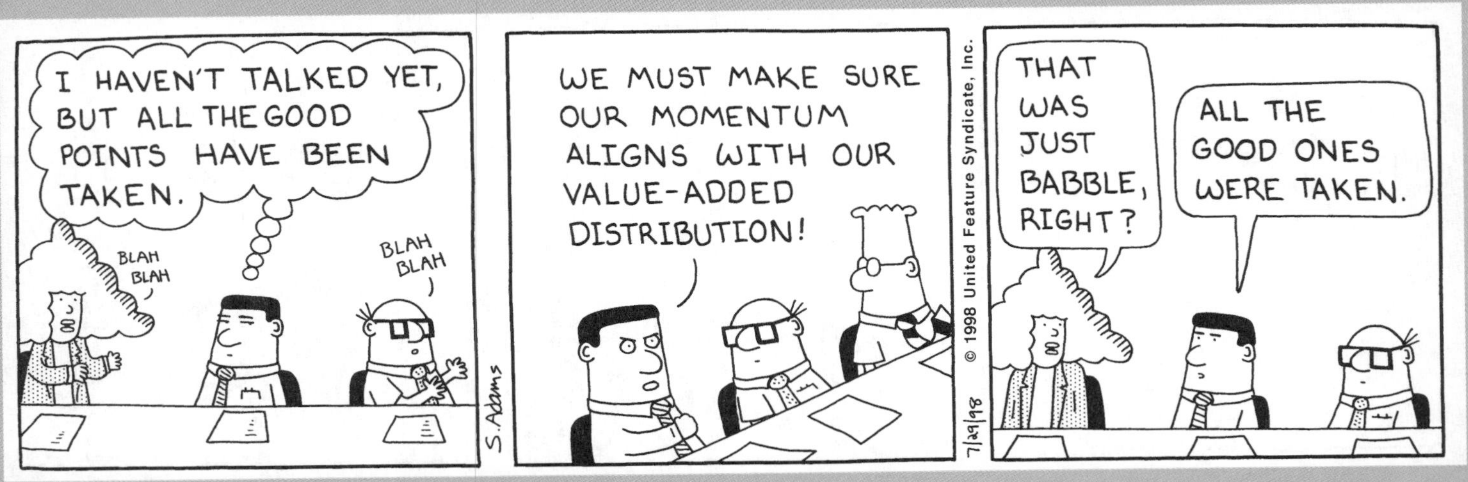
I HAVEN'T TALKED YET, BUT ALL THE GOOD POINTS HAVE BEEN TAKEN.
BLAH BLAH
BLAH BLAH
S. Adams
WE MUST MAKE SURE OUR MOMENTUM ALIGNS WITH OUR VALUE-ADDED DISTRIBUTION!
© 1998 United Feature Syndicate, Inc.
7/29/98
THAT WAS JUST BABBLE, RIGHT?
ALL THE GOOD ONES WERE TAKEN.

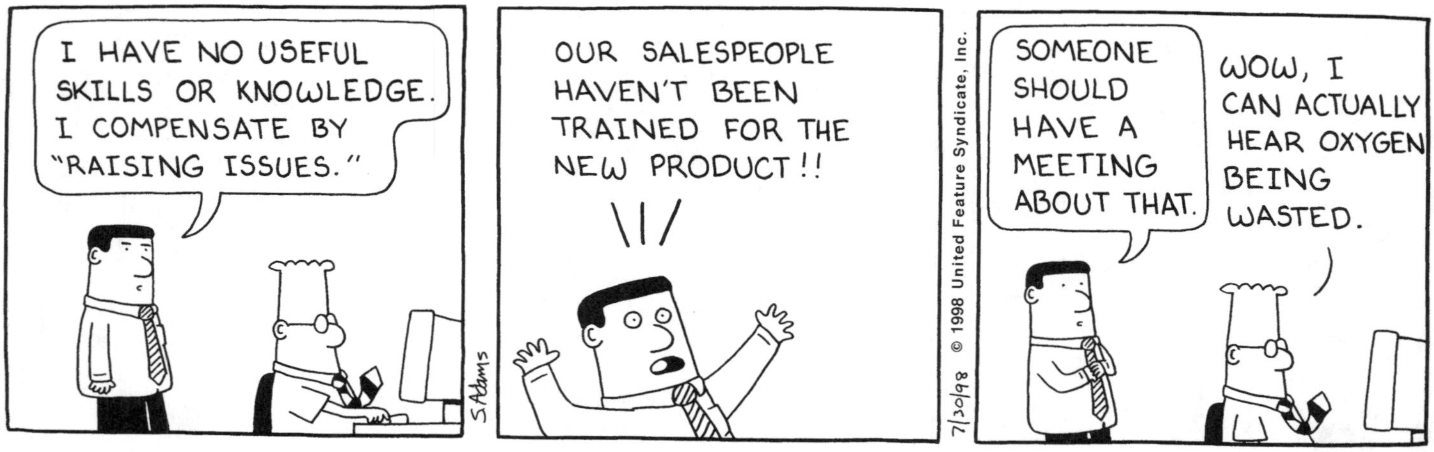
I HAVE NO USEFUL SKILLS OR KNOWLEDGE. I COMPENSATE BY "RAISING ISSUES."
OUR SALESPEOPLE HAVEN'T BEEN TRAINED FOR THE NEW PRODUCT!!
SOMEONE SHOULD HAVE A MEETING ABOUT THAT.
WOW, I CAN ACTUALLY HEAR OXYGEN BEING WASTED.
7/30/98 © 1998 United Feature Syndicate, Inc.

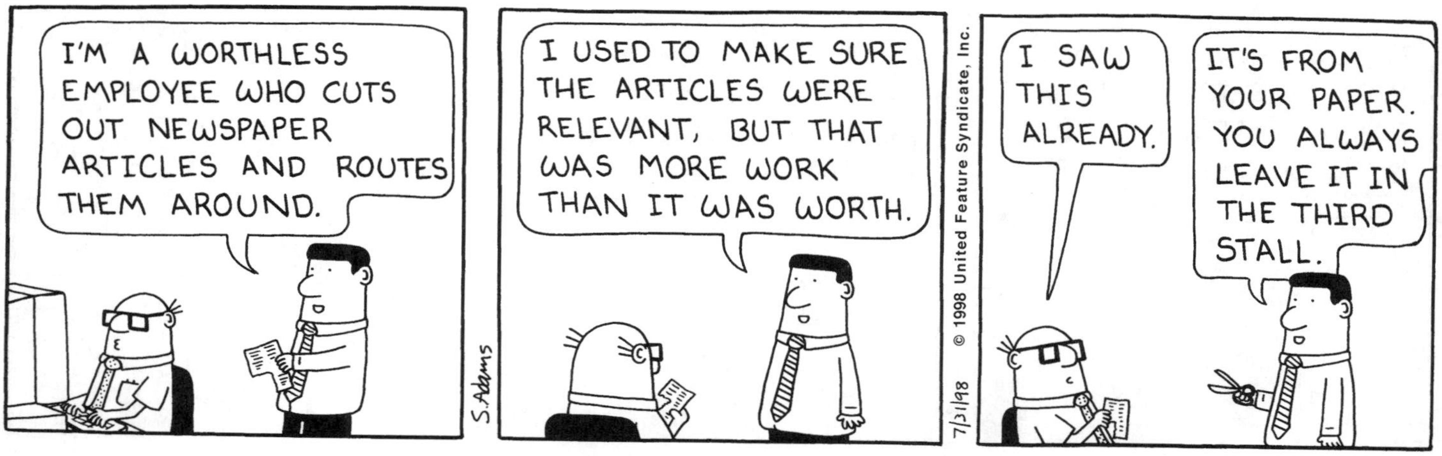
I'M A WORTHLESS EMPLOYEE WHO CUTS OUT NEWSPAPER ARTICLES AND ROUTES THEM AROUND.
I USED TO MAKE SURE THE ARTICLES WERE RELEVANT, BUT THAT WAS MORE WORK THAN IT WAS WORTH.
I SAW THIS ALREADY.
IT'S FROM YOUR PAPER. YOU ALWAYS LEAVE IT IN THE THIRD STALL.
7/31/98 © 1998 United Feature Syndicate, Inc.

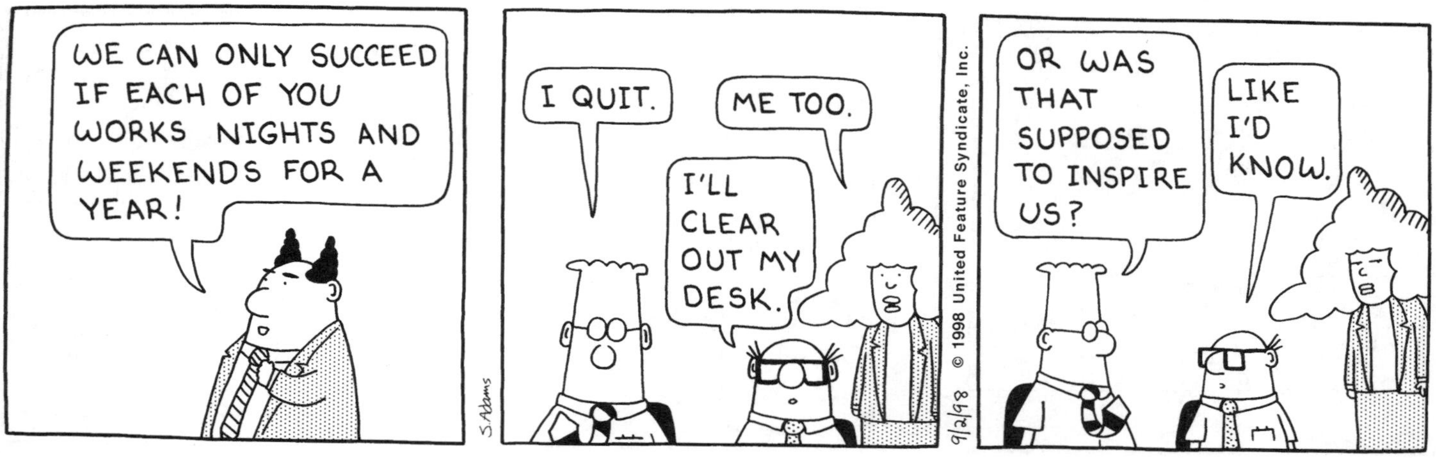
WE CAN ONLY SUCCEED IF EACH OF YOU WORKS NIGHTS AND WEEKENDS FOR A YEAR!
I QUIT.
ME TOO.
I'LL CLEAR OUT MY DESK.
OR WAS THAT SUPPOSED TO INSPIRE US?
LIKE I'D KNOW.
9/2/98 © 1998 United Feature Syndicate, Inc.

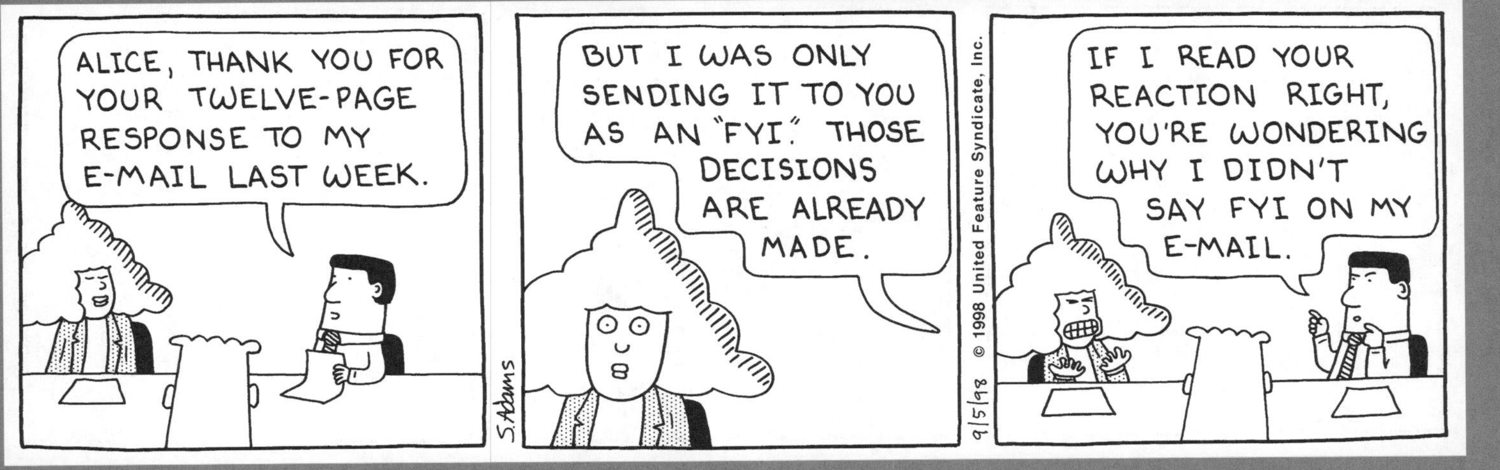
ALICE, THANK YOU FOR YOUR TWELVE-PAGE RESPONSE TO MY E-MAIL LAST WEEK.
BUT I WAS ONLY SENDING IT TO YOU AS AN "FYI." THOSE DECISIONS ARE ALREADY MADE.
S. Adams
9/5/98 © 1998 United Feature Syndicate, Inc.
IF I READ YOUR REACTION RIGHT, YOU'RE WONDERING WHY I DIDN'T SAY FYI ON MY E-MAIL.

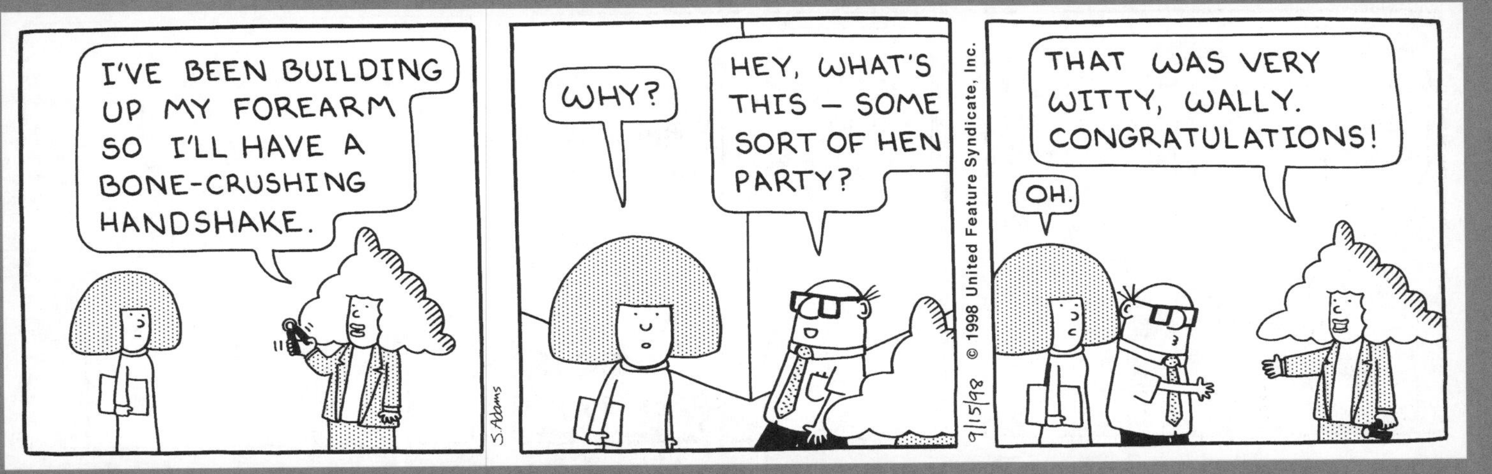
I'VE BEEN BUILDING UP MY FOREARM SO I'LL HAVE A BONE-CRUSHING HANDSHAKE.
S. Adams
WHY?
HEY, WHAT'S THIS — SOME SORT OF HEN PARTY?
9/15/98 © 1998 United Feature Syndicate, Inc.
THAT WAS VERY WITTY, WALLY. CONGRATULATIONS!
OH.

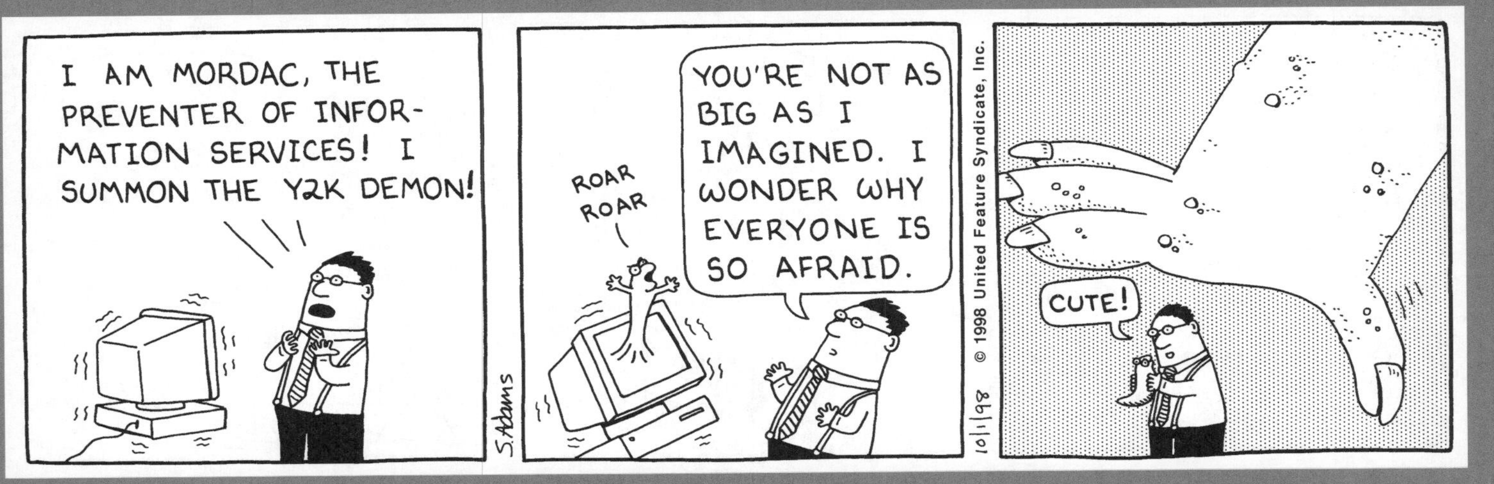
I AM MORDAC, THE PREVENTER OF INFOR-MATION SERVICES! I SUMMON THE Y2K DEMON!
S. Adams
ROAR ROAR
YOU'RE NOT AS BIG AS I IMAGINED. I WONDER WHY EVERYONE IS SO AFRAID.
10/1/98 © 1998 United Feature Syndicate, Inc.
CUTE!

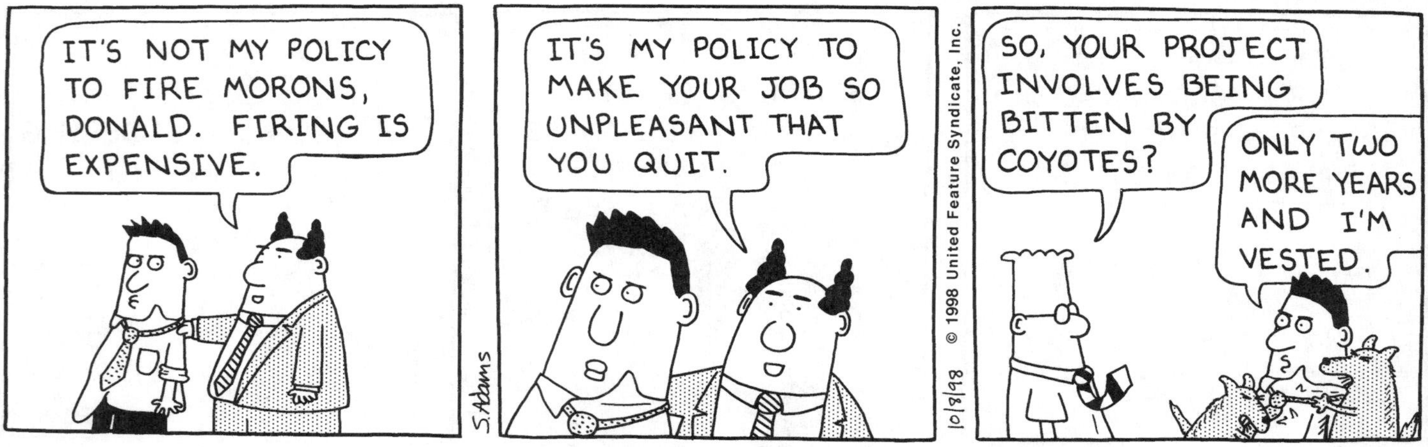
IT'S NOT MY POLICY TO FIRE MORONS, DONALD. FIRING IS EXPENSIVE.
IT'S MY POLICY TO MAKE YOUR JOB SO UNPLEASANT THAT YOU QUIT.
SO, YOUR PROJECT INVOLVES BEING BITTEN BY COYOTES?
ONLY TWO MORE YEARS AND I'M VESTED.
S. Adams
10/8/98 © 1998 United Feature Syndicate, Inc.

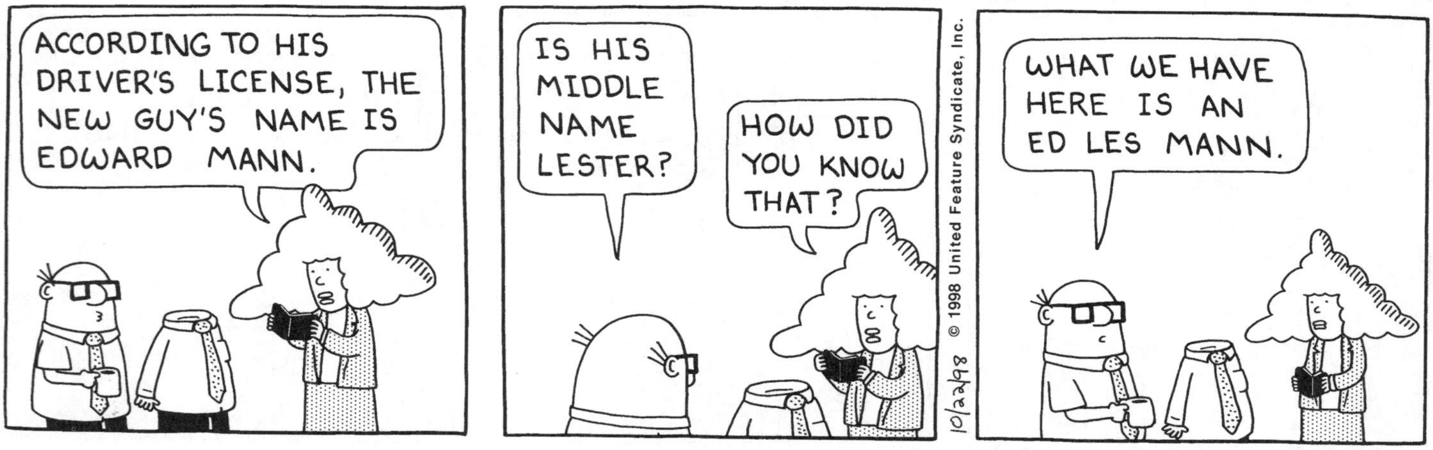
ACCORDING TO HIS DRIVER'S LICENSE, THE NEW GUY'S NAME IS EDWARD MANN.
IS HIS MIDDLE NAME LESTER?
HOW DID YOU KNOW THAT?
WHAT WE HAVE HERE IS AN ED LES MANN.
10/22/98 © 1998 United Feature Syndicate, Inc.

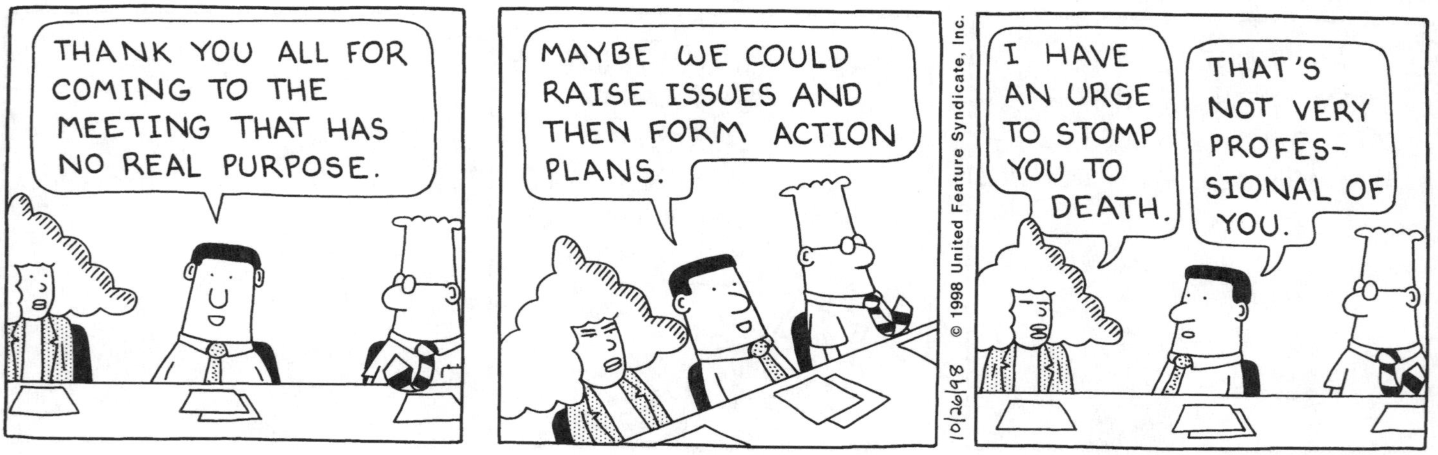
THANK YOU ALL FOR COMING TO THE MEETING THAT HAS NO REAL PURPOSE.
MAYBE WE COULD RAISE ISSUES AND THEN FORM ACTION PLANS.
I HAVE AN URGE TO STOMP YOU TO DEATH.
THAT'S NOT VERY PROFES-SIONAL OF YOU.
10/26/98 © 1998 United Feature Syndicate, Inc.

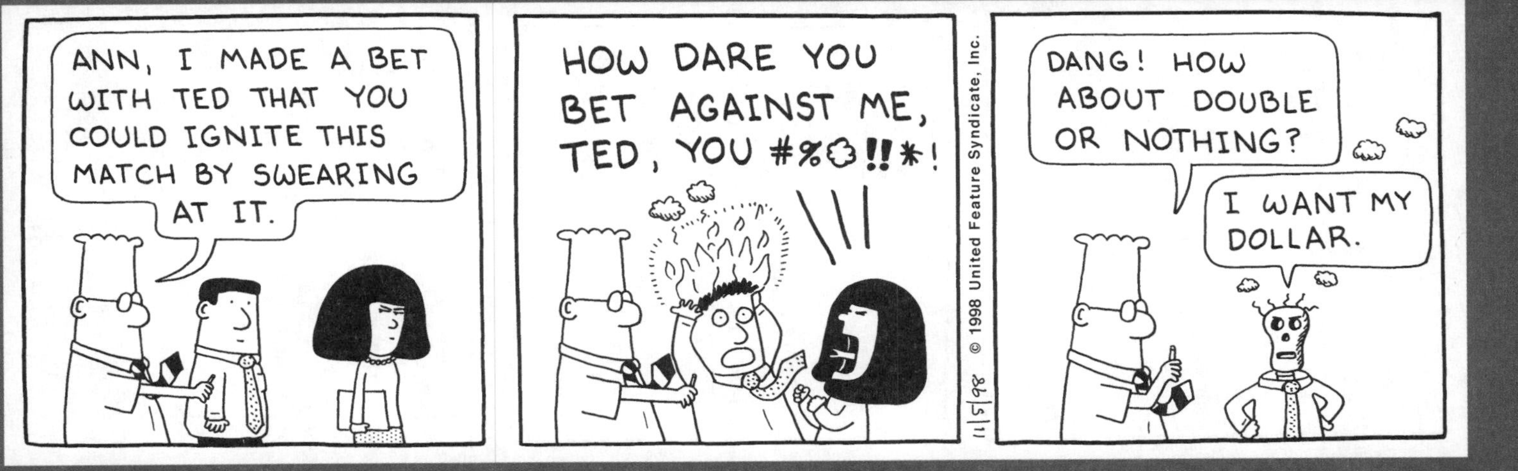
ANN, I MADE A BET WITH TED THAT YOU COULD IGNITE THIS MATCH BY SWEARING AT IT.
HOW DARE YOU BET AGAINST ME, TED, YOU #%!!*!
11/5/98
© 1998 United Feature Syndicate, Inc.
DANG! HOW ABOUT DOUBLE OR NOTHING?
I WANT MY DOLLAR.

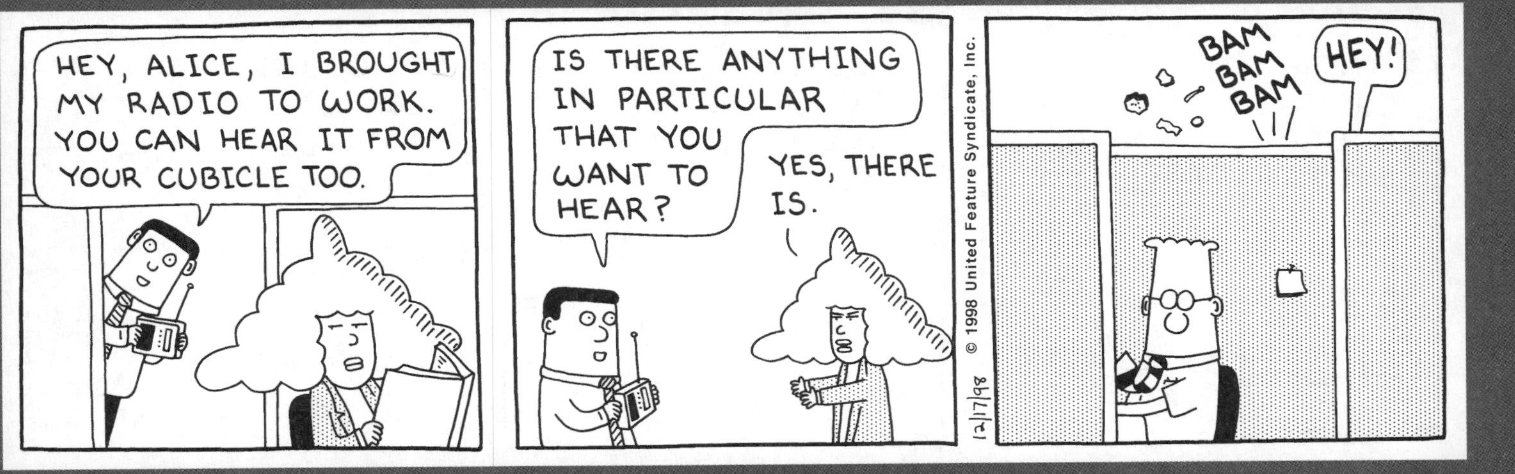
HEY, ALICE, I BROUGHT MY RADIO TO WORK. YOU CAN HEAR IT FROM YOUR CUBICLE TOO.
IS THERE ANYTHING IN PARTICULAR THAT YOU WANT TO HEAR?
YES, THERE IS.
12/17/98
© 1998 United Feature Syndicate, Inc.
BAM BAM BAM
HEY!

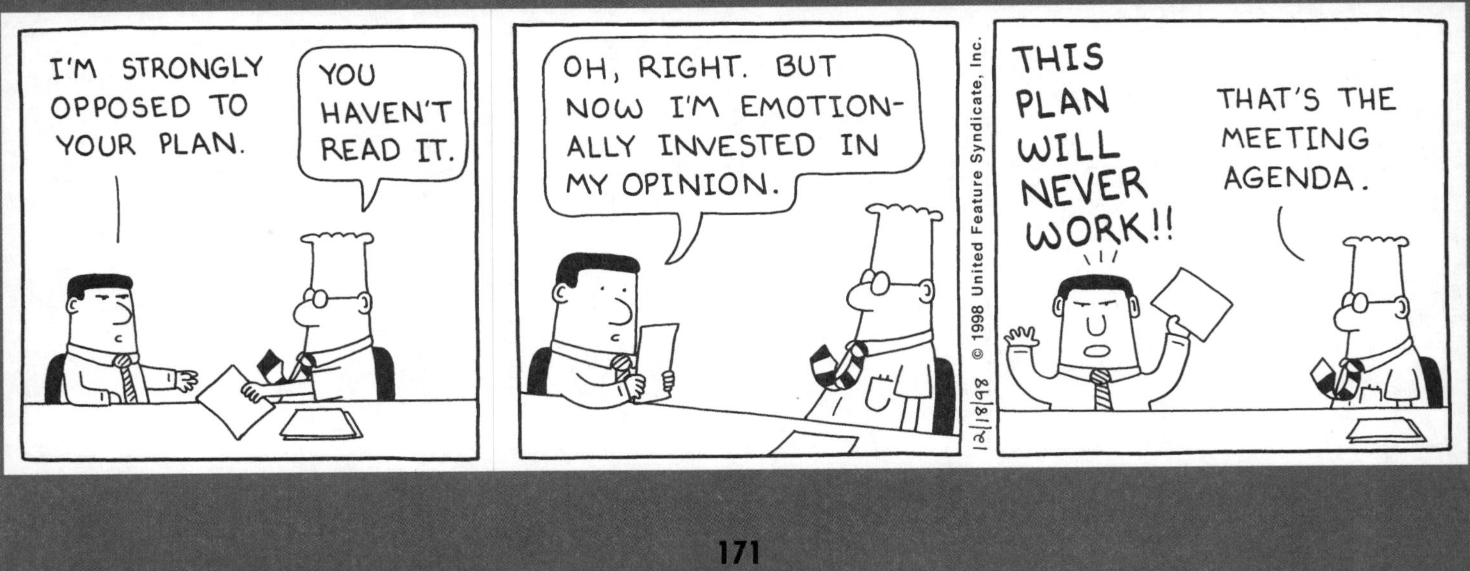
I'M STRONGLY OPPOSED TO YOUR PLAN.
YOU HAVEN'T READ IT.
OH, RIGHT. BUT NOW I'M EMOTION-ALLY INVESTED IN MY OPINION.
12/18/98
© 1998 United Feature Syndicate, Inc.
THIS PLAN WILL NEVER WORK!!
THAT'S THE MEETING AGENDA.

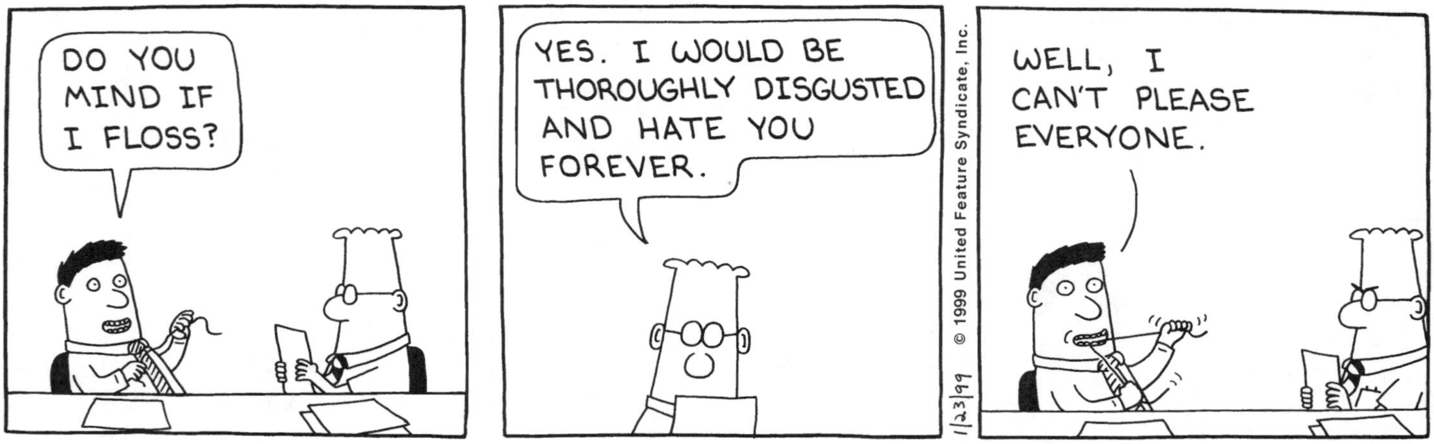
DO YOU MIND IF I FLOSS?
YES. I WOULD BE THOROUGHLY DISGUSTED AND HATE YOU FOREVER.
1/23/99 © 1999 United Feature Syndicate, Inc.
WELL, I CAN'T PLEASE EVERYONE.

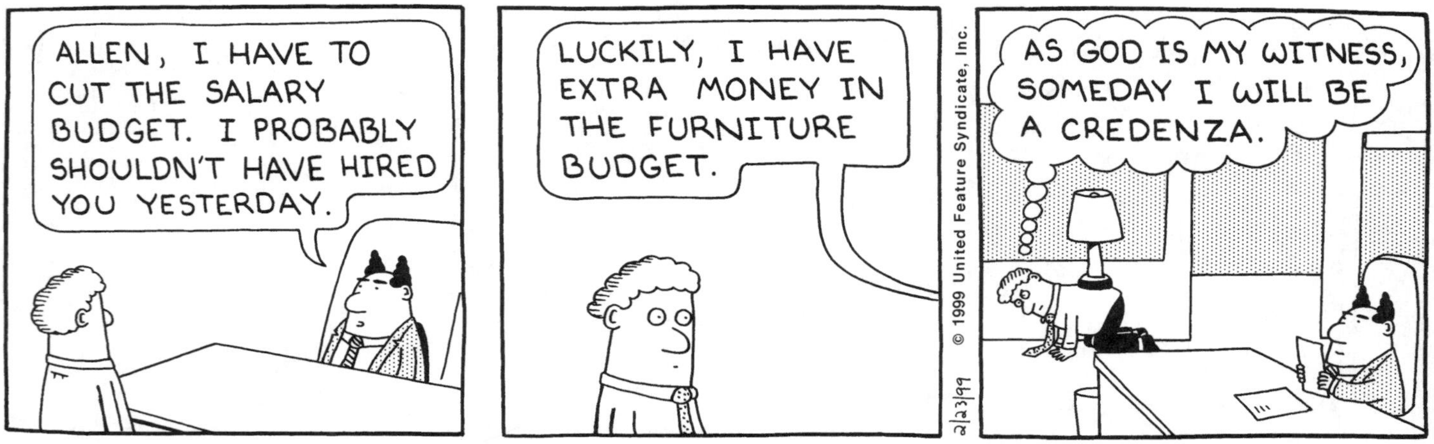
ALLEN, I HAVE TO CUT THE SALARY BUDGET. I PROBABLY SHOULDN'T HAVE HIRED YOU YESTERDAY.
LUCKILY, I HAVE EXTRA MONEY IN THE FURNITURE BUDGET.
2/23/99 © 1999 United Feature Syndicate, Inc.
AS GOD IS MY WITNESS, SOMEDAY I WILL BE A CREDENZA.

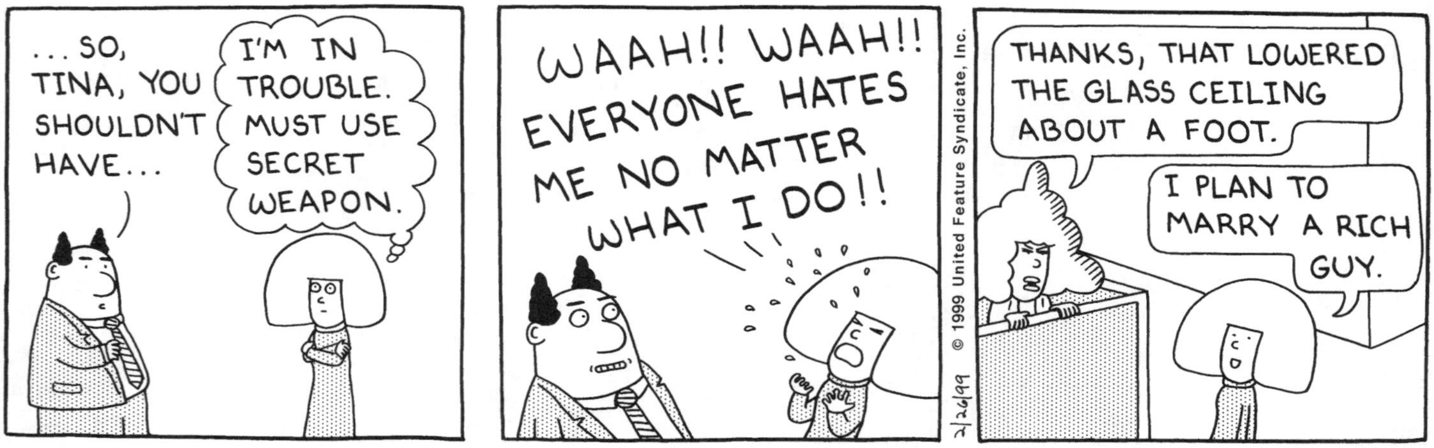
... SO, TINA, YOU SHOULDN'T HAVE...
I'M IN TROUBLE. MUST USE SECRET WEAPON.
WAAH!! WAAH!! EVERYONE HATES ME NO MATTER WHAT I DO!!
2/26/99 © 1999 United Feature Syndicate, Inc.
THANKS, THAT LOWERED THE GLASS CEILING ABOUT A FOOT.
I PLAN TO MARRY A RICH GUY.

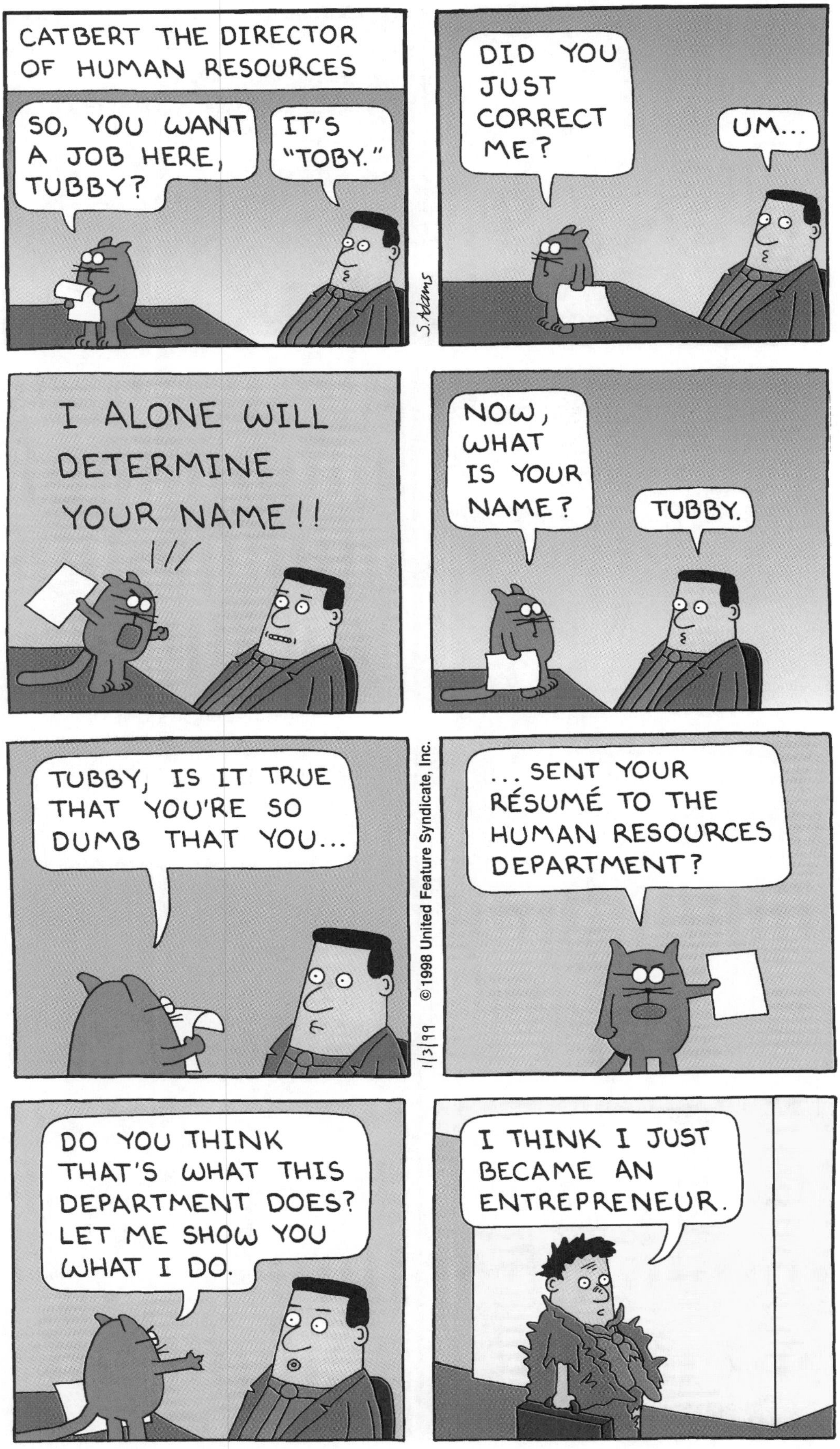
CATBERT THE DIRECTOR OF HUMAN RESOURCES
SO, YOU WANT A JOB HERE, TUBBY?
IT'S "TOBY."
S. Adams
DID YOU JUST CORRECT ME?
UM...
I ALONE WILL DETERMINE YOUR NAME!!
NOW, WHAT IS YOUR NAME?
TUBBY.
TUBBY, IS IT TRUE THAT YOU'RE SO DUMB THAT YOU...
© 1998 United Feature Syndicate, Inc.
1/3/99
... SENT YOUR RÉSUMÉ TO THE HUMAN RESOURCES DEPARTMENT?
DO YOU THINK THAT'S WHAT THIS DEPARTMENT DOES? LET ME SHOW YOU WHAT I DO.
I THINK I JUST BECAME AN ENTREPRENEUR.

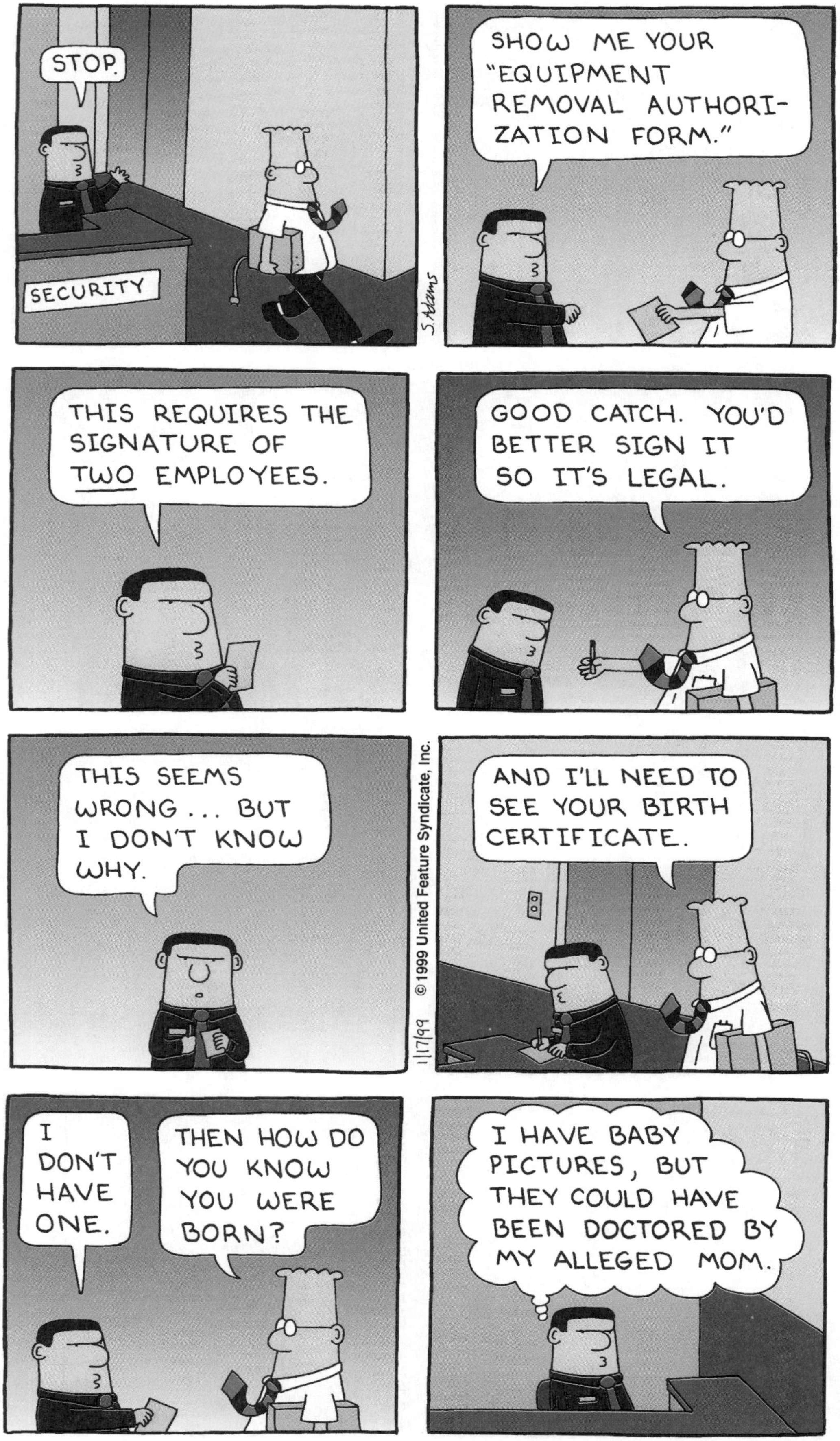
STOP.
SECURITY
S. Adams
SHOW ME YOUR "EQUIPMENT REMOVAL AUTHORIZATION FORM."
THIS REQUIRES THE SIGNATURE OF TWO EMPLOYEES.
GOOD CATCH. YOU'D BETTER SIGN IT SO IT'S LEGAL.
THIS SEEMS WRONG . . . BUT I DON'T KNOW WHY.
1/17/99 © 1999 United Feature Syndicate, Inc.
AND I'LL NEED TO SEE YOUR BIRTH CERTIFICATE.
I DON'T HAVE ONE.
THEN HOW DO YOU KNOW YOU WERE BORN?
I HAVE BABY PICTURES, BUT THEY COULD HAVE BEEN DOCTORED BY MY ALLEGED MOM.

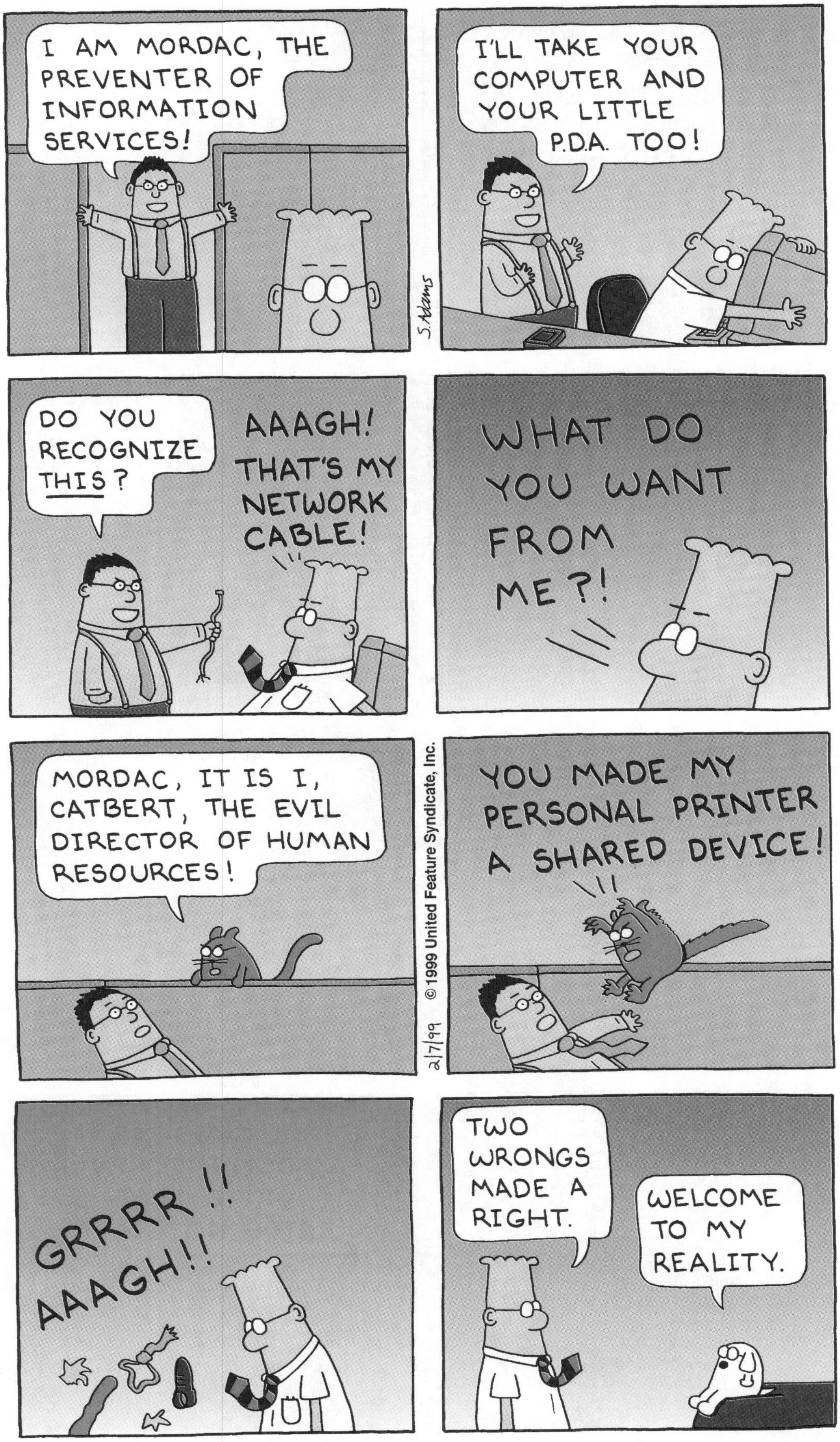
I AM MORDAC, THE PREVENTER OF INFORMATION SERVICES!
S. Adams
I'LL TAKE YOUR COMPUTER AND YOUR LITTLE P.D.A. TOO!
DO YOU RECOGNIZE THIS?
AAAGH! THAT'S MY NETWORK CABLE!
WHAT DO YOU WANT FROM ME?!
MORDAC, IT IS I, CATBERT, THE EVIL DIRECTOR OF HUMAN RESOURCES!
© 1999 United Feature Syndicate, Inc.
2/7/99
YOU MADE MY PERSONAL PRINTER A SHARED DEVICE!
GRRRR!! AAAGH!!
TWO WRONGS MADE A RIGHT.
WELCOME TO MY REALITY.

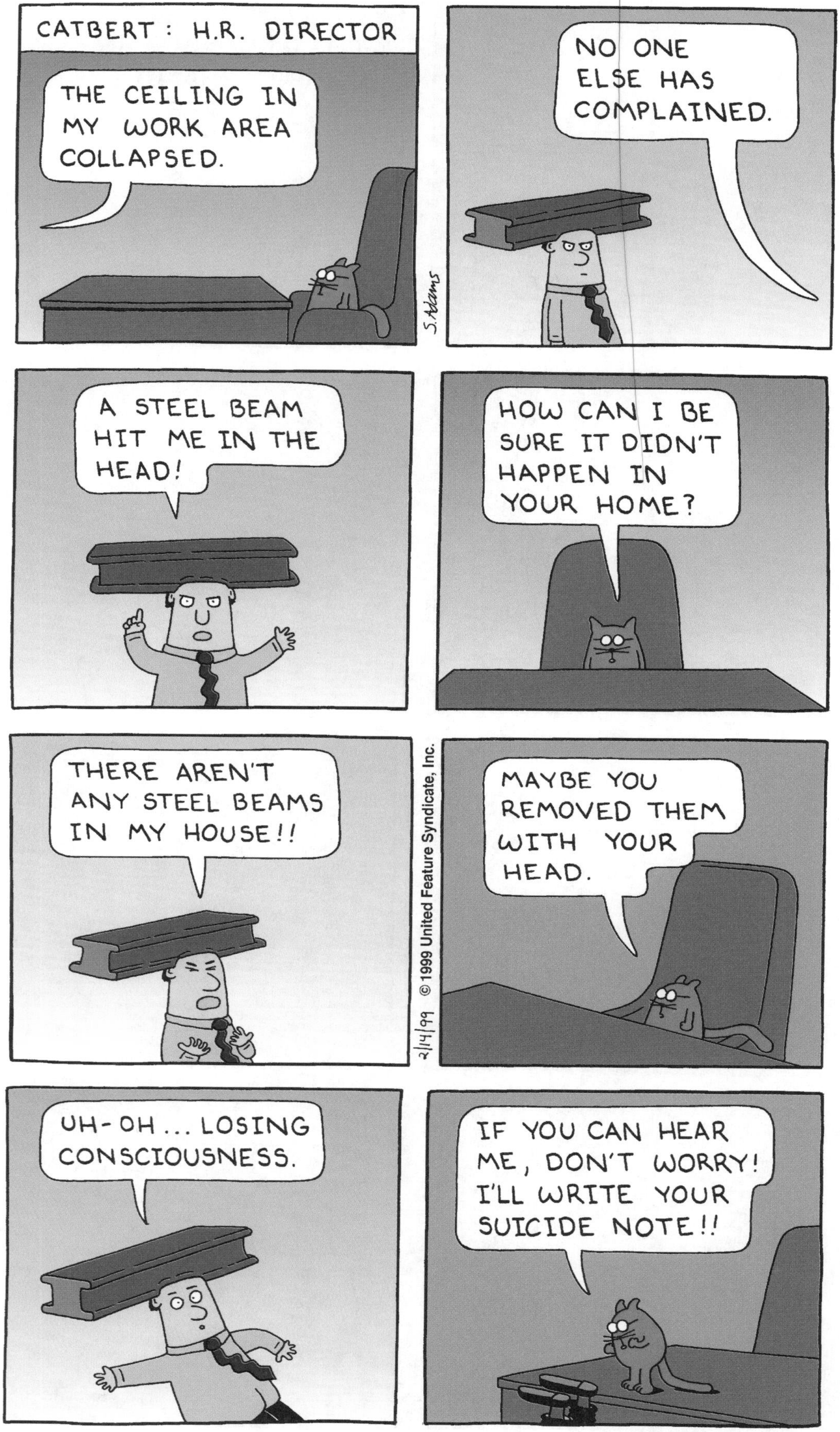
CATBERT : H.R. DIRECTOR
THE CEILING IN MY WORK AREA COLLAPSED.
NO ONE ELSE HAS COMPLAINED.
A STEEL BEAM HIT ME IN THE HEAD!
HOW CAN I BE SURE IT DIDN'T HAPPEN IN YOUR HOME?
THERE AREN'T ANY STEEL BEAMS IN MY HOUSE!!
MAYBE YOU REMOVED THEM WITH YOUR HEAD.
UH-OH ... LOSING CONSCIOUSNESS.
IF YOU CAN HEAR ME, DON'T WORRY! I'LL WRITE YOUR SUICIDE NOTE!!
S. Adams
2/14/99 © 1999 United Feature Syndicate, Inc.

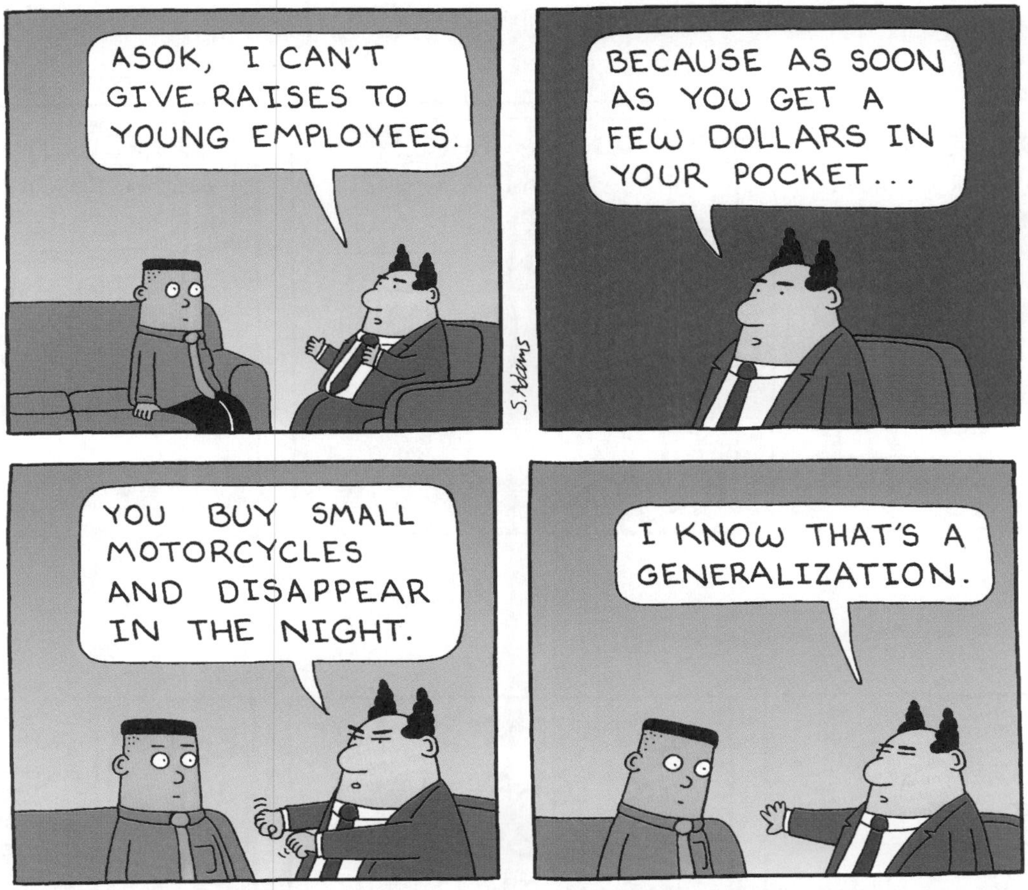
ASOK, I CAN'T GIVE RAISES TO YOUNG EMPLOYEES.
BECAUSE AS SOON AS YOU GET A FEW DOLLARS IN YOUR POCKET...
YOU BUY SMALL MOTORCYCLES AND DISAPPEAR IN THE NIGHT.
I KNOW THAT'S A GENERALIZATION.
S. Adams

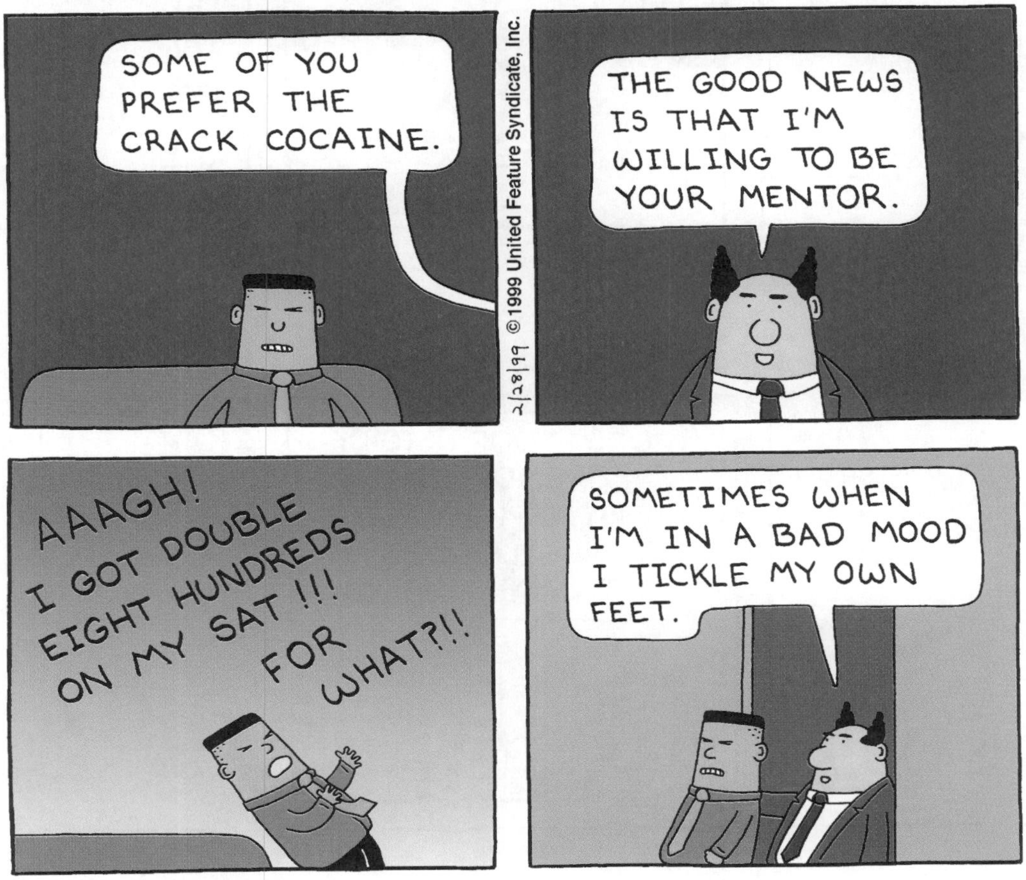
SOME OF YOU PREFER THE CRACK COCAINE.
THE GOOD NEWS IS THAT I'M WILLING TO BE YOUR MENTOR.
AAAGH! I GOT DOUBLE EIGHT HUNDREDS ON MY SAT!!! FOR WHAT?!!
SOMETIMES WHEN I'M IN A BAD MOOD I TICKLE MY OWN FEET.
2/28/99 © 1999 United Feature Syndicate, Inc.

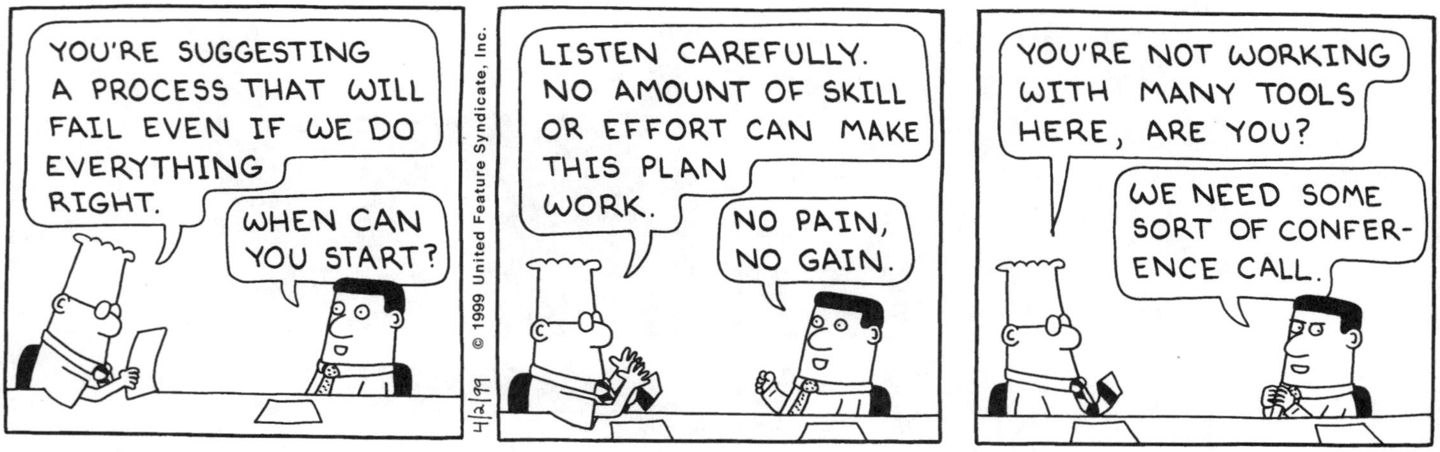
YOU'RE SUGGESTING A PROCESS THAT WILL FAIL EVEN IF WE DO EVERYTHING RIGHT.
WHEN CAN YOU START?
LISTEN CAREFULLY. NO AMOUNT OF SKILL OR EFFORT CAN MAKE THIS PLAN WORK.
NO PAIN, NO GAIN.
YOU'RE NOT WORKING WITH MANY TOOLS HERE, ARE YOU?
WE NEED SOME SORT OF CONFER-ENCE CALL.
4/2/99 © 1999 United Feature Syndicate, Inc.

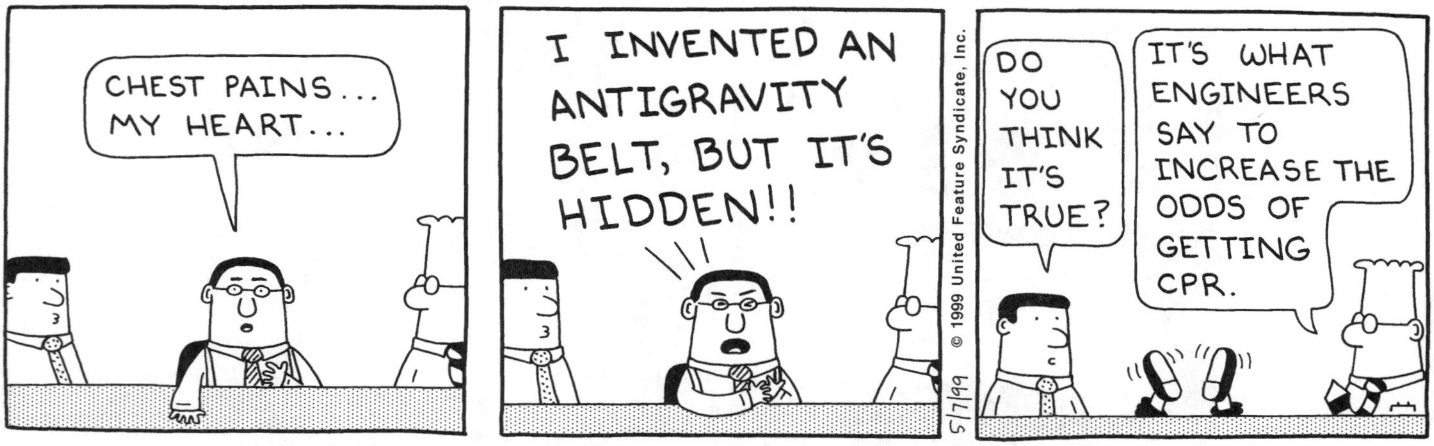
CHEST PAINS... MY HEART...
I INVENTED AN ANTIGRAVITY BELT, BUT IT'S HIDDEN!!
DO YOU THINK IT'S TRUE?
IT'S WHAT ENGINEERS SAY TO INCREASE THE ODDS OF GETTING CPR.
5/7/99 © 1999 United Feature Syndicate, Inc.

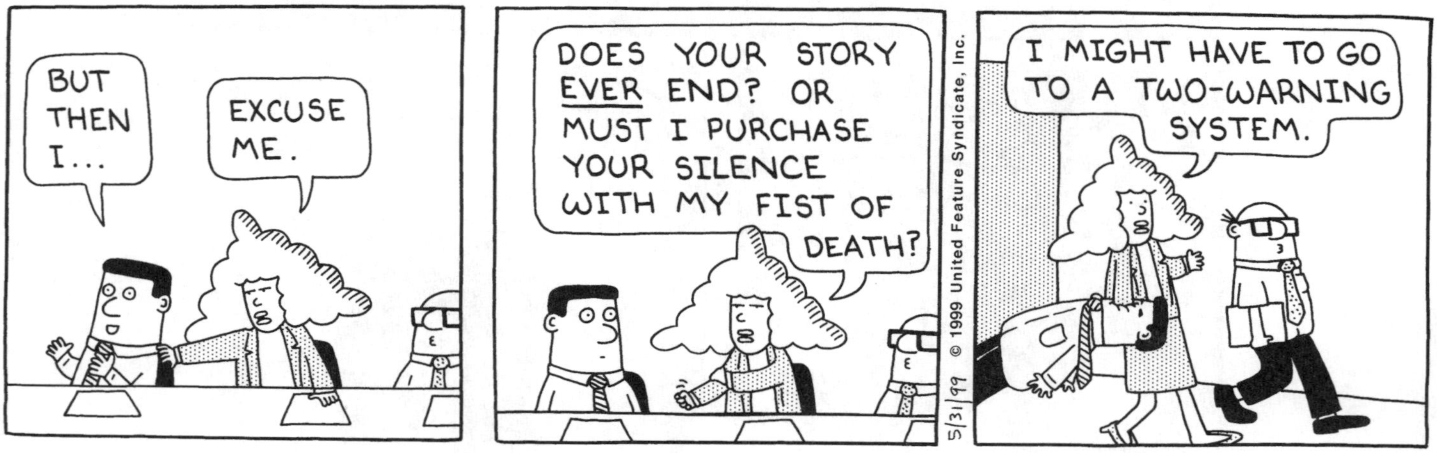
BUT THEN I...
EXCUSE ME.
DOES YOUR STORY EVER END? OR MUST I PURCHASE YOUR SILENCE WITH MY FIST OF DEATH?
I MIGHT HAVE TO GO TO A TWO-WARNING SYSTEM.
5/31/99 © 1999 United Feature Syndicate, Inc.

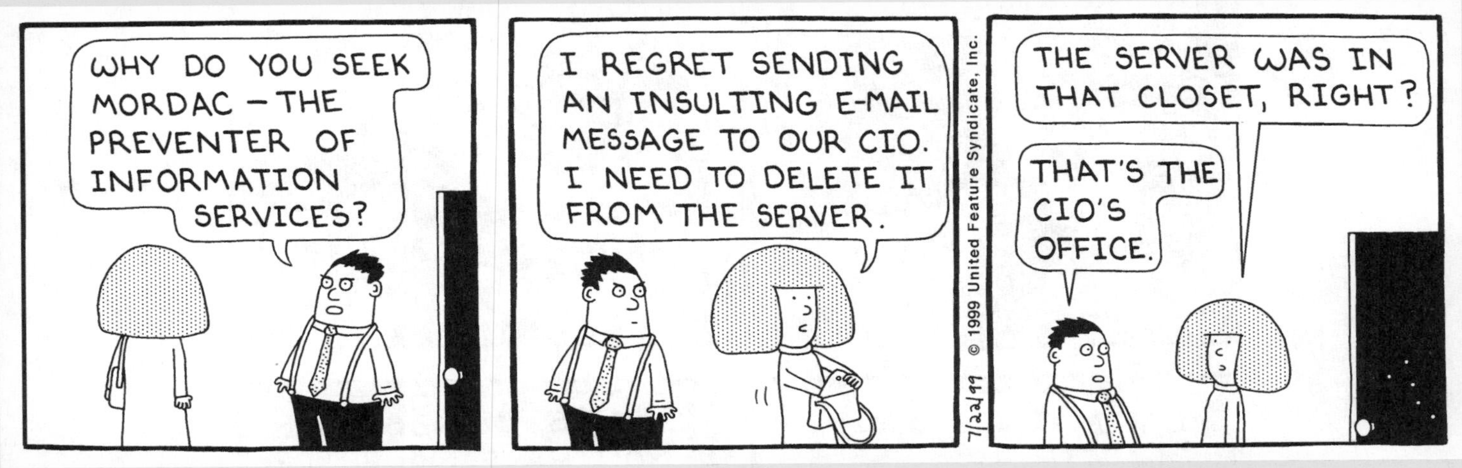
WHY DO YOU SEEK MORDAC — THE PREVENTER OF INFORMATION SERVICES?
I REGRET SENDING AN INSULTING E-MAIL MESSAGE TO OUR CIO. I NEED TO DELETE IT FROM THE SERVER.
7/22/99 © 1999 United Feature Syndicate, Inc.
THE SERVER WAS IN THAT CLOSET, RIGHT?
THAT'S THE CIO'S OFFICE.

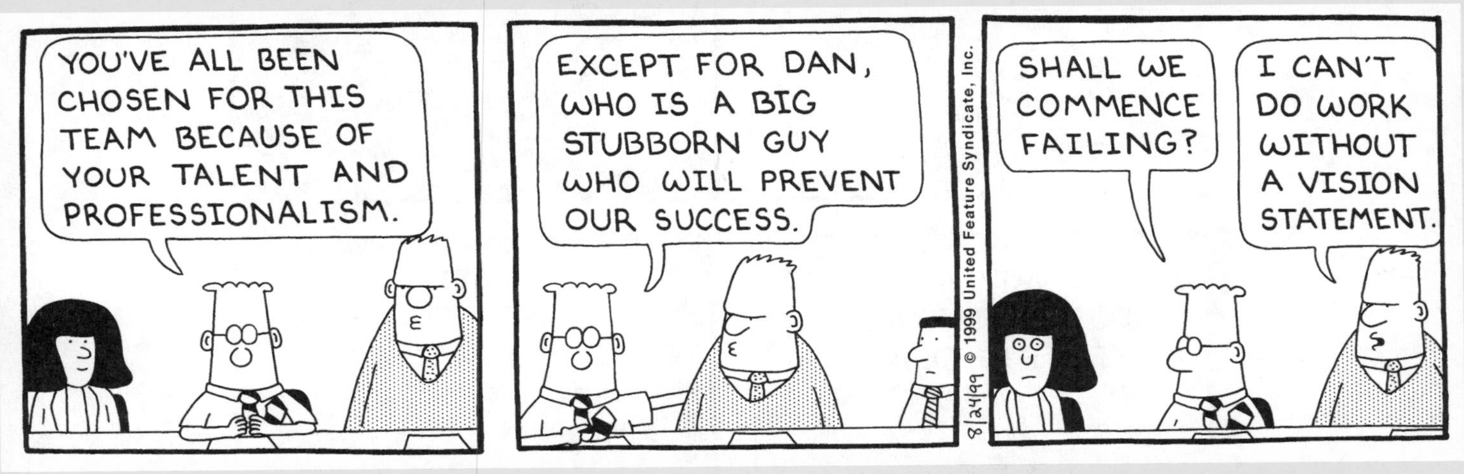
YOU'VE ALL BEEN CHOSEN FOR THIS TEAM BECAUSE OF YOUR TALENT AND PROFESSIONALISM.
EXCEPT FOR DAN, WHO IS A BIG STUBBORN GUY WHO WILL PREVENT OUR SUCCESS.
8/24/99 © 1999 United Feature Syndicate, Inc.
SHALL WE COMMENCE FAILING?
I CAN'T DO WORK WITHOUT A VISION STATEMENT.

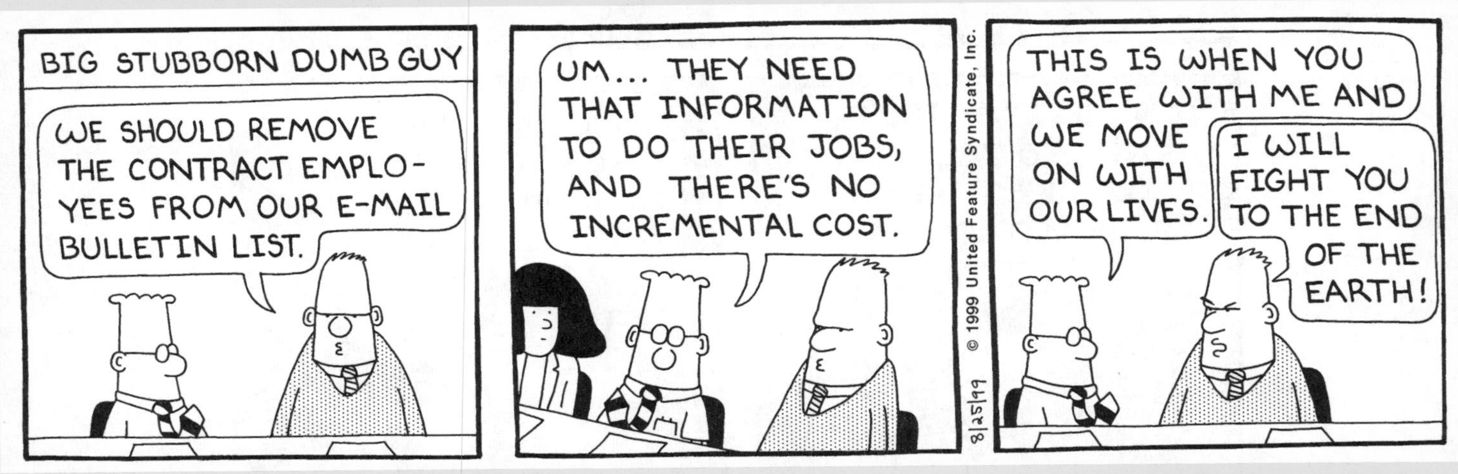
BIG STUBBORN DUMB GUY
WE SHOULD REMOVE THE CONTRACT EMPLO-YEES FROM OUR E-MAIL BULLETIN LIST.
UM... THEY NEED THAT INFORMATION TO DO THEIR JOBS, AND THERE'S NO INCREMENTAL COST.
8/25/99 © 1999 United Feature Syndicate, Inc.
THIS IS WHEN YOU AGREE WITH ME AND WE MOVE ON WITH OUR LIVES.
I WILL FIGHT YOU TO THE END OF THE EARTH!

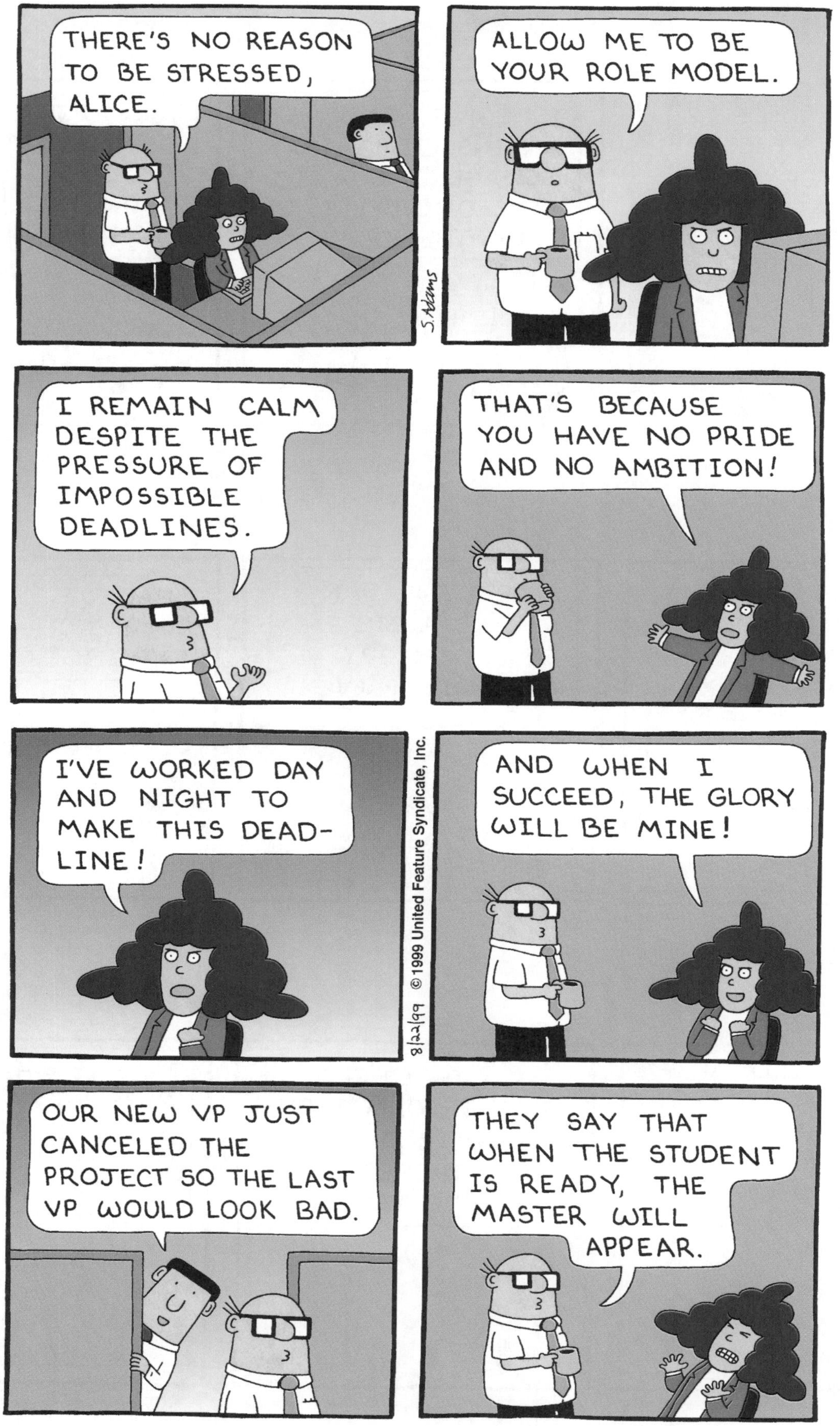
THERE'S NO REASON TO BE STRESSED, ALICE.
S. Adams
ALLOW ME TO BE YOUR ROLE MODEL.
I REMAIN CALM DESPITE THE PRESSURE OF IMPOSSIBLE DEADLINES.
THAT'S BECAUSE YOU HAVE NO PRIDE AND NO AMBITION!
I'VE WORKED DAY AND NIGHT TO MAKE THIS DEAD-LINE!
8/22/99 © 1999 United Feature Syndicate, Inc.
AND WHEN I SUCCEED, THE GLORY WILL BE MINE!
OUR NEW VP JUST CANCELED THE PROJECT SO THE LAST VP WOULD LOOK BAD.
THEY SAY THAT WHEN THE STUDENT IS READY, THE MASTER WILL APPEAR.

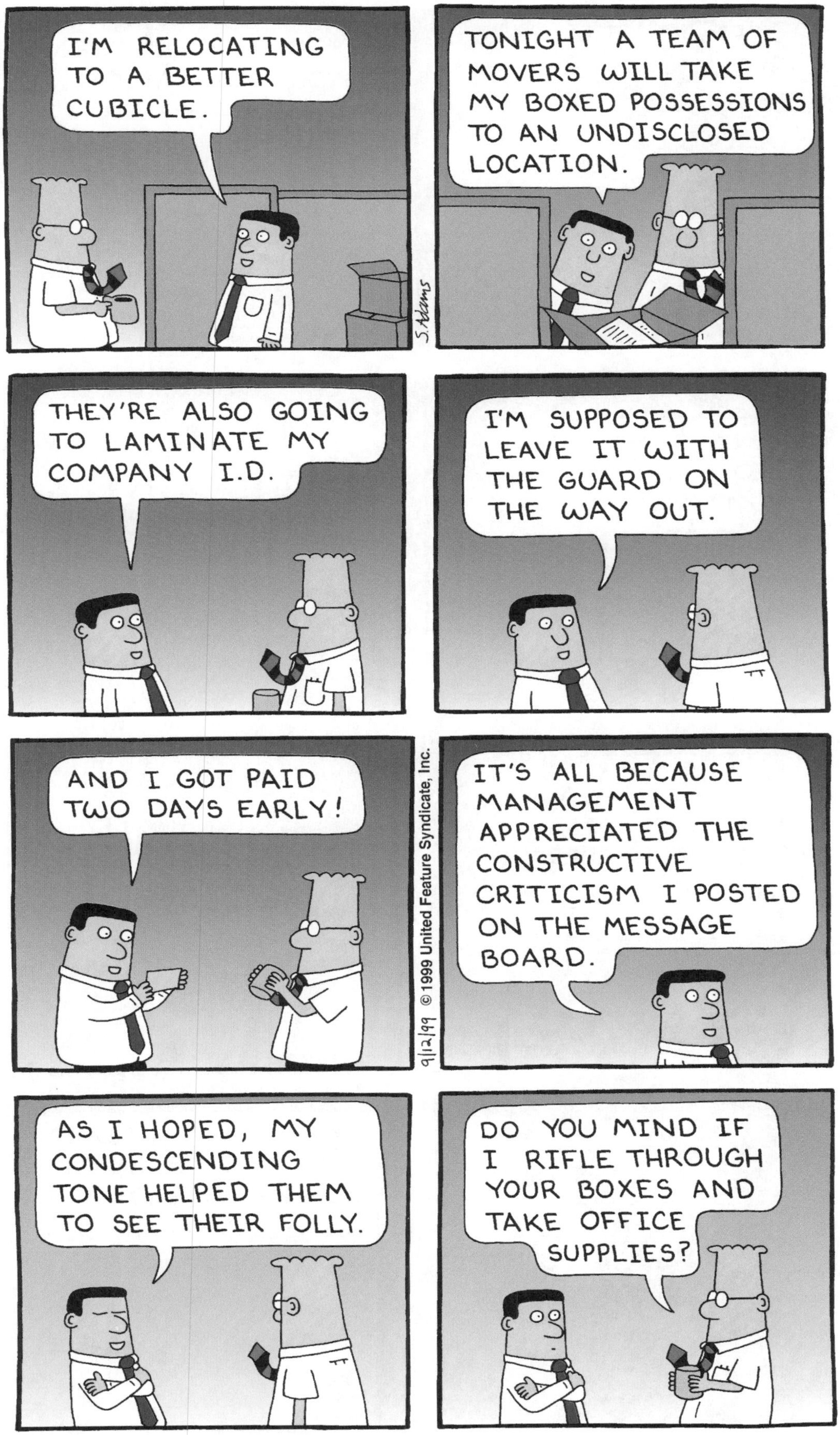
I'M RELOCATING TO A BETTER CUBICLE.
TONIGHT A TEAM OF MOVERS WILL TAKE MY BOXED POSSESSIONS TO AN UNDISCLOSED LOCATION.
THEY'RE ALSO GOING TO LAMINATE MY COMPANY I.D.
I'M SUPPOSED TO LEAVE IT WITH THE GUARD ON THE WAY OUT.
AND I GOT PAID TWO DAYS EARLY!
IT'S ALL BECAUSE MANAGEMENT APPRECIATED THE CONSTRUCTIVE CRITICISM I POSTED ON THE MESSAGE BOARD.
AS I HOPED, MY CONDESCENDING TONE HELPED THEM TO SEE THEIR FOLLY.
DO YOU MIND IF I RIFLE THROUGH YOUR BOXES AND TAKE OFFICE SUPPLIES?
S. Adams
9/12/99 © 1999 United Feature Syndicate, Inc.

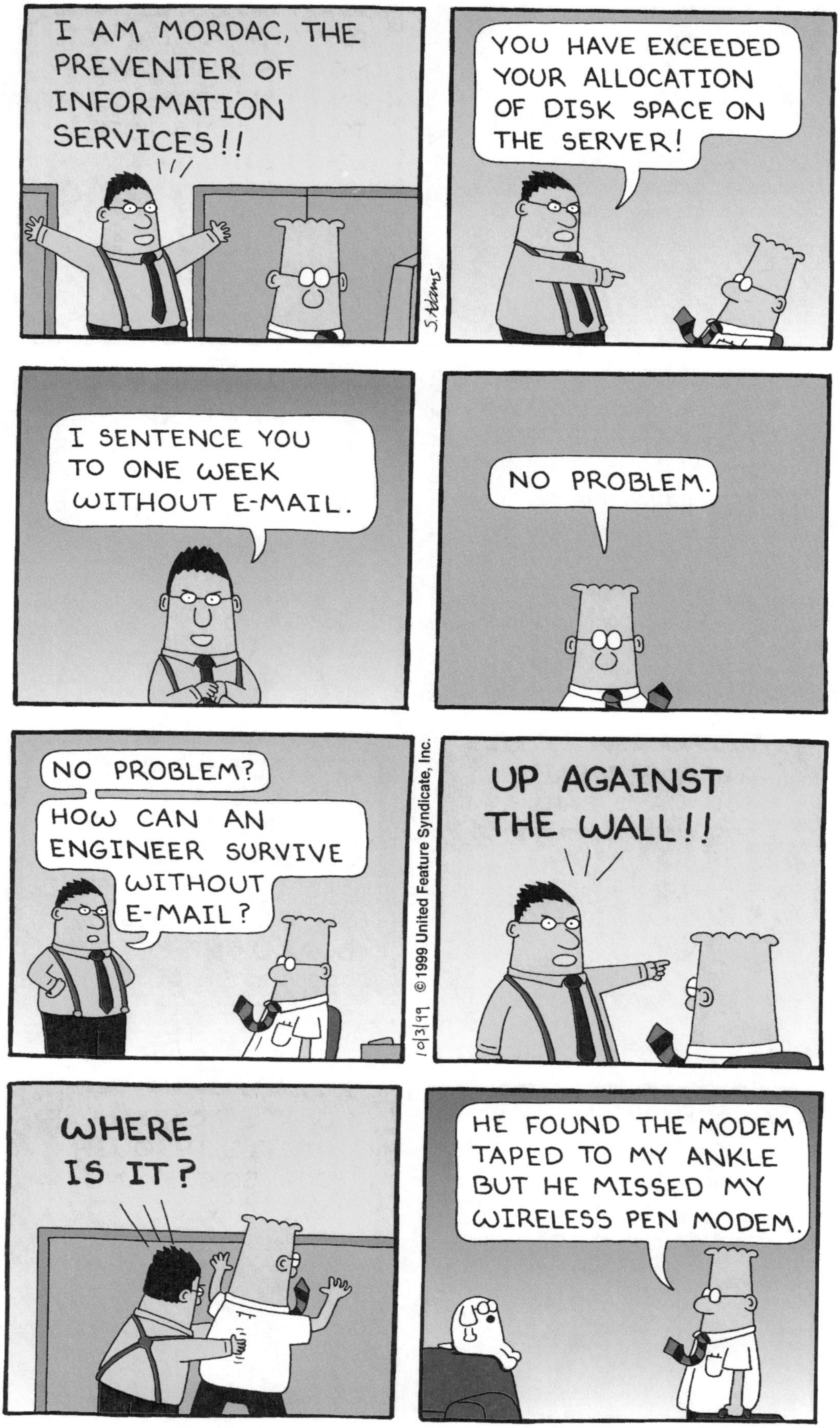
I AM MORDAC, THE PREVENTER OF INFORMATION SERVICES!!
YOU HAVE EXCEEDED YOUR ALLOCATION OF DISK SPACE ON THE SERVER!
I SENTENCE YOU TO ONE WEEK WITHOUT E-MAIL.
NO PROBLEM.
NO PROBLEM?
HOW CAN AN ENGINEER SURVIVE WITHOUT E-MAIL?
UP AGAINST THE WALL!!
WHERE IS IT?
HE FOUND THE MODEM TAPED TO MY ANKLE BUT HE MISSED MY WIRELESS PEN MODEM.
S. Adams
10/3/99 © 1999 United Feature Syndicate, Inc.

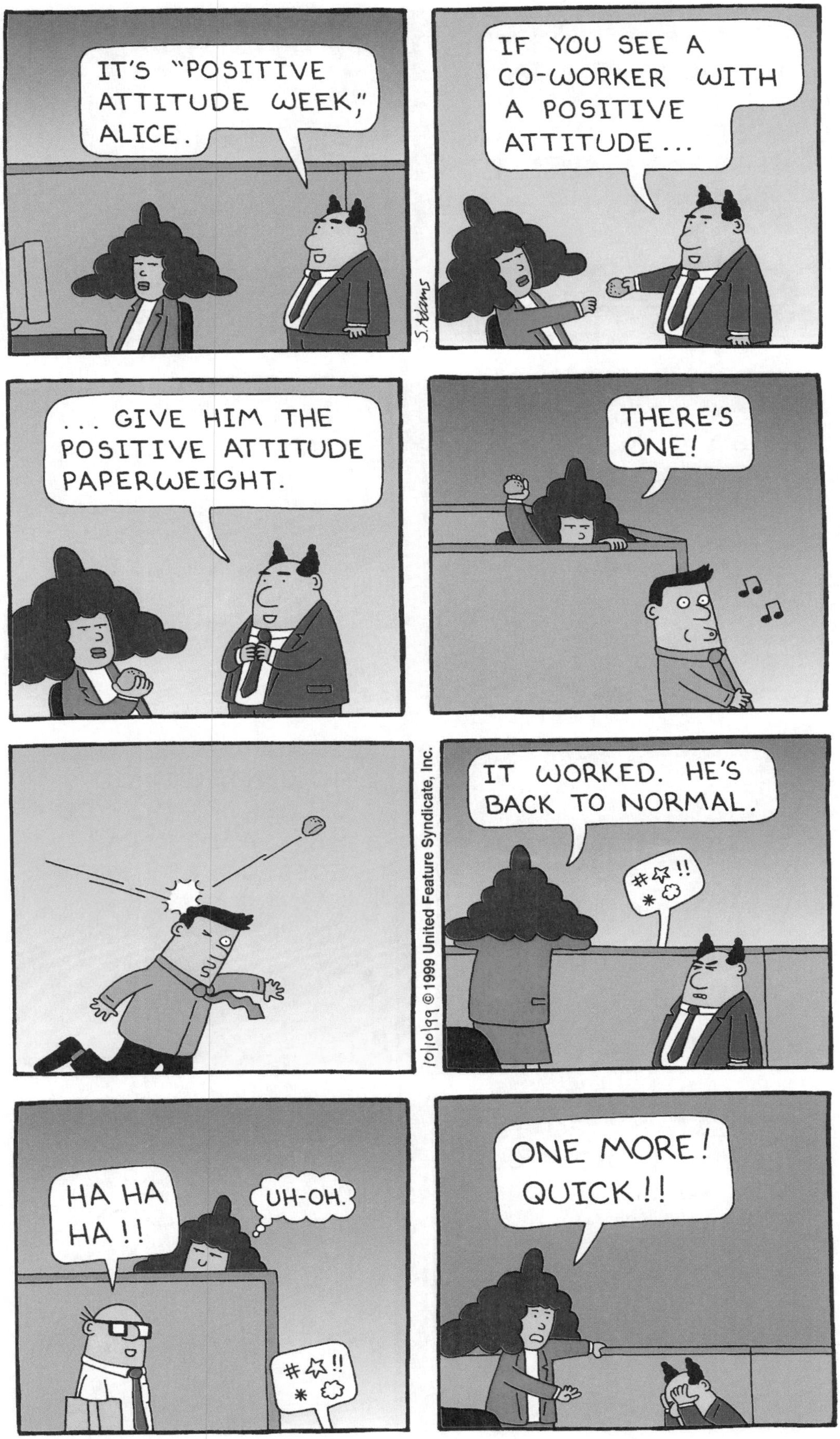
IT'S "POSITIVE ATTITUDE WEEK," ALICE.
IF YOU SEE A CO-WORKER WITH A POSITIVE ATTITUDE...
S. Adams
... GIVE HIM THE POSITIVE ATTITUDE PAPERWEIGHT.
THERE'S ONE!
10/10/99 © 1999 United Feature Syndicate, Inc.
IT WORKED. HE'S BACK TO NORMAL.
#☆!! * ✿
HA HA HA!!
UH-OH.
#☆!! * ✿
ONE MORE! QUICK!!

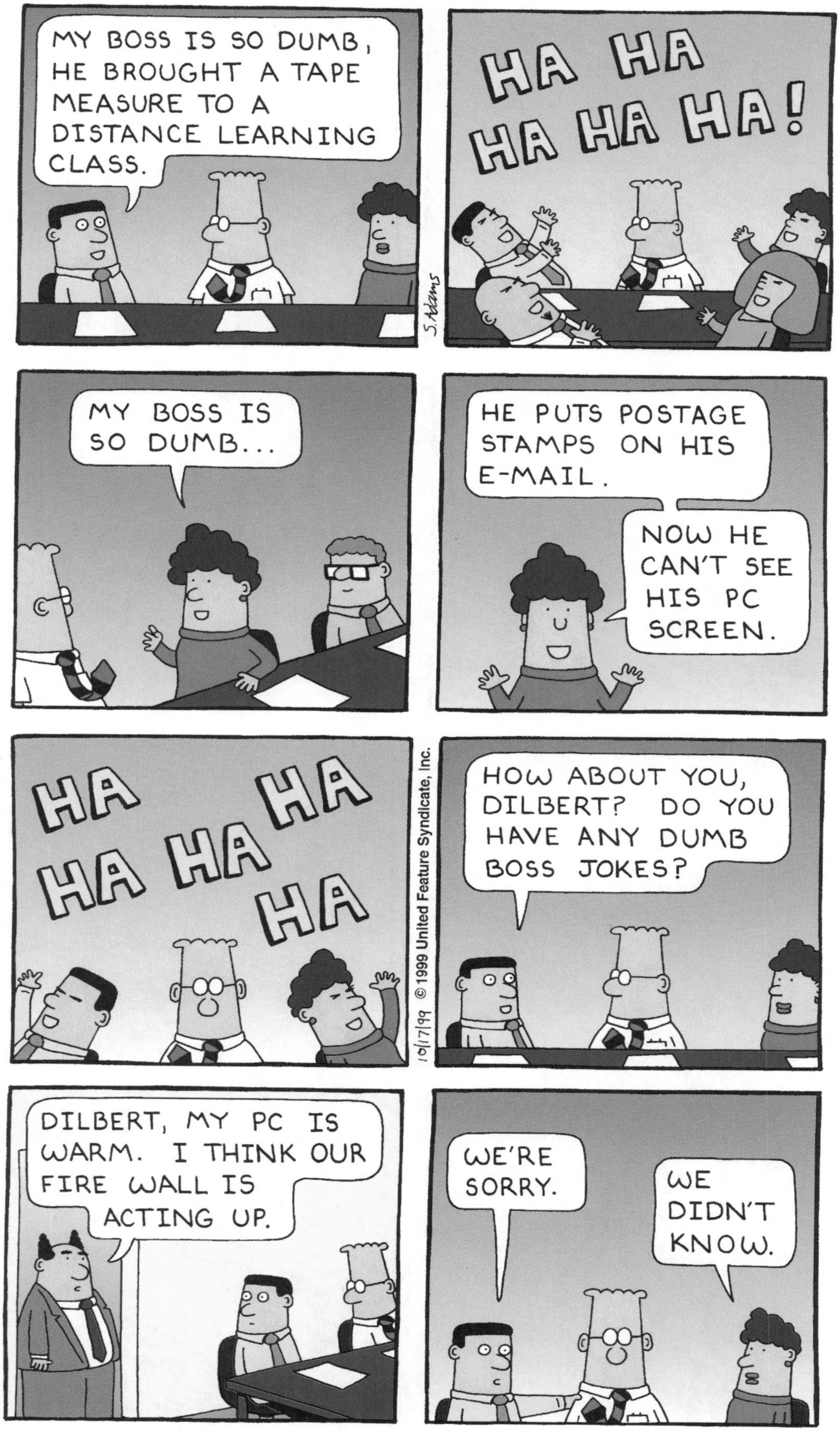
MY BOSS IS SO DUMB, HE BROUGHT A TAPE MEASURE TO A DISTANCE LEARNING CLASS.
S. Adams
HA HA HA HA HA!
MY BOSS IS SO DUMB...
HE PUTS POSTAGE STAMPS ON HIS E-MAIL.
NOW HE CAN'T SEE HIS PC SCREEN.
HA HA HA HA HA
10/17/99 © 1999 United Feature Syndicate, Inc.
HOW ABOUT YOU, DILBERT? DO YOU HAVE ANY DUMB BOSS JOKES?
DILBERT, MY PC IS WARM. I THINK OUR FIRE WALL IS ACTING UP.
WE'RE SORRY.
WE DIDN'T KNOW.

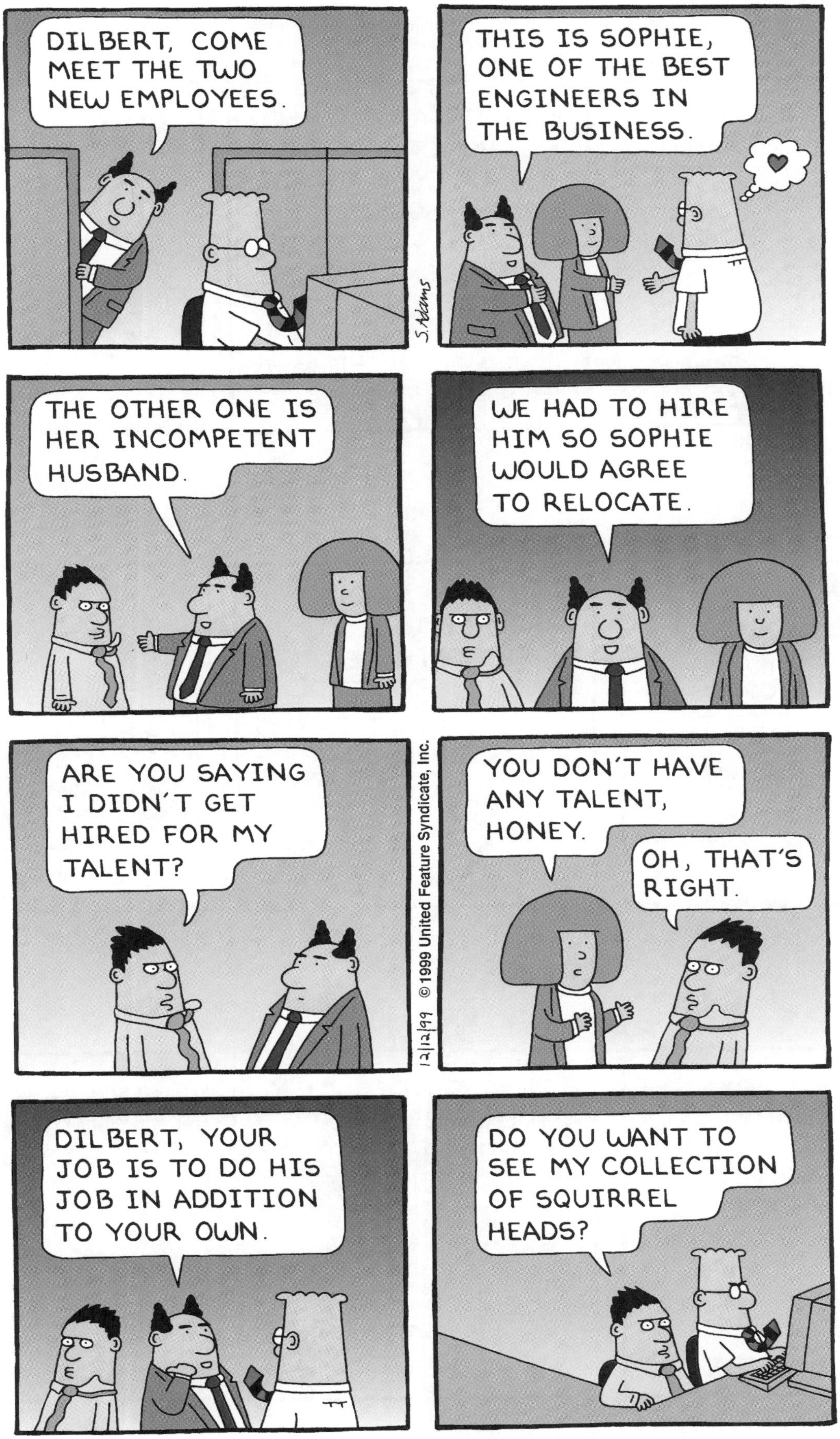
DILBERT, COME MEET THE TWO NEW EMPLOYEES.
S. Adams
THIS IS SOPHIE, ONE OF THE BEST ENGINEERS IN THE BUSINESS.
THE OTHER ONE IS HER INCOMPETENT HUSBAND.
WE HAD TO HIRE HIM SO SOPHIE WOULD AGREE TO RELOCATE.
ARE YOU SAYING I DIDN'T GET HIRED FOR MY TALENT?
YOU DON'T HAVE ANY TALENT, HONEY.
OH, THAT'S RIGHT.
DILBERT, YOUR JOB IS TO DO HIS JOB IN ADDITION TO YOUR OWN.
DO YOU WANT TO SEE MY COLLECTION OF SQUIRREL HEADS?
12/12/99

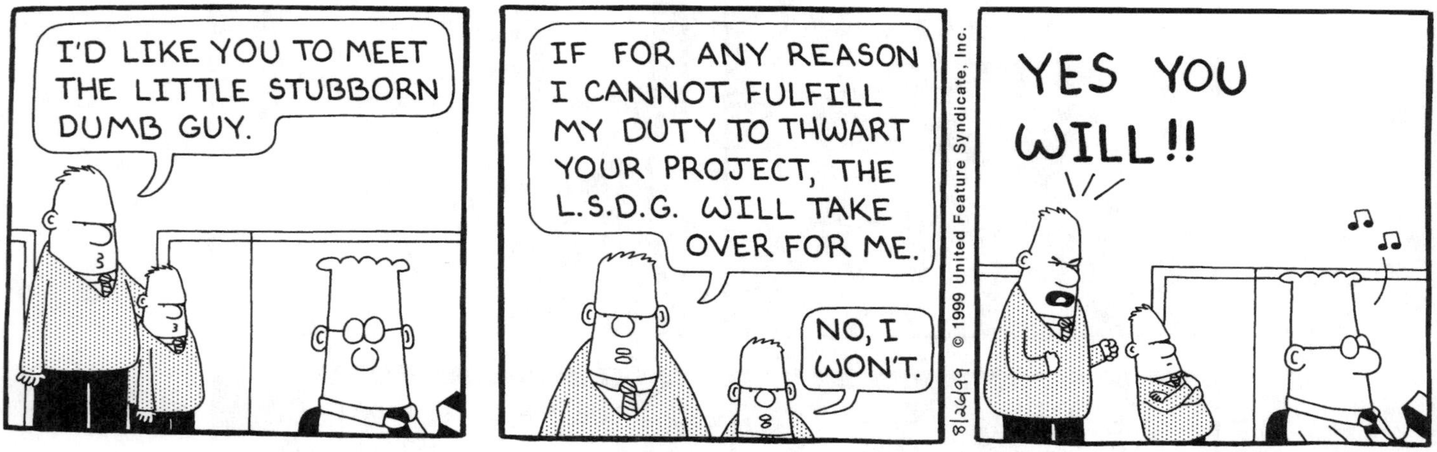
I'D LIKE YOU TO MEET THE LITTLE STUBBORN DUMB GUY.
IF FOR ANY REASON I CANNOT FULFILL MY DUTY TO THWART YOUR PROJECT, THE L.S.D.G. WILL TAKE OVER FOR ME.
NO, I WON'T.
8/26/99 © 1999 United Feature Syndicate, Inc.
YES YOU WILL!!

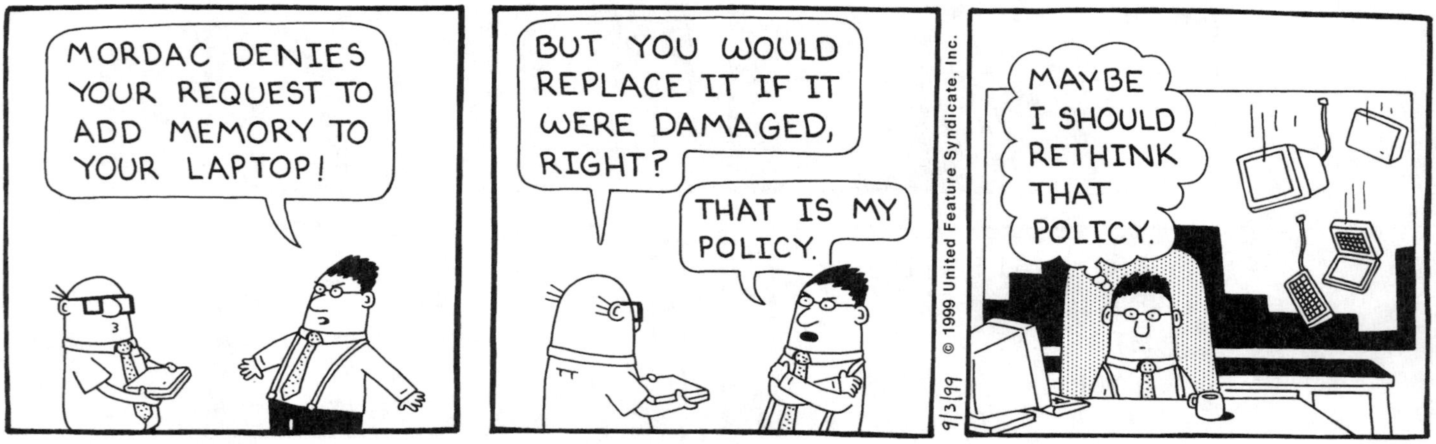
MORDAC DENIES YOUR REQUEST TO ADD MEMORY TO YOUR LAPTOP!
BUT YOU WOULD REPLACE IT IF IT WERE DAMAGED, RIGHT?
THAT IS MY POLICY.
9/3/99 © 1999 United Feature Syndicate, Inc.
MAYBE I SHOULD RETHINK THAT POLICY.

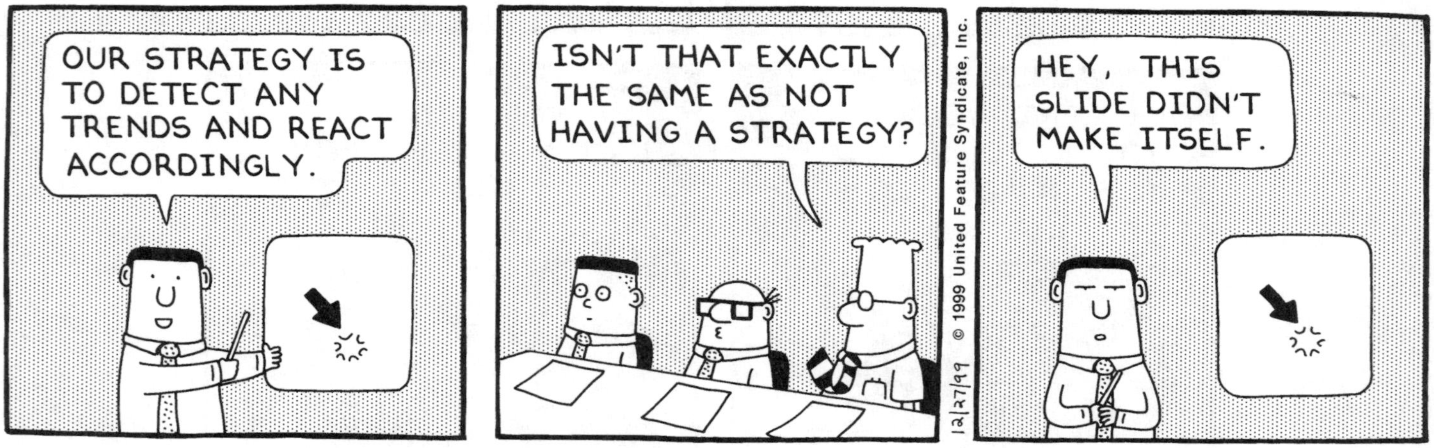
OUR STRATEGY IS TO DETECT ANY TRENDS AND REACT ACCORDINGLY.
ISN'T THAT EXACTLY THE SAME AS NOT HAVING A STRATEGY?
12/27/99 © 1999 United Feature Syndicate, Inc.
HEY, THIS SLIDE DIDN'T MAKE ITSELF.

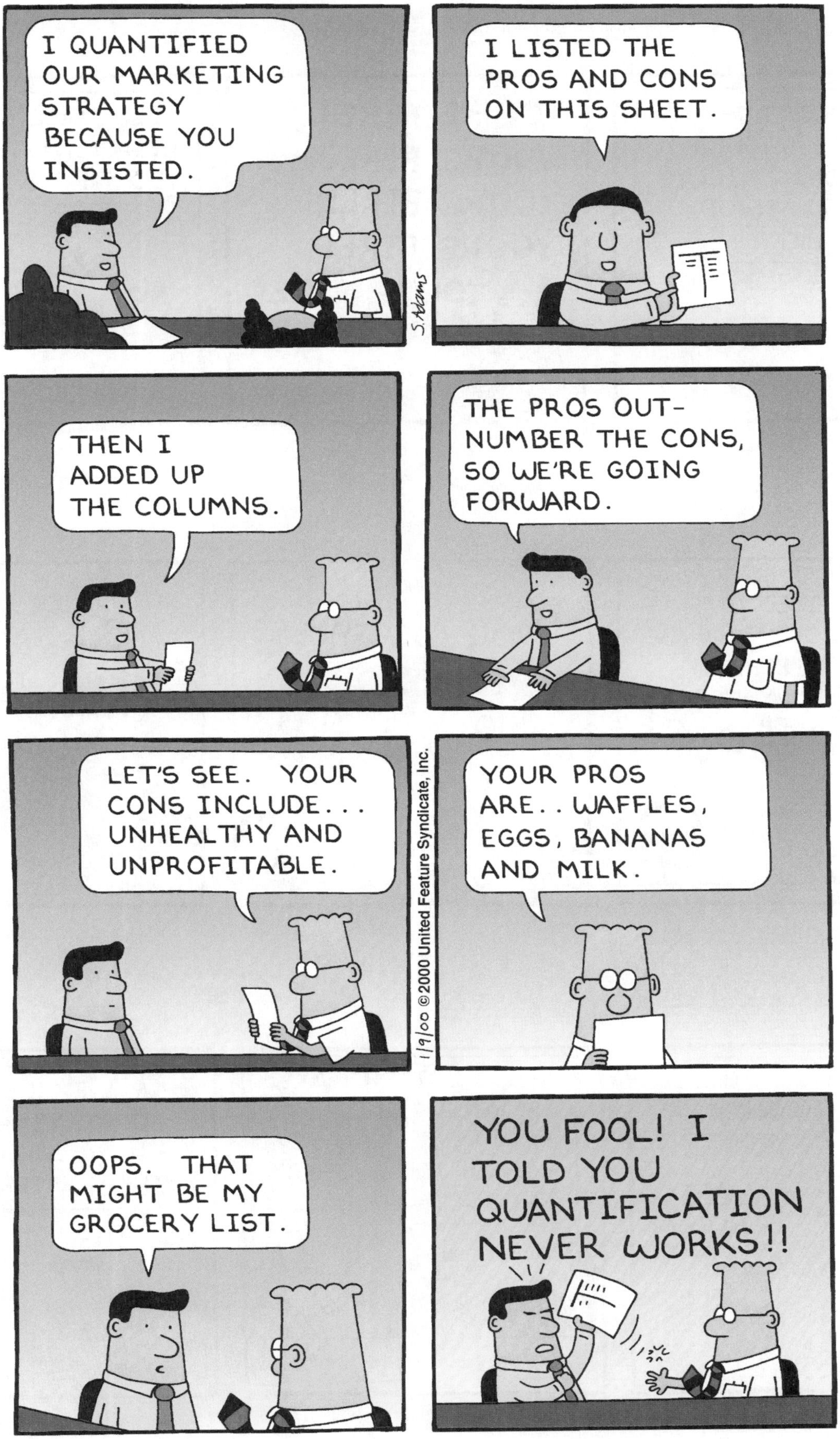
I QUANTIFIED OUR MARKETING STRATEGY BECAUSE YOU INSISTED.
S. Adams
I LISTED THE PROS AND CONS ON THIS SHEET.
THEN I ADDED UP THE COLUMNS.
THE PROS OUT-NUMBER THE CONS, SO WE'RE GOING FORWARD.
LET'S SEE. YOUR CONS INCLUDE... UNHEALTHY AND UNPROFITABLE.
1/9/00 © 2000 United Feature Syndicate, Inc.
YOUR PROS ARE.. WAFFLES, EGGS, BANANAS AND MILK.
OOPS. THAT MIGHT BE MY GROCERY LIST.
YOU FOOL! I TOLD YOU QUANTIFICATION NEVER WORKS!!

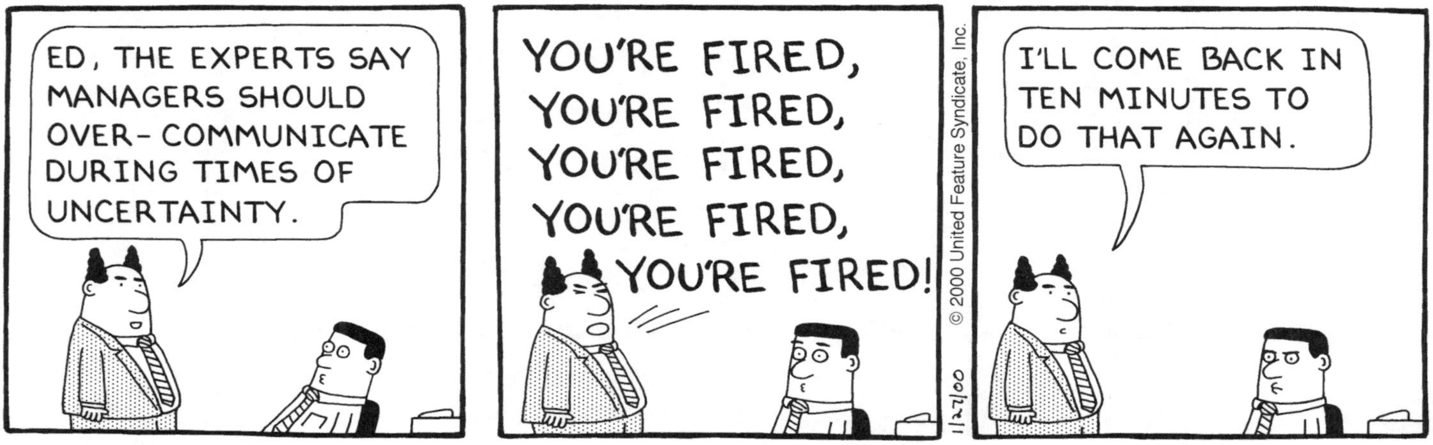
ED, THE EXPERTS SAY MANAGERS SHOULD OVER-COMMUNICATE DURING TIMES OF UNCERTAINTY.
YOU'RE FIRED, YOU'RE FIRED, YOU'RE FIRED, YOU'RE FIRED, YOU'RE FIRED!
I'LL COME BACK IN TEN MINUTES TO DO THAT AGAIN.
1/27/00

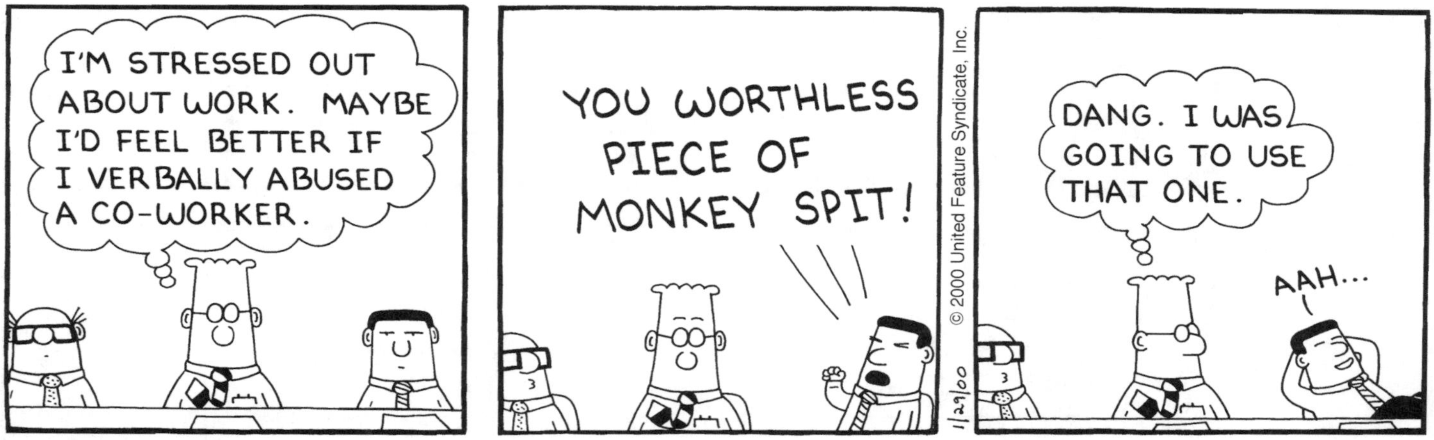
I'M STRESSED OUT ABOUT WORK. MAYBE I'D FEEL BETTER IF I VERBALLY ABUSED A CO-WORKER.
YOU WORTHLESS PIECE OF MONKEY SPIT!
DANG. I WAS GOING TO USE THAT ONE.
AAH...
1/29/00

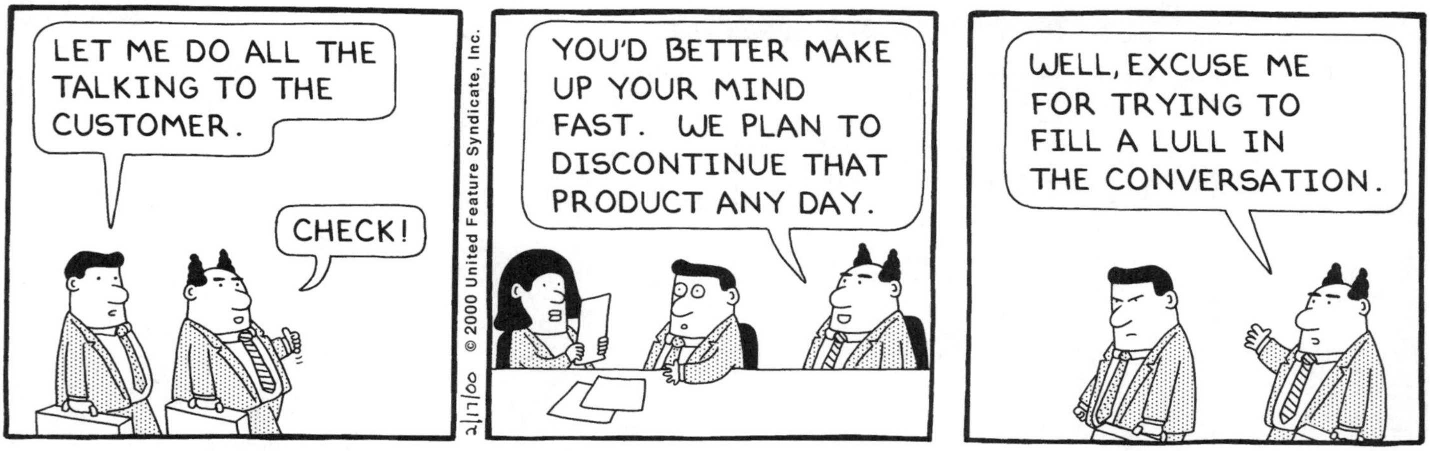
LET ME DO ALL THE TALKING TO THE CUSTOMER.
CHECK!
YOU'D BETTER MAKE UP YOUR MIND FAST. WE PLAN TO DISCONTINUE THAT PRODUCT ANY DAY.
WELL, EXCUSE ME FOR TRYING TO FILL A LULL IN THE CONVERSATION.
2/17/00

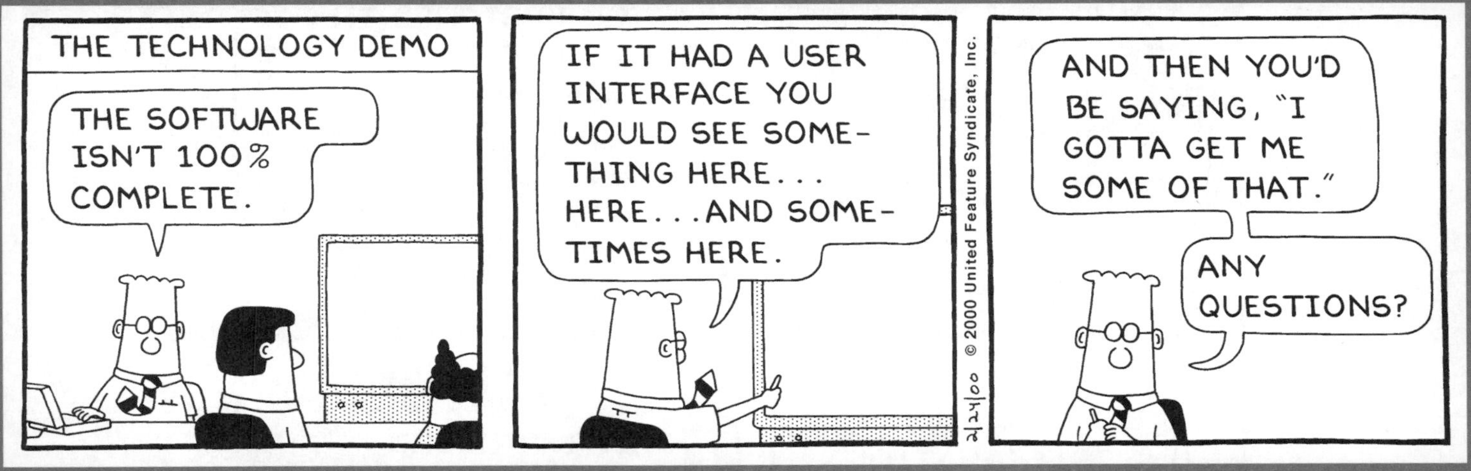
THE TECHNOLOGY DEMO
THE SOFTWARE ISN'T 100% COMPLETE.
IF IT HAD A USER INTERFACE YOU WOULD SEE SOMETHING HERE... HERE...AND SOMETIMES HERE.
2/24/00 © 2000 United Feature Syndicate, Inc.
AND THEN YOU'D BE SAYING, "I GOTTA GET ME SOME OF THAT."
ANY QUESTIONS?

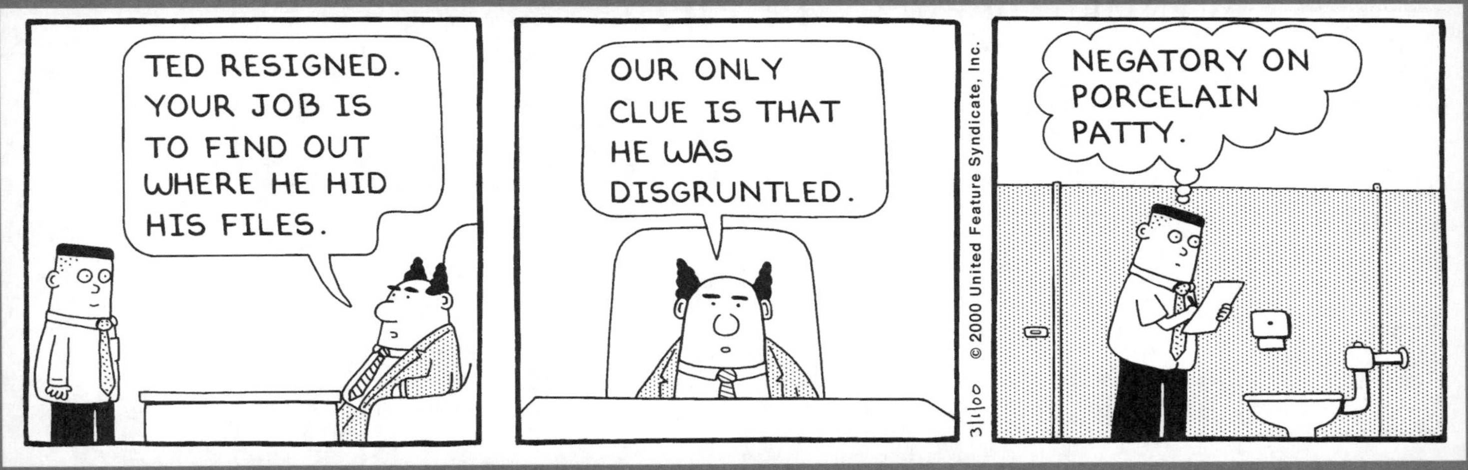
TED RESIGNED. YOUR JOB IS TO FIND OUT WHERE HE HID HIS FILES.
OUR ONLY CLUE IS THAT HE WAS DISGRUNTLED.
3/1/00 © 2000 United Feature Syndicate, Inc.
NEGATORY ON PORCELAIN PATTY.

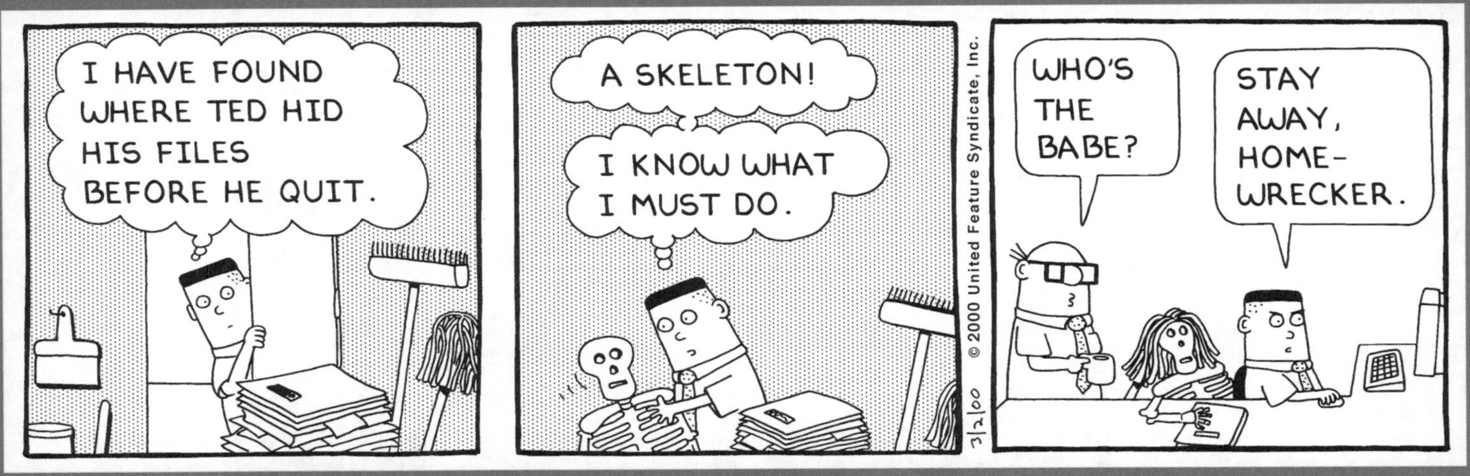
I HAVE FOUND WHERE TED HID HIS FILES BEFORE HE QUIT.
A SKELETON!
I KNOW WHAT I MUST DO.
3/2/00 © 2000 United Feature Syndicate, Inc.
WHO'S THE BABE?
STAY AWAY, HOME-WRECKER.

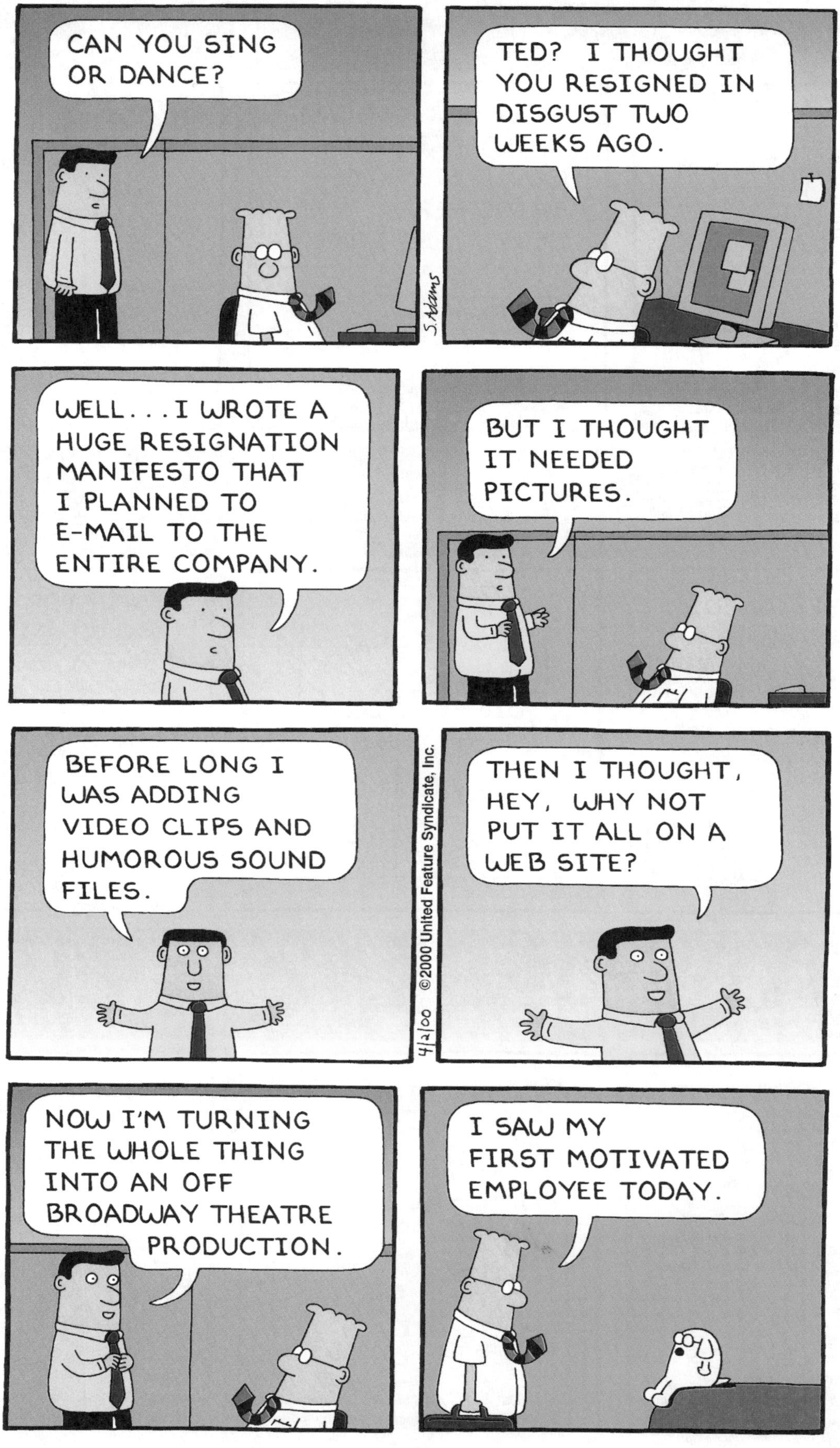
CAN YOU SING OR DANCE?
S. Adams
TED? I THOUGHT YOU RESIGNED IN DISGUST TWO WEEKS AGO.
WELL...I WROTE A HUGE RESIGNATION MANIFESTO THAT I PLANNED TO E-MAIL TO THE ENTIRE COMPANY.
BUT I THOUGHT IT NEEDED PICTURES.
BEFORE LONG I WAS ADDING VIDEO CLIPS AND HUMOROUS SOUND FILES.
©2000 United Feature Syndicate, Inc.
4/2/00
THEN I THOUGHT, HEY, WHY NOT PUT IT ALL ON A WEB SITE?
NOW I'M TURNING THE WHOLE THING INTO AN OFF BROADWAY THEATRE PRODUCTION.
I SAW MY FIRST MOTIVATED EMPLOYEE TODAY.

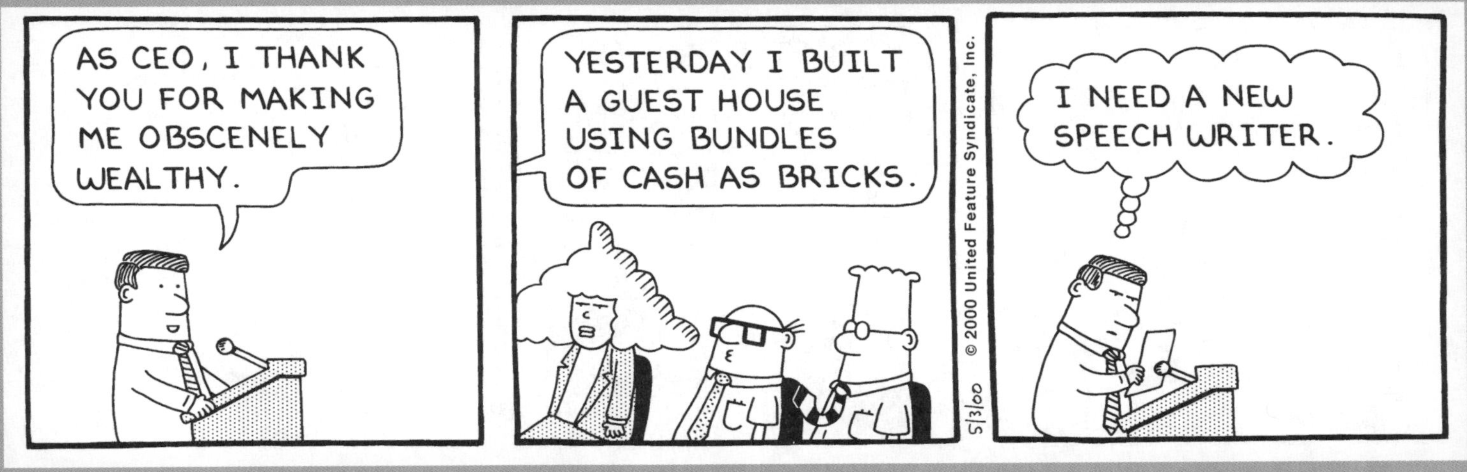
AS CEO, I THANK YOU FOR MAKING ME OBSCENELY WEALTHY.
YESTERDAY I BUILT A GUEST HOUSE USING BUNDLES OF CASH AS BRICKS.
5/3/00
© 2000 United Feature Syndicate, Inc.
I NEED A NEW SPEECH WRITER.

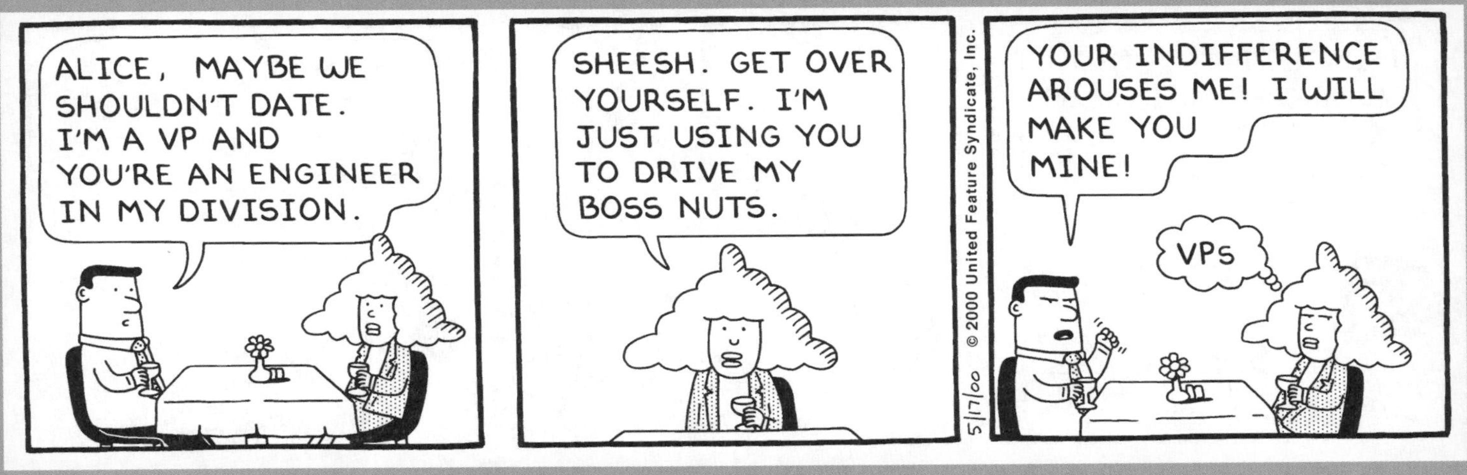
ALICE, MAYBE WE SHOULDN'T DATE. I'M A VP AND YOU'RE AN ENGINEER IN MY DIVISION.
SHEESH. GET OVER YOURSELF. I'M JUST USING YOU TO DRIVE MY BOSS NUTS.
5/17/00
© 2000 United Feature Syndicate, Inc.
YOUR INDIFFERENCE AROUSES ME! I WILL MAKE YOU MINE!
VPs

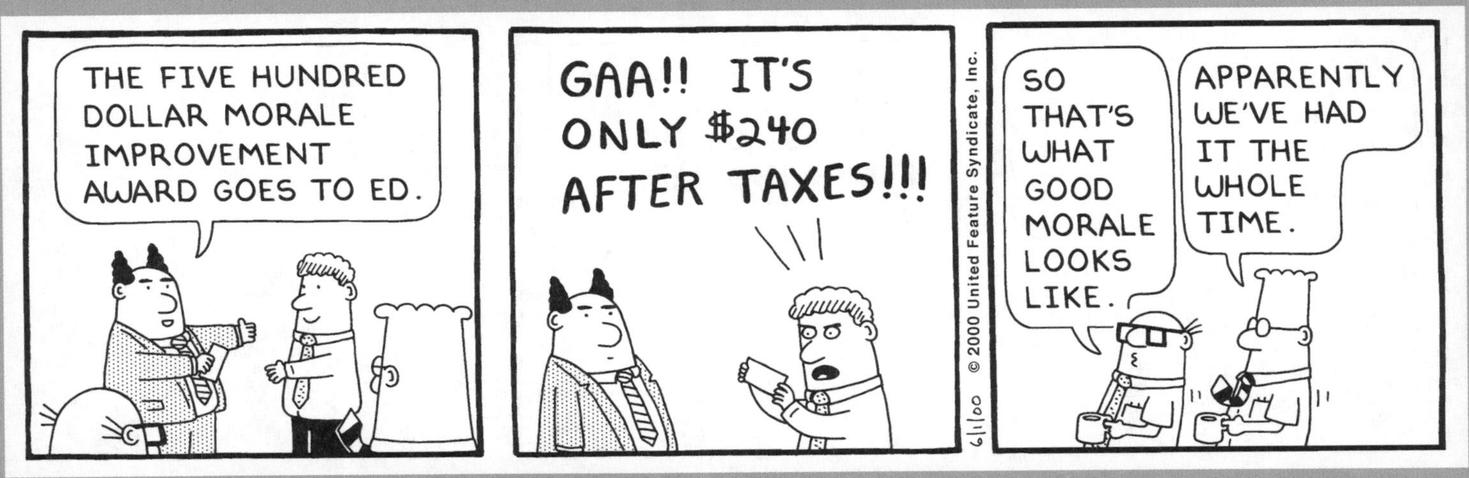
THE FIVE HUNDRED DOLLAR MORALE IMPROVEMENT AWARD GOES TO ED.
GAA!! IT'S ONLY $240 AFTER TAXES!!!
6/1/00
© 2000 United Feature Syndicate, Inc.
SO THAT'S WHAT GOOD MORALE LOOKS LIKE.
APPARENTLY WE'VE HAD IT THE WHOLE TIME.

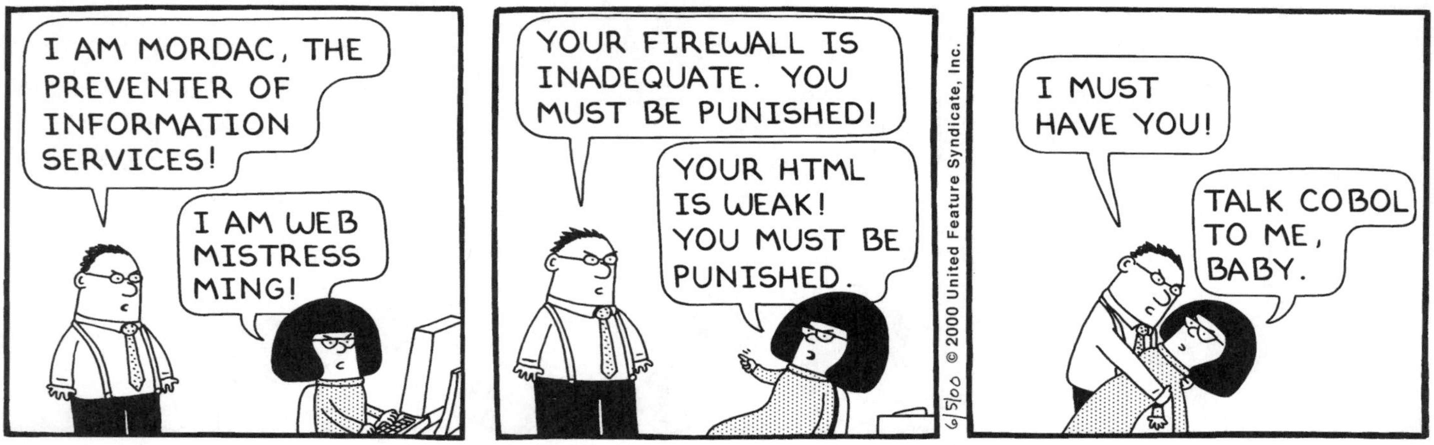
I AM MORDAC, THE PREVENTER OF INFORMATION SERVICES!
I AM WEB MISTRESS MING!
YOUR FIREWALL IS INADEQUATE. YOU MUST BE PUNISHED!
YOUR HTML IS WEAK! YOU MUST BE PUNISHED.
6/5/00 © 2000 United Feature Syndicate, Inc.
I MUST HAVE YOU!
TALK COBOL TO ME, BABY.

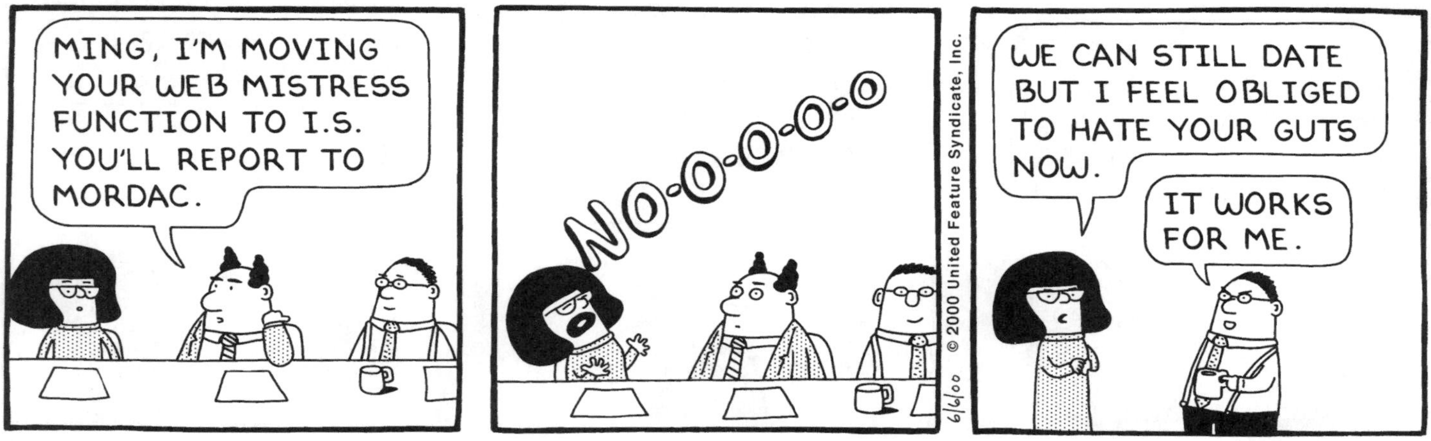
MING, I'M MOVING YOUR WEB MISTRESS FUNCTION TO I.S. YOU'LL REPORT TO MORDAC.
NO-O-O-O-O-O
6/6/00 © 2000 United Feature Syndicate, Inc.
WE CAN STILL DATE BUT I FEEL OBLIGED TO HATE YOUR GUTS NOW.
IT WORKS FOR ME.

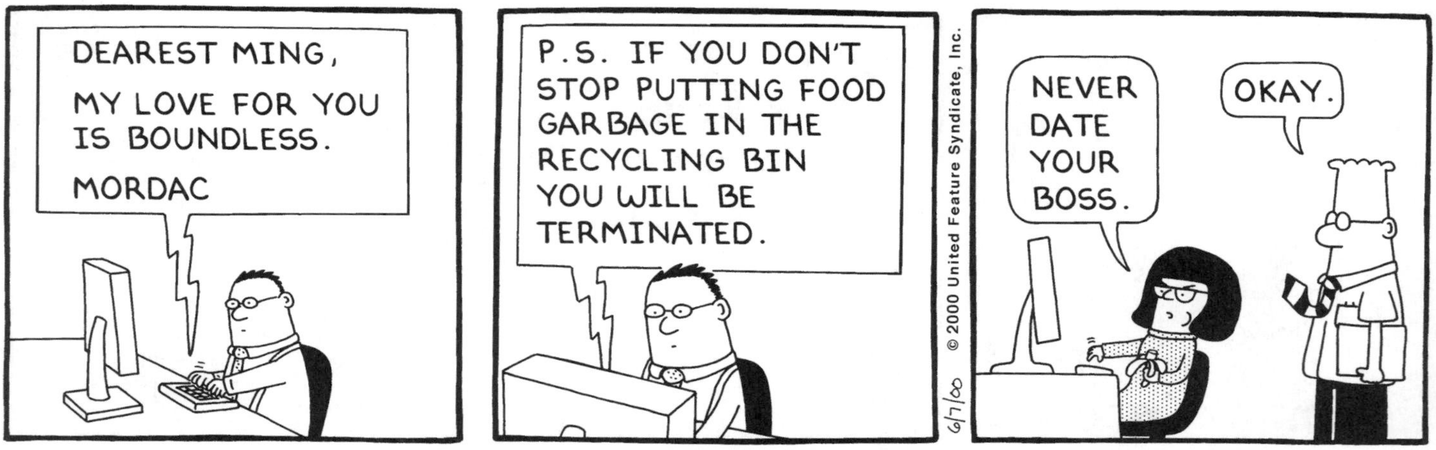
DEAREST MING,
MY LOVE FOR YOU IS BOUNDLESS.
MORDAC
P.S. IF YOU DON'T STOP PUTTING FOOD GARBAGE IN THE RECYCLING BIN YOU WILL BE TERMINATED.
6/7/00 © 2000 United Feature Syndicate, Inc.
NEVER DATE YOUR BOSS.
OKAY.

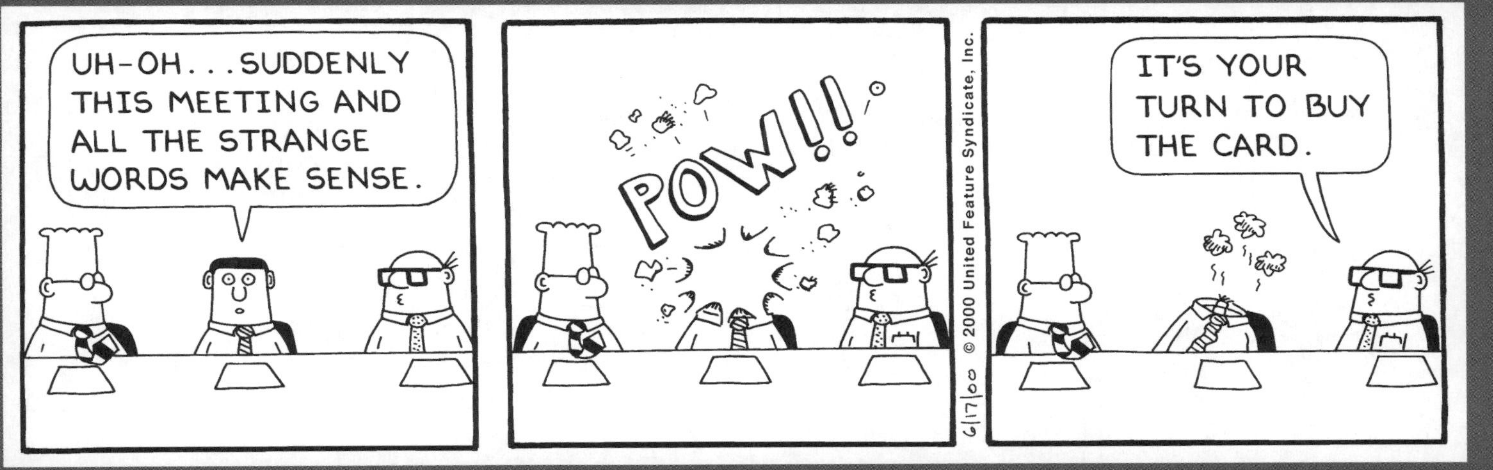
UH-OH...SUDDENLY THIS MEETING AND ALL THE STRANGE WORDS MAKE SENSE.
POW!!
IT'S YOUR TURN TO BUY THE CARD.
6/17/00 © 2000 United Feature Syndicate, Inc.

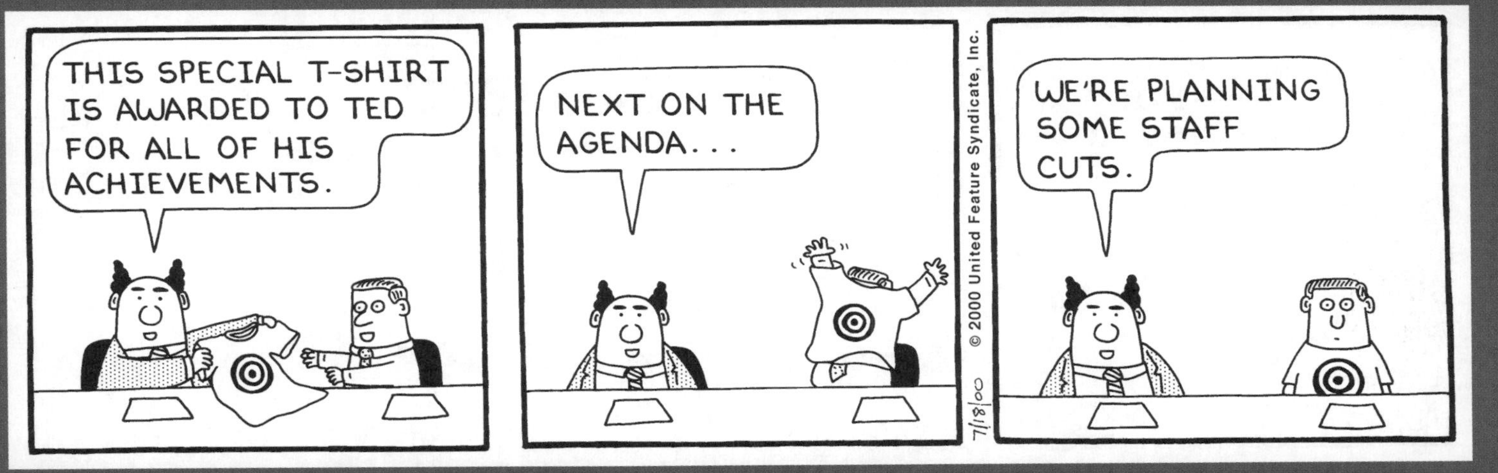
THIS SPECIAL T-SHIRT IS AWARDED TO TED FOR ALL OF HIS ACHIEVEMENTS.
NEXT ON THE AGENDA...
WE'RE PLANNING SOME STAFF CUTS.
7/18/00 © 2000 United Feature Syndicate, Inc.

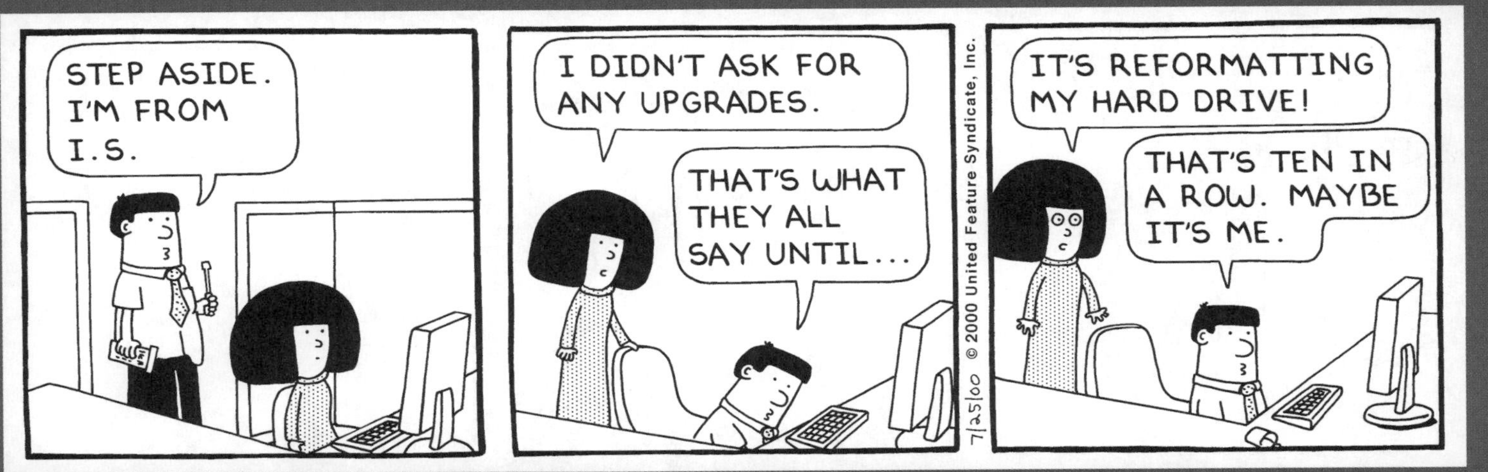
STEP ASIDE. I'M FROM I.S.
I DIDN'T ASK FOR ANY UPGRADES.
THAT'S WHAT THEY ALL SAY UNTIL...
IT'S REFORMATTING MY HARD DRIVE!
THAT'S TEN IN A ROW. MAYBE IT'S ME.
7/25/00 © 2000 United Feature Syndicate, Inc.

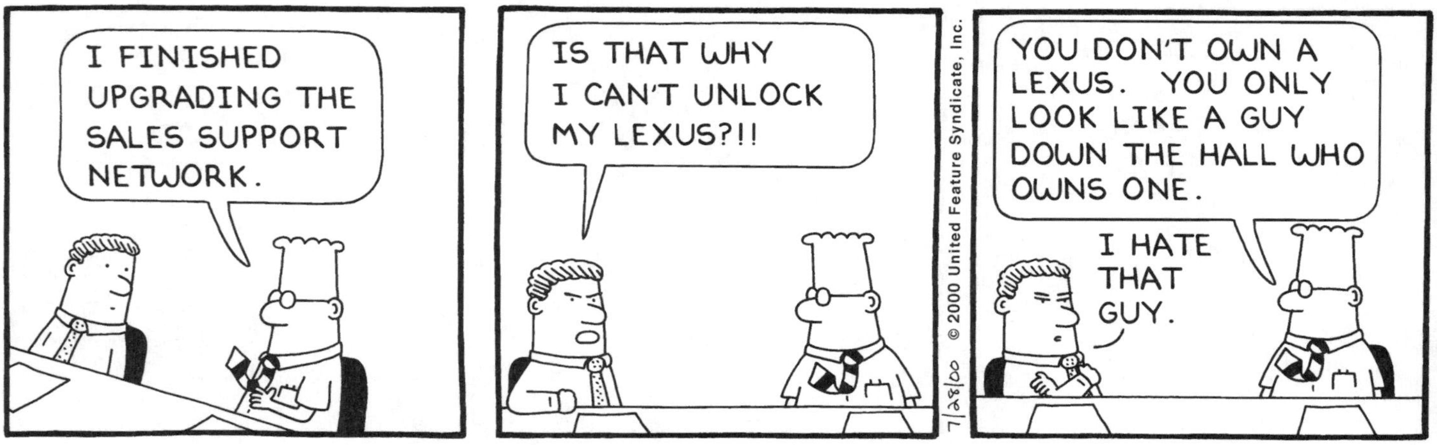
I FINISHED UPGRADING THE SALES SUPPORT NETWORK.
IS THAT WHY I CAN'T UNLOCK MY LEXUS?!!
7/28/00 © 2000 United Feature Syndicate, Inc.
YOU DON'T OWN A LEXUS. YOU ONLY LOOK LIKE A GUY DOWN THE HALL WHO OWNS ONE.
I HATE THAT GUY.

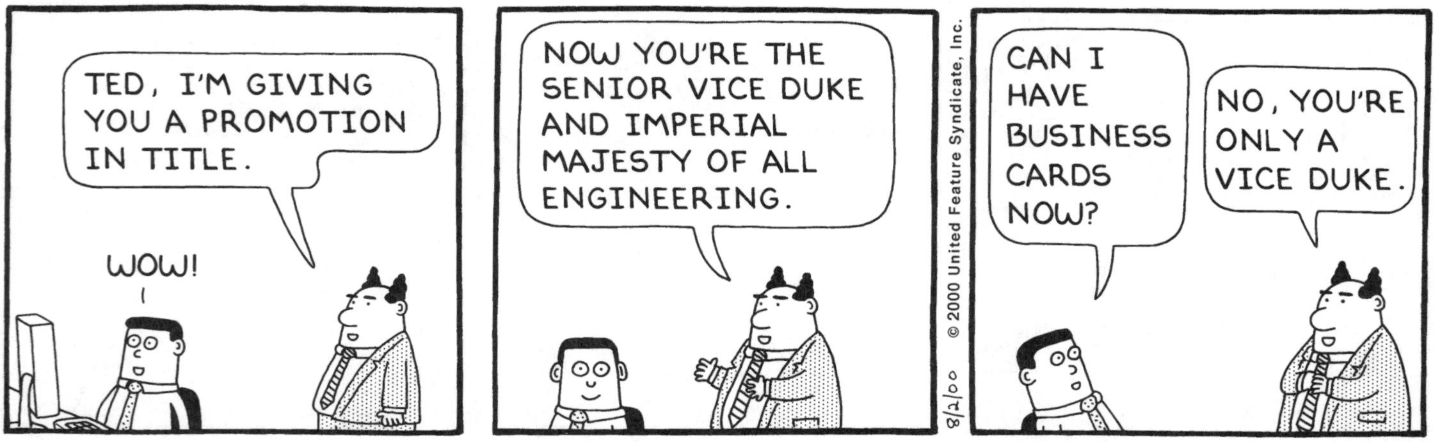
TED, I'M GIVING YOU A PROMOTION IN TITLE.
WOW!
NOW YOU'RE THE SENIOR VICE DUKE AND IMPERIAL MAJESTY OF ALL ENGINEERING.
8/2/00 © 2000 United Feature Syndicate, Inc.
CAN I HAVE BUSINESS CARDS NOW?
NO, YOU'RE ONLY A VICE DUKE.

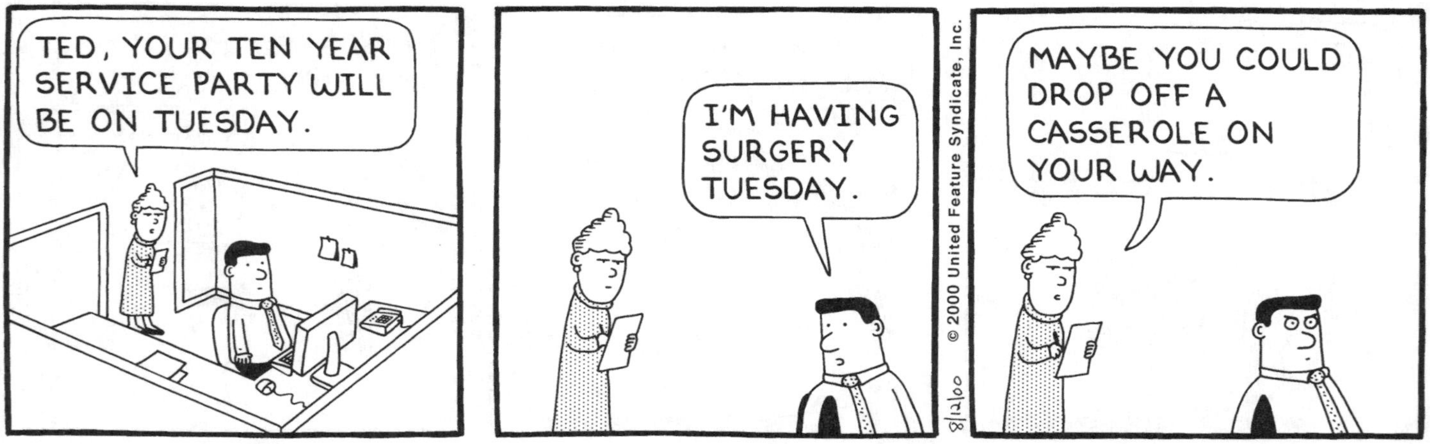
TED, YOUR TEN YEAR SERVICE PARTY WILL BE ON TUESDAY.
I'M HAVING SURGERY TUESDAY.
8/12/00 © 2000 United Feature Syndicate, Inc.
MAYBE YOU COULD DROP OFF A CASSEROLE ON YOUR WAY.

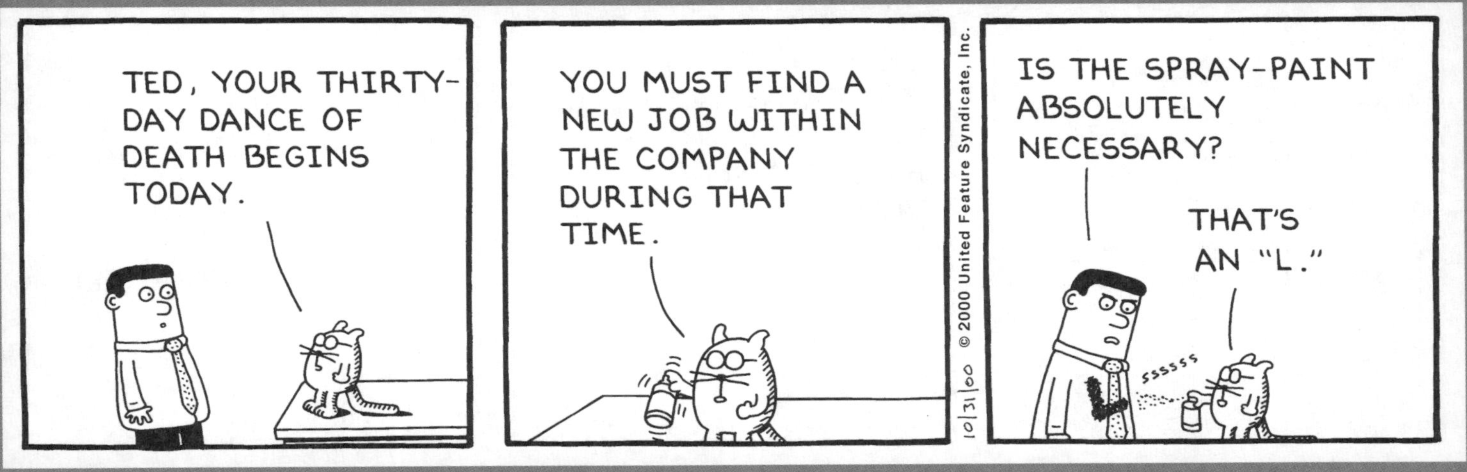
TED, YOUR THIRTY-DAY DANCE OF DEATH BEGINS TODAY.
YOU MUST FIND A NEW JOB WITHIN THE COMPANY DURING THAT TIME.
10/31/00 © 2000 United Feature Syndicate, Inc.
IS THE SPRAY-PAINT ABSOLUTELY NECESSARY?
THAT'S AN "L."
SSSSSS

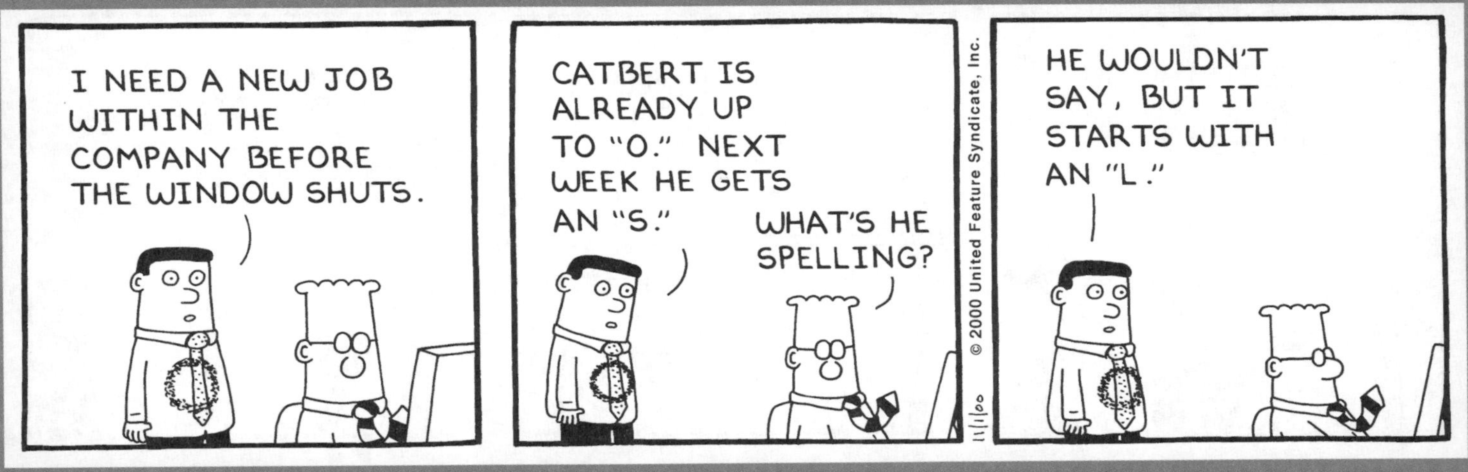
I NEED A NEW JOB WITHIN THE COMPANY BEFORE THE WINDOW SHUTS.
CATBERT IS ALREADY UP TO "O." NEXT WEEK HE GETS AN "S."
WHAT'S HE SPELLING?
11/1/00 © 2000 United Feature Syndicate, Inc.
HE WOULDN'T SAY, BUT IT STARTS WITH AN "L."

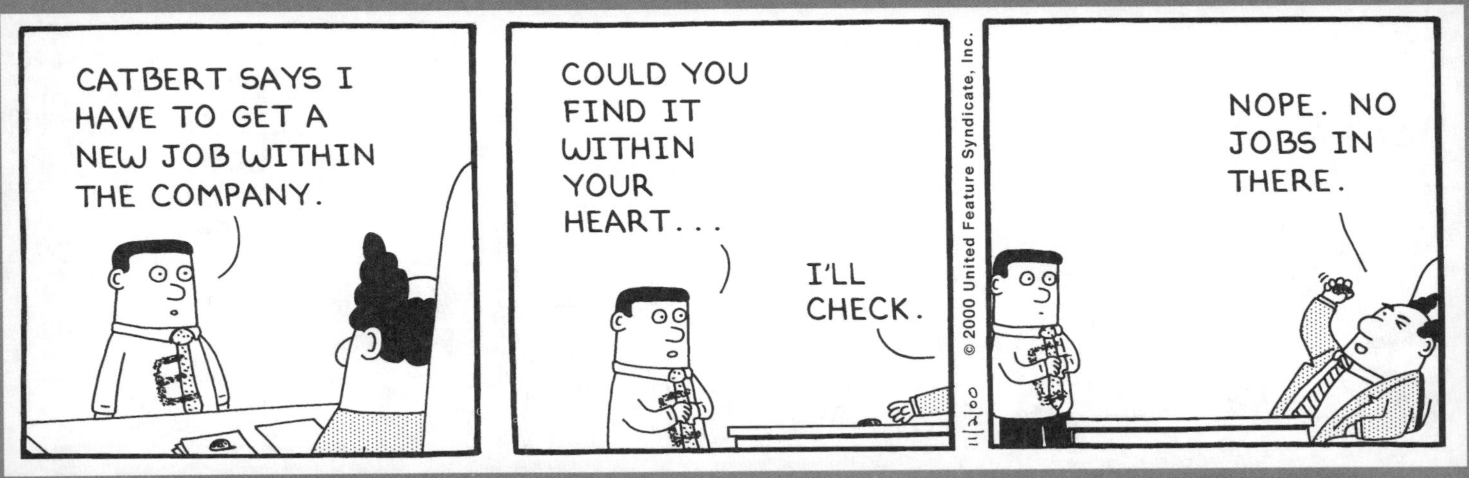
CATBERT SAYS I HAVE TO GET A NEW JOB WITHIN THE COMPANY.
COULD YOU FIND IT WITHIN YOUR HEART...
I'LL CHECK.
11/2/00 © 2000 United Feature Syndicate, Inc.
NOPE. NO JOBS IN THERE.

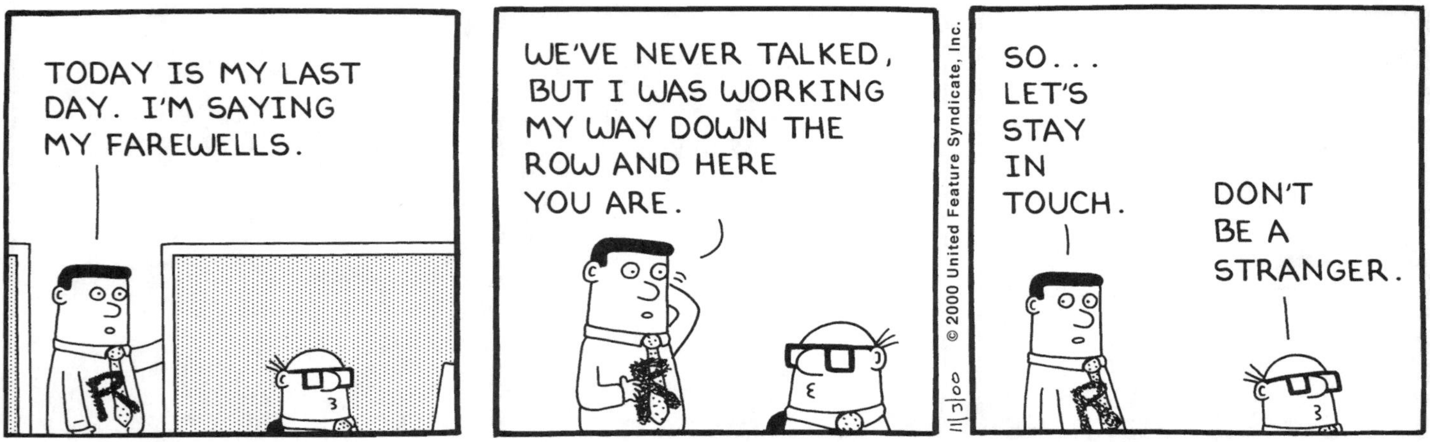
TODAY IS MY LAST DAY. I'M SAYING MY FAREWELLS.
WE'VE NEVER TALKED, BUT I WAS WORKING MY WAY DOWN THE ROW AND HERE YOU ARE.
© 2000 United Feature Syndicate, Inc.
11/3/00
SO... LET'S STAY IN TOUCH.
DON'T BE A STRANGER.

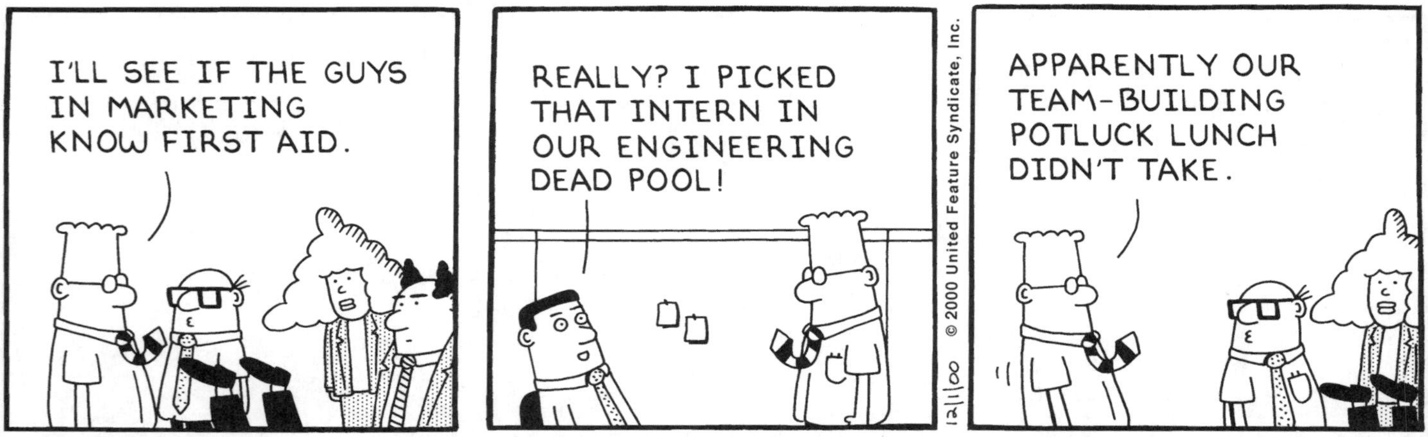
I'LL SEE IF THE GUYS IN MARKETING KNOW FIRST AID.
REALLY? I PICKED THAT INTERN IN OUR ENGINEERING DEAD POOL!
© 2000 United Feature Syndicate, Inc.
12/1/00
APPARENTLY OUR TEAM-BUILDING POTLUCK LUNCH DIDN'T TAKE.

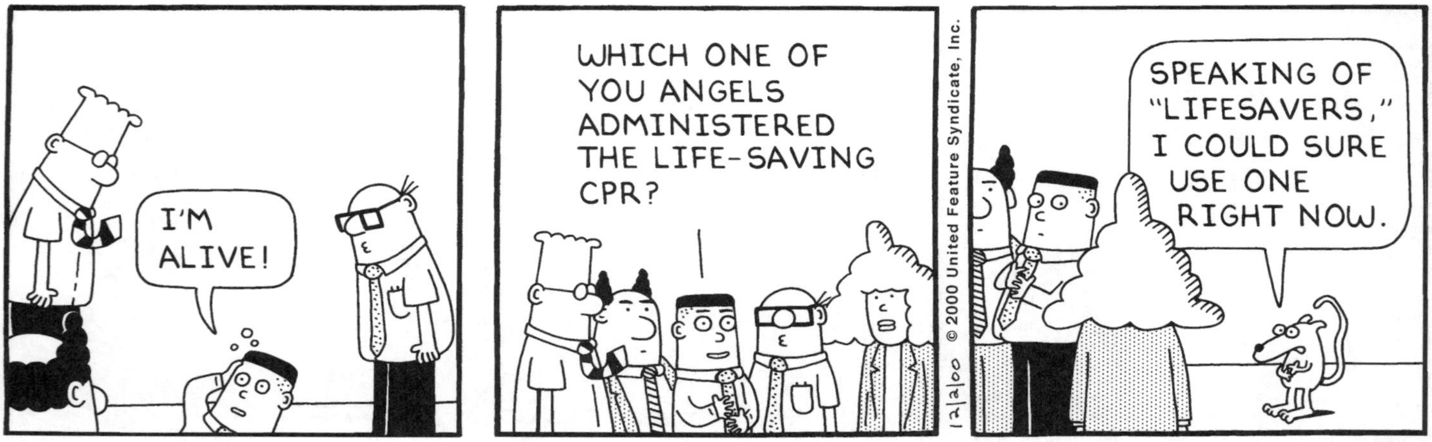
I'M ALIVE!
WHICH ONE OF YOU ANGELS ADMINISTERED THE LIFE-SAVING CPR?
© 2000 United Feature Syndicate, Inc.
12/2/00
SPEAKING OF "LIFESAVERS," I COULD SURE USE ONE RIGHT NOW.

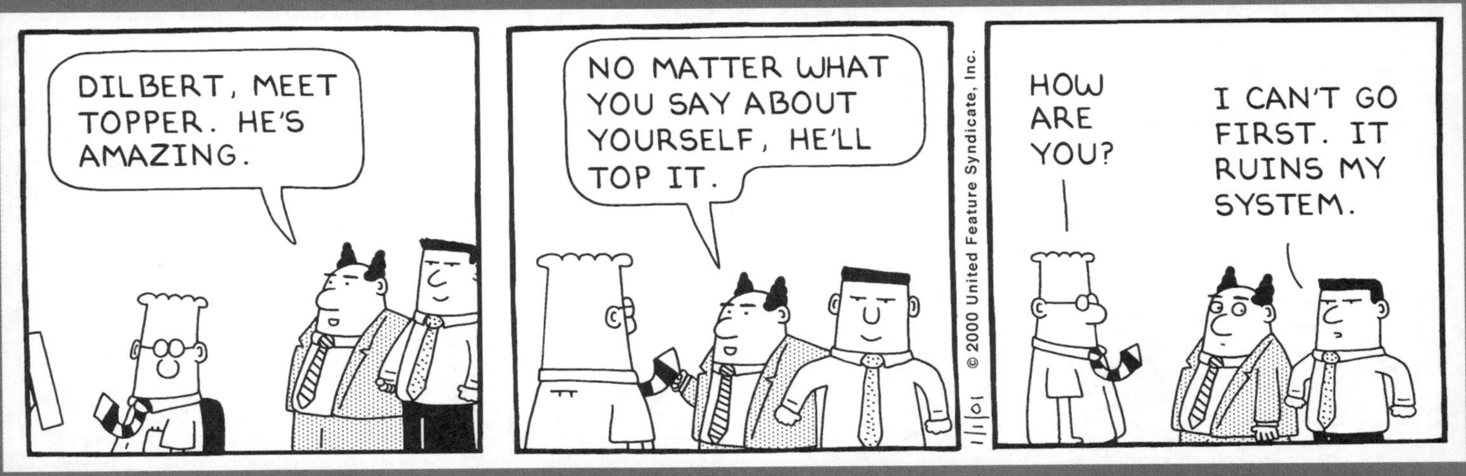
DILBERT, MEET TOPPER. HE'S AMAZING.
NO MATTER WHAT YOU SAY ABOUT YOURSELF, HE'LL TOP IT.
© 2000 United Feature Syndicate, Inc.
1/1/01
HOW ARE YOU?
I CAN'T GO FIRST. IT RUINS MY SYSTEM.

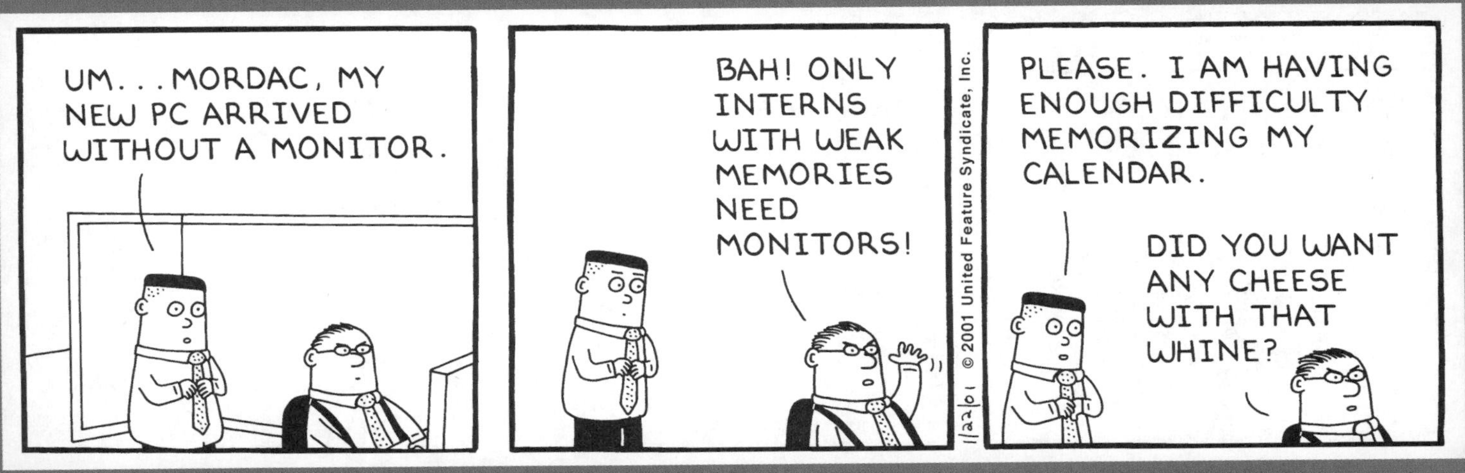
UM...MORDAC, MY NEW PC ARRIVED WITHOUT A MONITOR.
BAH! ONLY INTERNS WITH WEAK MEMORIES NEED MONITORS!
© 2001 United Feature Syndicate, Inc.
1/22/01
PLEASE. I AM HAVING ENOUGH DIFFICULTY MEMORIZING MY CALENDAR.
DID YOU WANT ANY CHEESE WITH THAT WHINE?

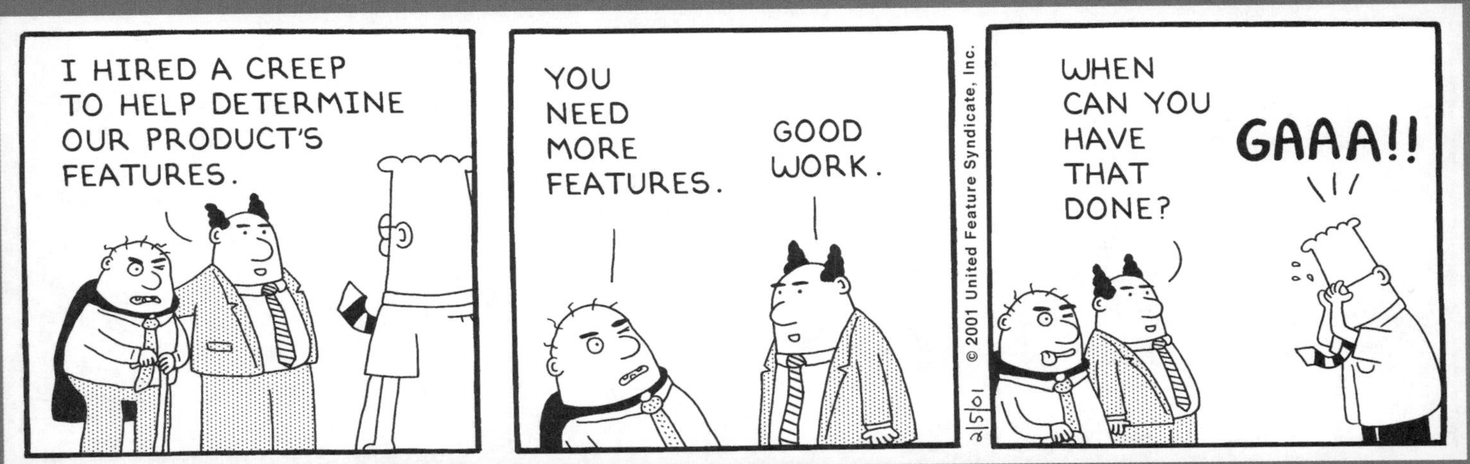
I HIRED A CREEP TO HELP DETERMINE OUR PRODUCT'S FEATURES.
YOU NEED MORE FEATURES.
GOOD WORK.
© 2001 United Feature Syndicate, Inc.
2/5/01
WHEN CAN YOU HAVE THAT DONE?
GAAA!!

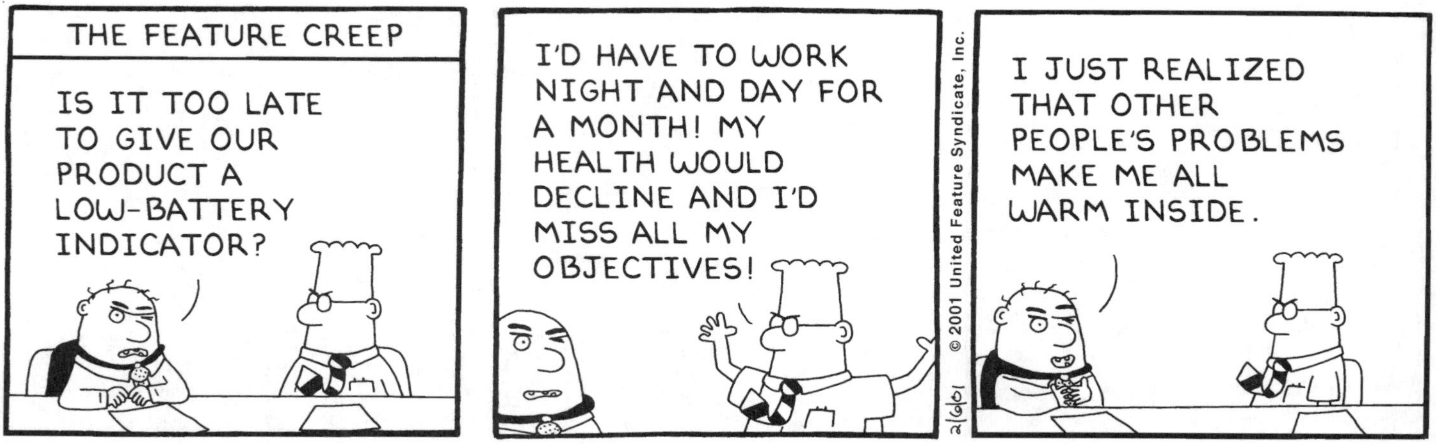
THE FEATURE CREEP
IS IT TOO LATE TO GIVE OUR PRODUCT A LOW-BATTERY INDICATOR?
I'D HAVE TO WORK NIGHT AND DAY FOR A MONTH! MY HEALTH WOULD DECLINE AND I'D MISS ALL MY OBJECTIVES!
© 2001 United Feature Syndicate, Inc.
2/6/01
I JUST REALIZED THAT OTHER PEOPLE'S PROBLEMS MAKE ME ALL WARM INSIDE.

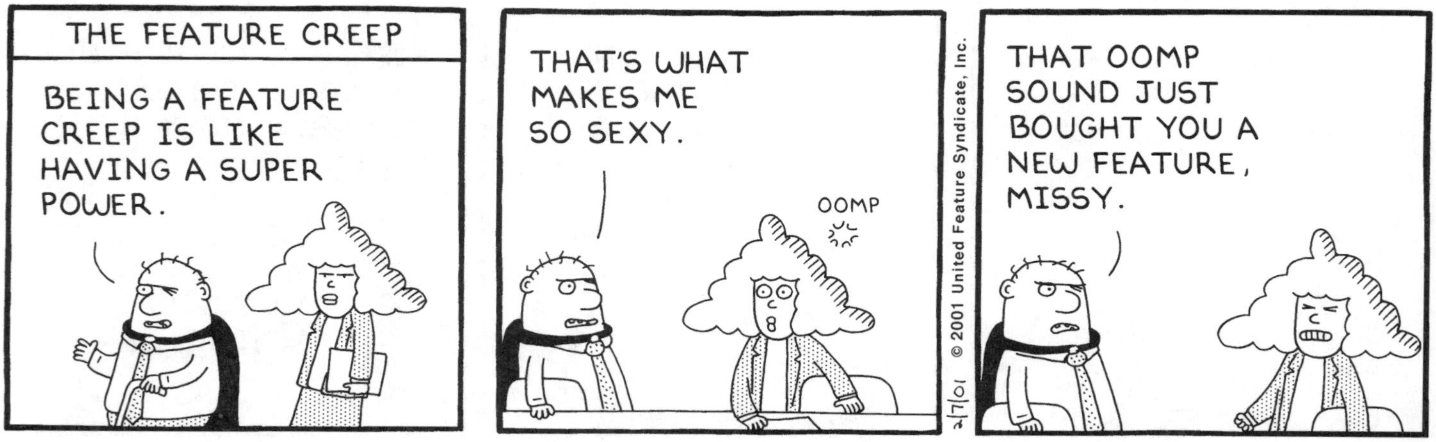
THE FEATURE CREEP
BEING A FEATURE CREEP IS LIKE HAVING A SUPER POWER.
THAT'S WHAT MAKES ME SO SEXY.
OOMP
© 2001 United Feature Syndicate, Inc.
2/7/01
THAT OOMP SOUND JUST BOUGHT YOU A NEW FEATURE, MISSY.

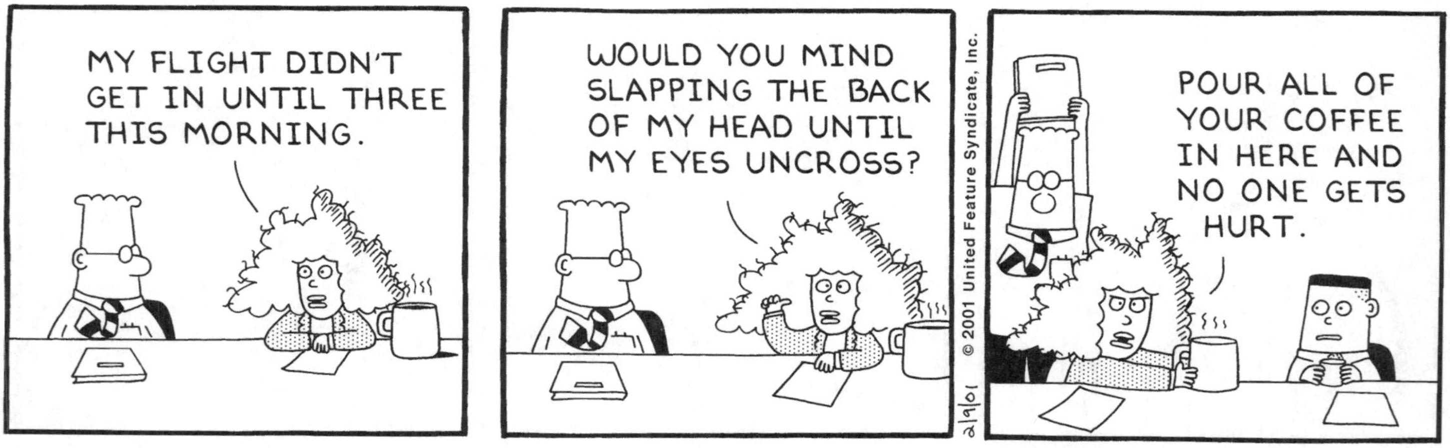
MY FLIGHT DIDN'T GET IN UNTIL THREE THIS MORNING.
WOULD YOU MIND SLAPPING THE BACK OF MY HEAD UNTIL MY EYES UNCROSS?
© 2001 United Feature Syndicate, Inc.
2/9/01
POUR ALL OF YOUR COFFEE IN HERE AND NO ONE GETS HURT.

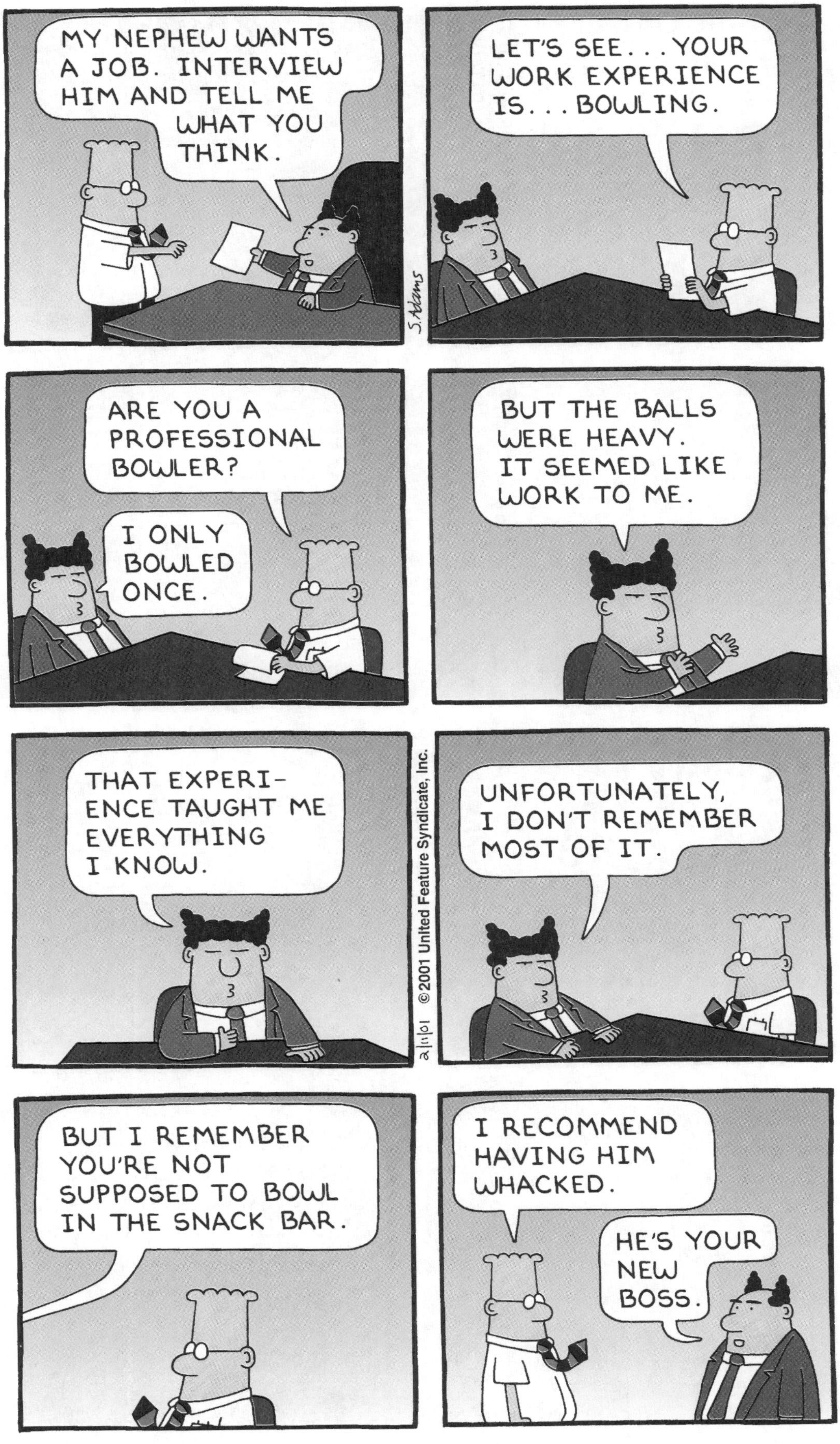
MY NEPHEW WANTS A JOB. INTERVIEW HIM AND TELL ME WHAT YOU THINK.
LET'S SEE. . . YOUR WORK EXPERIENCE IS. . . BOWLING.
S. Adams
ARE YOU A PROFESSIONAL BOWLER?
I ONLY BOWLED ONCE.
BUT THE BALLS WERE HEAVY. IT SEEMED LIKE WORK TO ME.
THAT EXPERI-ENCE TAUGHT ME EVERYTHING I KNOW.
UNFORTUNATELY, I DON'T REMEMBER MOST OF IT.
©2001 United Feature Syndicate, Inc.
2/1/01
BUT I REMEMBER YOU'RE NOT SUPPOSED TO BOWL IN THE SNACK BAR.
I RECOMMEND HAVING HIM WHACKED.
HE'S YOUR NEW BOSS.

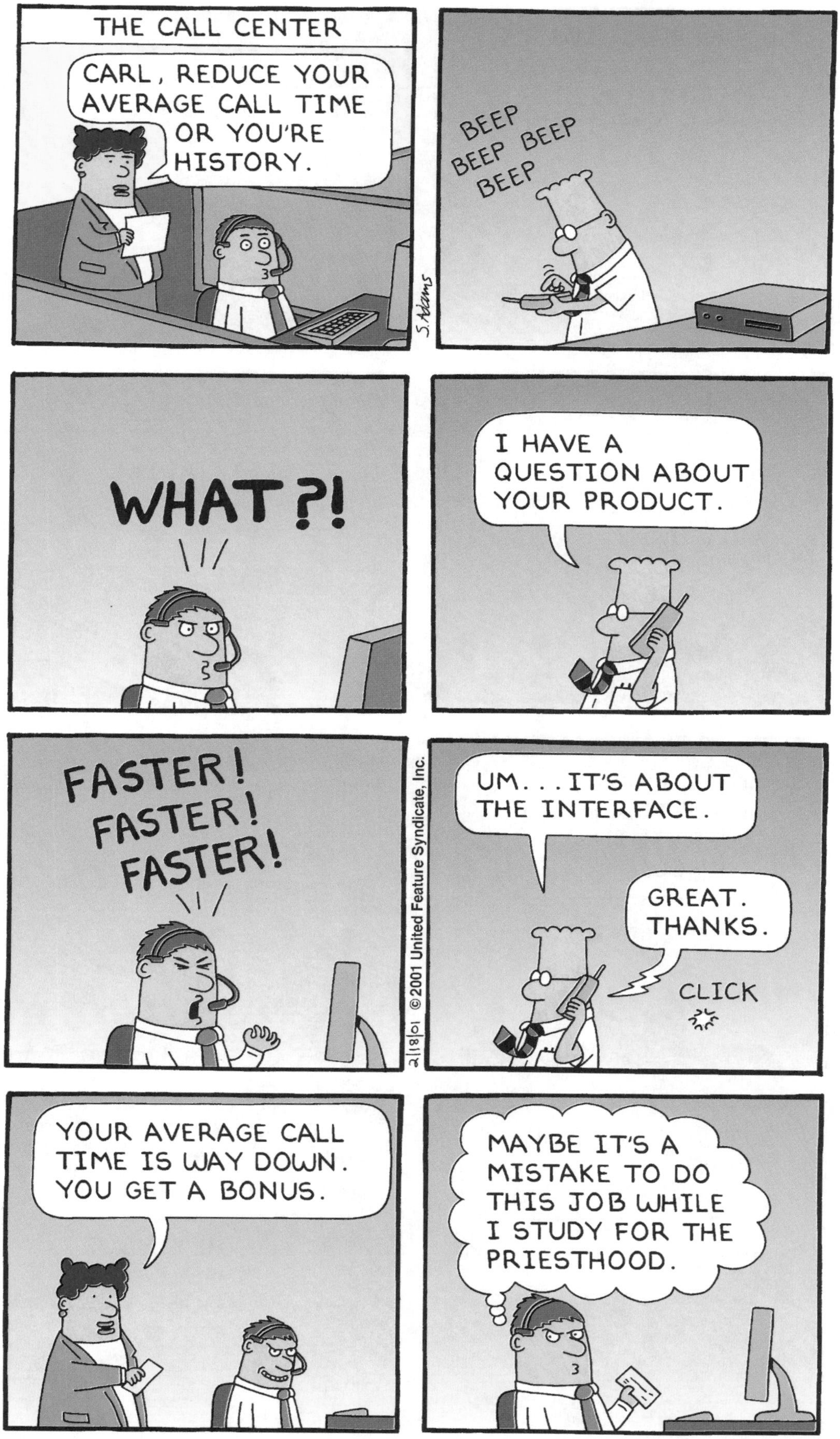
THE CALL CENTER
CARL, REDUCE YOUR AVERAGE CALL TIME OR YOU'RE HISTORY.
S. Adams
BEEP BEEP BEEP BEEP
WHAT?!
I HAVE A QUESTION ABOUT YOUR PRODUCT.
FASTER! FASTER! FASTER!
2/18/01 © 2001 United Feature Syndicate, Inc.
UM... IT'S ABOUT THE INTERFACE.
GREAT. THANKS.
CLICK
YOUR AVERAGE CALL TIME IS WAY DOWN. YOU GET A BONUS.
MAYBE IT'S A MISTAKE TO DO THIS JOB WHILE I STUDY FOR THE PRIESTHOOD.

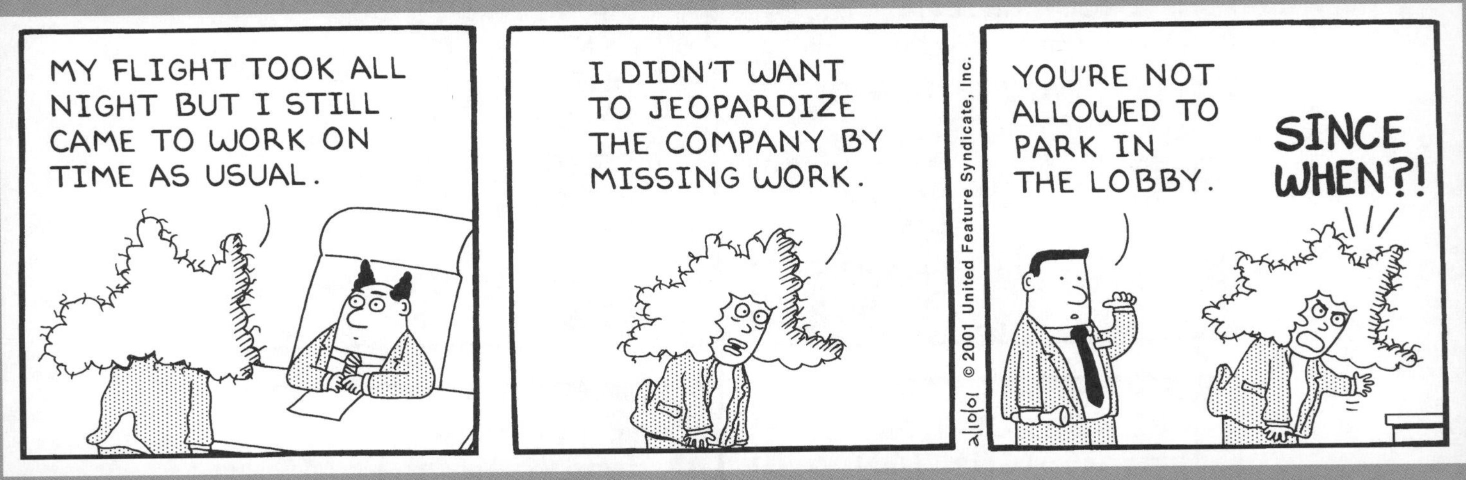
MY FLIGHT TOOK ALL NIGHT BUT I STILL CAME TO WORK ON TIME AS USUAL.
I DIDN'T WANT TO JEOPARDIZE THE COMPANY BY MISSING WORK.
2/10/01 © 2001 United Feature Syndicate, Inc.
YOU'RE NOT ALLOWED TO PARK IN THE LOBBY.
SINCE WHEN?!

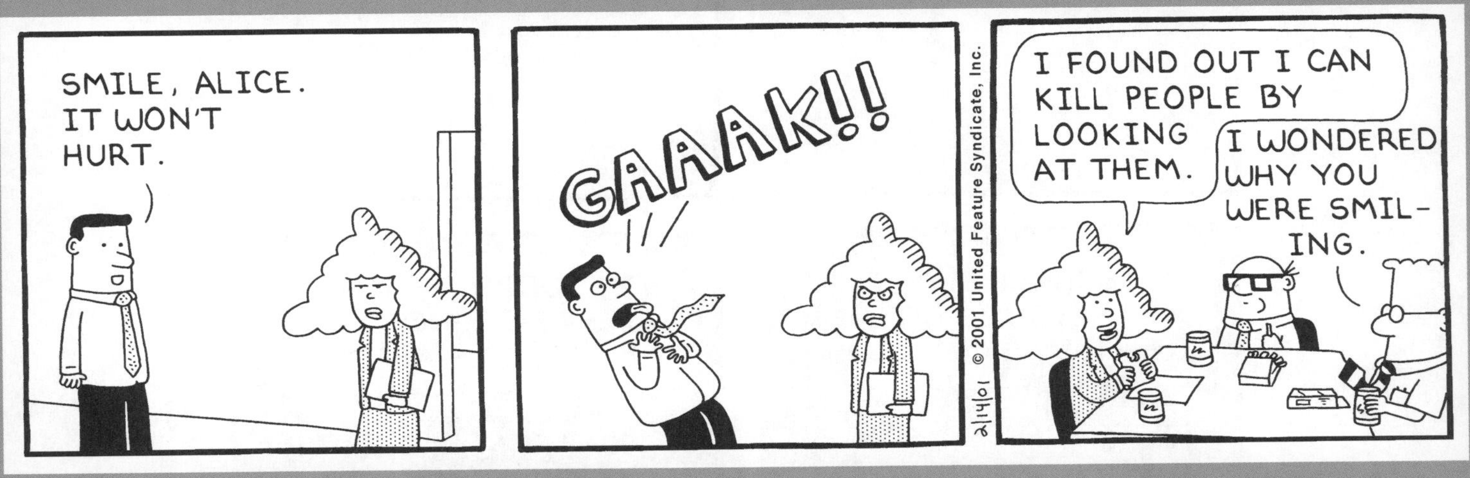
SMILE, ALICE. IT WON'T HURT.
GAAAK!!
2/14/01 © 2001 United Feature Syndicate, Inc.
I FOUND OUT I CAN KILL PEOPLE BY LOOKING AT THEM.
I WONDERED WHY YOU WERE SMIL-ING.

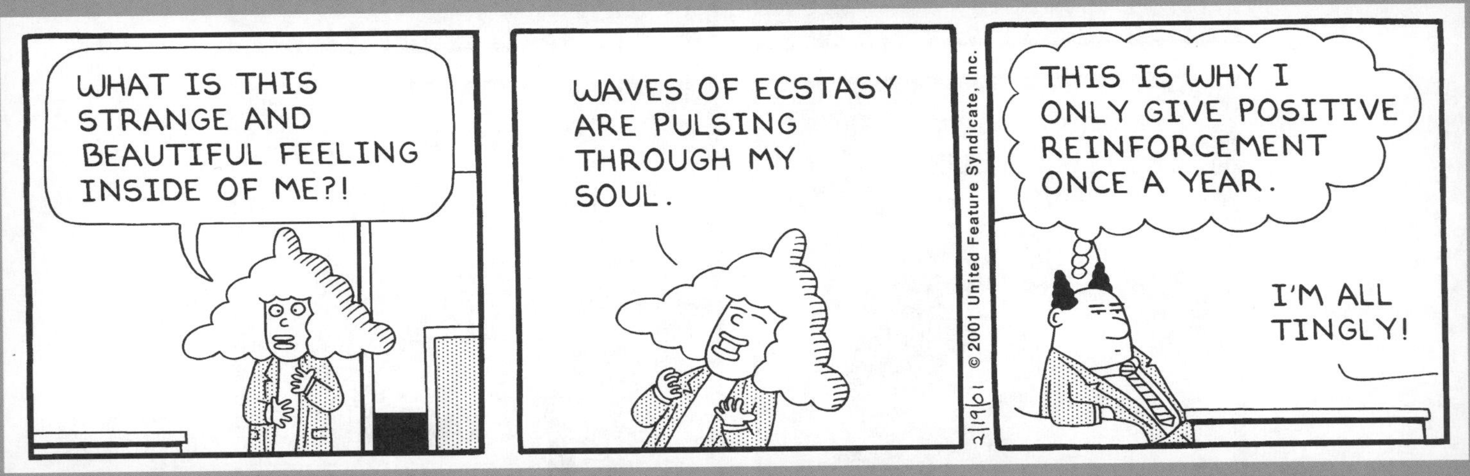
WHAT IS THIS STRANGE AND BEAUTIFUL FEELING INSIDE OF ME?!
WAVES OF ECSTASY ARE PULSING THROUGH MY SOUL.
2/19/01 © 2001 United Feature Syndicate, Inc.
THIS IS WHY I ONLY GIVE POSITIVE REINFORCEMENT ONCE A YEAR.
I'M ALL TINGLY!

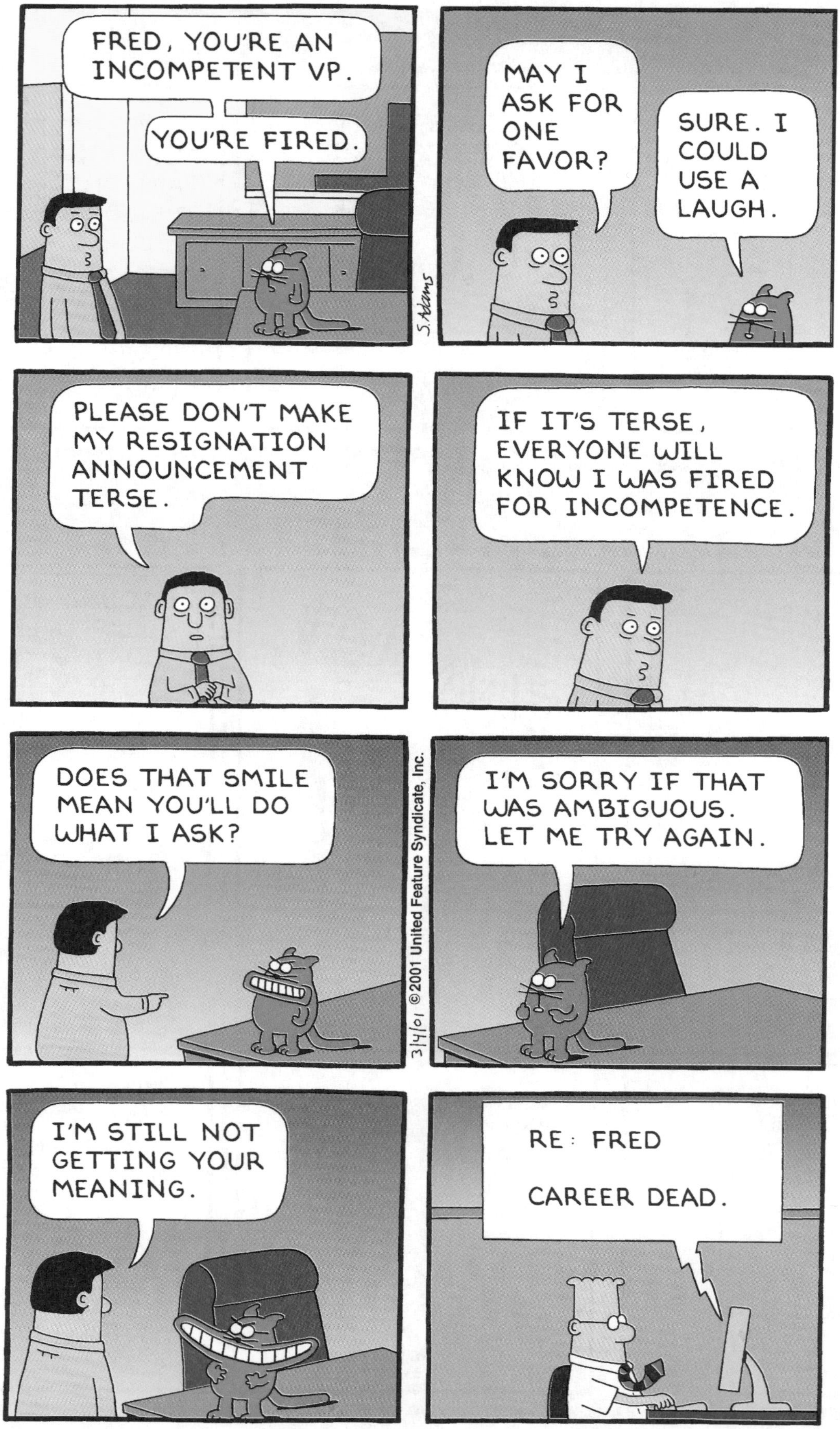
FRED, YOU'RE AN INCOMPETENT VP.
YOU'RE FIRED.
S. Adams
MAY I ASK FOR ONE FAVOR?
SURE. I COULD USE A LAUGH.
PLEASE DON'T MAKE MY RESIGNATION ANNOUNCEMENT TERSE.
IF IT'S TERSE, EVERYONE WILL KNOW I WAS FIRED FOR INCOMPETENCE.
DOES THAT SMILE MEAN YOU'LL DO WHAT I ASK?
3/4/01 ©2001 United Feature Syndicate, Inc.
I'M SORRY IF THAT WAS AMBIGUOUS. LET ME TRY AGAIN.
I'M STILL NOT GETTING YOUR MEANING.
RE: FRED
CAREER DEAD.

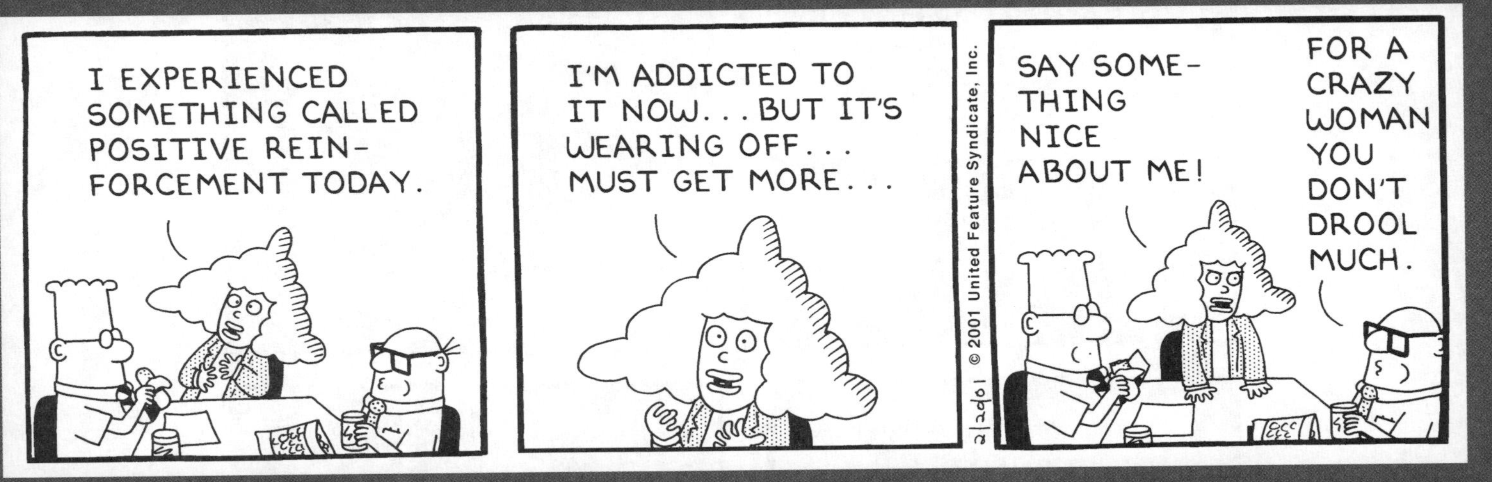
I EXPERIENCED SOMETHING CALLED POSITIVE REIN-FORCEMENT TODAY.
I'M ADDICTED TO IT NOW. . . BUT IT'S WEARING OFF. . . MUST GET MORE. . .
2/20/01 © 2001 United Feature Syndicate, Inc.
SAY SOME-THING NICE ABOUT ME!
FOR A CRAZY WOMAN YOU DON'T DROOL MUCH.

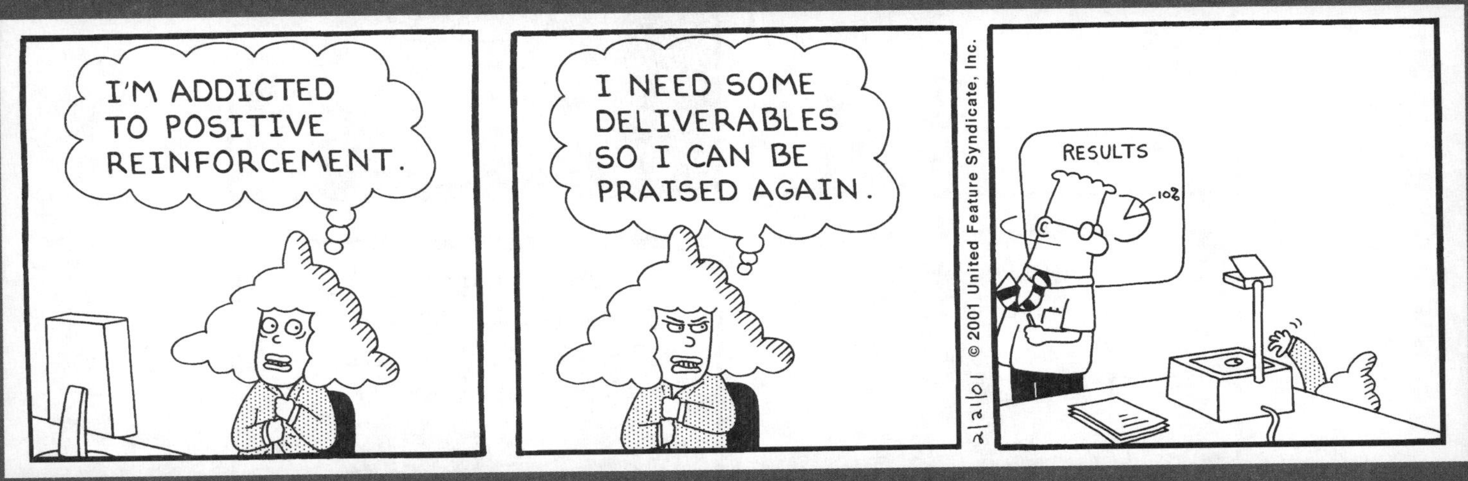
I'M ADDICTED TO POSITIVE REINFORCEMENT.
I NEED SOME DELIVERABLES SO I CAN BE PRAISED AGAIN.
2/21/01 © 2001 United Feature Syndicate, Inc.
RESULTS
10%

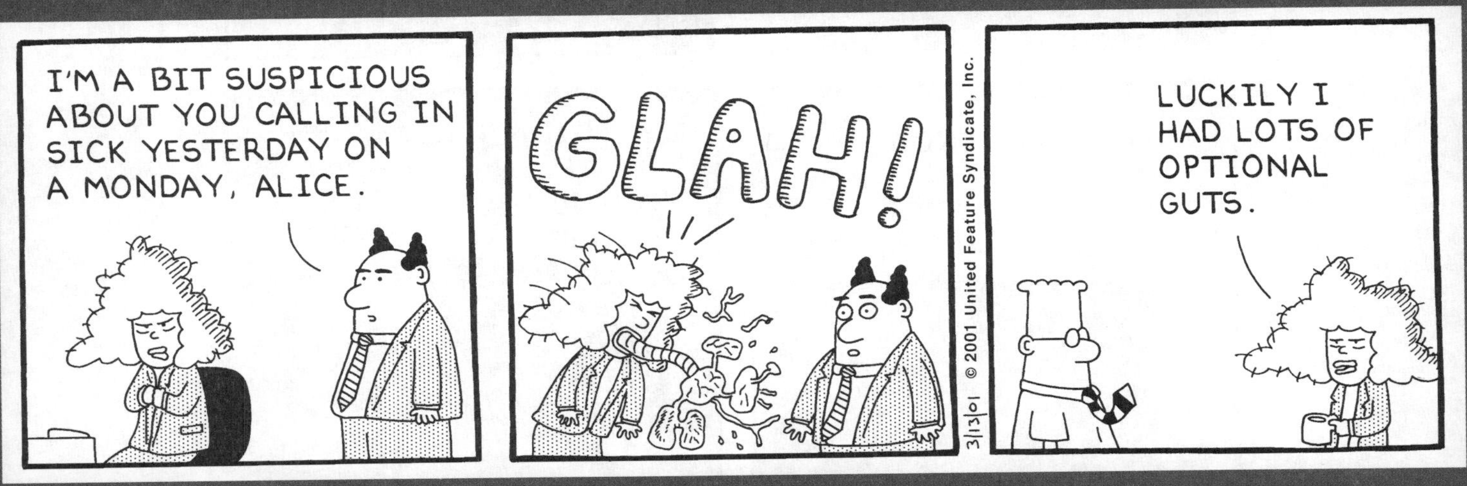
I'M A BIT SUSPICIOUS ABOUT YOU CALLING IN SICK YESTERDAY ON A MONDAY, ALICE.
GLAH!
3/13/01 © 2001 United Feature Syndicate, Inc.
LUCKILY I HAD LOTS OF OPTIONAL GUTS.

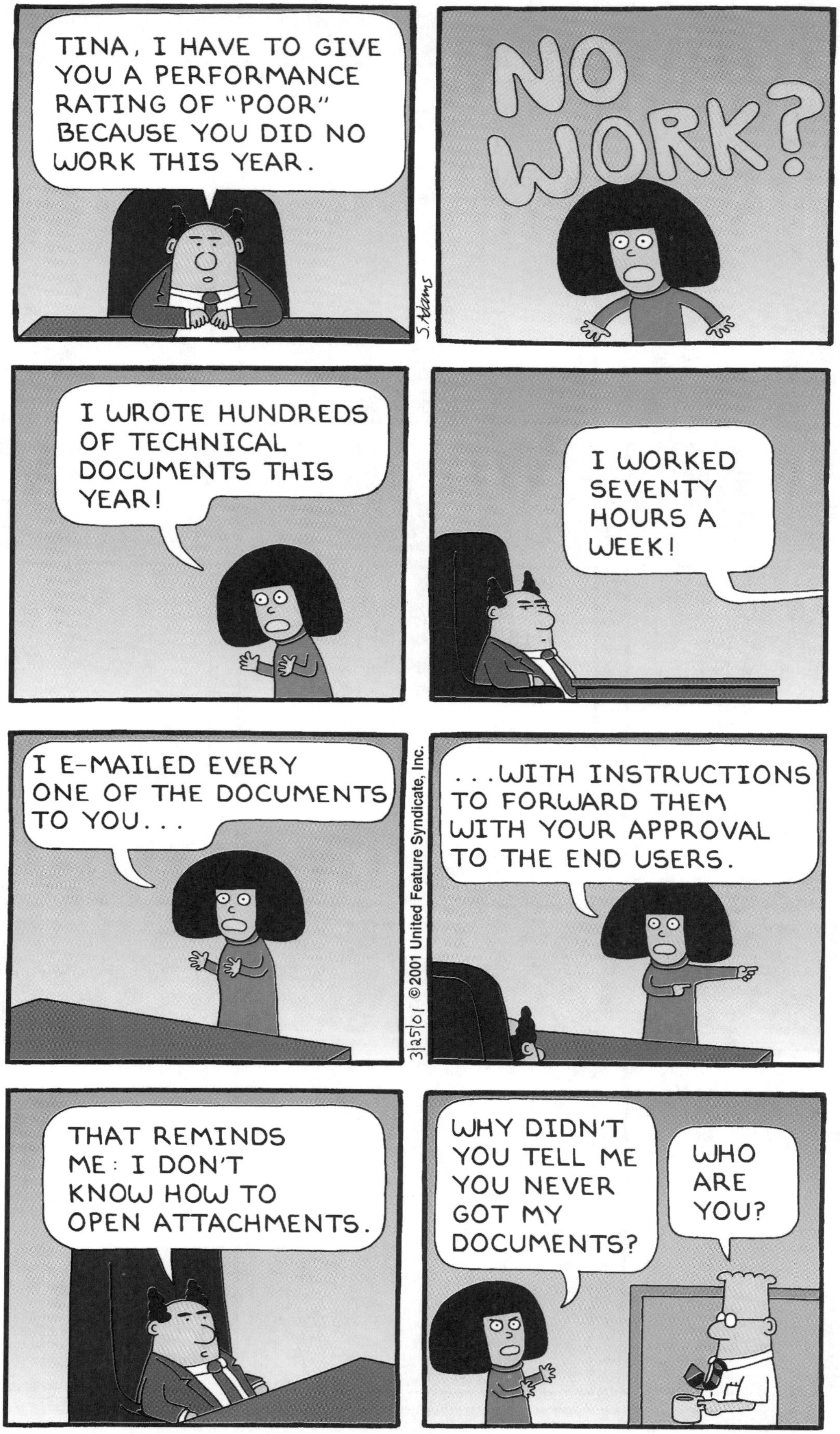
TINA, I HAVE TO GIVE YOU A PERFORMANCE RATING OF "POOR" BECAUSE YOU DID NO WORK THIS YEAR.
NO WORK?
I WROTE HUNDREDS OF TECHNICAL DOCUMENTS THIS YEAR!
I WORKED SEVENTY HOURS A WEEK!
I E-MAILED EVERY ONE OF THE DOCUMENTS TO YOU...
...WITH INSTRUCTIONS TO FORWARD THEM WITH YOUR APPROVAL TO THE END USERS.
THAT REMINDS ME: I DON'T KNOW HOW TO OPEN ATTACHMENTS.
WHY DIDN'T YOU TELL ME YOU NEVER GOT MY DOCUMENTS?
WHO ARE YOU?
S. Adams
3/25/01 ©2001 United Feature Syndicate, Inc.

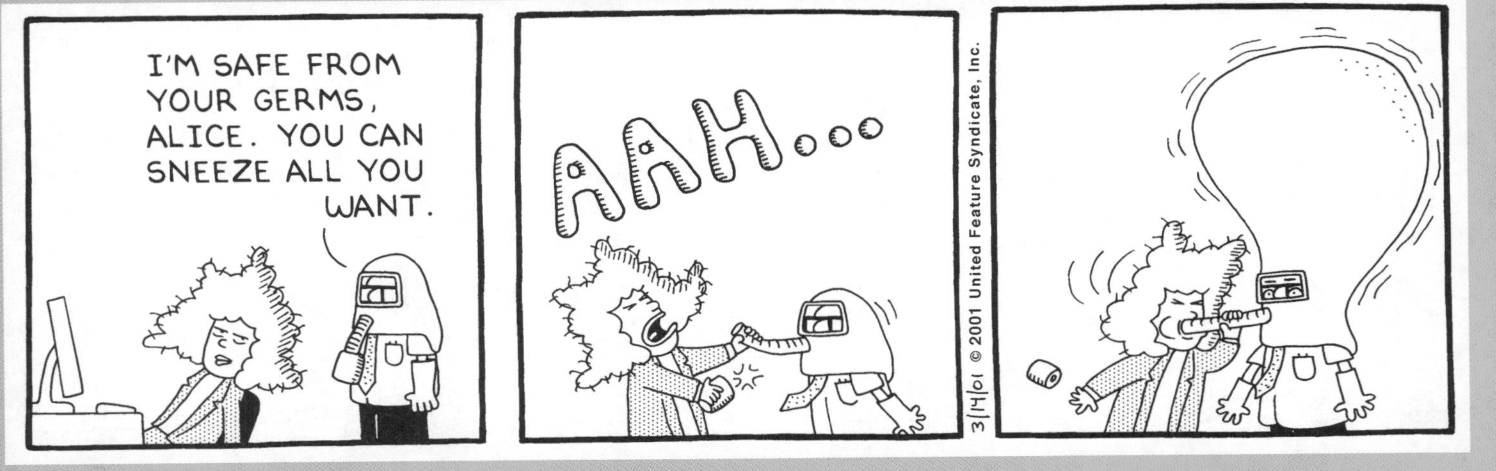
I'M SAFE FROM YOUR GERMS, ALICE. YOU CAN SNEEZE ALL YOU WANT.
AAH...
3/14/01 © 2001 United Feature Syndicate, Inc.

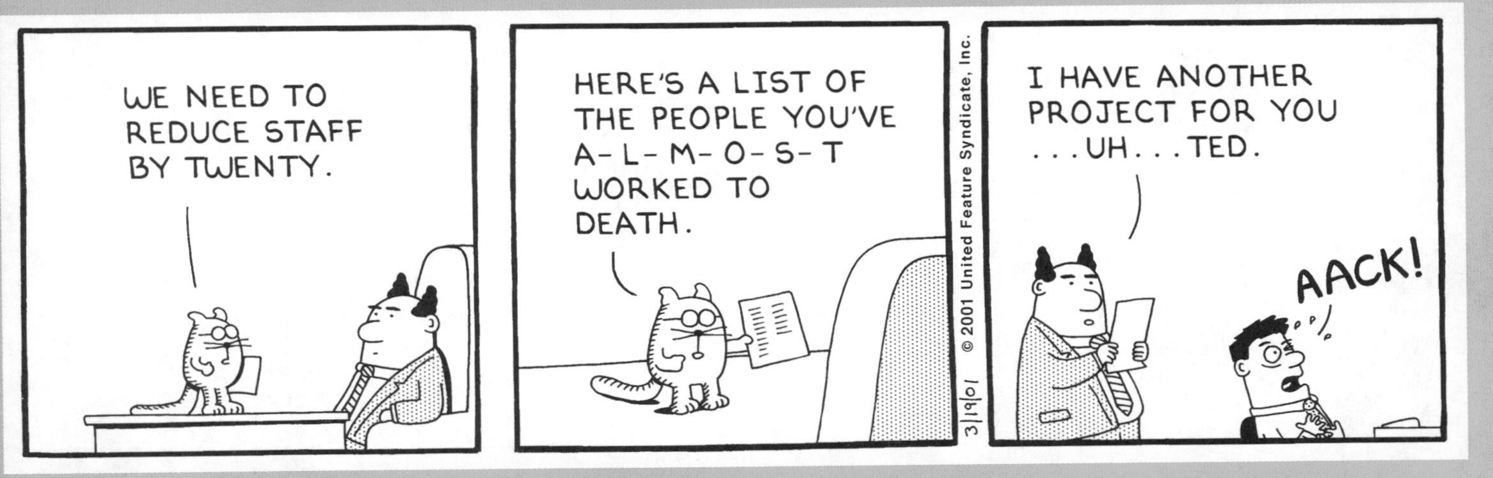
WE NEED TO REDUCE STAFF BY TWENTY.
HERE'S A LIST OF THE PEOPLE YOU'VE A-L-M-O-S-T WORKED TO DEATH.
3/19/01 © 2001 United Feature Syndicate, Inc.
I HAVE ANOTHER PROJECT FOR YOU ...UH...TED.
AACK!

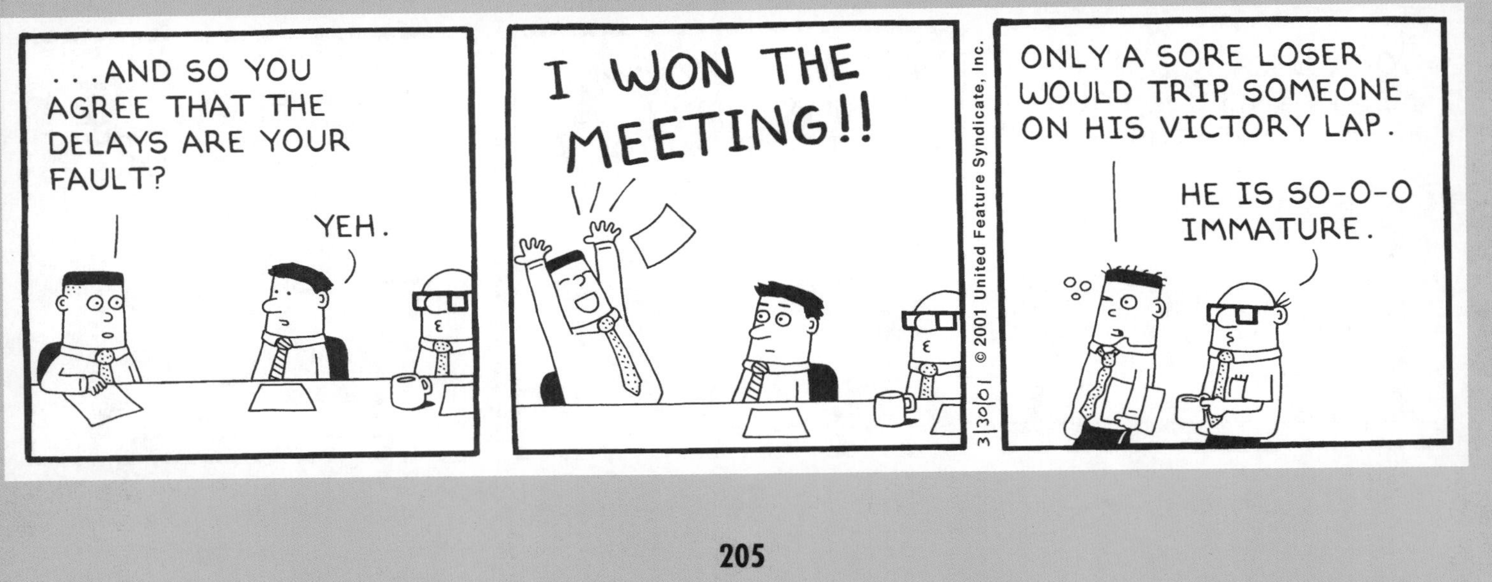
...AND SO YOU AGREE THAT THE DELAYS ARE YOUR FAULT?
YEH.
I WON THE MEETING!!
3/30/01 © 2001 United Feature Syndicate, Inc.
ONLY A SORE LOSER WOULD TRIP SOMEONE ON HIS VICTORY LAP.
HE IS SO-O-O IMMATURE.

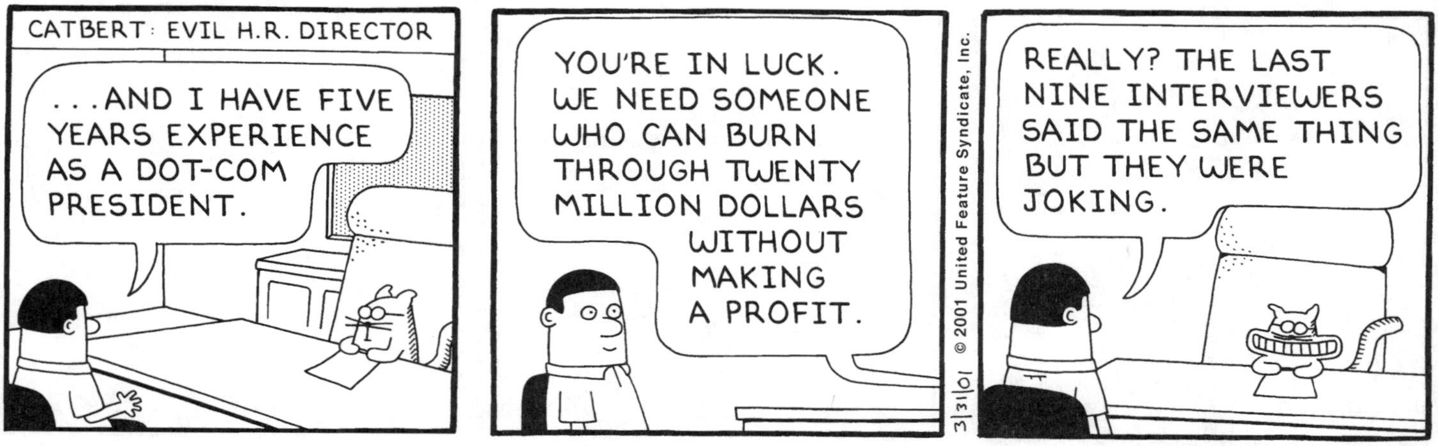
CATBERT: EVIL H.R. DIRECTOR
. . . AND I HAVE FIVE YEARS EXPERIENCE AS A DOT-COM PRESIDENT.
YOU'RE IN LUCK. WE NEED SOMEONE WHO CAN BURN THROUGH TWENTY MILLION DOLLARS WITHOUT MAKING A PROFIT.
3/31/01 © 2001 United Feature Syndicate, Inc.
REALLY? THE LAST NINE INTERVIEWERS SAID THE SAME THING BUT THEY WERE JOKING.

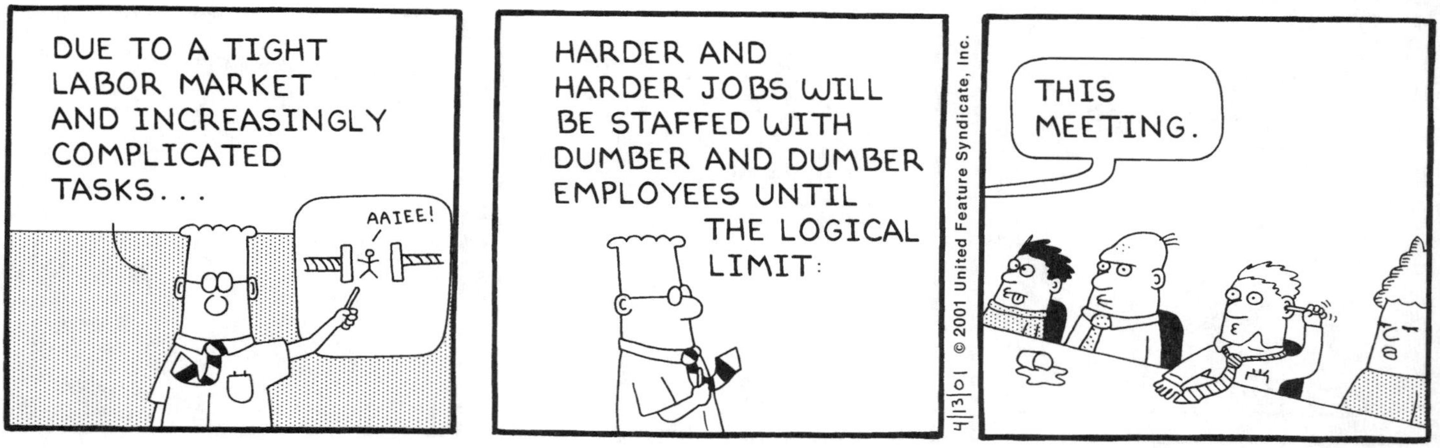
DUE TO A TIGHT LABOR MARKET AND INCREASINGLY COMPLICATED TASKS . . .
AAIEE!
HARDER AND HARDER JOBS WILL BE STAFFED WITH DUMBER AND DUMBER EMPLOYEES UNTIL THE LOGICAL LIMIT:
4/13/01 © 2001 United Feature Syndicate, Inc.
THIS MEETING.

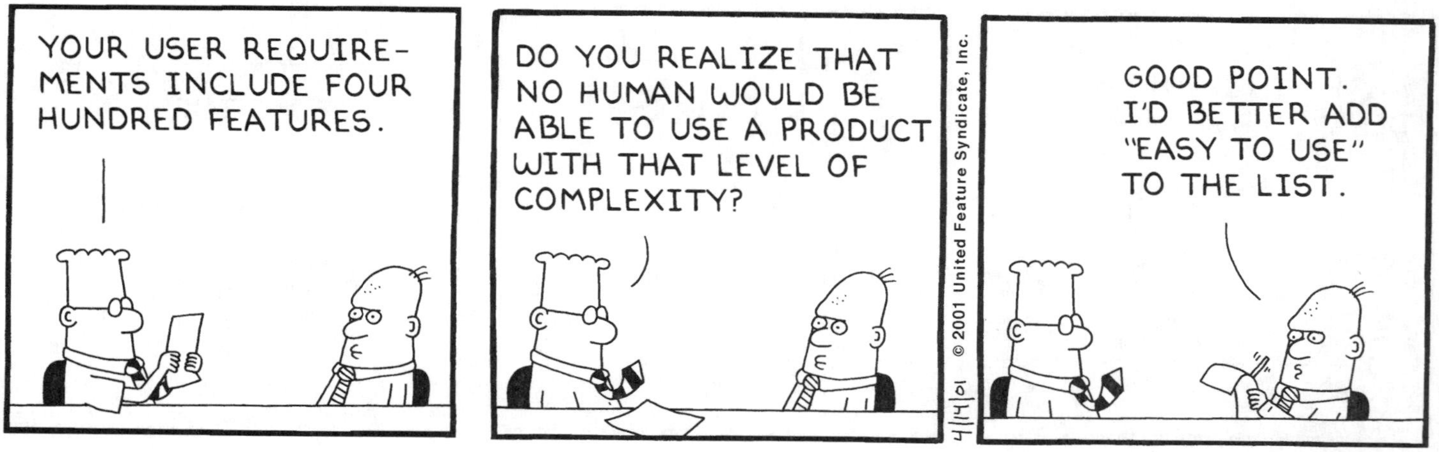
YOUR USER REQUIRE-MENTS INCLUDE FOUR HUNDRED FEATURES.
DO YOU REALIZE THAT NO HUMAN WOULD BE ABLE TO USE A PRODUCT WITH THAT LEVEL OF COMPLEXITY?
4/14/01 © 2001 United Feature Syndicate, Inc.
GOOD POINT. I'D BETTER ADD "EASY TO USE" TO THE LIST.

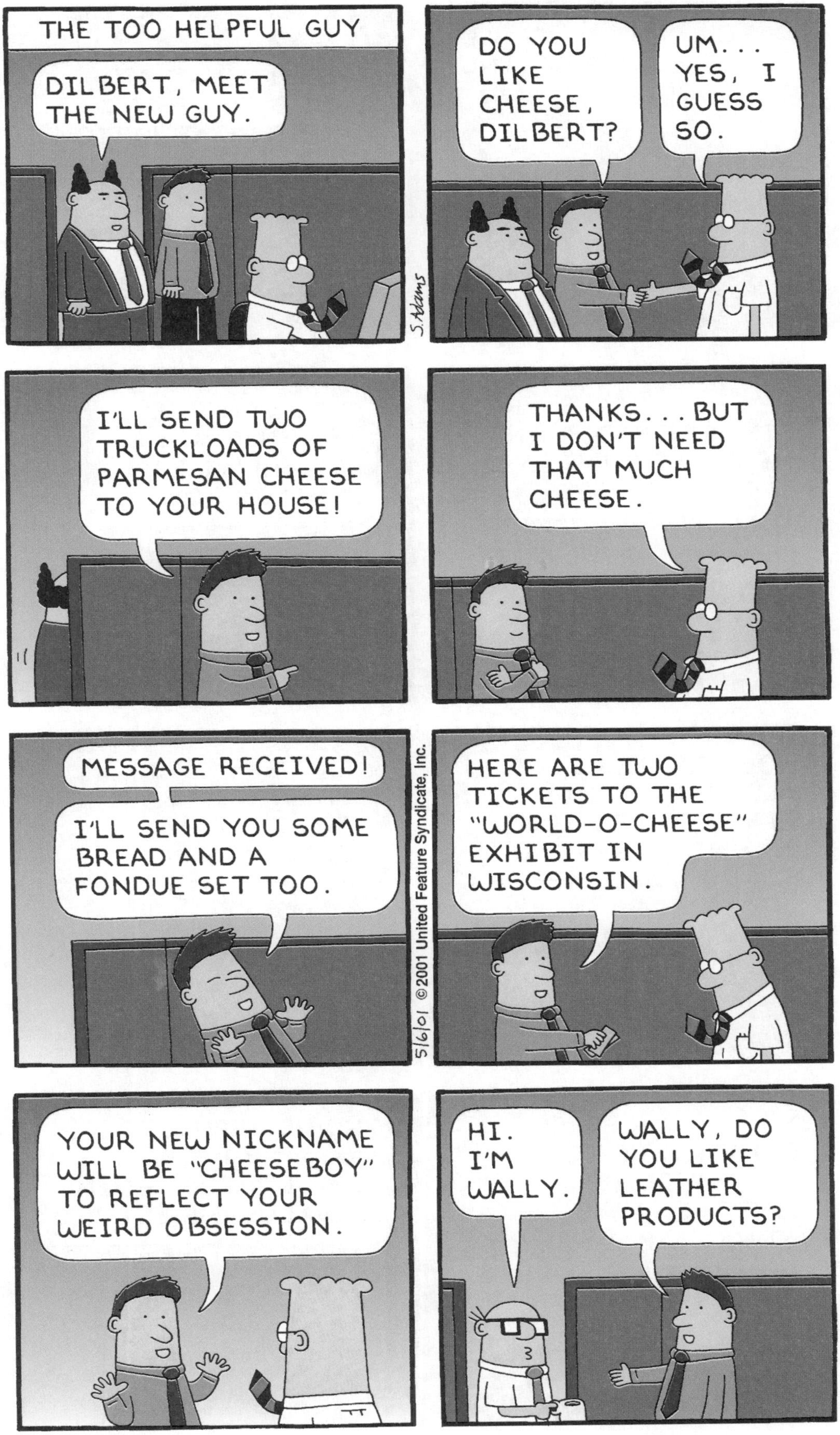
THE TOO HELPFUL GUY
DILBERT, MEET THE NEW GUY.
S. Adams
DO YOU LIKE CHEESE, DILBERT?
UM... YES, I GUESS SO.
I'LL SEND TWO TRUCKLOADS OF PARMESAN CHEESE TO YOUR HOUSE!
THANKS...BUT I DON'T NEED THAT MUCH CHEESE.
MESSAGE RECEIVED!
I'LL SEND YOU SOME BREAD AND A FONDUE SET TOO.
5/6/01 ©2001 United Feature Syndicate, Inc.
HERE ARE TWO TICKETS TO THE "WORLD-O-CHEESE" EXHIBIT IN WISCONSIN.
YOUR NEW NICKNAME WILL BE "CHEESEBOY" TO REFLECT YOUR WEIRD OBSESSION.
HI. I'M WALLY.
WALLY, DO YOU LIKE LEATHER PRODUCTS?

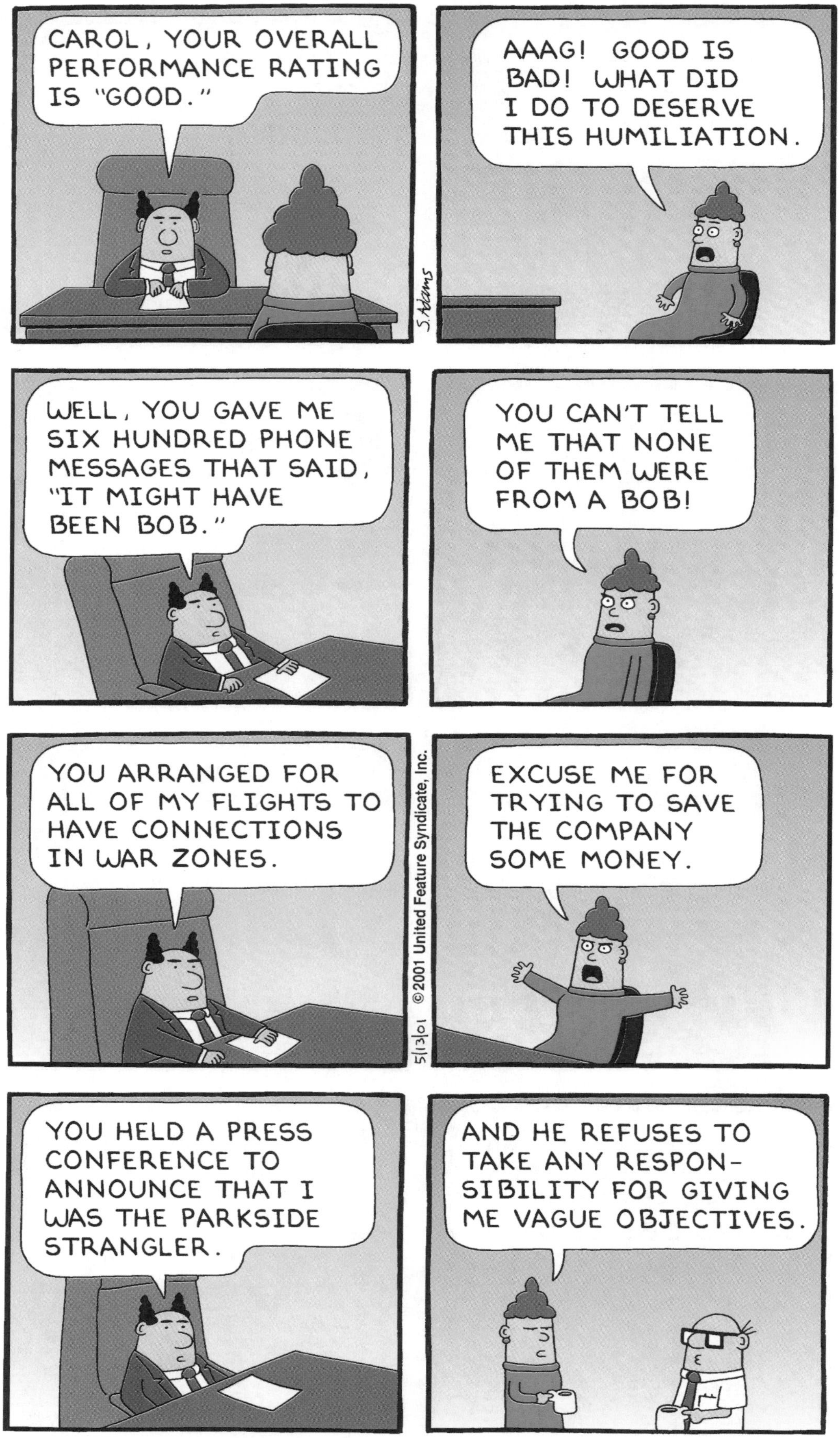
CAROL, YOUR OVERALL PERFORMANCE RATING IS "GOOD."
S. Adams
AAAG! GOOD IS BAD! WHAT DID I DO TO DESERVE THIS HUMILIATION.
WELL, YOU GAVE ME SIX HUNDRED PHONE MESSAGES THAT SAID, "IT MIGHT HAVE BEEN BOB."
YOU CAN'T TELL ME THAT NONE OF THEM WERE FROM A BOB!
YOU ARRANGED FOR ALL OF MY FLIGHTS TO HAVE CONNECTIONS IN WAR ZONES.
5/13/01 ©2001 United Feature Syndicate, Inc.
EXCUSE ME FOR TRYING TO SAVE THE COMPANY SOME MONEY.
YOU HELD A PRESS CONFERENCE TO ANNOUNCE THAT I WAS THE PARKSIDE STRANGLER.
AND HE REFUSES TO TAKE ANY RESPON-SIBILITY FOR GIVING ME VAGUE OBJECTIVES.

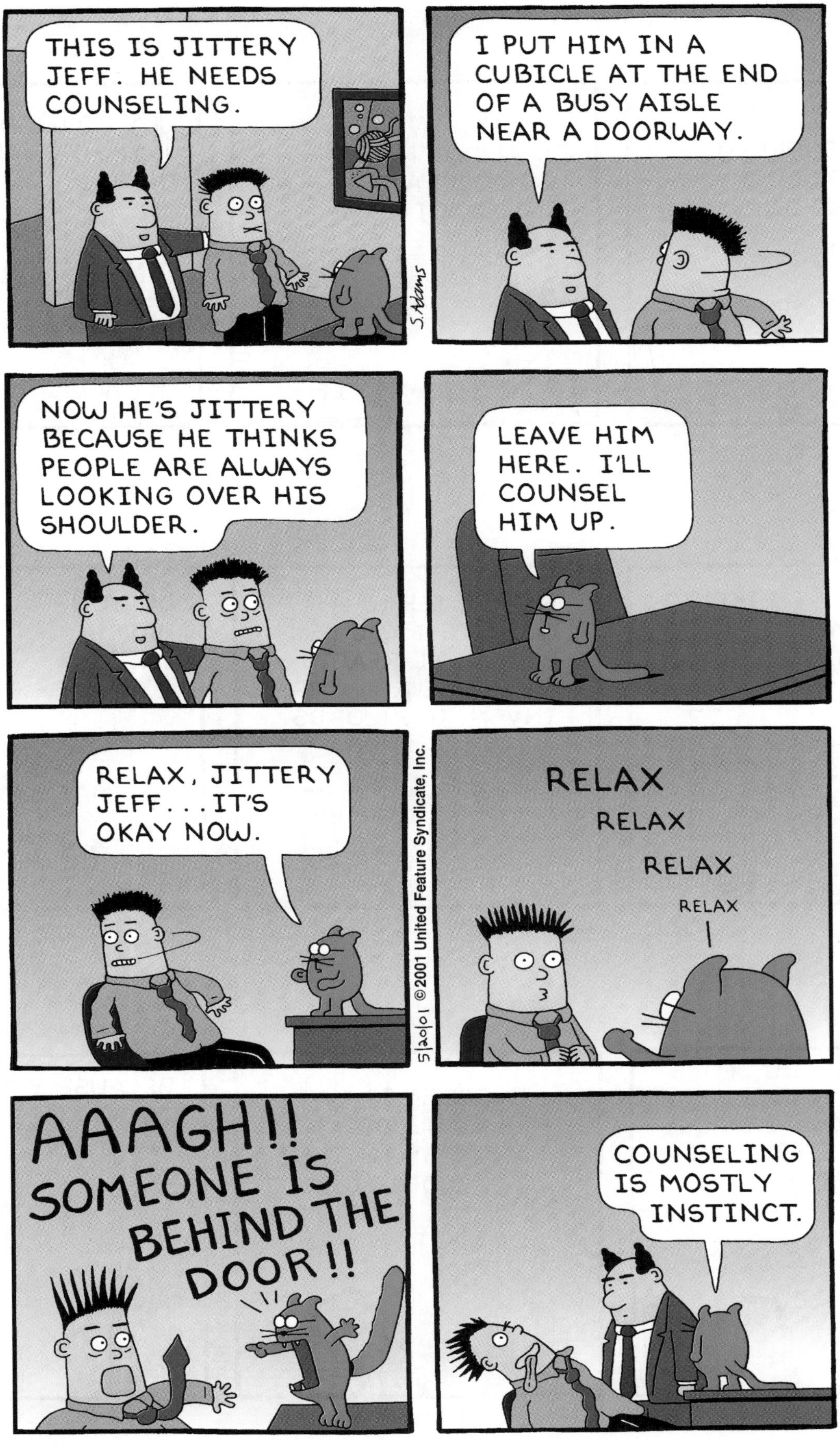
THIS IS JITTERY JEFF. HE NEEDS COUNSELING.
I PUT HIM IN A CUBICLE AT THE END OF A BUSY AISLE NEAR A DOORWAY.
NOW HE'S JITTERY BECAUSE HE THINKS PEOPLE ARE ALWAYS LOOKING OVER HIS SHOULDER.
LEAVE HIM HERE. I'LL COUNSEL HIM UP.
RELAX, JITTERY JEFF...IT'S OKAY NOW.
RELAX
RELAX
RELAX
RELAX
AAAGH!! SOMEONE IS BEHIND THE DOOR!!
COUNSELING IS MOSTLY INSTINCT.
S. Adams
5/20/01 ©2001 United Feature Syndicate, Inc.

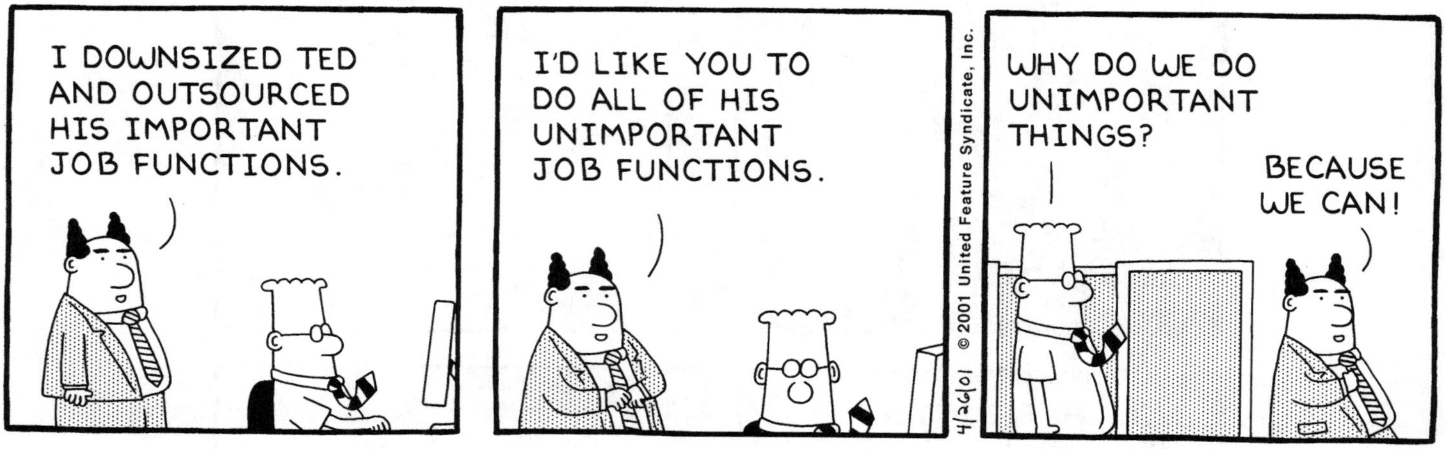
I DOWNSIZED TED AND OUTSOURCED HIS IMPORTANT JOB FUNCTIONS.
I'D LIKE YOU TO DO ALL OF HIS UNIMPORTANT JOB FUNCTIONS.
4/26/01 © 2001 United Feature Syndicate, Inc.
WHY DO WE DO UNIMPORTANT THINGS?
BECAUSE WE CAN!

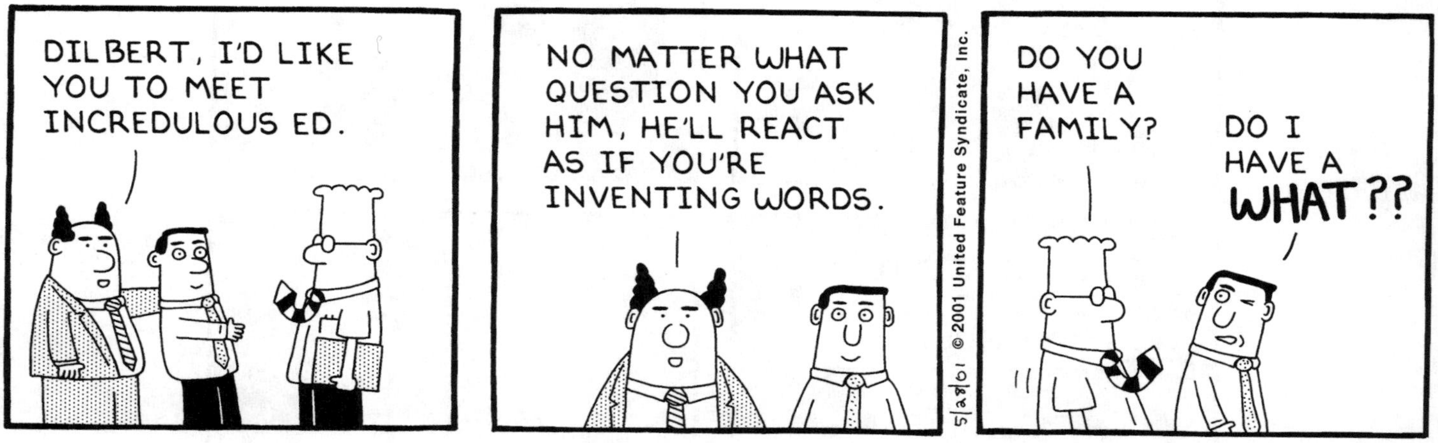
DILBERT, I'D LIKE YOU TO MEET INCREDULOUS ED.
NO MATTER WHAT QUESTION YOU ASK HIM, HE'LL REACT AS IF YOU'RE INVENTING WORDS.
5/28/01 © 2001 United Feature Syndicate, Inc.
DO YOU HAVE A FAMILY?
DO I HAVE A WHAT??

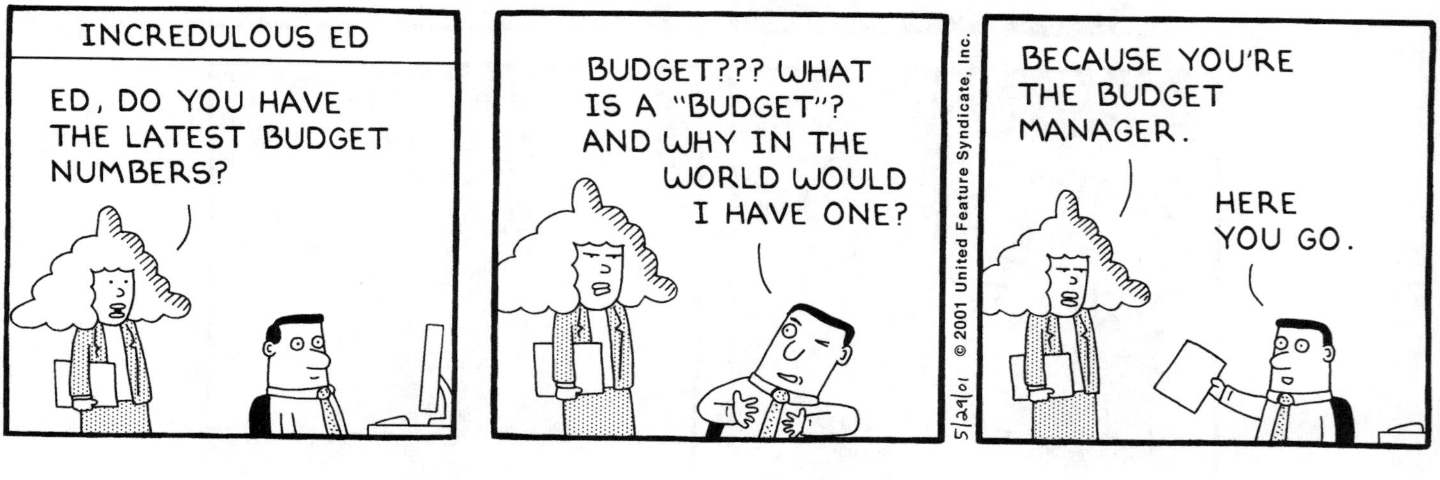
INCREDULOUS ED
ED, DO YOU HAVE THE LATEST BUDGET NUMBERS?
BUDGET??? WHAT IS A "BUDGET"? AND WHY IN THE WORLD WOULD I HAVE ONE?
5/29/01 © 2001 United Feature Syndicate, Inc.
BECAUSE YOU'RE THE BUDGET MANAGER.
HERE YOU GO.

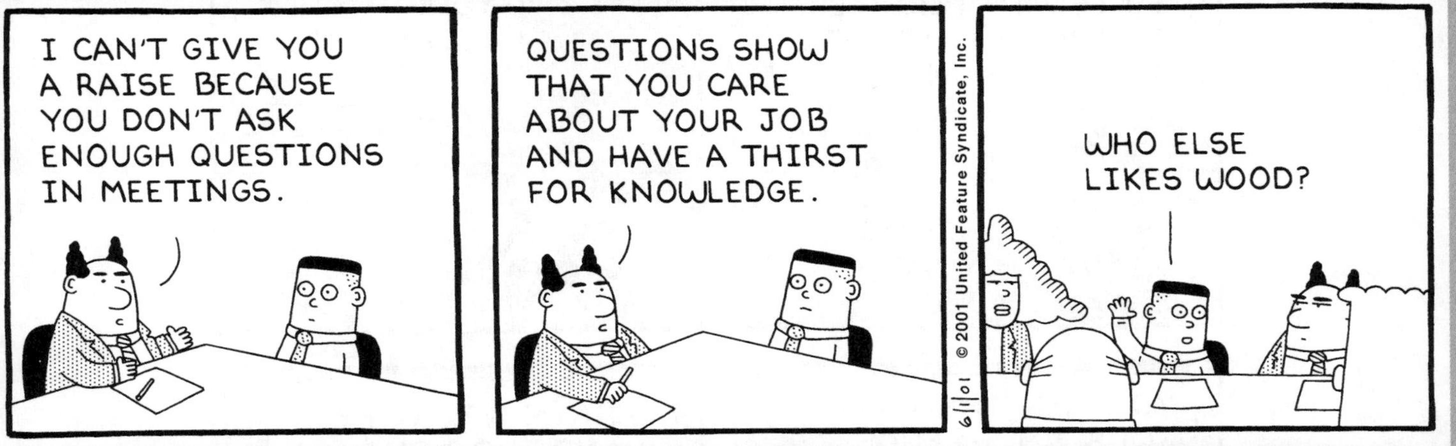
I CAN'T GIVE YOU A RAISE BECAUSE YOU DON'T ASK ENOUGH QUESTIONS IN MEETINGS.
QUESTIONS SHOW THAT YOU CARE ABOUT YOUR JOB AND HAVE A THIRST FOR KNOWLEDGE.
6/1/01 © 2001 United Feature Syndicate, Inc.
WHO ELSE LIKES WOOD?

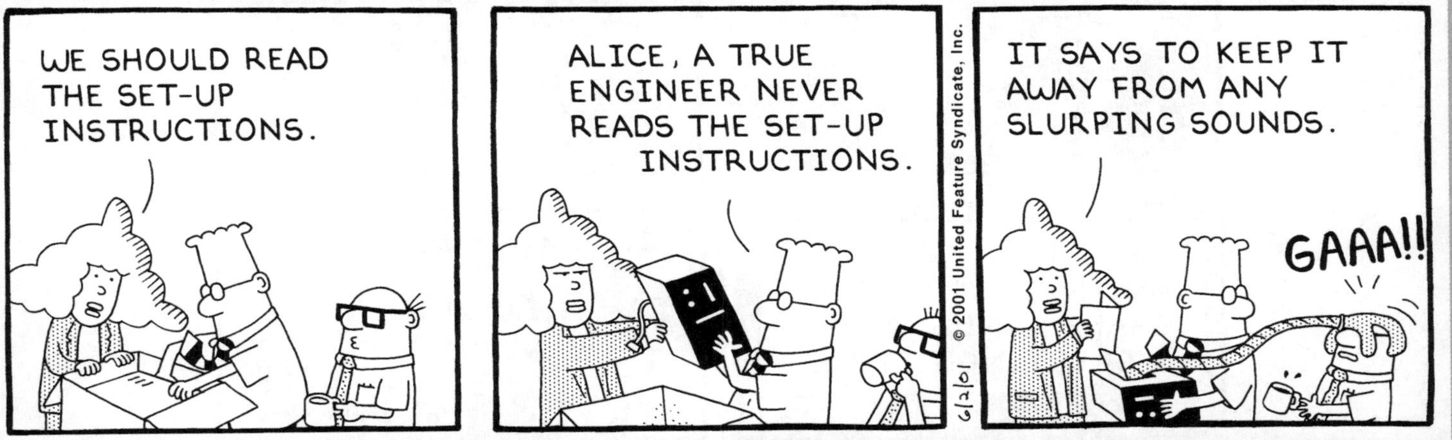
WE SHOULD READ THE SET-UP INSTRUCTIONS.
ALICE, A TRUE ENGINEER NEVER READS THE SET-UP INSTRUCTIONS.
6/2/01 © 2001 United Feature Syndicate, Inc.
IT SAYS TO KEEP IT AWAY FROM ANY SLURPING SOUNDS.
GAAA!!

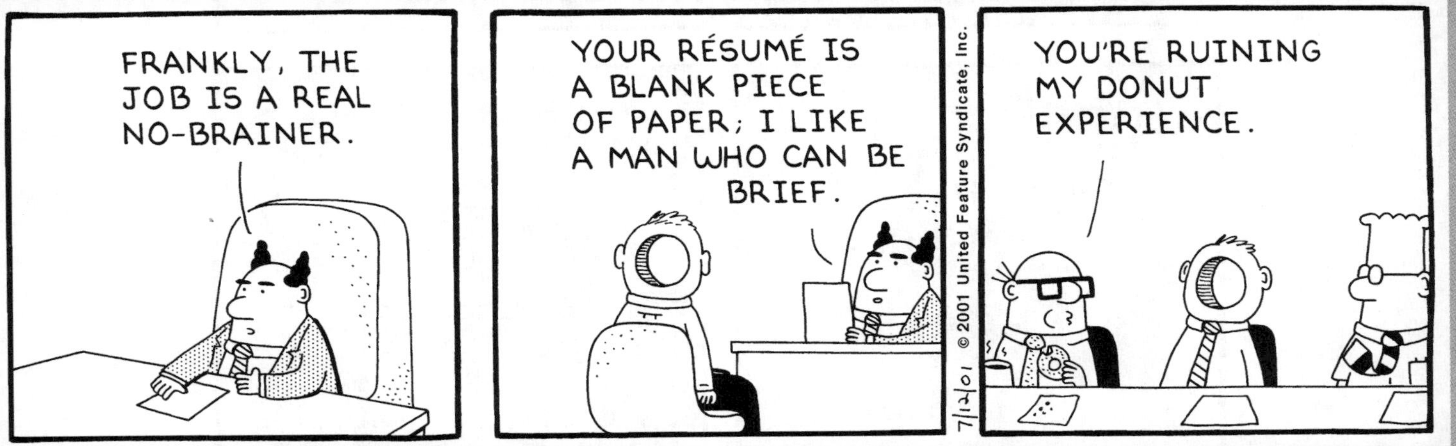
FRANKLY, THE JOB IS A REAL NO-BRAINER.
YOUR RÉSUMÉ IS A BLANK PIECE OF PAPER; I LIKE A MAN WHO CAN BE BRIEF.
7/12/01 © 2001 United Feature Syndicate, Inc.
YOU'RE RUINING MY DONUT EXPERIENCE.

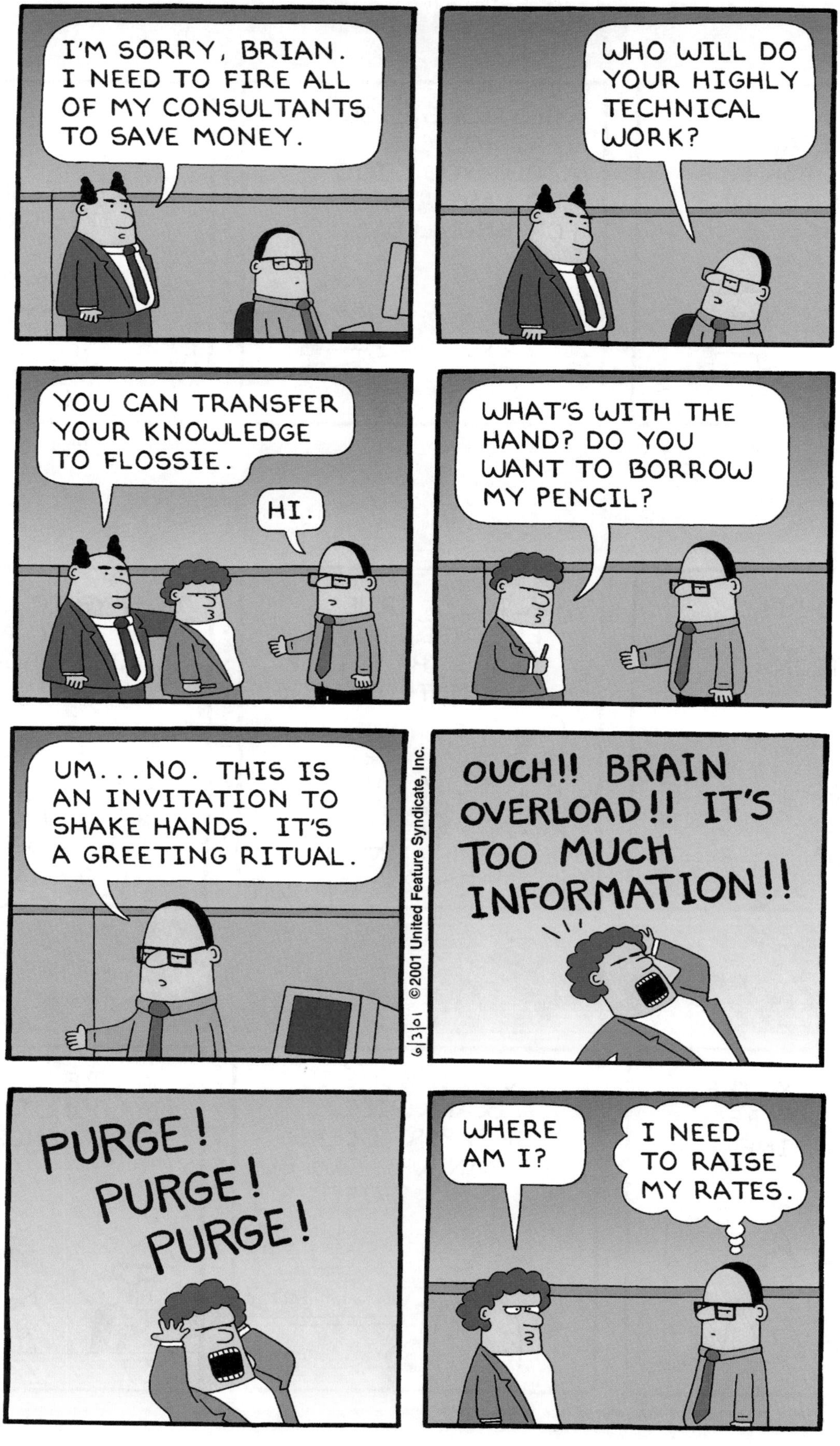
I'M SORRY, BRIAN. I NEED TO FIRE ALL OF MY CONSULTANTS TO SAVE MONEY.
WHO WILL DO YOUR HIGHLY TECHNICAL WORK?
YOU CAN TRANSFER YOUR KNOWLEDGE TO FLOSSIE.
HI.
WHAT'S WITH THE HAND? DO YOU WANT TO BORROW MY PENCIL?
UM...NO. THIS IS AN INVITATION TO SHAKE HANDS. IT'S A GREETING RITUAL.
6/3/01 ©2001 United Feature Syndicate, Inc.
OUCH!! BRAIN OVERLOAD!! IT'S TOO MUCH INFORMATION!!
PURGE! PURGE! PURGE!
WHERE AM I?
I NEED TO RAISE MY RATES.

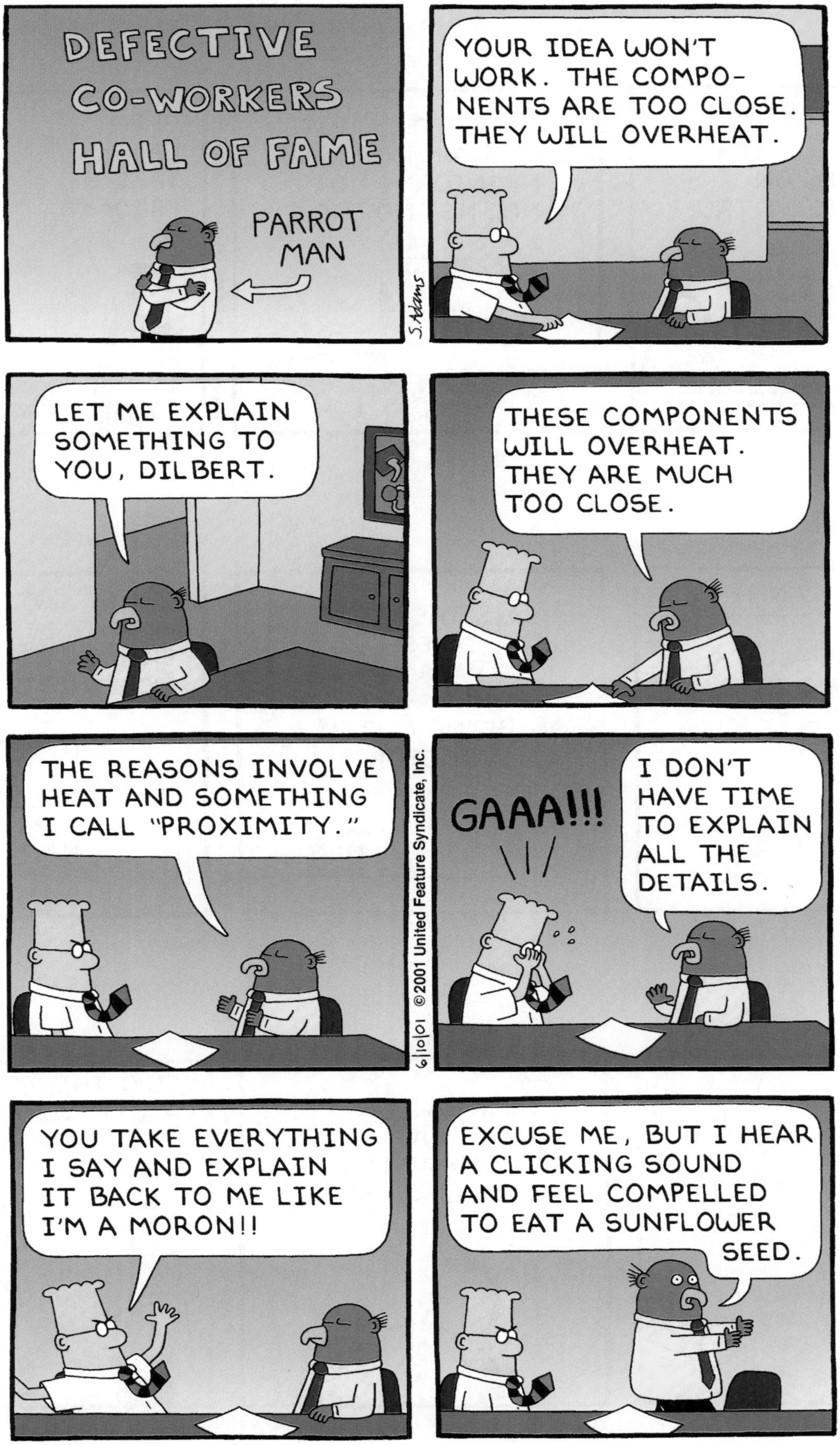
DEFECTIVE CO-WORKERS HALL OF FAME
PARROT MAN
YOUR IDEA WON'T WORK. THE COMPONENTS ARE TOO CLOSE. THEY WILL OVERHEAT.
S. Adams
LET ME EXPLAIN SOMETHING TO YOU, DILBERT.
THESE COMPONENTS WILL OVERHEAT. THEY ARE MUCH TOO CLOSE.
THE REASONS INVOLVE HEAT AND SOMETHING I CALL "PROXIMITY."
6/10/01 ©2001 United Feature Syndicate, Inc.
GAAA!!!
I DON'T HAVE TIME TO EXPLAIN ALL THE DETAILS.
YOU TAKE EVERYTHING I SAY AND EXPLAIN IT BACK TO ME LIKE I'M A MORON!!
EXCUSE ME, BUT I HEAR A CLICKING SOUND AND FEEL COMPELLED TO EAT A SUNFLOWER SEED.

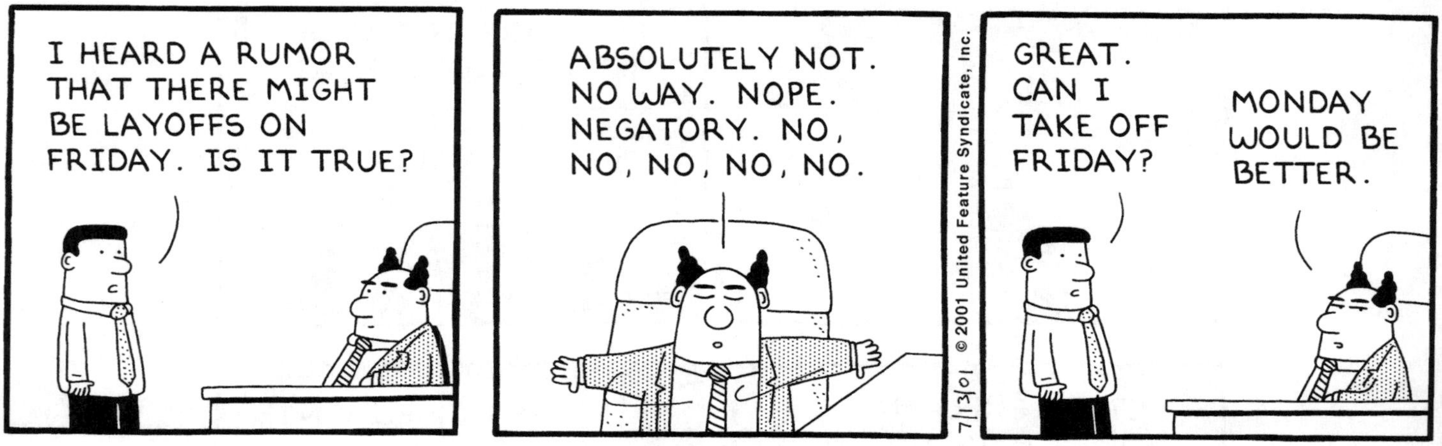
I HEARD A RUMOR THAT THERE MIGHT BE LAYOFFS ON FRIDAY. IS IT TRUE?
ABSOLUTELY NOT. NO WAY. NOPE. NEGATORY. NO, NO, NO, NO, NO.
7/13/01 © 2001 United Feature Syndicate, Inc.
GREAT. CAN I TAKE OFF FRIDAY?
MONDAY WOULD BE BETTER.

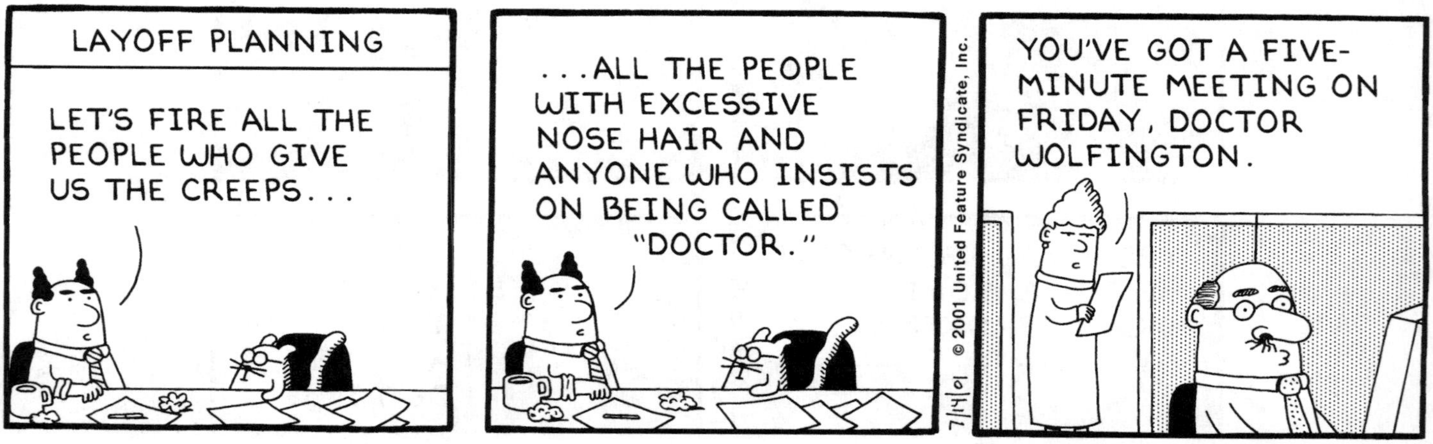
LAYOFF PLANNING
LET'S FIRE ALL THE PEOPLE WHO GIVE US THE CREEPS...
...ALL THE PEOPLE WITH EXCESSIVE NOSE HAIR AND ANYONE WHO INSISTS ON BEING CALLED "DOCTOR."
7/14/01 © 2001 United Feature Syndicate, Inc.
YOU'VE GOT A FIVE-MINUTE MEETING ON FRIDAY, DOCTOR WOLFINGTON.

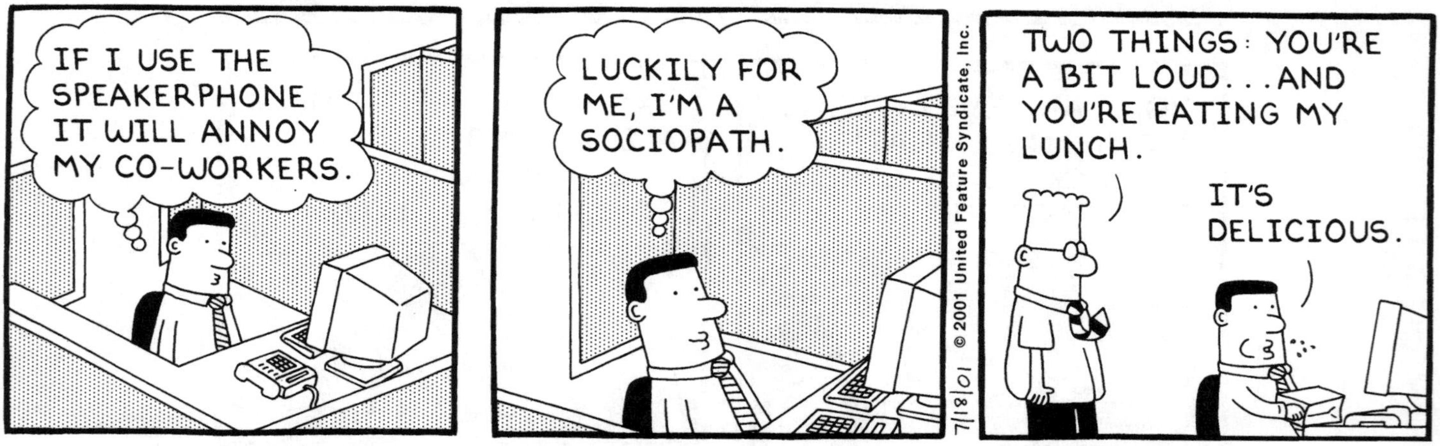
IF I USE THE SPEAKERPHONE IT WILL ANNOY MY CO-WORKERS.
LUCKILY FOR ME, I'M A SOCIOPATH.
7/18/01 © 2001 United Feature Syndicate, Inc.
TWO THINGS: YOU'RE A BIT LOUD...AND YOU'RE EATING MY LUNCH.
IT'S DELICIOUS.

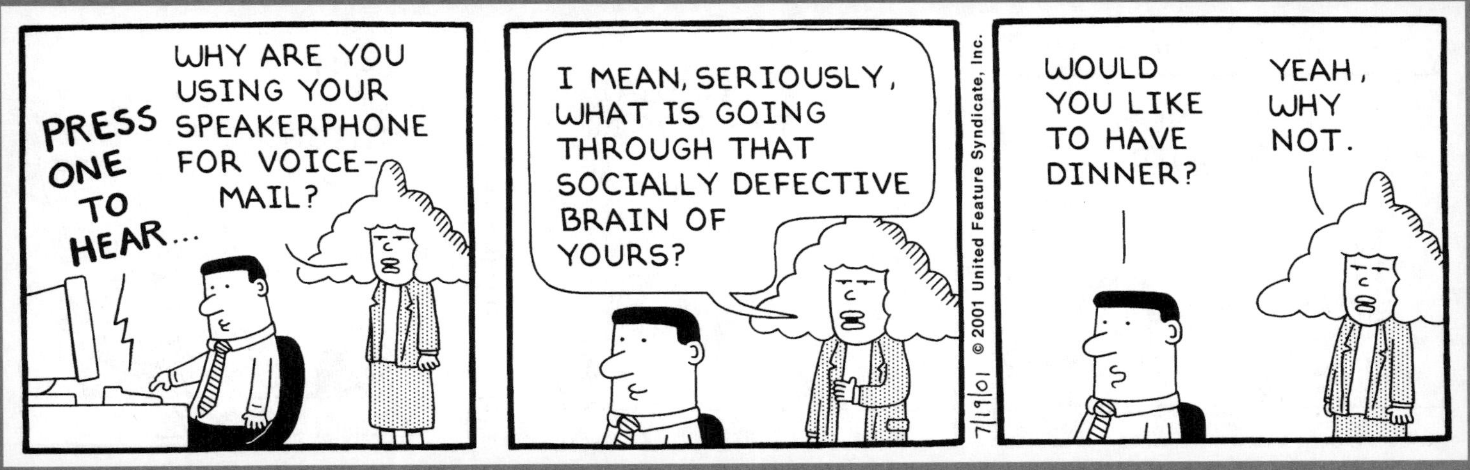
PRESS ONE TO HEAR...
WHY ARE YOU USING YOUR SPEAKERPHONE FOR VOICE-MAIL?
I MEAN, SERIOUSLY, WHAT IS GOING THROUGH THAT SOCIALLY DEFECTIVE BRAIN OF YOURS?
WOULD YOU LIKE TO HAVE DINNER?
YEAH, WHY NOT.
7/19/01
© 2001 United Feature Syndicate, Inc.

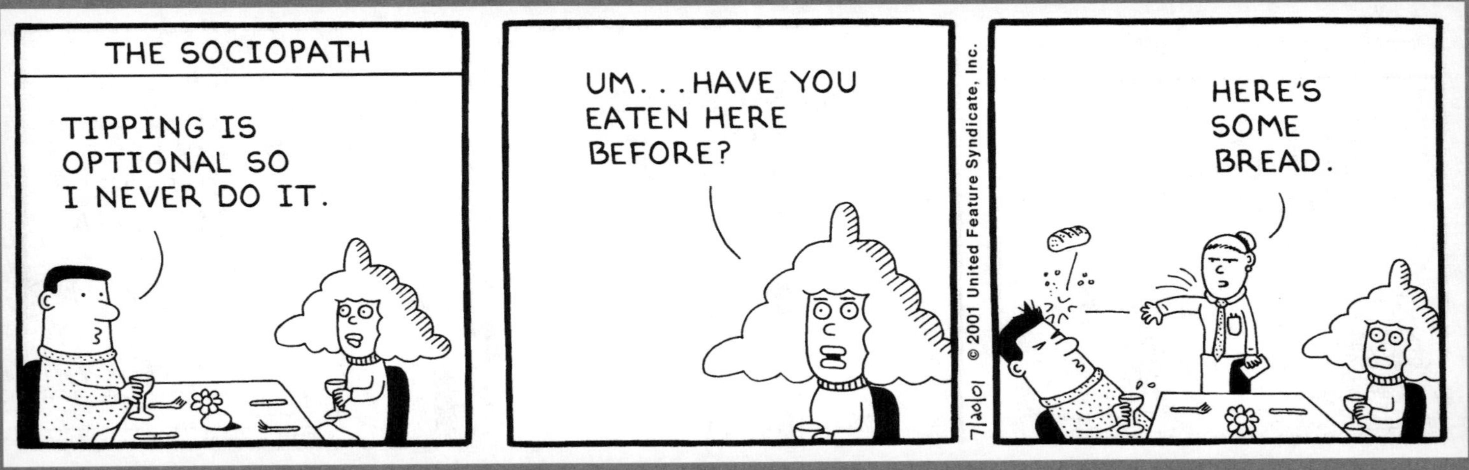
THE SOCIOPATH
TIPPING IS OPTIONAL SO I NEVER DO IT.
UM. . . HAVE YOU EATEN HERE BEFORE?
HERE'S SOME BREAD.
7/20/01
© 2001 United Feature Syndicate, Inc.

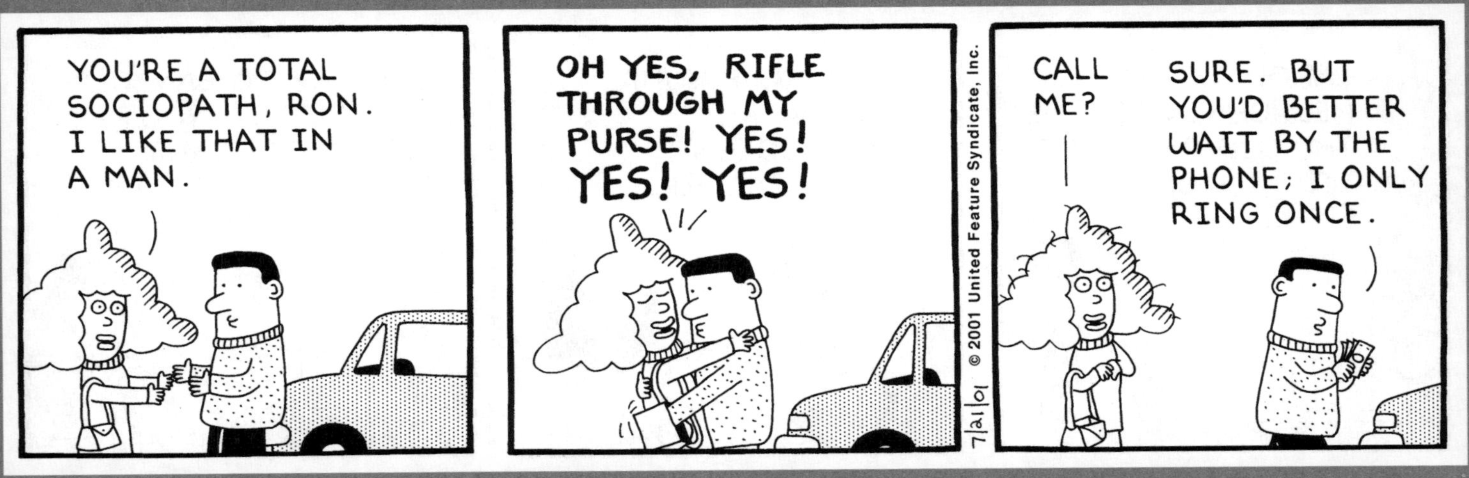
YOU'RE A TOTAL SOCIOPATH, RON. I LIKE THAT IN A MAN.
OH YES, RIFLE THROUGH MY PURSE! YES! YES! YES!
CALL ME?
SURE. BUT YOU'D BETTER WAIT BY THE PHONE; I ONLY RING ONCE.
7/21/01
© 2001 United Feature Syndicate, Inc.

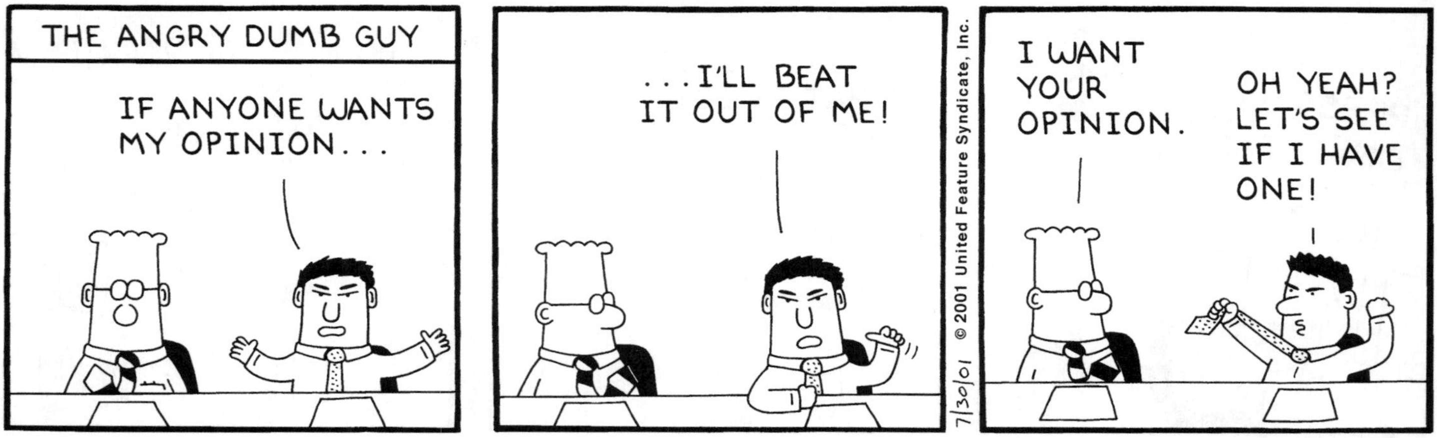
THE ANGRY DUMB GUY
IF ANYONE WANTS MY OPINION...
...I'LL BEAT IT OUT OF ME!
7/30/01 © 2001 United Feature Syndicate, Inc.
I WANT YOUR OPINION.
OH YEAH? LET'S SEE IF I HAVE ONE!

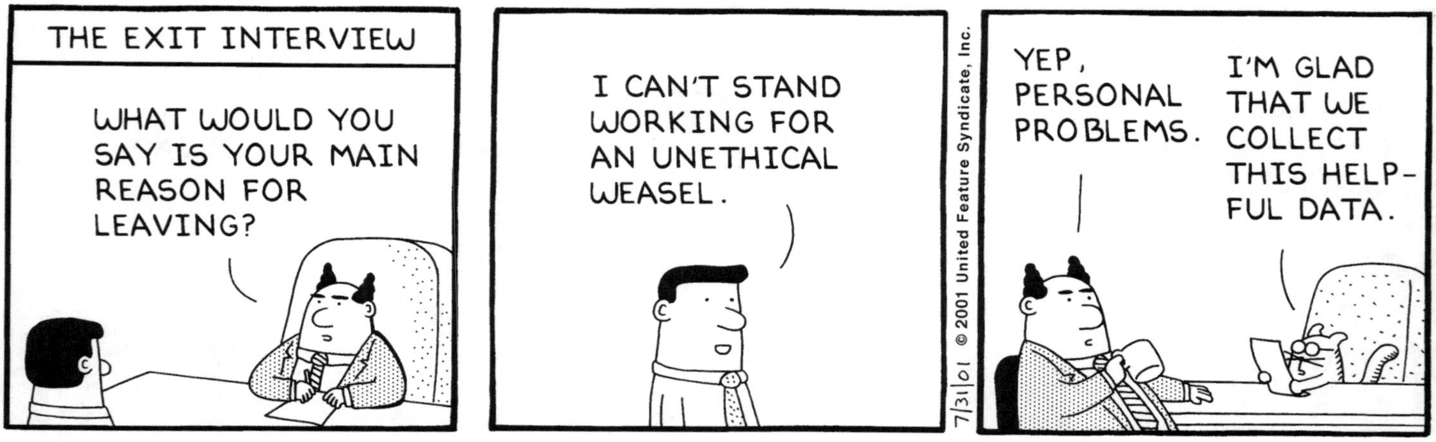
THE EXIT INTERVIEW
WHAT WOULD YOU SAY IS YOUR MAIN REASON FOR LEAVING?
I CAN'T STAND WORKING FOR AN UNETHICAL WEASEL.
7/31/01 © 2001 United Feature Syndicate, Inc.
YEP, PERSONAL PROBLEMS.
I'M GLAD THAT WE COLLECT THIS HELP-FUL DATA.

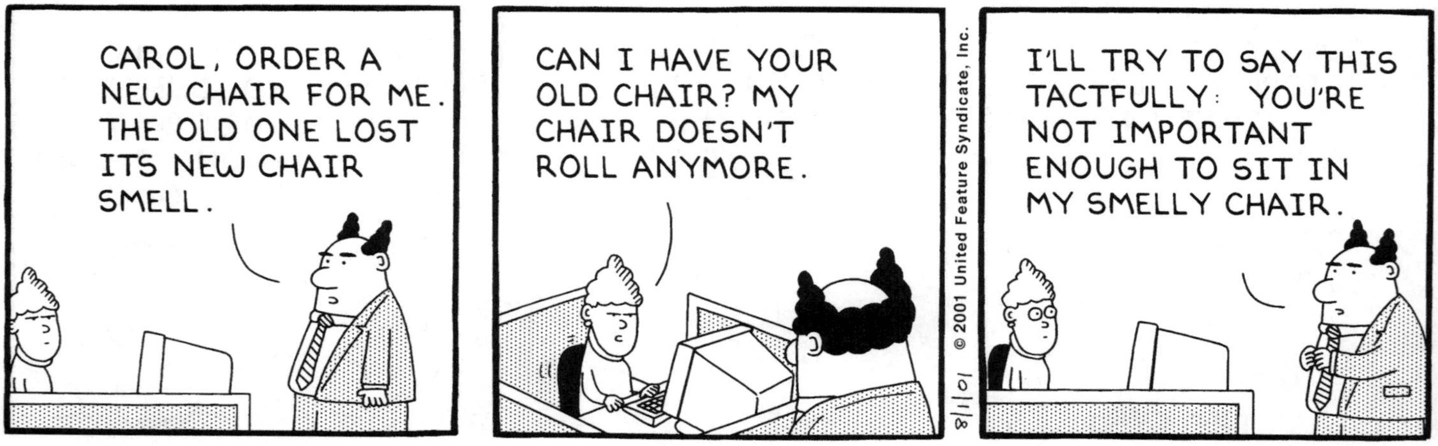
CAROL, ORDER A NEW CHAIR FOR ME. THE OLD ONE LOST ITS NEW CHAIR SMELL.
CAN I HAVE YOUR OLD CHAIR? MY CHAIR DOESN'T ROLL ANYMORE.
8/1/01 © 2001 United Feature Syndicate, Inc.
I'LL TRY TO SAY THIS TACTFULLY: YOU'RE NOT IMPORTANT ENOUGH TO SIT IN MY SMELLY CHAIR.

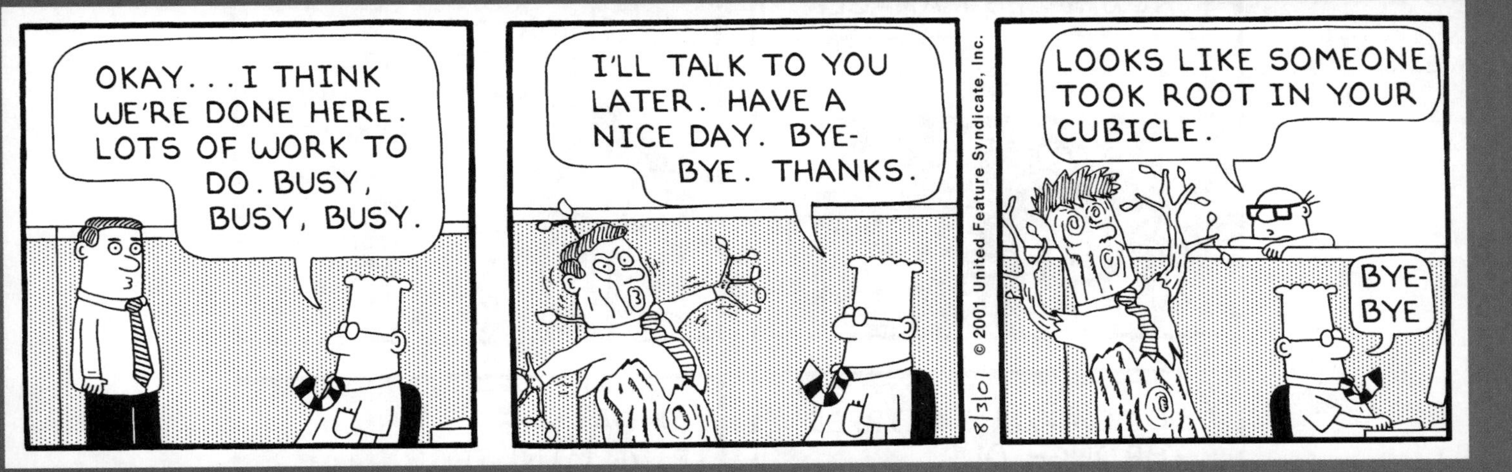
OKAY. . . I THINK WE'RE DONE HERE. LOTS OF WORK TO DO. BUSY, BUSY, BUSY.
I'LL TALK TO YOU LATER. HAVE A NICE DAY. BYE-BYE. THANKS.
8/3/01 © 2001 United Feature Syndicate, Inc.
LOOKS LIKE SOMEONE TOOK ROOT IN YOUR CUBICLE.
BYE-BYE

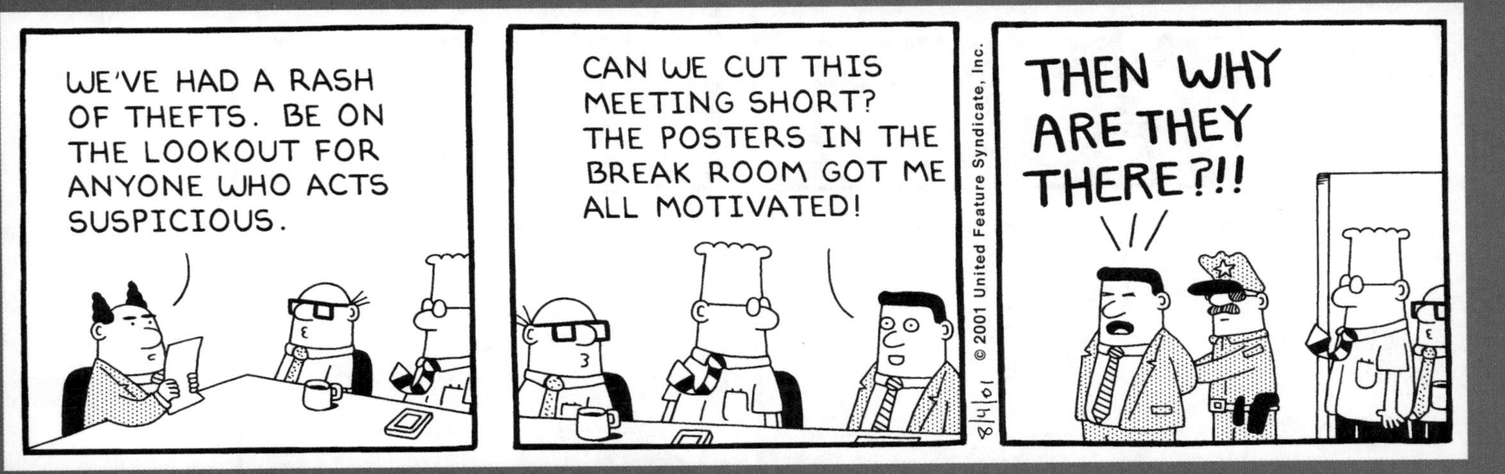
WE'VE HAD A RASH OF THEFTS. BE ON THE LOOKOUT FOR ANYONE WHO ACTS SUSPICIOUS.
CAN WE CUT THIS MEETING SHORT? THE POSTERS IN THE BREAK ROOM GOT ME ALL MOTIVATED!
8/4/01 © 2001 United Feature Syndicate, Inc.
THEN WHY ARE THEY THERE?!!

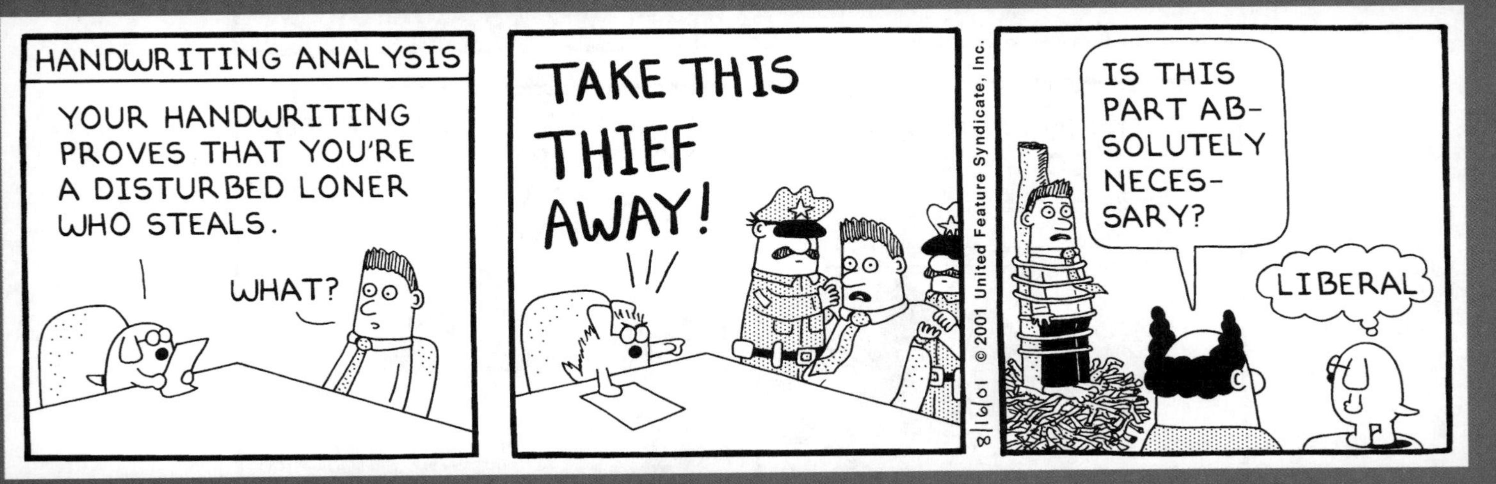
HANDWRITING ANALYSIS
YOUR HANDWRITING PROVES THAT YOU'RE A DISTURBED LONER WHO STEALS.
WHAT?
TAKE THIS THIEF AWAY!
8/16/01 © 2001 United Feature Syndicate, Inc.
IS THIS PART AB-SOLUTELY NECES-SARY?
LIBERAL

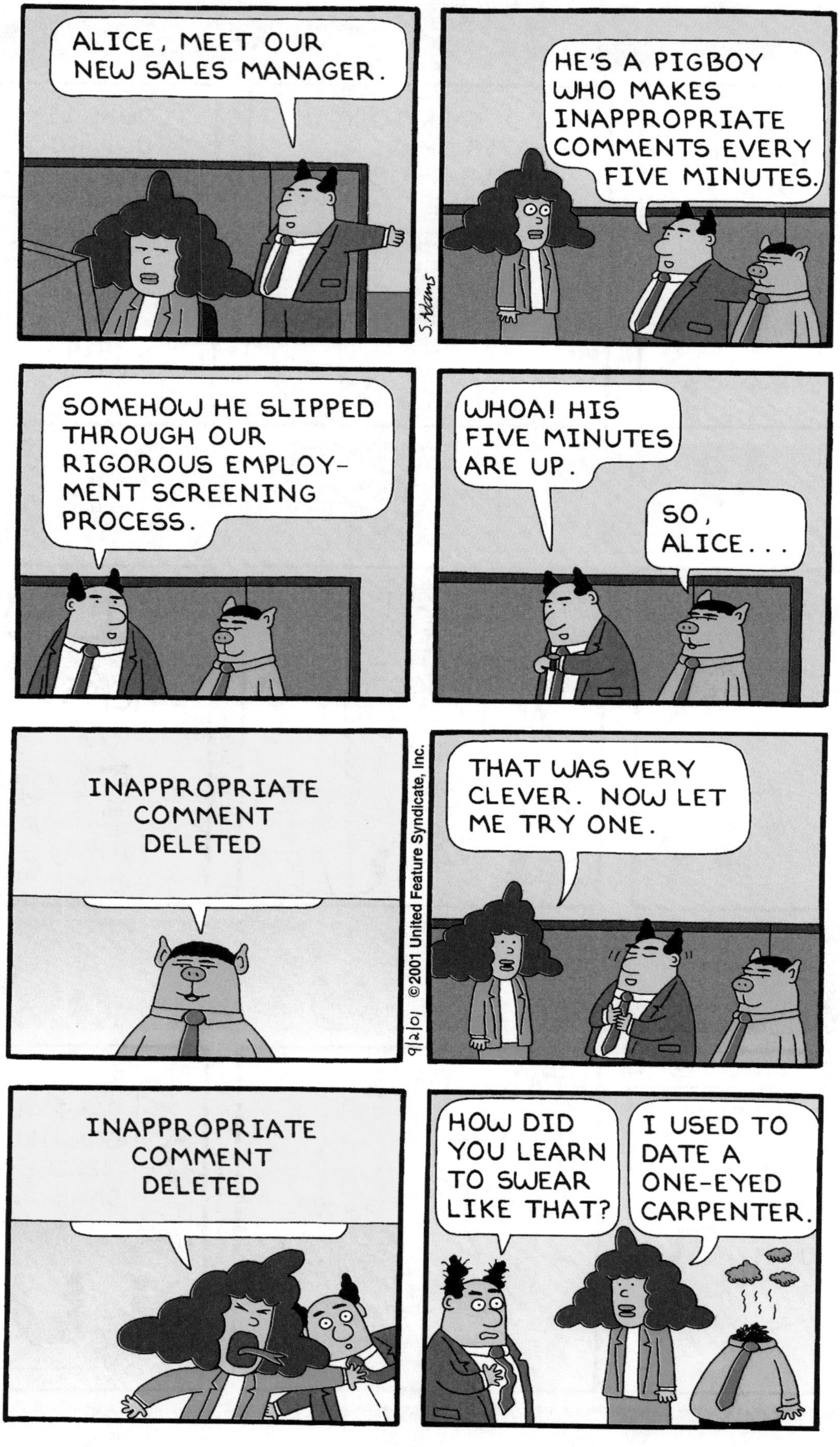
ALICE, MEET OUR NEW SALES MANAGER.
HE'S A PIGBOY WHO MAKES INAPPROPRIATE COMMENTS EVERY FIVE MINUTES.
S. Adams
SOMEHOW HE SLIPPED THROUGH OUR RIGOROUS EMPLOY-MENT SCREENING PROCESS.
WHOA! HIS FIVE MINUTES ARE UP.
SO, ALICE...
INAPPROPRIATE COMMENT DELETED
9/2/01 ©2001 United Feature Syndicate, Inc.
THAT WAS VERY CLEVER. NOW LET ME TRY ONE.
INAPPROPRIATE COMMENT DELETED
HOW DID YOU LEARN TO SWEAR LIKE THAT?
I USED TO DATE A ONE-EYED CARPENTER.

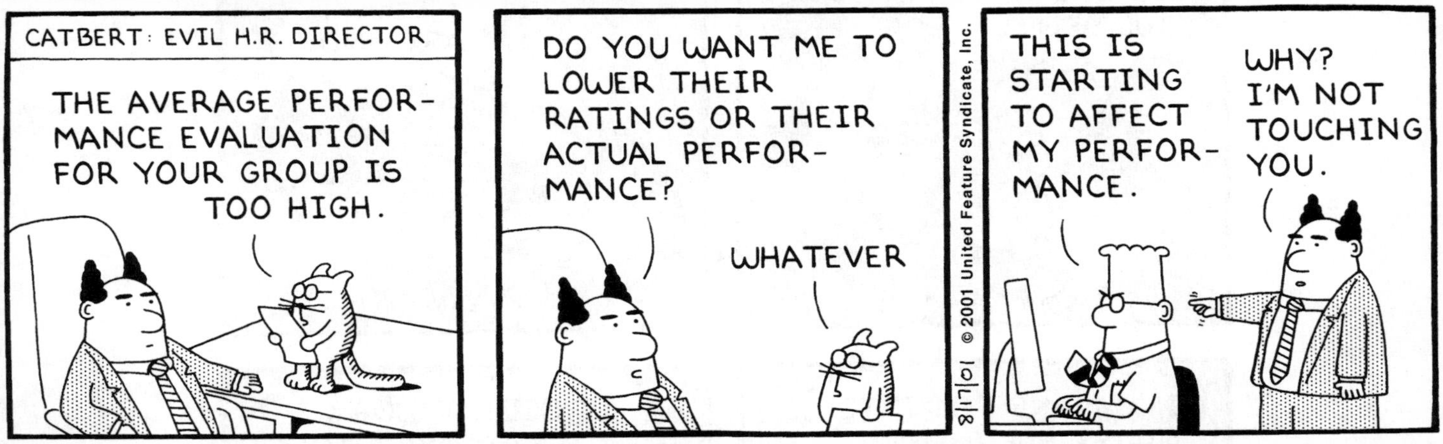
CATBERT: EVIL H.R. DIRECTOR
THE AVERAGE PERFORMANCE EVALUATION FOR YOUR GROUP IS TOO HIGH.
DO YOU WANT ME TO LOWER THEIR RATINGS OR THEIR ACTUAL PERFORMANCE?
WHATEVER
THIS IS STARTING TO AFFECT MY PERFORMANCE.
WHY? I'M NOT TOUCHING YOU.
8/17/01 © 2001 United Feature Syndicate, Inc.

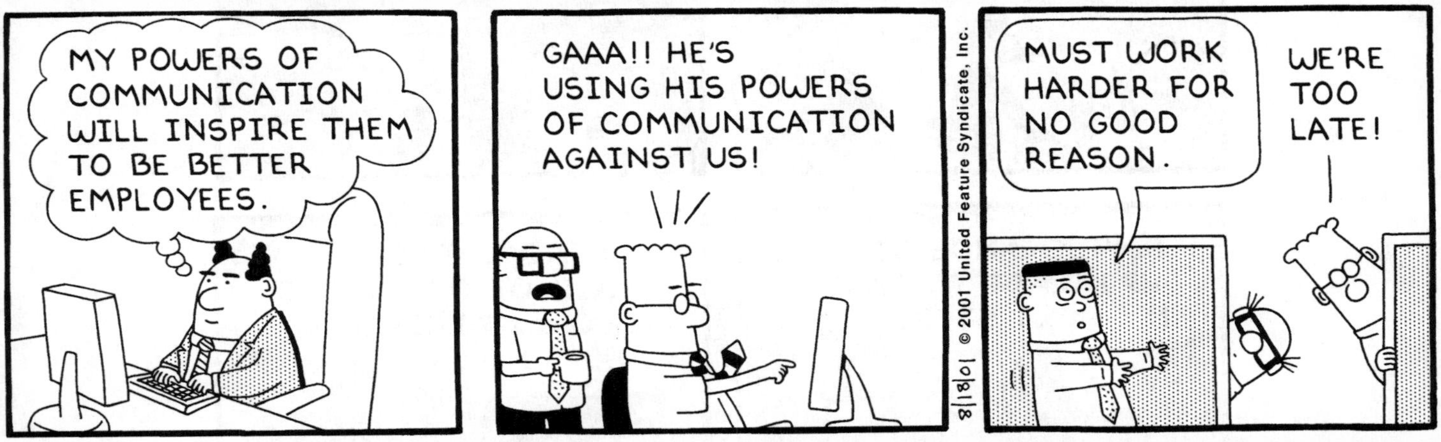
MY POWERS OF COMMUNICATION WILL INSPIRE THEM TO BE BETTER EMPLOYEES.
GAAA!! HE'S USING HIS POWERS OF COMMUNICATION AGAINST US!
MUST WORK HARDER FOR NO GOOD REASON.
WE'RE TOO LATE!
8/18/01 © 2001 United Feature Syndicate, Inc.

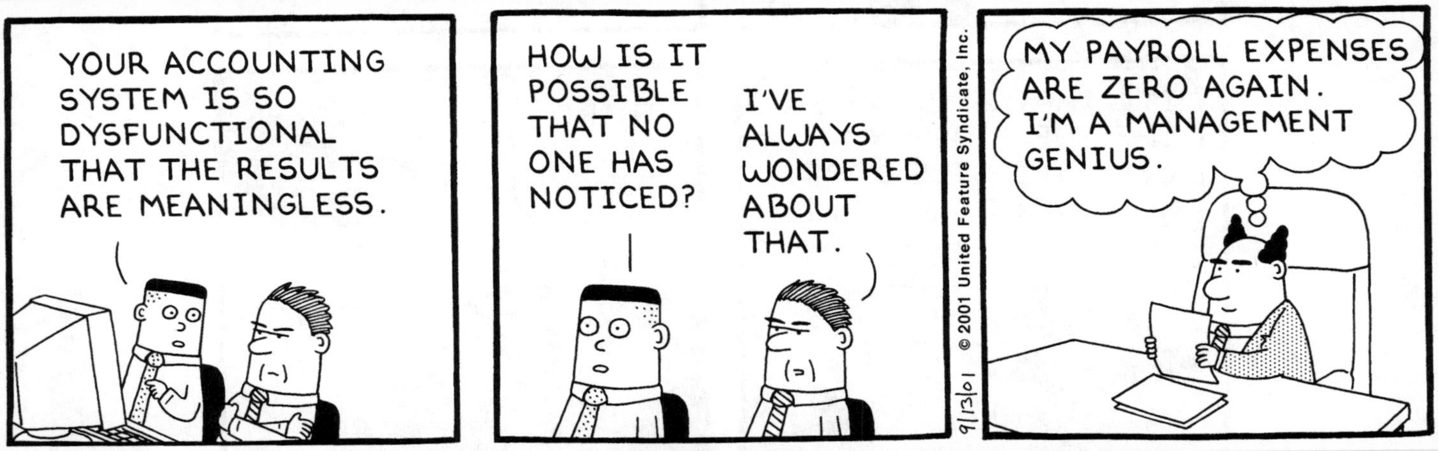
YOUR ACCOUNTING SYSTEM IS SO DYSFUNCTIONAL THAT THE RESULTS ARE MEANINGLESS.
HOW IS IT POSSIBLE THAT NO ONE HAS NOTICED?
I'VE ALWAYS WONDERED ABOUT THAT.
MY PAYROLL EXPENSES ARE ZERO AGAIN. I'M A MANAGEMENT GENIUS.
9/13/01 © 2001 United Feature Syndicate, Inc.

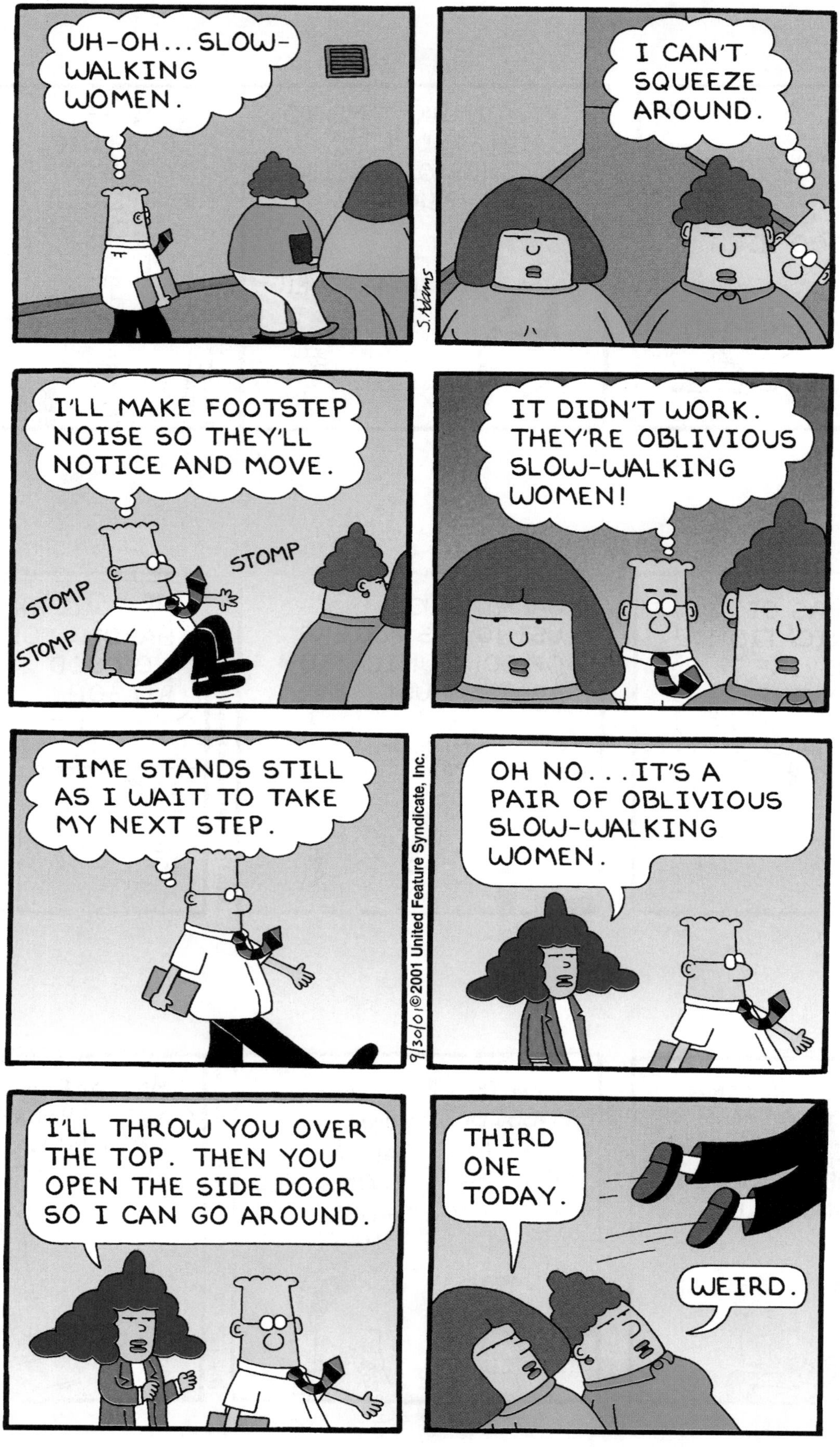
UH-OH... SLOW-WALKING WOMEN.
S. Adams
I CAN'T SQUEEZE AROUND.
I'LL MAKE FOOTSTEP NOISE SO THEY'LL NOTICE AND MOVE.
STOMP
STOMP
STOMP
IT DIDN'T WORK. THEY'RE OBLIVIOUS SLOW-WALKING WOMEN!
TIME STANDS STILL AS I WAIT TO TAKE MY NEXT STEP.
9/30/01 © 2001 United Feature Syndicate, Inc.
OH NO... IT'S A PAIR OF OBLIVIOUS SLOW-WALKING WOMEN.
I'LL THROW YOU OVER THE TOP. THEN YOU OPEN THE SIDE DOOR SO I CAN GO AROUND.
THIRD ONE TODAY.
WEIRD.

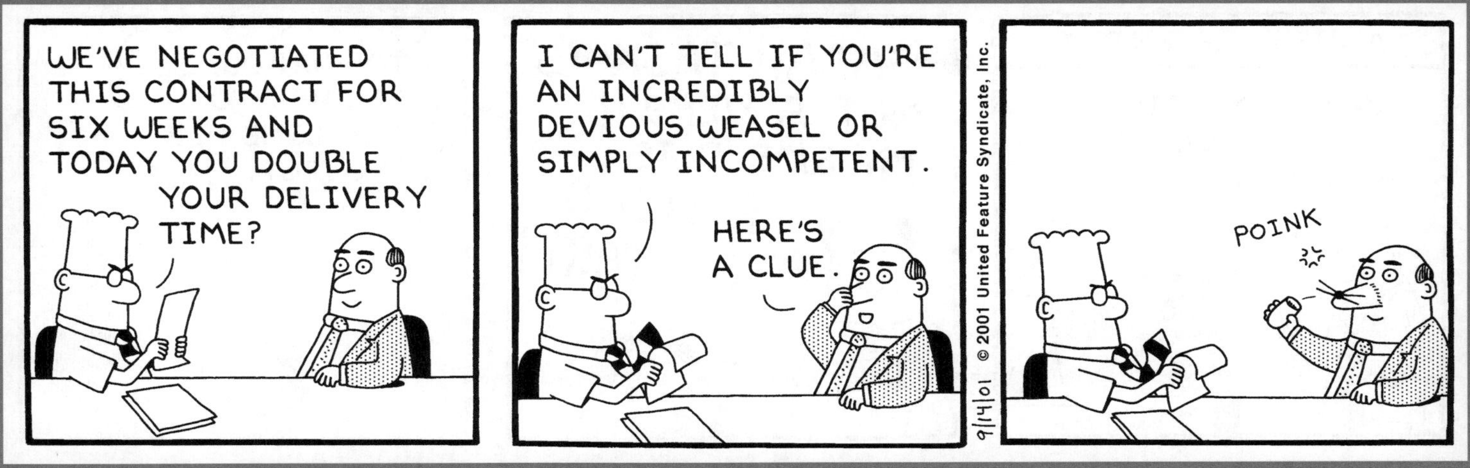
WE'VE NEGOTIATED THIS CONTRACT FOR SIX WEEKS AND TODAY YOU DOUBLE YOUR DELIVERY TIME?
I CAN'T TELL IF YOU'RE AN INCREDIBLY DEVIOUS WEASEL OR SIMPLY INCOMPETENT.
HERE'S A CLUE.
POINK
9/14/01 © 2001 United Feature Syndicate, Inc.

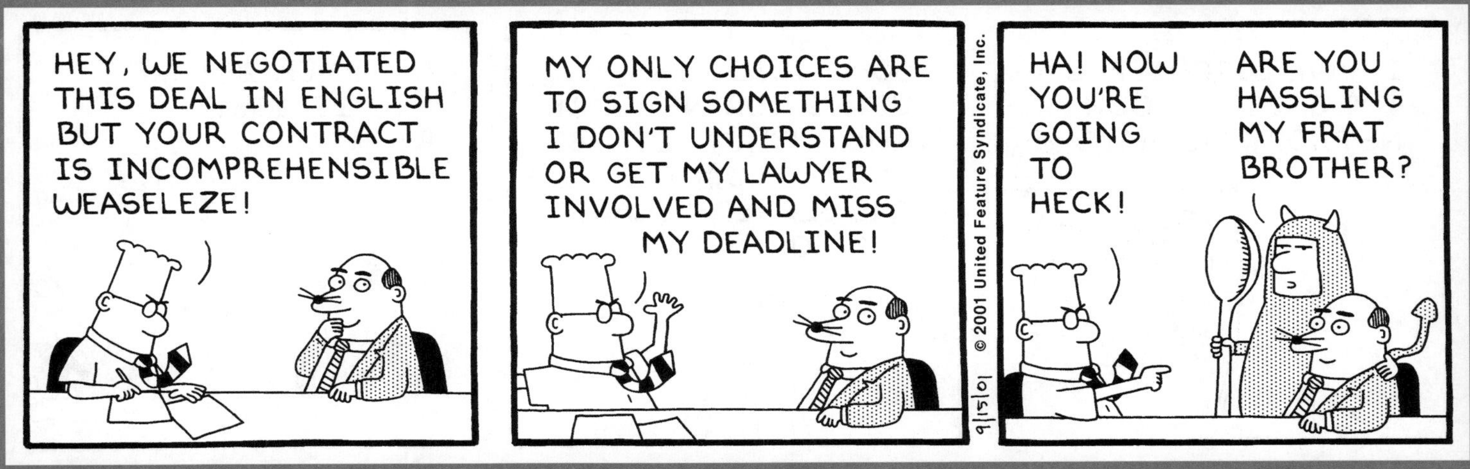
HEY, WE NEGOTIATED THIS DEAL IN ENGLISH BUT YOUR CONTRACT IS INCOMPREHENSIBLE WEASELEZE!
MY ONLY CHOICES ARE TO SIGN SOMETHING I DON'T UNDERSTAND OR GET MY LAWYER INVOLVED AND MISS MY DEADLINE!
HA! NOW YOU'RE GOING TO HECK!
ARE YOU HASSLING MY FRAT BROTHER?
9/15/01 © 2001 United Feature Syndicate, Inc.

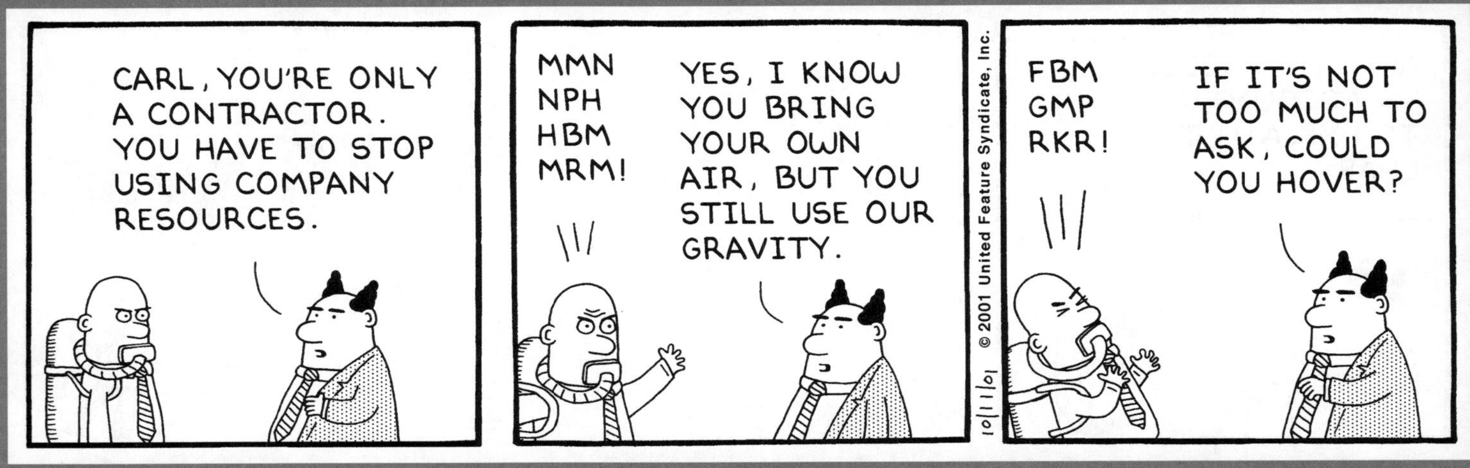
CARL, YOU'RE ONLY A CONTRACTOR. YOU HAVE TO STOP USING COMPANY RESOURCES.
MMN NPH HBM MRM!
YES, I KNOW YOU BRING YOUR OWN AIR, BUT YOU STILL USE OUR GRAVITY.
FBM GMP RKR!
IF IT'S NOT TOO MUCH TO ASK, COULD YOU HOVER?
10/1/01 © 2001 United Feature Syndicate, Inc.

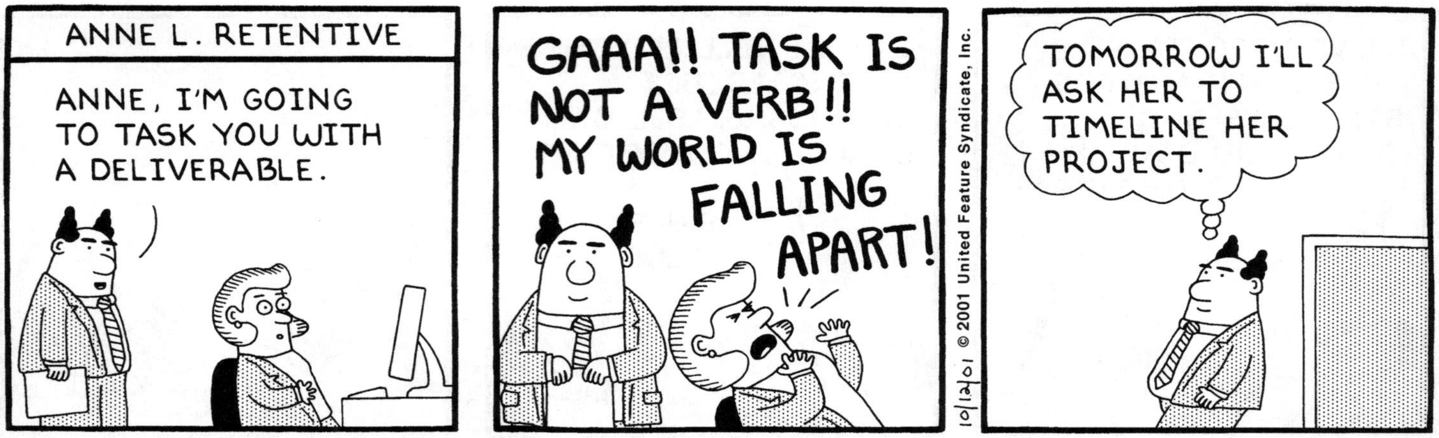
ANNE L. RETENTIVE
ANNE, I'M GOING TO TASK YOU WITH A DELIVERABLE.
GAAA!! TASK IS NOT A VERB!! MY WORLD IS FALLING APART!
10/12/01 © 2001 United Feature Syndicate, Inc.
TOMORROW I'LL ASK HER TO TIMELINE HER PROJECT.

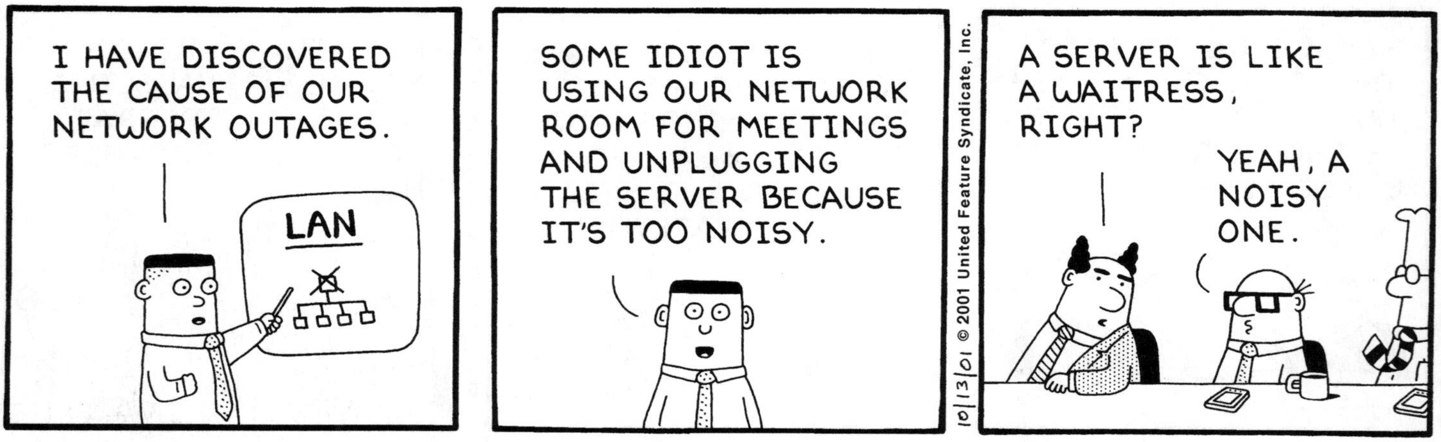
I HAVE DISCOVERED THE CAUSE OF OUR NETWORK OUTAGES.
LAN
SOME IDIOT IS USING OUR NETWORK ROOM FOR MEETINGS AND UNPLUGGING THE SERVER BECAUSE IT'S TOO NOISY.
10/13/01 © 2001 United Feature Syndicate, Inc.
A SERVER IS LIKE A WAITRESS, RIGHT?
YEAH, A NOISY ONE.

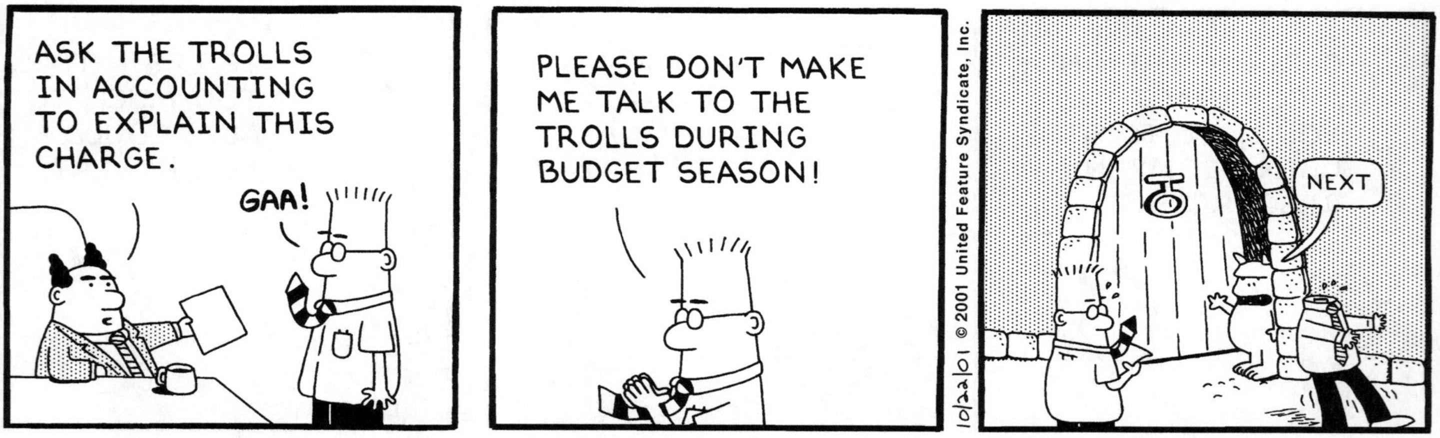
ASK THE TROLLS IN ACCOUNTING TO EXPLAIN THIS CHARGE.
GAA!
PLEASE DON'T MAKE ME TALK TO THE TROLLS DURING BUDGET SEASON!
10/22/01 © 2001 United Feature Syndicate, Inc.
NEXT

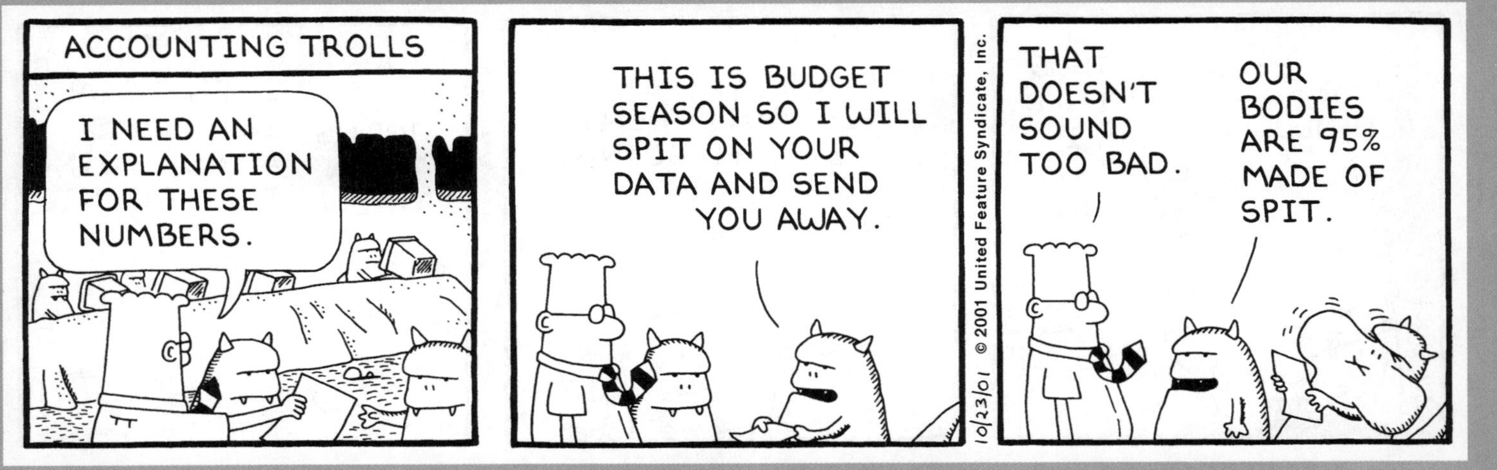
ACCOUNTING TROLLS
I NEED AN EXPLANATION FOR THESE NUMBERS.
THIS IS BUDGET SEASON SO I WILL SPIT ON YOUR DATA AND SEND YOU AWAY.
10/23/01 © 2001 United Feature Syndicate, Inc.
THAT DOESN'T SOUND TOO BAD.
OUR BODIES ARE 95% MADE OF SPIT.

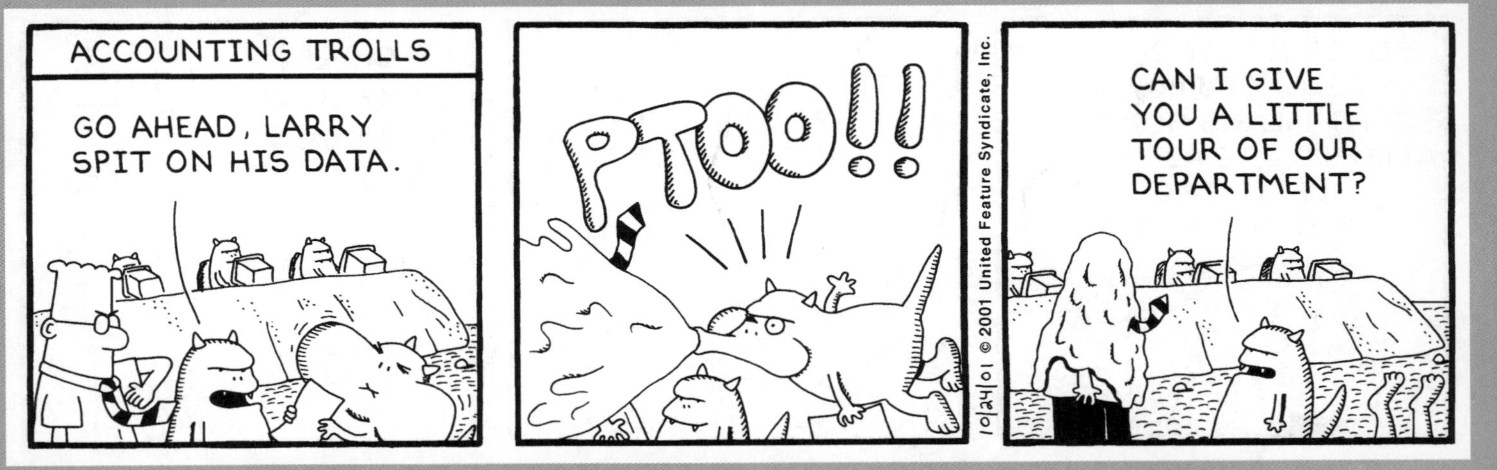
ACCOUNTING TROLLS
GO AHEAD, LARRY SPIT ON HIS DATA.
PTOO!!
10/24/01 © 2001 United Feature Syndicate, Inc.
CAN I GIVE YOU A LITTLE TOUR OF OUR DEPARTMENT?

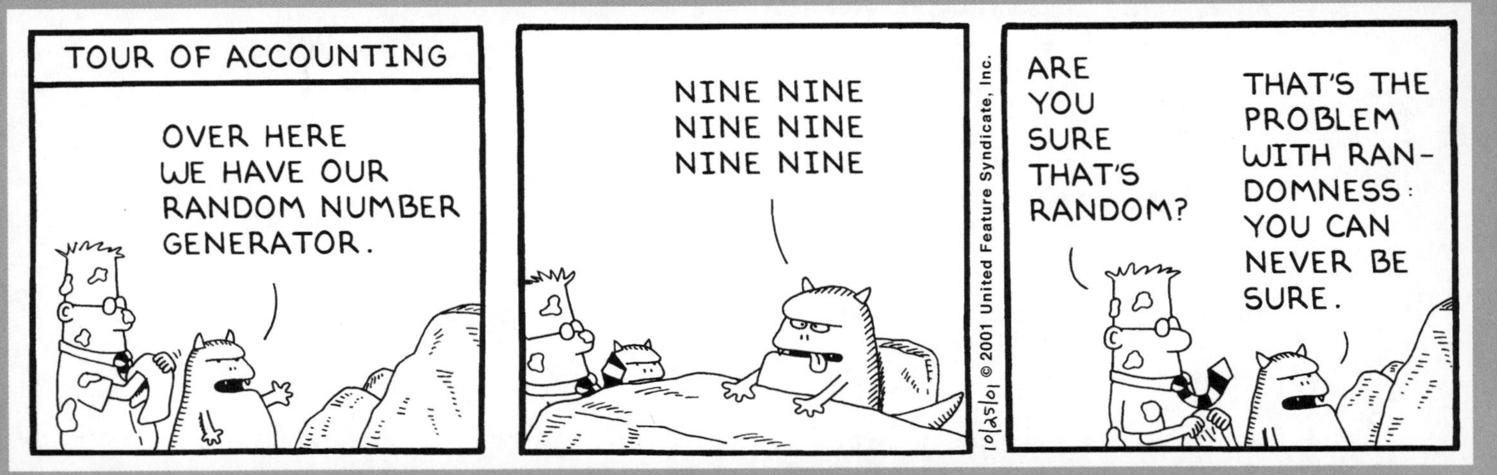
TOUR OF ACCOUNTING
OVER HERE WE HAVE OUR RANDOM NUMBER GENERATOR.
NINE NINE NINE NINE NINE NINE
10/25/01 © 2001 United Feature Syndicate, Inc.
ARE YOU SURE THAT'S RANDOM?
THAT'S THE PROBLEM WITH RANDOMNESS: YOU CAN NEVER BE SURE.

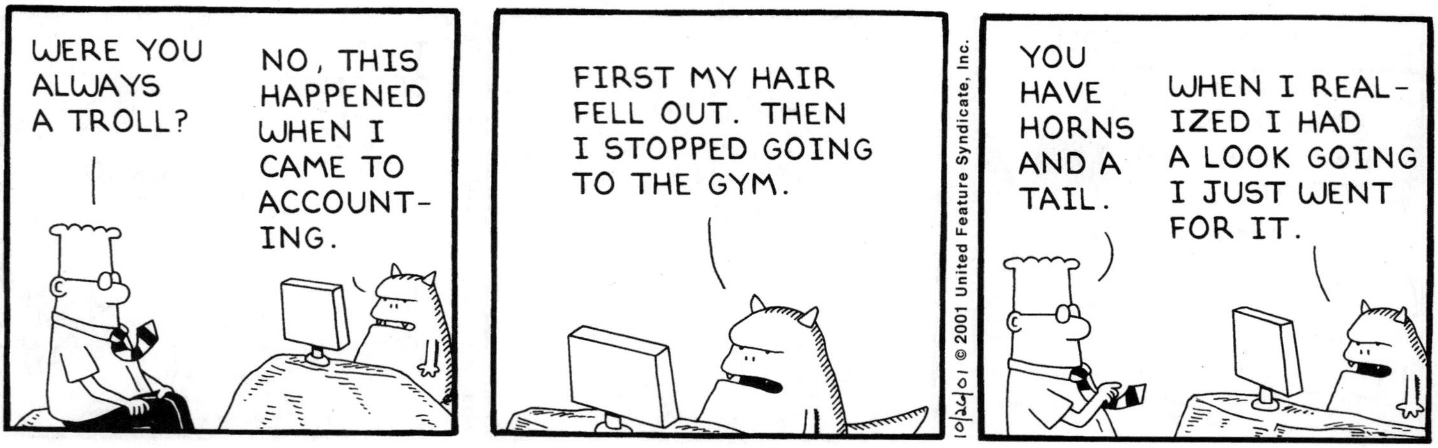
WERE YOU ALWAYS A TROLL?
NO, THIS HAPPENED WHEN I CAME TO ACCOUNT-ING.
FIRST MY HAIR FELL OUT. THEN I STOPPED GOING TO THE GYM.
10/26/01 © 2001 United Feature Syndicate, Inc.
YOU HAVE HORNS AND A TAIL.
WHEN I REAL-IZED I HAD A LOOK GOING I JUST WENT FOR IT.

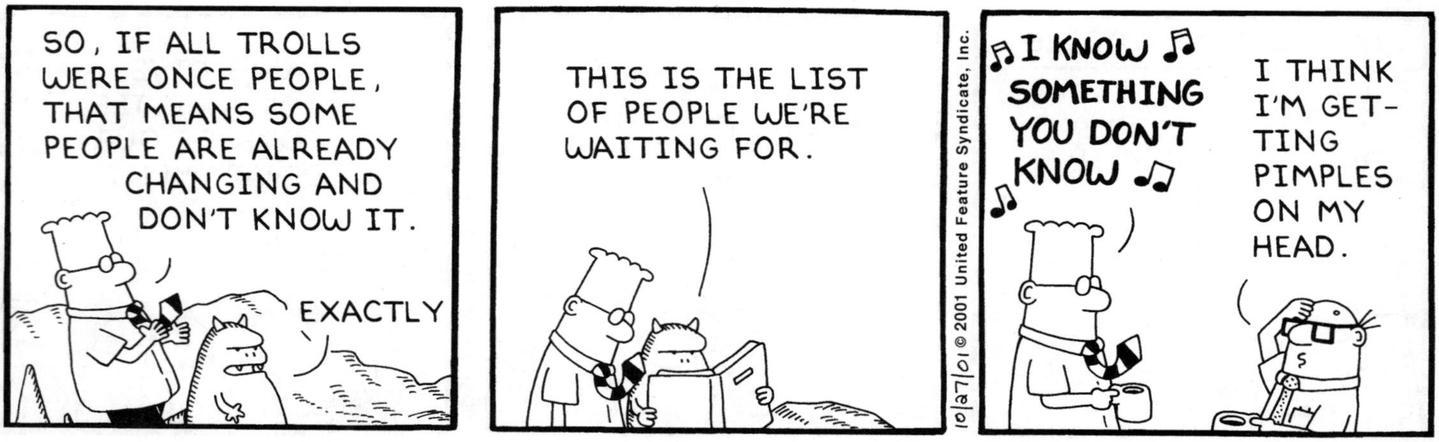
SO, IF ALL TROLLS WERE ONCE PEOPLE, THAT MEANS SOME PEOPLE ARE ALREADY CHANGING AND DON'T KNOW IT.
EXACTLY
THIS IS THE LIST OF PEOPLE WE'RE WAITING FOR.
10/27/01 © 2001 United Feature Syndicate, Inc.
♫ I KNOW ♫ SOMETHING YOU DON'T KNOW ♫
I THINK I'M GET-TING PIMPLES ON MY HEAD.

ELECTRICIAN'S EXAM

PREPARATION GUIDE

Ninth Edition

Based on the 2014 *NEC*®

by
John E. Traister

Revised and Updated by
Dale C. Brickner

Includes inside the back cover:

Includes Free Software Download

Inside the back cover of this book you'll find a software download certificate. To access the download, follow the instructions printed there.

- Contains all the questions in the book in interactive self-test software that makes studying almost fun.
- Each answer is explained, and shows the pertinent *NEC*® section at the click of the mouse.
- Use the study mode to get an immediate response on each answer.
- Use the exam mode for a timed exam — just like the real one, and see your grade when finished.

Craftsman Book Company
6058 Corte del Cedro, Carlsbad, CA 92011

ledgments

I am indebted to several individuals and organizations who helped in the preparation of this book. One group is the electrical examining boards throughout the United States. A list of these organizations appears in Appendix I of this book. The following were especially helpful in furnishing reference materials or else helping with the production.

National Fire Protection Association® (NFPA®)

C. Keeler Chapman, *Artwork*

Nicole L. Brickner, *Typist and Organizer*

Joe A. Fintz, *Final Exam Verification*

Ron Murray, *Code Consultant*

Floyd Richards, *Question Verification & Code Consultant*

Portions of this publication are reprinted with permission from *NFPA 70®*-2014 *National Electrical Code®*, Copyright © 2013 National Fire Protection Association, Quincy, MA 02169. This reprinted material is not the complete and official position of the National Fire Protection Association on the referenced subject, which is represented only by the standard in its entirety.

National Electrical Code® and *NEC®* are registered trademarks of the National Fire Protection Association, Inc., Quincy, MA 02169.

Library of Congress Cataloging-in-Publication Data

Traister, John E.
  Electrician's exam preparation guide : based on the 2014 NEC / by John E.
Traister, revised and updated by Dale C. Brickner. -- Ninth edition.
      pages cm
  Includes bibliographical references and index.
  ISBN 978-1-57218-303-2 (alk. paper)
  1. Electrical engineering--Examinations, questions, etc. 2. Electrical
engineering--Examinations--Study guides. 3. Electricians--Licenses--United
States. 4. National Fire Protection Association. National Electrical Code
(2014) I. Brickner, Dale C. II. Title.

TK169.T73 2014
621.319'24076--dc23

                        2014002984